1964

JOHNSON | GOL[DWATER]

WASH. 9
ORE. 6
IDAHO 4
NEV. 3
CALIF. 40
UTAH 4
ARIZ. 5
N.M. 4
MONT. 4
WYO. 3
COLO. 6
N.D. 4
S.D. 4
NEBR. 5
KAN. 7
OKLA. 8
TEXAS 25
MINN. 10
IOWA 9
MO. 12
ARK. 6
LA. 10
WISC. 12
ILL. 26
IND. 13
KY. 9
TENN. 11
MISS. 7
ALA. 10
GA. 12
MICH. 21
OHIO 26
W.VA. 7
VA. 12
N.C. 13
S.C. 8
FLA. 14
N.Y. 43
PA. 29
N.H. 4
MASS. 14
R.I. 4
CONN. 8
N.J. 17
DEL. 3
MD. 10
D.C. 3

ALASKA 3

HAWAII 4

Total Electoral Votes

JOHNSON: 486
GOLDWATER: 52

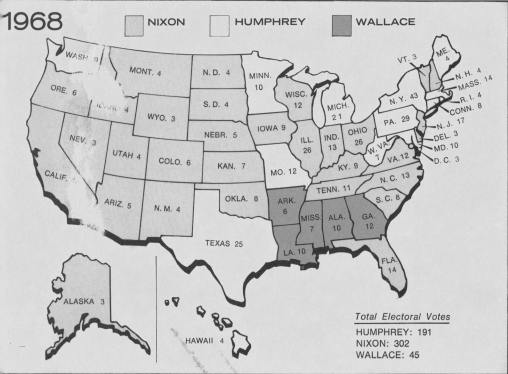

1968

NIXON | HUMPHREY | WALLACE

WASH. 9
ORE. 6
IDAHO 4
NEV. 3
CALIF. 40
UTAH 4
ARIZ. 5
N.M. 4
MONT. 4
WYO. 3
COLO. 6
N.D. 4
S.D. 4
NEBR. 5
KAN. 7
OKLA. 8
TEXAS 25
MINN. 10
IOWA 9
MO. 12
ARK. 6
LA. 10
WISC. 12
ILL. 26
IND. 13
KY. 9
TENN. 11
MISS. 7
ALA. 10
GA. 12
MICH. 21
OHIO 26
W.VA. 7
VA. 12
N.C. 13
S.C. 8
FLA. 14
N.Y. 43
PA. 29
VT. 3
ME. 4
N.H. 4
MASS. 14
R.I. 4
CONN. 8
N.J. 17
DEL. 3
MD. 10
D.C. 3

ALASKA 3

HAWAII 4

Total Electoral Votes

HUMPHREY: 191
NIXON: 302
WALLACE: 45

Map by Morgan

BOOKS BY

THEODORE H. WHITE

THE
MAKING OF
THE PRESIDENT
1968

THEODORE H. WHITE

THE
MAKING OF
THE PRESIDENT
1968

NEW YORK
ATHENEUM PUBLISHERS
1969

Endpaper maps by Ava Morgan

FOR

JOHN FITZGERALD KENNEDY

AND

ROBERT FRANCIS KENNEDY

*Saul and Jonathan, sweet and
beloved in their lives; nor in their
death were they divided; swifter
were they than eagles, braver than
lions. . . .*

DAVID'S LAMENT, SAMUEL II:1

". . . Behold men, as it were, in an underground cave-like dwelling, having its entrance open towards the light, which extends through the whole cave. Within it, persons, who from childhood on, have had chains on their legs and their necks; so they can look forward only, but not turn their heads around because of the chains, their light coming from a fire that burns above, far off and behind them.

"And between the fire and those in chains is a road above, alongside which one may see a little wall built, just as the stages of magicians are built before the people in whose presence they show their tricks. . . .

"Behold then, beneath and behind this little wall, men carrying all sorts of machines rising above the wall; and statues of men and other animals, some of the bearers probably speaking, others proceeding in silence. . . .

"Think you that such as those who live in the cave would have seen anything else of themselves, or of one another, except the shadows that fall from the fire on the opposite side of the cave?

"And if the prison had an echo on its opposite side, when any person present were to speak, think you they would imagine anything else addressed to them except by the shadow before them?

"Such persons would deem truth to be nothing else but the shadows of exhibitions."

PLATO: *THE REPUBLIC,* BOOK VII, 2

FOREWORD

THIS BOOK is an attempt to tell what happened on earth in America, in 1968, while Americans prepared to land on the moon.

Whenever they turned their eyes upward, on summer evenings or fall nights, the moon tantalized Americans. But the stories of the space adventure filled them with a pride, hope and faith in themselves that vanished each day with the rising of the sun. For by day, the imagination of Americans was largely earthbound, their thoughts turned inward, their emotions tormented by unending war and the vain quest for peace. They were little different from the people of Spain who were far more intent in 1491–1492 on the final struggle against the Moors in Granada than on the vision of Christopher Columbus, who persuaded the court of Castile and Aragon that the world was round, finite and in man's grasp.

From the very beginning, the arbitrary calendar year has had to measure two kinds of time, one measure for the community and the law, another measure for man and his plans. Does the calendar reach outward to frame man in his universe? Or does it reflect inward, on the season and cycles of man? The Egyptians, three thousand years before Christ, were perplexed by the same problem in working out the first primitive calendars. Should they rely on the Calendar of Thoth, which divided the year into four-week cycles, those same uncertain cycles that move a woman's body to her periods of fertility? Or should they choose the calendar of the sun, by whose turnings they could determine flood and ebb on the Nile— and thus manage affairs of state, setting the flood warnings, the sowing, the planting, and the tax season by that day in early summer when Sirius first appeared above the horizon, a flash before the rising of the sun. The Egyptians chose the sun and outer world as measure; and ever since, the 365-day year has been the measure of historians.

Historians may see 1968 as another such conventional measure framing man in his universe—the year that Americans gave earthbound men their first close glimpse of the moon and prepared for the effort of 1969. But they will do so only if America finally succeeds inwardly in mastering the passions and furies that threatened her civilization in the streets that year. And these passions and furies were susceptible to no conventional measure of time. They had begun long before the calendar signaled the beginning of 1968 and will sweep on long after. Of all the major events of 1968, only the march on the moon moved to a schedule set by reason. America's power to control events, it appeared, extended farther into outer space than within her own cities.

In his last speech from Geneva, on July 9th, 1965, a week before he died, Adlai Stevenson said, "We travel together passengers on a little space ship, dependent on its vulnerable supply of air and soil; all committed for our safety to its security and peace, preserved from annihilation only by the care, the work, and I will say the love we give our fragile craft."

This book is written in Stevenson's old-fashioned spirit. It rests on the thought that those who care for this little space ship, who try to manage it and set its course, require understanding; and the requirement of understanding leads inescapably to respect and sympathy. Never was this more difficult than in America, in 1968, as those who manage this particular compartment of the global space ship faced the problems of their people.

There is always something ridiculous about American politicians doing their business—their posturings, their dialogues, their threadbare rhetoric are all too familiar. The morning breakfasts, the grease of hot dogs and mustard on their chins at county fairs, the pumping of hands at factory gates, the dreary "fund-raisers," the required hypocrisies of presentation, the instant solutions, the slippery, underhand deals—all these, in 1968 as ever, degraded the best of men. And when on top of these time-worn rituals were overlaid the concern and agony of the American people—the death of their sons in far-off war, the fear that haunted the streets, the violence of mugging and murder, of mace and police clubs—1968 became grotesque.

Yet wherever else one turned in the world, either in 1968 or in retrospective memory, the process of politics was worse. Elsewhere, leadership was more inflexible and sterile, hunger worse and spreading, voices either more choked or more violent. In a world of rigid political orthodoxies, of states cramped by dogma, America, in all its confusion, still offered choices, still tantalized men everywhere with the thought that it might grope its way to solutions.

Against this scene, American leaders still seemed to me as worthy as, or more so than, most of their contemporaries abroad. They risked their lives, and two were killed in 1968, to make life for their fellow men better. There were, as always, a goodly company of crooks, scoundrels and hypocrites among them; but those who came to the top were deeply concerned men, trying their best to offer directions to peace and good-will.

1968 gave a writer little room for irony; there was too much bloodshed, too many people were hurt. The pursuit of novelty was also different than in other campaigns. Ten years ago, when I began writing of Presidential politics, I began with a cluster of candidates—a Kennedy, a Johnson, a Nixon, a Humphrey, a Stevenson. They were all still there in 1968, except for a Stevenson, whose mantle was assumed by Eugene McCarthy, who had nominated Stevenson in 1960. Never over any single decade of American politics, since the days of Clay, Calhoun and Webster, had the process seemed so stuck. Yet it was stuck only if one limited the story to the names of candidates. If one studied the people, all was different.

What was different was the entire nature of American life—not only the bursting condition of prosperity, not only the grind of unending war, not only the change in manners, not only the explosion of education, but all those movements of mind gathered together under the phrase "culture." Within this new culture was not only much good and elegance and concern, but also new ingredients of hate, indulgence and all-staining cynicism. The marvel of American politics previously had been its ability to channel passion into peaceful choice of directions. In 1968, hate burst out of the channel, and hate, whether from student ideologues, unabashed white racists or black extremists, incubated further hate, loosing lunatics, gunmen, rock-throwers and club-wielders. Roosevelt, in 1933, declaimed that the "only thing we have to fear is fear itself, nameless, unreasoning, unjustified terror." One might paraphrase this diagnosis and apply it to the politics of 1968 by saying that all we have to hate today is hate itself—nameless, unreasoning, unjustified hate.

A final word on the approach of this writer:

There are two ways one can go at the writing of history. It can be seen as a matter of aesthetics, as most European writers see it. In which case, if the writer is theologically sure of his own truth, he can decorate and adorn that truth by choosing from the myriad facts offered by events whatever he needs for convincing artistry. Symmetry, conviction, unconditioned eloquence follow easily on such inner assurance of what is right or wrong, or what must be shown as right and wrong. All events, in such histories, flow smoothly, irrevocably toward the conclusion the writer has known from the beginning. Or else history can be approached as journeyman reporters generally do: as a study of men making up their minds, prisoners of their information, captives of events, forced to decision when scissored by clash, acting either clumsily or gracefully when hit by the unexpected. This latter approach does not make for neat truths or cunning analysis. But that is the way history appears, as it happens, to those who must report its junction points. This book, like its predecessors, is, therefore, a reporter's book of a campaign; it tries to tell what happened to the American people in 1968, and how Richard Nixon came to be elected

President of the most powerful nation back on earth.

As a reporter, I must, as always, give my first thanks to my companions of the press—the countless men and women whose dispatches and observations have been made available to me, who have let me pick their brains or quote them, who have given me a "fill" on what I could not manage to see myself.

There are others to whom my gratitude requires specific mention by name. Foremost among these is Mrs. Dana K. Benenson, not only chief researcher and coordinator of this book, but also a stern executive and devoted partner whose spirit enriched the work from beginning to end. Christopher Chandler (of the *Chicago Sun-Times*) provided the best background of events at Chicago that I have read (though he is not responsible for my opinions), and should write his own book on that episode. Ray Jenkins of the *Alabama Journal* helped guide my thinking on George Wallace. Ralph Earle of M.I.T. provided useful information on student movements.

I cannot close without thanking Paul Hirschman, managing editor of Atheneum, for his enormous tolerance and spectacular efficiency in dealing with late-closing copy; and Carmen Nickel for her gleaning of the press. Nor shall I do more than mention the names of Simon Michael Bessie, President of Atheneum, and Nancy Bean White, my wife. Their contributions to this book are immeasurable, and their thought and help is woven into every paragraph.

New York, May, 1969

CONTENTS

PART ONE

PART TWO

PART THREE

PART
ONE

TET!—THE SHADOW ON
THE WALLS

I T WAS days before anyone could see the Tet offensive in perspective —perhaps weeks. But by then it was too late. For events lead a double life, and the appearance of events in politics is as important as their reality. Upon this contradiction between reality and appearance, all through 1968, American politics was to turn.

The first news of Tet seemed purely military, arriving as it did in the "E" ring of the Pentagon late Monday afternoon, January 29th, 1968, in a spurt, then a cascade, of action reports to the National Military Command Center. The National Military Command Center—or NMCC —gleams beneath its low ceiling with a continuous glare of harsh white light. But whoever passes its double-guarded entrance enters a world where all reality is reduced to symbols. When the gold curtains on the left are swept back, the sliding glassined wall maps mirror a globe of violence—divisions and missiles, ours and the enemy's, aircraft and submarines, movements and mysteries speckle and thread their surface. The translucent glass panels set in bakelite on the far wall illuminate the readiness or alert conditions of American force all around the globe—a missile homing in from outer space on New York would show here first. Day and night, in the subdued hubbub and clatter of messages, under the thirteen clocks that mark the time zones of the world, teams of seventeen officers monitor the American military dispersion, a general of the Army or flag-rank officer of the Navy always in command, a White House and a State Department observer always present. Constantly they test and re-test the open lines to all eight Specified and Unified Commands of the American military establishment that patrol the globe. Behind the wall maps are the three teletype receivers of MOLINK—the hot line to Moscow—and a Russian-speaking expert is never more than a few feet away. No less than 800 FLASH or IMMEDIATE messages surge through this room each twenty-four hours, recording the restless movements, large and small, of men and armies, the sporadic ticking of violence in a world that for twenty years has hovered on the edge of extinction.

Here, enshrined like myth, in January, 1968, was the visible symbol of American faith: that the power of the United States can be curbed by no one, that the instruments of American government need but the will to act and it is done.

In 1968 this faith was to be shattered—the myth of American power broken, the confidence of the American people in their government, their institutions, their leadership, shaken as never before since 1860.

But all this was not immediately apparent.

All through the late afternoon and early evening of Monday, January 29th, 1968, fragments of report had come stuttering into the National Command Center in Washington from MACV—the American command in Saigon—where it was already the dark early morning of Tuesday, January 30th. The enemy had struck at night, in the black, as he always did—but with the utmost precision and skill. At precisely midnight, Quinhon on the coast had been hit. At 12:35, Nhatrang, 100 miles south on the coast above the green deep waters of Camranh Bay, was hit, too. At 1:35, Pleiku, Kontum, Banmethuot were, according to the early reports, overrun; and then, at 3:30 in the morning (dusk when the news came to Washington), the mud-soaked Marine base of Danang, supposedly secure in the shelter of the Bay of Tourane, was under assault. Here, as the Vietnamese celebrated the Tet festival of the New Year while the night popped and sparkled with their firecrackers, came the thudding of enemy mortars, and six American planes blazed to the sky, showing the enemy his shells had found target. By evening in Washington the NMCC knew that seven major cities in South Vietnam were under attack and that the long-expected Communist winter-spring offensive was under way.

The news made only modest headlines the following morning. Names like Nhatrang, Pleiku, Kontum, Quinhon, Hoian, Danang had long since become unpronounceable staccato punctuations in a war which had become a blur that Americans did not quite understand.

The next morning, however, no blur could conceal the dimensions of what was happening. At three o'clock in the morning of January 31st, Wednesday, Saigon time, a Viet Cong suicide squad of nineteen men had blasted its way into the grounds of the American Embassy in Saigon, a diplomatic outpost built to be impregnable. All Saigon was under attack, its suburbs burning; the two major American airbases in South Vietnam, Bienhoa and Tansonnhut, were being mortared; and in the north that most beautiful of Vietnamese cities, Hue, with its moats and temples, its crenellated walls and history, its flowers and perfumed air, was, apparently, occupied in force by North Vietnamese main-force units.

These were not isolated raids; somehow the enemy had astounded the world and America with a force, a fury and a battlefield presence that gave the lie to all that Americans had been told for months. Aware that half a million men in one of America's great field armies were equipped with every device of miltary superiority, Americans believed that they were slowly, expensively, but surely winning a war in Asia. Yet here were facts in the morning papers, the blood, gore and flame in living color on evening television, and a tone in the reporting that reflected panic.

For Americans, a time of rethinking had begun. Had the government deceived its people? Or had the government deceived itself? And, in either case, whom could one trust? Trust was to be one of the major themes of the campaign of 1968. For those candidates for the Presidency who in January, 1968, were preparing to seek the confidence and mandate of the people, it was a time of reassessment of American purpose and their own postures.

Among those thus seeking a midway position between politics and reality that week was a guest at the Howard Johnson Inn at Nashua, New Hampshire, who registered Thursday night, February 1st, under the name of "Mr. Benjamin Chapman." All that week the so-styled "Mr. Chapman" had been in New York supervising the last details of his final, irrevocable, but hardly surprising open announcement of candidacy for President of the United States. On Wednesday, the day before, when Americans had learned that all South Vietnam was in flames, some 150,000 personal letters had gone out to every household in New Hampshire telling Hampshiremen of this candidate's entry in their primary, and signed with his true name: Richard M. Nixon. His aides had chosen the alias of "Chapman" for hotel-registration purposes only; the concealment would enliven the drama of his first appearance in the flesh in Manchester, New Hampshire, as challenger to George Romney of Michigan in the first round of the Presidential sweepstakes.

Thursday had been a cold day of drizzling rain in Manhattan, where Richard Nixon then lived; all commercial flights to New England had been canceled, and thus, at eight P.M., he had driven up the East Side of Manhattan to the Butler Marine Air Terminal, where a privately chartered Convair waited. At nine P.M. Nixon boarded with three young aides, Patrick Buchanan, Raymond K. Price and Dwight Chapin, amateurs all, completely inexperienced in Presidential politics. At 9:17, with wheels up, he began to leaf through his opening speech and the fifty-page briefing book his staff had prepared on New Hampshire politics. But for him, as for the nation, there were more important things pressing on attention, and so he began to chat with his young men, among whom, for the rest of the year, he would be always at his most relaxed and convivial. One of them remembers that he wanted to talk about Vietnam; the headlines of the previous forty-eight hours were beginning to seep in. Mr. Nixon was of the opinion that Vietnam would, indeed, be a key issue in the campaign—and in New Hampshire this issue, being one of foreign policy, would work for him and against George Romney, whose authority lay in domestic affairs.

Only one advance man greeted the yet-to-become 37th President of the United States at the Boston airport—Nick Ruwe, who proceeded to drive him in a rented car through the dark to the Nashua hideaway where, as "Benjamin Chapman," he would pass the night. The next day, at two in the afternoon, in the crowded Meeting Rooms A and B of the Holiday Inn in Manchester, he faced the first full press conference since he had bade farewell forever to the press, five years earlier in the Beverly-Hilton Hotel in Los Angeles.

This time the very first question was about Vietnam, and Mr. Nixon passed.[1] He, like every other American, was completely confused by the situation in the field. The next day, Saturday, he received the voters for the first time at St. Anselm's College just outside Manchester and their concern must have become quite clear to him. This correspondent, eavesdropping on the reception line, remembers the file-by of people, overwhelmingly middle-class and middle-aged, and how frequently the procession stopped as mothers flustered a question to the candidate. Mr. Nixon would pass the file along to Mrs. Nixon, saying quietly to his wife as he moved the line, "This lady has a boy in South Vietnam. . . . This young fellow's father is a sergeant in Korea. . . . We're going to see to it that boys of fourteen or fifteen, when they grow up, don't have to go off to any more wars like this. . . ." Mr. Nixon had, until this point, the national reputation of being somewhat of a hawk on Viet-

----

[1] "Q: What are you going to put forward to the American people as a policy towards Vietnam?

"A: . . . At this point I think it is very important to make quite clear that when American forces in Vietnam are under very devastating assault on a desperate —I would hope—last ditch effort by the Viet Cong, we must recognize that that effort by the Viet Cong and the North Vietnamese is not directed toward our forces in South Vietnam. It is directed toward the public opinion in the United States. I want to make very clear as one member of the loyal opposition and as a candidate for the Presidency that we may be divided on many issues but that the enemy . . . cannot and should not count on American division to gain politically in the U.S. what they cannot gain militarily in Vietnam. I begin with that proposition. I have had and will continue to have differences with the administration on the conduct of this war. . . . Our disagreement on the war in Vietnam is not about the goal. Our disagreement is about the means to achieve that goal . . . and I will be spelling out ways and means that that can be accomplished during the course of the campaign. . . ."

nam; but he sounded nothing like a hawk on the receiving line. In the next few days his staff began preparing a major new positioning speech on the Vietnam war which would clearly establish where he now stood. The nation craved new leadership, new answers.

The other candidates were similarly perplexed, wherever they were:

§ Hubert Humphrey, Vice-President and later Democratic standard-bearer, was in Washington. He had been excluded, for years, from both the war council and the strategy of his chief, Lyndon B. Johnson. The sterile intelligence reports which he, officially as Vice-President, did see had indicated that there was trouble brewing in Vietnam. But he had not been included, as had been members of the President's closest official family, in the analyses of December which had informed the White House of the dimensions of the enemy effort then building up. When, on January 30th, the Vice-President of the United States read of the sweep of the Tet offensive in the morning papers, it was as much a shock to him as to the general public.

§ Nelson Rockefeller of New York was that week preoccupied with other matters. His passion, involvement and enthusiasm for foreign affairs, the position, role and posture of America in the great outer world, had been the essence of his concern for over twenty-five years. His position on Vietnam had already changed—once a hawk, a deep-commitment man, his thinking had begun to alter in the fall of 1967; he was trying to think through a better way to use the instruments of American power in Asia. He had and retains a lordly superior attitude to technicians, who, he believes, are tools to be used by the leader for the leader's purposes. But as Vietnam exploded with the Tet offensive, his generation-long concern with the instruments of American foreign policy was obscured by more homely concerns. In the streets of New York the instruments of sanitation, the garbage men, were on strike, and New York was mounding with stinking swill and heaps of refuse. This lay on his mind as he approached one of his chronic clashes with John Lindsay, another putative candidate for the Presidency. Messrs. Rockefeller and Lindsay began the political year with a garbage strike, and saw the year out with a schoolteachers' strike. At home, as abroad, the instruments seemed unresponsive to leadership.

§ Among Democrats, the unraveling of the year was probably clearest to Eugene McCarthy. On the morning of Wednesday, January 31st, he attended an executive committee meeting of the Senate Foreign Relations Committee which discussed the Gulf of Tonkin resolution and the *Pueblo* incident; and in the afternoon he received, briefly, a group of his supporters from New Jersey to discuss his prospects in that state. But there seemed little substance to the McCarthy campaign at the moment. A man moved by conscience, he had offered himself two months earlier as candidate-martyr for the Presidency on a single plank: Peace.

Considered a fool by political reporters—whom he disdained—he had denounced the war as "immoral," and set off to lead a campaign much as Saint Francis of Assisi might have done. While he preached brotherhood, he left it to others to organize the cause. The deputy of this new Franciscan order and campaign manager at the time of Tet was Blair Clark, a one-time publisher and broadcasting executive, ever ready for combat, who had urged the candidate, against his own instinct, into the New Hampshire primary contest. Clark had hired a curly-haired, twenty-three-year-old dropout of the Harvard Divinity School, Sam Brown, to explore and rouse student sentiment against the war. Beyond this, at the time of Tet, there was nothing in the McCarthy campaign but a guerrilla potential, latent across the country, of professors, students and intellectuals, whose underground leadership had offered, and persuaded McCarthy to accept, a Merovingian role in their plan to bring peace. For many years students and professors of political science had been taught or had preached the doctrine of political participation—now, they felt, was the time to participate.

At the moment of Tet, however, the McCarthy campaign, the first announced candidacy, stood at ground zero. An occasional cluster of students—chiefly from Smith, Amherst and Harvard—had, in January, driven from Greater Boston to McCarthy headquarters in a store-front on Pleasant Street in Concord, New Hampshire, to paste labels on mailings and take in the skiing if the weather was good, and then returned to classes. No one took them seriously. A number of supposedly secret polls—three by Republicans, one by Robert Kennedy, one commissioned by the Democratic National Committee for Lyndon Johnson—reported McCarthy's probable percentage of the New Hampshire primary vote as low as 8, none higher than 11. Nor did the candidate seem to take himself seriously as he wandered through the snows of upper New Hampshire like a solitary troubadour, an Irish bard, singing his sad lay to the unhearing White Mountains.

Tet was swiftly to change this appreciation of Eugene McCarthy.

§ More slowly came the impact on another candidate, Robert F. Kennedy. Of the anguish of Robert F. Kennedy all through the last year of his life there will be much more to say later. The Democratic Party was his party, by inheritance and family; but that party had misled the nation, and thus came his torment. His loyalty to the Party went deeper into the spirit of the man than any outsider could imagine; but included in loyalty to the Party was an implied loyalty to its leader, Lyndon B. Johnson, whom he loathed. He had been under pressure of friends and self-seekers since 1967 to take the Party away from the President, but had resisted despite every enticement and blandishment. On the Tuesday morning of the Tet offensive he had previously agreed to breakfast with a closed inner circle of political reporters in Washington who link together as one of the prime transmission belts of political opinion. They met privately in "The President's Room" of the National Press Club, and one of the reporters—Peter Lisagor of the Chicago *Daily News*—brought with him the torn sheets of agency ticker-file on the outbreaks in Vietnam. Kennedy talked with the men off the record, and when they insisted on some public statement of opinion, he toyed with phrases. He still would not challenge the President for control of Party and nation. Tet was not entirely clear to him. His first formulation was that he would not seek the Presidency under any "conceivable circumstances." For the record, however, he changed that to a statement that he would not challenge Johnson for renomination "under any foreseeable circumstances." Within forty-eight hours those unforeseeable circumstances were manifest. Nine days later he stood before an audience in Chicago and declared that the Tet offensive had "shattered the mask of official illusion with which we have concealed our true circumstances, even from ourselves." That day, for the first time, he explored directly with Mayor Richard Daley of Chicago the possibility of un-horsing the President. Daley rebuffed him; but the rebuff was friendly, for Daley, too, hated the Vietnam war. Daley told him to play it cool, and wait. Notwithstanding Daley's advice, within six weeks Robert Kennedy would also be a candidate for the Presidency.

§ Almost alone in his understanding of what was happening in the field of combat was Lyndon B. Johnson himself. His misfortune was that he could not or would not make clear this understanding to Americans as a President should, or explain the mission, purpose and fate of their sons.

For months the White House had known of a coming crisis in South Vietnam. The enemy had begun mobilization for the Tet offensive six months earlier, in July. This slow, painful preparation, entailing the movement of 200,000 men by foot over hundreds of miles of jungle trails, could not be concealed from American intelligence. By December 16th a summary of the enemy's intentions and capabilities, based on massive documentation, had been prepared in a top-secret memorandum for the President's eyes alone, informing him in detail that Hanoi was preparing a climactic drive, with all its resources, to wipe out the South Vietnamese government, timed to coincide with a general uprising and culminate in the installation of coalition governments in Saigon and across the countryside.

The President had secretly acted on this information. He had earlier promised the command in Vietnam to raise American combat strength in Vietnam to 106 maneuver battalions (up from 90) by the end of 1968. Now, hastily, the 101st Airborne Division was packed in planes, and by Christmas 102 of the promised 106 American maneuver battalions were already deployed in the field. Where necessary, the President spread warning: on December 21st in the cabinet room of the Australian government in Canberra he personally briefed the Australian cabinet on the dark days ahead, the *kamikaze* tactics we might expect in the coming offensive, the American troops being flown out, the promised new division from Korea, the need of greater Australian exertion in the common cause.

Mr. Johnson, however, found it unnecessary either to inform the American Cabinet (except for those directly concerned with security) or the American people. All through the fall, peaking in November, a series of happy stories was told the American people as first Ambassador Bunker and then General Westmoreland reported to the nation that all was well. The opinion polls reflected these reports and, for the first time in over a year, Mr. Johnson's popularity and public confidence in the President began to climb. By January 28th, 1968, his rating in the polls stood at 48 percent—a figure he was never to achieve again. Some in the White House urged that the President, in his State of the Union message, take the American people into his confidence, that he warn them of what lay ahead; Mr. Johnson, on January 17th, chose, however, to report otherwise (". . . the enemy has been defeated in battle after battle . . . the number of South Vietnamese living in areas under government protection tonight has grown by more than a million since January of last year . . .") and drew national attention to a new peace tentacle and possible negotiation with the Hanoi government.

Mr. Johnson, thus, was the only man in American leadership who faced the crisis with complete *sang-froid*. He is always best in a tight, hard crisis, as he had demonstrated in the moment of his assumption of office in Dallas in 1963 and again in the Israeli crisis of 1967. Other members of the Cabinet were to learn first of the Tet offensive in the morning newspapers and be carried away by the gloom that swept the nation. But Johnson himself was firmer, cooler, more self-possessed than even his commanders in the field. He had received the Tuesday reports of battle almost simultaneously with those coming into the Military Command Center, and had spent a bad day on Wednesday while American troops battled for control of the American Embassy in Saigon against Viet Cong commandos. More than twenty-five combat reports had come to him from Saigon before, in mid-afternoon, Westmoreland had personally telephoned from Saigon to reassure the President that he (Westmoreland) was telephoning from the Embassy and the Embassy was cleared. Mr. Johnson then settled down to watch the progress of events of whose outcome he had no doubt. By Saturday, only four days after combat had broken out, while Richard Nixon in Concord, New Hampshire, was making the maiden speech of his campaign and demanding new national leadership, Lyndon Johnson could confidently report to a press conference in Washington that the enemy's military effort was a "complete failure."

That the Communist Tet offensive was indeed a complete military failure there could be no doubt in the following weeks. Few greater disasters have ever been visited on an armed force than that which Hanoi invited on its troops. Within one month some 42,300 enemy soldiers had been slaughtered, a third of the entire strike force, in one of the great blood-lettings of modern war. Not one of the twenty-six provincial capitals attacked by the Communists fell. The much-despised South Vietnamese troops found, suddenly, the skills, the will and the cohesion to fight back and began to shape up, for the first time in five years of war, as an army with a vitality of its own. In the bombed and lacerated cities of South Vietnam, scores of thousands of *attentistes* and middle-class Vietnamese who had waited without commitment to either side found they had no choice but to support their fragile government against insurrection and civil war. Enemy commando units, flung into action with no directives or guidance but to attack, found no way to flee, no route or method of withdrawal prepared to save them for another round of fighting. The longest-planned, the most meticulously prepared enemy effort of the long, long war had come to nothing—except, in Mr. Johnson's words in the same press conference, for a "psychological victory." And, Mr. Johnson continued, "when the American people know the facts, when the world knows the facts, . . . I do not believe that they will achieve a psychological victory."

But the facts were less important than the psychology, and psychology left the enemy in command. Of their "psychological victory," Mr. Johnson was to be the chief victim within two months. For, as the Tet offensive was slowly, inexorably crushed, he could not then envision either Party or nation repudiating its wartime chief.

On the third night of the Tet offensive, Wednesday, January 31st, the President had guests at the White House, and one of them remembers him that evening with complete admiration. Johnson had not been to bed for thirty-six hours; but now the Embassy in Saigon was clear and he felt the crisis was over; he wanted to relax, talking politics. He sat upstairs in the long-hall sitting-room of the private floor of the White House, an attentive and gracious host, drinking Fresca. The President was not worried about the situation in the cities in Vietnam—he felt that was under control; the condition of the Demilitarized Zone still weighed heavily on his mind, particularly the embattled Marine outpost of Khesanh; but, said the President, General Wheeler had sworn in blood, today, yesterday, three days ago, that the Viets couldn't take Khesanh. (As a matter of fact, they did not—and two Viet Cong divisions, almost 15,000 men, were wiped out by American air power.) The President was convinced that we were going to break the enemy's back this time—and then the President reflected on some of the great decisions of his administration and was led forward by the reminiscence to the Presidential campaign. He was proud of his intervention in the Dominican Republic—that had kept the Communists out of the Caribbean, we had nailed them, nailed them. But the hairiest moment, he remembered, was the Israeli crisis in the summer of 1967, when he and Kosygin had been on the hot line twenty-seven times; Kosygin had actually initiated the conversations with an ultimatum to the United States demanding it restrain the Israelis, implying the use of nuclear weapons. Johnson had outfaced Kosygin, deployed the Sixth Fleet in the Mediterranean at flank speed, and Kosygin had backed down. The President wished he could tell that story in the election this November, but it would embarrass Kosygin and he really wanted to get Kosygin to a summit conference and make a peace. So he couldn't use that story, much as it would help in the election, if it would spoil the chance of a peaceful summit—and he really got along fine with Kosygin, Kosygin was a country boy like himself.

As for the election itself—he wasn't worried about that. McCarthy would get some votes in the primaries, and Bobby (Senator Kennedy) wasn't going to give any trouble. Johnson wasn't worried about Bobby because Dick Daley, the best mayor in the country, was standing by the President. There was no way for any Democratic politician to walk out on a sitting President, no matter how rough the going was, and Dick Daley was firm. Dick Daley had come by a while ago and told the President how, in nineteen-an'-forty-eight, when Daley had been just a precinct captain and Ed Kelly had been boss of the Chicago delegation of the 1948 Democratic convention, Ed Kelly had decided Truman couldn't win and thus let the Chicago delegation make up its own mind. Only two of the Cook County leaders had stuck by Truman—Dick Daley and Jake Arvey. With people like Dick Daley on your side, said the President, you don't worry about people like Gene McCarthy and Bobby Kennedy. It was going to be a long summer and a long fall, but in the end the Democrats, as they always do, would kiss and make up, and all would be well.

One must sympathize with Lyndon Johnson, whose historic dimensions will appear only as he fades off into the sunset and sagebrush of South Texas. The Presidency was both an ecstasy and a torment for him, and for months, from 1966 on, he had talked, as every man does in private inner debate—now of quitting his job, now of scaling new heights. The two thoughts were always in his mind, to stay or to quit, contending against each other as the Presidential year of 1968 opened. But the outside world, starting at Tet, was to force him to decision.

Were there no outside world, if America inhabited a satellite planet, capable of controlling its own environment, its own circumstances, its own future, Lyndon Johnson might conceivably have gone down as the greatest of twentieth-century Presidents. But America does not—and one of the cardinal duties of the President is to educate not only himself, but his people, about the nature of the outside world and its challenges. He must understand not only the history of his own people as they change, but the history of other peoples as they, too, change about us. A President can trust no one and no theology except his own sense of history; all the instruments of government must be subordinate to this feeling of his for history; and when this supreme guidance is lacking, the instruments themselves are useless.

It so happened, however, that by the beginning of the year 1968 the instruments of American government had failed American purpose as never before. This was what had become obvious to the American people at the Tet offensive—staining the vast majority with that morbid, unhappy mood which lasted until election night. Americans questioned the very capacity of government to govern, and were to thrust forward, as by-products of this questioning, two new movements in American politics, both of them, for all their novelty, enormously old-fashioned— a peace movement on the left which believed that America had the capacity, all by itself, to sweet-talk the Communist world to peace; and later, as its counterpart on the right, the Wallace movement which believed that America had, all by itself, the ability to impose victory and settlement.

And it had all begun in a place named Vietnam, first visited by an American skipper named John White in June, 1819. Of John White's memories we have chiefly the account of his enormous frustration with a strange land and an Oriental bureaucracy, whose long-fingernailed mandarins plagued him from the day of his arrival to the day of his departure. One need not reach as far back as John White to begin the story of the election of 1968—but its roots, wherever one begins, go back to the clash of two civilizations, one American, the other Asian, neither understanding the other, which was to bring grief to both. John F. Kennedy in melancholy moments used to tell the story of the outbreak of the First World War—how, shortly after the long diplomatic negotiations of the summer of 1914 had ended in war, the German Chancellor, Bethmann-Hollweg, was approached by his aged predecessor, Prince von Bülow. "How did it all begin?" von Bülow is reported to have asked the Chancellor. And the Chancellor replied, sadly, *"Ach,* if one could only say."

So it was with Americans in 1968 as we contemplated a war we could not win—no one could explain how it had happened.

Vietnam had been there for a quarter of a century before 1968, a distant Asian menace, gnawing away at a dream of American statesmanship. And we knew all but nothing about it from the days of Franklin D. Roosevelt, who first perceived it as a problem in the new world he meant to shape, to the day of this writing.

Vietnam was only a place when John White first docked at Vung-tau—not a nation. It was a place under the vast umbrella of Chinese civilization where, for centuries, Annamite pioneers had been moving south into the unsettled jungles of the southern bulge of the Asian continent; their original language was a pudding of Thai-Khmer-Lao words, upon whose communicants the Chinese had imposed their culture and literature much as the Romans had imposed theirs on the barbarian Germans and Celts. Hating the Chinese, the Viets nonetheless were led to accept the values of Chinese civilization as their own—an imported contradiction to begin with, for in order to govern, they accepted the traditions of Confucian order with its disciplined mandarinate; yet to live with each other, they found it easier to accept the warmer, family-oriented tradition of Chinese Buddhism. Upon this uneasy folk, torn then as now by a civil war of their own between north and south, French conquerors imposed an imperium early in the nineteenth century—along with the built-in contradictions of French civilization, that strange unceasing clash between the logic of Cartesian thinking and Celtic individualism which creates the prickliness of French character. Translated into the politics of empire, the French presence made of Vietnam at once a prison and a museum. Exquisite French scholarship explored the ancient history and archeology of Vietnam; exquisite French cruelty made it the most savage colony in Asia. In my youth in Asia, I remember it as the place where I first saw grown men strike other grown men and watched the stricken cringe—white Frenchmen had the right to slap awkward native waiters who spilled soup, or slap native rickshawmen who argued about the fare. It was a place where the state monopoly's purchase of opium exceeded by five times French expenditures on schools, libraries and hospitals combined. It was a place where any yellow man seeking dignity could only hate white men.

Vietnam grew so slowly into an American problem that no man can identify when the fatal miscalculation took place. Americans, brought up in the pragmatic, responsible tradition of American history, commonly seek clear reasons and a clear chain of responsibility for events. When, for example, an American orbital shot goes wrong in the great space adventure, American practice traces the chain of responsibility from the top down to the precise individual or procedure that has erred. But in trying to understand Vietnam, no one could trace the chain of responsibility, no one could identify the single critical error with date and name. Americans had been brought up in a history that identified date and enemy: "Twas the Eighteenth of April, '75"; or "Millions for defense, but not one cent for tribute"; or "Remember the Alamo," or the firing on Fort Sumter, or "Remember the *Maine*," "Remember the *Lusitania*," "Remember Pearl Harbor." All American wars had begun with a date, a cause, a reason.

In Vietnam there was no phrase to which one could pin emotion; Americans were required to fight a war without hate. The real culprit—ignorance—could never be made clear.

For the ignorance, every branch of American government and every institution of American learning could share the blame. When, in 1950, the State Department had been persuaded to consider French Indo-China something more than a geographical expression, it was still regarded, in the diplomatic service, as a penal colony of the Paris Embassy—a distant Oriental Siberia to which were exiled superannuated, French-speaking American foreign-service personnel or ne'er-do-wells who could not make their mark in Europe. The two American consulates in Hanoi and Saigon together employed no more than seven Americans. The newly formed South East Asia desk, which was supposed to understand and judge all the ongoing revolutions in Burma, Indonesia, Malaysia, Thailand and Indo-China, had source materials and information that filled only one half of a file drawer in a four-drawer filing case. Harvard University, then, as now, the greatest center of East Asia research in the world, still left the study of French Indo-China to its French department. No serious course in Vietnamese language or history was given anywhere in America; for ten years up until 1966 the scholarly chambers of American Ph.D. factories produced not a single notable thesis on Vietnam.

Persuading the State Department's bureaucracy that we should indeed learn something about Vietnam came hard. The French language, State believed, was all that was needed; America dealt only with French colonial officials and their French-speaking native *compradores* in the big cities. Not until 1954, when we had linked our policy to the Geneva settlement of that year, did we send the first young American officer to Dalat to study the native language of the peoples in the countryside. One or two a year followed, men of very junior rank, until a training program was begun which produced two specialists in 1957, two in 1958, two in 1959, two in 1960, until in 1962, for some unfathomable reason, the bureaucracy decided we had had enough and trained none.[2] At that time,

[2] Not until 1964 did we begin an accelerated program to train officers for this prime area of American concern when 7 men were rushed through an accelerated course of six to ten months. Not until 1967 did the White House, in February, become aware of the need at the operational level and authorize the Foreign Service Institute to open a true Vietnam Training Center in Alexandria, Virginia. That program, beginning in April, 1967, began to recruit young men in batches of 10 to 20, to be rushed through an intense forty-two-week program, the batches sequenced to graduate at six-week intervals. Not until April, 1968, eight weeks after the Tet disaster, did the first group of 16 students come off the line to be rushed to Vietnam, where they have performed, as do their successors, magnificently. Up until April of 1968, thus, American statecraft possessed in all probably 40 men with a crude understanding of Vietnamese language and culture, with less than 20 of those in the field, responsible for guiding half a million American troops, of whom 25,000

of course, we were allied with, and our honor was committed to, the unspeakable dictatorship of Ngo Dinh Diem. For ten years—under the Truman, Eisenhower and Kennedy leaderships—Assistant Secretaries of State always agreed in principle to the need for more language officers and greater understanding of Vietnam; but the nether bureaucracy of State's personnel department could never crank principle into action. Not only were Americans totally ignorant of the war they undertook, but they were, apparently, unconcerned. Never through the long agony has any senior official at the State Department been solely responsible for a consideration of Vietnam; no officer with rank as lowly even as Assistant Secretary of State has ever been given the responsibility for the politics of that area of conflict as his sole concern.

Somewhere in this general ignorance lies the prime reason for the disaster—difficult to explain even to this day.

The generating cause of the conflict, however, was much clearer; and only a total breakdown of political leadership could have let that cause be so clouded as to permit the politics of 1968 to ring with the charge of "immorality" without instant rebuttal.

The cause in Vietnam was the cause of America for half a century, a cause made clear to the world by the Democratic Party of the United States. This holds that the world, to make progress, must change in peace; that recognized boundaries are sacred, to be changed by negotiation, not infiltration or invasion. If there is any fragile form of world order today, 400,000 American battle deaths in four wars in this century have created that world order. Ever since the end of World War II, whether in Azerbaijan in 1946, in Berlin in 1948, in Korea in 1950, in Lebanon in 1958, this has been the commitment on which the orderly world rests; this has been the shield under which even our former enemies, Germany and Japan, have learned to thrive.

It was a Republican, John Foster Dulles, who, in 1954, after the French defeat at Dienbienphu, extended this shield to South Vietnam, wisely or not. And from 1954 on, the defense of South Vietnam became part of the general commitment which America had made to all friends, allies, neutrals and enemies around the world. The commitment was made to a place, South Vietnam, and traced by a line, the 17th parallel; but of the nation which that line bisected, we were, as we have seen, totally ignorant—ignorant of its languages, its customs, its aspirations, its heritage; ignorant of the hate of its mandarin dictator, Ngo Dinh Diem; ignorant of the thinness of its social structure; ignorant of the nature of the enemy within the southern state and the Hanoi regime.

But the enemy not only knew its own people, it had learned by

---

had died in battle, through a war which all had long since agreed could only be won by political understanding.

study and reflection a great deal about Americans and their way of making war. Three hundred American military advisers in South Vietnam grew slowly to 600 in 1961 and trained a South Vietnamese army as they had trained a South Korean army for the last Asian war we had won. But the Communist enemy meant never again to mass troops on a line to be massacred by American fire power in positional war. For some twenty years the Communists of Indo-China had been at war— against French, against Chinese, against each other; and they had elevated the doctrines of partisan warfare of Mao Tse-tung to a level of sophistication that Americans do not yet recognize. In essence, their philosophy of war was to transform all society into an environment of hate in which no neutrals could survive; men, women, children, aged and young, must be fused with wrath, and embrace the tactics and agents of terror. There is no way of fighting such a war except by politics and counter-terror; American ignorance gave us no knowledge of Vietnamese politics, and American tradition shrinks from the tactics of torture, assassination and terror. Thus the quandary when John F. Kennedy came to power in 1961—a quandary which by 1968 seemed to offer Americans a choice only between surrender to the enemy, or exterminating him by a brutality of which we were incapable.

Lyndon Johnson's first involvement in Vietnam had come on a quick tour in the summer of 1961; as a Senator he had always been against involvement in land war in Asia, stubbornly opposing American participation in the French war in Tonkin at the time of their agony at Dienbienphu in 1954 when Richard Nixon, then an interventionist, supported an American air strike. From his first summer visit to Vietnam in 1961, Johnson reported privately to the President, John F. Kennedy, that "the participation of American ground troops in the war in Vietnam is neither desirable nor necessary." In this opinion he was supported by some of the most impressive names in American military life—General Matthew Ridgeway, the victor of Korea; Lieutenant General James Gavin, the most lucid thinker in the Pentagon in the decade of the 1950's; General Lauris Norstad, who had said, "The moment the first American arrives in Vietnam to shoot or be shot at, there's no way left open to us but escalation."

But from 1961 on, the guerrilla bands of the Viet Cong were spreading in South Vietnam by a process of terrorist metastasis; and as American military personnel rose to 16,000 by the fall of 1963, so too did enemy strength. Clumsily realizing that this war was a political war after all, American Intelligence, with the full knowledge of the Secretary of State and the President, first learned, then approved, of a plot to remove President Diem by *coup d'état*. On the weekend of President Kennedy's assassination, a full-dress review of the situation in Vietnam had been called at the White House; and Lyndon Johnson, presiding over his first major decision of state even as John F. Kennedy's body lay in the rotunda of the Capitol, could not, most understandably, reverse a policy on which America and his dead predecessor had been set for so many years. No history had ever explained Asia to Lyndon Johnson.

1964 was a year of election in America—and a year of speeding deterioration and gloom in South Vietnam as Communist control spread through the countryside and South Vietnamese military units, as large as companies and battalions, dissolved in defeat. It was thus, while the President's attention was fixed on the grand adventure of the 1964 election, that the instruments of American military strength and diplomacy seemed, by some momentum of past inertia, to move by themselves. They were provoked, to be sure—there could be no doubt that the Communists were closing for the kill in South Vietnam. In August came a first sharp clash: an American intelligence ship had been cruising in the Gulf of Tonkin, testing enemy intentions, and Communist torpedo boats took the high seas to attack. Despite later controversy, there could be no doubt then, and there is no doubt now, that the enemy initiated assault —American intelligence intercepted and decoded the orders radioed to the torpedo boats to attack. For months the bureaucracy had been considering and urging on the President some legislative authorization to enlarge America's power to respond. Hastily, thus, in mid-campaign of 1964, the President thrust forward a resolution, known later as the Tonkin Gulf Resolution, and, by a vote of 88 to 2, the Senate passed it; the House also consented by 416 to 0; and the President was authorized to take "all necessary steps including the use of armed Forces" to assist any nation that requested aid "in defense of its freedom" under the Southeast Asia Pact.

The election proceeded in America, and the war proceeded in Asia —the weekend before the election, Communists shelled and killed four Americans at the air base at Bienhoa. In the interregnum between the election and the inauguration, the enemy grew bolder, testing American response here, probing there, raiding elsewhere. The situation seemed, in the Pentagon, to cry out for retaliation. But first there had to be a basic policy decision, and only the President could give leadership.

Within the bureaucracies, wills and philosophies clashed, and clashed again. Shortly before the election of 1964, Under Secretary of State George Ball presented himself as the first heretic, and offered for consideration a sharply reasoned, eloquently persuasive, top-secret memorandum advocating the immediate liquidation of the war in Vietnam. Ball's proposal was discussed at several successive Saturday-afternoon meetings of Rusk, McNamara and Bundy; and rejected. Since the President was preoccupied with the election, Ball let the matter drop, not pressing it further. In State, in Pentagon, other task groups and study groups piled paper on paper, hoping the President would give them the guidance they sought. The President insisted, over and over again, that he had made up his mind to do "what was necessary." He could not, however, specify, as one counselor remembers, "necessary for what"; and when pressed on Vietnam, might ramble off into a pictorial essay on a completely different subject.

Secretary of Defense Robert McNamara and, the President's National Security Assistant, McGeorge Bundy had both, through the long election campaign, longed for the day when the President could give his full attention to Vietnam and provide the national decision they required. Together, finally, after the election they prepared for his new administration a seven-page memorandum known, in inner circles, as the Fork-in-the-Y memorandum. On January 25th, five days after his inaugural address, they delivered it. America, they said, was approaching a fork in the Y in Vietnam. One fork led to complete withdrawal and acceptance of the loss of South Vietnam; but it meant the shameful, precipitate withdrawal of the 23,300 American troops stationed there on December 31st, 1964, on any terms the enemy would permit. The other fork led to an increase in the commitment—for without increased American support *either* by ground troops *or* by air strikes on the north, South Vietnam could not be held. McNamara and Bundy required decision.

The President pondered for a few days and then dispatched McGeorge Bundy to Vietnam to review the alternatives in the field. Already in Bundy's mind there had been shaped the conviction that there was no middle course between defeat, entailing the loss of all Southeast Asia, or American participation in defense of that area against growing Communist boldness. Already, too, Secretary of Defense McNamara and Secretary of State Rusk, had come to the conclusion that the next Viet Cong or North Vietnamese attack on Americans or American installations must bring reprisal and retaliation.

They had not long to wait. On the night of February 6th, 1965, in the mountain town of Pleiku in South Vietnam an explosive charge planted by Viet Cong terrorists blew up an American army barracks, killing eight American servicemen. News arrived in the Pentagon between four and five in the afternoon. Again an incident. Should America retaliate or not? On the urging of McNamara, the President summoned a few members of the National Security Council for a meeting as soon after six as possible in the Cabinet Room of the White House. Hastily, McNamara, Deputy Secretary of Defense Cyrus Vance and Chief of Staff Earle Wheeler were detailed to find out the exact facts, the number of killed and wounded, and assemble the contingency plans listing American options. Such plans, for any conceivable crisis, are always kept in the huge vault, protected by fantastic electronic security devices, just off the Secretary of Defense's imperial-sized office. With these plans, Vance, Wheeler and McNamara drove to the White House in the Secretary's limousine to join the National Security Council. And though the options they brought ranged from no retaliation whatsoever through the bombing of targets in the north (grouped in clusters of importance to the number of ninety-eight) to the sending of ground forces, the span of alternatives before the American government was thus limited to those conceived by the uniformed bureaucracy of the Pentagon. This was a time for choice—but within a range defined by the instruments of government, not its policy-makers.

The meeting was a gloomy one; no one wanted war; but the issue was ill-joined. Present were Secretary and Deputy Secretary of Defense Robert McNamara and Cyrus Vance; Secretary, Under Secretary and Assistant Secretary of State Dean Rusk, George Ball and William Bundy; from CIA, its chief, John McCone, and its executive secretary, Bromley Smith; and several others. The President was quiet, breaking the meeting only with grave, insistent questions. McNamara led off by describing the situation and the options of retaliation; Ball demurred—he had long wanted to end the war by withdrawal and insisted that tactics would develop a life of their own. McNamara narrowed the question: Did we want to retaliate or not? Ball again demurred: Soviet Premier Kosygin was at the moment in Hanoi—a direct bombing while he was there would be an affront to his presence. McNamara detailed the clusters of retaliatory targets grouped by priorities. The President went around the room, probing each man for a view and a decision. The conversation moved by itself to the question of which of the targets open to them should be chosen from the panel of military responses. The question of South Vietnamese participation in the retaliatory air strike was raised. The President wanted to know McGeorge Bundy's reaction in Saigon; and, opportunely, at this moment—seven in the evening in Washington, seven in the morning in Saigon—McGeorge Bundy telephoned directly to the White House. He had been staying overnight in Saigon with Ambassador Maxwell Taylor, had been wakened at four by news of the bombing, proceeded directly to the MACV Situation Room, conferred there with Westmoreland and was now, on his own initiative, telephoning the White House. Vance withdrew to the Situation Room in the White House basement and took the call—a fuzzy, guarded conversation over an open line—and came back to report that Bundy agreed with the dominant sentiment: to strike in retaliation. It was, recalls one of the participants, never quite clear what we were doing; the general thought, at the moment, was one of tit-for-tat—one air strike in response to the blowing up of the Pleiku barracks. Another recalls it as an either/or situation—either use air power or send in combat troops, and it was better not to send ground troops.

After about an hour and a quarter, the President went around the room again, and all agreed, with the exception of Ball, that strike they must. The President withdrew to his Oval Office; McNamara, Vance and Wheeler were left alone in the Cabinet Room to draft the orders to Admiral Ulysses Grant Sharp, Commander-in-Chief Pacific, to strike. The President did not choose to read the draft; he trusted them; and they drove back to the Pentagon to flash the order to the Pacific Command.

On the afternoon of February 7th, in a tit-for-tat response, forty-nine American planes struck at barracks and staging areas of the Viet Cong, strafing and blasting in the vicinity of Donghoi in North Vietnam. Three days later another terrorist raid struck at the coastal city of Quinhon. In retaliation, the next day, 160 U.S. and South Vietnamese planes bombed a military installation of about 125 buildings in the area of Chap Le—forty miles north of the 17th parallel. No one remembers when tit-for-tat became the systematic bombing of the north, code-named Rolling Thunder.

Of those involved in high policy, only two seemed to have deep reservations about the bombings. One was Hubert Humphrey, who opposed the bombings as an affront to the presence of Soviet Premier Kosygin in North Vietnam; Humphrey had been absent from the meeting of February 6th, but had separated himself from its conclusions at the Cabinet meeting of the 10th, and again in a private session with the President on the night of February 11th; thereafter he was not to be able to see the President alone for several months. The second dissenter remained George Ball. Ball had been a Director of the Strategic Bombing Survey of 1945, which had analyzed the techniques our bombers used in pulverizing Germany. Thus, as the only theoretician of bombing in high civilian counsel, he knew that bombing must have a design. What was the philosophy of the bombing, he continued to ask, what was its purpose? But he could get no clear answer—some held it was to raise morale in Saigon; others that it was to interdict supplies; others that it was a delicate way of escalating crunch; others that it would weaken the will of the enemy. But no one knew.

The war now had a dynamic new appetite of its own; each measure taken required another to support it. On March 8th, since the air bases required ground protection, 3,500 United States marines landed at Danang to protect their fields. On April 7th, 1965, in one of the most generous gestures in any war, the President of the United States, in a speech at Johns Hopkins University, offered to begin "unconditional discussions" to stop the bombing and pour American funds to the amount of one billion dollars into the rebuilding of the war-ravaged country, North and South alike. The first of many tentacles of negotiation and peace were put out via the British and the Russians. But there was no response, and by May 5th, 8,000 more Marines had landed, to bring America's troop total to 42,000. A six-day bombing pause brought no response from Hanoi except for the increased pressure of Communist troops at the waist of South Vietnam. Knowing the logic of America's action better than Americans, the enemy sought to cut South Vietnam in two before the full weight of American manpower made that impossible. Though this logic was not yet apparent to Americans, each week it became more so. On June 8th, Robert McCloskey, the State Department's Press Officer, announced that American troops would engage in direct ground combat with the enemy—but McCloskey was a State Department career officer, far below the level of policy, a functionary, and few people could believe that the American government would ask its men to die in a new war without the President himself, as is the tradition, or the Secretary of State making the announcement.

That announcement was shortly to come, but to come in the bewildering manner that kept America ignorant of the dimension of its commitment for years. June had been a bad month in the field of combat, and early July was worse for Allied forces in South Vietnam. In mid-July McNamara flew to Asia to review the situation on the spot. Returning, he reported that it was no longer a question of either/or, air strikes or ground troops. If Vietnam was to be saved, it required both. All through the last ten days of July the leadership of the United States met under its many names—National Security Council, President's Council, Joint Chiefs—to ponder McNamara's gloomy report. Almost all participants conceal the sequence of the last ten days of decision; none will yet pinpoint the final moments of stress and debate. All, however, remember one dominating factor: the personality and motivations of Lyndon Johnson.

Barry Goldwater had bequeathed to Lyndon Johnson the greatest electoral victory any man ever won in an election of free peoples. With a rubber-stamp Congress overwhelmingly liberal in orientation, Johnson could envision remolding and restructuring American life as no President had since Franklin D. Roosevelt. By July, Johnson was halfway along in that fantastic burst of creative legislation called the Great Society, legislation which will shape the lives of all of us and those of children still unborn. Nothing must interfere with his great domestic adventure in legislation and dreams. McNamara, the wisest and most sensitive of the leaders of the Vietnam war, argued that we must not slip into the war—that it should be brought before Congress, that reserves should be called up, that the entire issue should be debated openly until a national understanding and mandate was achieved in Congress. He argued further that the costs of the war before them must be faced forthrightly—by tax legislation plainly conceived and openly passed to pay for the frightful expense of combat. Johnson could not see it that way; still gripped by his diplomatic and military instruments, he had been convinced that 125,000 troops and another six months or a year would see the war to a victorious end. Therefore—it should not be debated in Congress, for that would interrupt the passage of the Great Society legislation by a long summer filibuster. Troops could be raised, he was told, by increasing the draft quotas each month administratively, without calling up the reserves, and he chose that method, to avoid debate. Moreover, since the war would soon be over, its costs could be buried temporarily in the Pentagon's huge budget, whose arcane mysteries of spread-forward, hidden funds and incomprehensible billions passed any average citizen's understanding. Some could foresee the inevitable inflationary consequence of enormous war expenditures if the war went on too long; but Johnson was convinced it would not. And thus, in a press conference on July 28th, 1965, Lyndon Johnson declared that we would raise our manpower in Vietnam to 125,000 troops by the end of the year and stressed the United States' determination to prevent the South Vietnamese from having "any government imposed upon them by force and terror."

Years later, reviewing the slow, somber stretch of decision between the fall of 1964 and the middle of 1965, McGeorge Bundy ruefully remarked that somewhere along the way there had been "a shortfall in management." Later, too, Robert McNamara, wiser by years and more sensitive to the shortcomings of the instruments he directed, declared that if any errors or blunders had been made—and with enormous conscience and sorrow he acknowledged them—they were all made by late spring of 1965. After that, there was no way out.

One half the issues of the campaign of 1968 had been set. It was only fourteen days later, on the evening of Wednesday, August 11th, 1965, that a forty-minute episode—a brawl in the Watts district of Los Angeles between a drunken black driver and a white policeman—set the flare that lit up the other half.

I was to lunch the next day, August 12th, 1965, with a young man named Robert Finch,[3] whose career I have followed, with growing admiration, for years. Finch, the campaign director for Nixon in 1960, had followed his leader into that political never-never land reserved for discarded politicians. But he retained a reflective, almost romantic, interest in the politics of America which marked him as much more than a politician. Out of favor with fortune, detached, apparently closed off from political ambition, his talk of the problems of the Southland had an urbane scholarly quality, and whenever I paused in Southern California his was the most rewarding conversation I could find. On Thursday, when I met him for lunch, however, he was disturbed as I had rarely seen him. The night before, he said, there had been a police arrest in the Watts dis-

[3] Now Secretary of Health, Education and Welfare.

trict; Watts was on the edge of explosion, but no one understood—least of all Los Angeles' mayor, Sam Yorty. He felt that I, as a reporter, should get on top of the situation immediately—the disturbance might become very serious.

Driving away, I dismissed Finch's alarm as agitated localitis aggravated by his own long-held concern for Negroes. I had seen no report of the brawl in the morning papers; the news reports on the car radio seemed to reflect a very minor incident; most of all, the possibility of a major race catastrophe seemed to me impossible in the light of my past reporting in Los Angeles. I had reported Watts as early as ten years before. The long open avenues, the palm-shaded lawns, the clean white bungalows with their red-and-green tiled roofs did, indeed, frame a ghetto where children played in the streets. But it was a clean and sunlit ghetto, so incomparably superior to the rat-infested tenements of Harlem, or the huddles of Chicago's South Side fused with the summer stink of the stockyards, that here, in my opinion, Negroes lived closer to the standards of decency than anywhere else in white America. Politically, too, Los Angeles was a benchmark of progress in my reporting of the black condition. Years ago the black districts of Los Angeles had been patrolled by black policemen, called the Black Watch; since this was segregation, liberal opinion had called for and prevailed in the dissolving of the Black Watch, and Negro policemen were dispersed, on full equality, all across the city.[4] Moreover, Los Angeles was the only city I knew in America where Negroes were represented in government beyond their numerical proportions. With only 17 percent of the city's population, three Negroes had nonetheless been elected to the fifteen-man City Council of Los Angeles and two at least were remarkably able men. What conversation, observation and politics had shown me over the years was further buttressed by a survey of the Urban League, which the year before, in 1964, had surveyed sixty-eight large American cities. Their report, using ten key statistical indices—family income, education, delinquency, employment, etc.—held that Los Angeles ranked first among all American cities in opportunity and condition for black Americans.

It seemed thus entirely fanciful to think that the apparently contented blacks of Los Angeles would explode in a race riot. It was as impossible for me to foresee what was about to happen in the next two days as to foresee that four years later the same Robert Finch would sit as Secretary of Health, Education and Welfare, the man most respon-

[4] Later, during the riots, when an all-black police group was sought to enter and pacify Watts, the Los Angeles police were unable to identify from their rosters the precise distribution of white and black patrolmen around the city, so thoroughly had integration done its work. If, today, advanced opinion calls for Negro policing of Negro districts, it represents a full circle come about in fifteen years in our attitudes to the realities of America.

sible in the nation for correcting the conditions he had so early first sensed in Watts.

Three days later the full weight of my own ignorance sank in. Sitting on one of those green and jeweled lawns of Beverly Hills, high above the panorama of Los Angeles, I could see smoke plumes waving and swaying in the air as Watts burned. All of us on the tawny slopes that cup Los Angeles could watch, on portable television sets beside the pools, the beginning of a new chapter in American politics. Although only half an hour's drive separated us from Broadway and Central Avenues, we were as far away in understanding as if the fires, the flames, the shootings were going on in Vietnam 10,000 miles away.

The episode had begun on Wednesday in a way that has since become classic in American riots.

It was summer, and in Los Angeles the climate is at its best in July, when warm days are followed by blessedly cool nights. Some time in August, though, the temperature begins to bake, as it does everywhere else; and in 1965 the baking heat, delayed for a full week, had finally begun to clamp down about August 11th. Thus the streets were more than normally full of people and drifters when, at seven in the evening, white motorcycle policeman Lee W. Minikus was told by a passing Negro motorist of a drunken driver up ahead. Minikus gave chase, and pulled the reckless driver over to the curb at the corner of 116th Street and Avalon. The driver turned out to be a twenty-one-year-old Negro, Marquette Frye, indeed drunk, with his twenty-two-year-old brother, Ronald. Frye's mother appeared shortly, first scolding her drunken son, then turning her anger on the police when they began to prod, push and struggle with Marquette Frye, who was resisting arrest. As more police gathered to help, more Negroes appeared to watch, their sympathy all with the resister, who was soon bleeding. As the crowd's temper rose they began to yell and spit, and the police arrested a young woman for inciting to violence; when they took her off to jail, too, at 7:40, for spitting on them, the entire episode had lasted no more than forty minutes.

By now, however, the crowd had grown to an estimated 1,000 people; and the rumor started that the young female spitter, who had really been wearing a barber's smock, had instead been wearing a maternity dress—and that the cops had abused a pregnant woman. By 8:15 blacks had begun to stone automobiles and pull white people out of their cars and beat them up. By one A.M. a police command post in the area had apparently contained and dispersed the violence. The next morning, Thursday, the mayor of Los Angeles found it necessary to be in San Diego. But that excellent black sociologist Dr. John A. Buggs, of the Los Angeles County Human Relations Committee, sensing the explosive within his people, brought together a number of community leaders in the ghetto to plead with their people to "cool" it. Television, press and radio were already on the scene, however, and from the meeting they lifted what appeared to them to be the best story. Of whatever else appeared on television that evening, this passer-through remembers best, as do many Angelenos, a handsome teenage black boy, his face full of rage, promising that the riots were going to start again tonight, and that this time they were going to get whitey.

Whatever the influence of television in the early stages of the riot, by Thursday evening the story of violence was authentic enough for all. Looting broke out in Watts by Thursday afternoon; that evening a thin perimeter of police found itself unable to contain the few initial blocks of violence. By Friday, like a cancer in metastasis, rioting, burning, sniping had spread to dozens of pockets miles apart in the huge Negro community of Southeast Los Angeles. By Friday evening, as the National Guard rushed to the scene, the first killing had taken place—a Negro bystander, trapped on the street between police and rioters, shot accidentally during an exchange of gunfire. A few hours later the first two white deaths —a fireman killed under a falling wall, a sheriff killed by the accidental discharge of another sheriff's shotgun in a scuffle with rioters. From then, the riot built to its ultimate savagery, until 13,900 National Guardsmen, 934 police, 719 deputy sheriffs were needed to restore order.

For the first time that sickening drama of the streets, of which America was to have so many re-enactments in the following summers, was being played to its full and violent climax—death, ruin, bloodshed, 34 killed, 1,032 injured, almost 4,000 arrested, almost $40 million worth of property destroyed. There was to be more and more of this, even worse, for the next three years, as the issue of black against white, black violence against white structure, became the nightmare haunting every large city in the nation.

All of one's first observations were tragic; all raised questions; and none had any answers, or has answers even to this day.

§ There was, first, the sense of political absence. It was not simply that the Governor of California, Edmund G. Brown, was in Greece on vacation, or that the mayor of Los Angeles found it necessary to be in San Francisco on Friday, when his city was in peril. It was simply that no policy governed the state's approach to confrontation.

One could observe this best in the behavior of the military and martial instruments of California, seeking leadership, not finding it, unsure of tactic, doctrine, or what their own behavior should best be. The first request for National Guard support had been made by the Los Angeles police on Friday morning at eleven; but the Lieutenant Governor of the state, an elected official, shrinking, like all such elected officials, from the stigma of violence, had tarried in issuing mobilization orders. Mobilization of troops had not begun in the suburbs of Burbank and Glendale until five in the evening. The commander, Lieutenant General Roderic Hill, probably unconsciously expressed best the then-naïve state of the American mind by describing the move from marshaling point to Watts. He had had to move his 1,336 men across Los Angeles in the face of the Friday-evening weekend traffic through busy intersections, and had been slow. But, he said, "we didn't have authority to cross a red light." Street tactics for both police and National Guard forbade the use of tear gas; soldiers were forbidden to carry loaded rifles. By the time, at one o'clock on the morning of Saturday, the instruments of defense had begun their first sweep of the area, the civil peace had completely broken down and violence could be quenched only with greater violence.

How quickly should troops be sent to riot areas? Who should give the orders to fire? How fast should response come? At what level?

§ There was, next, the presence of television. One of the Los Angeles stations, Channel 5, performed a technical near-miracle from its flying helicopter. All Angelenos, black or white, could look almost directly down in their television sets and, from a few hundred feet up, through Channel 5's eyes, see looters carting off sofas, furniture, television sets, appliances, groceries as if in a barbarian carnival. The band of Los Angeles radio stations filled the air with reports, wild, unchecked, erroneous--snipers on the Harbor Freeway, outbreaks in a dozen different places, rumors of rovers about to invade white districts. Together they spread through black and white communities panic, hate, glee, rage, greed and lust for looting or shooting.

What should be the role of television and radio in a riot situation? When does reporting go beyond reporting and become a disturbance factor in itself? Can electronic reporting be curbed in the higher interest of domestic tranquillity? Should it be?

§ Another observation was provoked by my memory of several of the elected Negro Assemblymen and City Councilmen of Los Angeles knotted together, uneasily talking with one another outside Los Angeles City Hall. They did not dare penetrate the riot area itself; their authority among their own community had run out at the first outbreak of fire; and no one, black or white, had any bridge to the barbarians of the street who had usurped their role of leadership.

By and large, it has been my observation that the Negro legislators elected by Negro communities across the country—with the exception, of course, of Adam Clayton Powell—are men of first quality, of exceptional talent and ability, living demonstrations of the ability of black communities to pick their best in pride under conditions of tranquillity. But in crisis the fragile leadership of such men evaporates. It evaporates before an indefinable surge of black rage, a rage that unites, then terrorizes, all. No more than a handful of hoodlums stimulated the riots that engulfed the 650,000 Negroes of Los Angeles; among the 3,438 adults arrested in the riots, 1,042 had "major" criminal records; among the 514 juveniles arrested, 212 had "minor" criminal records, 43 had "major" criminal records. This small handful of barbarians had dominated for four nights the emotions and the streets of a black community of 650,000 people; and nowhere in that community was there any organic internal power of resistance, any capacity for defending its own homes against the fire-bombers, its own stores from looting, its own streets from violence, its own children from temptation.

Who, then, were the Negro leaders? No investigating commission[5] found any evidence of conspiracy, planning or organization in the Watts riots. No real rationale for the riots was found except rage—blind, primitive, generations-deep rage, reasonless, subduable only by force from the outside. Of this hidden rage, and the conditions that generated it, the white community in one of the most tolerant cities of America had been completely unaware and, in crisis, completely unable to cope with it. The established black political and community leaders had proven equally incapable of coping with this rage-in-crisis. But in the next three years an entirely new cast of Negro leaders was to appear, eager to whet the rage to a fine edge, ambitious to make of this old rage a new power base to divide America.

§ The last of my observations was to come more slowly. In Los Angeles, as in other advanced communities of America, the term "integration" had been for all men of conscience not only gospel, but a code-word covering all the practical proposals to bring harmony among our races; it was the name of the new partnership to bring our communities together. From the day of the Watts riots on, the term "integration" lost its force in politics, its savor to good people; and I was never to hear it used seriously again, in Los Angeles or anywhere else. Twenty years of American goodwill had sanctified the phrase; three nights of burning and bloodshed had stripped it of luster.

For the next three years Americans, black and white, would search for new terms of partnership under a whole new variety of phrases like "Black Power," "Black Capitalism," "Community Action." But underlying all such phrases, from Watts on, was the new recognition of rage,

---

[5] The report of the Governor's Commission on the Los Angeles Riots, headed by John McCone, *Violence in the City*, is the best full-scale story of the Watts riots. Published in December, 1965, by the State of California, its wise but melancholy conclusion at the time: "As a Commission we are seriously concerned that the existing breach, if allowed to persist, could in time split our society irretrievably. So serious and so explosive is the situation that, unless it is checked, the August riots may seem by comparison to be only a curtain-raiser for what could blow up one day in the future."

of hate, of fear, of barbarisms that might tear America itself apart. Under all the rhetoric of the campaign of 1968 lay this somber recognition, and it had begun in Watts.

It is impossible to understand any of the domestic politics of the United States, at a Presidential, a municipal, or a neighborhood level, without understanding how deeply, beneath surface euphemisms, goes the cleavage of race. There is an experiment commonly demonstrated to youngsters in their first introduction to science. The teacher usually takes a piece of paper and scatters iron filings over it. The iron filings lie helter-skelter, with no recognizable pattern on the surface. Then the teacher thrusts a magnet under the paper—and the iron filings instantly arrange themselves about the two poles, guided into place by the invisible lines of magnetic force. American politics at home had, for years, been similarly guided by the hidden polarity of races. But from 1965 to 1968 they were to become inescapably visible.

"Events are in the saddle and ride mankind" was to become one of the favorite intellectual observations on the campaign of 1968, as men in trouble recalled their learning and quoted Ralph Waldo Emerson.[6] The first use of the phrase in contemporary politics, however, was by George Ball, who in June of 1965, pleading vainly against the final decision to plunge ground troops into the swamps of Vietnam, had written for the President's eyes alone a private and top-secret memorandum, which he began with the quotation from Emerson. He urged, as he had so often before, that the government must get on top of events, must foresee rather than respond to circumstances. His dictum was as true in Watts as it had been for Vietnam eight weeks earlier.

Events were to ride American politics all through the years of Lyndon Johnson's administration, down, finally, to election day of 1968. Events were to reduce the personalities of candidates in the soul-searching of the year 1968 to marionettes; events were to shake America's confidence in its own self and purpose; events were to kill 35,000 Ameri-

---

[6] It is a matter of historical curiosity to this writer that two of the favorite catchlines of the 1968 campaign, whether their parentage was recognized or not, came from the New England transcendentalist. Few of the mob leaders of 1968 who spat upon and so defiled American political tradition realized, as they demanded the right "to do their thing," that they were quoting Emerson, who in 1841, in his essay on "Self-Reliance," had said: "If you . . . vote with a great party either for the government or against it, maintain a dead church, contribute to a dead Bible society, spread your table like base housekeepers—under all these screens, I have difficulty to detect the precise man you are, and of course so much force is withdrawn from your proper life. But do your own thing and I shall know you. . . ." Emerson also contributed the phrase "events are in the saddle and ride mankind," except that in his original phrasing he wrote it "things are in the saddle and ride mankind."

can men in Vietnam; events were to convert the greatest mandate, the greatest personal triumph of any election year, that of 1964, to the greatest personal humiliation of any sitting President.

The Watts riots of 1965 were to initiate a sequence of blood and disorder, spread by television, that would dominate the politics of 1968 three years later; the Vietnam decisions of 1965 were to initiate a sense of helplessness in American life which no candidate could cure. It was to be a long time before Americans realized that these were not just episodes of the day, or decisions of the week, but more than that—cleavage lines that would split all Americans apart as they approached their choice of a national leader.

These cleavages were still obscure in 1965 as Lyndon Johnson wrote the finest chapters of his record in the history books. But the vulnerability of Lyndon Johnson, even at his zenith in 1965, was already quite clear to Richard M. Nixon, the next President of the United States, as he observed the rivals within his own party and considered the stance which might give that shattered and humiliated group of men, the Republicans, an opportunity to offer alternative national leadership.

CHAPTER TWO

THE REPUBLICANS: RETURN FROM EXILE

F EW EPISODES in American history can compare with the return of the Republican Party and Richard M. Nixon to national leadership in 1968.

One must discard entirely the artificially narrow margins of the election of 1968, and go all the way back to 1964, to measure the turn of fortune. In 1964, Lyndon Johnson and the Democrats had shattered the Republican Party. The greatest electoral margin ever given any party anywhere, 16,000,000 votes, had washed away every traditional Republican stronghold—the industrial Midwest as well as New England, the Plains states as well as the Rocky Mountain states. In the big cities, the Republican candidate, Barry Goldwater, had carried less than 2 percent of the Negro vote; he had fared only slightly better among other ethnic minorities; he had lost the farmers, the old folks, the youth, wherever such interest groups could be picked out in the general pattern of voting. In Congress, Republicans faced the largest Democratic majority since Franklin D. Roosevelt's zenith in 1936; in the Senate, they faced a hostile majority of two to one; across the country, they held only seventeen of the fifty governorships in the nation. Not since the Whigs had any great party seemed so completely to have lost touch with reality; and their candidate of 1964, Barry Goldwater, had become a political pariah, so contagious with defeat that three months after his downfall not a single one of the rock-ribbed county committees of conservative Ohio wanted him as speaker at any of the eight traditional Republican Lincoln Day banquets across the state.

No formal measurement can, however, give the particular odor of self-doubt, self-hate and defeat that stank in the corridors of the Party from top to bottom. One tiny post-election incident seemed to me to give better the smell of disaster than any poll or analysis. During the campaign of 1964, I had come to know Karl Hess, chief speech-writer for Barry Goldwater, the putative Sorensen/Schlesinger of a Goldwater administration if such an unlikely event were to come to pass. Sober, intense, hard-working and an arch-conservative, Hess had been the intellectual laureate of Barry Goldwater's court as that dismal campaign dragged about the country in 1964. Senators, Governors, Congressmen, Republican leaders of high and low degree alike sought his favor to reach the candidate's ear. Came the election and disaster—and it was time for Hess to find a new job. By tradition, of course, political parties take care of their own, even in defeat, and Hess, an able writer, could by custom and talent expect a job in the office of any of those conservative Congressmen or Senators who had so loudly cheered Goldwater on. Not so, however. For weeks Hess trudged from office to office of those who once had paid him suit, looking for a post. But no Republican of any stripe would shelter a man so closely tied to Goldwater and defeat. As Hess's money ran out, so did the reach of his ambition. By spring of 1965 he was pleading for even the meanest of jobs—could not some Congressman or Senator get him on the payroll simply as an elevator operator in the Senate or House office building? But no one dared put his name even on so lowly a patronage list. By spring, reduced to the ranks of the unemployed and hungry, he began a night-school course in welding; and by summer Barry Goldwater's chief braintruster's skills were sufficient to earn a job welding bulldozers in a Washington machine shop, to which he traveled, night after night, on his motorcycle, to work the night shift until fortune might turn again.[1]

No one in 1964 had even the vaguest idea of what might happen to the Republican Party four years later. A brisk house-cleaning of the Goldwater-staffed Republican National Committee followed a month after Johnson's election; Messrs. Nixon and Eisenhower gathered with Barry Goldwater at a New York hotel in December of 1964, insisted on the immediate dismissal of the Goldwater appointee, Dean Burch, as National Chairman, and agreed, all three of them, on his replacement by Ray Bliss of Ohio, a thoroughly efficient political neutral. The Party leaders settled down to wait—eyeing each other with suspicion and hate, and Lyndon Johnson with fear. Describing the problems of his Party at the time to a group of New York editors, Mr. Nixon candidly stigma-

---

[1] Since, in the Goldwater mythology, pluck and perseverance always win in America, it delights me to report that for Karl Hess pluck and perseverance won out, too. At the bulldozer plant he discovered that metal-welding could be more than a job, and that his skills could make of metal, metallic sculptures. In his own time, he began to weld art forms; by 1967 he had qualified for a one-man show in one of Washington's fashionable galleries. Metallic sculpture is still one of Hess's hobbies and his abstract welded steels may be found in the capital's DeGains gallery; he earns his living now, however, as author of a newsletter and as Associate Fellow of the Institute of Policy Studies.

tized it as "religious, recidivist and reactionary." Split in spirit, parochial, bound together only by tradition and emotion, the Republicans, a hideously wounded and scattered group of men, looked to the future, in 1965, with no greater common purpose than simple survival. And no greater principle was offered to the nation by Ray Bliss, its custodian and new National Chairman, than the traditional chant of the loser in America—that the nation had to preserve the two-party system for the good of the Republic.

There was, thus, at the top of the Republican Party, effectively, nothing—leadership would belong to whoever snatched it in the next three years. And yet the property was of immense value. If Lyndon Johnson and the nation fared badly, the Republican Party might conceivably be the nation's only alternative choice for leadership in 1968.

No formal description whatsoever can fit the condition of the Republican Party at this time. Both great American parties are coalitions of such a broad and fluid nature as to be subject to no precision of description whatsoever. One must try, however. Fundamentally, the Republican Party is white, middle-class and Protestant. Here and there across the nation, various other ethnic groups are absorbed into this parent mass—as are Italian and Irish middle-class citizens in the Northeast, German and Scandinavian Americans in the Midwest. Two moods color its thinking. One is the old Protestant-Puritan ethic of the small towns of America, of the decent, sober, god-fearing, law-abiding men whom Nixon in 1968 was to call "the forgotten Americans." The other is the philosophy of private enterprise, the sense that the individual, as man or corporation, can build swifter and better for common good than big government. From middle-class America the Republicans get their votes; from the executive leadership and from the families of the great enterprises they get their funds.

Ideologically, historically and regionally, these larger patterns are, however, so split[2] that only metaphor can serve to describe the interlocked and contending parts; and it is best, therefore, to compare the Republican structure, as well as the Democratic structure, to a mobile. The Republican Party hangs suspended, as does the Democratic Party, from the roof-beam of American history, with branches, forks and clusters of dangling groups, all of different sizes, shapes, colors and weights, constantly seeking a center, an internal balance, as it sways in the breezes of politics or shudders in the great gusts of history.

In 1965, and for the next three years, the gusts of history that swept through America were to stir and shake every value that middle-class Protestant America had cherished for centuries. Riot, bloodshed and disorder were to stain every major American city; a mismanaged war in Asia was to shake the traditional discipline of patriotism, most of

[2] See *The Making of the President—1960*, pp. 59–61.

all among the college children that middle-class America had bred. The vast and visionary expansion of Johnson's Great Society, coupled with the cost of war in Asia, were to unleash a slow, then speedier, inflation that eroded the values of thrift and shivered the planning of all who worked on fixed-income salaries or looked forward to pensions. Most of all, manners and morals seemed unbound by the sweeping permissiveness of a Supreme Court which, apparently, found Bible-reading in schools illegal, but pornography permissible in or out of class. America was approaching a time when the clash of its two great cultures, the old and the new, was to burst in the political arena to fill the air with an entirely new rhetoric.

The gusts and storm winds were to shake the Democratic Party to a climax of unprecedented turbulence and violence by mid-summer of 1968. But as they began to blow, in 1965, all the clusters in the Republican mobile began to sway and bob in response also, seeking their center balance.

It was not until the end of 1966 that anyone could discern among the swaying parts of the Republican Party any systematic approach to the re-conquest of power nationally and the seizure of leadership internally. It is set that not until after the off-year elections between Presidential campaigns are all the cards dealt to the players in the quadrennial Presidential contest. In November, 1966, therefore, with all the off-year election returns in, with all the Governors, Senators, and new Congressmen in place, serious political men began to survey the scene and found among Republicans the first stirring of ambition.

First were the newcomers, and the election of 1966 had thrust up only two that were noteworthy enough to add to the one new Republican face of 1965.

1965 had been the year of John V. Lindsay. The rules of American politics establish three grand prizes in each state: one governorship and two seats in the United States Senate. When, as among Minnesota Democrats or New York Republicans, a party bursts with more than three major talents, the rules make their rivalry a prison. In New York, the two Senate seats were held by Jacob Javits and Robert F. Kennedy, blocking off all ambition in that direction; and the governorship was held, apparently forever, by Nelson Rockefeller. Thus, in 1965, Lindsay, with utmost daring, had chosen to run for the mayoralty of New York and, astoundingly, won. A Republican mayor of New York is almost a contradiction of political grammar; but a young Republican Protestant, a romantic and a moralist at once, gay and earnest at the same time, governing the world's most turbulent and boisterous city, had never happened in this century; and from the day of his election Lindsay was a Presidential potential. His trouble was that, as a New Yorker and a

Republican liberal, he was, simply, the most glamorous figure in a column of liberals whose Grand Marshal, nationally, was Nelson Rockefeller; Lindsay could not—or believed he could not—operate effectively, either as mayor or as Presidential contender, against the will of Nelson Rockefeller.

1966 offered another new figure, in the Midwest, who faced a problem similar to Lindsay's. He was Charles Percy of Illinois, forty-seven, bright, eager, handsome, who had won a surprising Senatorial victory over one of the authentically distinguished Democrats, Paul Douglas. But Percy had wrung his victory directly from the voters. And his influence in the Illinois Republican Party was even less than Lindsay's in New York's party, because he was the junior senator in a team whose senior, senior, maximum Senator was Everett Dirksen. Vibrantly attractive to young voters, Percy lacked the political machinery, the allies or the knowledge to translate his popular appeal to real power within his party.

More important was a new face in the West: Ronald Reagan. Reagan had just sent Governor Edmund Brown down to defeat in California by 993,739 votes—the same "Pat" Brown who had humiliated Richard M. Nixon by 296,758 votes four years earlier. Not only did his victory give Reagan a major power base in California, where the governor controls all, but another power base was also waiting for him— the Goldwater movement. Graceful and charming, the onetime movie actor was the only major figure in the Goldwater movement to survive with any popular appeal at all; smiling, deft, sincere, smooth with the press and handsome on television, this Mr.-Deeds-Come-to-Sacramento seemed to possess all the Goldwater virtues with none of his flaws.

Nor was Reagan loath to enter combat. Within ten days of his election, Reagan had gathered his inner circle together, on Thursday, November 17th, 1966, at his home in Pacific Palisades for a first discussion of the Presidency. There, too, was named a captain for the adventure—young Tom Reed, a distinguished physicist turned successful industrialist, now urged into politics by his conviction that Lyndon Johnson was an incarnation of evil. Reed, in the next two weeks, was to engage as counsel for the campaign the master architect of the Goldwater nomination of 1964, F. Clifton White of New York.[3] Together, the two were to draw up a meticulous master plan for seizure of the nomination, timed in five phases and date-deadlined from December, 1966, to nomination in August, 1968. That all their work was to come to naught, and to mean so little later, was less their failure than accident and tragedy. Reed and White had only begun to translate their plans to action when, in the summer of 1967, there was exposed in Sacramento a homosexual scandal which all but shattered Reagan's self-confidence, as well as his confidence in fellow men. One of the key lieutenants of his

[3] See *The Making of the President—1964*, pp. 131–138 *et seq.*

1966 campaign was discovered to be a homosexual. Not only that, but, now in a position of high trust in the Governor's office, the same individual was actively inserting other homosexuals into the Governor's staff. Shocked, Reagan purged his immediate staff, then withdrew to the circle of only his oldest friends, making his trusted personal lawyer, William French Smith, an amateur in politics, master of all his political enterprises and surrogate for all decision. The plans of Reed and White were put on ice. From this blow, the Reagan campaign never recovered. But in November of 1966 all that lay in the future, and, as the new leader of the Republican right wing, Ronald Reagan was too important to be ignored.

Thus, as the speculation began, men shifted their attention to the other two major and obvious contenders for the nomination: George Romney of Michigan, and Richard M. Nixon.

First, George Romney.

Romney had been there for a long time, waiting for attention. Indeed, it was Nixon who, in 1962, had first pointed to George Romney as Presidential timber; and for some years people had been examining the man, trying to penetrate what appeared to be a smoke screen of morality. For the first quality that surfaced, as one met and talked with George Romney over a number of years, was a sincerity so profound that, in conversation, one was almost embarrassed. In him the small-town ethic, the small-town morality of America's past seemed to be exaggerated to hyperbole. Yet, on probing, one discovered this morality to be pure, unfeigned and of innermost religious conviction. 1968 was to see two of the most religious men in American public life vie for the Presidency—Eugene McCarthy and George Romney. But Romney's religion—the Church of Jesus Christ of Latter-day Saints—framed his every phrase and reaction. He would not talk politics or do business on a Sunday; he neither smoked nor drank; he believed, again in all sincerity, that the Constitution of the United States was a divinely inspired document. When he talked of stopping moral rot, he meant it, as much as an evangelist would—and, indeed, for two years in his youth George Romney had been a Mormon evangelist in the streets of Scotland and England.

George Romney's religion did not make him a forbidding man, however; he added to it goodwill, jollity and warmth; and it was perhaps this human warmth that caused his only departure from the tenets of his church. His experiences with life, working his way up from humble origins (his father had been a potato farmer), had led him far from the harsh doctrine of the Mormon Church which consigns Negroes forever to outer darkness in the Hall of God; and it was on the issue of civil rights that he had come to acrimonious and blazing disagreement with

Barry Goldwater in 1964. He spoke quite simply of his migration through life to the conviction of brotherhood. "I come from a Rocky Mountain background," he said to me later during the campaign. "I didn't know any Negroes, America was still pretty simple, still pretty uncomplicated. I spent some time in Washington later and we had a Negro maid, but we didn't know any Negroes. It was only after I got to Detroit that I got to know Negroes and began to be able to evaluate them and I began to recognize that some Negroes are better and more capable than lots of whites. Whites and Negroes, in my opinion, have *got* to learn to know each other. Barry Goldwater didn't have any background to understand this, to fathom them, and I couldn't get through to him. I understand Barry and Ronnie Reagan, they come from the same background I did—they just can't understand what we have to do, how to reach Negroes with programs of their own, how we have to know each other." This conviction had by 1964 penetrated even the Negro ghettos of Michigan, where Romney racked up a substantial 15 percent of the Negro vote in Michigan in a year when Goldwater was claiming less than 2 percent, and by 1966 Romney's claim on the Negro vote had risen to over 30 percent, unprecedented for a Republican.

There was another quality which recommended Romney even more to political leaders: effectiveness. The man's record showed a knack for getting things done. He had taken a moribund automobile company—American Motors—and turned it around, making a fortune for himself, millions for his stockholders, and pleasing his union workers by a novel profit-sharing plan to boot. He had, in 1959, entered politics to become the driving force in a state constitutional convention that re-wrote and gave the State of Michigan one of the finest charters in the Union. He had been first elected Governor of Michigan in 1962 by 80,573 votes, ending a fourteen-year Democratic rule in the state; given his state effective government; been re-elected by 382,913 votes in 1964, the year of the Goldwater disaster; and climaxed his political career with a sweep to re-election in Michigan in 1966 by 527,047 votes.

Thus, Romney—governor of a great industrial state—clean, moral, effective, hard-driving, tolerant. All of these good qualities had their corresponding and complementary drawbacks, as we shall see. But, above all, he looked like a President. Handsome, silver-haired, robust, masculine, smiling or stern, he seemed cast for the part by Hollywood's Central Casting. Correspondents who liked him called him "Mr. Straight Arrow"; those whose flesh crawled at his pieties called him "Mr. Square," or worse. It was difficult to foresee how a man of these qualities could be so savagely massacred by the media as he was later to be.

His prominence, as he stood tall on the day after his re-election in 1966, came from more than these simple qualities, however. They came from the nature of things and the natural groupings in Republican leadership. On the one side was the national Congressional leadership of the Republican Party—a minority in Congress for all but four of the thirty-eight years between 1930 and 1968. Congressional Republicans have a built-in criticism complex; they are the nay-sayers of American life, conditioned to suspicion, petulance and resistance by a generation of ill-fortune. Barry Goldwater had been their candidate in 1964. On the other side, for a generation there had always been a rival force within the Party, the Republican governors. These men, burdened with the responsibility of governing, understanding all its infinite complexity in an American age of tormenting adjustments, had fought its Congressional wing for twenty-five years, and by 1966 governors like Rockefeller of New York, Scranton of Pennsylvania, Romney of Michigan, Rhodes of Ohio, Volpe of Massachusetts, Hatfield of Oregon, Smylie of Idaho had decided never again to let a simplist like Barry Goldwater of Arizona carry the banners of their Party to disaster.

With the election of November, 1966, it became obvious that, even without any deals, Romney was the natural candidate of the governors. Nelson Rockefeller had won a surprising, uphill battle for re-election as Governor of New York; but he *knew* he could not be the candidate in 1968—he was the man whose war with Barry Goldwater had torn the Party apart from New Hampshire to California in the 1964 primaries. Rockefeller was loud and adamant; he would not face a primary fight again in 1968 and go down in Party history as the Great Wrecker. Nor would William Scranton of Pennsylvania run. Scranton had been forced out of office in Pennsylvania by an antique constitution (whose revision he later masterminded) which at that time prohibited the re-election of a sitting governor. The most thoughtful man in any American statehouse, Scranton simply had no taste for power; he could wield it as well as any, but he did not enjoy it. And all other governors, except Reagan, either came from states too small—like Chafee of Rhode Island —or were too little known—like Evans of Washington or Love of Colorado—to head the parade.

It was not long before the obvious became real. The week after his own re-election in 1966, Nelson Rockefeller flew to the Dorado Beach Hotel in Puerto Rico, a luxurious family property, there to rest and ruminate. Nine days later there followed George Romney, who, after taking his usual Sunday respite from politics, lunched on Monday with Rockefeller and received from him the promise of all necessary support. There was always a persistent awkwardness in understanding between the Rockefeller and Romney staffs, but the substance of this understanding was clear enough: Rockefeller would provide all possible support to Romney, public and private—research from his copious establishment, speech-writers, key personnel if needed, money and the boon of his great name. Rockefeller had already, three days earlier, visited with newly elected Governor Raymond Shafer of Pennsylvania; among sitting governors, the master of the Empire State is now the acknowledged sage and leader. Shafer, as a novice in national politics, had offered to take guidance from Rockefeller in the President-picking of 1968, and it was agreed that the Pennsylvania and New York delegations would go to the Republican convention as a package. Thus Romney could count immediately on the support of three of the most powerful industrial states of the union—New York, Michigan and Pennsylvania. Romney's own prestige and Rockefeller's residual net of national contacts would certainly add much more to that. Whether Rockefeller at this time harbored any ambition for the Presidency is unknown; he stated, and I believe, that he was then through forever with Presidential ambition. Yet, as in Lyndon Johnson's renunciation, one could never escape the impression that a debate, never verbalized by the man himself, was continually going on between the conscious frontal lobe of the brain which said no, no, never again, and the posterior lobe of the brain which kept whispering—well, maybe, someday if, if, if . . . and if, why not?

From the Dorado Beach Hotel the Romney campaign broadened swiftly. Four weeks later, at the Greenbrier Hotel in White Sulphur Springs, West Virginia, the National Governors' Conference held its first post-election meeting. At a quite private breakfast Romney gave a chosen group of Republican governors a *tour d'horizon* of his thinking. He did not ask any of them to pledge themselves to his candidacy; if any so wished, fine; he hoped only that they would not pledge themselves to any other candidate without informing him first; he would, in the meantime, explore the possibility of being an active candidate and if, at any time, he felt he could not make it, he would consider himself duty-bound to come back and report to the others first that he could not. All present —Love of Colorado, Chafee of Rhode Island, Scranton and Shafer both of Pennsylvania, Winthrop and Nelson Rockefeller, Boe of South Dakota, and Evans of Washington—agreed, as did Henry Bellmon of Oklahoma and John Volpe of Massachusetts, both later to announce for Richard M. Nixon, the chief adversary of the Romney drive.

Affairs seemed to march briskly in the next few weeks for Romney. Eleven days after the Greenbrier meeting, a parley of the higher leadership of Romney's campaign took place at the Waldorf-Astoria Hotel in New York to draw up a strategic plan, including the assumption of managerial over-all responsibility by Leonard Hall, former Republican National Chairman, who at this meeting was the surrogate of Nelson Rockefeller of New York. Plan was soon translated into action. Returning to Lansing, Romney peeled off from his gubernatorial staff a task force headed by scholar Walter DeVries, to begin to mobilize the troops. Four blocks down from the old gray capitol in Lansing, Michigan, in a walk-up floor over a store-front on East Michigan Avenue, DeVries formed Romney Associates, the campaign staff, and crammed its book-shelves with every conceivable study or book on national politics, as well as with what may have been the finest collection of polls and poll-samplings in the nation.

There were reservations, to be sure, among the other governors, even among members of Romney's own staff, about the Governor's ability to stand up to national exposure. There was a cloying naïveté about his statements. He angered easily when his good faith was questioned. He could, for example, hand out to various newspapermen copies of his bitter correspondence with Goldwater in 1964, then become furious at its publication in *The New York Times* and wire his sincere regrets to Goldwater. He could call Charles Percy an "opportunist" and be saddened when Percy resented it. He would make a forthright statement one day, then, like a man making up his mind in public, contradict it or modify it on another. His press conferences were always handled with remarkable candor—which next day he would regret. Nor was he a gifted phrase-maker, a quipster; he handled the English language like a blunt instrument and could find no speech-writer to sharpen his thoughts to style. Most importantly, the Vietnam war was beginning to press on the nation, and Romney's credentials as an expert in world matters were of conspicuous concern to everyone. Even earlier in the year, in February of 1966, David Broder, then of *The New York Times,* had written in a perceptive article: ". . . if the Michigan executive has a major weakness today, it is probably his fuzziness on national and international issues. His advisers say adequate briefings at the proper time can overcome the problem, but his lapses are embarrassing." Within a few weeks of his re-election, the effort by the national press to nag Romney into some clear statement of his views on the world and the war was the chief handicap of his campaign.

Romney was more conscious of this than anyone else; he could sense the nagging of the press like the probing of a dentist's drill for a nerve. He had been pushed into the race, he felt, too early; even Nelson Rockefeller's public endorsement of his candidacy (with Senator Jacob Javits of New York as Vice-President) in May of 1966 had been a "shove" so early in the game that it was a shackle. He did not, he later insisted, have an answer for everything in the world from Nigeria (or did he mean Rhodesia?) to Vietnam and in between. It was too early to be in the saddle, the target of every question on every matter of American worry, the only clearly defined candidate and alternative to Lyndon Johnson in the nation.

But the overwhelming advice of the Romney staff and the Romney friends was to move. Their memories went back to 1964, and how Barry Goldwater had all but sewed up that nomination eighteen months in advance. Now, while the nation restlessly sought an alternative to

Johnson, now while the polls showed him to be the only Republican who could beat the President—now was the time to go.

Above all, the polls. Polls have always been of extraordinary importance to Romney and his entourage. Romney, like most businessmen who come to politics, has been trained to think in product, sales and measurement. Politics, however, is a business of no executive substance whatsoever, for its ingredients are dreams and images, words and fears, insubstantial products difficult of measurement. In politics, polls substitute as the measure of sales, and from the beginning of his career in politics Romney had depended on them. Though he might as a private man dream of a country where God reigned in every heart and the streets were patrolled by brotherly love, as an executive he had an appetite for polls second only to Lyndon Johnson's. Now in November, 1966, in the aftermath of his re-election, with TV exposure whenever he wanted it —and frequently when he did not want it—he watched his polls soar like a homesick angel or an arrow pointing straight at the White House. By the end of November, 1966, the Harris poll showed him the choice of 54 percent of American voters, Johnson as the choice of 46 percent. The Gallup poll confirmed these figures. From November, 1966, through the spring of 1967, Romney was to hold this lead in public opinion, and, with such a margin, his advisers insisted he put the hay in the barn while the sun shone. Using polling figures as arguments of persuasion, they proposed to pressure the grassroots politicians of the Republican Party into Romney's camp before Richard M. Nixon ever got his campaign off the ground. Thus, without any formal announcement, Romney's campaign was launched.

Which left Richard Milhous Nixon.

America had known many Richard Nixons—the boy Congressman, the Senator prosecutor, the pugnacious politician, the intemperate partisan scourge, the unremarkable Vice-President, the man of temper and taut nerves, the poor and persistent loser. What it had not yet perceived was the man of extraordinary courage, of dogged perseverance, the precise thinker and meticulous planner, the character changed by learning and experience. Thus the story of Richard M. Nixon must move through this book on two tracks—the technical planning of a modern campaign in America, and the movement of the man in spirit from disaster to triumph, seeking his own identity.

First, the man.

Of the man, one is almost forced to begin the story of his return with a paraphrase of Dickens' *A Christmas Carol.* "Marley was dead: to begin with. There is no doubt whatever about that. The register of his burial was signed by the clergyman, the clerk, the undertaker, and the chief mourner. . . . Old Marley was as dead as a door-nail." For, by the beginning of 1963, Richard M. Nixon was dead. No doubt whatever about that. Political clerks, clergymen, undertakers and mourners had all signed the register. Nixon was as dead as a doornail.

Nixon had been wounded by his defeat by John F. Kennedy in 1960, but not mortally so—he had run a respectable campaign, losing by the closest margin of any loser in twentieth-century American history. The choice before him, in the aftermath of that defeat, was the choice of identity he had faced all his life. He could return to California, the home place; or go to New York, where offers far more lucrative than any from California enticed him to come. Yet California was home, and he returned there, though forewarned by friends and aides that, if he did, there would be no escape from public pressure to run for Governor of California in 1962. The pressure proved indeed inescapable—Republican friends at home and from as far away as New York insisted he run, as the only hope of keeping the California Party out of the hands of the right-wingers who later captured it.

It was still the old Nixon who ran for Governor of California, the political loner, an introspective, self-observing man. On the day of his announcement to run in 1962 he locked himself in a room at the Beverly Hilton Hotel in Los Angeles to brood alone. "And no one," reported a friend later, "knew what decision he would come out with, to go or not—not Pat Nixon, not Rose Mary Woods, not Bob Finch. They all waited. That was part of Nixon's character at the time. He wouldn't do that now."

Thus the campaign of 1962, an ordeal on which all in the Nixon group now look back as nightmare. This correspondent, who briefly visited and toured with that campaign in 1962, remembers his speeches and statements—on the one hand, crisp, critical and unequivocal denunciation of the John Birch Society, which alienated the California right wing; on the other hand, the early invocation of his later law-and-order theme, deploring the rising California crime rate, which alienated the liberals. And at the end—humiliation by Pat Brown, to be crowned by the unforgettable morning after at the Beverly-Hilton, where, ignoring his restraining aides, and in a tantrum, he dashed down the corridor to blister the assembled press with his proclamation: "You won't have Nixon to kick around any more, because, gentlemen, this is my last press conference." Five days later, taking him at his word, ABC television network aired its half-hour-long show, "Political Obituary of Richard Nixon," graced with the presence of one of his earliest adversaries, Alger Hiss, and the former Vice-President was dismissed from history.

California and Los Angeles had, by this time, palled on Richard M. Nixon. "What was there for him to do in the evenings?" asked one New York friend who urged him back to the East Coast. "All there was in Los Angeles was to sit around and talk about maids, or discuss the new Symphony and Art Center. He was bored." By early 1963 the itch to be back in the stimulating world of Eastern affairs, with its windows on the world abroad and national politics, had become overwhelming. Two of his old friends—Elmer H. Bobst of Warner-Lambert, and Donald M. Kendall of Pepsi-Cola—were both clients of one of the oldest of New York's Establishment law firms, Mudge, Stern, Baldwin & Todd; they urged Nixon's name on the senior partners; and it was arranged that Nixon would join the firm, at 20 Broad Street, its name to become, shortly thereafter, Nixon, Mudge, Rose, Guthrie, Alexander & Mitchell. There, soon after his arrival, he signed off from politics in an interview with Roscoe Drummond: "I say categorically that I have no contemplation at all of being the candidate for anything in 1964, 1966, 1968, or 1972. Let's look at the facts. I have no staff. I am not answering any political mail. I am only making an occasional speech, writing an occasional magazine article. I have no political base. Anybody who thinks I could be a candidate for anything in any year is off his rocker."

Thus, by the spring of 1963 Nixon was installed in the heart of the Eastern Establishment, his office in the cleft off Wall Street, his home at the core of the Perfumed Stockade, on the fifth floor of the same apartment block that sheltered his antagonist, Nelson Rockefeller, on the eleventh floor.

The two apartments in themselves told something about contrasts in life-styles. Rockefeller's seemed light and airy; its mood changed from room to room—by turn stark modern, elegant soft, traditional solid, each setting a background for painting and sculpture. The art, lovingly collected and placed, ranged from primitive to latest modern, reflecting a curiosity refined by boldest taste and sustained by infinite resources. The Nixon apartment, six floors below, reflected more cautious tastes, in keeping with the more sober past of its owners. In the hallway were Chinese paintings, gifts of Madame Chiang; in the anteroom, light watercolors, dominant color yellow. Within, the Nixon apartment had the same high ceilings, but retained the mahogany-paneled style of New York in the twenties, the living room dominated by Oriental jardinières and vases, and furnished by Mrs. Nixon with light draperies and discreet upholstery. Nixon's den was snug and comfortable, with old-fashioned easy chairs and sofas. On the mantel of his den was an array of elephants, in teak, ivory, crystal, plastic, stone, which I have seen surpassed in only one other Republican home, that of the William Scrantons of Pennsylvania, inherited from the Governor's mother, Mrs. Marion Margery Scranton, who for four decades was Mrs. Republican of Pennsylvania.

The apartment of Richard Nixon told little, however, of inner lifestyle, nor could any outsider. Of so closely locked an inner man, it is difficult to report accurately the streams of identity and propulsion, even after the long conversations we had later. I had observed him from afar in the 1960 campaign with an attitude of suspicion and dislike which I cannot now withdraw; the intensity of the man offended me. But I was to see him occasionally now in New York, by chance. Once, I remember seeing him strolling solitary on Fifth Avenue on a cold December day. He had no topcoat, only a light suit jacket, and the habitual frown, I noticed, was gone from his face; he was smiling as if amused by some inner conversation. Occasionally I would see him at the annual glög Christmas parties of his friend Gabriel Hauge, of the Manufacturers Hanover Trust Bank, and he seemed entirely at ease, almost jovial. It was a personality infinitely more relaxed than the one I had watched in 1960. The Nixon I saw fleetingly still puzzled me; he had put on weight, which rounded his features—yet they were sharper than ever. The jaw jutted out, the nose was more pronounced, the bushy, thick hair of his earlier campaigns was slowly receding to a widow's peak, its curly wave more conspicuous. The lines on his face from nose to chin, the cheek folds themselves, were deeper, more furrowed; yet the more mature man seemed more attractive, less harsh than the man of 1960. But as a political reporter I had little interest in Nixon in his early years in New York; and though I tried continuously, out of residual curiosity, to keep my ear tuned to scraps and bits of gossip about Nixon, I had long since packed my files and clippings on him away to a forgotten corner of my cellar.

There seemed, however, adding up the gossip from afar, to be something of a "culture hunger" about Nixon, difficult to understand if one did not also come from a background of deprivation and earnest self-improvement. Nixon craved music, for one thing—not modern music, not the atonal universe of Schoenberg and Webern, or the polyrhythmic dissonances of Stravinsky, but the more familiar standards like the works of Beethoven and Bach; the melodic enticements through which most uninitiates seek an understanding of classical music. Nixon, friends told me, would occasionally play his records turned up full-volume when he worked. And he liked to play the piano, in a thumping, barrelhouse, fraternity-hall, Harry Truman style.

He had, as he has pointed out himself, time to read between 1963 and 1967, which he had never had time to do before. His bookshelves in his den, I later noticed, were full of Book-of-the-Month Club selections of which, it seemed to me when once I was alone there, the best-thumbed volume was John Hersey's *The Wall*. He had time to go to plays—not the benefit-party plays which are the curse of the New York theater, nor the openings with their cruel detached judgment of thumbs-up-or-down, but plays as plays where on the spur of the moment one calls, finds two seats, visits and goes home. His humdrum taste in food was well known before coming to New York, spaghetti and meat sauce being one of his favorites, cottage cheese and catsup being another. Now in New York he could sample the cuisine of the best restaurants of the city—the broadest, if most expensive, gastronomic range in the world. But he was, all in all, when he came to New York, still a tourist in famous places, unsure of standards, sampling what the great world of culture might have to offer.

It was in New York between 1963 and 1967 that he stopped being a tourist. "Between 1963 and 1967," said Robert Finch once, "there came a greater change in life-style than in all the years I'd known him between 1946 and 1963."

Perhaps the greatest influence on Richard Nixon at this time was the law firm whose roster of names he now headed. Nixon, Mudge, Rose, Guthrie, Alexander & Mitchell does not have quite the prestige of, say, Sullivan & Cromwell in the pecking order of New York law firms. But it is right there in the top ten, along with the two most prestigious Republican law firms, Dewey, Ballantine, Bushby, Palmer & Wood and Royall, Koegel, Rogers & Wells; along with the two most prestigious Democratic law firms, Paul, Weiss, Goldberg, Rifkind, Wharton & Garrison and Cleary, Gottlieb, Steen & Hamilton; along with the top antiseptic high-collar establishment firms like Cravath, Swaine, or Milbank, Tweed, or Shearman & Sterling, *et alia*. New York and Washington lawyers play an absolutely astonishing role in national affairs, unmatched by any other community of their legal brethren in this country or abroad. They are the midwives of great public, national and industrial affairs; the simple use of one of these names as counsel can be a calling-card that costs a minimum $100,000 a year as a retainer. Nixon's new firm was of this magnitude and impact; and thus, when Nixon joined them, his new associates offered him three things that were gradually to change his view of the world and of himself. They were, in order of ascending importance, the young and eager junior members of the firm, the presence of John Mitchell, and a sense of having made it.

Of the bright and eager young men, Leonard Garment's name came first. Garment, a specialist in litigation, with an exceptional sensitivity to words and arts, had such a conspicuously bright mind that the prestigious law firm had hired him directly on graduation from Brooklyn Law School in 1949. It is a long way from Brooklyn, with its quilt of nestling little Jewish communities, to the spires of Manhattan; but the aspirations, ambitions and wonderment at achievement that propel the sons of these communities are not too different from those of small-town America which moved Richard Nixon. Nixon, despite the fact that Jews have always overwhelmingly voted against him in every city of the Union, has a particular, long-lasting pleasure in Jewish associates, dating back to the days of his first campaign in California, when Murray Chotiner was his campaign manager. The persistent inclination of Jews to vote against him is a constant sadness to Nixon, for there is a sympathy of striving between them; affinity of respect flourished between himself and Garment. Garment, who had regarded Nixon with detached curiosity when Nixon entered the firm, found himself first intrigued, then mesmerized by Nixon's sober, intense work habits. They became friends; Nixon would go to Garment's home in Brooklyn and as Garment played the clarinet, Nixon would thump on the piano. Garment was enormously alert to the climate of New York's culture—the world of television, broadcasting, stage, literary intellectualism—and through Garment there passed into Nixon's acquaintance a file of new people, new liberals, names Nixon had never known before. And there were also two other young men who, joining the firm soon after Nixon's arrival, became his dedicated servants: Tom Evans, thirty-four, and John Sears, twenty-seven. When, as Nixon said later, "I was talked into this campaign by amateurs," he referred to these three young men among whom he had found a new loyalty and warmth. From his experience with them Nixon learned that even among strangers he could rouse the kind of affection without which the solitary man freezes.

Next came the presence of John Mitchell,[4] a magnitude of his own in the Nixon circle. Within the Nixon circle, there are five people who have critical influence on his thinking. Two are women—his wife, and his secretary, Rose Mary Woods. The other three are men: Robert Finch and H. R. (Bob) Haldeman of California—and John Mitchell of New York, latest comer to the group. Mitchell was and is a conservative, as is Nixon himself. But Mitchell is a conservative with a creative, professional twist. His legal clients were chiefly governments of states, cities and public authorities, and through Mitchell's clientele Nixon was to see a new aspect of government. It is important that one linger in this particular chamber of Mitchell's professionalism, for it was part of the education of Richard Nixon, and Nixon was fascinated by what he found there. Briefly—since it would be an aberration here to lead one through a history of public finance—Mitchell had come from a law firm that had specialized since 1873 in counseling governments on how to write laws and issue bonds to do in constitutional fashion what they had to do. Governments these days *have* to build public housing, clear slums, erect university halls and dormitories, increase medical services. But enormous legal technical care must be exercised in issuing municipal and state bonds, in employing the public credit to achieve these purposes. Mr. Nixon, in Congress and Senate, had been a persistent and rigorous conservative opponent of public housing, of liberal proposals for the use of public credit for public ends. But when he arrived in New York, he found himself associated with a lawyer who specialized in the blue-

---

[4] John Mitchell is now U.S. Attorney General.

printing of just this kind of use of public finance for welfare ends. Among John Mitchell's clients was the State of New York, governed by Republican Nelson Rockefeller, which was trying to raise $2.2 billion for metropolitan transportation through a new bond issue. Also on the roster was a Democratic client, the Democratic administration of the State of Wisconsin, which needed to borrow millions for the immediate building of dormitories and classrooms for its expanding state university system. Yet Wisconsin was trapped by an archaic constitution which forbade it to go deeper in debt than $250,000 and allowed it to go that far only in case of domestic insurrection or foreign invasion. Nixon was intrigued by Mitchell's successful effort to draft a law that would let Wisconsin, by legal subterfuge, do constitutionally the things that Wisconsin could not, politically, escape doing for higher education. Mitchell became not only an educational force in Nixon's life but a friend to be trusted almost more than any other.

Lastly, with his partnership in the new law firm, Mr. Nixon was beginning to make it. Its clients included such major enterprises, spreading across the fat of the industrial spectrum, as Studebaker-Packard, Pepsi-Cola, Mutual of New York, El Paso Natural Gas, Irving Trust Company, Hornblower-Weeks. Ordinary senior partners in the law firm made, variously, upwards from $150,000 a year, which is a good deal of money. With the spread-forward royalties of his book, *Six Crises,* Mr. Nixon found that he was making much more than $200,000 a year. He had come to New York a relatively poor man. In New York he found, as many others have found, that with the right connections and a certain knack anyone can make large sums of money—and it turned out that, once he had made it, money was not all that important.[5] This is why New York psychiatrists make so much money out of the rich of the East Side, who, after they have made their money, discover that there is greater purpose in life than money. Partnership in the law firm somehow released Nixon from that inner hunger, that outer pugnacity of the poor boy who had so offended so many people in the years between 1946 and 1962.

But release for what? There is in Nixon, privately and publicly, always a sense of striving, always a dogged, persistent, unshakable diligence that dates, in the old American culture, from the heroes of Horatio Alger, an emotional need of "doing it," of "making it," against all odds. But when one arrives, what then? When one learns that the towers of

[5] Mr. Nixon's net worth in 1968 was publicly announced as $515,830. His assets were listed as $858,190 and his liabilities as $342,360. His chief assets were in real estate, with holdings in Florida valued at $401,382 and a New York cooperative apartment valued at $166,856. He had cash in the bank of $39,385, and his personal property, including Mrs. Nixon's jewelry, was valued at $45,000. His civil service retirement benefits were put at a cash value of $18,605—but, as President, these benefits will increase somewhat in value.

the Eastern Establishment are occupied largely by people like oneself—what then? From his apartment windows in the Perfumed Stockade, Nixon could look out on the Knickerbocker Club (whose building was owned by Nelson A. Rockefeller, Jr.) and on the Metropolitan Club. He himself belonged uptown to the Links Club, the most Establishment of New York's Establishment clubs. Downtown, he belonged to the Recess Club and India House. Out of town, he belonged to Blind Brook, in Westchester, and Baltusrol, in New Jersey. When one thus lives under the same roof with Nelson Rockefeller; when one is head of a major New York law firm, as distinguished as any in the country; when one has all the creature comforts one can need, and creature comforts are not enough to satisfy the inner man—what then? Thomas Dewey, like Nixon a defeated Presidential candidate, had withdrawn completely from politics in 1954 to settle for a huge income as head of Dewey, Ballantine. But Nixon could not settle only for money. He had tasted national power as Vice-President, as Dewey had not; he had sojourned at the summit, and the vision of another world lingered on; it could not be forgotten.

When and where the appetite for the Presidency revived in Richard Nixon, one cannot say for sure. Certainly no one could have foreseen the assassination of John F. Kennedy in 1963. But with that assassination, with the Republican nomination in 1964 apparently up for contest, some of Nixon's friends could already see, in the distant perspective, a faint chance of using the Nixon equity either to choose the nominee or, if the convention deadlocked, to make him the nominee. All that was required was for Nelson Rockefeller and Barry Goldwater to kill each other off in the 1964 primaries, and there might be an opportunity for leverage. Robert Finch recalls a meeting with Nixon a few weeks before the Republican convention of that year, at Montauk Point, Long Island.[6] Goldwater had beaten Rockefeller in the California primary; Everett Dirksen had just declared for Goldwater; thus, the nomination was closed. Not only that, thought Nixon—Goldwater would surely lose to Johnson and by a disastrous margin. Nonetheless, Nixon thought, he *must* help the Party; it was the minority party, badly split, needing whatever crutch it could find. To associate oneself with it was like joining the bedraggled army of Napoleon as it set out on its raggle-taggle retreat from Moscow. But, to have any future claim on this party's loyalty, one had to be present, as at Agincourt. And Finch, for the first time since Nixon's defeat in the California race of 1962, realized that Nixon might be thinking once again of the Presidency. Nixon, at the same time, dispatched Leonard Garment to San Francisco, to be one of his observers

[6] Nixon is a restless man and one can almost trace his decisions by following his migrations around the circuit of his favorite hideaways—Key Biscayne in Florida; the Waldorf Towers in New York; Montauk on Long Island; Southern California.

at the Republican convention—Garment's first—just to get the experience. An awareness of Nixon's returning presence came later to other men —and thus we move from the man to the politics of the Presidency. For Richard M. Nixon, 1965 was a year of cautious revival. The Republican Party, as yet, had no recognized leaders—Dwight D. Eisenhower, an aging and ailing saint, could no longer campaign; and Barry Goldwater was still the kiss of death for any candidate outside the Deep South. Two governorships, the mayoralty of New York, and several minor races were all that marked the elections of 1965—but all Republican candidates in these races, except for Lindsay in New York, craved Party help. Nixon would supply it. Friends provided a fund for travel expenses; and he spoke in dozens of towns, often with as few as forty or fifty people to hear him, and to no press attention whatsoever except for a major episode in New Jersey. There, with his old pugnacity, he denounced Professor Eugene D. Genovese, of Rutgers University, an outright advocate of victory for the Viet Cong, and earned, once more, the hostility of the liberals.[7]

1966 was a much more inviting year for Nixon. The Vietnam war had begun to ache in every home and on every campus, riots had begun to flare in American cities in the summer festival of hate, and Lyndon

[7] Responding to his critics on the Genovese case, Nixon replied in a letter to *The New York Times* which is worth recalling: "Every American is for free speech and academic freedom. The question is how do we preserve that freedom? We do so by recognizing and protecting the right of individuals to freedom of speech. We do so by defending the system of government which guarantees freedom of speech to individuals. Unfortunately there are occasions—particularly in wartime —when the individual's rights and the nation's security come in conflict. Justice Learned Hand summarized it best when he said, 'A society in which men recognize no check on their freedom soon becomes a society in which freedom is the possession of only a savage few.' . . . No one has questioned the right of Professor Genovese or anyone else to advocate any controversial issue in peacetime. The question in the Genovese case is whether a professor, employed by a state university, should have the right to use the prestige and forum of the university for advocating victory for an enemy of the United States in wartime. The victory for the Vietcong which Professor Genovese 'welcomes' would mean ultimately the destruction of freedom of speech for all men for all time not only in Asia, but in the United States as well. The question at issue, therefore, becomes: does the principle of freedom of speech require that the state subsidize those who would destroy the system of government which protects freedom of speech? We are confronted in the Genovese case with this choice: The responsibility of the state to protect the right of freedom of speech for an individual. The responsibility of the state to defend itself against enemies whose victory would deny freedom of speech to all. . . . Reports from Hanoi and Peking conclusively indicate that the demonstrations against our policy in Vietnam encourage the enemy, prolong the war, and result in the deaths of American fighting men. . . . Where the choice confronting us is between the lives of American fighting men to preserve the system which guarantees freedom of speech for all, and the right of an individual to abuse that freedom, the lives of American fighting men must come first. We must never forget that if the war in Vietnam is lost and the victory for the Communists which Professor Genovese says he 'welcomes' becomes inevitable, the right of free speech will be extinguished throughout the world. . . ." Richard M. Nixon, October 27th, 1965.

Johnson's vulnerability was clear. The large men of the Republican Party—Rockefeller, Romney, Reagan—were all preoccupied by home-state struggles for their governorships. And thus, by default and history, Nixon was the Republican most available to do the Party thing. He was willing—and so were friends to help.

"Congress '66," the Nixon group of that campaign, was established early in the year with the specific purpose of enabling Nixon to help elect Republican Congressmen across the nation and roll back the Johnson majorities on the Hill. How or when it became the nucleus of Nixon's Presidential effort no one can quite identify by date. "We weren't politicians," said Peter Flanigan of Dillon Read, its inspiring spirit. "We didn't know who the proper Congressmen to support were in Missouri and California. We didn't know how to spend money and we wanted to help elect Republicans; so we put the money in the hands of a man who knew where it should go."

"Congress '66" began with a core of no more than ten people—centrists by political doctrine, old friends of Nixon by emotion and affection, chiefly civilians with little experience in political mechanics. It included, in addition to Flanigan, Hobart Lewis (an Executive Editor of the *Reader's Digest*), Richard Amberg (Publisher of the St. Louis *Globe-Democrat*), Maurice Stans, John Lodge and Nixon's three young law partners—Leonard Garment, John Sears and Tom Evans. It expanded gradually to a group of almost twenty-five men, with occasional out-of-state and California members, enjoying weekend meetings at the New York Metropolitan Club where they planned, advised and funded Nixon's campaign effort.

Primarily, their function was to raise money which Nixon could distribute to promising Republican candidates. From the Republican Congressional Campaign Committee came a grant of $30,000 to help the only national figure who could usefully stump for their candidates; from Miss Helen Clay Frick of Pittsburgh came some two dozen checks of $1,000 each to be passed on by Nixon to candidates of his selection. And, under the leadership of Flanigan, $60,000 more was raised directly from friends who wanted Republicans of center-stripe elected. "It wasn't," says Flanigan, "a Nixon-for-President group in the beginning. I suppose we all would have said at the beginning, it'd be nice—but he can't be elected. And then gradually it passed over to something else, like—it's nice working together, maybe he *can* be elected. And then the night of the election in '66, with those telephone calls coming in from all over the country—we knew we were in business."

Nixon was to travel some 30,000 miles and visit some 82 Congressional districts in his exercise. At no time, however, was his personal staff larger than two—twenty-eight-year-old Patrick Buchanan, on a year's leave of absence from Amberg's *Globe-Democrat*, and a gifted political public-relations officer, William Safire, who had come to devotion to Nixon as early as 1960.[8] But although Nixon's speeches were more graceful, his quips more humorous, although the loyalties earned from grateful candidates was solid money in the bank of politics, nonetheless Nixon perambulated week after week with scant attention from the national press, barely making, as Safire said, "the furniture pages in *The New York Times.*"

The turning point, if there was a turning point, came almost by accident. At the beginning of November, Johnson, returning from his Asian trip of that year, issued a communiqué on Vietnam. Reading the communiqué in his New York office that afternoon in the presence of Safire and Buchanan, Nixon decided it required a Republican reply, which was swiftly dictated, but apparently destined, as so many of his other statements that year, to oblivion. But it was a slack afternoon for news that day, and Safire, on a hunch, inquiring of *The New York Times,* was told by them that if the full text were ready by six, they might consider publishing it. The next day, the front page of the *Times* indeed ran the full Nixon story—to provoke instant and furious response from a televised Johnson press conference and the President's blast that Nixon was "a chronic campaigner" and "He never did really recognize what was going on when he had an official position in the government." With this attack, Nixon was, overnight, front-page again. The next day, television crews of the major networks were assigned to his travels; on the following Sunday, just before the election, he was given time by a major network to reply to the President as the Republican national spokesman—and to emerge before his Party as the architect of the Republican comeback that was to follow in the Tuesday election.

The election of 1966 was a major comeback for the Republicans; for Nixon it was personal triumph. All Tuesday evening, from a suite in the Hotel Delmonico, Nixon was on the telephone around the country, checking on the fate of his candidates. From California, where he had stumped for Finch, came the happy news that Finch, running for the first time for public office as Lieutenant Governor—Finch who had clearly parted with his conservative running-mate, Reagan, to take the liberal side of the censorship-pornography controversy—Finch was actually outrunning Reagan for a victory of 1,200,000 votes, the largest ever in any single state contest for office. From the Midwest, the Rocky Mountain states, the Plains states came further reports of triumph of the candidates for whom he had stumped. "It's a sweep, I tell you, it's a sweep," he was quoted as saying. He received the reports with a grow-

---

[8] Safire, a phrase-maker whose punch lines and cue lines studded Nixon's speeches all through 1968, is something of a scholar. His *The New Language of Politics,* published by Random House, is at once amusing, erudite and a mine of political folklore.

ing euphoria, a mounting happiness, until, at three in the morning, he decided to walk home, stopping off at El Morocco for a bowl of his favorite spaghetti to celebrate. Only John Sears was left to take the late returns in the hotel suite, and by four o'clock it was obvious that the Republican Party had picked up forty-seven seats in Congress—seven more than Nixon had predicted—and three in the Senate. When, at about this time, Nixon telephoned Sears for the last-last returns, Sears remembers Nixon clearly chortling, "We'll kick their toes off in 1968."

He was running.

It was the Sunday after election that "Congress '66" met for the last time, at the Metropolitan Club, in a two-hour morning meeting. Nixon presided: a decision, he said, had to be made; he would be thinking about the matter for the next few weeks. What were the views of the group? There was no doubt about the views of the group—Nixon must run. The question was how. Nixon would reflect. His reflections in the next few weeks were carried on within his law firm; with Finch of California, flying back to New York to consult; with Hobart Lewis of the *Reader's Digest,* who offered him the role of special writer for the *Digest* on the overseas trips that Nixon planned for 1967—this would reinforce his image on the American mind as a master of foreign affairs. And then, before the first of the trips overseas, came a serious initial planning session.

The first planning session—a two-day meeting on January 7th/8th 1967 in Suite 31A at the Waldorf Towers—is of interest for the age of those present, for their discussion, and for Nixon's own perception of the perspective of the next year and a half in Republican politics.

The group was young—Finch of California, forty-one; Peter Flanigan of New York, forty-four; Jeremiah Milbank of Connecticut, forty-six; Fred LaRue of Mississippi, thirty-eight; Peter O'Donnell of Texas, forty-two; William Safire, thirty-seven; Tom Evans, thirty-six. Nixon himself, aged fifty-four, brought the average age to 42.2. Nixon's Southern strategy was already obvious in the composition of the group.

Nixon, to begin with, accepted the odds for the nomination much as did the press. It was Romney even money to win the nomination, he said. The odds against himself and Charles Percy of Illinois were two to one. Against Reagan, four to one. As for Rockefeller—Nixon gave him zero chance.

A delegate count for the Republican convention—still eighteen months away in the future—had already been drawn up and was ready. State by state it went, starting with Alaska, 6 (ultimately at convention, 11), Arizona, 6 (correct), down the list to Wyoming, 12 (correct), for a total of 603 that Nixon might reasonably assemble if he held the South against the big industrial states of the Northeast, which, already, he had written off.

The first and basic problem was Romney. There was Romney out front and running. Percy, Nixon felt, could be ignored for the moment, for Percy's problem was also Romney. At some point, opined Nixon, the Eastern Establishment would try to ditch Romney as not being of their style, and shift to choose Percy—but Romney would not let himself be discarded that easily. How, then, to take on Romney? Nixon summarized the conversation at one point: some say I should do nothing —otherwise, in a deadlock, there'd be no chance to be king-maker. But I disagree, continued Nixon—you can't be king-maker unless you try to be king. It gets you power, it may help form the deadlock. If he, Nixon, were to sit still and do nothing, Romney would sweep through the delegate-brokers of the Midwest and nothing could stop him from getting the nomination. Whoever was going to be in the running had to start running now—delegates had to be sown now, in 1967, to be harvested in 1968.

On the other hand, Nixon was firm about not announcing his own candidacy. It was too early. Thus, discussion ran to decision: they would start at once to assemble names for a Nixon for President Committee; it would be headed by Dr. Gaylord Parkinson of San Diego, California. (Finch left the room to telephone San Diego, had Herbert Klein reach the doctor, reported back with Parkinson's consent.) A Washington office would be set up to raise the flag, as O'Donnell insisted (it was to be the most-beflagged office in Washington, a few hundred yards from the White House on Pennsylvania Avenue, hung with bunting and stars from early May until the convention ended), and a staff would be assembled for delegate search and care.

But Nixon himself? At one point Nixon asserted that he could not be re-packaged by any public-relations officer, no matter how skillful. That might work with a new man, but not with him. He would persist in his six-month personal moratorium of all discussion of politics as he traveled the world for the *Reader's Digest*. There would be a Nixon campaign, thus—but Nixon would not be in it until the time was ripe. For the moment, let the nation pay attention to George Romney. "I want him to get the exposure," said Nixon, "we have to keep him out at the point." The man who had been so thoroughly savaged by reporters and cartoonists over the years wanted their full talents for destruction concentrated on the personality of George Romney. It was, said someone later, looking back on George Romney's earnest and miserable exercise of 1967 and 1968, like seeing a missionary abandoned to the cannibals. And thus we return to George Romney as Mr. Nixon, through 1967, remained sheltered from the press.[9]

[9] For a good study of Nixon at this point in transition, see "The New New Nixon," by Nicholas Thimmesch, in the New York *World Journal Tribune*, April 23, 1967.

* * *

Governor James Rhodes of Ohio was later quoted with the cruelest epitaph on the Romney campaign. "Watching George Romney run for the Presidency," he said, "was like watching a duck try to make love to a football."

Yet there was nothing comic in the performance itself—only in the mirror of the media and the press through which the nation saw the performance. And the story of the Romney campaign is less one of politics than of the influence of the media in modern America.

Of this changing media-environment in the past decade of American life there will be much more to say later in this book. The American journalists who represent the media and report for its press, to whose brotherhood I have belonged for thirty years, are the most efficient, honest and accurate press corps, taken as a whole, in the world. Yet since time on air is always limited and space in print is always tight, all reporting must be the snatching of fragments of a continuum, chosen by each reporter's own inner judgment of which fragments reveal or symbolize a larger general truth. Reporters and media thus sit in judgment on candidates. But the media-men themselves are judged by critics in the thought-climate of New York and Washington who can make or break reporters' reputations, advance or destroy their careers by extraneous judgments on their style. And here, in these two great centers of Eastern thinking, a new culture of style, manners and elegant aesthetic cruelty has grown up which removes people like George Romney—and to a lesser extent Richard M. Nixon—as far from judicial consideration as a rabbi in Nazi Germany. In the new culture of American criticism, to be kind, soft or tolerant in judgment is to be labeled "square." Copy must have bite; TV shows must "march"; by these standards reporters themselves are judged.

Somewhere out beyond the Alleghenies the old culture of America still persists—people who think Boy Scouts are good, who believe that divorce is bad, who teach Bible classes on Sunday, enjoy church suppers, wash their children's mouths with soap to purge dirty words, who regard homosexuals as wicked, whose throat chokes up when the American flag is marched by on the Fourth of July. In its extravagant and hyperbolic form—as in Barry Goldwater's cosmology of demons—the old culture sees the Atlantic Seaboard, particularly the Boston-New York-Washington belt, as the locus of a vast and sinister intellectual conspiracy, a combination of capital and decadence, corrupting the moral fiber and legendary decencies of an earlier America.

The new culture, of which we shall talk later, is the child of prosperity and the past decade. Characterized by an exuberance of color, style, fashion, art and expression flowing from the enormous excess energies of American life, it defines itself best not by what it seeks but by its contempt and scorn of what the past has taught. Its thrust lies in the direction of liberties and freedom, but with an exaggerated quality of aggressive infantilism. In its exploration of the limits of sensibility, all laws, manners, mores, institutions which restrict such areas of individual expression as drugs, sex, obscenities and mob violence are generally held to be oppressive; and the greatest agent of oppression in the twentieth century is generally held to be the United States government. As parochial as the old culture, the new expressionist culture is as sure of its own moral superiority over the old as the old culture is of its superiority over the new; and in its extreme and paranoid form the new culture is as convinced of the conspiracy of a military-industrial complex pushing America to war and ruin as, say, the John Birch Society is convinced of a Communist conspiracy pushing America to slavery.

In the operational climate of American politics, the critical difference between the two cultures is that the new culture dominates the heights of national communications, subtly but profoundly influences those who sit astride the daily news flow in New York and Washington, and thus stains, increasingly, the prisms of reporting through which the nation as a whole must see itself.

George Romney of Michigan, despite the fact that he is a shrewd, efficient, hard-driving business and government executive, is, by style, a man of the old culture. In a state like Michigan, as in many other states of the Midwest, West and South, a man of the old culture campaigning on a state level, through state media, dealing with statehouse reporters who understand the idiom of the homefolk, can and does frequently win out. But when a man like George Romney ventures out on the national scene, he must operate in a totally different environment— the environment of the national press and media. In a Presidential campaign there is no such thing as an Off-Broadway production; wherever a microphone is held to his lips, or a camera crew assigned to him by the great national networks, a Presidential candidate is on Broadway; and the performance expected of him is entirely different from the quality of a performance in Grand Rapids, Michigan. There is a natural timberline in national politics beyond which certain kinds of men cannot thrive. Once George Romney began to press into the stratospheric environment of national media and attention, his Presidential image was to wither; and this withering was to be shown as a matter of cruel amusement to the nation.

There was much else wrong with the Romney campaign beyond the natural dis-affinity between Romney and the standards of the media. Although campaign management was headed up by Leonard Hall, former Republican National Chairman and a veteran of many national campaigns, many others had greater influence on Romney. And these were split between his old friends—personal acquaintances of long standing like J. Willard Marriott of the national motor-hotel chain, Max Fisher, an old supporter and Detroit businessman, Clifford Folger, a Washington banker—and his younger men. His younger men were always further split by the rivalry between the campaign staff proper and the Governor's in-state executive staff. No one was ever thoroughly or authoritatively in charge of the candidate, or ever effectively in control of his plans and campaigns. But most important of all was the gulf between the man and the national media, who could not understand each other —Romney's billboards in New Hampshire read THE WAY TO STOP CRIME IS TO STOP MORAL DECAY; he could not understand why newsmen found the slogan funny; and they could not understand what he meant by moral decay.

It was apparent from the very beginning of 1967 that press and candidate would not get along. The press was focused on George Romney as the only visible candidate; and the press had one great, inescapable concern: the war in Vietnam. It would have been wise for Mr. Romney to say flatly at once, and for many months thereafter, that he simply did not understand Vietnam, that he was not equipped to discuss Vietnam at that early moment. But he could not keep himself from answering questions—at length, in the most plodding prose, in open innocent confession of his non-understanding, over and over and over again, to the despair of his staff.

Romney began his adventure (not officially as a campaign but "to explore" whether he *should* campaign) with a trip to Alaska and to the Rocky Mountain states, areas of his greatest natural strength, in February of 1967. He left at the height of his popularity in the national polls: and shortly thereafter his polls began to slip. The attendant national press would insist on questioning him on Vietnam wherever he went; they were annoyed by the inefficiencies of the trip, and frustrated by the candidate's irritable reluctance to speak on something which he felt he could not yet discuss in public.

The trip was a failure, and the campaign staff immediately went through the first of its many reorganizations. A new public-relations officer, Travis Cross, a most amiable and civilized Oregonian with good practical national experience, was called in to replace the local Michigan State public-relations officer; and a young and prestigious Boston firm of political managers—Campaign Consultants Incorporated—was added to the campaign apparatus to re-draw the image. Since Vietnam now dogged Romney as much as it did Johnson, it was decided that he must address himself squarely to the issue, with a speech scheduled in Hartford, Connecticut, for April 7th, 1967. All through the next eighteen months this correspondent was to observe the writhing of every candidate, Democratic and Republican, to produce a Vietnam policy statement, always cooked up by bright young staffers and international-affairs ex-

perts most of whom had never been in Vietnam and knew little or nothing of Asia. Always the documents were pasted together in compromise,
with a posterior glance at Asian reality and a prime focus on American
public opinion. The Hartford speech of Romney was as good a disserta-
tion on Vietnam as any that later appeared; but it too was a compromise;
Mr. Romney himself leaned to the "dove" side on Vietnam, as did most
of his staff and the brains group supplied by Campaign Consultants. But
since Mr. Romney was so unsure of himself in foreign affairs, he sent
the next-to-last draft of his major statement on to New York to be approved by Nelson Rockefeller, at that point in time still a resolute commitment man, several substantial degrees to the hawk side of George
Romney. What emerged was a document neither dove nor hawk in which
Romney offered a multi-point program for Vietnam (its essential plank
"Peace with Amnesty") designed to establish, once and for all, George
Romney's profile as an independent man who thought deeply on foreign
affairs.

The effort might have succeeded but for the alertness of the White
House staff. Lyndon Johnson had first privately reacted to Romney's
draft speech with his characteristic irritation and indignation at any disagreement with government policy. But in a few hours it was pointed
out to him that the disagreements and differences were so minor that
Johnson could score best by *praising,* not denouncing, the Romney
speech—which Johnson that night hastened to do. And thus, smothered
in the public embrace of Lyndon Johnson, there vanished the project
to establish George Romney as an independent voice on Vietnam—sub-
jecting him again and continuously to the nagging of the press for an
alternative policy, the magic solution for which all America yearned,
Peace with Honor.

By now, in April, the national polls were reflecting the sag in Romney's popularity with the voters. By May, after the Hartford speech, he
dropped to being even with Johnson for the first time as the public rated
him no better than their President. If it was true that Americans did not
believe what Johnson was telling them, it seemed clear that they could
not *understand* what Romney was telling them. Down, down, down
went Romney's rating in the polls. The terrible race riots of Detroit in
July, 1967, paradoxically raised Romney's ratings the next month—
apparently his testy dispute with the President on the timing and use of
Regular Army troops separated him once again from the President, thus
heightening his popular esteem by a bounce-back from the President's
unpopularity. And then happened what is remembered as the "brainwashing" statement.

George Romney's "brainwashing" statement, if remembered at all,
will be remembered as a tiny episode in the pre-campaign of 1968; but
it was huge in public thinking at the time and will illustrate as well as

any other episode the relation between the reality of politics and its distorted reflection in the media. For what-it-is-that-makes-news is not taught in any course on politics as presented in schools. Not only did millions of Americans *know* that George Romney *stated* he had been brainwashed; millions of them *saw* him say it on their home TV screens. It is so difficult to deny the episode as fact that it is well, for the purposes of demonstration, to show how a slip of the tongue is inflated to a major statement of policy.

The actual story went this way:

Several weeks prior to the supposed "statement," Mr. Romney had been approached by a broadcaster in Detroit called Lou Gordon. Lou Gordon had previously been a Midwest garment-manufacturer's representative, a Midwest leg-man for the Drew Pearson column, but in an expression of his own identity he was a radio-TV personality in the Detroit area. As master of a "telephone-in" question-and-answer show on radio, he had major local prominence—for Michigan politicians he was a man who could give away air time free by exposure on his show. Gordon had supported Romney with friendly air time in campaigns of the past. Romney had actually filled in as guest-host on the show on one occasion when Gordon was off on vacation.

But now Gordon's career was moving forward; he wanted to become a national TV personality, a Midwestern Mike Wallace. He was to launch, right after Labor Day, a new television question-and-answer show which would be exposed at various times later, not only in Detroit but in Philadelphia and Boston. He needed a headliner for the launching of the show, and Romney was both a friend and a headliner. For Romney, a generous man, consent to the invitation was a simple response to another old friend—and also, since the show would be aired in Boston two weeks later, it was a free opportunity to reach the voters in New Hampshire, where he was entered in the primary.

Came the day for taping—Thursday, August 31st, 1967—and Romney by then had a busy schedule. Thursday morning he was engaged in a critical review of the over-all campaign in his Bloomfield Governor's Mansion with Len Hall of New York and other important staff members. The meeting ran late, so late that Romney's press aide, Travis Cross, had to be deputized to race Len Hall to the Detroit airport to catch a plane to Washington. Next on the Governor's schedule was a visit to the Michigan State Fair outside Detroit, which Romney must ceremonially visit, taking with him his grandchildren. At the State Fair a most human incident happened, further delaying the Governor; one of the grandchildren disappeared, and Romney, at the moment all grandfather and violently upset by the disappearance, would not leave until the grandchild was found. The schedule could wait. Could it be a kidnapping? State troopers fanning out over the Fair Grounds eventually found the happy child riding around and around in a Ferris wheel, and restored the child to Grand-father. By now upset and very late for the scheduled taping of the television show, Romney dashed into Detroit with, as one witness said, "cowflop and dirt from the State Fair still sticking to his shoes." Nor would the moralist Romney have been much comforted had he known that the Lou Gordon show was to increase its nationwide inaugural appeal by adding to the Governor's appearance other guests including, said the press release later, "a couple from 'The Swingers,' a national husband and wife swapping organization."

Composing himself, his handsome Presidential face earnest and serious as always, deprived of Cross's wise counsel, bereft of any aides or briefing, Romney swung into the question-and-answer session and, a few minutes later, still pulling himself together, responded to a question by Mr. Gordon thus:

Question: (on Vietnam) "Isn't your position a bit inconsistent with what it was, and what do you propose we do now?"

Answer: *"Well, you know when I came back from Vietnam, I just had the greatest brainwashing that anybody can get when you go over to Vietnam.* Not only by the Generals, but also by the diplomatic corps over there, and they do a very thorough job. And since returning from Vietnam, I've gone into the history of Vietnam, all the way back into World War II and before. And, as a result, I have changed my mind . . . in that particular. I no longer believe that it was necessary for us to get involved in South Vietnam to stop Communist aggression. . . ."

It was, said one of those present, a "tossaway line," and nobody thought it important. Romney himself did not even want to hear the play-back, being already late and tightly scheduled to sweep back from Detroit immediately after the television show to a state budget session in Lansing. Indeed, when the machinery of publicity cranked into action for the mini-build-up of the mini-show, the covering press release announced only that George Romney had said "he would not be interested in accepting the Vice Presidential spot on the Republican ticket."

The blossoming of "brainwashing" in the next ten days is a perfect illustration of the mechanics of public relations, media, publicity and politics. Mr. Gordon read the full transcript of his show Sunday, three days later. He decided then that "brainwashing" was more important than anything else in his show for attention-catching purposes. He tele-phoned the *New York Times* man in Detroit (Jerry Flint) to that effect, giving him a full transcript. Flint, four days after the actual taping of the show, reported the story to his desk, burying "brainwashing" down in his text. The man on the desk caught the "brainwashing" quote. On Tuesday, September 5th, the day after the telecast, on page 28 of *The New York Times,* a full five days after the blurt-out, the story came to national attention: ROMNEY ASSERTS HE UNDERWENT "BRAINWASHING"

ON VIETNAM TRIP. *The New York Times* is the bulletin board of the great TV companies; its news reports are the alert signal for the national evening news shows, and thus by Tuesday night the nation could see the thirty-second clip, requested from Gordon by the networks, in its homes. Shorn of background and circumstances, Romney was saying exactly what he was quoted as saying—the part presented as the whole, the fragment presented as reality.

Within the next day or two, happy Democrats of the administration made of the statement national controversy. John Bailey, Democratic National Chairman, first saw the opportunity and declared that Romney's statement had "insulted the integrity of two dedicated and honorable men"—General Westmoreland and Ambassador Lodge, who had briefed Romney in Vietnam. Robert McNamara weighed in with "I don't think Governor Romney can recognize the truth when he sees it or hears it." The Detroit newspapers, which had up till then ignored the tiny newsslip, weighed in with local pride; and the Detroit *News* prepared for its Sunday editorial pages a denunciation of George Romney, a demand that he quit the race as an incompetent, and a declaration that only Nelson Rockefeller could save the Republican Party.

It would have been well—but probably already too late—for Romney to have ignored the matter. But his pride was involved and he felt he was being abused. Wherever he went, thus, he must for the next six weeks, against all advice and pleading and urging of his staff, reply to the charge of innocence. And no one wanted an innocent for President.

Romney, perhaps, was the first to know that his hopes were over. He had planned to attend the floating gathering of the National Governors' Conference of 1967 on their autumn shipboard journey to the Virgin Islands. He appeared on the boat to join his basic constituents, the governors, like one of the walking wounded, pale, exhausted and dragging of foot. As the boat took off, a copy of *Time* Magazine was placed under every door with a joint cover-picture story on Rockefeller and Reagan, writing Romney off as a fool unqualified for high office. Three times on board the boat, closeted with Rockefeller in Rockefeller's cabin on the sun-deck, he pleaded with New York's Governor to let him off the hook. He was through, Romney insisted; Nelson must run for President. But Rockefeller would not—the plan was for Romney to run as the governors' candidate. He must go on with it.

On and on the good man went for the next few hopeless months, embrangling himself further with the press, whom he now regarded as a native American Viet Cong. He flew to Paris to polish his image as a foreign-affairs expert, at least on European affairs—and fell into additional befoulment with the press as he claimed that reporters had misquoted him and their little portable tape-recorders proved they had not.

He flew on to Vietnam, and the dispatches from Vietnam portrayed him as a blunt, crude, unfeeling politician campaigning for office in a land where men were dying. Romney could not win with the press.

Meanwhile, the New Hampshire primary of 1968 was approaching, and Rockefeller had put up one final installment of money to sound out the sentiment of New Hampshire voters. Three days after Christmas the Romney lieutenants secretly rendezvoused at the Port Authority Conference Room of the LaGuardia airport in New York to receive the results of the poll. Only one voter in eight among New Hampshire Republicans, said the private poll, picked Romney to be President. As a matter of cold figures, Richard Nixon, without having spoken once on Vietnam, was the choice of New Hampshire Republicans by 64.2 to 12.0 for George Romney—a five-to-one preference, a disaster. Further analyzing the secret polling results and weighing the volunteered comments of the sample, one of those present summarized the impression that George Romney had made. "I guess the poll shows," he said, "that New Hampshire Republicans think George Romney is too dumb to be President of the United States."

For two more months, with utmost bravery and great energy, George Romney campaigned through the snows of New Hampshire, stopping at bowling alleys, inspecting milk plants, hand-pumping in the sub-zero dawn outside factory gates, speaking to neighborhood groups, up early and to bed late. Yet one more major speech on Vietnam was forthcoming—a call for neutralization of that land—and several more polls followed. The last of the polls, taken by Romney's favorite polling firm, Frederick Currier's Market Opinion Research, was completed in the third week in February. Nothing had budged in Hampshiremen's minds; they were still for Nixon by six to one; the cause was hopeless. Thus, since he who lives by the polls must die by the polls, George Romney took his decision forthrightly, openly, bravely, and on February 28th called an end to it, leaving behind the impression of an honest and decent man simply not cut out to be President of the United States.

Thus, as 1968 turned the calendar pages of the nation toward the new year, it appeared that America would experience one of the dullest elections in all history—a choice between Richard M. Nixon and Lyndon B. Johnson. For the Democrats seemed equally unable to throw up a new face.

CHAPTER THREE

THE DEMOCRATS:
THE STRUGGLE FOR
THE INHERITANCE

NINETEEN-SIXTY-EIGHT was to be a year of torment for the Democratic Party of the United States; but its own history was to be its chief tormenter.

It is both curious and tragic that this should be the verdict, for the Democratic Party of the United States is the oldest and most successful political institution in the world. No Communist, Socialist, Liberal, Nationalist or Conservative party anywhere on the globe matches its long-lived vitality. All are junior, some by over a century, to this venerable party whose achievements in America have made captive the imagination of free nations everywhere, whose triumphs in arms have redrawn the boundaries of Europe and Asia, whose diplomacy has imposed new constitutions on nations illiterate and heirs to thousand-year-old cultures alike.

Yet no good history has ever been written of this majestic institution. Most American political scientists, oriented in recent times to a sterile behavioral explanation of political response, try to imprison it in statistics and analyses, and fail. Most European political scientists, nursed on theories, regard it from a distance as a native American freak, as once they did the feathered Indians and the roving buffalo. What baffles all writers is that this strange party has never possessed, until of late, anything remotely resembling a doctrine, an ideology or a code that could be put on paper to the taste either of scholarship or of historians. "The Democratic Party," said Ignatius Donnelly once, "is like a mule, without pride of ancestry or hope of posterity." From its very beginning, the Democratic Party has been guided chiefly by instinct and compromise to choose leaders who could somehow satisfy the tongueless yearnings, atavistic fears and blind urges of frightened and underprivileged men. No one can understand its torment in 1968 without looking back on its past; and that past carries us back to the eighteenth century.

The earliest traceable taproot of the Democratic Party goes back, in time, to the very birth of the American Constitution and Republic; in place, to New York City (whose history that party has largely shaped); and, in person, to a man called William Mooney. Of William Mooney, a Manhattan upholsterer and paper-hanger, we know very little except that he and a small group of kindred spirits were irked by the pretensions of the Society of the Cincinnati, an élite veterans' group organized by Alexander Hamilton and drawn from the officer corps of Washington's Revolutionary Army. The Sons of the Cincinnati, the Establishment of the day, whose membership was to be limited by heredity, seemed about to manipulate the new Federal Constitution of the Republic to their own aristocratic purposes. In those days in New York no man could vote unless he possessed £100 of property (the equivalent of $5,000 today); and of 324,000 New Yorkers, only 12,300 could cast ballots. Thus, only two weeks after the final adoption of the Constitution, we find paper-hanger Mooney assembling a number of *his* kind of veterans—enlisted men all—to form a rival group called the Society of St. Tammany, after the fabled Indian chief Tammany, the legendary discoverer of beans, tobacco, crab apples and corn. (Which is why, possibly, Democratic politicians still prefer to drink native American bourbon, made of corn, and Republican politicians still generally prefer scotch.) No learned paper, no philosophical manifesto or platform marked the founding of Tammany; a mumbo-jumbo of sachems, tepees and wigwams cloaked its ritual; its vitality came from groups of men who enjoyed friendship, boozing and volunteer firefighting in that order; but its chief purpose was to get out the votes. Clearly, it was an association of little guys against big guys, a first experiment in participatory politics; and within ten years Tammany votes controlled New York City, while Aaron Burr controlled Tammany.

It was the heroic figure of Thomas Jefferson who first gave shape to the Democratic Party as a national party. Jefferson, America's most distinguished intellectual of the day, was also one of its toughest pragmatists. Perceiving that the new Republic needed another national party to offset the dominant and conservative Federalist Party, Jefferson sought to create just such a party by adding the votes of impoverished farmers to the under-class of the big cities. The first of his missions to the big cities—purportedly a "butterfly hunting" expedition along the Hudson—took him to New York and to Tammany, from which came the deal whereby Aaron Burr, the treacherous boss of Tammany, emerged as running-mate to Jefferson himself in the elections of 1796 and 1800, and the national Democratic Party was formally born. Barely surviving the treachery of Burr in the tricky mechanics of the Electoral College in 1800, Jefferson, as third President, went on to set the mold for all Democratic Presidents since. As a politician, Jefferson was as cold and manipulative a dispenser of patronage as ever sat in the White House, a Party man to the core. But as a national leader, he set larger patterns—strong Federal government, executive leadership in Congress, expansion abroad, and reforms visionary enough to satisfy the yearnings of people who could not yet express their own needs.

Not until Franklin D. Roosevelt, more than a century later, did any Democratic leader match Jefferson in this combination of vision and gut-punching, of long thought and crisp immediate pragmatism. It was Roosevelt who, in the 1930's, put together all the urgencies and yearnings, the hopelessness and need of millions of Americans of different kinds, to create the grand coalition that has been the formula definition of the Democratic Party since. The coalition which Roosevelt formed was simple to describe: it was made of immigrants and their children in big-city ethnic blocs; of workingmen in their unions; of Southern rural machines terrified of Negroes; and of intellectuals. By definition, this formula held that the underprivileged, ignorant and fearful poured their pavlovian votes into the organizations and machines that mustered them to the polls; that the power-brokers who controlled these votes then assembled in blocs at a convention every four years to negotiate a candidate for the Presidency; and that the President, once elected, called on the intellectuals to shape the plans that would satisfy the needs and urges of the blind voters in the under-stratum.

This working formula, like all clichés, was true—for thirty years; and then, like so many clichés, was, in 1968, to lose its validity. It was to lose its validity because three grand but silent assumptions controlled its workings. The first assumption was that a Democratic President of the United States, once elected, so long as he met the immediate needs of the constituent blocs, was left free to conduct foreign policy and make war around the world with no protest from the voters. The second assumption was that politics was a trade limited to professionals. The third assumption was that government was responsible for the "share-out" of the nation's wealth, and that any Democratic administration would increase or stretch the wealth so that everyone would get his fair share of money, goods and comfort, and thus be content. In 1968 all three of these grand and hidden assumptions were to crumble; and Lyndon Johnson failed to grasp how completely the erosion of these assumptions would erode his leadership.

The first of the assumptions—that the President spoke for the nation in foreign affairs and received its automatic patriotic response in war—had run for half a century and changed the nature of the globe itself. From the year that Lenin's Bolsheviks seized power in Russia in 1917, to the present writing, Presidents of the Democratic Party of the United States have challenged the tyranny and pretensions of totalitarian parties everywhere around the world. Whether against Nazi dictators, Asian imperialists or Communist hierarchs, the Democratic Party has been the most persistent political adversary of aggression and insurrection of the twentieth century. Americans take this noble record in an age of upheavals quite cynically, for they see the record through the prism of domestic manners and pledges. Four Democratic Presidents came to power—Wilson, Roosevelt, Truman and Johnson—promising peace; and once elected, they went on to lead the nation into the four great wars of this century. This first assumption underlay not only domestic politics; it underlay world politics as well, giving the American President that diplomatic power which made him both initiator of world change and policeman of universal unrest. The crumbling of this first assumption, starting in 1965, is still too recent to be assessed in global meaning; but by 1968 it was fact.

The second of the assumptions—that politics was a professional matter left to the professionals—had begun to crumble years before Lyndon Johnson became President. But those of us who write about politics write about them in terms to which the people have become accustomed. Therefore, the Democratic Party continued to be described until 1968 as the politicians' party—a rowdy carnival of richly colorful characters who entertained the nation with their constant feuds, their quadrennial brawlings at conventions, and the neat verities they lent to reporting. The Democrats were controlled by "pros." From clubhouse to city hall, from state capitols to Washington, the professional politicians all agreed: amateurs had to be kept out. Politicians controlled nominations, from local judges and aldermen to Senators and Presidents—and the only gateway to November elections lay through their anterooms. Harry Truman was the perfect politicians' President—a man who played the game at home by clubhouse rules, yet understood the rules of reality that govern power politics in the world beyond the seas.

This condition of professionalism had begun, in fact, to change in the late 1940's; so great an adventure in so high a cause as the war against fascism *had* to change the quality of American life and politics. Thus, in 1948 Boss Jake Arvey of Chicago's Cook County machine offered the apparently worthless gubernatorial nomination for Illinois to a gentleman called Adlai Stevenson. Stevenson won; and by 1952 a cluster of five bosses—Arvey and Daley of Cook County, Lawrence and Finnegan of Pennsylvania, John Bailey of Connecticut, all of them supported by Harry Truman—combined to deliver the nomination for President to Adlai Stevenson. And with Stevenson, a new voice rang through American politics, a voice whose call penetrated all those people whom Elmer Davis once described as regarding politics "with wholesome apathy." With Stevenson, amateurs began to creep into politics all across the country, from California to Manhattan. Where the clubhouses would not let amateurs in, they formed their own clubs, learning as they went the legal mechanics hitherto known only to professionals. By 1960 John F. Kennedy had learned to use such amateurs, harness them to old organizations, and thus snatched his victory from a biased nation. What his brilliant administration might have done for America had it run its course, how it might have changed the Democratic Party, no one will ever know. But when it ended, Kennedy was only halfway across his bridge of dreams, and the work, both as President and as Party leader, fell to another man, Lyndon Johnson.

Lyndon Johnson had, however, been bred as a politician in the old Southern school where a loud voice and a personalized following substituted for the more mechanized structures of Northern machines. As a Southern politician, Johnson knew exactly what he was doing and the full measure of risk he assumed, as with great courage and tenacious goodwill he moved forward on the course of civil rights. But in the North and the West he could not understand how the mechanical structures with which he had dealt so long were changing.

The mechanical structures of the Northern and big-city Democrats were changing so rapidly as to baffle even political reporters. In 1960, when John F. Kennedy was on the move, a political reporter could still work a beat of known power-brokers. The Kennedys and John Bailey controlled New England; Charles Buckley, Dan O'Connell and Peter Crotty in New York could balance off Carmine DeSapio of Tammany; David Lawrence controlled Pennsylvania; Ohio's delegates could be brought to heel by a single conversation between John F. Kennedy and Mike DiSalle at an early-morning rendezvous at the Pittsburgh airport; Walter Reuther and Soapy Williams could deliver Michigan; the Indiana machine was solid; Daley was king in Illinois. And, similarly, as one moved west to the states of citizen politics, other recognized leaders of different style carried similar authority.

By 1968 this old political map of the Democratic Party was as out of date as a Ptolemaic chart of the Mediterranean. No one any longer controlled New York, the state which had given Lyndon Johnson a 2,669,543 plurality in 1964. When one telephoned the switchboard of the New York State Democratic Committee early in 1968, one heard the languid voice of the telephone girl, "No. He's not here. There's nobody here. No one comes in any more. You can leave a message if you want." The California Democratic Party had dissolved into a clash of feuds as bizarre and personal as those of the Shansi warlords in China in the 1920's. Here and there, of course, a few hereditary enclaves of the old machines, passed on from father to son, still existed. There was still an O'Connell machine in Albany; in Brooklyn, Steingut *père* had passed on to Steingut *fils* leadership of an organization that could still deliver, when pressed, a clean 50,000 votes; in Manhattan, one could still find on the West Side a third-generation McManus delivering the same but ever-diminishing votes that McManus *père* and McManus *grandpère* had delivered a generation ago. In Philadelphia, young Congressman Billy Green still controlled his own Congressional district in the metropolis where his father had controlled the whole; the mighty Kansas City machine of Boss Prendergast, whose gift to history had been Harry Truman, was reduced to control of scattered precincts and wards handed down, as elsewhere, from father to son, or uncle to nephew. But, over all, the machinery creaked and clanked, as if it had come ungeared.

Lyndon Johnson could be excused for ignoring this decay in the Party; a President of the United States cannot be expected to pay attention to details of party mechanics. His job is to deal with the problems of the world and let the politicians take care of the precincts; and his chief political deputy, Marvin Watson, a Southerner of limited political experience, assured him all was well. The President knew, to be sure, he had lost the South on the race issue. That was home country for him. But the structures of the North, he felt, were firm. All the Catholic Democratic governors of the Northeast were, without exception, with him. He was told the New York State machinery was with him. ("That Steingut," a White House assistant later lamented, "if you gave his crowd a pocketful of free subway tokens, they couldn't find their way to Bedford-Stuyvesant, or what was going on with the Negroes when they got there.") Johnson had Dick Daley of Illinois with him and that was indeed solid. He had also, most important of all, the AFL/CIO leadership of the labor unions—which was to prove, in the end, the most vigorous and resilient of the partners in the old coalition, delivering at the moment of greatest crisis in the late fall of 1968 its grandest and most successful exertion on behalf of the Party which had fostered its strength. Over all, at the beginning of 1968, when seen from the White House, the Party still appeared as it always had, except for the South. But the assumption of professional control was hollow—and the machinery of the Party could best be described in T. S. Eliot's phrase, "like broken springs in a factory yard, rust that clings to the form that the strength has left."

The fading of this second assumption was intimately linked with the fading of the third and last assumption—the importance and eternal validity of the share-out.

Fundamentally, success had undermined the third assumption. The share-out, which is as vital to Lyndon Johnson's personal philosophy as to the history of his Party, had worked so well that by 1968 no society anywhere on earth could boast a greater or more lavish sharing of wealth. But in an age of affluence and education the blind urges that had once created atavistic Democratic votes in slums, factories, ghettos, universities were no longer blind. Unemployment had been reduced to almost nothing among white workingmen; welfare took care of millions of unfortunates; about each American city sprawled mile upon mile of suburbs built with cheap Federal credit; avenues of communication were choked with the movements of prosperity; the channels of sanitation were clogged with the detritus of affluence. But in pursuit of the philosophy of share-out, the Johnson administration had come to consideration of the last group still clamoring for its share—the unfortunate and underprivileged black population of America. Here, however, was a cleavage line that the old philosophy of share-out could not straddle; for what the blacks clamored to share was not only money, jobs and material things but such intangibles as dignity and equality. And the sharing that was demanded in this quest was demanded not from the affluent so much as from white workingmen, who were asked also to share their schools, neighborhoods and places of amusement with the blacks. All through 1968 the working-class base of the Democratic coalition was to be torn almost as if by civil war, as white workingmen questioned the risk and the pace imposed on them in the adventure. The philosophy of the share-out as a satisfaction of the blind needs of the workingmen was to run its course in 1968.

The workingman's challenge of this assumption was, however, not to come to prime until the Wallace phenomenon in the late fall of 1968; so the historic role of first challenging the old philosophy, and thus beginning the real agony of the Democratic Party, fell to its most pampered and cherished beneficiary group: the student mass of the United States. What they wanted was something the old share-out had never envisioned: a share of the power.

It is well to linger over the student profile of America, for in student restlessness, of which we will have much more to say later, lie the greatest promise and the greatest threat to the national political process.

The first quality one must signal is simply that of mass. America boasts today, in totals and per capita, the largest student body in the world, and the bulge of its numbers can only be measured by looking back. In 1939, as America prepared for World War II, the country boasted only 1,350,000 students in all its colleges and universities. By contrast, at that time the blue-collar proletariat in two muscle industries alone—soft coal (388,300) and railways (988,000)—numbered 1,376,000 men. A generation later, railway workers and coal-miners combined had fallen to 715,900—yet the number of college and university students by 1968 had soared to a campus proletariat of 6,900,000.

By 1968 this campus proletariat outnumbered farmers by almost three to one, coal-miners by fifty to one, railway workers by nine to one. Students were, in short, the largest working-class group with a single interest in the United States—or any other country. It was inevitable that this huge and intelligent mass would eventually reach critical mass and exert itself as an interest group.

One must note, next, the changing texture of this mass and its leadership. Parents tend to think of college students as they are when they send them off to college—bright and cheerful adolescents in their late teens, hopeful, clean, aspiring. Yet the college community today covers an age spectrum that runs from eighteen to twenty-six, and leadership in the community lies not with undergraduates, but with graduate students in numbers and of motivations unknown a decade ago. These graduate students form, actually, the largest part of the instructorate with whom the youngsters come in contact. One cannot think of such graduate students—in law, in languages, in political science, in divinity, in engineering—as children. They are of the same age group which in World War II commanded companies and battalions, organized squadrons and bombing missions, mastered intelligence and analysis; they are of the same age group which, contemporaneously, leads other young Americans to battle and death in Vietnam; nor are they inferior in ability to their parents or contemporaries in Vietnam. With their young bodies, limitless energies and mature drives, student activists lead the kind of raw manpower which in other generations of history caused great and hostile nations to tremble.

The millions and millions of students in America are, to be sure, as different, individually, as are their parents. But, held together arbitrarily in campus compounds, they are subject to gusts of student fashion—frivolous or profound—which sweep the nation periodically from coast to coast. Over the decades, student fashions have englamored goldfish-swallowing, raccoon coats, military preparedness, anti-fascism; and it requires an impossible degree of cultural heroism for a fresh-faced freshman or sophomore to resist a dominant fashion presented to him by campus leaders as a challenge to manhood.

There is a last quality that should be signaled about the student mass, the quality that touches closest on politics—the intellectual climate and discipline of scholarship in which they are incarcerated. The normal scholarly process in any discipline follows a simple, well-known track. First, scholars analyze facts and conditions as they exist; then they contrast such conditions against an ideal, or theoretical, pattern of what should be; then they identify the gaps, the flaws, the faults, and try to devise solutions that marry theory with reality. In science, of course, one starts with physical facts, and theory must fit the facts, for physical facts cannot change. In social studies, one must start with a theory or a morality, and then the facts of life must be changed by activists to fit the theory. Man knows no other way of making progress, or changing his environment, than this. What separates the intellectual community from the political community is pace and timing. In the political community, all one can ask of a seasoned and responsible leader is that his direction be correct: the pace at which he moves is a matter of his skill and the resistances he finds on the way, his timing resting on the reach of his power, persuasion and the compromises he must accept. For the intellectual community, however, and the students who live within it, "pace" is a politician's pettifogging excuse for postponing the inevitable, for denying the truth. If a certain goal is accepted by the best thinking as an unchallenged good, why cannot it be made real *now?*

Rarely has any American administration more strenuously sought the best ideas of its time than did Lyndon Johnson's; rarely has an administration striven more vigorously to encase those ideas in law and program. And never has any administration been more completely repudiated by the community of thinkers from which it sought its ideas and guidance. To each new effort of the administration came the answer: *Faster.* To each promise for tomorrow came the response: *Why not now?* More money was appropriated for public housing in Johnson's administration than ever before; yet, since it takes five years from concept to slum-clearing to new-housing-ready-for-occupancy, progress seemed invisible, and across the country, students shrilled: *Now.* Under Johnson, the first serious experimental attack on poverty was started, a slow process. To which the roar came back: *Now.* Under Johnson, year by year, the Congress and the Party legislated the nation to civil rights and social equality, an even slower process, which brought, again, the roar: *Now.*

The loudest clamor of *Now* came, however, from student consideration of the Vietnam war. From 1965 on, Lyndon Johnson had been trying to find his way out of that war; and could not. And the roar that came from the campuses on this issue, was inspired, not only by the student concept of what was right and what was wrong, but by a sense of their own lives. A blunder of this magnitude, a moral affront (or so it seemed to the dominant campus activists) was not a distant condition, a mistake that could at some later time be rectified. It involved their own lives; they were the pawns in a losing game of international affairs. Educated, they could not be blind. Having been taught by so many teachers of government and political science that a citizen's duty *is* to participate, they meant to follow their learning.

Somewhere, thus, in the vast campus proletariat of America, in a huge mass not yet conscious of its own strength, was incubated the insurgency that ripped the Democratic Party apart.

* * *

The insurgency of 1968 was a skein of many threads. But if one must pull a single thread from the tangle, it is well to start with Allard K. Lowenstein,[1] a new type in American politics and, at the beginning of 1967, a man almost totally unknown outside the student world of American colleges. Lowenstein, at thirty-eight, and already almost two decades out of college (University of North Carolina, class of '48), was a type familiar in Europe but entirely new to American politics—the aging but permanent youth leader. Wiry yet frail, balding early, his eyes compelling behind their black horn-rimmed eyeglasses, a non-smoker and non-drinker, Lowenstein was a one-man excitement wherever he moved. Even alone in a room, in private conversation, his talk quivered with the intensity of convention oratory.

Lowenstein reminded one of a college football star, unable to shake off the remembered electricity of fall afternoons in the stadium and settle into the tedium of middle-aged life; Lowenstein's heart in 1967 still thrilled to his memories of campus politics and student movement. He had been a student leader at the University of North Carolina; had become president of the National Student Association in 1951, four years after its founding; was remembered later as the last president of the NSA before its subsidization by the CIA. The student association lay at the center of his life whatever, thereafter, he was to do—whether it was serving as a Congressional assistant to Senator Frank Graham on Capitol Hill, a leader of Students for Stevenson in 1952, an assistant to Mrs. Eleanor Roosevelt at the United Nations or a staff member for Senator Hubert Humphrey. Lowenstein's life had been spent in liberal causes—the cause of the anti-Franco rebels in Spain, the blacks in Southwest Africa, the Mississippi Freedom Democratic Party in 1964. But at the heart of it always was the student movement. A remembered romantic fervor, and long evening gatherings and bull sessions made his West Side apartment in New York a permanent student convention, an infinitely expandable continuing caucus of all the student leaders and NSA chieftains who followed him to leadership over the years. He was restless, impatient, unable ever to sit still; no man in America traveled further than did Lowenstein, or with greater enthusiasm to lecture to, preside over, convene or simply attend student gatherings. Nor, as over the years the student mass exploded into its many millions, with its new concerns, did anyone understand better than Lowenstein how powerful a force it might become in American politics, or where its leaders and resources lay.

At once a romantic and an executive, a distinct philosophic quality set off Lowenstein from a later generation of students—from the "rev-

[1] Lowenstein is now Congressman Lowenstein, elected in 1968 from New York's 5th Congressional District.

olutionaries," anarchists and radicals of the college generation of the mid-sixties. Whether from Frank Graham, Norman Thomas, Eleanor Roosevelt or Adlai Stevenson—all saints in the Lowenstein mystique— Lowenstein had come to the conviction that what had to be done to change America could, and must, be done within the traditional system of American party politics. Thus, in public, for those few politicians who noticed him, Lowenstein was a desperate, irresponsible, rabble-rousing student leaders; but within the student movement he was constantly engaged in a transcontinental internal battle with the newer, younger "revolutionary" leaders who thought of him as an Establishment fink.

We must see Lowenstein, therefore, in 1967 as a faintly preposterous character—a self-appointed, self-annointed voice of American youth, revolving from campus to campus, from California to New England, from the Bronx to Sherman, Texas, calling for revolt, while, at the same time, surfacing in Washington as a self-constituted one-man lobby pleading with whatever Congressmen or Senators he could button-hole for an end to war and the repudiation of Lyndon Johnson. "It was like looking for your father," recalled Lowenstein some time later, "but who was I? Nobody knew who I was. There was a credibility problem. I must have spoken to twenty Senators or Congressmen. Some thought I was a kook. Some of them listened. No one defended Lyndon Johnson or the war. I told them we had the strength, I told them there was a base in the student movement. But no major figure would take the lead —I couldn't find a trigger or a fuse."

It was early in August of 1967 that shape began to come to Lowenstein's one-man crusade against Lyndon Johnson's war. Five or six student leaders had come to visit Lowenstein's apartment (he was flying off on another of his personal crusades to Africa the next day), and in another of those long night sessions they had boxed the political compass. Johnson had to go, the young men decided. But it was impossible to form a third party, Lowenstein insisted. Therefore, Johnson had to be humiliated and driven out in the primaries. Since no insurrectionary candidate would at the moment risk the test, said Lowenstein, who talks always as if from a precise inner agenda in his mind, they must first prepare a base. A nationwide network of students to canvass in the primaries must be formed. Some roof-shelter, some national machinery must be prepared for the few Democratic Party politicians who, across the country, might dare to join them; and specific targets must be set: the Wisconsin and California primaries of the following spring. In the Wisconsin primary, which permits the alienated to vote a simple "no," Lowenstein hoped to get enough "no's" against Johnson to shock him into withdrawal. "I said," recalls Lowenstein, "we'll build the base first, the candidate will come along." Leaving behind $2,000 of his own money to pay for the travels of his deputies to the various student conferences of the summer, Lowenstein was off on his brief trip to Africa, while his lieutenants set about hopefully organizing something called ACT-68: "Alternate Candidate Task Force—1968."

One must rigidly summarize the complicated activity of this little cabal of unknown young men who meant to remove a sitting President of the United States from power. Their frame was discontent, a national discontent with war that was beginning to sputter not only in student groups but within the Democratic Party itself. All across the country, under varying names, bits and pieces of Democratic leadership—usually too lowly to fear reprisal, too insignificant to have been caught in the web of responsibility—had been surfacing in snatches of news paragraphs through 1967. In California, the California Democratic Council had already officially condemned the war; in Michigan, the State Democratic Chairman, Zoltan Ferency (shortly to resign), became an organizer of something called Concerned Democrats. Lowenstein's purpose was to harness the physical energies and vivid emotions of his student base to the skill, know-how and local prestige of established Party leaders, no matter how lowly. Lists had to be prepared of names—of church groups, student groups, Party groups. These must be presented in public; meetings in every state had to be called. By late August the California Democratic Council had promised enough money to hire the first full-time employees of a new national group to be called The Concerned Democrats. Their first recruit—a young man called Curtis Gans—was taken from the ADA (Americans for Democratic Action), and by September, Gans and Lowenstein were a working team, making a pattern of the Lowenstein trips around the country. Gans would prepare the lists and names, and Lowenstein would de-plane at the chosen place for his standard three-act road show: a public meeting, a private meeting of leaders, and a university meeting. In each state, ads paid for and signed by the participants would be published ("all political meetings, if you publicize them well enough, have an enormous effect on local politicians," says Lowenstein). By mid-October it was obvious that a nationwide base was actually there, yet still formless and unnamed, consisting of individuals working as individuals, or groups working as isolated groups, lonesome socially and regionally, needing a capping event, a public climax, to draw national attention, and, above all, a candidate.

Still without a candidate, but knowing their base to be jellying in colloidal suspension, Lowenstein and Gans decided that rhythm demanded they summon full national attention by a National Conference of Concerned Democrats, to be held in Chicago some time in November. The fact that it was postponed two weeks until early December was relevant only because Lowenstein believed that, with the postponement, he could at last deliver in the flesh a real candidate to oppose Lyndon Johnson.

Lowenstein had begun his hunt for a candidate with Robert Kennedy. ("You understand," said Lowenstein once, "I love Bobby Kennedy more than anyone else in political life.") But Kennedy had turned him down, saying, "I've tried to stop the war in every way I can, but Johnson can't be stopped." For Kennedy, of course, Lowenstein was a minor figure among many closer and more important urging him to run; he would have to make up his own mind in his own way. Lowenstein had tried Lieutenant General James Gavin, who felt Johnson could be stopped only in the Republican Party. Lowenstein had tried George McGovern of South Dakota in late September and been turned down by McGovern also. He had finally tried Engene McCarthy, but Senator McCarthy of Minnesota had felt that only Bobby Kennedy could lead the insurrection effectively. Lowenstein had lingered over McCarthy, however; McCarthy felt so deeply that someone *must* oppose Lyndon Johnson that he had not rejected Lowenstein out of hand, merely sent him elsewhere. It was not until late October, in a much later session, that Lowenstein, again describing to McCarthy the growing student base of dissent and its potential of action, heard him say, "How do you think we'd do in a Wisconsin primary?" "I was ecstatic," recalls Lowenstein, "it was like music, like an organ welling up in my ears." It was then that Lowenstein postponed his national conference until December, knowing that he would by then have a candidate to offer his troops at Chicago.

Chicago was to be a pivot point in the politics of the Democratic Party in 1968, a place name to be remembered as more than a place—as Munich in international diplomacy. And within the symbolic pivot there was to be always a physical pivot point: the crossing of Balbo Drive and Michigan Avenue, where two hotels, the Sheraton Blackstone and the Conrad Hilton, face each other. What bloodshed and violence were later to come there was unknown to the Conference of Concerned Democrats when they gathered on December 2nd, 1967, sharing the two hotels with the annual convention of the Home-Owner Builders of America. And the only appreciation one could make of this first meeting of the machinery that Lowenstein had prepared for McCarthy was that of a gathering of innocents.

Some 460 Concerned Democrats from forty-two states had gathered in the two hotels; but as this reporter, familiar with old politics, tried to read them or operate with them, he could find no jugular. Even their most important political names were inconsequential—obscure Congressmen and statehouse legislators, unknown county committeemen, dissidents and dissenters from the West Side New York reform clubs. The mass of the delegates was overwhelmingly young, overwhelmingly clean-cut, overwhelmingly middle-class; above all, earnest and ineffective, resembling more a student mock-convention than anything else. One found their press operation on the first day in a back chamber on the second floor of the Blackstone Hotel, after penetrating a happy Jewish wedding party. They did not know where, or how, they would meet in the Conrad Hilton across the street, until the California delegation, a veteran group of operatives, took over arrangements and overbore the surly management of the hotel. Their title described them best: the Concerned Democrats were Concerned Americans, all neat, well washed, bright and shining of face, few beards among them, fewer Negroes, no working-class types, and an extraordinarily large component of faculty and university types.

One remembers the faces of individuals that one was to see over and over again in the year 1968 as they learned national politics.

§ There was an innocent Harvard Divinity School student called Sam Brown, dream-walking, it seemed, as he tried to find a place where theology and politics coincided; such a boy, one felt, should absolutely be protected from the hurly-burly of carnal politics.

§ A pert professor's wife from Dartmouth, New Hampshire—Mrs. Sandra Hoeh—seemed irrationally sure that New Hampshire was only waiting for Eugene McCarthy to stop the war.

§ One had breakfast with a man called Donald O. Peterson, general sales manager of the Black River Dairy Products of Eau Claire, Wisconsin ("the pizza with the THIN GOLDEN CRUST," read his calling card, "several great flavors"), and one listened to the story of what had brought him here. He had been a young man from Minnesota when first called up and had become a navigator-bombardier on a B24 during World War II ("I learned then that bombing was absolutely ineffective"). He had become a vice-president of his dairy company in the years since; more importantly, he had become the Democratic county chairman in Eau Claire, Wisconsin. Even more importantly than that, he had become a father of two sons whom he loved, one of them twenty-one at the time and the other fourteen. "I felt," he said, explaining his presence at this meeting as a Democratic functionary, "that my sons meant more to me than the Democratic Party. Everybody's willing to let other people's sons go off to the war, but not their own. But I can't commit myself to allow them to go off to that damned war. What am I in politics for, if I can't take care of my sons?"

The conference seemed made up entirely of such amateurs, all drifting aimlessly about, stumbling over each other, full of earnest goodwill, pulled together by Allard Lowenstein's contrivings. All came to climax on Saturday evening, when, in the basement of the Conrad Hilton, both Lowenstein and McCarthy spoke. Lowenstein spoke first, a rooting-tooting, ranting exercise in the rhetoric of protest which deeply offended Eugene McCarthy, waiting in the wings. (Lowenstein, not knowing that McCarthy was waiting, had been trying to fill time with denunciation of Lyndon Johnson and the war, *sic:* "If a man fools you once, he should be ashamed. But if a man fools you twice, *you* should be ashamed.")

Then on strode Eugene McCarthy to speak to his troops—pale and handsome, subdued and pensive, as he was to be always throughout his campaign. A long minute of applause greeted him as he rose to speak, and the youngsters in the audience wriggled, waiting for him to go. But that was not McCarthy's style. The slow, dry voice began: "In 1952, in this city of Chicago, the Democratic Party nominated as its candidate for the Presidency Adlai Stevenson . . . his promise to his party and the people of the country then was that he would talk sense to them. . . ." Thereafter, as the youngsters stared up at him, he intoned his convictions, rousing them only once to a standing ovation with, "Finally . . . this war is no longer morally justifiable." He quoted Charles Péguy on the Dreyfus case, Toynbee on Hannibal's wars, and ended, his voice ringing with melancholy, "Let us sort out the music from the sounds, and again respond to the trumpet and the steady drums."

McCarthy left his audience cold. His style recalled Adlai Stevenson's famous gloss on the nature of oratory: "Do you remember that in classical times when Cicero had finished speaking, the people said, 'How well he spoke'—but when Demosthenes had finished speaking, people said, 'Let us march.'" The students had come that night to march—and had heard a philosopher. Only later did they learn to thrill to his new music, eventually to delight in his style and be willing to shed their blood for him.

That night, however, McCarthy refused to address the overflow student audiences waiting outside. To his staff he vowed he would never follow Al Lowenstein as speaker on any platform again; the stridency of Lowenstein's tone offended him. He declined all invitations to visit the state caucuses clamoring for his presence, and spent the evening chatting with friends at the Hotel Blackstone. To this reporter he had presented the image of a man running for President as martyr, stirred by conscience and of boundless courage, yet of little appetite for power. He seemed to be offering himself, a symbolic sacrifice for truth, as leader of all those children who believed helplessly, as he did. Few judgments of this reporter in the year 1968 were to be more wrong. For McCarthy was to make manifest all across the country how empty were the assumptions of the Democratic Party which he had represented for twenty years.

No one completely understands Eugene McCarthy, for the man lives by himself, a scholar, meditant and poet, an inner-oriented person who remains an enigma to those who love him most. Yet no one can thoroughly explain the McCarthy candidacy without an attempt to penetrate the McCarthy personality.

One picks up the first trace of the small-town country boy in Watkins, Minnesota, where he was born in 1916, a year before John F. Kennedy, his mother second-generation German, his father, Michael, a cattle-broker. Watkins, Minnesota, is still a hamlet surrounded by green fields, blue lakes and woodland; and McCarthy is still in large part a countryman, able to pause wherever he goes and observe the slope of hills, self-taught to name the trees and the flowers he sees about him. A studious, introspective youngster, he was nonetheless a star baseball player—a husky, handsome boy growing into virile, athletic manhood. He has remained a baseball fan ever since, the best raconteur of baseball stories, statistics and peculiarities on the Senatorial circuit. From high school one follows him to a small Benedictine college, St. John's, where as a straight A student he majored in English. St. John's is a place of easily worn but profound culture. From St. John's he took away a Catholic faith so deep, so permeating, that one feels gross in any approach to open discussion of religion with him. He carried away from St. John's also an abiding love of poetry and a taste for style in English. This elegant taste still makes him wince at the discourse of journalists who must write for people who read in haste, and jibe at that other Minnesota stylist of high rhetoric, Hubert Humphrey, whose tongue is that of the gospel and the revival meeting.

A brief nine-month novitiate at the Monastery of St. John's followed an early attempt to teach in the public schools; but, deciding he was not a *religieux,* McCarthy became a professor of economics at St. John's University (the quiet humanitarian community of St. John's has always been home place for Eugene McCarthy), then left during the war to become a civilian technician in the Army's military intelligence branch. It was when he returned to teaching again, at St. Thomas' College in St. Paul, Minnesota, that he was caught up in politics and the remaking of the Minnesota Democratic-Farmer-Labor party. By 1948 he had been elected a Congressman; by 1958 he had followed another Minnesota teacher, Hubert Humphrey, to the Senate; in 1960 he became a national figure with his delivery of the nominating speech for Adlai Stevenson at the Los Angeles Democratic national convention, that famous flight of never-to-be-forgotten eloquence: "Do not reject this man. . . . Do not reject this man who has made us all proud to be Democrats. . . . Do not leave this prophet without honor in his own party."

By 1968 one could examine a man whose intellectual reach was prodigious and whose Congressional and political experience was almost matchless. A shy man, but not a modest one, McCarthy could look at himself from the outside and with self-mocking candor detail his own merits, as once I heard him do in private conversation: "You can put it down that I'm the best-prepared man who ever ran for the Presidency of this country. I was born in a small town of 500 population in the Midwest, my mother's family were farmers, my father was in small business. I know small-town life and I know big-city life. I represented St. Paul in Congress for ten years. I served in the House on the Agriculture Committee and the Interior Committee, on Banking and Currency, Post Office and Civil Service and on the Ways and Means Committee for four years. In the Senate I've been on Foreign Relations, and Finance, and Public Works. I've written four books on politics and philosophy. Where would I be an outsider? You list them—I'm at home with the farmers and on Main Street, with labor and on Wall Street. I'm at home with the academic community and the business community. I can't think of anybody in the Senate who'd be at home with as many different groups as myself."

He was all this—and more, too. He could be gay and, at the homes of friends, delight them by singing "The West's Awake," a favorite Irish ballad. He was witty in a low-key, yet biting, style. One had to listen closely for the wit because, usually, it was mumbled as a self-amusement, and of a subtlety that only rarely puckered into such strokes as his orchestral description of the Democratic greats: "Roosevelt was a trumpeter, Adlai Stevenson was a French horn, Truman was a bass drum, and Johnson is an accordion player—did you ever find a critic able to review an accordion performance?"

The word "critic" was the clue to the man. For he was a critic of all things—of books and poetry and performances, of politicians, journalists and Presidents, of history and life itself. A wry amusement prickled his observations on the American political process—as if it were a burlesque, in which leaders were forced to prance as clowns and buffoons to attract a public; and he would play no such role. No one doubted that Eugene McCarthy bore love in his heart—but it was an abstract love, a love for youth, a love for beauty, a love for vistas and hills and songs. It was not a love for individuals, as individuals. His generosity was rarely wasted in praise of anyone—and no one on his staff escaped the flick of his mordant analysis. Of individuals he was forever suspicious. He felt John F. Kennedy might have consulted him during his Presidency, and brooded over slights years after the assassination ("He might have invited us to the White House, but he didn't"); he bore quiet and long-lasting rancor for Hubert Humphrey, a rancor somehow connected with the feeling that Humphrey had tried to use him as the house Catholic in Minnesota politics, an exposure that deeply offended his privacy and his glowing faith. He came later to enmity of Bobby Kennedy with an ultimate bitterness that not even Kennedy's death could erase. In the end, with rare stubbornness of spirit, he was always his own man—he belonged to no one, had no allies, few personal friends outside the fathers and faculty at St. John's, and lived by truths and perceptions of his own soul, with a courage that was to change American history. He owed no one anything, recognized no political obligations—not even to his own movement, or his own constituency. All through the year, one's admiration of the man grew—and one's affection lessened.

It was as a critic of history that Eugene McCarthy approached the year 1968. As a father, a scholar, an historian, as a man responsible to his conscience, but above all as a critic, he had come deeply, irrevocably, to the sense that the war in Vietnam was wrong. It was only three days after the closing of the Chicago conference that, talking to McCarthy, I heard him best explain the course that had brought him to where he stood.

"The central point," he said, "is what this war is doing to the United States itself, in terms of its potential to influence world history, what it's doing to us around the world today, this draining of the material and moral resources of the country from our really pressing problems. It's the old Roman problem—their policing of the Mediterranean world as Rome decayed at home."

He had come step by step to this central point. McCarthy had voted for the Tonkin Gulf resolution of 1964. But he had not considered it a vote for war. Until 1966 the war in Vietnam had been presented to the Senate as a holding action and he was willing to stay five or ten years on that basis. But when the war passed from being a holding action to a war of conquest, when at the same time the will of the South Vietnamese themselves to resist began to diminish, McCarthy's opposition to the war had begun to swell. The administration, it seemed to him, was moving from an earlier concept of nation-building in South Vietnam to a crusade to save all of Southeast Asia, then to save the United States itself, then to take a stand against a billion Chinese as the global threat. Policy began to sound to him more and more like a commitment to all-out war in Asia; policy-making, he felt, was contemptuous of the Senate itself and its constitutional role in foreign affairs. Key episodes studded McCarthy's memory: Robert McNamara's announcement of a new ballistic missile system pointed at China, an invitation to holocaust; the curt testimony of Under Secretary of State Nicholas Katzenbach which McCarthy felt to be an "outrage" to Senate dignity, a political abuse beyond reason of the Gulf of Tonkin resolution; and then, finally, in October, 1967, Secretary of State Dean Rusk's statement about "a billion Chinese" being the real menace. And, said McCarthy, "at this point, I thought I would call a halt."

Other influences were at work on him. Through his daughter, Mary, a Radcliffe sophomore, he could sense the enormous disillusion of the young people of the campus. Beyond his family concern, through his mail, through his travels, he could sense the anxiety of religious leaders, of concerned people he could not categorize. Speaking on his travels, meeting politicians around the country, he had found something close to "unreason" in Democratic concern. At Berkeley, where he spoke in the fall of 1967 and said that Dean Rusk should resign, the student response had been so loud, so grateful to him, that he was embarrassed. Many people had urged him to candidacy. Lowenstein did not occur in his recollections at all. He talked with many friends in Washington and in California, and in Boston to the Harvard-M.I.T. group, "just getting the feel." Then, finally, when it appeared that no one else would run, he had talked to Bobby Kennedy and told him that if he, Bobby, would not run, he, Gene, must. Thus to the press conference announcing his candidacy in Washington on November 30th, and then on to the Chicago meeting where the Lowenstein organization waited for him to lead.

"All the facts are on the table," he said as we talked in December. "What's called for is a decision. Do we escalate? Do we go on with additional militarism and by so doing set a similar pattern of policy around the whole world? Or do we say, here's the moment of choice. What's the price of peace? What's the price of war? And you've got to personalize the issues. You can't get into all the complexity of the issue by a Senate debate, or a Senate Foreign Relations Committee hearing, or running individual Congressmen on the ballot, or in a platform hearing. You've got to transmit the people a choice in personal identifications."

So he was running. One man plus the truth made a majority—so ran the old adage. But the truth required troops and organization.

It was impossible, ever, to make a neat diagram of the organization of the McCarthy campaign. He was not that kind of man, nor was it that kind of organization. Later, much later, I remember asking a young graduate student in physics, serving as interim press officer for McCarthy in Wisconsin, where the candidate actually was at that moment. He replied that it was an impossible question, for it was like trying to identify an electron—you could say either where it was or how fast it was going, but you couldn't say where it was and where it was going at the same time. The simile seemed more and more apt as the campaign wore on: the McCarthy campaign from beginning to end was a constellation of force subject to no diagram or organizational chart, resembling most of all an atomic chart of a nuclear field. The central nucleus was the gravitational force of Eugene McCarthy's conviction; about this nucleus, in concentric orbits but in paths of their own, whirled various electrons in quantum dances set by different equations of conviction. To manage such a campaign, no ordinary campaign manager would do, and thus McCarthy, a week after his December convocation in Chicago, had sounded out and then chosen Blair Clark as chief executive.

Blair Clark had flown to Chicago from London, donned a spurious press pass to observe the launching of the campaign, recognized its substance and seriousness instantly, and then, to the surprise of his friends, volunteered as campaign manager. Clark, Harvard-schooled, a classmate of John F. Kennedy's, a onetime publisher, a broadcasting executive (once vice-president of CBS News), a direct descendant of the Sons of the Cincinnati had all American history in his aristocratic blood, from the days of Lincoln to the days of Franklin D. Roosevelt, each of whom his forebears had served. In 1961, Clark had turned down an ambassadorship offered him by John F. Kennedy; but now he had come to conviction that the war in Vietnam was endangering not only the lives of his two handsome sons, but the fate of the Republic itself. He must act.

No more untidy a situation could have confronted any man than confronted Clark on his arrival in Washington in mid-December to take over. Two rooms in the Carroll Arms Hotel housed several volunteers with no definable function; the Lowenstein machinery had not yet been geared into program; several thousand dollars a day were arriving, unsolicited, by mail from citizens responding to McCarthy's announcement of his campaign; but the candidate himself was blithely uninterested in any details of organization or professionalism. "Events will march in our favor," he told Clark later as over-all directive for the campaign, and he did not want to be bothered with organization of the march. ("His attention span," remarked Clark ruefully, "is limited to a maximum of one hour and a half.") Clark, a compulsive executive but eccentric administrator, is a superb policy-maker. And two decisions made by Clark in the next two weeks were to set the frame of the entire McCarthy campaign.

The first was Clark's decision to go with youth. Operationally, Clark found useful when he arrived only Curtis Gans, thirty, of the Lowenstein movement, an able young man whose intensity, however, seemed to offend McCarthy. To Gans, in the first ten days, he added an administrative assistant aged twenty-one, Sandy Frucher; a researcher-writer, Peter Barnes, only four years out of Harvard, *summa cum laude* in history; a press officer, Seymour Hersh, twenty-nine years old. To these, in the next fortnight, he finally added Sam Brown, twenty-three years old. Brown had been telephoning Clark from Harvard for days for an appointment; in a quick talk, he proposed to Clark that the campaign invest $20,000 for mobilization of the nation's schools. Clark staked Brown with a personal check of $200 to proselyte for McCarthy at a Cleveland conference of the University Christian Movement; and a week later in Cleveland, Clark informed Brown that all signals were go—he, Clark, would guarantee the $20,000 needed; Brown would recruit five student leaders to circulate the campuses; and they were off.

The next problem was to give focus and rhythm to the campaign. There was no doubt that the McCarthy announcement had twinged nerves all across the country—nerves just as responsive in Wall Street as in the enclaves of far-out left-wing kookery. In California, in Wisconsin, in Massachusetts, in New York, self-starting nuclei of diverse citizens were already climbing aboard the McCarthy campaign, itching to ride driver's seat in a Presidential campaign in their home states. Fanatics and zealots across the country were trying to kidnap the McCarthy name for their causes. Students everywhere were organizing in McCarthy groups, clamoring for leadership. Money to finance the campaign hung, as obviously pregnant as rain clouds, in the air—it needed only to be tapped.

To tap, to harness, to control the energies, the emotions, the rival cliques, the moneys of concerned citizens, it was necessary that somewhere, very soon, a controlled start be made, a visible open beginning of the adventure. Thus, as December turned the corner into January, while the Tet offensive was known only to the staffs of General Giap and President Johnson, a date for kick-off had to be set. As late as December 27th, McCarthy was saying in Washington that the New Hampshire primary was "not particularly significant." Foreboding and instinct had led McCarthy to suspect that a primary contest in New Hampshire was a trap baited by Bobby Kennedy to snare him. On a long train trip from Washington to New York, however, on a rainy day when planes were canceled, Clark and McCarthy discussed the matter in the dining car. McCarthy preferred to start the campaign in Massachusetts, a more representative state than supposedly hawkish New Hampshire; he felt it might be wise to go abroad, *à la* Romney, while waiting for the Massachusetts primary. Clark demurred. The campaign could not be delayed; if the case was not good in hawkish New Hampshire, it was not good anywhere; press and partisans were insisting that McCarthy make his move. Clark felt it should be made at once, in New Hampshire.

Thus, on January 3rd came the formal announcement that the Minnesota Senator would indeed enter the primary of the Granite State. Nine days later, Friday, January 12th, Professor David Hoeh rented a store-front headquarters, for student volunteers, in Concord, New Hampshire, the first of hundreds later to flourish in the country, a quarter of a mile down the hill from the capitol of the state.

There was little that a reporter could technically note about the candidate in those weeks before the Tet offensive, except sound and style. McCarthy's bases were the universities and schools of the nation as he roved from campus to campus from California to Wisconsin to Oregon to New Hampshire. But his style was new; no speech conceded a single phrase to popular taste or the common dialogue of politics. One had to listen closely to the dry, hesitant, low-pitched tone in which he gave the same speech over and over again, to catch the nuggets of thought or, more particularly, in response to questions, the crack of his wit. Of

John Bailey, the Democratic National Chairman: "John Bailey didn't really decline or fall, he started so low that couldn't happen to him." Of Presbyterian John Foster Dulles' pactomaniac diplomacy: "John Foster Dulles accepted a kind of moral responsibility for the whole world. He was the greatest covenanter in history." Of the war: "Escalation is a word that has no point of interruption. By the time you raise the question, the flag has gone by." Of how he would handle the Pentagon if he were President: "I would go to the Pentagon. If not, I would at least try to get diplomatic representation there."

The man was difficult to define as a political leader. He would visit New Hampshire, but would not see politicians. He would ask favors of no one, make no promises, was bored by advice. He would pause, unrecognized and solitary, to eat at a roadside restaurant or the Sheraton-Wayfarer Inn, and no heads turned. At the height of the campaign, when he was late for a reception, a brace of reporters dutifully tried to track him down and found him eating in a hotel dining room alone with poet Robert Lowell; he waved them off, poets being more important than politics. And his main headquarters at the Sheraton-Wayfarer in Manchester, a grisly, paper-cluttered two-room suite made bedlam by amateurs all engaged in their first campaign, contained only one man who made sense: Richard N. Goodwin. A veteran of the Presidential campaigns of 1960 and 1964, Goodwin was, with young Curtis Gans and a New York banker, Howard Stein, directing the media campaign. Matching the official Johnson effort dollar-for-dollar, Goodwin was trying to identify unknown Eugene McCarthy in voters' minds by saturating the air waves. For the last three days of the campaign, McCarthy spots were booked every half-hour all through the evening on every radio station in the state, with a matching TV effort buying prime time as far away as Boston to blanket the overspill of the suburban belt. Goodwin could give an overview of the campaign, but his sharpest advice was, "Don't bother with us *here.* Go on up to Concord and see the students. That's where the action is." [2]

[2] I recall how unexpected the student adventure in New Hampshire was to political professionals. I retain in my files one of the most expensive and detailed political analyses, privately commissioned, which, in the first week in January, 1968, had this to say: "The 'Youth Quake,' while it has strongly affected other areas of the nation socially, economically, and politically, simply will not be apparent in New Hampshire, confined as it is at this moment to the pre-teen and teen years. Similarly alienated youth will be more conspicuous by their absence than their presence, not only because the youth population is numerically small but also due to the inner-oriented, tradition-bound nature of New Hampshire society. Except possibly for Dartmouth College, neither is there any evidence that the candidates will be confronted with the problem of dealing with "hordes" of youthful political activists either as supporters or opponents. Necessarily, this will mean that the candidates need not be inordinately worried about bridging the generational gap, but should be prepared to talk on a peer level on those issues which are of daily and direct concern to New Hampshire voters 35 years of age and over."

It was not until the end of February that I did, at last, return to New Hampshire to see the action; for by the third week of February the polls, both private and public, had begun to quake, and, remembering New Hampshire's seismic instability in primaries from the Kefauver upset in 1952 through the Lodge upset of 1964, I drove north from Manhattan to Concord.

In the state capitol I visited Governor John King, under whose administration New Hampshire had reached a point of such robust good health that its unemployment rate was the lowest in the entire nation. King was a Johnson loyalist; a veteran; an American Legionnaire; a reasonable and intelligent commitment man on Vietnam. His state was considered hawk—its war casualties had been low (only 100 killed in Vietnam), its defense industries were booming. But King was worried. The Johnson staff in Washington had imposed on his organization, against his wishes, an unprecedented loyalty pledge—signed tickets, with numbered stubs—to be circulated among loyal Democrats by which they bound themselves to vote for Johnson. It was not the thing to do with independent Hampshiremen. And the kids, those out-of-state students— they were having an effect. King had upped his estimate of the McCarthy vote far beyond anything in the Washington guesses: he thought McCarthy could get as high as 25 to 28 percent of the primary! Go see the kids.

One wandered down the stairs of the lovely capitol building to pass the oil painting of New Hampshire's war hero, General John A. Dix, his Union blues still clear, his epaulets shining, his sword in his hand; it seemed as if he quivered in indignation, or might read aloud his famous legend, written in gold beneath: "If anyone attempts to haul down the American flag, shoot him on the spot." [3]

Down the hill, a quarter of a mile away, at 3 Pleasant Street, were "the kids." At first one noticed the red-white-blue bunting, as at every political headquarters—and then, nothing was the same. A huge portrait of Douglas MacArthur adorned the walls; but underneath, his message read: "*Anybody who commits the land power of the United States on the continent of Asia ought to have his head examined.*" Another read: "*God isn't Dead, He's just Lonely,* BUT *he just might commit suicide on March 12th, it's up to* YOU."

Then, one noticed the operational signs. A bulletin board: "*Housing*

---

[3] I have always taken a particular delight in visiting American state capitols, from Sacramento to Madison to Jackson to Harrisburg to Boston. They are all of them halls of martial valor, bristling with a patriotism and pride in heroes that in 1968 seemed forlornly anachronistic. My favorite inscription, noticed in 1968, was on the grounds of the capitol in Lansing, Michigan, on the pedestal of the memorial to our veterans of the first war with Asian guerrillas, the Filipino insurrection. It read: "Through steaming tropic jungles they fought/ beneath a sweltering sky/ Through shot and shell while their comrades fell/ and 'Remember the Maine' was their battle cry."

Desired—Departures—No Housing Needed"—and lists of names.

Then areas designated: *"Election Day Activities Center"*—*"Quiet Zone—Telephone Canvass"*—*"News and Notes for New Voters."* Then one noticed a new political, technical aptitude: charts of factories and factory gates for leafleting workingmen; maps of New Hampshire, crosshatched into canvassing zones; voting precincts in big towns broken down with previous results and registration figures. Suddenly, all that had been taught the bright young students of political science, children trained on computers and methodology, had leaped from the classroom to reality. They knew what they were doing. They were skilled. They were organized (*"Happiness,"* read one sign, *"is a nine o'clock staff meeting that starts at nine o'clock"*). And they were happy. Girls with sleek Ivy League blond hair bustled in and out, smiling, laughing, but precise. Booted in black shiny leather, as was the style that year, their mini-skirts and plaids flickering over their pretty legs, they might have arrived for a ski weekend. But they had come to stop the war. Well-mannered, hesitant, they spoke softly, with the "um . . . ummm . . . ummmmm" interjections of Ivy League girls, yet they were on crusade. Groups broke up and re-formed in different configurations; telephones rang; boys lugged in cartons of literature and dumped them on tables for sorting. It was oddly reminiscent of the jovial Chinese Communist guerrilla headquarters I had once known, thirty years ago, before victory, conquest and power had made monsters of the guerrillas. I mentioned the similarity, and a handsome dark boy leaned over to say yes; then he broke into excellent Chinese. He was a graduate student of Chinese history and politics from Columbia, but had abandoned that campus at Christmas vacation to work for McCarthy. Yes, they were a kind of guerrilla grouping, he said, and Ben Stavis of New York was finding American politics very much to his liking.

So were all the others. They had begun to arrive early in January, when volunteer headquarters had opened in Concord, more out of curiosity and conviction than hope. The Amherst-Smith-Mount Holyoke complex in northern Massachusetts had been the first to hire buses for weekend trips. Then Harvard and Yale boys heard the news that the good cause was to be fought, that the action was in New Hampshire, and girls were there, too. Girls excite boys, boys excite girls, and all hated war. They came with sleeping bags and ski boots—like a Boy Scout camp-out, bringing with them the youthful talent for improvised organization. A new crest had been reached on the weekend of Washington's birthday, when from Washington and Baltimore three chartered buses—there were later to be hundreds more—set out for New Hampshire to do battle for McCarthy and Peace. From the Greater Boston area almost 300 university students hitch-hiked that weekend or found transportation of their own to canvass voters. "We were learning how to transport large numbers of people over long distances," recalled one of the organizers later, "but we were scared, oh lord, how scared we were, we were really shook." A few days later there leaked in *The New York Times* the grim news that General Westmoreland felt he required 206,000 more troops to bring the situation in Vietnam under control; and on a score of campuses young men and their girl-friends instantly translated this figure into draft quotas and read its meaning in their own lives. By the first week in March the McCarthy student movement was a force-in-being, with its own logistics, staff and command, independent of the national campaign except for money. Housing headquarters had been set up; ministers and rabbis lent the basements of churches and temples for sleep-ins; there were song, hootenannies, good fellowship and work to do the next day. As word spread, so did the number of headquarters spread. There were fifteen such student headquarters across New Hampshire by the time I caught up with the action in the first week in March. A Yale graduate student in political science was coordinating election-day activity and poll-watching; an Amherst French major had translated McCarthy literature into French to reach the 100,000 Hampshiremen of French-Canadian descent (almost one sixth of New Hampshire's population). Two busloads of Yale majors in Romance languages were now canvassing in Yale French in Manchester and northern New Hampshire. A senior in art history was director of canvassing. Bearded students had sacrificed their beards so as not to alarm the citizens on their rounds; blue jeans and sweatshirts were also proscribed; if students refused to sacrifice beards, they were relegated to back rooms, where they stuffed envelopes. All were as neat, tidy and wholesome as their parents had ever hoped they would be.

And they were shaking New Hampshire to its roots. Between 2,000 and 3,000 such students—no one had an exact count—had already been in New Hampshire. Midyear exams were now over, and 1,500 more were expected for the final pre-election burst of activity. They had already spoken to 30,000 families or individuals in their door-to-door rounds, left leaflets at 10,000 more homes and hoped, before election, to have reached 60,000 New Hampshire homes—or almost half the total in the state.

"What is happening," wrote Mary McGrory of the Washington *Star,* "is that violet-eyed damsels from Smith are pinning McCarthy buttons on tattooed mill-workers, and Ph.D.s from Cornell, shaven and shorn for world peace, are deferentially bowing to middle-aged Manchester housewives and importuning them to consider a change of Commander-in-Chief. Some of the best young minds in the country are sitting in the cellars of Manchester, Nashua, and points north, poring over precinct lists, drawing up baby-sitting rosters for summa cum laudes of the Ivy League." And Hampshiremen and their wives loved it. It was shaking even professional politicians. Joseph Whelton, chairman of the Nashua Democratic City Committee had already joined the McCarthy group openly, and he explained it this way: "These college kids are fabulous. There are so many people who have kids of their own of the same age, and they can't talk to their own kids, it's another generation. These kids knock at the door, and come in politely, and actually want to talk to grown-ups, and people are delighted. They want to listen. I had ten kids staying at my house last weekend, and Mrs. Stanley had sixty sleeping in hers."

The organizational leadership was spread over half a dozen graduate students fully qualified to command battalions in action; but the motive and the force came from sources deep in the student view of the world. It was a romantic view; an exciting view; and yet, disturbing. These were the best in American life. But with sadness, one realized that their view of America was warped by a new mythology. They distrusted America, saw only its evil. "Think of what we've grown up with," said Sam Brown. "We've recognized the true nature of the United States. We saw the United States attack Cuba, it attacked the Dominican Republic, it attacked South Vietnam. The Communists are now a fragmented force; the United States is now the great imperialist-aggressor nation of the world."

It is well to linger over Sam Brown, whom I was later to see grow to full executive responsibility over the year. Curly-haired, slim, pale-cheeked, brown-eyed, soft and gentle of voice, he was armored with unshakable righteousness; and from thousands of similar young people of his goodwill and his unconscious arrogance, his purity of spirit and his remarkable ability, stems much of the perplexity of future American politics.

Such young people as Sam Brown are throwbacks—they come of a strain of American life that goes back probably to the Abolitionists, explosive with morality. Born in Council Bluffs, Iowa, twenty-three years earlier, Sam came of what anyone in Council Bluffs would consider a "best family." His father is not only a good businessman, owner of a local shoe-store chain, but a music-lover, a member of local hospital boards, chairman of the school board, a Republican and a Rotarian; his mother is a preacher's daughter, active in the Methodist church. Sam had gone to Redlands University in Southern California, where first he was president of the Young Republicans, then president of the student body. His first reflex of rebellion had come when the university had banned Communist speakers from the campus and Sam, protesting the ban, was branded a Communist himself by the trustees. That summer—1964— Sam became involved in the National Students Association, thus meeting Al Lowenstein and becoming alert to politics. The summer of 1964 was also the summer of the student crusade in Mississippi and Sam felt the

Democratic convention at Atlantic City that year sold out the students' cause by its compromise on seating the Mississippi Freedom Democratic Party.

In the fall of 1965 Sam enrolled at Rutgers University to take a master's degree in political science, and fell under the influence of a luminous teacher, the late Paul Tillett, socialist, atheist, humanitarian. A dedicated student and dedicated teacher find magic in each other, and the two—Tillett and Brown—talked and talked. One night-long session, at three in the morning, both found themselves in tears. Tillett cried because, after his intense career in law and history, he had not yet found a way to help *other* people; how, how, how—that was the essential question—could one really help other people? Sam "learned" that government really did not know how to help people. "I had to go back and think. It made me think about how is it we go about helping people, and that drove me to divinity school."

Sam went on to Harvard Divinity School, and for a year and three months studied what they teach of the ways of God at divinity school; he turned in his draft card, sent back his deferment, refused to participate in the war of the United States; yet his local Council Bluffs draft board still refused to challenge him. Thus, he decided he must challenge the war outright, and the McCarthy movement was the way to challenge it. War was evil. The United States was an imperialist aggressor. One must follow conscience. Thus to his persuasion of Clark that the students *could* be mobilized, and to his arrival in New Hampshire on February 12th as a theologian who had left divinity school to become the director of the student *putsch* in New Hampshire and, ultimately, an executive of prime promise. Sam abhorred violence, loved knowledge. But, he said in the Pleasant Street headquarters that morning, "Study in universities is irrelevant. The war is on our minds. The rhetoric of the government is outmoded—the problem is how you affect government."

All in the little headquarters listened to Sam quietly that morning as he explained what brought them there. "We aren't," he said, "the see-you-in-Chicago crowd," explaining their differences of opinion with those student leaders who were already planning to rock Chicago with the bloody violence of the August confrontation. "That crowd isn't with us, they want to tear it all down." He and his group, said Sam, were going to go the regular way, all the way. Whatever happened, they were not going to disband after the New Hampshire primary; they could continue on to Wisconsin, on to Indiana, on to Oregon, on to California—and on to Chicago.

Election day in New Hampshire was, for once, clear and crisp; and the results were clean and crisp, too.

By 11:40 on the evening of March 12th it was obvious that Eugene

McCarthy would do far better than the Gallup polls had predicted in January (12 percent); better than Johnson's private poll had told him in February (18 percent); better than Governor King had predicted in the first week of March (25 to 28 percent). The vote was coming in strong, with McCarthy running slightly over 40 percent and Johnson, a sitting President, in a closed Democratic primary, was running under 50 percent. Someone reported to McCarthy in his cottage at the Sheraton-Wayfarer in Manchester that three dead men had been voted in the third ward of Manchester. "They were ours," said McCarthy, "it was the Resurrection. They came back from the grave for this." Someone asked him whether he had talked yet with Robert Kennedy (who would call at 12:30 with his congratulations, a courtesy that McCarthy was never later to reciprocate on nights of Kennedy victories), and McCarthy said no, but he *had* talked with poet Robert Lowell. He went out to greet the young, who had made this victory, and they began to chant "Chi-Ca-Go, Chi-Ca-Go," for they felt now they could storm any heights. McCarthy replied, "If we come to Chicago with this strength, there will be no violence and no demonstrations but a great victory celebration."

Final returns in the Democratic primary of New Hampshire of March 12th, 1968, were to show the results even closer than they appeared that early morning of celebration. In the Democratic tally President Lyndon B. Johnson received 49.5 percent of the vote (27,243) and Eugene McCarthy 42.4 percent of the vote (23,280). But when McCarthy write-ins on the Republican side were also tallied, lo, the suburban Republicans of southern New Hampshire had also been tugged off base by Eugene McCarthy. Combining Democratic and Republican votes, McCarthy had received 28,791 votes for President; and Lyndon Johnson, combining his votes, had received 29,021—the embattled President led the mystic Senator by only 230 votes in what was supposedly one of the most patriotic and warlike states of the Union.

The next morning McCarthy permitted himself the closest approach to euphoria that his somber nature would admit throughout the campaign. In Manchester, at his victory press conference, his tragic view of the world was momentarily rosy. "I think I can get the nomination," he said. "I'm ahead now." Then with the puckering of his wit, his appreciation of the reality: "We'll be able to finance our Wisconsin campaign after what happened here yesterday, we'll be able to pay our hotel bills."

The euphoria lasted only a few hours. From Manchester he drove to Boston to catch a flight to Washington. He indulged in an early-morning Martini. He was still elated in his own way and prowled the aisles talking with warmth to the reporters, whom he regarded generally as amusing animals. When the plane arrived in Washington, the first man aboard was Jerry Eller, his Senatorial administrative assistant, carrying an imprecisely torn roll of carbon copy from a news ticker. Robert F. Kennedy had issued, overnight, a statement that he was "reassessing" his position in the Presidential race. A press conference greeted the victorious candidate as he alighted from the plane, the questions focused on his relations with Robert F. Kennedy. Charles Bailey of the Minneapolis *Tribune,* who had accompanied him on the plane, wrote, "The happy man was put away somewhere now and the black Irishman was very much dominant." The press conference broke up when a pack of students began chanting "McCarthy, McCarthy," and McCarthy drove away knowing that at his office was a message that Robert F. Kennedy was waiting to talk to him.

The McCarthy movement was yet to reach its crest, three weeks later in Wisconsin. But one of his students spoke best their feeling of the movement. "We woke up," she said four days later, "after the New Hampshire primary, like it was Christmas Day. And when we went down to the tree, we found Bobby Kennedy had stolen our Christmas presents."

This bitterness at Robert Kennedy was to corrode the McCarthy movement all through the following months; but Robert Kennedy had a rendezvous with his own conscience and his own responsibility which no cynical outside view could appreciate, and no one else's wounded feelings deter.

An even more important public figure was, however, in that mad March month, about to reassess his role and responsibility in American life. That figure was Lyndon Johnson, living alone in the agony that is uniquely reserved for the President of the United States. Johnson now was about to decide whether he was a politician or a President, whether the shadows that politics cast on the cave wall truly reflected the realities of power for which a President is elected.

PART
TWO

INTERPASSAGE

Now, in March of 1968, American politics became unhinged.
The reader must try to push himself back to the tumbling events of the spring of 1968 to recall how the pace of events overtook the decisions of leaders.

History wears, as one of its many robes, the study of men under the pressure of circumstances. But in the twentieth century, swift communications speed circumstances in a cascade of events without sequence or thread; those who must act or lead must absorb these events faster than the mind can sort them out. Never was this more true than in American politics in the spring of 1968.

In 1968 it was as if the future waited on the first of each month to deliver events completely unforeseen the month before. Thus, on January 1st of 1968, no one could foresee the impact of the Tet offensive at the end of the month. On February 1st, no one could forecast the student invasion of New Hampshire, or the withdrawal of George Romney. On March 1st, no one could forecast the entry of Robert Kennedy into the race, or Lyndon Johnson's withdrawal on March 31st. On April 1st, no one could foresee the assassination of Martin Luther King, or the riots that followed, or Rockefeller's entry into the race. On May 1st, no one could foresee Robert Kennedy's stunning victories in the primaries of Indiana and Nebraska, or his defeat in Oregon—or foretell the course of negotiations for peace in Paris. On June 1st, no one could foresee the assassination of Robert F. Kennedy in Los Angeles; and at no time could anyone wisely predict that at Christmas, Americans would be looking directly down on the moon.

Other events came in waves—no less pressing for being more difficult to define. The underlying crisis of the Western trading world provoked the great gold crisis of mid-March. The dollar quivered. Students rioted in Paris, Berlin and New York. The stock market—the best indicator of investor anticipation and greed—slithered about, sinking through the early months of the year, then soaring the morning after Lyndon Johnson's renunciation. The fevers of inflation began, steadily, then more rapidly, to flush and overheat the entire system, stimulating an orgy of spending and of speculation. Even girls' fashions seemed unable to make up their mind as skirts, simultaneously, went up to mid-thigh and descended to mid-calf.

Chronology is, generally, the safest guide to events, particularly in an American election. In an American election, classically, the tale should be told as a simple three-act story—first, the preliminary maneuverings and primaries; second, the conventions; third, the electoral climax. But 1968 offered no such simple story. The form I have adopted in the next few chapters is, therefore, arbitrary and not chronological; since events overlapped each other, and each family of events seemed to spread over several interlocking decisions of leadership, I have tried to group them not in sequence by date, but clustered about a dominant personality or a dominant disturbance.

March was, of course, a mad month, and the climate of emotion that introduced it was best caught by James Reston of *The New York Times*.

"Go across the full length of this great country," he wrote in the first week of March, "and what do you find? Material progress beyond the dreams of kings. Vast soaring commercial palaces of glass even in the middle cities. The bulldozer and the pneumatic drill, energy, noise, change, the fantastic beauty of the Los Angeles Art Center and the slums of Watts. The lowest national unemployment rate in many years and the highest Negro teen-age rate of unemployment and crime on record.

"The paradoxes are endless: We have probably never had so much moral concern or moral indifference at the same time in our history. Business . . . is filling the central cities with some of the finest architecture of the age and the suburbs with some of the most vulgar monstrosities in the long sad story of commercial construction. . . . It is impossible to go across this country without being impressed by the fundamental decency and fair-mindedness of the American people. They want to do what's right when they are really confronted with the hard facts. . . . The mysteries about Vietnam are beyond comprehension. The people are worried about Harlem in New York, and Hough in Cleveland, and Watts in Los Angeles, but most of them know little more about life in these places than about life in Saigon.

". . . When the people turn to their institutions for help, they feel abandoned. The churches are divided about the war, and even about the Negro revolution. The universities are in turmoil. . . . The Johnson administration asks for confidence and trust for policies which are not succeeding either at home or abroad, so there is no trust or confidence and the people are left to their own doubts and suspicions.

" 'A demoralized people,' Walter Lippmann wrote in 1932 at the height of the economic depression, 'is one in which the individual has become isolated. He trusts nobody and nothing, not even himself. He believes nothing, except the worst of everybody and everything. He sees only confusion in himself and conspiracies in other men. That is panic. That is disintegration. That is what comes when in some sudden emergency of their lives men find themselves unsupported by clear convictions that transcend their immediate and personal desires.'

". . . The country, one feels," continued Reston, "is looking for a new lead, for somebody who will come forward with a new philosophy and it is not finding the answer in Johnson or any of his political opponents.

"Washington is now the symbol of the helplessness of the present day. . . . Yet the political opposition offers no alternative that commands the confidence of a majority of the people. The main crisis is not Vietnam itself, or in the cities, but in the feeling that the political system for dealing with these things has broken down."

Thus the mood at the beginning of March, its central figure Lyndon Johnson; and so one must start with him

CHAPTER FOUR

LYNDON JOHNSON: THE RENUNCIATION

O F THE PARADOX of Lyndon Johnson historians will write many books, and many will find him a very great President indeed. Few men have done more good in their time, and no President has pressed more visionary ideas into law. Yet few have earned more abuse and roused less love, loyalty and affection from those he sought to help.

The popular impression of Lyndon Johnson—egomaniac, untrustworthy, a coarse man, mean of spirit, unforgiving—will fade. The bitterness of his associates will be better understood ("Lyndon Johnson," said one of his close personal aides on resigning, "is a man who distrusts his friends and despises his enemies"). But the historic verdict must hang on his conduct of office as President—and here the war in Vietnam overshadows all. For it was in his conduct of that war that he showed himself to be the poorest politician to sit in the White House in modern times; and it was only when in March, 1968, he was finally confronted with the choice between being politician and being President and renounced both that any greatness first became faintly visible to his contemporaries.

As a politician, leader of a nation at war, Johnson could not lead. The greatness of the chain of Democratic politicians that ran from Wilson through Roosevelt through Truman was that each, as President, when faced with reality abroad, could explain it politically to Americans at home and carry into combat a unified nation, willing to offer sons in death for the cause the President proclaimed. This is the greatest of all political talents—to be able to call on people to give up their lives for their country. It requires romance, eloquence, courage, wisdom and a magic of personality. Lyndon Johnson, though abominably mismanaging his war, led a cause of which no American need ever have been ashamed. The cause was world peace; his immediate objective was the frustration of an aggressor in an orderly world where, supposedly, change by violence was to be outlawed. Yet Johnson could never explain this cause to his people. The battlefield valor of Americans in Vietnam was left to be taken for granted by their countrymen, exposed to denunciation at home, then left without defense by the President while critics proclaimed it "immoral." Thus was valor squandered because Lyndon Johnson, President, lacked the political skill to give it meaning.

What was lacking in Johnson, above all, was a sense of the flow of history, of his own place in it, and of the place of Americans in the sweep of time that had brought them to world dominance. History, once past, can be fixed and frozen in dates and episodes; charted almost mechanically in forces rising, clashing, interacting; or traced by the ideas that govern decisions. But history while it happens is fluid and unpredictable, dependent on the intuitions of leaders who must break with the learning of the past and discard ideas that time has outworn; and who must explain their actions to their people and earn their trust while doing so. For an American President, leadership in the making of history is particularly difficult because of the immense increase in education of a people who insist on explanations; and because the sweep of change within American lifetimes has come so fast.

No better measure of the sweep of change in American life in this century can be found than the life of Lyndon Johnson, nor is there any better starting place than in his own education; for his education was little different from that provided for most of the 90,000,000 Americans by the dominant culture of the early century. In his high-school text on civics, Lyndon Johnson could read: "The child who has not learned obedience is handicapped for life. If he does not obey at home, he is not more likely to observe the laws of the state, even though he helps elect the men who make them. Boys and girls who study our Government will quickly discover that obedience to authority is as necessary in a government by the people as in a monarchy." So, up the ladder, as the book went on: "While we usually think of governor and government as they are connected with state or nation, government is necessary in the home, at school, in the shop, or on the farm—in short, anywhere that groups of people are working together. Someone must guide." Though the book had various passages of parochial observation (e.g., "Presidential elections excite the country and are not good for business. For these reasons some think they should not come as often as they do"), it went on quite soberly to describe the shapes rising in the future of an America whose population was to double in Johnson's lifetime. Of the problems of the cities, which he, as President, would first raise to prime national discussion, the same textbook read: "We have discovered city problems which were never dreamed of by city dwellers at the time of Columbus. Perhaps those who live in the future may wonder why we were not aware of other city problems in addition to those we talk about but often do not solve." And in his Southern history book he was taught, as so many other Southern children, then and now, of the Negro as a creature essentially inferior in ability and character to white men.[1]

Of the outside world, Johnson's geography books taught the same

[1] Lyndon Johnson's school history was entitled *A History of the United States,* by Hall, Smither and Ousley, published by the Southern Publishing Company, Dallas, Texas, 1920. The paragraph on reconstruction deserves, I think, quoting in full as a mirror of the world in which young Southerners grew up in the 1920's. Reconstruction was taught thus:

"The great problem facing the South was the negro. Thousands of the former slaves were without homes and they refused to work, thinking that the soldiers of the North would take care of them and give them 'forty acres and a mule.' The South recognized such a condition as a distinct menace to government, to property, and to person. The southern men, who knew the negro's character, understood that the way to help him was to require him under direction to care for himself. Ordinary prudence demanded that the negroes be controlled and disciplined until they could learn to use their freedom and in this way only could the negro be benefited and society protected. The southern legislatures, therefore, passed laws, the so-called 'Black Codes,' against vagrancy and undertook to compel the negro to work. Contract laws were also passed and an apprentice system was adopted by which minor negroes were bound out to service. The purpose of these laws was to initiate the negro gradually into his freedom. There was nothing new in such legislation; in many of the northern states similar laws were on the statute books and were enforced. Subsequent events proved this legislation on the part of the south to have been wise and beneficial, but unfortunately many people in the north, who had little understanding of the negro's real condition, regarded it as an effort to deprive him of his freedom and as evidence of a rebellious spirit on the part of the south."

I am indebted to *Life* Magazine's library services, and a research chain of many people, particularly Carolyn Sackett and Holland McCombs of *Life,* for tracking down first a classmate of Lyndon Johnson's who remembered their schoolbooks, then procuring the list of textbooks approved by the Texas School Board for use in Johnson's school during his formative years, then finding the copies themselves.

At least one other passage from his schoolbook on civics, quoted above, calls for reproduction as giving much of the fragrance of an earlier America. The book is entitled *Our Government,* by Davis and McClure, published by Laidlaw Brothers, Chicago-New York, 1922. The passage reads:

"PROBLEMS NOT YET SOLVED. As long as Americans continue to be an active and forward-looking people we shall have great problems in the solution of which all must share. Some wish to make changes very slowly. These may be called 'Conservatives.' 'Progressives' wish to move more rapidly. Those who desire sudden changes sometimes even by violent means are often termed 'radicals,' while those who believe in the good old days and that the future can never be better than the present are sometimes made fun of as 'old fogies' or 'moss backs.' Most of the constructive work of the world is done by those who are not extremists—conservatives and progressives. When new plans of government are proposed it is usually not best to be too radical and certainly not wise to insist that nothing new is safe. 'Be not the first by whom the new is tried, nor yet the last to lay the old aside.' "

limited wisdom that other schoolbooks taught an insular America. Of Southeast Asia he could read, "Siam is a monarchy, the king being assisted by a council of ministers and by a legislative body of noblemen. The poorer classes are still kept in a kind of serfdom by the local governors. . . . French Indo-China resembles Siam both in climate and character of people. Its forest-covered hills yield valuable teak and ironwood, and in its valleys are extensive fields of rice and millet. Silk, cotton, tea and spices are other products and there are also extensive coal beds. . . ." Of China, the same geography book had this to say: "The Chinese are followers of Confucius and his doctrine is everywhere taught. . . . One of the doctrines of Confucius is ancestor worship which leads them to regard new customs as bad. . . . By law, the punishment for striking a parent is death. Strangers, therefore, who represent new customs have never been welcome."

And of the world of physics, he could read in his science book about the dawn of something no one in the 1920's understood: ". . . Until recently the atom of hydrogen was supposed to be the smallest mass of matter that could exist separately: there was no means by which the atom could be divided. Sir J. J. Thomson has shown that there are minute particles called electrons . . . the prevailing view among physicists is that the atom of matter consists of a central sphere of positive electrification, surrounded by a number of negative electrons, moving around in minute orbits. . . . These atoms radiate energy slowly."

This entire view of the world, shared by so many millions of Americans, was to change in Johnson's lifetime; and from such ideas, step by step, he was to wrench himself away by main force and under the pressure of events.

Yet in the wrenching process, the education of Lyndon Johnson took a tight, controlled path. An early life of hardship, poverty and striving in South Texas brought him to Washington, D.C., by 1931, at the early age of twenty-three, and from then on, Congress and the mechanics of Congress were to be his life. It was there his true education took place; all the episodes of American life in the next thirty-seven years were to be part of him; but they were episodes as presented to the men of Capitol Hill, made concrete only by legislation. For Johnson, a law once passed was itself a new reality; and laws as he knew them were passed by managing the formal votes in the closed universe of Congress. As Congressman and Senator, Johnson's skill lay in uniting the most diverse groups, in weaving together majorities of all the fragmented power blocs represented at the Capitol, sent there from power sources he did not understand, but whose managers he could *manage*. The sweep of history, the grand perspectives of change were shaped in the White House; loyal to his administration, he nursed specific bills through the House or Senate; he scored each bill as it passed. From his first arrival in Washington until his departure after five years of the Presidency, his scoreboard was a legislative scoreboard. Except that, as President, Johnson played not only in a different league, but a different game, as if he were trying to score a football game with a baseball scoring card. The sacerdotal, priestly, almost mystic quality of the Presidency eluded him.

"He never understood the difference between the Hill and the White House," said Professor John Roche, historian and White House aide, whose loyalty to his chief never flickered. "The trouble was that the tactics of a Senate Majority Leader automatically created a credibility gap as President. If something like a Social Security Bill came up in the Senate, he used to be able to say to [Senator] Harry Byrd, 'I'll tell you what, you make your speech, and you can make a motion to recommit, but then when the final vote comes up, you go with it, huh?' and simultaneously he could say to Paul Douglas, 'You make your motion, and you make your speech, but when the time comes, this is the way it's got to be, and you go with it, huh?' and both of them thought Lyndon was with them, and he got his bill through. That's the way you do business in the Senate; but when you're President, newspapermen start comparing different versions of what you say, and they check Source A against Source B against Source C. Lyndon has no sense of historic inevitability as a President should."

A spirited Presidential campaign is probably the best way of educating any man in the quality of Presidential pronouncements. A Presidential pronouncement is a contract not with Congress, but with the people, which cannot be changed, cannot be fixed, cannot be manipulated by any deal with intermediary power-brokers. Johnson came to power and Presidency by the accident of assassination; he retained it in 1964, a year when the Republican Party, by choosing Goldwater, gave him a pass; his majority was imperial-size, imperial in quality, intoxicating. When a President promises that American boys will not be sent to die in Asian wars, as Johnson did in 1964, he must explain why history forces him to break that promise if such is, indeed, the case. Johnson did not see it that way. With his background of legislative loyalties to all Presidents of the past, he felt that unquestioning loyalty must flow to him, too, as prerogative of office. "Dear Jack," he wrote to John F. Kennedy in the first Christmas of their administration, in a warm, spontaneous, hand-written note, "where you lead, I will follow—Yours loyally, Lyndon." When he came to the Presidency, he felt all others should do the same—not understanding Kennedy's wider concept of leadership.

As President, Johnson believed he need concern himself chiefly with legislation on behalf of the people. For him the great goals of American life had been fixed in his youth by Franklin Roosevelt, his hero; the war had interrupted the construction of the New Deal; he would finish it. It is almost impossible to appreciate, at this close date in time, the monumental outline of Johnson's achievements in legislative architecture, within whose halls American life will proceed for a generation. With the passage of his Civil Rights Bill, the work of Reconstruction, suspended for one hundred years, was resumed. With his education bills, a century-long battle to make the government of the United States responsible for educating young Americans was won, and in his five years in office, Federal expenses on education rose from $4 billion a year to $12 billion. The beauty of our towns and countryside became, for the first time since Theodore Roosevelt, prime on the agenda of the nation. The urban problem, never formally discussed in national politics, became central to the political dialogue. Twenty million aging Americans had the financial blight of illness, the impoverishment of disaster, lifted from them by Medicare.

One could go on, as Lyndon Johnson was wont to go on in the closing days of his administration, calling the long roll of his accomplishments—yet he was personally despised. It was as if an enormous political body-odor suffused all he touched or did and people held their noses when they contemplated Lyndon Johnson.

Partly, there was a snobbery about it. "We come from the wrong side of the railway tracks," said a White House aide. "Take us all— Roche, Califano, Cater, McPherson in the White House staff. We all are self-made men. Look at Wilbur Cohen—Wilbur is homely. He looks like a little pawnbroker. But there's no finer man in all the country for that job than Wilbur. So Johnson said the Hell with them and made Wilbur Secretary of HEW." Johnson himself knew that he ran against Americans' image of their President and the dazzling silhouette of John F. Kennedy. To Hugh Sidey of *Life,* he once blurted, "I don't believe that I'll ever get credit for anything I do in foreign affairs, no matter how successful it is, because I didn't go to Harvard." And, on another occasion, "I wonder if anybody with my background can hold this country together." Parched for praise, he became embittered, coining at least one probably lasting aphorism: "Cast your bread on the waters, and the sharks will get it."

Other men of common clay had sat in the White House and survived criticism of their manners; other war Presidents had outlasted the denunciation of armchair strategists and amateurs of *Realpolitik.* Yet Johnson's manners, his training and his conduct as a war leader added up to something genuinely alarming as President-politician: people doubted his word. Deception in war is always necessary; but the purpose of deception in war is to deceive the enemy, not one's own. When the purposes clash, a President of the United States requires an area of concealment, an area of no comment, a deftness and dexterity in non-communication which dictators need never acquire. Johnson could never acquire this dexterity, and thus there emerged one of the operative clichés of political discussion: the credibility gap. Which meant that the press believed the President lied to the nation.

The distrust of the President was slow in growing. The first incident of press distrust could be dismissed as a reversion to his old habit, as Senate Majority Leader, of manipulating press reports by leaks and false implications for later maximum effect. Within weeks of his assumption of office, he had led the country to believe that his first budget could not possibly be brought below $102 billion; then he triumphantly emerged as a master budgeteer by pruning it to $98 billion. Other manipulations occurred. By summer of 1965 the phrase "credibility gap" had reached Vietnam, and GI's were reported wearing buttons saying *"Ambushed at Credibility Gap."* By 1966, denials had become outright deceptions. He promised in 1966 to campaign in California for Governor Pat Brown against challenger Ronald Reagan. Then he changed his mind. Instead of so stating, the White House flatly denied that any such promise had ever been made, which all newspapermen knew to be untrue. Thus, men paid attention to what he said and began to check his statements. He declared in February, 1968, at a press conference that "I have no intention of seeing him [General William Westmoreland] leave" his command in Vietnam; four months later he declared that he had made the decision to relieve Westmoreland as early as January. He declared all through the closing months of 1967 (see Chapter One) that the war was going well in Vietnam; and later insisted he should be given credit for having seen the Tet offensive in advance as early as the fall, when his public statements were otherwise. "Credibility gap" approached a mythic quality when in Korea he told the assembled troops, "My great-great-grandfather died at the Alamo," although his great-grandparents had not arrived in Texas until ten years after that massacre.

In a sense, one could regard Lyndon Johnson as a *naïf*. For all his wiles and guile, he had a raw, unsophisticated sense of the Presidency, a belief that what he said must be so because he, as President, had said so, or been told so. Truman, too, had been a *naïf* on reaching the Presidency; yet, under the tutelage of such men as Dean Acheson, had achieved greatness. Johnson felt he needed no tutelage from anyone; and Johnson was a Harry Truman with lust. His personality was not only vivid; it invited exaggeration. Johnson's manners and speech were of an earthiness unknown in the White House since the days of Andrew Jackson; and his phraseology was so colorful that those who heard it could not resist quotation and embellishment, ignoring its shrewdness of observation. Thus, of his troubles with the press, a friend remembers him saying, "I feel like a hound bitch in heat in the country. If you run, they chew your tail off; if you stand still, they slip it to you." Of his problem in Vietnam he once said, "Every time I stop the bombing of North Vietnam, they run those trucks of theirs right up my ---." Of peace-making he said, "I got earphones in Moscow and Manila, earphones in Rangoon, and earphones in Hanoi, and all I hear on them is 'F--- you, Lyndon Johnson.' " Of his distrust of the Germans and the Nazis: "We trusted them once and when they pulled out their knockwurst, it turned out to be a gun."

All these were matters of manners. But the manners invited and opened the way for an abuse of the man, at every level, that surpassed in viciousness anything any modern President had had to live with. The abuse finally obscured the truth, the dimensions and achievements of Lyndon Johnson, beyond any fairness, decency or responsibility.

Night-club comics and intellectuals of the new culture, Republicans and his own Party rivals, vied with each other to demean and make ridiculous the President. From Las Vegas to Greenwich Village, comedians exaggerated his Southern accent, hilariously mimicking an imaginary Johnson talking with or about Negroes, or his self-confusion with God. On the campuses, and then on streets, the buttons of the youngsters read *"Hitler is Alive—in the White House," "Sterilize LBJ: No More Ugly Children," "King Lyndon the First,"* and other phrases of an obscenity unprintable. Placards were printed and posted showing Lyndon Johnson in Nazi uniform; others bore the legend *"Lee Harvey Oswald Where Are You Now That We Need You?"*—a joking invitation to kill, sported usually by people who decried violence most loudly. *How to Be a Jewish President* was published to large sales, a picture-book callously and thoughtlessly anti-Semitic and anti-Johnson at the same time. Satire itself became unhinged, for satire, to be effective, must be a comic rearrangement of truth with a biting edge; satire without truth is meaningless. Yet the country's wits and taste-makers gave roaring coast-to-coast applause to a wildly graceless "satire" called *MacBird,* in which Johnson was portrayed as the assassin of John F. Kennedy and the plotter of the death of Robert Kennedy; the death of the one murdered President, the death of the noble Adlai Stevenson became a frolic, a joke, whose obscenity was held together only by its hatred of Johnson. The high point of the juvenile effort came as the Kennedy figure of the play was taken from the Johnson ranch and lifted high into the air, a marionette to be shot at. Then the shots rang out—a joke. "As the shots ring out," said critic Walter Kerr, who had gone expecting to see a drama, "we realize that the author has indeed made herself unique in our time. She has attempted to wrap the assassination firmly in the arms of a vast burlesque merriment. The arms won't fold, they freeze." *MacBird* was a success—so much so that the *Wall Street Journal* reported that one Washington official appeared at a staff meeting to find his three chief aides gleefully reading aloud parts of the satire. Political jokes were resurrected from as far back as the days of Herbert Hoover and pinned on Johnson; bedroom jokes of the President's life with Lady Bird were of a pornography to match those about Franklin Roosevelt's life with Eleanor.

Student leaders declared, and the press reprinted over and over again, their claim that they would never let Johnson speak out loud in public in a big city anywhere in the United States; he would campaign only at military bases. The Secret Service was now, even before the assassination of Robert Kennedy, intensely worried. By the beginning of 1968, crackpot letters threatening the President's life had jumped from an old average of 100 a month to an average substantially above 1,000 a month. In Syracuse, doing a pre-check on a Presidential trip, the Secret Service found demonstrators preparing paper cups of urine to throw at him, and buttons reviling the Johnson daughters in slogans of absolute filth printed up for the demonstrators to wear.

Waking thus, day after day, year after year, to the acid shower of criticism, the man had become by 1968 an individual embittered in all his thinking. Isolated in the White House with a corporal's guard of devoted loyalists, he had developed what one of his staff members described as "Johnson's porcupine psychology," or, in his own words, a philosophy of "hunkering our heads down and taking it." As the campaign of 1968 approached, we find him, thus, almost a prisoner of his own bureaucracies, both governmental and political.

His Party officials had already been uneasy as they looked ahead from the fall of 1967 to the campaign of 1968. Though the President was a lavish man in national social goals, he could, in private, be either unpredictably generous or narrowly parsimonious. To the Democratic Party, which he considered as much a personal property as his ranch, he was uncommonly niggardly. In 1966 he had slashed the budget of the Democratic National Committee to the bone, eliminating even the vital voter-registration division, a decision the Party was bitterly to regret in 1968. His callous humiliation of John Bailey, the nominal National Chairman, a veteran of great experience in the political wars, was a matter of Washington gossip. The Party headquarters over which Bailey presided in Washington is traditionally a service center for visiting politicians. But it could offer no services, no appointments, no favors. Johnson ran an administration so clean that no man he chose in five years of office was tainted with petty chiselling, fraud or graft. Of all his major appointees, only Abe Fortas' fiscal behavior was ever questioned.

So secretive and personal was Johnson, however, in his appointments that Federal patronage for politicians dried up almost totally. Of the political and amateur leaders who had labored so successfully in the Citizens for Johnson-Humphrey movement in the 1964 victory over Barry Goldwater, only one was ever invited to office by the President; nor did any but a handful ever receive an invitation to those White House receptions, dinners or dances which the wives of politicians so desperately crave. Of the restlessness in his Party he learned but little; his closest political deputy for Party matters was a fellow Texan, Marvin Watson, a steel-company executive, whose understanding of the political climate north of the Mason-Dixon line was as near zero as it is possible to come.

Occasionally, in the fall of 1967, hardy staff members or bold old friends of former days would try to slip a memorandum in to the President describing the troubles brewing. In September of 1967, Professor John Roche sent the President his report: "I believe that we are going to have a real battle for survival next year. . . . I would suggest the following points for your consideration. . . . Obliterate the memory of the 1964 election. If you had spent the fall months at the Ranch, relaxing, you would probably have gotten about the same vote. . . . Concentrate on explaining to the American people the philosophical (which does not mean abstract) basis of their greatness. . . . Avoid *defensive* explanations of how much has been accomplished. . . . Build an effective national political organization. . . . Forget (not forgive) the whole Kennedy caper—the point has been made to Bobby that if we go down, he goes with us. . . . Above all, as you said to the Cabinet on Wednesday, break the Administration out of the 'siege' mentality which is a form of defeatism. . . . The 1968 campaign is going to be a real slug-fest and your supporters should get in training. In County Mayo where my grandmother came from, the slogan was: 'Stand firm boys, and when a head comes over the wall—hit it.' I think we have got to cut loose in the same joyous way. Let's leave all the self-pity to the Republicans—and give them ample justification to weep." The Roche memorandum was followed by a much longer, more analytical memorandum from the President's old friend James Rowe in early November; and by yet another from Postmaster-General Lawrence O'Brien. The need of explaining the political unrest to the President was urged by chief of domestic staff Joseph Califano on all visiting governors and politicians; but they quailed when they entered the Presidential presence.

Sluggishly, his mind preoccupied with other matters, the President finally responded. In November he gathered a group of his old political friends together at the White House and heard them talk out the campaign for the first time. His old friends were men of another era, and they talked, indeed, of the problems they could foresee—the war being the greatest of the problems—and of the standard time-hallowed techniques: how to get the vote out, who would head up the women's committee, what labor should do, how the farmers' vote should be cultivated, money-raising, primaries (the President had not yet made up his mind whether to let his name be entered in primaries or not). Then, all of them took comfort in recalling Harry Truman's campaign of 1948, that upset victory for an earlier underdog President, and the meeting trailed off in nostalgic reminiscences without decisions.

A few weeks after this first conference on campaign planning—and still six weeks before Tet—I talked to Lawrence O'Brien, then Postmaster-General, who had participated. It had been an old-fashioned conference, thought O'Brien, and all the old rules of politics had to be rewritten, he felt. New forces were changing the country; the middle class now included all of the working class, too—why, Walter Reuther now had strikes without pickets, no passion. Workingmen used Labor Day to clean out the basement or fix up the playroom, and the traditional political kick-off of a Democratic campaign before the auto workers in Detroit on Labor Day meant nothing; last time the unions couldn't even fill up Cobo Hall. There were also going to be about 14,000,000 new voters registered in this campaign, said O'Brien—2,000,000 of them Negroes, 12,000,000 of them youngsters—and therefore you had to put youth on the top of your list of political priorities. These were the uncommitted children of the middle class, seeking new causes. You had to go out after them and bring them in. Yet even O'Brien's perceptive analysis was oriented only to the clash with the Republicans in the November elections of the next year; to him, as to other Democratic politicians, it was unthinkable that a sitting President of the United States could be un-horsed within his own Party either by primaries, conventions or riot in the streets.

That perception was to come later.

To tell of Lyndon Johnson's renunciation is made particularly difficult because of two directly contradictory versions of that decision—both of them probably true. There is first his own version—that he had decided to leave office six months before his announcement and was awaiting only the opportune moment to make it known. Then there is the version of a number of his closest White House associates who insist that he made up his mind only in the last forty-eight hours before renunciation. The truth of both stories probably reflects the inner struggle in Lyndon Johnson's own mind as the pendulum of decision swung back and forth, and back and forth again, to make one version of the story true at one time, the other at another time. Yet it is the second story—

of a powerful man arriving finally at his own sense of what is right, not out of pique or weariness, but out of conviction—that illustrates best the agony and drama of the Presidential burden.

The Presidential version of the renunciation can be easily told. Any number of staff men at the White House can remember the President saying as early as 1966, "I got my resignation right here in my pocket," and tapping his breast, or mumbling about how he wanted to get out of the job. But few took him at his word. Perhaps his first serious sharing of this vagrant thought with an outsider can be dated in October, 1967, a few weeks before the White House campaign-planning session of November. At his ranch in Texas, Johnson dictated a draft memo of resignation to his press secretary, George Christian, and instructed Christian to share it with his old friend Governor John Connally of Texas. But no decision was made. Again, in December, his mind full of the thought of the oncoming Tet offensive, the matter of renunciation came up as Johnson flew around the world from Australia to Rome to America. His companion then was another old friend, Horace Busby, who, with astonishing candor and deep affection, urged the President to withdraw. By mid-January, Busby and Christian had collaborated on another draft statement of withdrawal, to be appended to the State of the Union message scheduled for delivery on January 17th; Johnson read the statement, folded it up in an inside pocket, then thought better of it and was silent.

If others besides this little group and Mrs. Johnson knew of the inner thought in the President's mind, they are unknown to the record. A new Secretary of Defense, Clark Clifford, was coming aboard, giving up one of the most lucrative law practices in Washington, prepared to serve not just a lame-duck administration, but to go all the way, through the campaign and beyond to the vistas of peace and 1972. The Democratic Party was slowly, belatedly, readying for action; the President permitted his oldest political friend, James Rowe, to direct a new Citizens for Johnson-Humphrey; and the White House staff began to prepare the positions and strategies of re-election for an inattentive, but acquiescent, candidate.

It is thus, in the month of March, that one must see events coming to intolerable pressure in the Presidential mind. Over all lay the continued vilification, the unending abuse of the man. Yet he must perform. As war leader, he was obsessed day and night with the course of combat and the blood-costs of the battle overseas. As director of the economy, he could not escape the ominous, then nearly devastating, growth of the world's pressure on the Western currencies; by mid-March the very stability of the American dollar, the value of gold, was to hang suspended by only a thread. And at home, as politician, he was being urged to battle on the domestic front by men who were reporting a native student Viet Cong loose within the Democratic Party itself. Both press and his own political intelligence were reporting the student uprising in New Hampshire, the surge of anti-Johnson sentiment across the country since the Tet offensive.

It was in the first week in March that such events and developments began to grind toward the decision yet untaken in the President's mind. Even those most deeply involved cannot yet say where or how the decision to take a public stand came. But it began, as so often great events have in American history, with someone saying to someone else at the White House, "The President ought to say something, he ought to talk out."

A Presidential speech is a major affair of state; it is written usually in the White House by those the President trusts most. Then, if it concerns national policy, drafts circulate through the State Department, Defense Department, Treasury Department, and the Joint Chiefs of Staff; and as all their various points of view clash, are absorbed or eliminated, policy emerges—the President's policy. Not words, but ideas and decisions shape a President's speech. Thus, when in the first week of March the assignment to write a speech was given to Harry McPherson of the White House staff, it was as if the lead end of a reel of unseen film had been slipped into a projector—it would unwind from the first frame to an unknown climax in the weeks ahead.

By March 10th, two days before the New Hampshire primary, McPherson had finished a first draft, a set of raw thoughts for internal government discussion, embodying what the President felt he had to say. The draft had three main themes. The first expressed the pressure on the President of the war itself, and the request of the military command in Vietnam for 206,000 more troops in the coming year. The second expressed the pressure of the Treasury—the Treasury wanted an immediate 10 percent surtax raise in the income tax; and, to the Treasury, the call to arms seemed the most opportune moment to call on the nation to sacrifice its dollars also. ("If the Treasury had its way, it would have been a forty-five-minute speech devoted exclusively to taxes," said McPherson.) The third theme came from the President's emotion—a call for unity to a nation in crisis; this is a tough time, therefore, chest out, chins out, faces to the guns; the draft peroration ended with Colonel Travis at the Alamo.

By the end of the third week in March the speech had already passed through six versions as the various bureaucracies pulled and hauled to insert their ideas into the Presidential mouth as national policy. Several Presidential round-tables with Rusk of State, Clifford of Defense, Rostow of National Security, Fowler of Treasury, McPherson as drafter had brought the administration no nearer to any major agreement on policy. All had been frozen into position by months and years of wrestling with the problems of Vietnam, except for Clifford.

And it was the change in Clifford's view of the world, as March wore on, that was to change the policy of America and Lyndon Johnson's role as leader of his people.

Clifford had become Secretary of Defense on March 1st, with the reputation of being a smooth-talking hawk. But Clifford, a devout patriot, a fine mind, a probing questioner, was now the first fresh intelligence to join the weary war-command of America in high place. When, at 10:30 on the morning of March 1st, Clifford had been sworn in as Secretary of Defense of the United States, the event had followed by only a day the return from Vietnam of the Chairman of the Joint Chiefs of Staff, General Earle Wheeler, bearing the most somber of tidings: that the MACV Command in Saigon was about to request 206,000 more troops for prosecution of the war in Asia, a package of at least three full field divisions plus supporting air, sea and logistic elements. With this request, on his first day in office, began Clifford's review of foreign policy; and in policy he found his Pentagon to be frighteningly split. On the one hand was his uniformed bureaucracy, rigidly supporting the needs of the troops and command in the field. On the other hand was his subordinate net of civilian supervisory chiefs, Secretaries and Under Secretaries of Army, Air Force, Navy, who, theoretically, had policy guidance over the armed forces. But time and inertia had eroded the ancient American tradition of direct civilian control of the military branches; Secretaries and Under Secretaries of the armed forces had been reduced to little more than civilian procurers of hardware and funds for the generals and admirals they supposedly controlled; their influence on strategy and tactics was nil. Across the broad stretch of the civilian superstructure of the Pentagon, their simmering discontent with the conduct of the war in Vietnam had reached a point of almost open rebellion. What advice reached the President reached him only through the Secretary of Defense; through his National Security Assistant, Walt Rostow; through his Secretary of State, Dean Rusk; through his military commanders. Robert McNamara, Clifford's predecessor, had become increasingly disillusioned with the war, particularly with the net military values of continued bombing in the north. He had been replaced by Clifford, in whom the President had hoped to find a more resolute man. But Clifford, seeing no conflict between his loyalty to the nation and his loyalty to the President, had begun on entering office by probing for facts and perspective.

Clifford's questions at the Pentagon all had a simple thrust: How would the generals go about winning the war? If they got another quarter of a million troops, what would their strategy be? How long to victory, and by what route? And what about the costs? The answers that came back from the generals added up to a single statement: given the governing diplomacy of the war, and its political framework, even the requested 206,000 additional troops could not guarantee victory. Unless North Vietnam, Laos or Cambodia was invaded in order to stop infiltration and the enemy's flow of supply, escalation would result only in counter-escalation. Clifford is a broad-gauge man. Probing costs, he was told that the additional troops would add another $12 billion annually to the cost of the war; economists told him this could not be imposed on America without wage-and-price controls. Through his web of contacts in the highest levels of American business, with those corporate groups who form the bony structure of what is commonly called "the military-industrial complex," Clifford was also absorbing another input: even the military-industrial complex was adamantly opposed to escalation. Above all, Clifford, a man whose political experience dated back to Harry Truman, sensed that a matter of the highest, yet quite simple, politics was involved. The Pacific nations whose frontiers America was defending were themselves unwilling to make a greater effort; the South Vietnamese government was unwilling to intensify its exertion; why should American families be forced to sustain the entire cost in blood and treasure? The military judgment of the need would not wash politically.

In this appreciation of politics at home, Clifford was not alone. Politically, in the inner circle of the White House, Clifford had the support of Harry McPherson. McPherson—young, cultivated, a man of quiet style and great honor—had come to the White House in 1965 from service on the Pentagon civilian staff. He knew not only the language of the military; Texas-born and Texas-bred, he also spoke, when he wanted to, in the President's native idiom; and as speechwriter-in-chief to the President, he was also point man on the internal political front. The reports coming to McPherson of the domestic political upheaval in New Hampshire, and the even greater disaster impending in Wisconsin, now impelled him to address the President on domestic politics. Interrupting himself in the course of his major speech-drafting project on Vietnam, he delivered to the President on March 18th a crisp memorandum on the domestic political situation, full of gloom and foreboding. McPherson's was the view of a young man, fresh on the national political scene. But the next day, Tuesday, March 19th, the President had to absorb the opinion of James Rowe, that master scholar and practitioner of politics since the days of Franklin D. Roosevelt.

Rowe was and is a liberal of great credentials, ready to defend the cause at home or abroad. Hitherto an inflexible champion of the commitment in Vietnam, he now had a new view. He had risen that day from the regular weekly lunch of the leaders of Johnson's campaign for re-election—Lawrence O'Brien, William Connell, Richard Maguire, Marvin Watson, several others. Now he felt impelled by loyalty to break through the curtain Watson had spread between the President and reality and speak frankly.

Rowe observed, in his personal memorandum, that Watson had been startled by the unanimity all the politicians present showed on the Vietnam war: the President must do something "dramatic and exciting" before the Wisconsin primary.

All the politicians at the lunch had reported that was what they were hearing from other politicians talking to people in the streets. The President had become the war candidate; he had to do something to re-capture the peace issue. The fact was, hardly anyone was any longer in-terested in winning the war, and everyone wanted to get out.

Rowe recounted the dismal political situation, and how greatly "dove" sentiment had grown in the country since the Tet offensive. The President had actually won the local delegate fights in New Hampshire and Minnesota—but everyone had taken his contested victories as crush-ing defeats. What would be the reaction, asked Rowe, if the President actually lost in the Wisconsin primary—which was probable.

It was essential, concluded Rowe, that the President "regain the initiative" and stand forth as the "Peace with Honor" candidate, not as the "Win the War" candidate. It required, repeated Rowe, something dramatic. But he did not suggest what.

Three days later on Friday, March 22nd, the President gathered a few of those he trusted most in the family dining room of the White House to discuss the Vietnam speech once more. Present, as usual, were Clifford, Rusk, Rostow, Wheeler and McPherson. For the first time, they openly debated a call for a bombing limitation. Would a limitation of bombing at the 20th parallel entice the Viet Cong to negotiations? The group toyed with the idea, but rose with the consensus that a halt limited only at the 20th parallel would not be enough to satisfy the enemy; and came to no conclusion. The next day, March 23rd, General Wheeler flew halfway around the world, at the President's request, to meet secretly with General Westmoreland at Clark Field in Manila for ninety minutes and review his military requests. McPherson, the same day, on his own initiative, composed and sent to the President a memorandum raising again the previous day's proposal of a bombing halt at the 20th parallel—this time suggesting that it be communicated to the enemy only as a first step in de-escalation, to be followed by others if a corresponding de-escalation was observed on the other side.

Events of the next week moved faster. On Monday, March 25th, there gathered in Washington at the President's request a secret meeting of the *"genro"* of the nation, those soldiers and elder statesmen, wise in war and diplomacy, who had well served it in other times but were now out of government—former Secretary of State Dean Acheson, former Chiefs of Staff Omar Bradley, Maxwell Taylor and Matthew Ridgeway, other notables like McGeorge Bundy, Arthur Dean, Robert Murphy, Henry Cabot Lodge, Douglas Dillon (all Republicans) and Cyrus Vance, Arthur Goldberg, Justice Abe Fortas and George Ball (Democrats).

On Monday evening, March 25th, the group dined at the State Department and were briefed by such in-power responsibles as Rusk, Clifford, Rostow, Wheeler and Richard Helms of the CIA; McNamara was also present at the dinner. After dinner, the group proceeded to the Operations Center of the State Department, where they were briefed by such middle-echelon officials as Philip Habib of the State Department, Major General William Depuy of the staff of the Joint Chiefs, and George Carver of the CIA—men who, in normal governmental procedure, are denied direct access to the Presidential ear. It was the briefing of this second group that shook the elder statesmen.

On Tuesday the group met in the morning at State for another discussion with Rusk and Clifford, at which meeting Clifford expressed himself firmly against yielding to the staff demand of the Pentagon for the 206,000 troop increase; and then the group went on to lunch with the President at the White House. The lunch was dominated by a forty-five-minute talk given by General Creighton Abrams, who impressed all as being singularly able; and thereafter the President declared that everybody who was still in the official family should go back and go to work, and he would speak alone to the elder statesmen in the Cabinet Room.

The discussions must have been shattering for the President. Roughly the same group had gathered earlier, in November of 1967, and at that time Ball had been almost alone in his opposition to the war. Now, Bundy, as the spokesman authorized to summarize their opinion, began by saying that he, Bundy, previously so firm for the commitment, had now finally come to agree with George Ball. Dean Acheson followed—he, too, had swung to the side of negotiation. So, too, had Arthur Dean. General Omar Bradley was next with a shock statement—he, too, had swung; it was Bradley's opinion that the President had to "lower his sights" in Vietnam. So, too, felt Cyrus Vance, a Presidential favorite. Only three hawks remained—former Chief of Staff Maxwell Taylor, Robert Murphy, Justice Abe Fortas. The dominant sentiment of the elders was that America was bogged down in a war against Asian guerrillas which could not be won except by escalation and the dreadful risk of war against China. It was time, most felt, to suspend bombings and move to negotiations at the conference table. Ball insisted that suspension of bombings at the 20th parallel would be inadequate, for it did not meet the chief political consideration of the enemy. A brief unpleasantness ensued between Ball, on the one extreme, and Fortas, on the other ex-

treme. The President rose from the afternoon meeting stunned. Disillusioned, he immediately inquired who had briefed them; and was appalled
that what had been told them by the middle-echelon intelligence officials
had not previously been made known to him.

Many tracks of influence were now converging on the President
at once in this week of hidden decision. On another track, matters
less profound in world importance but equally immediate were also
hurtling at the President. For the President, as political leader of the
Democratic Party, also had another rendezvous with history: the Wisconsin primaries approaching on April 2nd. From top to bottom, the
structure of the Democratic Party had been shaken by the impact of
McCarthy's spectacular showing in New Hampshire; its leadership had
now begun to rally for what they now recognized as a major internal
crisis. The President himself, too, was finally moving to the politics of
politics which he had so long ignored for the larger problems overseas.
His Party machinery had gone operational immediately after the New
Hampshire clash, stimulated by the President's sudden combat relish—
Bobby Kennedy had entered the fight on Saturday, the 16th, and that
caused Johnson's glands to race. On Sunday, March 24th, he had
authorized Lawrence O'Brien, his Postmaster-General, to call together
the entire Cabinet—with the exception of the Secretaries of State and
Defense, who by tradition are above politics—at the Postmaster-
General's ornate offices to mobilize the Cabinet itself for the domestic
clash. O'Brien gave them their instructions—they were in a fight to
save the administration, all of them; Secretaries of Agriculture, Labor,
Post Office, were to saddle up, now, to defend the administration in
its own Party primaries. O'Brien himself was taking off for Wisconsin
on Wednesday the 27th to lash the disheartened loyalist Democrats of
the Badger State to repel the McCarthy assault. The President was now,
finally, cracking the whip. As the O'Brien group met on Sunday, White
House aide Joseph Califano, domestic legislative chief, was flying back
from an interrupted vacation in Puerto Rico—he had been summoned
by a direct Presidential phone call to address a meeting of Queens
County leaders of the New York State Democratic Party and rouse them
to start getting with it. Califano was also directed to set his White House
staff to work on an immediate compilation of the first full campaign
documentation of Lyndon Johnson's achievement as source material for
a defense of the administration. (Califano was to return from New York
on Tuesday, the 26th, the same gloomy Tuesday of the elder statesmen's
turnabout, to report to the President that his prospects in the Empire
State were poor.) Meanwhile, during this last week the bureaucracy of
the Democratic National Committee was moving at emergency speed
also. From its lean coffers a last $200,000 was appropriated for a final
weekend media effort; and twenty young men were hastily mobilized to

fly off to Wisconsin in a desperate effort to offset McCarthy. (Some of those recruited were still at the Washington airport, their tickets already purchased, at the moment on the following Sunday when Lyndon Johnson's renunciation made their mission meaningless.)

Thus, Tuesday, March 26th—the dismal views of the senior statesmen of the nation; the President's shock at what they had heard, which he had not, from the briefing officers; gloom from Califano on New York politics; gloom from Wisconsin.

One cannot know what went on in Lyndon Johnson's mind at this point; but a superficial snapshot of the President that Tuesday evening is, perhaps, in order.

A certain lack of reverence for Lyndon Johnson in my previous writings had annoyed the President, and I had not set foot in the Oval Office since the death of John F. Kennedy. Thus, I had been most pleased when I was told I could see "Mr. Big" that Tuesday evening, March 26th, 1968, and I went there in the protective companionship of James Rowe. I had no idea, then, of the burdens and anguish pressing the President that day.

I was shocked as, after a minute, he rose from his back desk and approached us. When I had last spoken to him, during the exuberant campaign of 1964, Lyndon Johnson had bestrode the nation's politics like a bronco-buster. Now he seemed exhausted. His eyes, behind the gold-rimmed eyeglasses, were not only nested in lines and wrinkles, but pouched in sockets blue with a permanent weariness. His forehead was creased, not only in the red wrinkles of the elevenses, which never unknit, but with layer upon layer of brow wrinkles above them, which kept folding and unfolding as he spoke. He spoke in an undertone, with a softness, a tiredness that did not begin to lift until the very end of the hour-long conversation. The contour of his large body reflected his exhaustion as he slouched in a large rocking chair, his feet lifting to a carpet-covered footstool, his slate-blue suit rumpled, his hand jingling something in the left pocket; nor did he ever stir to those famous gestures that accompany a classic Johnson performance.

Our conversation began with anticipated frostiness as he curtly rejected all questions on politics, on Robert Kennedy, on Eugene McCarthy, on the Vietnam war. Rowe, a friend of both of us, tried to mellow the air by suggesting that I was a man trying to write histories of Presidential campaigns, and that it was a good idea for us to talk so I could get it right. The President nodded curtly, and we moved on to other things. I wanted to tell the President's story to the people. Well, said the President, they accused him of lack of communication, but anyone who *wanted* to could find out what he was doing. He wasn't concealing anything. The press just didn't print it. What had the war done to his domestic plans? I asked. It wasn't the war, he replied, the

war was costing only seventeen billion dollars a year—go ask Mc-
Namara for the figures—it was the tax cut that was squeezing. If he
hadn't cut the taxes in 1964, he'd have an extra twenty-five billion
dollars a year now to do what had to be done; and all he was asking
Congress for now was to give him back half of that twenty-five billion.
If he had advice to give to another President, it was never to cut taxes;
he'd learned; he'd never ask for a tax cut again; they never give it
back to you, the way the economists say they should—cut taxes in a
downswing of the business cycle, put them back in an upswing. Then,
on to a disquisition about economists, academia and the intellectuals.

As he warmed, I slowly began to grasp that he was reviewing his
whole administration, trying to place it in history, not in the context of
a political campaign. There seemed to be two benchmarks in his own
measure of achievement—Kennedy and Roosevelt. What had Kennedy
done, he asked, except for three things—the test-ban treaty, the
manpower-retraining act, and a third bill (which I have now forgotten)?
The name Roosevelt was more important. A poor painting of Roosevelt
hung in the place of honor in the room where we talked, but Roosevelt,
for Johnson, was alive, the master. Roosevelt's name threaded all
through the conversation as he went on to review what he had accomplished. Even in recollection, there is a thrill to the memory of this
President measuring himself. He had willed good things to happen; and
they were happening now because he so willed it.

Education was first in his mind. He had passed more than forty
education bills—more than in all the preceding years of the Republic
put together—against all opposition. That B'nai Brith—they had given
him an award one day and denounced his education program the next
day. The Catholics—he'd had to buy the Catholics' approval for his
education programs with those free books he gave their schools. Even
the Protestants had given him trouble, they thought he was giving away
too much to the Catholics; the Baptists thought he'd sold out to the
Pope. But there it was—he'd got education on the Federal programs;
and figures, statistics, facts churned out of him in a magnificent description of what his programs meant for the future.

And beauty. Lady Bird was so interested in that. He'd gotten the
first clean-air bill through Congress, and now the country could get to
work on pollution. And this was the first year since Teddy Roosevelt
and Gifford Pinchot they'd put more land back into the public domain
than they'd taken out. And his parks weren't like Teddy Roosevelt's,
off there somewhere in Montana and Wyoming where only the rich
could go. He was putting his parks down right near the big cities, like
New York and Philadelphia, where a poor guy could "load his six kids
in a jalopy and get there and back in a couple of hours."

And medicine. Those health centers were going up all over the country where everybody, even a poor man, could get the best medicine there was. This year, he said, we'd treated 35,000 pregnant women with German measles—did I realize what that would have cost, taking care of 35,000 deformed kids, crippled by German measles in pregnancy, for the rest of their lives? And Medicare, that was for the old folks, he said; only the old folks or people taking care of old folks could understand what Medicare had meant. He was reminded of a journalist, always writing nasty things about him, Johnson, every day in his column, but when the journalist's old mother got sick and Medicare took care of her, even that "mean old son-of-a-bitch" (the only near-profanity in our talk) wrote him to say how wonderful Medicare was. He wished he could bring in a bill to take care of the little kids, so that a poor woman would have care for her child as soon as she missed her period; he wanted to call it "Kiddicare"; but it was an election year and people would attack it as political.

Thus, on to other matters—housing, and the urban crisis, and all he'd tried to do, and succeeded in doing. He didn't know what they were going to say about his administration, but "if you could give everybody a chance at a job, get them enough to eat, give them a decent roof over their head, a decent place to live in and a place to go on vacations, and then if you defended their liberties, and they had the patriotism they should have got from their fathers . . ." His sentence trailed off at this point and ended: . . . well, that's what he'd set out to do.

"And how much time did a President have anyway?" he asked rhetorically. A President has only four years' run from the Congress, he answered. Even Roosevelt—Roosevelt did all he was going to do in his first four years, except for that minimum-wage bill he got through in 1938. The best anybody could hope for was a run of four years, and he himself had had a good four-year run. They'd never repealed any of Roosevelt's legislation, and they weren't going to repeal any of Lyndon Johnson's legislation. For, however little time he might remain here, he'd had a good run of it, and thirty years before that in Congress—he'd had his say in a lot of good things that came out of Washington.

"I guess not many Presidents have been understood in their own time," he said. And with that, Rowe and I left. As we wandered out through the South Lawn, we discussed the valedictory quality, the underlying melancholy, of his somber talk; neither one of us conceived that the President was this week about to give up his power and authority; and Rowe said, "That's the way he is—up one day, down the next. I've seen him that way before."

The next few days were to be, for Lyndon Johnson, intensely worse. On Wednesday, March 27th, the machinery of high policy continued to turn, accelerating of its own momentum. Sometime between ten and eleven there gathered at the State Department, once again, the same responsibles charged with delivering to Lyndon Johnson the statement on Vietnam he would make to the nation: Clifford and Rusk, Rostow and Bill Bundy, and McPherson. McPherson cannot recall whether at this point he was on the sixth or seventh draft of his speech, but as the group discussed it, it was obvious that Clark Clifford had come to decision in his own mind. There was something all wrong about this speech, said Clifford, it just would not do; he reviewed his own re-examination of the Pentagon and his feeling that American policy must now point to negotiation. McPherson weighed in with his own assessment of the political front at home. Bundy was sympathetic to McPherson and Clifford. Rusk offered no objection to Clifford's thought, and Rostow was silent. McPherson, in recollection, admonishes that the meeting be remembered with no dramatics; there was no confrontation, no argument; only the result was dramatic. The meeting lasted until sometime between two and three in the afternoon. But it came to the conclusion that McPherson should redraft the speech once more and insert for the first time a statement that American bombing would be limited in the north, drawn back to the 20th parallel. Thus, on Wednesday evening McPherson returned to his office on the second floor of the White House and typed, until early in the morning, a version of policy styled Alternative Draft Number One, in which the President would propose that the course of the war be turned about, that American bombing be restricted, that negotiations be openly invited. Civilian authority had slowly reasserted itself over the instruments.

The President received the new McPherson draft on Thursday, then telephoned that he wanted to discuss various phrases on page three—of the new draft! Somehow, all the pressures, all the weight of the months, the years, the preceding days, had moved him in his own mind, his own decision alone, to take the first open step toward negotiation, to see if a first step of American self-restraint would bring peace closer. There were to be five more drafts of the new policy before the final text on Sunday, March 31st. And in each new draft the President must have sensed his choices narrowing:

The same speech would be studied by two totally different audiences, as if he were speaking to an auditorium filled half by the Women's Christian Temperance Union and half by drunks from Stag Night at the Elks. Only a President can sense the multiple rings of attention to his words, the ripples they set up in different universes. It would be in the best interests of America to make a last ultimate plea to North Vietnam to make peace; this the President now saw. But if he continued to stand as candidate for re-election, as an intra-Party opponent of Eugene McCarthy in the Wisconsin primary, then whatever he said would be taken as a cheap political maneuver addressed to local politicians in Sheboygan, Madison, Eau Claire and Ashland, Wisconsin, as a program jerry-built to score points in the Tuesday primary. If he remained a candidate, whatever he said would be dismissed at home and abroad as a vote-catching gambit in parochial politics. Whereas his real purpose was peace, for this is what the President of the United States owes the American people. He could not be both politician and President at the same time.

By now the speech had been scheduled for prime time on national television on Sunday evening, March 31st, at 9:00 P.M. Time was tight, and new input hammered him. On Friday the President had been in touch with Lawrence O'Brien, who called from New York. O'Brien had for months been urging negotiations in Vietnam; now, reporting on his visit to Wisconsin, he could not conceal from the President the full dimensions of the impending political disaster there. The President urged O'Brien to call the State Department and get a full fill-in on what was happening. Input from the uniformed Pentagon leaders was stubborn; they, in the loyalty of the service, had to make sure that, whatever the change in policy, the men in the field would not be abandoned. Clifford was equally stubborn that policy must be changed. But the President was now, finally, on Clifford's side; and when the drafting group met on Saturday afternoon, Johnson had already, forty-eight hours earlier, passed the divide on Vietnam policy.

The drafting group met in the Cabinet Room, working over the final, final draft of the speech (number twelve or thirteen) line by line, paragraph by paragraph, until nine in the evening. Present were Dean Rusk, Clark Clifford, General Earle Wheeler, Walt Rostow, William Bundy, Harry McPherson and George Christian, White House Press Secretary. The President sat in his usual seat, where he had sat on the evening of February 6th, 1965, when the first bombings had been launched as policy. Shirt open, his necktie unslung and askew, he was the President. Clifford and Wheeler had operated masterfully in the last few days to bring the Joint Chiefs around; but the minimal technical demands of the military simply had to be satisfied—which was to fill out with a few thousand more troops the service units the war in Vietnam did require at the moment. This announcement, however, had to be phrased so as to be conspicuously subordinate to the general statement that America *was* going to de-escalate the war; that American bombings *would* be held back below the 20th parallel; that this was the major all-out try to negotiate an end to the war at the conference table. It took an hour to write that single paragraph.

By now the entire speech had changed shape as the perception of realities had changed. Secretary of Treasury Fowler's insistence on an immediate tax rise had been cut to a few paragraphs. Instead of being a ringing call to arms and perseverance, the speech ended with a look back on what, actually, had been accomplished in giving Southeast Asia (and Indonesia, Burma and all the other states of the turbulent area) time to organize against Communist aggression. By now the original peroration, with its evocation of Colonel Travis at the Alamo, was obsolete. Clifford said, "Oh man, that last part just won't do, we've got to change that." McPherson asked the President what to do about the ending; the President replied: don't worry too much about the peroration, I may have one of my own to put on the end of the speech. As they rose from the five-hour meeting, McPherson approached Clifford and said, "Clark—what's up, is he going to say *sayonara?*" Clark looked at McPherson as at an idiot, in complete disbelief, and said, why, don't even think about that.

The next day, Sunday, March 31st, was an all-day wait for word from the White House. Richard M. Nixon had previously scheduled his own major policy statement on Vietnam for an hour-long nationwide radio address on Saturday; with much frustration, he had to cancel his speech pending the President's statement. Eugene McCarthy's leaders in Wisconsin, learning that the President was demanding nationwide time on TV for an address, appealed to the FCC for equal nationwide time. They saw the scheduled speech as a political abuse of power, an attempt to register on a few thousand votes in the Wisconsin primary, which they were now sure of sweeping.

At the White House, few knew what was happening or about to happen. Sunday morning the President went to visit Hubert Humphrey at his apartment, just before the Vice-President's scheduled departure for Mexico City; he showed Humphrey a draft peroration of renunciation, and they hugged each other. Yet Humphrey, as he left for Mexico, was still not sure that the President actually meant to give up all.

The President then returned to the White House. He had come to affection for and some dependence on Mrs. Elizabeth Carpenter, Mrs. Johnson's press secretary, a lady of good humor, who normally marked up the reading copies of his speeches into syllables and paragraph stresses for reading ease. Mrs. Carpenter sat down to mark up the reading copy for his delivery on television. She had no sense of what the peroration might be, for it was not on her copy; and besides, since she was so close to Mrs. Johnson, she felt in her bones that the campaign was on. On Friday night, only two days earlier, Mrs. Johnson had come to a women's group of politicians and pledged herself, personally, to all of them to do whatever was needed to re-elect the President: to go anywhere, stump anywhere, appear anywhere in the campaign that was now, very late, taking off from scratch.

At this point, we have three rooms at the White House. Mrs.

Carpenter was marking up a final text, draft number unknown, limiting American bombing in Asia and inviting negotiations. In another room of the White House were gathered the senior politicians of the Democratic Party planning the campaign and the final last-minute effort in Wisconsin—Marvin Watson of the President's staff, John Bailey (National Chairman) John Criswell (National Treasurer), James Rowe, Larry O'Brien, and the man who had just, secretly, been named to be the over-all campaign manager for re-election, ex-Governor Terry Sanford of North Carolina. And in a third room, the Treaty Room, the President joined Horace Busby and finally polished the last phrases of his renunciation.

This correspondent had left Washington that week, after seeing the President, to join the McCarthy campaign in Wisconsin. And in Wisconsin one could see naked the end of the historic Johnson mandate of 1964.

Nothing more forlorn, politically, occurs in my memory of the 1968 campaign than Johnson headquarters at 800 North Plankinton in downtown Milwaukee. In a barren store-front headquarters, silent as a funeral parlor, half a dozen people sat at long tables in a large complex of rooms listlessly turning over papers. No telephones rang. One infuriated black man stalked in during the hour I was there, indignant at some insult—and was pampered lavishly because he was a state assemblyman, one of the few to come out openly in support of Johnson. Of four senior Democratic officials flown out from the East during the week to inject vitality in the campaign, two had given up by Saturday and flown home.

Headquarters was now commanded by two remaining loyalists; Leslie Aspin, whom I had met in Washington as a White House specialist in Vietnamese affairs, who believed in the cause of commitment; and Kenneth Birkhead, of the Department of Agriculture, a Johnson loyalist to the core. Aspin and Birkhead were quite candid: it was lost. The machinery was there—but it did not work. The Secretary of Agriculture had flown through the state that week—and been heckled and booed. The administration had exacted public pledges of loyalty from sixty-three of Wisconsin's seventy-two Democratic county leaders—but some of these were now flagrantly housing, sheltering and feeding McCarthy student volunteers in their homes. The AFL/CIO was exerting every pressure from Washington on local labor organizations; but where, normally, labor's COPE can staff up to ten headquarters in a Wisconsin campaign, now it staffed only three. In Milwaukee—no volunteers at all, nothing but a sullen, apathetic morbid quiet; they might get some votes in the Polish and Negro wards. "But what the Hell have we got to sell?" asked Birkhead. "We're the guys who are saying more taxes, more troops, we need to go on with the war, and more austerity at home." In outlying Wisconsin it was worse; in Dane County, seat of the University of Wisconsin, worst of all. "We sent a man into Dane County to recruit for Johnson and all we've heard from him since is a few faint beeps, like the last radio signals from the beach of the Bay of Pigs." And all over Wisconsin swarmed the student volunteers, with twelve headquarters in Milwaukee alone, forty-one headquarters around the state, thousands ringing doorbells, hundreds stuffing mailers into envelopes. "My own son," said Birkhead with wry pride. "I haven't been able to get him to get a haircut for a year, or wear a clean suit. Handsome kid. Then he comes in with a new haircut and asks me for fifty-five bucks for a suit; he said he needed a new suit to go up to campaign for McCarthy in New Hampshire. But he isn't campaigning in Wisconsin because he doesn't want to embarrass me personally."

As we walked out through the silent place, three days before primary day, Birkhead pointed out a grave man, slowly, and all alone, filling envelopes with mailers. "That's an Assistant Secretary of Health, Education and Welfare we've brought in from Washington. You might say that what we haven't got in quantity we make up in quality." Then, as I left, he added, "I suppose you can say our campaign peaked too soon—like in November, 1964."

Student headquarters at the Wisconsin Hotel, a mile away, was explosive in its contrast. Wisconsin was to be the peak, the high-water mark, the Pickett's Charge of the McCarthy movement. Eight thousand students were now roving over Wisconsin. Every town of more than 5,000 had its student platoons, sleeping at friendly homes and in church basements; and still, on this last Saturday, they were pouring in, 800 from Michigan alone. By two A.M. on Sunday, student headquarters were sending back other arriving busloads simply because they could not be used. And now the students were veterans; they had learned to tap the post office of each town for its general-delivery lists; volunteer specialists had broken the lists down by street, block and district; had made "hardboards" of names and addresses, assigned eighty calls to each volunteer; and had, by now, rung over 800,000 doorbells in Wisconsin and were hoping to make the figure 1,250,000 out of Wisconsin's 1,500,000 homes by primary day. Brown and Gans still commanded; but their staffs were specialized: a young computer scientist from Boston tabulated canvassing results; Ben Stavis, having finished his oral exams in Chinese at Columbia, was now statistical chief; others specialized in housing, or in transportation, or simply the feeding of their young army. And discipline prevailed; when reporters sought to read their polling totals and results, a curt reply cut them off, as if the staff had been indoctrinated with the phrase "Revolutionary vigilance, comrades, vigilance." By Sunday their tabulations of their canvassing were running thus: in the 1st Congressional, with 43,000 people polled, 60/40 for McCarthy over Johnson; in the 2nd, 70/30; in the 3rd, 67/33; in every district of the state's ten, they were ahead by a similar margin except for the 4th Congressional (Milwaukee's South Side, Polish and Negro), where Johnson barely held a 51/49 lead.

This, then, was the view from the field as Lyndon Johnson's name was listed for the last time in his long career on an election ballot in the United States.[2] At McCarthy headquarters on Sunday morning, extrapolating their polling results to a national level, the student high command estimated that they had in the making the greatest landslide of the century—except for the hazard of Lyndon Johnson's scheduled nationwide broadcast that night. What would Johnson say? What rabbit could he pull out of the hat?

Candidate Eugene McCarthy was out campaigning at his usual university audiences that Sunday morning with rare self-certainty. (At Whitewater State University, for example: "I don't wish to sound over-confident, but I think the test is pretty much between me and Nixon now.") But Blair Clark and Richard Goodwin remained behind at head-quarters in Milwaukee to prepare for whatever emergency the Johnson speech would create.

I joined the two, shortly before the broadcast, in a hotel suite, interested this time chiefly in Goodwin's reaction. Clark had recruited Goodwin for McCarthy in January, and for two and a half months, in uneasy partnership, they had constituted the decision-making apparatus of the McCarthy campaign. Neither was bound by great affection to Eugene McCarthy or to the other; but whereas Clark's motive was simply to stop the war, Goodwin's was intensified by the affection he once had held for the President, and the conviction he now felt that the man must go.

Goodwin, along with Bill Don Moyers, had in 1964–65 done more to shape the legislation of the Great Society than any other man in Lyndon Johnson's administration.[3] Goodwin had well and ably served John F. Kennedy; but, whatever contribution he had made or might make to history, none would be greater than his service to Johnson in the early creative days of the Great Society. He had been Johnson's favorite speech-writer, author of the first Johnson peace proposal at Johns Hopkins on April 7th, 1965, as well as the Great Society speech of 1964 and the Civil Rights ("We Shall Overcome") speech of 1965. It

---

[2] On primary day, April 2, 1968, in his last contest for office, Johnson was to receive only 253,696 votes or 34.6 percent, as against Eugene McCarthy's 412,160 or 56.2 percent. Of the total combined ballots of both Republicans and Democrats (1,262,000), Johnson's percentage was only 20.1. Four years earlier in the race against Barry Goldwater he had drawn 62.1 percent of all Wisconsin votes in November.

[3] See *The Making of the President—1964*, pp. 389 *et seq.*

was he whom Johnson had chosen to edit the volume of his major speeches and statements, to package the Johnson philosophy in a master volume that had reached galley-proof stage before bitterness had come between them and publication, consequently, had been canceled.

Goodwin had resigned in 1966, tired of Washington life and disturbed by the steady escalation of the Vietnam war. He had, briefly, attempted to begin an academic life in New England, but politics was too deeply in his blood for that; and when the campaign of 1968 called, he responded. He had become in his years with Kennedy and Johnson a new-style professional of politics, the coiner of ideas and phrases, a man at home in and skilled at the new political use of television and film, a strategist of programs. Like other new American professionals—so many his imitators—almost European in their intensity, Goodwin was a man *engagé,* a non-compromiser, and had staffed the McCarthy campaign with others like himself, similarly engaged by program, not patronage. But of all those engaged emotionally by McCarthy, none was more so than Goodwin, and none with greater complications. Goodwin had been originally a Kennedy loyalist; he had enlisted with McCarthy at the outbreak of Tet only because Robert Kennedy had told him he would not run; and this evening was torn and uncertain of his loyalties between McCarthy and Kennedy, who had just entered the race. Goodwin was held in Wisconsin both by his devotion to the students who saw him as a leader and by the ferocity of his feeling about Johnson and the war. Yet he was disturbed—so long as the battle had been between McCarthy and Peace on the one side, and Johnson and War on the other, his course had been clear. But with Kennedy in the race, his course had, in the past fortnight, become acutely difficult. For the moment, Johnson was still the prime motivator of Goodwin's behavior; Johnson, felt Goodwin who knew him well, had come to an egomaniac confusion of self with national interest, a man capable of magnificence but capable of immense national harm also.

Now Goodwin watched the President come on-screen.

The President on-screen was quite different from the President I had seen five days earlier in his office. Whether inner peace had descended on him when he took his decision, or whether cosmeticians' art had smoothed away his wrinkles and concern, one could not discern on the tube. But the weariness of his mien was gone, he was poised, smooth and collected as he steadily read on through the final, final McPherson draft. It was a full thirty-five minutes before, just at the end of his speech, his countenance changed:

"For thirty-seven years," said Lyndon Johnson, "in the service of our nation, first as a Congressman, as a Senator, and as Vice-President, and now as your President, I have put the unity of the people first, I have put it ahead of any divisive partisanship. . . . There is division in the American house now. . . . Fifty-two months and ten days ago, in a moment of tragedy and trauma, the duties of this office fell upon me. I asked then for your help and God's that we might continue America on its course, binding up our wounds, healing our history. . . . What we won when all of our people united just must not now be lost in suspicion and distrust and selfishness and politics among any of our people. And believing this as I do, I have concluded that I should not permit the Presidency to become involved in the partisan divisions that are developing in this political year. . . ."

What was coming?

". . . Accordingly, I shall not seek and I will not accept the nomination of my party for another term as your President. . . ."

With this, as though touched by an electric cattle-prod, everyone in the room came erect, babbling, so that the last few words on television were lost. And Goodwin, in glee, was striding about. "It only took six weeks," he was saying, "it was six weeks earlier than I thought."

Thereafter McCarthy headquarters dissolved. Somewhere in Waukesha, fifteen miles away, McCarthy was addressing a student audience. But the young people in Milwaukee, at the Schroeder Hotel, McCarthy headquarters, boiled through the corridors looking for celebration. I remember one student who could not have been more than eighteen years old, dressed in a brilliant yellow sweater, his hair thoroughly tousled, running up and down the corridors all by himself, loping and dancing and screaming, yelling in a solitary Indian dance. He had helped force the resignation not of a Dean, but of a President of the United States.

McCarthy himself did not arrive at his personal suite on the nineteenth floor until almost an hour later, and he was perhaps the most composed man in the nation's politics that evening. His wife, Abigail, had already, minutes after the ending of the speech, called the White House switchboard and reached the President. She had said hello to him, then said that she knew how much this must have cost him; Harry Truman had done the same; but she wanted him to know that the McCarthy campaign had never been based on lack of friendship; they had had a difference on the issues, that was all. The President had been very gracious and said, "No one man can stand in the way of history" and then turned her over to Lady Bird. Lady Bird, Mrs. McCarthy reported, had been "more prickly."

This had happened by the time McCarthy arrived at the hotel from Waukesha to reflect on the new perspective of his campaign. His mind moved over the events of the previous hour; he had been finishing his speech at Waukesha, he recalled, when a voice out of the crowd shouted, "He's not running, he's not running!" and then correspondents leaped on the stage to question him; McCarthy recalled it was "like Orestes being smothered by the Eumenides." Coca-Colas were being brought into the room at this point, and someone dropped some silverware with a clatter. "Come on, kids—relax," said McCarthy, and as he relaxed, so did everyone else. McCarthy's verdict was a neat one, generous this time, thoughtful—that maybe LBJ decided he couldn't make peace and run for President at the same time, so he decided to make peace. "It was more than a political decision," he reflected. "I don't think they could stand up against five million college kids just shouting for peace—there was too much will-power there." The TV correspondents were clamoring outside the door for appearances. But McCarthy was not to be hurried. "Just tell the TV stations to put on a little music until I get there. Or maybe they should read a little poetry. This is a night for reading poetry—maybe a little Yeats."

It was after midnight before McCarthy came back to his suite, having done the rounds of the national television networks, then given a press conference, much delayed. (To one newsman, McCarthy's aide Jerry Eller growled, "Let the newspapers wait. They've ignored us for four years.") His staff now wanted to discuss specifics of the campaign, whom to call, what to do, scheduling over the next week or ten days. But McCarthy was in a rambling mood and moved on quickly to a poetic discussion of civilization in terms of geology and the moraine line on the hills, how as one comes down from the snows to the timberline, one finds the otter, and the bear, and the other animals of the slopes; then after that, one finds the Indians, and then the white man. The victory of the evening was taken in poetic stride also; it was like Moses in the desert striking the rock for water with a branch of a tamarisk tree. It turned out the rock was fragile. Later McCarthy wandered down the corridor with Blair Clark to the room of his favorite correspondent, Miss Mary McGrory, whose quotable recollection of great verse embraces a span larger than anyone else I know, and devoted himself entirely to poetry. McCarthy quoted from Yeats and from Robert Lowell and from the Welsh bard Vernon Watkins. He then began to recite his own poetry, as Clark typed out the passages of the unpublished texts on a portable typewriter.

There was little poetry in Washington that evening, for it was not part of the script of history that Lyndon Johnson of the Pedernales should be brought down by a poet from Watkins, Minnesota. Of Lyndon Johnson's evening in Washington, Yeats had already written:

"We are closed in, and the key is turned on our uncertainty."

CHAPTER FIVE

THE INEVITABILITY
OF RICHARD M. NIXON

ALL THROUGH the spring months, Richard Nixon moved on a calendar of his own.

Students mobilized in February and March; Romney withdrew; Kennedy entered; Rockefeller dropped out, then entered again; ambition refreshed itself in Ronald Reagan; the assassinations happened, the first an act of racial barbarism, the second totally incomprehensible; men died by the thousands in Vietnam; riots stained the nation at home.

But Nixon persisted, undeviatingly, in the course he had set himself in the beginning; and so we must turn back to January to pick up the unfolding of his primary strategy first, next his media strategy, then his delegate hunt and organization, and finally once more to the man himself.

The nation's turmoil of spirit seemed best reflected in the open war in the Democratic Party; yet the placid quality of the Republican contender's campaign reflected his different reading of the turmoil— that millions of Americans yearned for quiet. It was in these spring months that I was talking to Ray Price, the soft-spoken writer who so deeply influences Nixon's thinking on the liberal side, and he explained the thrust of his leader's thinking. "We're in a period when people want a change, but they're all caught in this terrible complex of fears, almost unstructured fears, amorphous fears. They live in a welter of frustrations, and this is a year for the outs, for the people who associate themselves with stability. But it's got to be a dynamic stability, not a status-quo stability, and that's what we're trying to communicate in our general posture."

To communicate a promise of stability and a sense of dynamism at the same time is one of the most delicate of all political feats. In his later election campaign Richard Nixon rested his thrust on stability rather than on dynamism and, thus, refusing the dynamics of either the left or the right, almost lost the election. But this was the theory and philosophy of his inner court, and the yet unwritten script of his administration-to-be. "Nixon," said Price at another time, "is neither a conservative nor a liberal, he is a centrist." And it was, retrospectively, as a centrist that he faced the succession of tactical problems which presented themselves in his takeover of the Republican Party in 1968.

The situation was clear as early as January of the year: The country was torn, the consensus of Lyndon Johnson had dissolved, the administration had lost the confidence of the American people, the apparently hopeless war went on. The situation insisted on alternative national leadership. Historically and practically, the alternative had to be a candidate of the Republican Party. But the Republican Party was also split. How, then, to capture the Republican Party? More specifically—how was Nixon to capture that Party without tearing it apart as Goldwater and Rockefeller had done in 1964? No one could claim greater credit from the Party's non-commissioned officers than Richard M. Nixon. Had it been a vote within an army, the Party regulars would have chosen Richard Nixon as their corps commander. Yet he was a corps commander who had not won a victory on his own since 1950, eighteen years before.

Cherishing Nixon as they did, the Republican leaders cherished victory more. The object of politics is to gain power; and in this year of opportunity they could not afford to squander the chance on a permanent loser. Thus, the first tactical problem of the Nixon camp was to erase, as he stated it, "the loser's image." This meant fighting in open primaries, an outdoor sport, the first celebration of whose rites would be, as always, in New Hampshire. Only after Nixon had proved himself in New Hampshire, in Wisconsin, in Nebraska, in Oregon, would his delegate apparatus have the leverage to pry open the hidden loyalties that remained his among the major delegate-brokers of the Republican Party. All the primaries would be important; a single loss would spoil all plans; but none would be more important than the opener, in New Hampshire, on March 12th. Thus, it is useful to follow him outdoors as he stumped that snowbound state, and hear the voice in which he began the action.

It is cold—sleet on the roads, snow on the hills, fishermen's cube huts on the icebound lakes—when Mr. Nixon arrives in New Hampshire, and the Tet offensive in Asia is reaching its climax.

New Hampshire is Republican. On the Democratic side of the political ridge, McCarthy's student commandos are preparing to groin the President of the United States. But there are only 89,000 registered Democratic voters in the little state, as against 148,000 Republicans, and the Republicans are a good cross-section of Republicans across the nation. Right-wing, reactionary Senator Styles Bridges once ran this state with club, mace and merciless discipline; since his death in 1961 the Republican Party has dissolved into the fragments that reflect its national fragmentation. The relentless reactionaries, whose mouth and voice is the execrable Manchester *Union Leader,* are a minority; so, too, are hereditary conservatives of the north country, a vanishing pocket of Yankee twangs and Yankee pride where Republicans still see Democrats as Catholics and rebels; more important are the civic Republicans in Concord and the Connecticut River Valley, liberal both in state and in national elections; and most important of all is the thick belt of suburbia that stretches south from Manchester to the Boston metropolitan complex. Thus, the Republicans—farmers, old folks, Protestants, above all, suburbanites. Most of the disorganized Republican leadership is neutral, at odds within its own house, for New Hampshire Republicans feud as easily as Massachusetts Democrats; but Nixon's cause is led by State Senate President Stewart Lamprey and a twenty-eight-year-old state legislator named David Sterling—and, between them, the two have enlisted a majority of Republicans in both houses of the legislature for the former Vice-President. Opposing such men, for Romney, is a bright young progressive, a Dartmouth professor named William Johnson, campaign manager, trying to build a Romney citizen organization.

But Nixon has the weight and presence. It is visible. The polls show it. And his campaign is planned that way: "no baby-kissing, no back-slapping, no factory gates," the candidate has decided; he runs as President. His opening press conference, with eight television cameras and reporters from all over the nation, is a deft, smooth performance. "I believe," he says, "I am better qualified to handle the great problems of the Presidency than I was in 1960. . . . I recognize," he continues, "I must demonstrate to the American people . . . that I can win and that I am prepared to meet that challenge. I have decided that I will test my ability . . . in the fires of the primaries and not just in the smoke-filled rooms of Miami Beach." He gets full marks from the attendance.

There follows in the afternoon of the same day a friendly, non-professional press reception, and this is indeed a different Nixon, care-free, jovial, circulating among the reporters, hoisting drinks with them, quite candid in his talk, a thought-provoking contrast with the tense, up-tight man so elusive and so hostile in 1960. He climbs onto a chair to talk about his press policy in the forthcoming campaign—I notice for the first time how physically agile he is, teetering on his toes on the seat of a chair much too small. There will be no press secretary this time, he says; Herb Klein, his old companion of 1960, will be an adviser; Pat Buchanan will be the "press contact." There will be direct access to him for special interviews whenever special correspondents find it necessary; there will be some kind of statement every day for the dailies; special arrangements for television men; and he jokes about the name-dropping we will hear, apologizes for all the times we will have to listen to the same "B-speech": "I know some of you will be able to deliver it better than I before I'm through." A reporter asks him why he wants to be President; he teeters on the chair before answering, then parries by asking why anyone would want to be a reporter. "All I can say is anybody who wants to be a reporter . . . well, I think covering a Presidential campaign is worse than running in one."

Then, the next day, to greet the public at St. Anselm's College in Manchester, his first crowd of the 1968 campaign. Meticulously organized and 2,000 there—signs posted by the campaign staff pointing the direction to the school, lady volunteers pouring tea, coffee, fruit punch, serving marshmallow cakes. The features of all his future audiences are already there: sedate, middle-class, neatly dressed people, no workingmen or their families. It has the feel of an extended wedding reception (and, indeed, Julie and David are there, too, bowing in a reception line of their own), a family affair. The family feeling grows as one circulates: this is the Republican family. Some of the ladies and men still carry 1960 campaign buttons, recalling that lamented effort. Others carry *"Ike and Dick"* buttons of 1952 and 1956; several old ladies carry baby pictures of Julie and Trish going back to sixteen years ago. The *"Ike and Dick"* buttons are very prominent, mementos of a safer past, of the promise and then the delivery of tranquillity; there is nostalgia here, a reservoir of affection for the man, for the Party, for his inheritance from Eisenhower. One circulates, trying to strain an apt quote from these small-town people, suspicious of reporters with notebooks. The notebook harvests very little except: "He's strong . . . that's why I'm for him," "I like the way he talks . . . he sounds strong," "He's got the experience . . . he was with Ike," and, again and again, the negative on Romney: "I was that close to him the other day I could touch him. He's a good man, but he doesn't seem to know what he's doing," "I don't think he knows foreign affairs," "He hasn't got the experience."

Then to Nixon's first formal speech, the campaign kick-off, scrawled and re-scrawled, revised and re-revised on his long yellow pads, until finally, at the New Hampshire Highway Hotel in Concord, he speaks to several hundred Republicans eating their roast beef, and begins:

"The finest hours in our nation's history have been triumphs of the American spirit," followed by his challenge to Lyndon Johnson, who once urged the nation, "Let us continue." Continue what? asks Nixon.

"When the strongest nation in the world can be tied down for four years in the war in Vietnam, with no end in sight; when the richest nation in the world cannot manage its own economy; when the nation with the greatest tradition of respect for the rule of law is plagued by rampant lawlessness. . . .

"I don't think America can afford four more years of Lyndon Johnson in the White House. . . .

"We need leadership that recognizes that the real crisis of America today is a crisis of the spirit. What America needs most today is what it once had, but has lost: the lift of a driving dream."

And so to bed that night, up the stairway to the second floor, barred off by a piece of raveled string and an awkwardly scribbled cardboard sign: *"Reserved for Mr. Nixon and Staff Only."*

There is little now, little later, to report of Mr. Nixon outdoors. After George Romney has withdrawn in February, there is even less hard news one can report in following Nixon. One follows him, say, a week before the primary, in a six-city tour of southern New Hampshire—Hampton, Exeter, Raymond, Plaistow, Nashua, Salem (over the entrance to the Salem Methodist Church hangs the sign: PEACE ON EARTH). The lovely white snow and the hills crested with feather-tipped trees are marred by tourist motels, trailer camps, gas stations, garages, furniture stores, bowling alleys—beauty here, as elsewhere, desecrated. This is solid suburban Republican country: even the bus driver is a Republican, and he is indignant at the McCarthy students roving his state ("Did you see them? Did you see them? Those girls in pants and sandals? Those girls are sleeping with those boys").

Mr. Nixon, in a blue suit, is ruddy, healthy, husky. Even though Romney has dropped out, he wants the largest vote possible to forestall what he is sure will be a Rockefeller counter-attack. Now his themes, in the standard speech, are all of them building toward what will be his best oration of the year, the acceptance at Miami. He is hitting the war, recalling how Eisenhower brought peace in Korea ("We ended that war, we will end this one and win the peace"). We have blundered in Vietnam—we failed to use our military power effectively, failed to use our diplomatic power wisely, failed to develop the social and economic potential of South Vietnam; and we failed to inform the American people. "End the War and Win the Peace"—and the youngsters in the crowd cheer. You notice that people in the crowd cheer at different punch lines —the old people clap when he says spending in Washington must be cut down, prices must hold the line, the dollar must be saved. The thin fringe of blue-collared workingmen who occasionally show up in his overwhelmingly neat middle-class audiences breaks into applause only when he talks of law-and-order and an end to violence. But law-and-order is still a minor theme in Nixon's speech at this point; it will grow later.

This is the first stanza of his campaign, and, faintly, but very definitely, there is a familiar echo of 1960. One catches it at first without recognition: "I say this is an important election and this is an important state. . . . I say we must get on with the unfinished business of America. . . . We did not become great because of what government did for the people. . . ." Suddenly, a phrase makes the source clear: "This country must move again, how long will it take the United States to move?"—and one is hearing the echo of the phrases of John F. Kennedy in 1960, the rub-off deep somewhere in the memory of his defeated rival. Somewhere it has been written that no human contact ever takes place without leaving some permanent mark, however microscopically small or apparently undetectable, on the two personalities in contact: hunter and hunted upon each other, lover on lover, child on parent and parent on child. The mark of John F. Kennedy was seared into Richard M. Nixon in 1960; it continues to surface even now, as he runs for President in 1968.

Then it is over in New Hampshire: a clear, smashing victory. Nixon receives 80,667 votes in New Hampshire's Republican primary, more votes than any candidate in any Presidential primary in that state's history. His margin over his write-in opponent, Nelson Rockefeller, is seven to one. In the Democratic primary he receives four times as many write-ins as Robert F. Kennedy. The total vote is the largest ever in any New Hampshire Presidential primary; and Nixon's share is larger than all other Democratic, Republican and write-in candidates put together.

With such superlatives as these, the Nixon organization is in business; the delegate round-up can now go forward with a Nixon the winner, not a Nixon the loser.

And from here on one could ignore Mr. Nixon on the outdoor primary trail and concentrate on the campaign as programmed indoors; for from the very first day of Mr. Nixon in New Hampshire, the public Nixon was also operating as the programmed Nixon.

As programmed indoors, the Nixon campaign, from primary to election day, was a new perception of American politics, a new appreciation of the environment of communications.

Half a dozen names form the constellation of Richard Nixon's communications group—Leonard Garment, Frank Shakespeare, William Safire, Herbert Klein, Harry Treleaven, H. R. Haldeman. These men, collectively, had greater importance and greater impact than any other communications group in any Presidential campaign; but the governing philosophy can perhaps best be traced to H. R. Haldeman.[1]

Haldeman likes to describe himself as a "political mechanic," the "no-man" of the Nixon entourage ("Dick says," Haldeman once told of himself, "that there have to be a few ess-oh-bees in any organization, and I'm his"); in self-description, Haldeman denies any concern with issues, and says he deals only with organization and program. To take him at this self-description would, however, be a mistake; both in the campaign of 1968 and in current politics, Haldeman was and is, in one of Richard Nixon's favorite phrases, a man of "extra dimension." Crew-cut, Arrow-collar handsome, green-eyed, low-key, Haldeman, now forty-two, is at once a very courteous and a very tough former advertising executive (J. Walter Thompson) whose interests range broad beyond advertising. Interested in art (Chairman of the Board of Trustees of the California Institute of Art), in education (a Regent of the University of California), he is interested most of all in politics; and in politics, for ten years, his cold, total, yet critical devotion has gone to Richard M. Nixon.

To the campaign of 1968 he brought a perception based on his sad memories of the Nixon campaigns of 1960 and 1962, as later sophisticated by his experience in mass-marketing as an advertising executive. The scene of American politics, he felt, had totally changed and the traditional marketing of candidates had become obsolete. Thus, in his much-quoted basic memorandum to Nixon at the end of 1967, he laid down the following theses: Americans no longer gather in the streets to hear candidates; they gather at their television sets or where media assemble their attention. A candidate cannot storm the nation; at most he can see and let his voice be heard by no more than a million or two people in a Presidential year ("The reach of the individual campaigner," says Haldeman, "doesn't add up to diddly-squat in votes"). One minute or thirty seconds on the evening news shows of Messrs. Cronkite or Huntley/Brinkley will reach more people than ten months of barnstorming. One important favorable Washington column is worth more than two dozen press releases or position papers. News magazines like *Time* or *Newsweek,* picture magazines like *Life* or *Look* are media giants worth a hundred outdoor rallies. Therefore the candidate must not waste time storming the country, personally pleading for votes—no matter what he does, he can appear in newsprint or on television only once a day. The inner strength and vitality of the candidate must not be wasted; if you do more than one thing a day, you make a mistake. If you test a man's physical strength too far, you push him beyond the realm of good judgment; both candidate and the following press must be given

[1] H. R. Haldeman is now Assistant to the President by rank; but in function he is the key man in the President's private entourage, the keeper of the gates, controller of all access to the Presidency of person or memorandum.

time to stop, rest, reflect and write. The importance of old-style out-door campaigning now lies less in what the candidate *tells* the people than in what he *learns* from them—with the important secondary value that outdoor exertions do provide the vital raw-stuff for television cameras. To his basic memorandum, Haldeman could always add some particularly poignant memories of 1960: "We started Nixon off in 1960 sick and under medication and then we ran his tail off." He meant not to do it again.

The Haldeman memorandum—with its obvious new insights and disturbing implications—framed the Nixon campaign from January of 1968 down almost to its last weekend in California in November of 1968. It was to be a campaign based on the great media of public influence; through them, Nixon would reach the people.

Let Frank Shakespeare pick up the story from there.[2] Shakespeare, forty-three, a CBS executive on sabbatical, onetime executive vice-president of its most lucrative owned-and-operated station (WCBS in New York), was the active manager of Nixon's television presence.

"What was the attitude to Nixon at the end of 1967?" asked Shakespeare in the fall of 1968, reviewing the course they had come. "The Party felt that Nixon was experienced, he was able, but he wasn't electable; and he wasn't electable because he couldn't handle TV. The country was moving to the right; the ablest conservative they had was obviously Nixon, but Nixon had to prove he was electable. He could win the primaries in the small states without using TV; but then that wouldn't prove anything; he had to win it, using TV, to prove to the Party chiefs that he could win a national election.

"Now," continued Shakespeare, who knows his media structure, "you could do it mechanically, packaging him. Or you could do it through content and personality. Now, which should we do—package him, or present him as he is? And because of the Nixon-Kennedy debates, we couldn't choose packaging, we had to do him as he really is. So we took what we call the Hillsboro approach, to show him spontaneous, with no rehearsal, in a serious posture, with a mixed bag of questioners, letting him get down to the one-to-one approach where he's most relaxed, and which is what TV is all about."

Hillsboro, New Hampshire, is a little town with a beautiful Congregational church, an electronics plant, several small yarn mills, a woodworking plant, and an almost exaggerated New England profile. Thus, Saturday and Sunday mornings of that first weekend in New Hampshire, while those who wanted to shake his hand waited for him until afternoon or evening at St. Anselm's or the New Hampshire Highway Hotel, his major effort was spent with a cross-section of hand-picked New Hampshire Republicans of all walks of life at the Hillsboro Town Hall. A color

[2] Frank Shakespeare is now Chief of the United States Information Agency.

teletape truck had been rolled up from New York, and for two mornings Mr. Nixon answered questions from members of the panel, while Treleaven and Garment, as producers, monitored the recordings from the truck outside. Nixon had been "grouchy" when first pressed into the new form. But with newsmen banned from the sessions, he began to relax, to enjoy the procedure, and, finally, would not stop. With the Hillsboro tapes, cut and chopped into five-minute segments, the media directors of the Nixon effort had their answer; he was crisp, direct, real and convincing. They could present snatches of Nixon, packaged but genuine, wherever they wanted both in New Hampshire and across the nation.

Other sophistications were added to the technique as the year wore on—particularly Nixon's radio addresses, in which he would address himself to issues, and his regional round-tables after nomination, where he could score in specific marketing regions. But the larger frame of his media program was set in New Hampshire in the first week of his campaign: Nixon would be shown real, yet controlled; he would reach the nation by spots, not by head-on commercial half-hours; media, not barnstorming, would carry the campaign message. This technique was not to change until the last ten days of the campaign when Nixon was finally forced into the stress of adversary appearances on television.

The New Hampshire primary was also the signal for another indoor system of the Nixon campaigners to go operational. For, in nominations, the name of the game is delegates and Mr. Nixon's delegate systems had, for months before the New Hampshire primary, been All Systems Go. Now they were going.

The smoothness that marked the Nixon delegate operation of 1968 came partly from experience, but even more from the fact that the Republican Party was waiting for him.

From 1967 on, no matter how high or low Romney or Reagan or Rockefeller rose or fell in the various national polls of all Americans, one polling result remained consistent: in polls limited only to Republican voters, Nixon outran any rival. And in every survey of Republican committee and county leaders, the delegates-prospective and delegate-brokers of 1968, Nixon continually ran far ahead of any other Republican rival. He was of the fiber and bone of the Party. For sixteen years, from 1952 on, through every Presidential and off-year election except 1962, he had campaigned for Senators, Congressmen, Governors, appearing in rain, snow, sun, storm, at fund-raisers, testimonials, Party gatherings. Only his image as a loser restrained Republican leaders from committing to him at once, for self-interest always restrains emotions. Once New Hampshire had ruptured the loser image, it was only necessary for Nixon's captains to shake the trees—and delegates would fall into their baskets; and the regional apparatus of Nixon was ready.

The delegate search had begun even in silent 1967, while Nixon was yielding public attention and exposure to George Romney. A number of men succeeded one another as leader of the effort: first, the mercurial Gaylord Parkinson of California, who, believing in Party unity, could not understand the resentment of the higher Nixon campaign staff when they came to believe he was sharing their secrets with California's Governor Ronald Reagan. After the excision of Parkinson came former Governor Henry Bellmon of Oklahoma; and when Bellmon left, direction of the campaign fell to Robert Ellsworth of Kansas and John Sears of New York, novices in national politics but more than willing to learn.

By the end of 1967, at their Washington offices, Sears and Ellsworth could already rack up rough charts of convention strength. New England was questionable territory; Governor John Volpe of Massachusetts toyed with the idea of making himself a regional favorite son and, in no uncertain terms, made known he could easily be deterred by offer of the Vice-Presidency—either from Nixon, Romney, Rockefeller or Reagan, it mattered not. The solid bloc of industrial states stretching across the Midwest was similarly confused—Pennsylvania, Ohio, New York, New Jersey, Minnesota, all chancy. Illinois looked better for Nixon, but its politicians, like those in the other big states, waited to see Nixon run in the primaries. The South was up for grabs. No one had the lock on that bloc of votes, as Goldwater had had so early in 1964; the Southern leaders, like the Midwesterners, waited on the primaries. But almost all the Rocky Mountain states were safe; so were the Border states, already solid for Nixon. California would be yielded to Ronald Reagan without a fight. And, as early as December of 1967, Nixon had passed the word from New York to Washington: no muscle tactics. If the nomination came his way, it must come in goodwill, not as it came to Goldwater in 1964, who locked up his delegates early, arm-twisting his way to a majority and then tearing the Party apart at the convention. Thus, the directive—go easy; scout; be ready; a nomination won by an intra-Party fight would be useless in the November election.

By February, Nixon had escalated the delegate rhythm, naming Richard Kleindienst of Arizona as his director of field operations. Kleindienst, a successful Arizona lawyer, had been one of the chief deputies of the Goldwater coup in 1964, second only to F. Clifton White. Now in 1968, though he could still use muscle when necessary (at the Republican convention his suppression of the mini-revolt over the Vice-Presidency was to earn him the title of the "Genghis Khan of Miami"), Kleindienst had learned to speak quietly and had perfected his techniques of delegate control and analysis even further than in his 1964 exercise. Around and around the country he quietly moved his candidate, to each of his eight delegate regions, starting in Denver a few days after the first victory in the New Hampshire primary in March. By

May there remained only one uncertainty on Kleindienst's sheets—the South. For the Reagan candidacy was reviving again, after its abnormal quiet, and only a combination of Reagan strength in the South *plus* the Rockefeller strength in the urban North could frustrate a nomination that was all but certain now for Nixon. Yet the South these days is no longer one, but twain; there is the Deep South, racist and Wallacite, living in its nightmare of fears; and the Middle South, or Border South, where here and there one can detect under its permanent conservative frost a first feeble spring of human tolerance.

It was here, at the end of May, that the candidate himself was required to intervene, to define precisely the limits of what later came to be called "the Southern strategy," yet to firm it up. Nixon had proceeded smartly from his New Hampshire victory in March to an almost unopposed Wisconsin victory on April 2nd, to a spectacular write-in in Pennsylvania, to another victory (unopposed) in Indiana on May 7th, to a smash victory in Nebraska on May 14th, to wind up, finally, in Oregon on the 28th, where at last he was faced with real opposition from the Reagan forces.[3] Oregon was critical; a strong showing by Reagan here would enlarge Reagan, in Southern eyes, to a Southern-oriented candidate with a national potential.

An episode the night of the Oregon primary seems to me as almost perfectly illustrative of the vivid emotions of the Democratic clash in contrast to the cool and placid quality of the Nixon campaign.

I had been traveling in California that day with Robert F. Kennedy, and was on his plane flying back to Oregon, where we arrived at the Benson Hotel in Portland at about 10:30 P.M. By that time the television networks had told Oregon and the nation that Kennedy had lost his race in the Democratic primary to Eugene McCarthy, the first election defeat any Kennedy had suffered anywhere in thirty consecutive primary and election contests dating back to John F. Kennedy's first entry in 1946. Yet, defeated as he was, Kennedy still had the magic—a crowd milled at the hotel entrance, screamers screamed, middle-aged men, teen-agers, mothers, all alike calling to him, "Don't quit, Bobby! Bobby, we're with you!" as they sought to touch him. With his wife, Ethel, the

[3] One of the thoughts offered by those closest to Nixon is that it was only in Oregon that law-and-order became the prime theme of the Nixon campaign. Robert Kennedy was, at that moment, also campaigning in Oregon, and by now Kennedy had caught the strange, shapeless fear of violence in the American mind. Kennedy had thus re-oriented his campaign to stress his record as chief law-enforcement officer at the Department of Justice, as the Attorney-General who had sent Jimmy Hoffa to jail, imprisoned Mafia leaders, and given common hoodlums a hard time. The feedback of the Kennedy campaign became apparent to Nixon only in his final telethon, in the contest on the Republican side of the Oregon primary. As the telephone calls piled up that evening for Nixon, he remarked, astonished, "Do you know a lot of these people think Bobby is more of a law-and-order man than I am!" From then on, law-and-order became the prime theme of his campaign, and was to remain so to the end.

defeated candidate plowed his way into the hotel lobby, and I, following him, in fear, as always, of being trampled down by his hordes, was separated from the candidate. Trying to catch my breath after the shoving and jostling, I wandered with my bags through the strange hotel to a half-empty downstairs restaurant called the London Grill, to find a moment of quiet and pull myself together.

There, in a corner, was a familiar face, the Republican victor of the evening. Richard Nixon and his wife, Howell Appling (campaign manager for Oregon) and his wife, and another couple sat together at a corner table eating their dinner—with no one else even close, or watching, or approaching the group in the dining room. By that evening Nixon had all but locked up his control of the Republican Party and was almost in full possession of the only alternative political choice of the American people. Yet whereas normally the victor of a major election is overwhelmed and pestered to death by the gawkerie of people on election night, he sat entirely alone with his little group; and since the conversation seemed to be neither private nor animated, I approached, was welcomed, and sat down. Mr. Nixon was gay. I questioned him on the returns, and, as usual, he knew them and read them with the sensitivity of an old professional. The two great winners of the evening, it seemed to him, were himself and Eugene McCarthy. ("I'm going to have to learn more about Eugene McCarthy," he said.) Rockefeller had done poorly, although the write-ins were still being counted. More important to him was Reagan's poor showing; Reagan had made a massive TV effort; defeat had now eliminated him as a viable national candidate to be put forward by the South. Then, with the quick anticipation of his mind, he said, "I'm going on to Atlanta, Teddy, I'm going to wrap up the whole campaign there. Come along with us." I could not accept, for I was watching the approach to the climax of the McCarthy-Kennedy struggle in California that week, and I decided I would have to reconstruct the Atlanta gathering later.

At Atlanta, Mr. Nixon went on to meet with the Southern leaders— Senator Strom Thurmond of South Carolina, Senator John Tower of Texas, and other considerable individuals of the Republican Party of the South. Since so much has been made of this Georgia meeting and of its later binding imperatives on the Miami convention as well as the present course of the administration of the United States, one should note now what the principal figure recalled some months later: the meeting was not presided over by Strom Thurmond but by Peter O'Donnell, Texas Republican State Chairman. At issue were two things: first, the convention votes of Southern delegates at Miami, and, second, the philosophy of a Nixon administration.

On civil rights, which was the chief concern of the Southern Republicans, Mr. Nixon agreed that the Supreme Court phrase "all deliberate speed" needed re-interpretation; he agreed also that a factor in his thinking about new Supreme Court Justices was that liberal-interpretationists had tipped the balance too far against the strict-construction interpreters of the Constitution; and he averred, also, that the compulsory bussing of school students from one district to another for the purpose of racial balance was wrong. On schools, however, he insisted that no Federal funds would be given to a school district which practiced clear segregation; but, on the other hand, he agreed that no Federal funds should be withheld from school districts as a penalty for tardiness in response to a bureaucratic decision in Washington which ordained the precise proportions of white or black children by a Federal directive that could not be questioned in the provinces.

More specifically, as he "wrapped up" the campaign on June 1st, Mr. Nixon noted that Strom Thurmond seemed most interested in national-defense policy; and he gave reassurance to Senator Thurmond that he, too, believed in strong defense. The Southerners, in general, wanted to be "in" on decisions, not to be treated like pariahs on the national scene as Negroes had previously been treated. On this, too, Nixon gave reassurance. No particular veto on Vice-President or Cabinet members was requested, although Mr. Nixon assured them they would be in on consultations. To their desire that he campaign heavily throughout the South, Nixon could not give entire assurance—Deep South states like Mississippi and Alabama he felt were lost, but he *would* stump the Border South. The Southerners wanted some clearance on Federal patronage; they agreed that a new administration ought, indeed, to include large personalities from the South; and some would have to be Democrats, since the Democrats are still the Establishment in the South. But the Southerners wanted no appointments that would nip the growth of the Southern Republican Party; they did not insist on veto, only on consultation.

All in all, Mr. Nixon could please and reassure the Southern chairmen; and when he left, his nomination was secure. There would later be the threat of Nelson Rockefeller; but the Rockefeller threat was one jaw of a trap which could be effective only if the other jaw, Ronald Reagan, could operate. With the understanding at Atlanta, the Reagan move was blunted and the convention could safely be turned over to Richard Kleindienst, who now had a clear field for his talents.

From Oregon on, Kleindienst was foreman of willing workers in a clear design. One hundred twelve delegates had been won, by statute, in primaries. The Rocky Mountain states, with their 108 delegates, were also locked. The Atlanta conference had locked up the South and Border states under Strom Thurmond's harsh discipline for another 394. There seemed very little doubt as to the outcome. By the end of the Atlanta meeting, Kleindienst, with his precise delegate files, could draw up the first hard estimate of his candidate's strength at the forthcoming convention. Three days later the key members of the Nixon high command—Haldeman, Mitchell, Kleindienst, Klein, Garment, Flanigan, Ellsworth—met at Key Biscayne in Florida and reviewed their holdings. Kleindienst's guess was that they could count on 757 votes in Miami (not too gross an overestimate at that moment before the Rockefeller campaign took off) and the nomination was solidly locked up. They must therefore set post-convention targets now. Thus, Kleindienst would remain in charge of delegates and focus on the Miami convention, organizing the eight regional directors, command posts, floor communications, tactics. Nixon and the other members would focus on the post-Miami problems, the planning of campaign strategy and the winning of the general election itself—a luxury not to be permitted to his ultimate rival, Hubert Humphrey.

The concept that governed both convention tactics and election strategy was simple: the nomination must be won without splitting the Party, the election must be won without splitting the nation. Inherent in this concept was a strategy of blandness; and in the strategy, a flaw—for unless he could expand his base from his minority-party Republican loyalists, Mr. Nixon would emerge ultimately as a minority President. Yet, without passion or dynamism, he could not expand the base. Artistically, the flaw translated itself as boredom. Another synonym, however, for boredom is "unexciting," and millions of Americans in their year of stress wanted precisely that—an "unexciting" Presidency, a calm and soothing regime which would not prod them with the increasing perplexities of America and the world, nor with the dramatics that seemed, increasingly, to be substituting for politics in their country.

The very smoothness of the Nixon campaign machinery promoted this sense of non-excitement. By Key Biscayne in June, the organization that had finally emerged to cap the Nixon drive reflected a good deal of the campaign. It was exciting chiefly to *aficionados* of political technique as an almost perfect model of what a campaign should be—at once spankingly efficient in all substantive functions, yet simultaneously tailored to the personality of the candidate as well.

All substantive functions were captained by a top-management team of John Mitchell, chief, and Peter Flanigan, deputy. To these two men reported all division chiefs, with their own pyramids descending beneath them. Maurice Stans, loyalist to Nixon over five campaigns,[4] commanded a team that descended through six regional finance chiefs to embrace all the financing and money-gathering of the organization; the media division was headed by Leonard Garment as philosopher and operated by Shakespeare and Treleaven as executives; press was headed by Herbert Klein as chief and Ronald Ziegler as operational outdoor

4 Now Secretary of Commerce.

man; organization was headed by Richard Kleindienst, followed by Ellsworth, Sears and Evans.

The personal staff was similarly neat. Here, at the top of the pyramid, was Haldeman, who guarded the candidate's door, approved of every appointment, decided on every piece of paper that reached the candidate personally; just as intimately, but without executive or policy authority, Dwight Chapin, personal aide, and Rose Mary Woods, executive secretary, also had total access to the candidate's presence. Haldeman controlled not only the candidate's body and time, but through another deputy, John Whitaker, chief of scheduling and advance work, oversaw all movements. Another personal stream also reported through Haldeman—research and speech-writing. By mid-May of 1968 the research team had already fleshed out from its three regulars (Price, liberal; Buchanan, conservative; and Safire, generalist and phrase-maker) to include specialists on foreign affairs, urban affairs, economics. Other names dangled off to infinity from both the management chart and the personal chart, and each man had a fixed place, except, of course, for Finch, closest of all to the candidate.

That there was no place for Finch on the organizational chart was also significant. Finch's function ran beyond any title. As Robert Kennedy might have been defined in 1960 simply as "brother" to the candidate, and Bill Moyers in 1964 simply as "conscience," Finch could best be defined by the true use of the word "friend."

Finch had, of course, official credentials. As candidate for Lieutenant Governor of California, his victory in 1966 had been won by the largest majority of votes for any statewide candidate in any state contest in the nation. He had served Nixon as campaign manager in his California race in 1962, after having advised against making it. He had served Nixon as campaign director in 1960 at the age of thirty-five. But he was most important to Nixon as a window on the world.

Tall, craggy-faced, sandy-haired, a chain-smoker, Finch looked like a grown-up Eagle Scout, which, of course, he had been. His early career traced the story of the all-American boy—star football player in high school, editor of the high-school newspaper, president of his student bodies at high school, at college (Occidental), at law school (University of Southern California), winner of the National College Speech Contest with a speech on Andrew Jackson.

Yet there was a warmth about him, a vivid concern for people in his politics, which had roots entirely outside this background. One could trace it in his talk about his father, whom he adored, and out of whose life Finch had learned compassion. His father had been a war hero, earner of the DSC, and life had been refracted for the boy through his father. The war hero had come home to run for the Arizona legislature and won a seat; but he had also been a cotton farmer, and five bad crop years had forced him off the land, out of Arizona, to become a school-supply salesman in Southern California. Ever after, his father would nostalgically reminisce about the wonders of politics and government. His father's combat unit had been an all-Negro battalion in World War I; when the Finches moved to California and lived in the Inglewood district of Los Angeles (now all-Negro), Negroes came to their house constantly, asking for help, references, jobs; Negroes were a family concern. His father had died at the age of forty-three, when Finch was thirteen—a lingering, painful death of cancer, in and out of hospitals, and Finch remembers "this proud man being humiliated by this terrible thing and what it did to my mother and my sister." From the trauma of his father's passing, Finch took away several things—a concern with the problems of the ill and medical care; a concern with the conditions of Negroes in America; and a boy's romantic memory of his father's fascination with politics and yearning for public service.

Finch had met Nixon first in 1946, when both arrived in Washington for the first time—Nixon as an unknown freshman Congressman, Finch as an assistant to California Congressman Norris Paulsen, much more famous than Nixon. Their offices were on the same corridor, and, both of them lonesome, they talked for hours: about Nixon's problems—as member of the Herter Select Committee and about the Marshall Plan, or as member of the House Un-American Activities Committee and how does a witness get a chance for fair response. They talked also about Finch's problems—what he should do in life, how he should point, and Nixon urged Finch back to California to study in a California law school if he wished to pass the bar there. Their friendship continued, grew closer as their families grew closer, and when, in 1958, Nixon set out on the planning for the 1960 campaign, Finch abandoned his law practice in Los Angeles to come to Washington again as manager of the Vice-President's office.

1968 was a harder time for Finch. Having established his own identity in California politics, he was fascinated by the problems of its universities and racial confrontations; his perspectives were now Californian, the governorship or a Senate seat the long hope on his horizon. Nor could he abandon his responsibilities in California, leaving the state and the Republican Party to be dominated by Ronald Reagan, from whose politics Finch dissociated himself. Yet Nixon needed Finch, too, as chief confidant and closest friend. Thus, throughout the spring months and down to the convention, one must see Finch as an almost unseen presence in the Nixon camp, his transcontinental flights unnoticed, the long and constant telephone conversations between Sacramento and New York unrecorded. Among the Big Three of the Nixon camp it was clear that Mitchell controlled the organization, Haldeman controlled the person, and Finch dominated the thinking. Mitchell was a conservative; Haldeman a neutral; Finch was a liberal.

What was most interesting about this structure was its contrast with the Nixon structure of 1960—a confused, ramshackle, over-centralized and constantly cross-feuding body of men. It illustrated as well as any analysis what had happened to Nixon—he had come to understand himself better, and the men around him understood him better, too.

Each expressed the change in a different way.

Haldeman said, "We've learned a lot since the 1960 campaign. Nixon gets irritated by petty annoyances. In 1960 we ran it badly and he was always angry with the need of dealing with petty details that were handled badly. He has no time for small talk, or the ordinary kind of bull when people sit down together. He's best when he's dealing with problems—you have to keep people off his back and let him deal with larger things. . . . Basically, there are ordinary people and extraordinary people, and he's one of the extraordinary ones; it's the way his mind works, the way he can soak up a whole range of opinions."

Mitchell, who has known Nixon since 1946, said, "When he came to New York in 1963, he was completely shattered. He'd been a comparatively young man when he shoved off from Whittier, California, to Washington, and all his life, until he came to New York, he was looking back over his shoulder at the jungle of California politics. In New York he felt his public life was all behind him, and for the first time in his life he let down his guard and began to look at other people, other events. It broadened his whole concept of American life. In California he'd always looked up at the chairmen of the board of the Eastern Establishment, and now he was dealing with them. In New York he had a place of merit, a responsibility of his own. People who've arrived, they don't worry about gimmicks, defenses, angles, Any country boy who gets here, they too lose their phobias, their problems. He was relaxed."

Finch said, "He's still a solitary. But he's lost the syndrome of 1960 and 1962. He doesn't want to be loved; he's not looking for adulation the way he used to; it's a case of cold respect, he wants respect; that's the lesson that came to him from the 1962 campaign, and if he's come to that point, he offers the potential of being a great leader. But that's a judgment that history will have to write. . . ."

Whatever judgment history will make on Richard Nixon must wait for years, and will rest on his record in the White House; that judgment must concern itself with the drama of government and policy. But already in 1968 one could see that, though there was to be little drama in Richard Nixon's campaign, there was a drama in the man, in his turning-about in himself; yet it was a drama too dense for easy analysis.

Here was a man who in 1960 had been attacked as vicious, untrustworthy and unstable. His campaign managers in 1960 had considered their greatest handicap his "image of pugnacity." Now, in 1968, he was being attacked as dull, smooth and programmed, his greatest danger "the image of complacency." I myself in 1960 had found him banal, his common utterances all too frequently a mixture of pathetic self-pity and petulant distemper.[5] I had never found him untrustworthy, questioned his courage or doubted his intelligence. But before that lay years of reporting which could not be forgotten. Nixon had fought a tooth-and-fang campaign in his first try for Congress in 1946. His behavior in that campaign, accepted practice in the turmoil of California politics, reached an even more intense peak of ferocity in his campaign against Helen Gahagan Douglas for the United States Senate in 1950. In Washington he had, indeed, proven himself an internationalist and a responsible in foreign affairs—but in domestic affairs always a conservative. What bothered a reporter most was his failure to disassociate himself publicly from the animal savagery of Senator Joseph McCarthy of Wisconsin. Nixon's pursuit of the spoor of Alger Hiss in his investigation of conspiracy had been finally validated by Hiss's conviction on the charge of perjury; but he had worn that credit as triumph, not as tragedy, and accepted the cheers of the bloodthirsty indiscriminately when he might have, with his credit for the Hiss case, made surgically clean the real difference between dissent and conspiracy.

As Eisenhower's Vice-President he had been the knife, the enraged partisan warning the nation against monolithic Communism, implying, over and over, that somehow treason had run free through the twenty years of Democratic administration, slashing constantly by innuendo at great patriots like Dean Acheson ("Isn't it wonderful," he said shortly after Eisenhower's election, "to have finally a Secretary of State who's on our side of the table?"). And always, in the campaign from 1952 to 1960, his behavior would break in sentimentality—his Checkers speech in the 1952 campaign came to mind, his weeping reunion with Eisenhower the next night, his rhetorical style, the constant use of the word "folks," his strange debate with Nikita Khrushchev in the model kitchen in Moscow.

There should, and must, be a statute of limitations in politics; and thus, just as I had in 1960, when I came to cherish John F. Kennedy, tucked away his early denunciation of Communist conspirators in the China division of the State Department, so, as I approached the campaign of 1968, I tried to tuck away the records, files and utterances of Richard Nixon of the 1950's.

Yet they could not be so easily tucked away. The Nixon of 1968 was so different from the Nixon of 1960 that the whole personality required re-exploration. Something had transformed his thinking; it was important to try to read all over again the quality of his mind.

[5] See *The Making of the President—1960*, Chapter Ten and Chapter Twelve.

Most important, perhaps, in my reassessment of Richard Nixon was the genuine devotion he had called forth from men I respected—men like Finch, Garment, Mitchell, Haldeman, Price. I had never been able to fathom the call of Nixon on men of such abilities. Now, as I tried to follow their thinking and pursued Richard Nixon in person, I began to catch an echo of what stirred them and, to my surprise, found in myself a slow and ever-growing respect for him.

Reporters, said one of his aides, always keep asking what the real Nixon is like—they forget, went on the aide, that whenever Nixon sees a reporter, he's all wound up, he's working, he's not the real Nixon.

I remember the remark because during a series of conversations we had that winter and spring of 1967–68 the first real glimpse I had of the man came quite by accident. I had already made a first call on him at his apartment on November 10th, 1967, and that conversation, though cordial, had been wary, brisk and businesslike. A few weeks later, catching the second section of a shuttle flight from Washington to New York, I found a cluster of empty seats in the rear lounge of the already full Constellation. A minute or two later down the aisle bustled Nixon himself, catching the plane just before it took off. There were only two seats left, one across from me, one beside me, and Nixon, making the best of the unexpected meeting and smiling, waved his aide, Dwight Chapin, to the facing seat, then sat down beside me, pulling open his black briefcase to work, as he usually does on a plane flight.

He opened the briefcase, in which were three of his yellow legal pads, and then, instead of working on them, showed them to me: page after page had been written on, then scratched out. He must have written twenty openings for this speech—a short one, he said—and he still didn't have it right. He couldn't make a good extemporaneous speech, he said, he had to work on it. I said I suffered from the same weakness, and we began to talk about writing; he was enormously interested in writing habits: how, when, at what times of day did I work—where? From that to a common concern of all writers—the tax incidence on authors, whereby, whatever the returns or however long it might take to write a book, the tax fell all in one year, with little leeway except the standard spread-forward. Nixon was professional now and the professional lawyer's mind was incisive—probing, stabbing, reaching into point after point of the law, the grasp on detail easy and the constitutional background of patent and copyright law clear in his mind. From that to the more serious problem of writers and politicians—how to get it all down on paper, how to absorb information. What papers did I read? Did I clip and file? Which did I think were the best papers in the country? How many could I read a day?

It was an interrogation, and he led, from question to question, until I brought up a favorite subject of mine, which is the reach of the mind—

the concept of the mind as a muscular system of lenses that reaches out to pull fragments of fact together in a new pattern or new connection of reality. I mentioned the legends about Sir Isaac Newton's genius, his enormous powers of concentration as he worked the muscular lenses of the mind, and with that Nixon pinned me. He wanted to hear more about Newton, all about Newton. I mentioned John Maynard Keynes's famous tercentenary essay at Cambridge on Newton's genius, and he signaled Chapin to make a note of the essay, he must read it himself.[6]

We must have talked of Isaac Newton for a full ten minutes of the short trip, and then, with that sensitivity I came later to recognize, he withdrew the pressure of his questioning and began to ramble anecdotally and analytically. He was fascinated by the way things worked. A stewardess came down the aisle to offer us coffee and he mused about the marvel of their training, how airlines could take untrained girls, put them through several weeks' training and make them exquisitely competent technicians, efficient hostesses with well-modulated voices; it was wonderful what you could do with almost anybody with modern training methods. Then to a favorite anecdote of his of a long plane ride with Harry Bridges of the Longshoremen's Union in the old Boeing Stratoliners; then, on the way into New York, with more privacy, he was talking politics—clear, detached, lucid summaries of the problems of all the candidates. Of Bobby Kennedy's candidacy and the trap Bobby was in as a Democratic candidate locked in under a sitting Democratic President—he couldn't see how Bobby would work his way out of that one. Of Romney's candidacy—Romney had been ill-advised; Romney's strength lay in domestic affairs, not foreign affairs, he should have dodged Vietnam and stuck to domestic themes in his campaign. Of polls—he believed in issue-analysis polls, they were useful; personal-standing polls, he felt, were a waste of money—"if you're ahead, don't look behind; if you're behind, it only discourages you." And then, as he drove me home, he was pleased that he had, in his few short years in New York, found an access exit from the East River Drive that got one to midtown minutes quicker and with less traffic than the formal exit I had been using for fifteen years.

It was a new view of the Nixon personality—in which the trait uppermost was a voracious, almost insatiable curiosity of mind, a hunger to know, to learn, to find out how things work, to understand and explore detail. "One of the troubles with Johnson," he said to me much later, "is that Johnson just doesn't listen to anybody. When you go in to see him, he does all the talking from the moment you get in; he doesn't ask questions. I like to listen."

[6] For the record, I must signal that Mr. Nixon had pulled me far off base and I was running together, out of failing memory, the Keynes essay on Newton and the E. N. da C. Andrade essay on Newton, both to be found in the *World of Mathematics* series edited by James Newman. A better study has since appeared, *A Portrait of Isaac Newton*, by Frank E. Manuel (Harvard University Press, 1969).

He had spent a great deal of time in the years in exile doing just that—listening. I remember that when I visited him the first time and asked him the standard questions, he toyed with the terms "new Nixon" and "old Nixon." There was no new Nixon, he insisted—it was only that in the past eight years, while Rockefeller and Johnson had been so busy, he had had time to read; all his eight years as Vice-President he hadn't had time to read a thing. He'd been reading some things recently by this fellow Moynihan, for example—very good stuff; did I know Moynihan and what did I think of him? [7]

Not only was he reading, he was writing. At the time of our first meeting, in November, 1967, he and Price were almost finished with the final draft of a book. He wanted to launch his campaign with a book (an idea that later fell by the wayside); but he didn't want it to be a book of specifics, or politics, or programs. The idea was to write a book about the whole last third of this century, the long-range perspectives of change—change in weapons systems, change in power relations, in cities and urban affairs, in race relations. We needed new perspectives before we could get new programs. It was not "a collection of speeches," he insisted, showing me his yellow pads, it was an attempt to think through problems.

It was always difficult to recapture a conversation with Nixon unless one took notes—for there were several Nixons. The Nixon on the plane, a jovial, relaxed anecdotist, was one thing. The Nixon in a formal interview was another. And then there was Nixon when his thoughts raced away with him—and his speech became choppy, allusive, almost chaotic, as the thinking outran the words and came out in bursts, jerks, and clusters of phrases from an inner pressure to say too much too quickly.

An attempt to recapture a typical Nixon thought-ramble with all his concepts churning at once might, to the best of my memory, go like this. I asked him, the first time we talked, about the origins of his famous feud with Nelson Rockefeller and the answer, as I recall it, took off:

He couldn't really understand it. He had always supported Rockefeller in the Eisenhower Cabinet, supported Rockefeller in his running conflict with John Foster Dulles, supported Rockefeller in his plan for reorganizing the Federal government; did I think Rockefeller would make a good Secretary of State?

But, continued Nixon, getting back to the feud, he couldn't really put a finger on its origins. Perhaps he ought to tell about Lee Kuan Yew, the Prime Minister of Singapore: On one of his trips abroad, Nixon had queried Lee about the split between Russia and China. Lee Kuan Yew had replied that it was not a split over ideology, there was really no question of ideology involved; it was just that Russia and China

[7] Daniel P. Moynihan is now White House Assistant for Urban Affairs.

were huge super-powers, they had natural conflicting interests, they were too big to live harmoniously on the same continent. All he could say about Rockefeller was that they were both of them, himself and Rockefeller, very large quantities, too big to be contained by the same Party; it wasn't personal dislike. But the thought of Lee Kuan Yew lingered, and Nixon cast up another thought that evidently bothered him. Lee Kuan Yew had carried the Asian analogy on to Japan and had warned Nixon that America must pay attention to Japan; Japan was simply too great a power to be docile forever, the Japanese would not go on forever simply making transistor radios and supertankers and eating rice. Japan had great interests of its own. From there, an explosive and fascinating thought about the Presidency itself occurred to him. The job of the President was above all foreign affairs. "I've always thought this country could run itself domestically," he said, "without a President; all you need is a competent Cabinet to run the country at home. You need a President for foreign policy; no Secretary of State is really important; the President makes foreign policy."

Thus, a typical, choppy Nixon ramble. But there were larger quantities one could discern when one added up all recollections: two things fascinated him above all. The lesser was the minutiae of American domestic politics, at which he is one of the great experts, with a relish for every detail from the relative cost of nighttime radio to network television, to the political weight of Tom Dewey, the personality of George Romney, the reason why Rocky couldn't win in Indiana ("eating blintzes is O.K. in New York, but in Indiana you have to project a different image"). But the larger interest, continuously obsessive with him, was foreign policy. He could not say why he was so interested in foreign policy ("perhaps because I was brought up as a Quaker. People say I'm a hawk, but I want peace"). His interest in foreign policy, his concern with America in the outer world, was certainly greater than Franklin Roosevelt's or Lyndon Johnson's when they reached power, and fully equal to that of John F. Kennedy. At these two extremes, his conversation was best: party politics and foreign affairs.

I visited him again in New York, early in the afternoon of March 12th, the day of the New Hampshire primary. I found him in his nervous mood—legs crossing and uncrossing; hastening to light the guest's cigar; his sentences tumbling. It was a rainy, slushy day in New York, but in New Hampshire the weather was good. Stewart Lamprey had called from New Hampshire saying that the voting was extremely heavy—what did I think it meant? It could mean, I said, either a very heavy McCarthy write-in or a very heavy Rockefeller write-in, probably a McCarthy surge. He said that Rockefeller ought to get at least 30 percent of the vote in the Republican primary to have a chance, and then, since we were alone, he candidly retracted. "I guess I'm playing political gamesmanship with you, he won't do that well." But I ought to remember, he admonished me, that he himself, Nixon, had taken 15,000 of the New Hampshire primary votes in 1964 without lifting a finger and, in fairness, I ought to admit that Rocky should do at least that well.

It was the first test at the polls in 1968, and he was understandably unsettled, but soon the unsettled mood passed and he was Nixon the anecdotist and, again, thoughtful. He had taken a beating in the press this week for not stating a Vietnam policy in New Hampshire; but he didn't think he *ought* to state a Vietnam policy; it could only bind his hands later if he were elected; and it might undermine whatever negotiations Johnson was trying to bring off with Vietnam at this very moment. We talked of guerrillas, terrorists and insurrectionary warfare, and then he said that if he were elected President, the very first thing he'd do would be to try to get in touch with Red China. There had to be an understanding with Red China. In ten or fifteen years it would be impossible to run the world if Red China weren't part of it.

Thus, back and forth, between the probable results and impact of the New Hampshire primary on the Republican Party and the great external world. The two chief problems immediately, it seemed, were whether Rockefeller would challenge him in the Oregon primary—and how could we liquidate the war in Vietnam. It was important that we get out, but that we not be defeated. How do you liquidate that war with honor?

It was at this passage in our acquaintance I came to believe that one must respect this man: there was about all he said a conviction and a sincerity. Why did he run for President? I had asked. And he could not answer, as no other major Presidential candidate has ever been able to answer. He had all the money he needed now, $200,000 a year, and he lived in this affluent apartment—with a wave of the hand, he displayed the affluent apartment. But it didn't excite him. He didn't need that much money. He supposed it was just because it was in his blood; he liked politics.

Thus, by the late spring of 1968 my reportorial observation on Nixon had deeply changed from that of 1960—chiefly because he had changed too. There was in all he said, even in discussing the most hostile personalities, a total absence of bitterness, of the rancor and venom that had once colored his remarks. I had learned, as I had not known before, how diligent and untiring a worker he was—and how phenomenally driven to get to the bottom of things. There remained to bother me several other matters: the peculiar fatalism of the man, the Kismet with which he looked forward to the happening of events; the ability of the man to stand up to the strain and heat of violent decision; and the nature of his dreams, which, in a President, are the most important qualities of all.

All of these unsettled questions—his fatalism, his stress-capacity, his dreams—were not immediately relevant, however. His campaign, as he saw it, would be to offer the nation a sober alternative to the leadership of the Democrats. And thus, of course, one has to go back to the Democrats, whose uncivil wars were dominating the nation's attention.

CHAPTER SIX

ROBERT F. KENNEDY: REQUIESCAT IN PACEM

T HE gash that Robert F. Kennedy tore in the story of 1968 aches still—aches in personal memory, but more in history itself. Of all the men who challenged for the Presidency, he alone, by the assassin's bullets, was deprived of the final judgment of his party and people. Wistful and pugnacious, fearless and tender, gay and rueful, profound and antic, strong yet indecisive—all these descriptives of him were true. Yet none recaptures what stirred the passions that made him the most loved and most hated candidate of 1968, nor the quicksilver personality who, when pensive, looked like a little boy, or, when hot-in-action, like a prince-in-combat.

For he was more than himself; and he knew it. To explain why this was so, and the blaze he lit in the mad spring months of 1968, one must start with that pedestrian phrase, "the Kennedy movement." However difficult it is to define, the Kennedy movement is a romantic reality— and thus one of the hard political forces of America today as it was when, in the spring of 1968, it exploded at the call of its then-leader, Robert F. Kennedy.

Technically, of course, one can specifically date the transformation of the political resources of the Kennedy family into what is called a "movement." It began at the moment when John F. Kennedy's body was buried in Arlington and his memory rose to become legend. One could dissect the Kennedy movement almost as one dissected the anatomy of the grand Rooseveltian coalition: there were the common millions who had come, simply, to enjoy the presence and grace of the handsome young President on the home screen or in their midst; there was the very real gratitude of millions of Negroes, given hope; there was the respect of thousands of thinkers who could not forget a man who had so effectively used talent and ideas; there was the corps of eminent men—

executives, writers, diplomats, politicians—who had known their first taste of greatness and responsibility in the thousand days of the Kennedy administration and remained, a shadow corps of loyalists, yearning to govern again.

But the legend was stronger than this analysis suggests; the legend rested on more primitive elements. The strongest force in the movement came from an atavistic craving—the simple craving of people for heroes. In the remorseless strangulation of American politics by new technologies and infinitely complicated problems, the vent of a personalized loyalty gave millions of Americans who responded to the name Kennedy the same emotional satisfaction felt by those English yeomen who had fought for York or for Lancaster. An indefinable but nonetheless substantial power came to the movement from the equally simple hunger of people for style and elegance. And there was a time element also: when Dwight D. Eisenhower was succeeded by John F. Kennedy, it was as if a generation of fathers had been put aside and a new postwar generation of Americans had taken over. Accident had interrupted the Kennedy administration and its promise, placing Johnson in the White House; but the surge to power of a new generation ran on nonetheless.

There could have been no Kennedy movement without John F. Kennedy; but there could also have been no Kennedy movement had not Robert Francis Kennedy been large enough a man to keep it alive. Without the younger Kennedy, the older brother would have been remembered as Tiberius Gracchus might have been by the Romans if Tiberius' assassination had been an isolated episode—as a single glorious moment in the expansion of freedom and opportunity in that republic. It was the life—and violent death—of Gaius Gracchus, his younger brother, that made them remembered as "the Gracchi," and identified them with a cause that outlived their time in the forum.

From the death of John F. Kennedy, in November, 1963, the principal question in American politics was, thus, whether his administration had been an isolated episode—and whether his younger brother Robert was creative enough to make of that administration more than a memory. For Robert Kennedy provoked controversy far beyond any controversy provoked by his older brother. JACK WAS NIMBLE, JACK WAS QUICK, read one sign I saw as Robert F. Kennedy tried to enter on his inheritance, BUT BOBBY SIMPLY MAKES ME SICK. Of the man Robert Kennedy, Americans had only a distorted public image at the time of his brother's death. And millions recoiled from him.

The first quality that surfaced when Bobby Kennedy was discussed was his "ruthlessness."

The tag had been applied to him as he first came to public notice in his brother's Presidential campaign and administration. There was no doubt that he had been for his brother the enforcer, the "rod," the crackdown man, whether it was against Russian diplomats who lied to the administration, or politicians who ran out on a deal. If one had to choose an enemy, Robert F. Kennedy was not a man anyone would like to have as an enemy. He fought hard, bare-knuckled, savagely. To break one's word to Robert Kennedy was to put oneself in peril—for a welsher he had little forgiveness. Whether it was hack politician, book-writer, steel magnate—once a man broke his word to Robert Kennedy, Kennedy's retaliation was certain. He could also be intemperate and impulsive. Robert Kennedy made up his mind on the right-or-wrong of any given issue quite slowly, but once he did he could be the image of wrath—his forefinger pointing, his fist pounding in his palm, his eyes ablaze. His insistence on immediate action, a quality of youth, angered a broad spectrum of Americans. It angered businessmen who never forgave the Attorney General who, they believed, had authorized the FBI to rouse sleeping newsmen in their homes during the steel-price crisis; it angered liberals who felt that no sin of Jimmy Hoffa justified the wire-tapping and relentless pursuit of that corrupt union leader to jail; it angered intellectuals and writers who could not understand Kennedy's quarrel with William Manchester, who had been authorized to write an approved story of the assassination of John F. Kennedy and who Bobby believed had broken his word.

The rigidity of his convictions was so stubborn that to the outside world he appeared dictatorial. Within the inner circle of the Kennedy administration, however, this rigidity was often an amusement. I remember a late-afternoon visit to the White House during the Kennedy administration when, sitting in the Oval Office, I tried not to eavesdrop but was unable to resist tilting my ear to a series of important telephone calls that interrupted the President. A Federal judgeship in the Southern states, at the frontier of civil rights, was obviously at issue. President Kennedy was balancing calls between the hold buttons on his desk telephone until he reached his brother, the Attorney General. When he reached the Attorney General, Bobby must have been crisp, tart and emphatically negative. The President flicked his hold buttons and told the Southern Senator hanging on the decision that he would have to get back to him later. Then he noticed I had been listening. "You know," he said, "you know what the trouble with this administration is?" "No, sir," I said. "The trouble with this administration," continued the President, "is that the Attorney General has so much higher standards for judges than the President." It was not quite that, of course; but whatever the Attorney General felt he would express with a vehemence which, in echo, always made him sound like Savonarola.

Thus, "ruthlessness."

The second quality noted publicly was Robert Kennedy's exuberance, enlarged in print until he became the master of the revels of

Camelot. The revels were indeed real. His taste in friends was so broad that any of the great parties at Hickory Hill was a memory that seemed untrue and impossible the very next morning. Mountain-climbers and astronauts, generals and ambassadors, Cabinet secretaries and machine politicians, movie stars, singers, writers, staff secretaries, pretty girls, and august figures of the American past all mingled at his home. But however such revels were distorted in second-hand report, one remembers them as gaieties, not bacchanals—their purpose was to bring great figures of responsibility to simple human warmth, to lubricate high policy by frolic. Some of the remembered scenes were odd. This correspondent remembers an evening when he was teased into an Indian wrestling match with an equally middle-aged Russian diplomat, and Ethel Kennedy crying out most undiplomatically at a fleeting moment of successful exertion: "Our side is winning, our side is winning." One remembers Senator Edward Kennedy being lured into a mimicry of the West Virginia politicians he had met in 1960, then swiftly turning on the parlor with a parody of American political idioms and stump rhetoric that ran from coast to coast. One remembers Secretary of Defense Robert McNamara and his wife, Margaret, being enticed into singing their high-school songs. One remembers the Attorney General late on another night challenging anyone in the room to a push-up match and besting Kenneth O'Donnell, ex-Harvard football captain and his onetime classmate, in push-ups from the floor. Kennedy was a physical-fitness man; he rarely drank anything but beer, or smoked anything but an occasional cigar. His "highs" came from sheer animal delight in action. One remembers leaving Hickory Hill very late one night at some period when the house was being reconstructed. Scaffolding surrounded it, and the Attorney General was seized by the impulse to challenge anyone to hand-climb with him. Off he went, swinging from rung to rung like a circus acrobat in the moonlight; and then, climbing down, scorning the rest of us because no one would venture to contest him. Wherever he went in Washington, as he moved among his friends, there was joy and gaiety, an indefinable but enormously important contribution to the temper of the capital.

These were the qualities of Robert Kennedy most in the public mind when, on John Kennedy's death, the memory of his administration fostered the "movement." Missing in this appreciation of Robert Kennedy were several other qualities of personality that had surfaced first in the administration and then, later, in Robert Kennedy's years of displacement from power. They were his sheer, stunning executive ability; his intuitive sense of the use and nature of American power; and his sense of personal identification, unique among American politicians, with the victims and casualties of American society.

His executive talent had been noticed only by a small handful of men in the years of his brother's administration, when he was over-shadowed in action by the larger transactions of the President. But one should linger over this talent, for his stewardship of the Department of Justice as Attorney General was, without doubt, the ablest of modern times. He took office as the attitudes of American jurisprudence toward written law were changing, and as the clash of the races in America was coming to climax. Through such times the Attorney General, an inex-perienced lawyer, had to find and cleave to the thread of legalities, yet permit change to happen; and all the while he was directing an obsolete staff of the Department of Justice in the most delicate duties they had ever performed.

Within months of his swearing-in in 1961, black "freedom riders" were loose on their challenge to ancient racism in the South; and no law, nor any legitimacy, gave the Federal government the right to protect them. One remembers Washington slowly becoming aware of his execu-tive talents during these weeks of peril. What code gave the Federal government the right to act? If the Attorney General did choose to act, how would he find the manpower? How—out of the few hundred middle-aged men who bear the title of Marshals of the United States scattered across the country—could he assemble an effective force? Could he legally recruit Treasury Agents, prison guards of Federal prisons, immi-gration border guards, to pacify the turbulent South? The simple admin-istration and coordination of such bodies was a puzzle; yet it was all accomplished in a matter of weeks. And at the moment of crisis, when white mobs in Montgomery, Alabama, threatened to burn down a Negro church in May, 1961, the Attorney General was ready and presided over every detail of the counterstroke—the assembly of men, the provision of planes, the installation of communications. He was to demonstrate his flair for action over and over again as Attorney General—at the Univer-sity of Mississippi in 1962, at the University of Alabama in 1963.

This executive quality of Robert Kennedy flowed from the best principles of leadership. He had impeccable taste in men, chose ex-traordinary lieutenants. He listened; no man seemed more indecisive over longer periods of time than Robert Kennedy as he consulted, con-sulted again, aired his thoughts with friends and deputies, probed, ques-tioned and re-questioned, trying to find the jugular of his problem. But then, when he acted—decision was his alone. Those who had known Kennedy as the political muscle of his brother's 1960 campaign were astounded by his quality in office. He could decide to plunge the De-partment of Justice into the reapportionment problem, hear his advisers and lawyers out, and then prepare and argue his own brief before the Supreme Court, fully aware, as a politician, how fundamental a change he was advocating in the structure of the nation. He could, as executive, hammer together all the jealous, and conflicting, anti-crime agencies of the U.S. government—FBI, Narcotics Bureau, Treasury Agents, Crime Division of the Justice Department—in the first co-ordinated assault on the underworld of organized crime. He became the scourge of the Mafia and labor racketeers. (His spectacular energies, it should be noted, were never fully geared to the problems of industrial concentration. He remained, until he left office, dissatisfied with the operation of the Anti-Trust Division of the Department of Justice, but never moved actively to make his mark on it.)

All these talents were subordinate, however, to the quality that made him the prime explosive force of 1968.

This was his sense of power.

Where others might see power as administrative, or as a subject of intellectual criticism, or as a brokerage of favors, honors and punishments, Kennedy saw power as real and breathing. He knew the nature of American power even better than did the President of the United States, Lyndon Johnson. Politics, for him, was the handmaiden of policy, and the Presidency was an art form. Of the use of power he had learned much from his father, but even more from his brother, John F. Kennedy. He had been the closest man to the President during his brother's administration, and this apprenticeship had taught him to see national purpose across the fences of the parochial Cabinet departments. In great moments of stress, as in the Cuban missile crisis of 1962, his executive instincts married to his intuitions could be superb.[1] Most importantly, he saw power as creative—the wondrous things one could do, or call into being, if one were President, the changes that could be brought about, the ills that could be rectified, the use of men and the writing of laws to make the lives of other men better.

This naked power-drive in Robert Kennedy contributed more than anything else to the paradox in public appreciation, to the adoration and hatred he roused wherever he went.

For millions of Americans, the power-drive was sinister. It was not right, felt such millions, that any man should inherit the leadership of a nation by patrimony, family wealth or descended prestige. Had he not been the son of Joseph P. Kennedy, the brother of John F. Kennedy, what then would Robert F. Kennedy have been? How much serious attention could he have roused if his name were simply Robert Francis? Was a Kennedy dynasty, a single family, to claim by family right the prize all other men in American history had been required to struggle for?

For other millions of Americans, this power-drive was what drew their loyalty. They knew that government was not, for him, an abstraction; for him government was the way one did things that people could

---

[1] As a parable in the wise use of power, see *Thirteen Days*, by Robert F. Kennedy (W. W. Norton, 1969).

not do for themselves and his power-drive was fueled by concern—concern for the poor, concern for the underprivileged, concern about the way life in the cities of America was snarling into fear and chaos. His apprenticeship in government and the inheritance of the movement may have come to him by kinship. But this kinship had given him a very personal attitude toward the government of the United States. It was not that it belonged to him, as personal property. But he could not abide seeing it mismanaged. His concern about its errors, its shortcomings, its blunders was entirely detached from his personal ambitions, which were also, in fact, very substantial. But it was these moral and political concerns which, all through the years from 1964 to 1967, made him so restless, so unpredictable, so fascinating a character. And of all these concerns none went deeper than his concern about Lyndon Johnson's conduct of the Presidency at home, and his conduct of the war in Vietnam abroad.

The unfurling of these concerns was not slow in coming—it was as if the heat of American politics and policy were incubating them, as in a hotbox, forcing them to the surface faster than was natural.[2]

Before leaving the United States in 1966 for a year abroad, I spent a brooding, rather sad farewell breakfast with Robert Kennedy, and found him still numb with the melancholy that had suffused him since the death of his brother. The Presidency was not then even remotely on his horizon or in his conversation. But overseas, as newspapers from home arrived, one could see more clearly, with distance, what was happening to him. In February, 1966, Kennedy expressed his first open concern about the war in Vietnam, his first public breach with Lyndon Johnson. KENNEDY BIDS US OFFER VIETCONG A ROLE IN SAIGON, read *The New York Times,* and inside were excerpts of his speech in space and length usually given only to Presidential statements. KENNEDY URGES VAST SLUM DRIVE, read another headline. Then: KENNEDY BIDS U.S. AID LATIN CHANGE. DIVORCE LAW CALLED UNFAIR BY KENNEDY. KENNEDY DENOUNCES APARTHEID AS EVIL. KENNEDY HAS A 35-MINUTE AUDIENCE WITH POPE PAUL. KENNEDY CHEERED IN OLE MISS TALK BY CROWD OF 5,500. KENNEDY FEARS AIR STRIKES MAY DELAY PEACE EFFORTS. Senators of national eminence and decades of service in Washington might yearn for a single paragraph on an agency wire. But a void in the public dialogue of America had come about and Robert F. Kennedy had been elected by the press and public to fill it. Whether he willed it or not, a political gravity was drawing him into Presidential

---

[2] For two excellent accounts of the Kennedy campaign in 1968, the reader is referred to *85 Days—The Last Campaign of Robert Kennedy,* by Jules Witcover (Putnam, 1969), and *The Unfinished Odyssey of Robert Kennedy,* by David Halberstam (Random House, 1969).

consideration—and his problem all through 1967 was to decide his own role, to measure himself.

1967 was a bad year for Robert Kennedy. As a man of action, he craved clean-cut decisions. But as a realist, he could see no way to decision. Several long conversations with Kennedy in that year made me think his the most unenviable position in American politics. Over and over again he would cover the same ground. The same considerations were always in his mind, and they added up to paralysis. First, there was the personality of Lyndon Johnson, a man who governed the United States in a style that deeply disturbed him. Next was the war in Vietnam, which he called a waste, an extravagance, an excess, a diversion of all the country's resources to a folly which was crippling it to deal with problems at home. But then came the problem of actually challenging Johnson—how could a Democrat, within his own party, eliminate a Democratic President who wanted to be re-elected? Kennedy felt he could count on almost all the delegates of New England, New York, Michigan and Wisconsin. But how about Pennsylvania, California, Ohio? Above all, Illinois, where Dick Daley controlled? And even if he got those industrial states at the convention and went on to rip the nomination away from the President, he would have torn the Party apart for years, perhaps forever. Moreover, if he did, he would be branded Kennedy the ruthless, the wrecker, the mean, hard, "vindictive Bobby." And if he did win the nomination and campaigned all-out on peace, he would be in no position after election to negotiate with Ho Chi Minh later on any terms except surrender. That, he said, was "unacceptable."

Thus Kennedy through 1967 and down to late fall—his concern over the conduct of the United States government in Vietnam and at home always uppermost in his mind, but his pragmatic sense of politics telling him that the nomination could not be taken from Lyndon Johnson without destroying the Democratic Party. From outside came the pressure, increasing month by month—pressure from self-seeking men hoping to use his name and leadership as leverage for their own politics, pressure from fine-spirited men trying to persuade him that he was the only political figure who could end the bloodshed in Asia. And within his own mind, always, Bobby Kennedy the realist executive, who knew that Johnson could not be overthrown, was at war with Bobby Kennedy the artist of power, who could not tolerate the misuse of American power. How—that was the question—how could American policy be turned about? But not even those closest to him agreed on the answer.

In late October, 1967, Kennedy authorized Pierre Salinger to call the first meeting of the dynastic loyalists at the Regency Hotel in New York. The group was in an exploratory mood. Richard Goodwin was clearly in favor of Kennedy making the race against Johnson; Ivan Nestingen of Wisconsin supported him. The others—Senator Ted Kennedy, Ted Sorensen, Kenneth O'Donnell, Stephen Smith, William Vanden Heuvel, Joseph Dolan—were more uncertain, of varying degrees of enthusiasm and restraint, in favor of deferring decision until they had sounded the mood of political leaders around the country. "We accomplished nothing," said one of those present, "except to authorize Joe Dolan to scout the politicians; to take a secret poll in New Hampshire and call another meeting after we got the poll results. Our only firm recommendation was that Bobby ought to get a haircut—he was looking too much like a long-haired kid."

A second meeting followed on December 10th, called by William Vanden Heuvel, with Kennedy himself present. Again the group boxed the compass and now the discussion was more of a set debate: Arthur Schlesinger (absent from the first meeting) lined up with Goodwin in firm support of immediate candidacy. Salinger was inclining to the view that Kennedy should indeed make the race in 1968. O'Donnell urged that Kennedy run, but not as an individual seeking office, only as a leader crusading against war. ("He must impale himself on the poignard of the war," O'Donnell had said much earlier, "even if it means his political death. The war has to stop.") Senator Ted Kennedy and Sorensen firmly believed that a race against Johnson in the primaries would produce no result except to damage Robert Kennedy's effectiveness as the leader of the anti-war force in the party and country. When the meeting broke up, Kennedy remarked, "We haven't decided anything—so I guess I'm not running."

The entry of Eugene McCarthy into the race further complicated Kennedy's thinking. He did not like Eugene McCarthy for the simplest of reasons—Gene, he thought, would not make a good President. Gene, he said, was vain and lazy. And, continued Kennedy, if he supported Gene on the peace issue, it would mean as complete a breach with Johnson as if he ran himself, tearing the Party apart in the same way.

The pressure on Kennedy through the winter was relentless, wherever he went. He spent the week after Christmas with Pierre Salinger, skiing at Sun Valley—and told Salinger that his own future now no longer mattered, the country could not stand four more years of Johnson. He flew to California from Sun Valley. In California, Jesse Unruh, boss of the California legislature, applied the pressure—hard; Kennedy had to run, said Jesse—better that the Democratic Party be defeated standing for peace than that Johnson win standing for war. In Los Angeles, Kennedy was briefed by the Rand Corporation's experts on Vietnam, with their enormously discouraging view of the conduct of the war. He flew back to Washington to find the restraint of his own brother, Senator Edward Kennedy, much diminished: If Bobby wanted to run, Teddy felt he could no longer argue against the project.

Robert Kennedy was still set against running until the end of January, when he declared, once more, that he would not run against Lyndon Johnson "under any foreseeable circumstances." (See Chapter One.) But with the unfolding events of the week of the Tet offensive, any residual loyalty to Johnson's leadership of the Party vanished.

A week later Kennedy was in Chicago, breakfasting with Mayor Richard Daley. Kennedy had long known that Daley was "dovish" on the war. Now Daley told him that he, Daley, felt that Johnson should have "cashed in his chips" and ended the Vietnam war several years earlier. Yet Daley did not want to break openly with Johnson, nor did he want Robert Kennedy to split the Party. How about a commission appointed by Johnson, suggested Daley, to review the entire course of the war—a commission of such national eminence as to give the administration moral authority for a switch in Vietnam policy. Would that please Bobby? Kennedy did not recollect his own answer in telling the story. But there had been a nice punctilio in his dealing with Daley, the courtesy of a man bred in the ethics of the old politics. Had he asked Daley for outright support? I asked. No, replied Kennedy, you can't do that to any man, it's not fair. If I announce, said Kennedy, then I have the right to ask Daley for support, and to ask McNamara too; but unless I announce first, I've no right to ask them to support me on an iffy decision I haven't made myself.

For weeks thus, after Tet, storm swept the mind of Robert Kennedy, the agony of indecision worse than the hazard of open combat. He felt the base of the Kennedy movement crumbling; thousands of students whose loyalties he felt were Kennedy legacies were hitch-hiking north to New Hampshire to join McCarthy in what they considered the struggle for peace; even the ever loyal Goodwin had left camp to join McCarthy in New Hampshire. Kennedy's indecision was now a public drama; he shared it in consultation with characters as diverse as Jesse Unruh and Walter Lippmann. He shared it with old friends still loyal to Johnson, men like Lawrence O'Brien and Robert McNamara; he shared it with those who had left his leadership to join McCarthy, men like Richard Goodwin and Allard Lowenstein; he shared it with friends, newspapermen, governors, politicians. History and events had trapped him. Having himself refrained from challenging Johnson for fear of tearing the Party apart, he had seen the Party torn apart nonetheless by Eugene McCarthy. And if now he tried to seize control of the insurrection from Eugene McCarthy, he would appear doubly ruthless, unconditionally a self-seeker. Yet Eugene McCarthy, he felt, would prove as inadequate a President as had Lyndon Johnson.

One remembers abrupt conversations with him during this period: the stab of a telephone call late at night and the sharp question, without introduction, "Should I run for President?" and then, without waiting for answer, the tumbled, tormented thinking: "I sit here reading my mail in the office, and it's about the sewage system in Dunkirk, New York, or upstate parks. Shouldn't I be doing something more than that?" A pause. "They keep telling me I should run, my friends, my sisters; Ethel thinks I should run." Another pause, and then, "But that's not so bad, it's what I hear from myself at five o'clock in the morning—the country can't stand four more years of this."

More substantially, as March approached, one could sense the executive mind turning to the problems of action. "Should I enter the primaries?" he asked one night. "It's too late to enter Wisconsin. That leaves Oregon and California; what do you think about California?"

With California came the crunch of decision. In politics there is always the apparent reality, important for its impact on the public mind, to be balanced against the substantive reality, vital in the sequence of decision. Were Kennedy to announce at the beginning of March that he was entering the race, the apparent reality would be that he was greedily snatching the fruits of Eugene McCarthy's hard-won battle in New Hampshire. But if he did *not* announce early enough in March, he would be forfeiting all the delegates of California.

The substantive reality was the complicated California electoral laws:

California law stipulated that three citizens of the state must file by Tuesday, March 5th, an official statement of intention to offer a delegate slate in order to deliver formally signed petitions by April 5th. Any three citizens could file the preliminary statement; but the task of finding, naming, balancing the names of 344 individuals as delegates and alternates for Kennedy by April 5th was a formidable one, normally requiring months of time. If Kennedy *were* to take the primary route to nomination, he could not avoid the battle in California. In California, time was running out very fast; the prize of its delegation was too large and tempting to lose by default. And Jesse Unruh, at this point, telephoned Kennedy with the results of a private poll: Kennedy would get 42 percent, Johnson's stand-in (Lynch) would get 28 percent, Eugene McCarthy would get 11 percent of the California Democrats. So read Unruh's poll at the end of February.

Kennedy received Unruh's telephone call late at night on March 2nd, ten days before the New Hampshire primary. On March 7th he asked his brother, Teddy, to inform Eugene McCarthy privately that he, Bobby, was reconsidering his course and might find it necessary to fight in the spring primaries. Teddy, fearing McCarthy might make mischievous use of such a message later, did not deliver it. Bobby reached next for Dick Goodwin, now high in McCarthy's council, to deliver the message; and Goodwin, as messenger, but not as intermediary, passed the word to McCarthy in New Hampshire the weekend before the primary. McCarthy listened coolly and told Goodwin to relay his reply—why don't you tell him that I only want one term, and he can have it next time, and that would be the arrangement. This concept of the Presidency as something to be handed on was to perplex Bobby until the day of his death. The interchange of messages gave Bobby no instant guidance as to course; and meanwhile, in his own inner circle of friends, opinions and positions were shifting with each day's news, public and private, domestic and foreign.

One must approach the final week of Robert Kennedy's decision with all its elements clear in mind. At issue was the conquest of power in America by a man who had held it, understood it, and yearned for it, not so much as personal gratification but in order to do things. With the power he might alter the course of war; with the power he might enlarge the national community to include all those groups so long excluded, whose deprivations were seared on his thinking. But the power he sought could come to him only by the choice of his Party first and then by the choice of all the people; but no course to power that he could take would fail to divide the Party in bloody bitterness, leaving it shattered when he came later to face the Republicans in the general election. And there could be no privacy during the agony of this decision; friends and enemies alike were all involved, all pressing on him, all revealing their versions of the frenzy as they saw it—some as an attempt at *coup d'état,* some as bedroom farce.

The final sequence begins on Sunday, March 10th, when Robert Kennedy is on the West Coast. All day he has been trying to reach historian Arthur Schlesinger, in Boston; through his wife, Ethel, Kennedy has relayed a message to Schlesinger that he will enter the race if Eugene McCarthy can be induced to withdraw; thus the peace forces would not be split. He wants Schlesinger's opinion. On Monday, March 11th, Schlesinger calls back. Schlesinger is not only historian-in-residence to the Kennedy movement, but bound to Robert Kennedy by such affection and personal loyalty that he cannot help being candid; Schlesinger, as historian, also has the ability to divorce himself from the long sweep of scholarship and focus tightly on the hard moment of quick decision. He opposes Kennedy's fanciful proposal. He urges that Kennedy come out for McCarthy openly in tomorrow's New Hampshire primary. This, thinks Schlesinger, will make it easier for the pro-Kennedy members of McCarthy's staff later to urge McCarthy's withdrawal *after* New Hampshire and *before* the convention. Schlesinger does not anticipate the size of the next day's showing by the Minnesotan. Kennedy considers the advice, then calls Schlesinger back with equal candor: he feels that Eugene McCarthy is simply not *fit* to be President, and he cannot support him in good conscience.

An even more important input is swaying Robert Kennedy's thinking that day. A chain of accidental events has led, on this day, to a visit to the White House by Ted Sorensen of the old loyalist staff. Like Schlesinger, O'Donnell and Salinger, he, too, has set peace in Vietnam as the primordial political consideration of the year. But Sorensen remains among the most consistent of the loyalists in opposing any direct challenge to Lyndon Johnson within the primaries of the Party across the country. Sorensen calls on Johnson as the President is balancing his reconsideration of the Vietnam war against the political mood of the nation. Sorensen, sure of his principal's motives—he has conferred with Robert Kennedy, now back in Washington, before calling on the President—tells the President it is not personal ambition that makes Bobby want to go but his desire to turn the course of the war. Could the President make clear to the world that negotiation, not escalation, is the American policy? The resignation of Dean Rusk could be such a public signal of change in policy. The President, in response, rambles through a long study of the personalities in his Cabinet and entourage. Sorensen sets off on another tack: could not the President appoint a commission to review Vietnam policy? The President observes that Dick Daley has just made a similar suggestion. But Johnson will not commit himself. Sorensen leaves the White House and telephones a report of the conversation to Kennedy.

The next day is the Tuesday of the New Hampshire primary, and Robert Kennedy goes to speak at a dinner in the Bronx, then on to watch the returns in his New York apartment with William Vanden Heuvel. The McCarthy sweep is greater than expected, and Kennedy and Vanden Heuvel drive across town to a fashionable restaurant to meet Arthur Schlesinger and Tom Johnston (Kennedy's Executive Assistant) and take counsel. Schlesinger is now more firm. Kennedy, he says, must endorse McCarthy—on the theory that McCarthy cannot possibly get the nomination but, with Kennedy's help, can demonstrate Johnson's vulnerability to all. Then, at Chicago, the professionals, having been convinced that Johnson is a loser, will go to Bobby—and McCarthy will be obliged to support Kennedy. That night Kennedy also telephones McCarthy's jubilant headquarters in New Hampshire to reach Goodwin and check the final returns. A happy and excited Goodwin tells Kennedy that he cannot be neutral any longer—Kennedy must now either enter the race himself or support McCarthy.

Wednesday the decision-making process dissolves. Robert Kennedy has left New York for Washington, planning to meet Eugene McCarthy in his brother's Senatorial chambers. As he descends in Washington, he replies to the press that, yes, he is "re-assessing" whether he should run. The news is carried by agencies and TV around the country, and speculation boils. The loyalist high command, now joined by Robert Kennedy's personal Senatorial staff, is scheduled to meet in New York, at the Fifth Avenue apartment of his brother-in-law Stephen Smith at four P.M. TV is now disgorging, hour by hour, fragments of news, shreds of gossip, speculation, comment on Kennedy's public indecision. Will he go or won't he go? Those who are supposed to be deciding learn chiefly by the television set what is being decided both in Washington and New York. No one knows all the elements involved; and even when the leader flies in from Washington to New York, quite late, to join his council of war, they are still confused. To Arthur Schlesinger, Kennedy confides McCarthy's suggestion on the Presidential succession. To Vanden Heuvel, Kennedy confides the story of Sorensen's Monday visit to Johnson—Kennedy feels that if he can turn Vietnam policy about, if Johnson will yield on negotiations, then he, Kennedy, has no need to run this year. Vanden Heuvel agrees.

The scene in the duplex Smith apartment is now quite confused; the TV sets are going, with their cascade of snatched fragments of news and comment. Those who wish to wait for more sober decision are overwhelmed by those who believe that decision has already been taken. The old loyalists and the young ideologues are all of them action men by instinct, and they divide themselves by habit into task forces. Upstairs, a special California task force starts on the long-distance phones to California, for the mechanics of the California election laws make the organization of that state the most urgent priority; a New York State task force is also on the telephones; other lieutenants of the operation are on the phone to Wisconsin, to Nebraska, to Indiana, to Massachusetts, mobilizing the Kennedy reserves of loyalty and personnel. But only the putative candidate knows all that is going on.

It is quite late at night when, finally back at his suite at the UN Plaza, Kennedy receives a critical telephone call. Sorensen has been in Rochester all day on business of his own, but has received a message from the White House. The President, says Sorensen, wants to act on the suggestion of naming a commission to review all Vietnam policy and now seeks names. Kennedy interrupts to fill Sorensen in on the last few hours' secret events. He, Kennedy, had this evening telephoned Daley in Chicago to say he was running. Daley had called President Johnson, and then relayed Johnson's message back to Kennedy. The President's response to Daley had confirmed Sorensen's information: the President has decided to appoint a commission to review Vietnam policy and is only waiting for Sorensen to suggest the names. In Daley's report to Kennedy, Secretary of Defense Clark Clifford has been appointed to coordinate the details. Already Senator Edward Kennedy has reached Clifford and an appointment has been made between Robert Kennedy and Clifford for eleven o'clock the next morning, Thursday. Now, says Kennedy, he wants Sorensen to accompany him on the delicate visit. Sorensen assents and they agree to rendezvous the next morning at one of the Pentagon entries.

The next morning Sorensen and Kennedy fly separately from New York and meet at the Pentagon unobserved. Like a corporal's guard, they pace back and forth outside the Pentagon before their meeting with Clifford. Sorensen, as tough a politician as he is a fine writer, is still insistent that Kennedy make no challenge in the primaries of 1968. Such a challenge will come to no good end, thinks Sorensen; he feels foreboding from the beginning. Kennedy listens as they prepare to meet Johnson's spokesman; Kennedy wants peace in Vietnam above all; but he tells Sorensen that this meeting will result in nothing.

The meeting—which lasts almost two hours—occurs at the midpoint of Clifford's re-examination of the Pentagon (see Chapter Four). And Clifford is receptive, sensitive, not at all hostile to the delicate conversation. The idea of a nationally eminent commission to turn policy on Vietnam about appeals to him. Robert Kennedy stresses that he is making no deal—he is not trading off a political candidacy for a change in policy. But he makes equally clear: if the administration really wants peace, he has no need to run. Clifford says he will report the President's reaction to this discussion to Kennedy or Sorensen by late afternoon. As they leave, Sorensen will later recall, Bobby's spirits rise. He is in elation. It is a way of getting out of the whole thing—if there is to be peace, he need not run.

Kennedy and Sorensen now lunch with a group of dove legislators—McGovern, Metcalf, Thompson and Morris Udall—and they urge him, almost unanimously, not to do this thing to Gene McCarthy, not to split the peace wing of the Democratic Party. Sorensen and Kennedy leave, and they wait for the Clifford phone call. It comes at 5 o'clock—Clifford talks to Sorensen at Kennedy's office while Kennedy listens in on an extension. The President has said no to the Kennedy proposal of a special Vietnam commission.[3]

It is that night, Thursday, that Robert F. Kennedy makes his decision—he will run; and Friday he is off from Washington early to tell a *kaffeeklatsch* of 175 lady civic leaders at Kings's Point, Nassau County, that he will announce his plans in Washington the next day. As he is leaving, he tosses the remark that "there are a lot of problems" and is queried if he has resolved them. "Yes, I have," says Kennedy, as he drives off. He has been on the telephone earlier, at nine o'clock, to tell the key members of his staff that he is running. In New York, Stephen Smith is already negotiating with the New York State politicians for their delegates, who will, certainly, be crucial at the convention. Salinger is organizing the California names. In Washington, left behind on Friday as the candidate flew to New York, is Sorensen, drafting the announcement statement.

[3] The President was, of course, in the next few days to see merit in the proposal; but, as President, he was to summon the commission in his own name, as his advisers, divorced from politics; and their meeting on March 25/26th was, indeed, the turning point of policy. (See Chapter Four.)

On this Friday, March 15th, all the cross-ties and cross-links in the Democratic Party's many factions are vibrating in intercommunication. On the McCarthy side, Richard Goodwin and Blair Clark, peace men both, are convinced that a fratricidal war between McCarthy men and Kennedy men in the primaries can only benefit Lyndon Johnson. They reach Senator Edward Kennedy and suggest that he join them in a flight to Green Bay, Wisconsin, where Eugene McCarthy will be that night. Clark and Goodwin wish to postpone the confrontation. Their thought is that each of the two rivals will run uncontested in primaries in states they agree to yield to each other until they come to California on June 4th; in California they will meet head-on, and the winner will take all. Without committing himself, Edward Kennedy consents to accompany them and explore whether the primaries can be contested without McCarthy and Kennedy disemboweling each other. In early evening the trio takes off from Washington for Wisconsin to see McCarthy. Robert Kennedy is returning to Washington this Friday evening to make the final decision of his announcement—but he must be host this same evening at a party at Hickory Hill scheduled weeks before. The party holds a cross-section of Washington's beautiful people—James Whittaker the mountaineer, Art Buchwald the philosopher, Rowland Evans the columnist, George Stevens the movie-maker, and others. Arthur Schlesinger and William Vanden Heuvel, hastily alerted in New York, fly down to Washington to add their advice to the final counsel on launching the campaign; and the press conference of announcement has been scheduled at the Senate Caucus Room for ten o'clock of the next day, Saturday.

It is not until eleven in the evening that the serious planners are able to sequester Robert Kennedy from his guests and hold conference on strategy and tactics. Whether Kennedy wishes it or not, Oregon and Nebraska will place his name on their primary ballots. But should he make an all-out transcontinental fight in other states, too; and, if so, how? Sorensen, Dutton, Schlesinger, Vanden Heuvel are for avoiding pitched battle with McCarthy; Adam Walinsky and Jeff Greenfield of the Senator's personal staff, activists and ideologues separated by a generation from the older men, are all for making an outright battle of it; Allard Lowenstein, midwife of the McCarthy campaign, is also present. They are all waiting for word from the Ted Kennedy-Clark-Goodwin flight to Green Bay; they argue about Sorensen's draft of tomorrow's announcement; and come to no decision.

Downstairs, the happy party floats through its gaieties to the end, the piano playing, singers singing. Upstairs, the serious participants finally turn in, trying to sleep. It is about five in the morning when Teddy Kennedy returns from Wisconsin and wakes Schlesinger to report the results of the expedition, the effort to divide the primaries and avert a head-on clash. He tells Schlesinger, "Abigail [Mrs. McCarthy] said no." He wakes Vanden Heuvel next and repeats, "Abigail said no." At about this time Robert Kennedy, dressed in knee-length pajamas, begins circulating the upstairs bedrooms, waking his guests, asking what he should do. Should he announce candidacy but skip the primaries? Or should he announce candidacy and challenge McCarthy directly in the primaries?

At seven o'clock in the morning, with the campaign announcement only three hours away, a group of haggard men assembles in the downstairs breakfast room: to wit, Arthur Schlesinger and Ted Sorensen, historic guardians of the seals of the Kennedy legitimacy; William Vanden Heuvel, personal confidant of the Senator; the Senator's younger brother, Senator Ted Kennedy; and Fred Dutton of California. They are unanimous. The perspective of this morning's announcement must point to the convention, it must not pit Kennedy against McCarthy in fratricidal strife, primary state by primary state, across the nation. They wait on Bobby Kennedy and someone asks where he is. Sorensen replies that he is probably wandering around the upstairs bedrooms, waking people up to find out whether they agree with him. Then Kennedy appears, opening the French windows, and walks in. He listens to the group. "I am *not* going to come out for McCarthy in the primaries," he said, "I'm going to do it myself. I'm going."

Two hours later, in the Senate Caucus Room, where, eight years, two and a half months earlier John F. Kennedy announced his candidacy, Robert Kennedy rises and says, "I am announcing today my candidacy for the Presidency of the United States. I do not run for the Presidency merely to oppose any man but to propose new policies."

The next ten days were disaster. For months all Kennedy's emotional energy had been invested in stalking decision within himself. No preparations at all had been made for a national campaign. Aside from his personal staff as Senator, no command existed. The shadow staff of Camelot was dispersed at dozens of private occupations and careers. And the first reflex of Robert F. Kennedy was action—for action seemed the only release his imagination could contemplate after his winter of private torment.

He lingered only briefly for questions at his Washington press conference on Saturday, and then, like a bullet shot from a gun, was off. A plane to New York. A St. Patrick's Day lunch at Charley O's restaurant. The Donegal Piper Band waiting for him, playing "The Minstrel Boy to the War Has Gone"; people smothering him, screaming at him, snatching at him, so that the New York police had to wedge him almost bodily into the line of march. And the march (with Nelson Rockefeller watching the parade that day from his upstairs window at Fifth Avenue and 62nd Street, trying to make his own decision whether to enter the race or not) surging up the avenue, the cheers and the boos, zealots trying to touch him in adulation, and the haters booing him, one young New York Irishman breaking through the police lines trying to slug him. A mixed opening.

The next week was worse. His bitterness at Johnson, his hatred of the war, his fear that his appeal to the student masses had been out-matched by Gene McCarthy—all these emotions had pressed on the voiceless Kennedy for weeks. Now, in a frantic back-and-forth flailing across the country, all the pressures and emotions fused without plan: from Kansas to Washington to Alabama to Tennessee, to New York to California, to Oregon, to Idaho, to Utah, to Nebraska, to Colorado, to Indiana, to New Mexico to Arizona, he flew in a single week, his major stops everywhere in the universities and colleges, where he sought to halt the erosion of his student support.

"Our country is in danger," he shrilled as he opened at Kansas State University, "not just from the foreign enemies but above all from our own misguided policies. . . . [The Vietnam war] has divided Americans as they have not been divided since your state was called 'Bloody Kansas.' . . . I regard our policy there as bankrupt. . . . I am concerned that at the end of it all there will only be more Americans killed, more of our treasure spilled out; and because of the bitterness and hatred on every side of this war more hundreds of thousands of Vietnamese slaughtered; so that they may say as Tacitus said of Rome, 'They made a desert and called it peace.' " Wherever he went, as thousands of students cheered, more and more the war took on the aspect of a personal vendetta between himself and Lyndon Johnson, until in Los Angeles he described the President as something even more than reckless or stupid—as sinister, a man "calling upon the darker impulses of the American spirit."

Carried away by his own emotions and their echo among the volatile cheering young, he could not quite grasp how television outlined his figure on the forty-second and one-minute snatches of evening news shows where the larger, national, mature audience saw him: hysterical, high-pitched, hair blowing in the wind, almost demoniac, frightening. In short, the ruthless, vindictive Bobby Kennedy again, action without thought, position without plan.

The dimensions of the campaign, and its meaning, were more easily discernible from headquarters in Washington than with Kennedy on the road—particularly after the renunciation of Lyndon Johnson.

There was, as one entered the hugh offices on L Street in Washington, the sense of the past recaptured. The call had gone out, and the veterans of the Kennedy movement were pouring in: from New York, Sorensen, giving up a lucrative law practice on one day's notice to take an unpaid leave of absence for the duration. From Boston, Kenneth

O'Donnell, who, within a week of the announcement, gave up his business there, an audio-visual educational enterprise which was promising his family, after years of hard work and near-penury in government service, the first taste of comfort. From Los Angeles, Pierre Salinger, who in his years of absence from politics had discovered a magic money-making touch, and was now abandoning business to go back to his cigar-smoking youth as a Kennedy outrider. From the government, Lawrence O'Brien, giving up a Cabinet post and already in the field organizing primary contests. From New York, Donald Wilson, giving up his position as Associate Publisher of *Life* Magazine, to supervise advertising and press media for Kennedy. From his studio, William Walton, forgoing his painting to organize the structure in New York. And later, after seeing McCarthy through the Wisconsin primary, Richard Goodwin, enlisting again for Kennedy to oversee television exposure in Indiana and California.

These men had seen John F. Kennedy through his 1960 campaign and had staffed and directed his administration. For them, the Kennedy name was a cause; they had a responsibility; the 28,000 pieces of mail received at the Kennedy offices in the first six days after announcement was the echo of what they had helped call into being eight years before.

Then there were the younger men, chiefly on the road with the candidate, his personal staff of speech-writers, Adam Walinsky, Jeff Greenfield, Peter Edelman. For them, also, the Kennedy movement was a cause—yet a cause with an intensity, a personalized focus, a bite and an edge that separated them from the men who had learned compromise in power.

Both groups were liberals. But with a difference. For those who had served with John F. Kennedy, the prime motivation of their action in 1968 was the war in Vietnam, the war which had sabotaged the slow, steady progress toward Kennedy goals which they had once helped to set. With a longer view of history, able to measure the road that America had come and sensing the mood of 1968 as different from the mood of 1960, men like Schlesinger and Sorensen saw Robert Kennedy as the natural leader to set the country on proper course in a new time. "We came in," said Sorensen at one point, "after eight years of Eisenhower doing nothing. The country needed new programs. Today the country has had a bellyful of programs." Men like Sorensen, tempered by responsibility, saw politics in terms of directions and adjustments, politics which must move but must not crush.

For the younger men, passion was of the essence; they had enlisted with Robert Kennedy not to carry on, but to change. He was not only their leader but, as they thought, the vehicle of their ideas, or a lever with which to pry open the structure of American politics.

Of all the young men, the most passionate and intense was Adam

Walinsky. For him, this campaign was a new crest in a bloodless revolution. The new radicals, said Walinsky one night in Indianapolis—and Walinsky considered himself one of the new radicals—had abandoned the old liberal ethos of centralization, the thought of Washington as the source of all national good. People had to be heard; people had to be met at the grassroots. Bobby, in Walinsky's view of his chief, had begun his separation from the old theories as early as 1965—with a first speech on education, advancing the thought that, just as schools test pupils, communities should be able to test their schools. A series of three speeches on the urban crisis had followed in 1966 elaborating another theme— that the welfare programs of the Federal government were no answer to the problems of the poor, but a positive destructive factor; the poverty program, for example, had hired thousands of middle-class people to tell poor people how not to be poor, a corps of "government-paid bitchers" competing to escalate their demands. All these thoughts, said Walinsky, were not new—they had come from the slow growth of observation on the part of Robert Kennedy once he had left the executive branch and observed the nature of executive power from the outside. But how does Kennedy's attack on central government differ then, I asked, from Barry Goldwater's in 1964? Simple, answered Walinsky—Barry wanted to leave local institutions as they were, with local power as it was; we want to transfer more power to local institutions and change them at the same time.

There was a conflict here in attitudes—between those who saw the Kennedy movement as part of the great sweep of American liberalism, and those who saw it as a force of revolution. For both, the spokesman was Robert F. Kennedy. Until the renunciation of Lyndon B. Johnson, both influences on Kennedy could gear smoothly in opposition to the Vietnam war. They could go together thereafter, grating against each other, until Hubert Humphrey announced his candidacy for the Presidency on April 27th. With the entry of that old-fashioned liberal into the race, the precise line and theme of the Kennedy campaign became confused; nor could anyone decide on its course except the candidate himself, whose immediate target at this point was winning the Democratic primary in Indiana.

Indiana was a strange state for a Kennedy of this generation to find his theme. His grandfathers would have been more at home there, for the Indiana Democratic Party (just as the Indiana Republican Party) belongs in a Yellowstone National Park of primeval political fauna; with the exception of the Illinois Democratic Party, it is the sturdiest political anachronism in the Middle West. The state's 23,000 patronage employees are required to contribute 2 percent of their gross salary to the coffers of the dominant, appointing Party. The Party pyramids from closed precinct caucuses to closed county caucuses, to eleven Congressional district conventions, to a state committee of twenty-two members that controls nominations, booty and appointments down to the lowest levels. This was the ancient crust of control on which Lyndon Johnson had counted before withdrawal; between them, Eugene McCarthy and Robert F. Kennedy were to wreck this control. But Kennedy's exercise was more interesting, for the pressures on him were greater; McCarthy's tug was on the new, growing, educated middle class; Kennedy's was on the old solid Democratic votes of the minorities and the working class, whom he had to enlighten.

All the pressures, all the advice, all the streams of influence met in the court of the candidate, for Kennedy traveled, not with a staff, but with a court; and each of its forty or fifty members, from longest-haired New Left to prettiest young girl reporter, from oldest Boston Irish politician to former members of the Kennedy Cabinet, thought that he or she, individually, was the person closest to Robert Kennedy. The force of his personality absorbed the advice both of liberals like Sorensen and Schlesinger and young hot-bloods like Walinsky; he could balance advice on Indiana from writer John Bartlow Martin (Hoosier-bred and steeped in local folklore) against advice from Gerard Dougherty, just out of Massachusetts and organizing the volunteers in South Bend as if they lived in Springfield; he could harken as well and as courteously to a Jack New-field, historian of the New Left, as to a Joseph Alsop, of the old patriotism. All were embraced in his affection, in his respect—yet finally, in Indiana, he, as candidate, had to synthesize their views; and by the last two weeks one could see them all fused in the standard speech.

The standard speech, as it evolved, was, finally, what Robert F. Kennedy himself, in all his various personae, thought. He would stand in the back of his open car or be squeezed through the mobs to the platform and, with his cowlick tumbling over his forehead, begin with a quip or a quote, usually some sally about his "ruthlessness" and how he had come here to defend himself against the charges; and then into the importance of beating the Indiana machine which was supporting Humphrey: "Under the law there is tremendous power in the people. . . . The fact is the *people* of this state are going to decide; they have to vote, and that's why I hope you don't waste that vote. I'm running for President of the United States, not Vice-President. This isn't a question of back-room politics, it's a question of who the people of Indiana want for President."

From there he would strike out into law-and-order—"I was the chief law-enforcement officer of the United States. I promise if elected I will do all in my power to bring an end to this violence. We needn't have to expect this violence summer after summer," and then more on the need for law enforcement, balanced against the need for opportunities in the ghettos and the end of injustice. Some local note would follow this, and then the theme of moving the government out of Washington, giving the people the chance to work out their own destinies. Then into his anti-Vietnam passages, delivered with tremendous force to tremendous applause, but reasoned and conditioned nonetheless: "I'm not in favor of unilateral withdrawal from Vietnam, that would hurt us in Southeast Asia. But we have the right to expect an honest government in South Vietnam, we've got the *right* to expect that out of every three dollars for refugees that are taxed from the people of Indiana, more than one of those three gets to the pockets of the refugees. We've got the right to expect them to draft their eighteen-year-old boys if we're going to draft our eighteen-year-old boys—that's what I'd do, I'd clean up that government of South Vietnam." From there he would work to world peace and glide into his various perorations: There were only five more days (or four more, or six more) to win it here in Indiana, and everyone had to get out and work. "Will you help me?" he would ask. "Do you know how?" And the crowds would roar yes. "Then if you know how, what are you college students doing here listening to a politician make a speech when you should be out canvassing?" And sometimes as the closing line, a quotation from George Bernard Shaw: "Some people see things as they are and say: why? I dream things that never were and say: why not?"

His public mood gradually grew more and more gay and, once away from the reflex bitterness at Lyndon Johnson that had conditioned his first ten days, he could begin to make people laugh. People who came to see the ruthless one, or had seem him storming only on TV, would be entranced by his banter. Interrupted by a crying baby in the audience, he might say, "Are you competing with me?" Then, after the baby continued crying and the mother would rise to leave, he would say, "Don't leave. Please don't leave. People will say I'm ruthless." Asked about Humphrey after his entry into the race, Kennedy quipped, "I think it was opportunistic of him to come into the race so late—in fact, I think he's very ruthless."

With farm audiences, particularly, he mocked his own weaknesses. A tiny piece of paper blew out of his hand in a Nebraska town; Kennedy watched it go, and quipped, "That's my entire farm program, give it back quickly"; and the farmers roared. He would describe his background: "I, too, come from a farm state." (Boos and cheers.) "The state of New York . . . leads the world in the production of sour cherries." (Cheers.) "Besides I have five dogs—am I getting through to you?" And when all else failed, there was always the family. "Other candidates will be coming through here, telling you how much they will do for the farmer. I'm already doing more for the farmer than any of them, and if you don't believe me, just look down my breakfast table or my lunch table any day of the week. We are consuming more milk and more bread and more eggs, doing more for farm consumption—than the family of any other candidate. I challenge the other two Democrats to do as well by the day of the primary, and I challenge Richard Nixon to do as well by next November."

Audiences never learned to recognize Robert F. Kennedy as an executive. What they came to know was a man who was in communication with them, a man who might take politics seriously, but not himself: the very opposite of the ruthless Bobby. And with Johnson's resignation his bitterness at the President wore off, too, and he could tell the audiences that the President had advised him, "Go west, young man, go west" —then a pause and the tag-line, "But I was in California at the time."

Beneath the frolic and the stump rallies remained, however, the substance of what Robert F. Kennedy had come to think. His programmatic speeches—the best-reasoned of the Democratic campaign—were rarely if ever reported, because programs bore readers, and newspapers have little space for what bores readers. His programs were quite specific: he was for a fundamental change in American draft laws, a no-exemption lottery instead of Selective Service. He was for negotiation in Vietnam but not for surrender. He was for imaginative use of the income tax to stimulate private enterprise for public welfare. He was against overcentralization of government in Washington. He was for law-and-order. He was for equality for all minorities. In short, in terms of program, what he was advocating was not too different from what Richard Nixon was advocating. The difference between them was one of spirit. Whatever Robert Kennedy said rang with a passion, a cry, a call on emotions. Kennedy could, by a single appearance, rouse frenzy, rouse love, rouse hate; and from such love and hate there was to come, a month later, the bullet that was to end his life. One had to follow Robert Kennedy to sense the response of passion to passion.

"There he is, there he is!" would come the squeal of the girls as he emerged from hotel or from car, and with a convulsion the mob would close on him, squeezing, touching, jostling, yelling, hallooing. As his cavalcade picked up speed, the screamers, the jumpers and the boppers would begin to bounce, dance, jiggle. His routes, posted by advance staff, would be lined with such crowds as one normally, in other years, might see in late October or early November. The matrons on their porches with their aprons, pin-curlers in hair; the old ladies of Indiana, with their white pinafores over blue dresses, teeter-tottering in tennis shoes to catch a glimpse of him and mothering him from afar ("He looks so tired, the poor boy, why do they make him work so hard?") Blue-collar workingmen thickened the crowds, a rare sight in daytime political campaigning, and one saw them shyly wipe their hands on overalls or shirts before offering hands to the candidate to shake. One grasped for analogy: Along the highway, as the car swept along, he was, obviously, The Kennedy, of the Family and Blood Royal, the Prince Coming to Town. In a working-class district he was Robin Hood. At night, in such places as Gary and South Bend on the final weekend, he was the Prince, Robin Hood and Pied Piper all combined. One remembers the children in the streets who followed him. At night, as photographers' lights popped like firecrackers, his cavalcade would cleave through a crowd as a ship does through water, sweeping up in its wake the adolescents and even younger ones. They followed as fast as they could run, loping, panting, singly and in clumps, keeping up as long as they could, until, exhausted, they would drop out and others, fresh, would pick up the relay, chasing, chasing as if something indefinable there at the head of the vanishing caravan was tugging all the children after them.

But it was in the ghettos one could best see the passions he aroused. For in the Negro ghettos of Indiana (as in the Mexican and black districts of California) analogy changed again. In the ghettos he was the Liberator, come to free the oppressed. For, above all other themes in his campaign, beyond any program, the fire that burned most hotly in him was for the underprivileged—for the minorities, for the Negroes, for the Appalachians, for the Mexican-Americans. The enemies of Robert F. Kennedy had already made him a saint in the black wards of America; a hundred TV visions had captured the fire of his impatience, his swollen, throbbing sympathy for people who ached, hungered, or were sick and untended, or had no jobs. The blacks knew it; and they clotted as they waited, old and young, Uncle Toms and Aunt Jemimas, Black Nationalists, cold-eyed extremists, solid black workingmen and their families. They would boil up like a volcanic cone about Kennedy's car, shouting, "Bobby, Bobby, please! Oh, Bobby, Bobby!" in a sighing, near-sexual orgy of exultation. Kennedy would waste little rhetoric in the ghettos; the fury and indignation he felt at the condition of blacks in America he spent rather at university campuses or excoriating white audiences for their indifference. His speeches at black rallies were short; they knew what this campaign was all about—it was for equal opportunity ("That's it, man"), it was for jobs for everyone ("That's it, man") and for school equality ("That's it," would come the chant). And he was going to change it all and they were going to help him change it; only it was going to be a change without violence ("That's it, too," one heard an occasional shout when Bobby laid law-and-order on the line in a black district). But how were they going to change it? By getting out and voting. How many people were registered? Up with the hands! Shame on you! Get registered. How many were going to vote? Up with the hands. And get your husbands to vote, and your neighbors, and your friends. Vote—

Touring a deep ghetto with Robert Kennedy was like being in the eye of a hurricane, and as dangerous. There were the hands always outthrust to touch him or to get the autograph. "Bobby, sign it for me, Bobby, please, please, *please, Bobby.*" "Bobby, Bobby, if you win, will you come back?" He would clamber up on the slippery red leather back-rest of his open car, and there, balancing, would talk through a bullhorn. The hands would reach for him, grabbing for a thread, a shoelace, a shoe; in the near-hysteria, anyone in the car with Bobby would become a bodyguard, protecting him. If he stooped to shake a single black hand, six more would clutch at him, at his fingers, up his wrist, to the elbow, tugging. One learned to protect him, not by clubbing down on the gripping hands, but by thrusting up to break their grip. For they would not let go. Once, a few days before the end of the Indiana campaign, the clutchers seized him and pulled so hard that in tumbling over the edge of the car he had instinct enough only to throw his elbow over his eyes to protect them; and slammed his jaw on the door of the car, breaking a front tooth and cutting open his lip. They loved him; but the frenzy of their love was a danger in itself, for an accident was always instantly possible, anywhere, as the black youngsters climbed over the car, got into the seat with him, and crusted themselves on the hood and fenders. When the car tried to pick up speed and they tumbled to the ground, rolling over like bouncing balls as they fell or jumped from the vehicle, there was always, constantly, the danger that a child would be run over—and the frenzy might turn instantly to hate at the sight of blood.

Over and over, his staff warned Kennedy of crowds; over and over, those who traveled warned of how close to the edge of violence he brought himself by exposing himself to mobs, friendly or otherwise. Yet he would not listen. When it came to blacks, or Mexicans, or Indians, or any underprivileged, there was no cold Bobby—he was the Liberator, on horse, screaming with every fiber of his being that this was the purpose of power and government, to take care of them; and he was careless of whatever danger, political or personal, might lurk on the way.

The old machinery in Indiana could offer no resistence to such emotions, make no counter-call on any loyalties, and, outflanked by Kennedy on one side, McCarthy on the other, it collapsed. The vote came in neatly, as predicted by all, on May 7th, 1968. The first percentile, a few minutes after seven, showed the break: 53 percent for Kennedy, 26 percent for Branigan, 22 percent for McCarthy. The early lead shrank substantially in the next quarter of an hour to 45 (Kennedy), 29 (Branigan) and 26 (McCarthy). And then fixed itself, within an hour, very close to its final percentage: Kennedy 42 percent (320,485), Branigan 30.7 percent (234,312), McCarthy 27.4 percent (209,165). Kennedy arrived late at his hotel suite to watch the final returns, and stood for a moment watching television as Eugene McCarthy conceded defeat. What mattered, McCarthy was saying eloquently, as Bobby watched, was what a candidate stood for—not whether he came in first, second or third. "That's not the way I was brought up," growled Bobby Kennedy, talking back to the image on television, "we were brought up to win."

The Kennedys were indeed brought up to win. But never did any Kennedy face a more delicate, difficult or uphill battle in any of their election contests in Massachusetts, in New York, or across the face of America than did Robert F. Kennedy in 1968; and one must use a number of different prisms to view all his interlocked problems.

There was the grand strategy of personal rivalries to be solved first. He must, felt Kennedy, say no word of criticism in public against Eugene McCarthy, his face-to-face opponent in the primaries. Although he disliked Eugene McCarthy, he knew an attack would backfire. McCarthy, for students, was the knight *sans peur et sans reproche,* and Kennedy would need all their good-will and energy once McCarthy was downed in the primaries. Those energies and that good-will would be essential on his side of the convention in August. Thus, in the direct primary fights, he must focus his attacks on the absent third contender, Hubert Humphrey, denouncing him as surrogate for Lyndon Johnson even though he liked Humphrey. But he could not attack Humphrey too bitterly either, for after the convention he would need Humphrey's support in the general election. Yet he must best both Humphrey and McCarthy so clearly in the primaries that there would be no doubt among the old-fashioned delegate-brokers in the structured states of the East and Midwest that Kennedy was, beyond doubt, the man who could win for them in November.

The strategy of assembling delegates was equally complicated, and that was entrusted to headquarters back in Washington. No projection of the late-starting campaign, not even the most optimistic, could foresee in early spring more than 800 of the 1,312 delegate votes that Robert F. Kennedy would need for a majority at the Chicago convention—and that optimistic count assumed he could win most or all of the delegates in California, New York, Indiana, Oregon and those New England states not already sewed up by McCarthy. This came only to 600. Other delegates would be corralled one by one in such key states as Pennsylvania, Ohio, Michigan, New Jersey, for in none of these industrial states could any power-broker deliver an entire delegation *en masse,* as could Richard Daley in Illinois. No one knew which way Daley would finally go as between Humphrey and Kennedy; nor could one judge the final preference of any of the lesser delegate-brokers across the country. Like Daley, they would all be watching Kennedy's show of strength in the primaries, and convention tactic with all of them was very simple: hang loose, don't commit, wait and see. Watch Bobby's crowds, ask yourself who can do more for your local ticket in November right there in Akron, in Pittsburgh, in Providence, in Seattle—Humphrey? or McCarthy? or Kennedy?

Primary and convention strategy locked. The primaries—if they were won—would give Kennedy bargaining power at the convention. But the use of that bargaining power depended on another series of ifs: if the war continued or grew in unpopularity, if Humphrey could not dissociate himself from the war, if McCarthy's resentment could be mollified after his defeat, if any substantial number of state leaders stayed uncommitted on the first ballot—then, if Humphrey could be stopped on the first ballot, the McCarthy votes must crumble and go to Kennedy on the second ballot; then it would be Kennedy all the way as the old-timers, wanting their piece of the Kennedy action, would hasten to come over to the movement.

No one can guess now what might have happened had Robert Kennedy lived. Retrospect leads to no conclusion, for one must look back across the victory of Richard M. Nixon, the violence of the Chicago convention, the act of assassination itself. As one tries to unravel a never-to-be future from the record of the known past, one cannot say how each contemporary "if" would have affected the next "if" in the play of events.

"If" Robert F. Kennedy had survived his California victory and then carried off the lion's share of New York's delegates in the next primary test; 'if" he had come to Chicago with his claim on the loyalties of the new politics, and his respect from the leaders of the old politics, would he not then, certainly, have been the only possible compromise between the legitimacy of the old and the aspirations of the new? But "if," as this correspondent believes, a Kennedy candidacy would certainly have emerged from Chicago, would not the Republicans have foreseen that possibility—and, in Miami, might they not have chosen a Rockefeller or a Reagan over Nixon? And "if" Robert Kennedy had emerged triumphant from Chicago, could he then have beaten a Rockefeller, a Reagan or a Nixon?

Through all this cloud of "ifs," however, a profile emerges. Kennedy was, in 1968, a bridge. He knew and recognized the enormously potent political force of the young all across the country. Hack politicians everywhere, appalled by their own children returning from college with long hair and wild new ideas, sensed even in their own families new swells rising. The old men could not possibly understand the new politics of participation; but they required some respect and gratitude for what they themselves had done in community, state and country. Kennedy, who came of a family of their lineage and tradition, understood them. He understood both the old and the new; he could understand the nature of a political deal as Gene McCarthy never could, the mutuality of obligation in politics; yet he also understood what bothered the young, the Negroes, the intellectuals. He might have healed his Party. But the "ifs" trail off from there, echoing without answer in the corridors of history, just as they do in the case of his brother, President John F. Kennedy, leaving us only with a return to an older concept of history: that the choice or loss of a great leader may affect mankind far more than those remorseless "engines of history" which Marx saw as the moving thrusts of change in his Hegelian dialectic.

As Robert F. Kennedy saw it in the spring of 1968, all the "ifs" of the campaign depended on him, and him alone. He must voice himself clearly enough in the primaries to rouse the people.

He railed bitterly against the new descriptions of his campaign in the Eastern press and liberal journals: they were styling him the "new, conservative Kennedy." Didn't those people read, he would ask, hadn't they read his speeches over the last two years? He hadn't changed, the country was changing. Law-and-order? That was what the *people* wanted him to talk about. Everyone—even the labor unions. The labor people were telling him that their unions were more worried about riots and crime than they were about wages and hours. That's what he'd learned campaigning himself—law-and-order was important, why shouldn't he talk about it?

He was equally sensitive to criticism of his reckless expenditure of energy in the primary campaign. "Is there any other way," he would ask an old friend, "is there any other way of breaking through at the convention except by doing it the primary way?" This convention could not be won in the back rooms; and thus, there was no other way. He must be everywhere at once, up at dawn each day, to bed after midnight, proving his qualities as President not in executive posture, but as stump-speaker and rally-rouser, to the utter exhaustion of body and vitality.

From Indiana the campaign had to move directly to Nebraska, where, a week later, on May 14th, Kennedy, in a state overwhelmingly farm-oriented, with only 2 percent Negro population, swamped both McCarthy and Humphrey with his first clean majority win (51.6 percent). Then, in the last two weeks of May, the Oregon, California and South Dakota primaries were upon him simultaneously, requiring him to dart back and forth across the continent and up and down the Pacific Coast. In Oregon, on May 28th, he met the first defeat of any Kennedy at the polls; McCarthy won by 44.7 percent to 38.8 percent. "Oregon," said one of Kennedy's staff, "is all one great white middle-class suburb. It's a good state. It has no problems. We frightened them." And after Oregon, California became his rendezvous with destiny; for California he had to have, and, thus, the exhausted man redoubled his exertions.

All the last ten days of his effort are clouded in memory by omens of violence; and in retrospect in these clouds Robert Kennedy was a lightning rod.

Somehow in an increasingly violent world, May saw a new high of outbursts. Martin Luther King had been dead only a few weeks, and the memory of that tragedy lingered. Students were rioting in Paris against evils they could not define, tearing up the paving stones in Paris to make barricades. Students were rioting at Columbia University. The daily news those weeks paraded episodes: a riot at Stanford University; a riot at the University of Colorado; riots elsewhere; in northern California, the last week of his life, unknown saboteurs blew up three utility towers in the San Francisco Bay area, depriving 30,000 homes of power and light.

Disturbances in campaigning were mounting; they were not yet of the ferocity they were to reach in Humphrey's fall campaigns, but were already alarming. Sometimes they were silly—as when a group of student marauders in Los Angeles thought it bright to wedge a car into the campaign motorcade, then stall it there, between the candidate's car and the following press buses as if, physically, they could separate Kennedy from the attention of the press that followed him. Placards at Kennedy rallies ranged from the normally hostile to the outright sick: SELL-OUT WITH BOBBY, read adversary placards at a Santa Barbara rally, WE WANT A MAN NOT A NAME. DID 20,000 AMERICANS DIE FOR A COALITION IN VIETNAM? WHO KILLED YOUR BROTHER?

Against this background on every nightly show in California stormed the Kennedy. Not the elegant cool John F. Kennedy as America remembered him. But the exhausted Robert F. Kennedy, his emotions rubbed raw, disturbing the tranquillity of the evening with his vision of America and the passionate hope of making it a country without miseries. For at the end, apart from the smooth, romantic TV media presentations in which he was professionally packaged, the Kennedy the TV news showed was talking from the heart: about the war in Vietnam, and how it had to be brought to an end; about law-and-order; but, above all, about the sorrowing millions of underprivileged. He had seen too many children with bellies bloated by hunger in Appalachia, in Mississippi, in the highlands; he knew of the grape-pickers and knew that Cesar Chavez was not just a labor leader, but a symbol of the unformed yearnings of Mexican Americans who were neither black nor white; and when he spoke of the plight of the American Indians, of adolescents who hanged themselves before maturity out of sheer desperate misery, he quivered visibly.

Thus California saw, in this last week, a man whose intensity disturbed their peace. Californians might, for example, see a forty-second snatch of a Robert F. Kennedy rally in the deep Negro stretches of Watts, and the emotions he roused threatened peaceful citizens all the way from

Beverly Hills to Pasadena. They could see him one night in an exhausted outburst to a minority group; and then, by the most deft and artistic intercutting, be switched by their television sets to Washington, where a carnival demonstration showed war-whooping Indians in their feathered headdresses, screaming and shrilling as they made an attempt to assault the Supreme Court of the United States itself. Robert F. Kennedy always made fine copy and gave occasion to great filmic artistry; but there could be no doubt about the nature of his public image: he was the disturber. He meant what he said. If he were elected, he would perform as he promised and the country would change.

It is difficult to remember the last few days of the campaign and his life except as whirlwind and motion; yet on everyone who followed Kennedy there knocks the remembered moments of his kindness. This correspondent remembers best the candidate's amusement and sympathy when I, already exhausted by too much emotion and campaigning across the country, took to bed. He would walk down the corridor from his fifth-floor suite and tease me for not being up and ready to go at whatever hour it was—six, seven or eight in the morning. But then, relenting, would sit for a few minutes by the side of the bed to give a full account of yesterday's campaigning, and a promise to be a good leg-man on today's exertions of Robert Kennedy.

But he himself was already stretched to the limits of physical and emotional exertion. Advisers argued with him to knock it off—the national campaign was bigger than California, more important, it needed his attention and mind. His polls in that last week in California turned upward, and in his final weekend debate with McCarthy he scored well; friends urged him to relax, to slow the pace. But he would not. Politics to him were people. Though he knew as well as any man the modern technology of politics, of polls, medias, throwaways, spots, costs, promotions, canvassing, when it came right down to it, he really enjoyed the presence of people and their response to his message. The grabbing, pulling, screaming ecstasy made him feel alive. When he spoke, his hands were always moving, reaching, pleading, begging the people to come with him. In formal interviews or appearances on television, his voice might be controlled; but if one watched the hands, they were always writhing, trying to grip the people. He had, in California, in a poorly managed campaign, let his passion outrun his energies—but he was carrying it off, nonetheless, by simple will of spirit.

On the last Monday before the primary, he had risen as usual at seven and barnstormed California from north to south until late at night, in San Diego, out of sheer emptiness of any further vitality, he was forced to break off a speech at a rally and sit down. He could run no further on that lap. He was tired.

*   *   *

He slept late the next morning, on the day of voting, at the white beach home of Evans and John Frankenheimer by the Pacific. Six of the youngest children—with their dog and a friendly monkey—had been flown out from Hickory Hill to be with him on this day of rest, and Ethel slept late, too. When I arrived, about noon, he was playing with the boys, and it was no time to talk politics. We walked along the beach, kicking rubbery dark green kelp on the sand, and talked of the pollution of this beautiful coast and the disappearance of the great old kelp beds; we compared the Pacific to the Atlantic and he preferred Cape Cod. The sun would not break through, a chill mist hung heavy on the ground; but he stripped off his flowered sun-shirt and plunged in, nonetheless. A huge roller came in from the sea, and the bobbing head of one of two children went under. Bobby dived. For a moment one could not see them in the surf until he came up with David, whom he had pulled from the undertow. A large red bruise now marked his forehead where he had bumped either sand or the boy; he chided the boy gently for going beyond his depth, but the boy was safe.

Since the pool was less dangerous for the children, we all now came up to the poolside, where Ethel, equally tired, her hands placid in her lap, watched as he growled, teased them, let them rough-house him. He threatened them jokingly: "Mummy's so tired that she's going to rest next week, and I'm going to have to take care of you myself. How do you like that?" They laughed, for they would have loved it.

There was no full week free at any time in 1968 for him to be alone with his family, and the next week, as scheduled, would have been just as bad. If he won, the schedule was going to give him just two days of rest in California—Wednesday and Thursday. Early Friday he would be off by jet to an afternoon rally at Niagara Falls, New York; another jet the same afternoon would carry him to Long Island to catch the workers of Republican Aviation coming off shift; then would follow two rallies at shopping centers nearby; then into Manhattan (with just time enough to change to black tie) to attend the Firemen's Ball of the Hotel Commodore. The next day, Saturday, up early for a rally in Manhattan, then to Westchester for several more, then—and then, on and on, through every one of New York's forty-one Congressional districts, without another day's rest until the primary on June 18th. New York was enormously difficult—no statewide primary, no candidates' names on the ballot, delegates elected by Congressional districts and the McCarthy people well organized. He would have to do it the hard way, district by district, delegate by delegate, morning, noon and night; he needed as many of New York's 190 convention votes as he could get to show his coattail-pulling power to the professional politicians of the Midwest.

But all that, he thought, was yet to come. Only once in the lazy hours by the pool did he talk politics as, suddenly, he porpoised up from the water and began to talk about McCarthy and Humphrey. He liked Humphrey and felt Humphrey was trapped; if he (Kennedy) could do really well here in California today, that would affect the vote in New York; and if he did well in New York, that would affect all the Midwestern states too, no matter how many delegates Humphrey thought he had sewed up. Gene McCarthy intrigued him more; the two men could never understand each other. They simply did not like each other, but he wanted McCarthy's student youngsters with him after the victory here in California today; his people were already talking with McCarthy's student leaders, and he knew all the splits in the McCarthy camp. He repeated again McCarthy's offer to step aside after one term as President and turn the office over to him. "Can you imagine that?" said Bobby, and ducked under the water again.

He was tense through the early afternoon, moving from place to place about the house and the pool, until a first flash of news came through. CBS had done some early sampling of voters as they left the polls, and its analysts now guessed the vote would be Bobby 49 percent, McCarthy 41 percent, the Lynch-Humphrey slate 10 percent. He sat there in the mist, in blue pullover and flowered beach-trunks, and offered no visible reaction to the news. Ethel asked whether that was good enough. In turn, he asked what the results were from South Dakota, also voting that day. If rural South Dakota as well as urban California both went for him on the same day, that would be *really* good. It would influence results not only in New York but across the nation. Richard Goodwin and Fred Dutton had joined us by the pool before the first news came in, and one of them offered the thought that if the 49 percent in California could be pushed up to 50 percent, a clean majority, it would be total breakthrough. With a spasm, Kennedy became crisp executive again. How many precincts were there in California? 20,000? And 1 percent more of the vote was only 30,000 votes? That meant that an extra two votes per precinct and he would have a clean 50 percent! Was everybody out working? he wanted to know. Could they put on the extra push in the precincts to get those extra two votes to the polls? Make sure the entire organization is working all out—right now! Then, slowly, he relaxed, as the warmth and taste of victory came over him. He yawned, stretched his arms, suddenly drowsy, and said he thought he would take a nap. "We ought to get back early to the hotel," he said, "say, about seven o'clock." He was sure, now, it was going to be an early win, requiring an early appearance; and thus he left, relaxed and confident, to rest.

It was the last time any stranger would have a chance to see Robert F. Kennedy alone. By eight o'clock the Royal Suite on the fifth floor of the Hotel Ambassador was overflowing with people. He had acquired in his four years as Senator and his eleven-week campaign a host of hangers-on, all bound to him by affection and loyalty, each pressing on his privacy, all of whom he had invited to come spend the evening with him and watch the returns.

Californians and Bostonians, staff members and old friends, family and strangers all were there; including one early arrival from McCarthy headquarters, a young student leader rushing over to enlist with Kennedy even before the final count was in. They wandered back and forth through the six-room suite, Kennedy circulating among them; at one point he bounded from the telephone into the large living room, his glee absolutely uncontained. He held his hand up in the victory sign and said, "I just want to give you one precinct of Indians in South Dakota—878 for Kennedy, two for Johnson, zero for McCarthy! How about that?" By nine o'clock, in what later turned out to be a gross overestimate, CBS made its first projection—Kennedy 52 percent, McCarthy 38 percent, and the room began to boil, as the drinks were poured, and the guards at the end of the corridor unsuccessfully strove to keep the suite sealed against the suddenly gathering throng. Pierre Salinger spread word to friends that as soon as the public victory ceremony downstairs was over, Bobby and Ethel and a handful of old-timers would join at the Factory, a night club, for a private celebration. Hunted down by jubilant well-wishers from room to room, Kennedy momentarily sought privacy in his bathroom with Sorensen and Goodwin to discuss what their approach should now be to the McCarthy movement. There, his mood was otherwise. The day's reports from New Jersey and Ohio back East were bothersome; he was troubled by the failure of his lieutenants to make headway there; and the New York primary was going to be more difficult than anticipated. The elation of the evening's victory was already fading and deep concern about the weeks ahead showing.

But the script of election night unrolled as it had so many times before for the Kennedys in so many places. First, the ritual appearance before each of the three great networks; then the wait for the defeated candidate to concede; then the effort to clear the rooms of self-important strangers who inevitably seep into a political celebration; then the final girding for descent into the bearpit, into whatever ballroom or hall in whatever hotel has been designated as the victory room in which the candidate will thank his workers. Those experienced in politics, or who travel long on campaigns, grow weary of such ritual and, above all, of the stamping, yelling, crowding, sweating masses of workers and curiosity seekers who squeeze into the tight space to hear, see or touch the victor in the flesh.

Thus, only a few of the old guard went down with Kennedy. The rest saw him off down the hall, entwined in the serpentine of television cables and crew men, the photographers winking their flashes as they fell backward trying to snatch pictures as he strode forward, a swollen, moving bumble of people; the moving serpentine is a signature of political importance.

We lingered upstairs, watching him on television five floors below, heard him finally say "On to Chicago and let's win there," and then we slowly prepared to join him at the Factory after he had extricated himself from the crowd.

Below, the advance men, as always, had prepared a plan with two alternates. He could leave the platform, turn left, reach the main corridor of the Ambassador, thence to the stairwell and out to his car. But that would be crowded. Or he could turn right, go out through the kitchen, then come back to the stairwell and go down. No one *decided* which way he should turn as he left the platform; but he turned right to go out through the kitchen. His passion had aroused the best and the beast in man. And the beast waited for him in the kitchen.

They said mass for him at St. Patrick's Cathedral in New York, a most beautiful church, and it was entirely appropriate that they chose St. Patrick's for Robert F. Kennedy. Not because he was New York's Senator, but because St. Patrick's has always been that church in America most deeply involved in politics. On the land which the Church had bought in the upper meadows of Manhattan in 1810, it had decided in 1850 to build a Cathedral and, in 1858, laid the cornerstone. Catholics heard the first mass at St. Patrick's in 1879—and from then on it was known as "the powerhouse" to politicians, a force in the life of the city and the nation. St. Patrick's had stood for both good and bad in American politics. But part of its tradition was change, as was the Kennedys'. And so it had become one of the great symbols of life in the world's greatest city, which is the coarse, yet closest, attempt of men of all colors, skins, faiths and tongues to live together in community. Thus, for Robert F. Kennedy, Richard Tucker, trained as a synagogue cantor, sang in St. Patrick's. The mass was read in English. Andy Williams sang "The Battle Hymn of the Republic," the original freedom song of the Protestants, and the congregation slowly found voice and joined in the singing, a slow, melodious dirge.

We crowd-counted, as political people always do, as the cortege wound away from the Cathedral through New York City. So many of us who followed could not quickly adjust from the manners of last week's political cavalcades to the procession of death. And the crowd was better than good—at least half a million; all of them, somberly, with him. It was only, however, when the funeral train that was to bear him to Washington emerged from the tunnel under the Hudson that one could grasp what kind of man he was and what he meant to Americans. Kenneth O'Donnell said, as he glanced from the windows of the train, "Now you can see what the Hell it was all about—he could really turn them on."

For 225 miles from the Hudson to Washington, he had turned them on. There were the family groups: husband holding sobbing wife, arm about her shoulders, trying to comfort her. Five nuns in a yellow pick-up truck, tiptoeing high to see. A very fat father with three fat boys, he with his hand over his heart, each of the boys giving a different variant of the Boy Scout or school salute. And the people: the men from the great factories that line the tracks, standing at ease as they were taught as infantrymen, their arms folded over chests. Women on the back porches of the slum neighborhoods that line the tracks, in their housedresses, with ever-present rollers in their hair, crying. People in buildings, leaning from office windows, on the flat roofs of industrial plants, on the bluffs of the rivers, on the embankments of the railway cuts, a crust on every ridge and height. Pleasure boats in the rivers lined up in flotillas; automobiles parked on all the viaducts that crossed the line of the train. Brass bands—police bands, school bands, Catholic bands. Flags: individual flags dropped in salute by middle-aged men as the train passed, flags at half-staff from every public building on the way, entire classes of schoolchildren holding the little eight-by-ten flags, in that peppermint-striped flutter that marks every campaign trip. He turned them on, black and white, rich and poor. And they cried.

There, as one passed through New Jersey, Pennsylvania, Maryland and Delaware, to Washington, was the panorama of American industrial might. There were the famous brand names of all America's skills from steel and chemicals to pickles and mustards. There were the old red-brick factories of the last century and the new industrial architecture of glistening turquoise, orange, blue, red-tiled electronic plants, their workers no longer uniformed in blue overalls but in sterile white smocks. There, for example, was the Ford plant, and a delivery yard of almost a quarter of a mile of gleaming new Mustangs, shining on racks in their glossy colors, promising pleasure for the pleasure society; and the medicinal plants, with all their secret wonders, too. It was a nation of unlimited skills and crafts but plagued by the madness of violence.

It should have been a four-hour trip by train; accidents, crowds, and fatalities in the crowds delayed the trip, stretching it to eight and a half hours. Thus, slowly, almost grotesquely, then with relief and acceptance, the atmosphere in the funeral train changed. It could not have changed without the bravery and grace of behavior of Ethel Kennedy, her black veil turned back, proceeding through the cars of the cortege to speak friendship and comfort to his grieving friends. One finally understood aboard the train the purpose of an Irish wake: to make a man come alive again in the affection and memory of his friends. The memory of Robert Kennedy came back and the range of his friendships slowly transformed the mood from stark tragedy to an abashed yet real joy in this companionship brought together by one man's personality. There were the elder statesmen of other times, the Averell Harrimans, the John McCones; also the Douglas Dillons, the Robert McNamaras; there were the blacks of every range of his experience and devotion: Mrs. Martin Luther King, Bayard Rustin, the Reverend Abernathy, young John Lewis; there were those who had flown in from other countries: the Duke of Devonshire and Lord Harlech; there were the political leaders, Republicans and Democrats alike: the Javitses, the Lindsays, Senators Morse, Douglas, Yarborough, McGovern, and so many others, too numerous to count; there were the men of the scholar elite—Arthur Schlesinger, Walter Heller, McGeorge Bundy, Richard Neustadt, John Kenneth Galbraith; there was the old crowd, the early command: O'Brien, O'Donnell, Powers, Bruno; there were the new frontiersmen, Goodwin and Sorensen; there was his inner staff: Angie Novello, Walinsky, Greenfield. And famous writers, famous TV stars, famous athletes, beautiful ladies, and just plain friends. All journeying to Arlington, where the Harvard band would play "America the Beautiful" for Robert F. Kennedy, class of '48.

The cortege detrained in Washington four and a half hours late. But the people had waited for him, as they would have waited for no other Senator in the nation. Only a Presidential ceremony and sorrow could have held them there that long. For seven miles along the route they waited, having positioned themselves for hours through the hot sun. And now in the dark, spontaneously they made ceremony for him. As the cortege passed through the streets of Washington, the files on either side flared in firefly spots of matches held aloft, in cigarette lighters burning as torches in honor; some had brought candles. Silently, without a sound, the cortege rolled up from the station, then through the grounds of Capitol Hill, then down Constitution Avenue by the Department of Justice, a moving twinkle of flashbulbs bursting always just ahead of the coffin so those behind could tell where the procession was headed. Service guards lined the road, all at attention, and as one passed by Resurrection City, where 2,000 poverty-stricken were encamped in demonstration, one noticed the guard reinforced by policemen in riot helmets to quench an outbreak. A pause just beyond Resurrection City so that a choir on the floodlit steps of the Lincoln Memorial might sing a hymn—and then over the bridge and up the knoll to Arlington Cemetery, where John F. Kennedy lay. The green slope glistened in the night. President Lyndon Johnson waited there, as did Vice-President Hubert Humphrey, both in grief. The flag-draped coffin was brought forward in the candlelight of the mourners, and the brief ceremony ended quietly without noise, fanfare or taps.

It is difficult to remember Robert F. Kennedy either as friend or man of state and, at the same time, fit him into the pattern of 1968 politics. He had disturbed those politics, fought lustily and robustly, given his adversaries as much trouble and as many hard knocks as they had given him.

Yet it is even more difficult, at this early time, to position him by himself in American history. Had he lived, history would surely have accorded him his own place, for he was distinct as an individual. But, as it is, what Robert F. Kennedy left behind cannot be separated from what was left behind by his brother, John F. Kennedy. Together they created a movement and gave it form. They must go down in memory together; and I think each would have had it so.

Perhaps it is best to see them not in the perspective of the single decade of the sixties, but over a century, in the sweep of the generations that carried the Kennedys from Ireland to Boston and out into America. Perhaps the beginning memory lies a hundred years before our times, in that passage of American experience which Thoreau best captured in his "Cape Cod." Walking south from Boston in the fall of 1849, the Concord philosopher came upon a shipwreck at Cohasset, fifteen miles south; the beach was crowded with helpless Irish immigrants—mothers, children, fathers crying for those who drowned in the storm, within sight of the promised land, the promise denied. The Kennedys came to America at just that time before the Civil War, handkerchief migrants, outcasts in snow-cold Boston. And there, with the rest of the Irish, they suffered and shivered, hungered and strove, and rioted their way up to the light. Those of us born in Boston, whose parents came after the Irish, who were schooled by Irish schoolteachers and kicked about by Irish cops, knew both the sweet of what they could give and the rough of what they had learned.

The Kennedys passed through four generations, taking what they could of the city and country; Joseph P. Kennedy, the father of the present generation, studied at the Boston Latin School, where Franklin and Emerson had schooled, then went on to see how it looked from Harvard. From Joseph P. Kennedy, financier, multi-millionaire, ambassador, his sons learned to see it from on top, but with a wisdom that surpassed his shrewdness; they learned, on their own, that it was as important to give as to take. Somehow, over a century of experience, the family had come to the knowledge of high citizenship: that they were responsible for what happened in their country. The story of the Irish in America should be written only by one of them—how they came, in state after state, to feel that they must have a say in control, that they, too, must participate in the decisions of politics. John F. Kennedy and Robert F. Kennedy reached for the top; they assumed responsibility for an entire nation, sought and fought for what they considered, rightly or wrongly, was good for all. As such, they left behind all narrower ethnic, regional or economic interests and became part of the greater American history. This was the hope of the founding fathers and those who wrote the Declaration and Constitution: that under their concept of men as equal in opportunity, all those who might enter this land would eventually assume, personally, responsibility for the general welfare and the common weal.

This is where they sat in the scroll of American history—knowing its past and remembering its sufferings, understanding its power and the mechanics of its government, purposing to make it better for those who came after, as others had made it better for them. Though they were men of different style, they shared the same love of learning, and delighted in the same turn of phrase. One remembers best of the countless speeches of both men from California to Maine, from Cadillac Square in Detroit to New York's garment district, a passage they both shared and equally believed in. Either one, at any time, any place, when lost for words or for specific program would go into what we reporters used to call "the Dante sequence." Both quoted it in the same way: "Franklin D. Roosevelt, accepting his second Presidential nomination, said, 'Governments can err, Presidents do make mistakes, but the immortal Dante tells us that Divine Justice weighs the sins of the cold-blooded and the sins of the warm-hearted on a different scale. Better the occasional faults of a government living in the spirit of charity, than the consistent omissions of a government frozen in the ice of its own indifference.' "

To them, indifference was the greatest sin of all; and neither was indifferent to any human cause, at home or abroad. Their voices mingle still in my memory, ringing at a score of streetcorners, the high-pitched tenor and timbre of sound so much alike, quoting Roosevelt quoting Dante. Their call was to the heart; that is why people voted for them.

CHAPTER SEVEN

—

APPETITE FOR APOCALYPSE:
THE ISSUE OF LAW-AND-ORDER

So Robert F. Kennedy was dead. There he lay now in Arlington beside his brother. Lawmakers burst into debate over gun control, philosophers analyzed the nature of violence, and the nation was described as grieving.

Yet "grief" suddenly seemed like a faintly obsolete word. Nor would "shock," "rage," "dismay" do either. Such anthropomorphic words have been, for generations, the most convenient shorthand of political observation, inviting writers to describe millions of people as if their emotions were fused by a single spasm of "agony," "despair," "vengeance," or "sorrow"—as if, indeed, they were one community. But it is impossible ever to describe a great nation as if it were a community—and in 1968 the essence of the matter was that the old faith of Americans in themselves, as a community of communities, seemed to be dissolving. "Grief" would not do as a word that bound. Questions were more relevant: What kind of people were we? What kind of people were we becoming? Where, out of what evil of spirit, did American violence spring? What enemies, what hidden assassins lurked in the old-fashioned, friendly crowds that once had cheered candidates on their way? Out of what shadows, in which once-quiet neighborhoods would leap the mugger, the killer, the rapist? What ties bound us one to the other as kin? The murder of Robert F. Kennedy, following only eight and a half weeks after the murder of Martin Luther King, had come midway through a year pocked with bombings, arson, demonstrations and random shootings—and had been preceded by three years of riot, crime and summer terror, in a climate of ever-rising hate and fear, to prepare the way for the great concern that now dominated the second half of the campaign of 1968.

In politics, this concern was called the issue of "law-and-order." But the very term "law-and-order" enraged millions of good, self-styled "liberals" across the country. The phrase "law-and-order" had descended through American politics wrapped in the rhetoric of the right; it smacked of night riders, of vigilantes, of union-busting, of the witch-hunts and Red-hunts of A. Mitchell Palmer. "Law-and-order," insisted the orthodox liberals, was a code word for racism, as if whoever used the phrase now was determined to club blacks into submission. Blacks in the ghettos of Chicago and New York clamored to their city governments for more and more police, more and more protection. But any white man who used the phrase was suspect of covert bigotry. "Law-and-order," chanted the liberals, was the justifying slogan for repression, a repression they felt imminently about to close on the ever expanding freedoms sanctioned by the most permissive Supreme Court in American history. "Law-and-order," finally, felt most liberals, was so explosive and dangerous a phrase that to talk of it in public was tantamount to indiscriminate support of police brutality and the beating of innocents, while defending the sheriffs of Alabama and Mississippi, the FBI and the House Un-American Activities Committee all at once. In short, to millions of Americans of good faith, there was no legitimacy to the issue of law-and-order at all.

Yet no politician and no political reporter could accept such a dictum. Wherever candidates paused to speak, wherever people gathered to listen, there could be no doubt in any bystander's mind that law-and-order was indeed a legitimate issue. The two surest-fire applause lines in any candidate's speech were always his calls for "law-and-order" at home and "peace" in Vietnam. This is what the American people—poor and rich, white and black—wanted to hear. None of the major candidates—except Eugene McCarthy—felt he could ignore this prime concern of the people. All alike were trapped between editorialists who denounced their use of the phrase and people who cheered the call. The candidates smarted at the criticism, but persisted, for violence was the background condition of American life.

No one traveling the country in 1968 could be unaware of how changed this condition was from the condition of life in the campaign of 1964. This reporter's personal notebooks, reflecting only one man's travels, begin in the summer of 1967—with the outbreak of the Newark riots in July; pick up a few weeks later with a huddle of Marines, black and white, in Vietnam, listening to an Armed Forces Network broadcast of the bloodshed in Detroit; return to a Governors' Conference in the Virgin Islands with the governors discussing mobilization tactics, response time, and riot training for their National Guards; note the outbursts in the New York schools in the fall; record a dawn explosion in Washington —and I recall waking and peering out in a January night down Sixteenth Street from the Jefferson Hotel to find the Russian Embassy had been bombed and the street blocked off by police cars. My notebooks record a return to New York and a garbage strike; record in April of the year the first defense of the capital of the United States by the United States Army in fifty years. They record the traumatic peak of violence at Chicago; record again the pitiless harassment of both Hubert Humphrey and George Wallace as they traveled about the country in street savagery I had never known before in American politics; they note with particular personal regret that Hippies of the Boston Common were defecating and urinating in the entryways of the beautiful old private homes that still line the northern rim of Beacon Street; they record in the week of the election itself the breakdown of the school system of New York with more than 50,000 teachers on strike and over a million children deprived of school.

Any other reporter's notebooks of the campaign year of 1968 might record similar or different details; but wherever one went, there was no escape. For what was happening in America in 1968, and had been happening in crescendo for three years before, was a crisis of the American culture—not a series of episodes, or any localized breakdown of law enforcement, or grave, underlying conspiracy. It was simply that the times were different. The traditional standards of American conduct and behavior were, beyond any doubt, changing. And in the issue of "law-and-order" were wrapped up so many separate concerns that they must be peeled away, one from the other, if any reasonable analysis of the confused American mood of 1968 is to be sought.

Crime, riot, demonstration, bloodshed and assassination all run together in the common mind. Yet since crime is the most easily definable of the intertwined concerns—and since "crime" is accepted by all as a legitimate subject of study—it is best to take up crime first.

Crime in the United States is indeed rising—but by how much we do not know, for the exploration of police statistics is a specialized skill, as much a matter of flair and fancy as the exploration of baseball statistics or combat reports from Vietnam. All national figures on crime must be approached with inflexible skepticism, however, for they are gathered by the FBI from more than 4,000 local reporting police agencies of different standards of integrity, indifference and dishonesty. Experts break down crime, as does the FBI, into seven main categories—murder, rape, assault; larceny, burglary, robbery and automobile-stealing. Of these the fastest-rising figures are those of automobile theft, but they bother the nation least. Although the theft of automobiles had almost tripled in the past eight years, to one million a year, automobile-stealing is usually a youthful prank and is rarely accompanied by violence. It is murder, rape, mugging, robbery that rouse fear.

It is easiest to observe the changing pattern of criminal violence by choosing a single city, New York, which has probably the most reliable large-city crime statistics in the United States. And it is best, in New York's statistics, to button down on the figures for murder, which are most likely to be solid. In murder, the cadaver remains to testify to violence, and, thus, murder must be reported, unlike so many other forms of crime such as rape or assault, frequently unreported by victims out of shame, fear or hopelessness. It should be noted at once that New York is the safest of the big cities of the United States, ranking tenth in murders per 100,000 among the ten largest cities of the nation. (Houston's murder rate leads those of all other large cities in the nation.) But the trend of the murder figures even in New York are terrifying. In 1953, of every 100,-000 persons in New York, murder ended the life of a statistical 4.5, or a total, in the city, of 350. By 1968, this rate had almost tripled to 11.1 per 100,000! No less than 904 persons were killed in the nation's safest large city, and the single year 1968 had shown a 21-percent jump over the 745 murders of 1967. Across the nation, since national figures include suburban and rural areas, the national incidence of murder drops sharply, of course, to about 6 per 100,000—which means that out of 200,000,000 Americans, we can expect 12,000 to be murdered each year at the present rate.

The most illuminating contrast to life in America, and the best thread for exploration, are the murder figures of those of our parent culture—the British. The figures on murder for the 49,000,000 people of England and Wales (Scotland has separate statistics) came, in 1967, to a total of only 161 people! In other words, all of England and Wales, with six and a half times the population of New York City, had a murder total less than a fifth that of New York City. If the English killed at the same rate as Americans, they would be murdering thirty-five times as many of each other as they do today.

The contrast raises, of course, the question: why? And since sociologists argue *ad nauseum* why murders take place, why any human being should want to deprive another of life, it is best to take the easiest and most plausible answers that come to the surface and accept them as working truths.

Basically, the British are an unarmed people; they are permitted hunting guns, but the short rod is most difficult to obtain. In America, anyone has been able to buy both long and short rods, and in the last three years the sale and importation of guns of all kinds in the United States has risen by phenomenal proportions: production and importation of guns totaled 45.6 million from 1951 through the first half of 1968—but the total annual demand was only 2.4 million in 1951; it had jumped to 4.1 million in 1966; to 4.7 million in 1967; and in the first half of 1968 the annual rate hit 6 million! Today, there is believed to be one killing weapon for every two men, women and children in America, leaving out the old-fashioned kitchen knife, the hammer, the club, the razor blade, as well as primitive rock and fingers. To this gun-bristling and frightened American population there has descended a code which, in recent years, has been driven by television to the point of obsessive drama. In America, the only authentic folk mythology is the horse opera, the winning of the West by pluck, luck and gun. Every child exposed to television knows that, on occasion, even the most decent citizen in town, the man in the white hat, will strap on his gun (as his wife, sobbing, clings in an effort to restrain him), then stalk the marauder down Main Street and shoot to kill. All have seen the Bible-bearing householder slowly sight down the rifle from his cabin window (or from behind the rock) and slowly draw bead on the Indian, the rustler, the bandit, the bully—and then squeeze the trigger. Thus, by the code of the old West, the nation's folk drama, the quarrel is settled.

This code and the Constitutional availability of guns descends to all Americans from their past. This old heritage is, however, unbearably aggravated by the rhythm of speeding urbanization. Urbanization brings people closer together than nature meant them to live, and in all rapidly urbanizing countries, from Japan to Germany, the murder rate is rising. Abroad as at home, in any city of the world, crime statistics contain one absolutely universal truth: if you are murdered, the chances are three out of four that you will be murdered by an acquaintance of your past, or a neighbor who lives close to you. And big cities create strange neighbors. In the big cities today, the neighbor is the menace: he is the man who lives on the same apartment block as you do in the slum and keeps his radio going on a hot summer night while your wife is trying to rock the baby to sleep; he is the old man who shoots up your boy for yelling under his window, or sending his ball through it; or the boy who shoots up the old storekeeper to get enough cash for a quick fix or a quick date.

Urbanization in America brings us, of course, directly to the problem of the blacks in the big city.[1] It is the black population, ripped from the natural social discipline of small towns in the South and the West Indies, that is driven to explosion by the tensions of the big city and the hopeless anonymity of the ghetto culture. Two facts should be noted about black communities in America—first, that in almost every city of the country, the most violent, rape-ridden, drug-ridden, murder-ridden areas are black precincts. And second, that in each city there are other Negro precincts which have become real communities, and these real communities are among the safest, cleanest, best precincts in the entire city. Part of the public's difficulty in appreciating the black condition is that whenever any television exploration of the plight of the black in America begins, the producer immediately dispatches a crew to the most violent, ramshackle block in the worst slum of the city, presenting this grisly fragment as the whole. So far as I know, no television production has ever shown Negroes at peace, in natural decency, in any of the dozens

[1] See *The Making of the President—1964*, Chapter 8.

of tranquil Negro neighborhoods that increasingly speckle the urban and suburban panorama of America.

It is the prevalence of violence in the poor black precincts, however, which gives to "law-and-order" the racial edge that disturbs conservatives and liberals alike. Out of New York City's seventy-six residential precincts, for example, six black precincts in three districts (Harlem, South Bronx, Bedford-Stuyvesant) account for one third of all violent crimes in the great city. In the middle-class suburbs, where law-breaking means automobile-stealing, pot at the local high school, embezzlement, or adultery, crime is rarely violent; in suburbia, therefore, the racial edge to law-and-order is blunted, and a distant sympathy for the black condition can be aroused. But in the cities, where the process of urbanization boils, crime is more violent, and becomes a menace to one's own life. Thus it takes on the cast of a peculiar, savage condition brought about by Negroes. Those blacks who live in black ghettos are most in danger; but those who live close to black precincts are also in danger—of mugging, beating, knifing, looting; and those who live close to the black precincts are by and large the white poor, the white working class, largely of recent immigrant stock themselves. It is idle to explain sociologically to such people that all urbanizing groups, even white Appalachians, are apt to become dangerous when subject to the cold, mechanical discipline of the strange new city. The whites are afraid of Negroes. And as white workingmen and their wives in big cities cheered George Wallace on through the campaign of 1968, the issue of crime and its control became webbed, sickeningly, with racism.

Debate about crime in America has risen as the crime rate has risen. Yet all the common proposals advanced—gun control, drug control, better policing, more money for law-enforcement techniques, better schooling and housing for the underprivileged—are advanced within an arbitrary frame, as if crime were something to be managed administratively. And it is in listening to the working police, who must administer the crime laws, that one senses the narrowness of the frame of discussion. For the blue-coats, when pressed about their inability to control the rising rate, shift responsibility to the courts, which they style weak, lax, indulgent or politicized. And it is when one goes on to examine the police complaint against the courts that one comes upon the governing condition, which is cultural rather than administrative.

The courts of America—the most liberal in the world in this decade —are indeed politicized, as all courts should be. But they are even more sensitized by the general cultural atmosphere of the country. And in America, by 1968, the nation was living in a cultural climate in which the rising rate of crime was only one reflection of an entirely new set of values. In this new climate the ancient balance between individual and state had been tipped farther than ever before: the individual was now the center point of concern, his expression of self the highest good; and the state was his enemy. In this climate, the courts now saw their highest duty not as the defense of state or of order, but defense of the individual *against* the state at extremes of judgment unprecedented in jurisprudence.

Many new conditions—still only vaguely definable—led to the current crisis of American culture: the unremitting torment of the Vietnam war; the dazzling prosperity fostered by the Kennedy-Johnson administration, followed by the inflationary surge of the three years 1965–1968; the movement of Negroes and the restlessness of student populations; such new technologies as those of the pill, the bomb, the new drugs; above all, the growth of television. Yet all have combined to stimulate a profound intellectual re-examination of the structure of our society, a questioning of its inherited traditions, of duty, of discipline within a community, of moralities, and of each individual's responsibility to other men and to the law.

A culture is normally shaped and changed at the frontier of accepted thought by the avant-garde of its thinkers in religion, art, literature, drama, scholarship. Ages pass before the thinking of the avant-garde, tested by time, becomes the dogma of society—before, for example, the fresh and dangerous thinking of John Stuart Mill or Adam Smith becomes a century and a half later the concrete dogma of conservative businessmen.

Today, however, time speeds; and in the brilliant flourishing of American thought (the dominant intellectual force in the Western world today), ideas, fancies, theories churn from tentative concept to fashionable acceptance almost overnight, faster than society can absorb. The natural urge of all thinkers is to explore the unknown; but in America, flushed with its prosperity, this urge to explore the unknown has led to what may be called the Age of Experiment in American life—experiment at every level. Where the physical scientists with the resources of government slowly roll back the unknowns of space and the inner atom, the social scientists with the resources of academia roll back the unknowns in man's relation to man, and the artists roll back the unknowns in the individual's exploration of sensation. All these men of the American avant-garde are alike sterilized, however, by a clinical detachment of observation which rises above the right and wrong of older, slower-changing moralities. And it is from the subordination of moralities to the imperatives of experiment, the elevation of self-expression over self-restraint, that rises the cultural crisis—of which the new violence is only a part.

One can examine the cultural crisis at almost any level, but the sweep of the panorama is dismaying:

The leaders of the avant-garde in American culture define themselves not by programs, but by negatives; they move without purpose and against what is past—prisoners of the past, not liberators. On stage, on screen, in letters, they have created a world without heroes. It has been more years than anyone can remember since a critically acclaimed American novel celebrated an affirmative hero (except a black hero), or the stage applauded (except in musical comedies) a hero who set out to achieve and, struggling to achieve, caused the triumph of good over bad. Out of cynicism and despair, the new avant-garde has come to despise its own country and its traditions as has rarely happened in any community in the world; American institutions, customs and laws are regarded as the greatest system of restraints on that individual self-expression which it sees as the highest right of man. And, by these standards, no exploration of sensation in film, criticism, novel or drama can be condemned simply for qualities of hate, depravity, sickness, violence or obscenity.

Whether obscenity is right or wrong; whether homosexuality is good or bad; whether mind-expanding drugs are dangerous or not; whether killing is reprehensible or not—few voices in the established critical mood of the country dare exercise a moral judgment on the phenomena. Violence in the abstract is deplored; but in art, in cinema, in drama, in literature, violence is judged by style, and atrocity is examined as curiosity. From such critical leadership there seeps down to disturbed minds at the mass level an implied permission to explore their own nightmare fancies as well; and in the streets, brutality and violence color the outline in blood.

This revolution in critical standards has created, in large areas of American thinking, a system of values almost as stylized as those of George Horace Lorimer, whose *Saturday Evening Post* was the mightiest guardian of American manners in the 1920's. A new babbitry of permissiveness has replaced the old babbitry of conformity; style rather than content fascinates.

The growth of the critical attitude to American life to its present intensity is almost unique in the history of any country's thinking. But the time-conjunction has sped the attitude and authority of criticism in America far beyond the traditional realm of arts and letters. Politics is in fashion; and politics also is studied as style. The thought that thousands of good dull men in public life may honestly be trying to govern well, and that many of them are succeeding, is regarded in the critical climate almost as absurdity; leadership in public affairs is regarded with cynicism and suspicion; and the action of leadership is examined as a pageantry for artistic comment, devoid of any moral judgments. One could read early in 1968, for example, in *Ramparts*, a slick magazine ballooned by carnival promotion to major campus influence, this summary sentence of evaluation of the Pentagon demonstrations of 1967: "Objectively speaking, perhaps the best thing that could have happened on October 21st would have been for somebody to have been killed. For American soldiers to have shot unarmed American civilians exercising their right of free speech would have been a blow from which the administration could never recover. Yet, almost totally, the Pentagon either prevented violence or convincingly argued that the fault was the protesters.' " Or again, after the frightful month of killing and violence in July, 1967, the most elegant and best-written literary journal in America, the *New York Review of Books*, with no sense of obscenity, could, in a moment of critical tension, adorn its front page with a precise, full-scale model of how to make a Molotov cocktail: fuse, clothesline; stopper, gas-soaked rag; contents, two thirds gasoline, one third soap-powder-and-dirt. Yet month after month thereafter it could mourn violence and killing with no sense of hypocrisy.

The standards of the new criticism might, in the old days, have been limited to the regional cultural centers of New York and Los Angeles, where they reign. But it was in precisely these two states that was born the greatest of all the new media of American culture, television, which fused all America into one audience. And by 1968 television, the chief prisoner of this new court of high criticism held, in turn, all America captive.

It is, perhaps, necessary to give a short retrospect on the growth of television and its impact on politics and public affairs. Public-affairs television is a hybrid descendant of many influences—of the old movies, of the newsreel, of the commercial adman's cultivation of appetites, but, above all, of the tradition of the old radio news with its short, staccato announcements. If one had to choose the Mirabeau and Danton of the revolution in television as an instrument of public affairs, one would, certainly, have to choose Edward R. Murrow and Fred Friendly of CBS. But if one had to locate the precise date of television's breakthrough to dominance in American political life, one would have to choose, certainly, the fall of 1963, when, on September 2nd, the half-hour evening news shows were established on the national networks—a date as significant in American history as the Golden Spike that linked the Union Pacific and Central Pacific to give America its first continental railway in 1869.

Television news shows up to the fall of 1963 had been limited to fifteen minutes. The great television nets maintained large domestic news bureaus only in Washington and New York, and filled their quarter-hours with short domestic news clips out of these two centers, or visuals of historic events out of their far-flung overseas centers. But the half-hour news shows were a quantum jump; and as the networks passed to the half-hour news shows, it became artistically and commercially necessary to fill the expanded time with events presented entirely differently from the style of quick announcements. The administrative response to fill the time came in the creation of fresh news bureaus all across America-at-home—in the Midwest, in the South, in the Far West—with all these bureaus required to feed significant nightly pictorial representation of what was happening at home. But the artistic response was a seeking of drama. To hold audiences for half an hour, excitement was needed—excitement in casting of characters, excitement in the streets, excitement in change. The process of building, creating and healing is all too often long, slow, incremental and undramatic; it is when the normal pattern of life snaps, when the web of civilization breaks, that drama is created; and the growth of the half-hour evening news shows depended on an exploration of the snapping points, the artistic or critical or commercial arrangement of such fragments of crisis to draw viewers. By 1968 the networks had learned to draw audiences of 40,000,000 or 50,000,000 to their nightly news dramas; and these new shows had become, for the masses, the mirror of the world.

Excitement is the great unwritten imperative of television, an imperative which cannot be changed by any man or repealed by any law. The nightly news shows must "march." Of the bravery and integrity of the good men who run television, there can be no question.[2] But one irrevocable cowardice binds all men in television—television dare not be dull. The logic is simple: if a television show is dull, then it loses its audience; if it loses its audience, it loses either sponsorship or executive protection; if it loses these, the producer goes broke or is removed. Whether television feeds on excitement, breeds excitement or provokes excitement is a matter of intricate debate. Whatever the answer is, there can be no doubt that television *spreads* excitement, and any producer, knowingly or not, recognizes that the law of his survival requires that he speed the spread. Drama and clash, the new and the strange, are what television must find or create to survive. In a critical culture where television is judged by its dramatic quality, where the right of experimentation and protest has become an absolute standard, where great new waves of American citizens are penetrating the political process from which they have been hitherto excluded, one clash whets audience appetite for another, one dramatically successful presentation of violence stimulates a competitive desire to display more.

This appetite for sensation in America of the 1960's, of which television is only the chief satisfier, is an appetite that feeds on itself; and it runs through every stretch of our culture, until, taken as a whole, it would seem that the culture has an appetite for apocalypse: a pushing of the liberty of self-expression of every man until the instruments of government must respond with repression, or crumble altogether.

[2] This writer has, over the past seven years, been repeatedly associated with the Columbia Broadcasting System and independently responsible for several major television productions. In whatever criticism follows, he assumes his own share.

* * *

Though old-fashioned crimes like rape, mugging, murder, and assault have always been staple news-fare for catching attention, and though, indeed, their incidence was rising, what seemed most to stimulate the slow growth of concern of Americans in the years leading to 1968 was something else. It was the intrusion on their attention of newer forms of violence and a newer rhythm of contagion. For the new forms of violence came not so much in classical "crime waves" as in a chain of sputters or outbursts, spread across the country instantly by press and television, in a feedback where disturbance created disturbance. What one read in the morning, or saw at night a thousand miles away, might be hometown news the next day, or a scream beneath one's window. A madman murdered eight student nurses in Chicago in 1966; two and a half weeks later another madman shot down and killed fourteen people a thousand miles away on the campus of the University of Texas. In December of 1966 a vandal tried to destroy paintings in the United States Capitol in Washington; three weeks later the episode was repeated when a band of vandals succeeded in slashing the murals which hung in the City Hall of St. Petersburg, Florida. In the spring of 1967 school vandalism broke out seriously in New York—within weeks vandalism in schools had spread to Cleveland, Detroit, Cincinnati and other cities. Episodes seemed to leap from city to city—the invasion of mayors' offices, the sniping at trains and automobiles. In a single city like New York, there would come a rat-tat-tat of kindred crimes—a hippie and a girl friend would be found brutally murdered in that sad and squalid sanctuary of the disaffected, the East Village, in October, 1967; in November another student would be killed by marauders for refusing a cigarette request; in December another youth would be stomped and tortured to insensibility in the East Village. One could fill page after page of a book like this with chronologically linked chains of senseless brutality, each incident triggered by a report of another—senseless outbursts at amusement parks, on moonlight cruises, at football games, in subway cars or stations. None of them fitted into the old pattern of motivated crime; all seemed to be an animal twitching of human beasts in whom the delicate membrane of restraining morality had been ruptured, whose barbarism, though deplored, nonetheless insisted on explanation and attention. Such a rainfall of episodes, splashing in the morning papers or in the evening television news, drenched American life—but it was background sound, a disturbing blur not central to one's attention.

What was, however, central to the attention and the cry for "law-and-order" was political violence—and the disconcerting applause or justification it received from so many responsible and highly placed oracles of public opinion and politics.

It was as if an historic inattention had swept those observers who should have been on the watchtowers of history—their minds were fixed in gaze on the recent past, like the minds of old generals fixed on the last war. The riots that intrigued political historians, generally, were those of the first half of the century—the riots of St. Petersburg in 1905 and 1917, the riots in France and Germany in the thirties, the riots in China in the twenties. All these had been directly and immediately political; the purpose of the Bolsheviks, Communists, Fascists, Nazis, Socialists had been quite clear. Thus, one could deplore them, but they could be analyzed and understood in the passage of history. The American riots of the 1960's baffled political historians for lack of a clearly defined purpose. More parochially, American political scientists and historians found difficulty in framing the perspectives of the new American forms of mass violence because of the set of American history. For generations, violence had threatened America most from the native American right—the menace always perceived on the lunatic fringe of reaction where Ku Klux Klan, American Nazis and Minutemen muttered, rumbled and mobilized as phantom marauders. But when the real marauders, in the 1960's, took to the streets, they came not from the "right" but from the "left" in the most liberal American administration in history, while the thinkers were looking the other way.

Moreover, both conscience and mind of sensitive observers were disturbed in judgment, for under every reaction of such men was an underlay of guilt; the chief actors in the new political violence had grievances which all men acknowledged. Yet their unreasonable behavior passed the ability of men of good-will to satisfy, and passed the capacity of the ordinary law-abiding citizen to tolerate.

These chief actors were the blacks of America and the students of America, the two largest underprivileged groups in the nation. The rush and sweep of their disturbances over the years leading to the campaign of 1968 cannot fairly be compressed except in full and independent volumes describing the forces. Yet the rhythm of acceleration in those years cannot be ignored if one wishes to make any sense at all of the politics of 1968. And with an attempt to describe the rhythm, one passes to narrative again.

The swelling of the black unrest as America approached 1968 proceeded on two planes at once—both of them beginning in Watts in the summer of 1965. (See Chapter One.) For Watts began not only a train of episodes in the streets of America; it also provoked a deep re-examination of the most advanced thinking of the previous decade. There had been other riots like Watts in American history—in East St. Louis, Illinois, in 1917, in Chicago in 1919, in Detroit in 1943. Each, traditionally, had been followed by a commission of inquiry, a study, a report; little had been done—and then the rage and terror whispered off, to pass away like a summer tantrum. In the decade of the 1960's, this was not to be; and all previous standards of American political judgment were to prove invalid in containing or giving peaceful vent to black rage.

By every traditional index of progress—of wages earned, of housing, of entry into high public service, of education, of integration in the armed forces—the black community was, in the 1960's, moving forward more rapidly than ever before in American history. The rise in Negro family income was faster than the rise in white family income; the education of Negro youth had almost closed the gap on the education of white youth; the number of non-white families earning more than $8,000 a year was, by 1968, double the figure of 1960, or 27 percent of the total; among married Negro men the unemployment rate for 1967 had sunk to 3.2 percent. The fitful and sluggish response of white guilt to the black condition which had begun in the 1950's had, in the 1960's, under the prodding of inspired black leadership, begun to propel Congress faster and faster to rectification of injustice. With the passage under Johnson of the Civil Rights Acts of 1964 and 1965, the demands and life-work of such great black leaders as Roy Wilkins and Martin Luther King seemed well on their way to climax. "What do you want?" used to run the litany of black oratory in black audiences in the early sixties, and back would come the shout: "Freedom." "Let me hear it again. What do you want?" and the audience would scream, "Freedom." "When do you want it?" the orator would bellow, and the audience would rise, yelling, "Now!"

By 1968 such oratory was all but obsolete. The massive legislation and administration measures of Washington between 1960 and 1965 had fleshed out every hope voiced by recognized black leaders of the previous decade. But for the black man in the ghetto, there was something he wanted even more than freedom. No one could quite define it, and black leaders and sociologists themselves disagreed on what was required. Whether it was integration, or black separatism, or black power, or a fuller share in the national prosperity, it was something that surpassed the power of legislation to cure either overnight or in a decade. It was and remains something no white man can, perhaps, understand—a hunger for the personal dignity of which the black American had been deprived for so many hundreds of years, an ability for mother and father to look at a black child and dream dreams for him, the promise to the black young that they can work anywhere, enter anywhere, whether school, shop, factory, restaurant or vacation resort, standing erect and with pride. The promises of administration, the laws of Congress could not give this; they could whet the appetite—but not satisfy it. And thus the condition of mounting rage from which, starting in 1966, summer emerged marked as the season of riots on the American political calendar as clearly as football is marked on the sports calendar.

The second year of turbulence began in March of 1966 in the perpetual summer of Southern California with a minor disturbance in Los Angeles—a group of black students stoned a white teacher's car, began to beat up other white people, and a spasm of looting followed. But the police reacted quickly this time, only two were killed, and the disturbance was squelched overnight. Washington followed, with its first outbreak in April; then California with three more in May; then, with school out, riots spread to the Northern cities. Cleveland was off first in 1966, at the end of June; then, in a single fortnight, Omaha (Nebraska), Des Moines (Iowa) and Chicago (Illinois) with two killed. A week later, Cleveland (Ohio) again, with four killed; and then, by the rhythm of contagion, all across the land: Brooklyn, Baltimore, Perth Amboy, Providence, Minneapolis, Lansing, Detroit, Muskegon, Dayton, Atlanta, San Francisco, St. Louis, and on and on. By year's end in 1966, the nation had known forty-three outbursts of black rioting.

1967 was off to a late start—but it made up for it in intensity and escalation. It was not until April, 1967, that the summer ritual of barbarism resumed, and then, in four weeks, Omaha, Nashville, Cleveland, Louisville and Washington all flared. Now, too, new sounds, a new ferocity began to accompany the pictures stretching in color across the land on the web of television. In Jackson, Mississippi, a black student spokesman of SNCC proclaimed: "An eye for an eye, an arm for an arm, a head for a head, and a life for a life." In Prattville, Alabama, Stokely Carmichael: "We came here to tear this town up and we're going to tear it up." In Cincinnati, in June, 1967: a five-day orgy of Molotov cocktails and fires in the night (the worst record of arson in Cincinnati history since fire records were begun), punctuated on the third day by the arrival of H. Rap Brown to declare that no peace would come "until the honky cops get out," and later that day, "SNCC has declared war."

By July the number of outbreaks had passed the fifty mark; then with the Newark riots, it got worse. Newark, which sits on one of the most beautiful natural sites in America, is one of those opportunities for planning that American city-development has squandered; a greasy, slum-ridden, overcrowded, shapeless place, it has been successively inhabited by Protestants, Irish, Italians and Jews and, in this decade, has become the second-largest city, after Washington, D.C., to find itself with a Negro majority. As whites have fled, in a rout, Negroes have poured in so fast that in the seven years between 1960 and 1966 the city shifted from 65 percent white to 52 percent Negro and 10 percent Puerto Rican. The shifting population had by 1967 created new tensions, new demands—and for years the study of Newark's race relations has been a favorite indoor sport of social workers and social surveys. Indeed, by the time Newark blew, in 1967, the Federal government's anti-poverty program was investing more money per capita in Newark's black communities than in any other big city in the North. But money was not the answer. For weeks in June, 1967, the City's Board of Education had grappled with a flamboyant Black Muslim, self-styled Colonel Hassan Jeru-Ahmed, demanding a share in school control; school-board meetings had been violent and disturbing; race tension was high. On the night of July 12th a Negro taxi driver was arrested by police and dragged to a police station; a crowd gathered; a Molotov cocktail was thrown, and the cry of fire went up. A protest march gathered, broke up, began to loot, was subdued by police. The next night, Thursday, the 13th, looting began on a larger scale; by two in the morning the mayor had called for New Jersey's National Guard. By Friday, with the National Guard, the State Police and the City Police all in place, firing began. Where or how the first shot was fired, no one seems to know: the National Guard was badly managed; but the cities and states of America were only just learning how to mobilize for civil disorder; riot training was not yet a standard order of drill. By Monday, July 17th, when the National Guard was withdrawn, one could total up the score—twenty-three people killed, among whom were one white detective, one white fireman, six Negro women and two Negro children.

For the next week the nation knew not a single day of uninterrupted peace: Plainfield, Fresno, Des Moines, Erie, Cairo, Minneapolis, Durham, Englewood, East Harlem all erupted, until, on July 23rd, Detroit exploded in the worst of the disasters: City Police, National Guard, State Police, finally the Regular Army of the United States were required to quell Detroit's passion. By the time Detroit had been pacified, after six days of death and destruction, the final toll had reached the highest of any domestic disturbance in fifty years: 43 persons killed (33 black, 10 white), property damage approximately $45,000,000. On and on went the bloody scroll of the summer of 1967 until the cold had cramped the blacks back into their crowded tenements and hovels. By then the summary of race violence had counted 164 riots, and 83 dead.

All that can be known, historically, of these riots of 1967 is embodied in the U.S. Riot Commission Report. The report includes some of the finest narrative historical writing in any government document anywhere. Its analyses baffle one, and its recommendations are platitudes; yet it is a major document, and its confused analysis of the morphology of riots is the best conventional wisdom can provide us. Riots, says the report, begin with a background of tension, out of a growing bitterness of the black community in the given city, a bitterness generally unrecognized by the dominant white community. This background of grievance develops as the growing black community rubs up against the structures of white authority; white authority, apparently inflexible, insists that rural or uneducated blacks meet the standards of the host city, itself unwilling or incapable of adjusting to black manners or black mores; but all blacks, educated or uneducated, are subject to the same suspicions and same humiliations at the hands of authority, the most hated symbols of which are the police or the schools. The final precipitating act just before any riot is usually a police arrest; and the instinctive reaction of the black community is to protect whoever is arrested. If the initial outburst —which usually takes place in the evening—is not immediately quelled or mediated, emotion sets a fuse to events: fires, looting, then shooting ensue. Those who loot are generally the young—53 percent of those arrested in the 1967 disorders were black youths between fifteen and twenty-four years old; and most of those involved in active rioting were youngsters brought up in the North, not the South, and therefore less willing to accept the white man's authority. And, though the riot report does not say so, those who suffer most, those who die, those whose property is ruined are overwhelmingly black. With the outburst of a riot, the inner bonds even of the black community dissolve, and the gay and carefree youngsters one sees loping in their white shirtsleeves through the fringes of any riot area, in carnival glee, as they innocently snatch and run, are a menace to black and white alike.

The train of episodes and violence in the black ghettos of America, rising in crescendo from 1965 to 1966, from 1966 to 1967, was visibly the chief rupture between black Americans and previous American political traditions. But parallel to the street episodes an equal drama was developing in the thinking of Negro leadership, an even more significant rupture with the past.

For over a generation, the goals of black leadership and white liberals had been summed up in one catchword: "integration." "Integration" meant many things to many different people, but, over-all, it assumed that the one primordial step needed to make of Americans one community was the wiping out of all the legal and institutional barriers that segregated Americans by the color of their skins—in schools, in voting processes, in unions, in politics, in government, in housing. By 1967, even in the South, the last bastions of resistance were under unremitting pressure from the Federal government. Across the country, every major university scoured the ghetto high schools for promising Negro adolescents who could be lured to their ivied halls, while great corporations combed the universities for promising black talent. A Negro sat on the Supreme Court of the United States; two major cities (Cleveland and Gary) had elected Negro mayors; and over 200 Negro legislators sat in state assemblies and city councils; six Negro Congressmen and one Negro Senator sat in Washington. Integration had fostered a Negro leadership which seemed to be moving steadily toward its rightful privileges and responsibilities in American life.

Except that the term "integration" had lost its savor; and even those black leaders who were its expression would not defend it aloud, nor dared advance it in debate with a new black elite coming to prominence. For the new black elite, the fashionable and emotive phrase was "Black Power." The phrase had first gained currency in Mississippi, in June of 1966, when uttered by Stokely Carmichael, the student leader, as he marched with James Meredith in demonstration through the heartland of prejudice. Seized from then on by militants, intellectuals and media alike, the phrase dominated public discussion of the race confrontation though it defied precise analysis.

"Black Power," taken as a phrase alone, reflected a very real need of the black community—control of life in the black community by blacks, an appreciation by blacks of their own culture and own values, black communities patrolled by black police, black neighborhoods served by their own commerce. Other ethnic groups had similarly organized themselves within the larger American community in the past, as every American politician knew. And since the Negroes, having suffered more, required more help in achieving control of their communities than other groups, it was not impossible that somehow laws could be redrawn, cities could be remapped, an orderly transfer of power could be arranged.

But "Black Power," as it became part of the general dialogue, was advanced most vehemently by those who felt that its achievement required an overriding necessary ingredient: hate. "Integration" had rested on good-will and an appeal to conscience. "Black Power" based itself squarely on bitterness, and sought to wrench from white guilt or supposed white cowardice by violence what it could not get by law. So much suffering, so much injustice dyes the entire fabric of the black past in America that the most creative and imaginative resources must be commanded to open to this underprivileged tenth of the nation an equality of opportunity based on respect and good-will. Yet in the years 1966–1968 a new black elite insisted that Black Power was something to be won not *within* but *against,* and at the expense of, the larger white community. No morality, insisted this new elite, bound them to the general community in any common peace or shared decency. As a generation of black youngsters and students began to mature in this thought, convinced that hate and violence were the chief fuels of their own progress, the perspective of a swelling counter-hate among the whites became ever more real.

Thus, as a political obbligato to bloodshed and riot in the street came the sound of new voices and the call of a new doctrine. Nor could any white outsider ever tell who spoke for the black community, who led the black community—whether it was the men in high office whom Negroes had elected, or the men who gave the rioters in the street the moral sanction to revert to barbarism.

However it was, the visions of bloodshed in the street, coupled with the new voices of Black Power, were to change entirely the political climate in the black community of America between 1966 and 1968.

In May of 1966, Stokely Carmichael, twenty-four, had been elected chairman of SNCC. SNCC had been founded under the fostering influence of Martin Luther King in 1960 as the Student Non-Violent Coordinating Committee, and the word "non-violence" was operative through the first five years of its life. Its first inspiring leader, a saintly young man called Robert Moses, had held it to its course through the savagery of Mississippi and through the summer student organization of that state in 1964, which he called into being. But with Carmichael, a militant advocate of violence, a change in rhetoric took place, as if the word "non-violence" were an invention of Booker T. Washington, the discourse of the Uncle Toms of the old plantations. Carmichael's utterances curdled good-will, yet made marvelous national drama. "When you talk of Black Power," he was quoted, "you talk of building a movement that will smash everything Western civilization has created." Or: "If a white man tries to walk over you, kill him. One match and you can retaliate. Burn, baby, burn." At the height of the summer violence of 1967, from Cuba, he was alleged to have said, "In Newark, we applied war tactics of the guerrillas. We are preparing groups of urban guerrillas for our defense in the cities. The price of these rebellions is a high price that one must pay. This fight is not going to be a simple street meeting. It is going to be a fight to the death."

By summer 1967, Carmichael had been replaced as the leading spokesman of black violence by an even coarser racist, H. Rap Brown. As the riots of 1967 built to their July-August crest, one could read of H. Rap Brown declaiming in Cambridge, Maryland: "Burn this town down. But don't tear down your own stuff. When you tear down the white man, brother, you are hitting him in the money. Don't love him to death. Shoot him to death." Or, in Washington, D.C.: "Black people have been looting. I say there should be more shooting than looting, so if you loot, loot a gun store." Or again, exhorting a group of Negroes in Jersey City: "Wage guerrilla war on the honky white man."

Guerrilla warfare was indeed the most apt, though crude, comparison one could use in describing the perspectives such men set.

Guerrilla warfare requires a grievance of the oppressed, and an instigating action. It requires, also, some nearby tangible, emotional satisfaction. In China the early guerrillas had learned how easy it was to link high cause with immediate yield by sharing the landlord's grain stocks and then dividing up his land. In urban riots in America there was always the immediate carnival joy, the Bedouin impulse to grab, as youngsters were given moral let to snatch what they wanted from appliance stores, furniture stores, supermarkets, liquor stores, gun stores. The new rhetoric of Black Power gave a cause and moral absolution to those who took what they wanted and ran.

But guerrilla warfare requires, finally, an ultimate ingredient:

terror. And it requires that the terror be applied as much within the movement itself as against the enemy outside. By the end of 1967 and through 1968 into 1969, a disciplined terror began to develop, the tool of minority leaders among Negroes, exercised indiscriminately, against white authority and black rivals alike.

By the end of 1967 one could note that the older institutions of Negro protest—the NAACP, the National Urban League—were declining both in numbers and in prestige. Even SNCC was by 1968 declining. New names and new organizations were crowding to attention. There were, for example, the Black Panthers of Oakland, California—who, with guns in hand in May, 1967, invaded the galleries of the California Assembly, in session in Sacramento. There were, for example, the RAM's—the Revolutionary Armed Movement—unearthed in New York in 1968 with a cache of weapons and charged with a precise plan to blow up public installations. Other ethnic groups were specifically challenged: the growth of virulent anti-Semitism among some of the newer Negro leaders sent shivers down the backs of millions of American Jews. But most threatened of all were the established Negro leaders of older organizations, the elected Negro leaders of the political process, the ordinary Negroes who, whether knowingly or not, were threatened with loss of freedom of choice.

By 1968 terror had become a tactic by which militants pressed their will on more moderate Negroes; the Washington offices of SNCC were themselves to be fouled by gunplay in a contest for power that year; Boston was to witness Negro terrorists killing other Negroes; by 1969 gunplay and killing were to invade even groups of campus blacks, as at the University of California at Los Angeles. But as one entered 1968, even after the violence of 1967, one could not predict all this.

The black violence of 1968 began early—with two killed and forty injured in a riot in Orangeburg, South Carolina on February 8th; another explosion followed in Durham, North Carolina; a week later, trouble in Omaha, as usual. More ominous was the sputtering of the guerrillas, the Black Panthers in the Bay Area of California; then, like a fantasy out of some fanatic mind, arson in several of Chicago's largest department stores in March; followed, just the next day, with arson or attempted arson in four of New York's department stores. Then, one read that Martin Luther King was in Memphis, Tennessee, organizing the striking sanitation workers (overwhelmingly Negro) for a march against the city's garbage department.

Martin Luther King. What went on in his mind, in his heroic peregrination at the head of the black march to freedom in America, no one will ever know. He stood there in profile against the American experience, still so young at thirty-nine, with the wisdom of a veteran of the greatest of America's domestic struggles.

Like Robert F. Kennedy, he was a bridge between two worlds. He had come to prominence as a Christian pastor—and as a man of the church he spoke for the only authentic institution of the blacks in America. Out of the church and those who responded to its call, Martin Luther King had created his Southern Christian Leadership Conference —a group which took as much from the wrath of the Old Testament of Isaiah, Amos and Hosea as from the compassion of the New Testament. King had shown the world the resilience of black leadership, the depths of black courage. But his demonstration of this force provoked, by its own success, both imitators and rivals in the black community who would lead in other directions. Martin Luther King was thus a multiple link—he could link the black community to the larger American community, could link his demands to the legislative process, could link his people behind him, could link to and draw in line the newer, violent leadership on the black extreme. The strain on the link, in the single man, must have been enormous.

King had been passing, in his own journey of experience, almost imperceptibly from Christian love to forceful militancy. What law could do had, by 1968, largely been done, chiefly by his leadership and that of Roy Wilkins of the NAACP. Yet blacks needed more: there could be no dignity in poverty, and so King had become more and more concerned with the secular condition of ghetto misery; he had become more and more concerned with the cold mechanics by which big cities, though proclaiming equality, indifferently left blacks imprisoned in slum squalor; he had become concerned, too, with the war in Vietnam, and was attempting to link the cause of withdrawal from Vietnam with the aspiration of the black. He had begun to mobilize and lead demonstrations for causes more pragmatic than civil rights. The extension of his experience in 1968 had led him to a new level of activity. His major effort for the spring of 1968 was to be an encampment of the Poor People's Campaign in Washington, D.C., a march of poor blacks, and whatever whites and other minorities they could draw along, to press Congress for sweeping new economic and social legislation. It was a force maneuver designed to cow the legislative conscience in Washington into submission. But before he began his Washington program, King would pay attention to the black sanitation men of Memphis, Tennessee, who were insisting on higher wages, as were the white sanitation men in New York. He was the symbol of resistance.

So, in the first week of April, 1968, he had come to lend his presence and authority to the protest in Memphis.

Martin Luther King stood there at six o'clock on Thursday evening, April 4th, on the second-floor balcony of the Lorraine Motel, chatting over the rail with friends in the courtyard below. He asked one of them, a musician, to play "Precious Lord, Take My Hand" at a rally in support of the garbage men he was about to address. Then, from somewhere a shot was fired, precisely accurate as is the pattern of modern American assassinations, and his head was all gushing with blood. It is doubtful whether we shall ever know completely why, or how, or by whom was managed the planned killing that destroyed Martin Luther King—any more than we shall ever know who planned, paid or organized the killing of Malcolm X, even though we hold the alleged slayers of both men in prison. Murder is usually a motivated act which rises from greed, temper or passion. Assassination is a symbolic act, the assassin having no reason to hate except for the symbol of what the victim stands for. Assassination snaps a symbolic link.

Martin Luther King was dead an hour after his shooting—at five minutes past seven, Memphis time. Within three hours his symbolism had become apparent in death across the nation in a perfect demonstration of the contagion of outburst which modern communications bring.

Violence broke first in Washington. It began in the long thin rectangle which stretches north from Pennsylvania Avenue, the main artery of Washington, to Florida Avenue and encompasses its chief downtown shopping area. It began as deeply disturbed Negroes decided that the shopping area must close its doors that very evening in homage to their champion so brutally killed. At the center of it was Stokely Carmichael, gun belted to his body, asking courteously that shopkeepers, theaters, restaurants close their doors at once in respect. All so approached did. Like a vigilante stalking at the head of his band, Carmichael led his gathering troops from emporium to emporium, precise and intelligent—insisting that there must be no violence until all were ready. "Go home and get your guns," he was quoted as urging them, trying to disperse his followers. But he could not control them; they scattered over the area to express vengeance in their own way. By ten the first tinkle of broken glass had begun to sound; minutes later, looting had begun.

It had begun, too, all across the nation—in Boston north of Grove Hall and all down Blue Hill Avenue; in Detroit, in Chicago, in Philadelphia, in San Francisco, Toledo and Pittsburgh—and everywhere uncontrolled, by either white or black. Spread thin, the forces of law-and-order could only appeal to superior authority; everywhere, National Guards were mobilized and the Federal strength was beseeched. By afternoon of Friday, in the national capital, the police were helpless; at two minutes past four President Johnson signed orders calling in the Army of the United States; and within an hour helmeted troops, their rifles tipped with bayonets, were in place. The looting and fires had reached within two blocks of the White House by the time that a company of trained riot troops took up positions on the White House grounds; at the Capitol, a light-machine-gun post was set up on the west steps, overlooking the approaches from the Mall; and the nation woke on Saturday to see pictures of its soldiers on the steps of Congress, in full battle gear, defending the hallowed spot for the first time since the Civil War.

The bloodshed occasioned by the death of Martin Luther King was to persist for a full week. It was to strike more than 100 cities. More than 50,000 Federal and National Guard troops were summoned to cope with the disorder, in one of the greatest internal military exertions of Americans against Americans in their history. Almost 20,000 people were arrested; and 39 people died.

The event was almost too large to grasp, politically. It had to be reduced for each man to more human terms. Of that evening, this confused reporter remembers only the sorrowing voice of Roy Wilkins on television, ejaculating in disconnected phrases: "looting . . . not sorrow, not anger . . . looting . . . Martin's memory is being desecrated. . . ." And the mourning, rocking lament of a black friend with whom I watched the television reporting: "Why? . . . Why does this happen at home? . . . What's home coming to?" For home in America is as much home to blacks as to whites; and violence menaces them as much as it does Americans of any color.

The assassination of Martin Luther King came two days after the Wisconsin primary, four days after the renunciation of Lyndon Johnson, two weeks after the withdrawal of Nelson Rockefeller. It happened one month before the Indiana primary, just as the politics of the season were beginning to jell, and marked the crest of the year's black violence. After this first cataclysm of April, there were to be no more major black outbursts for the rest of the year—although an ominous new pattern of pre-planned sniping and organized ambuscades for police continued into the early fall.

But by summer 1968 the police had learned something of riot tactics in racial disturbances; except in the case of a paroxysm such as followed the death of King, they were ready. Police stations now bristled with an array of formidable, non-lethal weapons—with mace, with tear-gas, with special tactical patrols, with new communications, with helicopters. Both National Guard and Federal Army were revising doctrine, drilling troops in mob-control, perfecting barricade and communication discipline; and the armed defenders of the law everywhere stood continuously at semi-alert. Many deplored the changing quality of internal readiness—more cheered; but none could deny that the change in posture of American government was new, and was, alas, a complete break with the traditions that had previously governed our municipalities.

These preparations had, however, been made chiefly against illiterate and poverty-stricken blacks. Black violence was something the police could understand; over and over again, one could question police and hear a rough-and-ready sympathy for the black youngsters. "How can you shoot a fifteen-year-old kid running down the street just because he's taken a radio from a store?" asked one Chicago cop, reminiscing about the riots of 1967, shortly before Mayor Daley's "shoot-to-kill" order in 1968. Moreover, most police forces in the large cities had already been thoroughly integrated; white and black officers served together; and if the white cop had no particular affection for the Negro, he was marked in the big city by no particular race hatred such as was true of him only twenty years ago, and as is still true in the South. For the tactical police forces, black violence, black riots, black outbursts are a familiar condition, a professional problem which they believe they can handle more efficiently in the streets than their masters can handle in the forum of politics.

But when it came to the other great new source of violence in the United States—the violence of the student masses—the police were as baffled as their masters or political thinkers. The agonized outcry of the Negroes was rooted in a savage American past. But the outcry of the students was a defiance of the future—a screaming for identity against the machinery of an American life which increasingly locks them into a world they cannot comprehend.

The swift sweep of the student masses to the largest single interest group in America, we have already touched on. (See Chapter Three.) But before we can understand the intensity of student protest, or the rhythm of its development in the years leading to 1968, it should be set against the general background of American life as it is presented to them.

The education industry is, at the moment, the largest single employer of productive time of any industry in America. Yet it does not process steel, oats, cattle, oils—it processes human beings. It absorbs as raw material unshaped and unformed teen-agers, on the threshold of maturity, trembling in their first search for identity, and feeds them through four or eight years of high-pressure processing in a network of giant plants that rival the largest of General Motors, Ford or United States Steel. California has 266,396 students in its college system, 97,046 in its university system. New York has 259,548 students in its university system, and another 157,326 in its city university system. Individual campuses in some state college systems are industrial complexes of over 20,000 workers.

The first trauma in the life of any young American normally comes at the moment of his admission to this quasi-industrial center. Thirty-five years ago the Educational Testing Service of Princeton tested only 35,000 youngsters seeking admission to college, and it could provide two or three examiners who would leisurely scrutinize essay questions in the College Board examinations for the measure of an individual youth's ability and personality. Today the same service must test over 1,500,000 youngsters seeking admission to college each year; and can do so only by preparing examinations which are coded by machines that produce a machine-stamped report, machine-measuring four years of life in percentile numbers.

Youngsters grasp the implication of such sterile numbers only vaguely. They will be taught in college that the exploration of the individual, the development of one's own talents, is the great purpose of life; they will be taught to think independently, to question premises, to express themselves in projects and do their own thing. Yet the outer perspective of American life beyond the campus runs contrary to such teaching, and has been running contrary for twenty years. Opportunity for self-expression in independent careers dwindles. The number of self-employed and free-enterprisers has been diminishing in America since 1950; by 1960 the percentage of self-employed to all employed had fallen lower than ever before in American history; by the late 1960's, the percentage had fallen yet further. Practically all the increment in employment in the first six years of the Kennedy-Johnson administrations came in the public, non-profit sector of American life—in government bureaucracies, local, state or federal; or in schools, hospitals and social service institutions. The great corporations, concentrating at an ever more furious rate, hold just as little opportunity for creative self-expression or individual leadership. And even the traditional areas of creativity—writing, journalism, television, design—diminish in the numbers they absorb.

American universities are shaped to train an elite—not an administrative elite, as in Europe, but an elite in service to its people, an elite that can lead and change matters. The whole thrust of the American past has been to open leadership to all by opening higher education to all; and it is near-heresy to challenge this thrust, to question whether too many leaders, too many young people trained to expect to lead, may not in the end consider themselves betrayed when they emerge to find the available posts of leadership narrowing as their own numbers expand. Scores of thousands of students, for example, study international affairs; yet the State Department absorbs only 150 new Foreign Service Officers a year, and American industry only a few thousand overseas. More young people in New York, for example, are probably studying Far Eastern history than are apprenticed out as carpenters; yet New York needs carpenters more than Far Eastern experts. Two streams of American experience contradict each other in American colleges. By one tradition, each youth must be able to decide as an individual in which discipline he chooses to be processed; but the processing he receives ignores the industrial tradition; the universities do not provide a market for his talents as leader when he graduates.

Students enter a mammoth industrial complex to be trained for leader-ship—yet emerge four or eight years later to find that they are expected to subdue their hopes and become administrative cogs in huge industrial or governmental complexes.

If this is the general condition, several other conditions aggravate it, the chief of which is the draft, the intake apparatus of the most impersonal and mammoth complex of all—the American military. The draft policies of the United States have been obsolete for so long as to make World War II's Flying Fortress look like advanced design. Selective Service, unchanged since World War II, was designed for total mobilization of an entire nation in a total fight for survival of civilization. What is required now, for American defense, is something entirely different—a policy to provide technical manpower for its stra-tegic nuclear arm, as well as a truly selective service to provide the limited manpower needed for garrisoning and policing the *limes* of the orderly world. America's youth now lives, therefore, under a system of random, incoherent, confusing conscription in which service, possibly death, is a matter of almost pure chance. The system unsettles all with its sporadic call-ups; it hangs over every college talk, every plan for the future; and service and death, since they come by accident, deprive duty and life of meaning. An almost obscene condition of thought is stimulated in which the best and highest-motivated of the young accept fraud, hypocrisy, evasion, influence and dishonesty as part of the game. (The only more obscene political condition that I know of in this country is its method of financing elections.)

Add to this general condition of numbers, of crowding, of mass processing, of draft pressure, the intense work schedules of students, work loads of hours and demand rarely encountered in adult life. Add again to this condition the menace of the Vietnam war never adequately explained to the young men who must fight. Add again the upheaval of guilt and conscience occasioned by the Black Revolt—and one finds a mass in search of meaning, ready to respond to the first clear call that explains their marginal condition in American life and promises redress of their grievances.

This explosive campus proletariat has been growing in America for fifteen years. But it is only in the past four or five years that a minority of student leaders has learned to manipulate this mass, to offer it a new vocabulary, a new rhetoric providing a deceptive facsimile of political reality which now, for thousands of the best young minds in the country, is the language of truth itself. One must steep oneself in this new language before one can understand the new forms of action it invites, and the hard street tactics of violence which have developed from it.

A glossary might start, for example, thus:

Democracy is a phoney word to be sneered at unless carefully modified by such phrases as *democracy of the streets, democracy of direct action* or *participatory democracy.* Otherwise, *democracy* is a trick played on the people by the *establishment.*

Establishment is, of course, one of the most fashionable words in American politics today, and was to be heard as frequently from Barry Goldwater's thinkers as from the Students for a Democratic Society. *Establishment* in the new lexicon is the synonym for any group of leaders anywhere—in the press, in the government, in business, in education, in finance, in the Senate, in the House. On certain occasions, when discussing an entrenched political organization, as in Chicago, New Jersey or Indiana, the establishment becomes *the machine.* Most hated of all establishments is the *military-industrial complex* which dominates the American government, manufactures napalm, and sends boys off to die for gross corporate profit. (The inventor of the warning phrase *military-industrial complex,* that thoughtful scholar and historian Malcolm Moos, now President of the University of Minnesota, is himself frequently attacked as a member of the establishment.)

The glossary becomes operational when it moves on to its action words. Action opens by insistence on *dialogue.* A *dialogue* is begun (usually by a self-appointed delegation meeting with an official) when demands (*non-negotiable demands*) are presented and *communications channels* opened. The best ambiance for *communications* is something called *creative tension,* which is designed to reveal buried hates and unspoken prejudice. The rhythm of *dialogue, creative tension* and *communications* reaches its climax in what is called *confrontation,* a riot condition. In *confrontation,* force (styled by the provokers of confrontation as *non-violent* force) is arrayed against the force of the *establishment* (usually styled *police brutality*); and as shoving, pushing, cursing and obscenity rise, bloodshed frequently follows, imposed by the *pigs* (a term which scarcely endears demonstrators to the police), and the cruelty of authority is exposed.

In this new rhetoric, normal contradictions of thought vanish. Thus, the old virtues of tolerance and free speech becomes *repressive tolerance,* a sinister effort by the *establishment* to smother the truth by indulgence; this, apparently, justifies the denial of free speech to those who disagree. To steal, seize or destroy offices or files becomes *to liberate.* The old Marxist adverbial phrase *objectively speaking* becomes, in the new rhetoric, a transitional phrase to any statement that cannot be factually proven; when a speaker begins a paragraph with *objectively speaking,* it means that any construct of the imagination he thinks *should* be true is indeed so. The word *non-violence* is turned inside out. If what can be won by the massing of bodies, the occupation of buildings, shoving, and the use of brawn is yielded immediately, it proves the validity of *non-violence*. (Stone-and-bottle-throwing can be classed, in this vocabulary, as non-violent.) If the non-violent aggressors are resisted, then those who resist are styled violent and brutal. Eric Sevareid was recently reminded, in one of his broadcasts, of his European experience: "They [the student activists] have the same approach," he said, "as the early Nazis and early Communists. 'We are right,' they say, 'we are progress. If you resist us, or defend yourself, you are the instigators of violence.' "

Discussion in the new language has the quality, frequently, of a game of intellectual tag—the man who can first pin the proper label on the enemy wins. The best label to pin, for example, on any adversary is *racist*. Once that tag is pinned, no denial can wipe it away, and moral sanction has been set up for any action that follows the pinning of the label. It is important, always, in any issue or confrontation to establish this moral sanction first; however large or small are the procedural obstacles on the way to the confrontation, the moral sanction arms the demonstrator to violate them, and his strength is as the strength of ten because his heart is pure.

The rhetorical style is important—because the rhetoric imprisons minds, the rhetoric identifies grievances, abrades restraint, leads to action.

The student mass is, of course, like all masses, made up of individuals; but one must see the student individuals as passing through an experience as traumatic as the Negroes' in the city slums. It is only necessary for an activist minority to engage the emotions of a resentful majority to have a force at its command; and in the general resentment of the student masses, the dynamic of action calls youngsters to support demonstrations or resistance of fellow students in any form; to "chicken out" is to be a coward. The larger intellectual courage of resisting the heroes of the new thinking, or refrain from action until purpose is clear, is rather too much to expect of a seventeen-, eighteen- or nineteen-year-old whose manhood is challenged and whose conscience is troubled.

Thus began the student movements which were to affect the content of American politics in 1968 as much as the Black Revolt.

From 1960 on, we can trace this movement by a series of episodes —episodes rising continuously in their temper of protest, paralleled at each step by a rising mastery of tactics in organization, confrontation and, ultimately, violence.

It was early in the 1960's that two new student groups, of a type not known since the Depression, made themselves prominent. Until that time, intercollegiate Young Democrats and intercollegiate Young Republicans, Young Conservatives, Young Liberals, Young Communists, as well as Student Councils and even the National Student Association, founded in 1947, had limited their concern and activities almost entirely to the campus. The first of the new groups to enter national politics may be dismissed easily—it was the Young Americans for Freedom, a far-right group that soared swiftly to attention in the Goldwater campaign of 1964, then quickly, unexplainedly, became dormant; it lacked apparently the skill to engage the conscience of the larger masses of fellow students in its goals. More important was the Students for a Democratic Society, whose manifesto, the Port Huron Statement, written by founding father Tom Hayden, proclaimed in 1962, in a rhetoric that he and the student movement have long left behind, that "We regard men as infinitely precious and possessed of unfulfilled capacities for reason, freedom and love. . . . We oppose the depersonalization that reduces human beings to the status of things. . . . Vague appeals to posterity cannot justify the mutilations of the present. . . . As a social system we seek the establishment of a democracy of individual participation, governed by two central aims: that the individual share in those social decisions determining the quality and direction of his life; that society be organized to encourage independence in men and provide the media for their common participation. . . ."

The spirited rhetoric of the Port Huron Statement called to students at a time when civil rights had become the chief concern of every man of good-will in American politics; but for students, civil rights had an even more direct appeal. The black students in the South were already in the field; their sit-ins in 1961 had been the first match to the tinder of resistance; white students were their allies. By 1964 the passion and indignation that the Students for a Democratic Society voiced had found expression in two large episodes. The more dramatic was the rioting on the campus of the University of California at Berkeley—the first violent confrontation of students of the left with the police of the nation. Though the direct issue was described as one of "free speech," the incubating factor was the effort of many students to identify themselves and the Berkeley campus with the national shame at the condition of the blacks in the state of Mississippi. More significant in 1964, however, was the participation of almost 1,000 students from all across the country in the actual invasion of the state of Mississippi. Their gallantry was that of innocents, their tactics were primitive; by the time they had called the nation's attention to the condition there, they had paid with three dead, foully murdered. What the students learned from the Mississippi adventure was chiefly the strength of their own courage; and later, when they carried their cause to the Atlantic City convention of the Democrats in 1964, they learned how to use physical demonstration in the presence of television to score their point on national attention.

In 1965 and 1966 the concern of student leaders moved on to the Vietnam war—and here they discovered larger resources of support, even as they learned newer tactics of protest. The "teach-ins" of 1965

—an insistence on knowing why Americans were being sent to war—spread like an intellectual rash across the nation's campuses; and in their spread, student leaders discovered that they could engage the sympathy and concern of large numbers of their own faculty; they, not the administrations or authority, were the vehicles of truth. By 1967 the issue of Vietnam had been carried from the colleges to the streets. Techniques were being learned—of house-to-house canvassing, of street demonstrations in draft protest, of the parrying of police mobilizations. Thousands of students were engaged in the loosely linked series of episodes called "Vietnam Summer," climaxing in a major demonstration at the Pentagon.

The Pentagon demonstrations of October, 1967, were largely theater; but for the mobilizers they provided a tactical training ground, teaching street control, street communications, the bussing of large bodies of manpower, and the movement and manipulation of such bodies in the presence of television. In the handbook of protest, they were the high point until then of the strategy of confrontation.

Confrontation is drama; drama is a commercially valuable quantity; political confrontation provides television with free drama; by the laws of its nature, television cannot ignore free drama. Maurice Valency recently wrote: "When Plato warned in *The Republic* that the frenzy of the theater is potentially dangerous to the state, he was thinking, obviously, of the irrational excitement of the audience under the spell of dramatic illusion. . . . The art of the Greeks was supremely rational. It is only in comparatively recent years that irrationality as such has been elevated to the rank of an artistic principle." It is doubtful whether any of the students involved in the protests of 1964–5–6–7 had recently read Plato. But those who led them had an instinctive sense of what Plato meant, and they were veterans in the artistry of confrontation. Tom Hayden of the Students for a Democratic Society was, at twenty-eight, older than the Leon Trotsky who, at twenty-six, was chairman of the St. Petersburg Soviet of 1905; David Dellinger, leader of the National Mobilization Committee, was, at fifty-three, older than the Lenin who, at forty-seven, led the November insurrection that toppled the Czar; and just as Lenin and Trotsky were shrewder than the Czarist garrisons they brought down, the students' leaders were shrewder than the police commands they were to provoke in 1968 on the new fronts. They spoke a new language, understood new dimensions of force and emotion, and, in the cultural climate of America, commanded the heights of attention and the valleys of sympathy. Thus 1968 approached on the student front.

One of my earliest memories of 1968 is of a visit to the January conference of the Student Mobilization Committee, one of a number of student meetings across the country which were preparing for the Chicago riots. I registered first in the Ida Noyes Hall of the University of Chicago, and my impression was of the forlorn and wistful appearance of the arriving youngsters, and the bizarre decorations of those sad seekers of identity who had traveled far and arrived overnight or at dawn for this rendezvous with history. There was the youngster in the Australian campaign hat, his chest festooned with buttons (*"Viva Che . . ."*); the youngster in the black stovepipe hat; the barefoot girls walking about, despite the rain that fell continuously outside; the wanderers with their rolled-up blankets slung over their shoulders. As morning wore on, the file of registrants began to thicken with the children of the Chicago middle class, from local and suburban universities, open-shirted or necktie-less, white, clean and respectable. Some of the faces were, despite the generation gap, dimly evocative, faintly recognizable—such as the countenances of the prim young ladies, high-nosed and be-spectacled, almost fragile but quivering with dedication. I had seen young American ladies like these thirty years before in China, of precisely the same cast and bearing—but as missionaries saving the heathen. Some cause, in each generation, invites the young ladies of America to devote themselves to good works—be it abolition, missions or temperance. Now the cause of this generation was peace.

All had come to fight for peace, to stop the war in Vietnam. But if peace was the cause, little else made sense, for the heroes of their cause were killers. REVOLUTIONARY LITERATURE HERE, read a big red banner, and under the banner were stretched the literature tables. VICTORY TO THE VIETCONG, read the poster on the Trotskyite table. *Concentration Camp on the Campus* was one of the more popular pamphlets on the SDS table, and a girl strolling away with the pamphlet in her hand was saying to her friend, "Look, this one really tells you what they're doing to us." There was a Black Students table, a DuBois Club table, a Youth Against War and Fascism (Communist) table. Other tables were covered with literature from Hanoi, and China; one table was surmounted with the Chinese Red Star flag. Above all—Che Guevara. Buttons with Che's legend ("Wherever death may surprise us, let it be welcome if our battle cry has reached even one receptive ear, and another hand reaches out to take up our arms"), pictures of Che, posters of Che sold almost as religious trinkets to devout church-goers.

The opening meeting was held in the University of Chicago chapel. The chairman opened the meeting by explaining with a snicker that the chapel had been built by John D. Rockefeller, "May his soul ascend," and then after the responsive laugh, "I ask you all now to stand for a moment of silent tribute to Che Guevara!"—and, reverently, all stood, bowing their heads for the man who had promised the world

a hundred Vietnams, who had taken his gun to strange countries, sought
to kill, and been killed by those who defended themselves against him.

There followed then a speech, a perfect sample of the new rhetoric,
from a mild-mannered professor of law named Arthur Kinoy, described
as a "noted civil rights leader." He began moderately enough, but then
slowly began to boom, to exhort, to warn, his voice rising passionately
to near-shrieks and descending to hollow, sorrowing whispers. The burden of his message: the government of the United States was preparing
the machinery of repression to snuff out all liberty; concentration camps
were being built; the courts were violating the law; the cause of Rap
Brown, the noted black racist, was the cause of the students, for the court
order against Rap Brown was a new, fascist form of "preventative arrest."
Gradually, as his decibel count rose, so did the violence of his rhetoric,
as he pounded, shrieked and escalated his prose. The government
of the United States soon became in his discourse "The Powers
That Be," to be replaced in mid-course by the phrase "The Rulers,"
and, finally, to be styled simply "The Enemy." He concluded that there
was only one way to fight The Enemy, the government of the United
States, and that was by taking the offensive—by resistance. And then,
in a whisper, he ended by saying that he was only a lawyer, they were
his clients, he could tell them what to do—but they must do it themselves, the rest was up to them.

He was succeeded by a balding "student" leader who launched on
another warning—the *Pueblo* had just been seized by the North Koreans.
He wanted to warn of the war plot of the United States government
—this was just a trick to escalate the war and invade North Korea or
Red China. "Remember the *Maine,*" he told them. And remember the
Lusitania. And remember Pearl Harbor. All these were tricks by the
establishment to suck America into a war—and at this point I left.

There was not much to be learned by attending such open meetings.
All who came were given complete freedom to speak; meetings, arguments and disputations stretched on endlessly; yet one could not help
hearing the echo of the phrase "repressive tolerance." The more speaking, the more wild rhetoric, the less would openly be decided. And on
the second day, when I asked one student what had been decided about
the demonstrations scheduled for Chicago, I was told, "About the march
on Chicago—we didn't talk much about that. I think the Continuations
Committee will decide that on a higher level, and then tell us."

I went on from the Chicago conference of the Student Mobilization
Committee to New Hampshire to encounter the McCarthy students in
the field. (See Chapter Three.) And the contrast made obvious that
two rival leaderships challenged the student masses to enter politics.
There was the McCarthy-Lowenstein-Brown doctrine of participation,
by which students were invited to enter the process of politics, seize the

machinery of state and then turn it to their own policies. However much one might disagree with the policies they sought, their leadership fitted into the American tradition of peaceful change for defined purpose. And then there were the other students of the SMC-SDS-Hayden doctrine, which summoned students to smash the machinery of state or of existing institutions and thereafter, in the ruins, decide what they would build in their place. The latter, a minority within a minority, were less conspicuous as the year opened; but their skills, in 1968, were to be transferred from campus to convention to campaign to make of politics a nightmare; and their art of demonstration, causing bloodshed and riot, was to call for new judgment, different entirely from the judgment on the ghetto riots already disturbing American minds.

One should linger over the state of this art as it had evolved on campuses before its transfer to the forum of politics in 1968; and the best description of the state of the art may be called Searle's scenario, after Professor John R. Searle, professor of philosophy at the University of California at Berkeley.[3] Searle's scenario, which summarized the campus unrest of 1968, postulates three stages. Stage One is the picking of a procedural issue on which the college administration cannot give in, but which is somehow related to a Sacred Cause—Civil Rights, Freedom of Speech, the War in Vietnam. Demonstrations must violate as many rules as possible to assure punishment. Stage Two: When punishment is provoked, then the university authorities themselves become the target of the protest, because if they have defended orderly procedure in opposing, say, an anti-war strike, they can be tagged as being for the war itself. As sympathetic students rally to defend the sacred cause, the number of demonstrators will grow, and TV will pick the leaders and dignify the uproar. Stage Three: The administration is forced to call the police. Widespread revulsion follows, sympathetic professors become active in the protest, and no liberal dares oppose it. By now, with police on the campus, with bloodshed splashed on TV screens, it is made obvious that the "administration" has somehow failed—and if the scenario works perfectly, a student strike becomes general, the president is fired, the faculty is divided, the campus closed. Technically, this is called the "radicalization of the student mass."

It was at Columbia University in New York, in the spring of 1968, three weeks after the black riots of April, that American students first showed their potential for disturbance, in an almost perfect rehearsal of Searle's scenario. The rule to be violated was an obscure rule of the university administration, flatly enunciated six months earlier in Septem-

---

[3] Professor Searle, who has manned both sides of the barricades in recent years, is author of "A Foolproof Scenario for Student Revolts," published in *The New York Times Magazine* of December 29th, 1968, easily the best study of the pattern, as well as delightful reading.

ber: that there would be no indoor demonstrations without permission on university grounds. But the Students for a Democratic Society, led by a youth whose glands had outrun his learning, had chosen issues which none of the moralists of the campus dared oppose—chief among them a severance of Columbia's ties with national defense, and the suspension of construction on a gymnasium hard by Harlem's Negro ghetto. Forbidden to demonstrate indoors (at the Low Library), the students, after a confused milling about, first seized Hamilton Hall, where they imprisoned the acting undergraduate Dean, Henry S. Coleman. Rapidly they seized four more university halls, including their president's office, where they ransacked the files and broke up the furniture. By now the issues were no longer the rules, but had become Columbia's complicity in the war in Vietnam, and Columbia's imperialism in the adjacent Negro "colony" of Harlem. Vacillating and uncertain, unwilling to shed blood, the administrative forces dallied for six days until, on the night of April 29th, police were finally summoned—and in a bloody, violent, shrieking night, as bluecoats swept the campus, with TV attendant at every step, 711 students were arrested and 148 persons were injured, of whom 20 were police. A reprise of this violence occurred three weeks later, on May 22nd, with an even more intense police reaction that brought 177 arrests and 68 injuries. By May, however, learning at Columbia had come almost to a halt—the administration had in effect suspended the school year; student body and faculty were bristling with internal hostilities; what had been a community had been radicalized into systematic hates by confrontation; and in August, Columbia's president, Grayson Kirk, resigned. By August, however, center stage in the drama of confrontation was in Chicago, for which Columbia had been only a dress rehearsal.

The significance of the Columbia rioting was not, however, in its scope, its target, its wild brutalities and counter-brutalities. Its significance was, I think, caught best in the afterthoughts of Jacques Nevard, once a foreign correspondent in Asia, now Deputy Police Commissioner of New York, who was required to explain the people to the police and the police to the public. The Columbia students, recollects Nevard, with a cosmopolitan sense of irony, were quintessentially the children of the bourgeoisie. Their fathers, by class tradition, employed the cops; traditionally, the cops were there to protect them, their property, their neighborhood from the "proles." Cops did what they were told. But now, at Columbia, the cops were against them—cops were telling them, the pampered children of the bourgeoisie, what they *must* do. A cop may argue, plead, menace; but at some point a cop's duty is to say, "Now—get out," and he puts his hand on the arm of the resister. When a cop grips, he grips hard, squeezing or twisting the muscle. "If," says Nevard, "you've been brought up in the Spock generation, and when a cop puts his hand on you it's the first time in your life anyone has put his hand on you in anger, you're frightened—you scream, jerk, kick and bite. These were upper-middle-class kids faced with the revolt of the hired hands. The shock was perhaps greater on the part of the cops—here they were faced, for the first time in history, with the rejection of society by people who were brought up to inherit that society; nothing in any policeman's experience had prepared him for that."

Of the students who occupied buildings, rifled files, destroyed the life research of at least one professor, few were in any doubt that they were breaking the law. And it is here that their form of violence differed in political quality from the violence of the blacks in their ghettos. Negroes and poor white workingmen know they cannot break the law unpunished; when out of passion or desperation they break the law, they accept its penalties, but do not question its legitimacy. Few of the students at Columbia, however, had any knowledge of the consequences of breaking a law; and when the law imposed its reflex penalties, it was the legitimacy of the law itself they challenged. And thus, in all the turmoil of debate on law-and-order in 1968, it was the student protest that gave the issue its sharpest definition: what, in the present American culture, is the duty of citizen to law, and law to him?

These questions run to the beginning of American history, for American history begins with a contradiction, and this heritage, in 1968, was to haunt us.

In its chartering document, the Constitution, two high and conflicting purposes were set out for the American government. In its preamble, the document told Americans that we, the people, establish this Constitution "in order to form a more perfect union, establish justice, ensure domestic tranquillity, provide for the common defense." But then it went on, adding as an afterthought, and under pressure, a Bill of Rights guaranteeing the undefined rights of assembly, petition, freedom of speech, press and thought. And thus, by derivation, the right of demonstration and confrontation. In 1968 the first guarantee, of domestic tranquillity, was to be challenged by the later guarantee, of assembly and confrontation—and no one could say which had priority over the other.

The question and contradiction had not truly arisen before, because underlying both the Constitution and the Declaration of Independence were earlier American roots going back to the Mayflower Compact, all of them based on the concept of government by consent of the governed.

The black violence between 1965 and 1968 could escape from

the apparent contradiction by the blacks' history in America. They had been dragged to America in chains, without consent. They had made no compact and were bound by no historic agreement to codes that reduced them to beasts in servitude. All others had come willingly, because they found the opportunities in the new world better than in the old, and consented to be governed by laws that they had made together. It was precisely one century before, in 1858, that Abraham Lincoln had best expressed the black dilemma of 1968. "Now when by all these means," he said in a speech at Edwardsville, Illinois, "you have succeeded in dehumanizing the Negro; when you have put him down and made it forever impossible for him to be but as the beasts of the field; when you have extinguished his soul, and placed him where the ray of hope is blown out in darkness like that which broods over the spirits of the damned; are you quite sure the demon which you have roused will not turn and rend you?"

But the revolt of the students was entirely different in character, novel not only in American history but in world history. They, the group to whom society offered most, repudiated what society offered; the order that society spread before them as the future appalled them; the increasing wealth, food, shelter, leisure that the American system offered might nourish the dreams of the working class, but it nourished few dreams of individual expression or personality to those who saw themselves as tomorrow's leaders. Tearing at the system, like beasts clawing at cages that confine them, they saw laws as barriers to be torn down, while other millions of Americans saw laws as barriers for protection.

Violence scarred and lacerated American politics through 1968. Crime and killing, robbery and looting, perversion and let, riot, sniping, assassination all pounded on Americans as they considered their choice of President. But it was the revolt of the student proletariat that gave most shape and form to the issue of law-and-order: Who would control the instruments of government? How could the instruments of government change the structure of American society, of learning, of industry, of municipalities so that the last third of the century would not be swallowed up by the centralization and discipline that new technologies required? And if the instruments of government could no longer open society to individual expression, should the laws be smashed because one disagreed with the way they were used?

Vietnam would sooner or later be settled, at more or less tragic cost. But the issue of law-and-order was elevated in 1968 to the threshold of Constitutional crisis: What kind of people were we, what kind of people did we seek to become, what kind of new communities did we need to create, what restraints were required on expressions of purpose or communication that nourished violence? Though such questions never entered the political dialogue of 1968, sooner or later the issue of law-and-order, of duty and discipline, of structures and purpose, would require re-examination of the Constitution itself.

CHAPTER EIGHT

MIRAGE AT MIAMI: ROCKEFELLER VERSUS NIXON

H ISTORY past seems to be ribbed as starkly as a cathedral. But history present is never quite so clear.

Thus, it was not at all clear, as the Republicans prepared to gather in August at Miami, that Richard Nixon had foreclosed their nomination two months earlier, on the day of his meeting with Senators Strom Thurmond and John Tower in Atlanta, Georgia, on June 1st, 1968.

And if it was not all clear, it was because Nelson Rockefeller, Governor of New York, was brandishing his lance across his party and the nation in full-throated war cry. Appreciation of Nixon's smooth control over the convention and his victory is impossible unless one studies the power, the perplexity and the spring vacillation of Nelson Rockefeller, the most majestic and considerable quantity in his Party's national affairs for a full ten years.

As 1968 opened, to friends and enemies alike Rockefeller's intentions had been the great mystery of the Party's future. Rising high above all lesser figures on the national Republican scene, he was almost a force of nature, like a slumbering volcano, wreathed in clouds, occasionally emitting smoke which soothsayers attempted to interpret. Were he to explode again in 1968, the entire landscape of politics would change.

One must see Nelson Rockefeller in silhouette against the background of his Party. Rockefeller is a man who believes in aggressive, innovative managerial government in a Republican Party which distrusts government. What he shares with fellow Republicans is basically the old belief that the ethical engines of work, study, thrift, perseverance and striving flourish best in the American system of free, private enterprise. Rockefeller, however, also believes that government must act, at whatever cost, positively, to service this free-enterprise system, and that the roots of the system lie in individual opportunity which government must enlarge. The rank-and-file of the Republican Party believe that the less action government takes and the less interference it imposes on private enterprise, the better government is. Rockefeller has contempt for the stodgy majority of Republicans of this breed—but loves the Party as if it were his own family heritage. The lesser Party leaders fear Rockefeller—and many loathe him.

By 1968 Rockefeller's ten-year record as Governor of the Empire State had left no doubt about his sense of government. He had been seen as a curiosity when first elected in 1958 after a flamboyant, blintzes-and-pizza campaign that had made his rival, Averell Harriman, seem wooden. His first year as he learned the job had been unexciting, marked chiefly by a solid Republican budget-balancing performance. Then, gradually, as he began to warm to the challenges, program after program slowly began to take shape, of a scope and vision that no other state in the union could match. He had singled out education as his first target, financing education out of ever rising taxes in ever rising prosperity. By 1968 he boasted that the number of state university students had multiplied fourfold in his decade and guaranteed student loans had soared from 5,000 to 100,000. Housing and hospitals, minimum-wage laws and civil-rights laws, consumer-protection laws and narcotic-control laws had followed one after the other. All of central Albany was being torn down to build a mall which would make it the most beautiful state capital in the nation; the first State Council of the Arts had been set up. By 1968 the architecture of his vision stretched far into the future: $1 billion had been raised to clear the polluted waters of the Empire State's great rivers; $2.5 billion had been authorized for a master plan to rearrange, rebuild and coordinate all the transportation services that radiate out of New York; another $1 billion was under debate for an Urban Development Corporation, to stimulate $5 billion of private capital to clear the slums of the core cities. New Yorkers and their children would thank him for generations.

Not only did Rockefeller approach government as a responsibility and a challenge in problem-solving. It was, for him, hobby, sport and obsession. Inviting friends to dinner at his home, he might, immediately after coffee, haul out the red cardboard folders in which he carries his papers, and spread out on the floor the state's master program for parks—explaining in detail his plan for Troy, Syracuse, Utica as if he were rearranging the furniture in his living room, which he loved to do also. Government was a personal excitement. Not content with passing the largest state rat-control appropriation in the nation, he would direct the family's Rockefeller University, spangled with Nobel prize-winners, to launch immediately a study of the biology of rats, hoping they might come up with a rodent birth-control scheme. Lounging by a pool-side, he might suddenly set off on a gorgeous imaginary tour of New York City, Long Island and the lower Hudson Valley as they would be twenty years hence when his transportation program was finished: in his imagination, high-speed trains darted from Riverhead, Long Island, seventy-five miles away, to downtown Manhattan in less than an hour. Subways served the great airports. Zoning in this new world of high-speed, coordinated metropolitan transportation would be lifted from the suburban communities and become part of an over-all state plan for great industrial parks, quiet residential communities and open spaces for recreation.

Such achievements, by 1968, were known to every other Republican governor of the nation, the best of whom sought to emulate him. But of all big spenders in the nation, Nelson Rockefeller was the biggest spender of all—in his decade in New York, spending in the state budget had almost quadrupled from $1.79 billion annually to $6.41 billion projected for 1969. Rockefeller's dreams dazzled large-scale planners—but the costs shocked ordinary Republicans. Rockefeller recognized their shock; but he saw them as the backward, primitive members of his political family; he did not enjoy talking to them and preferred to keep them at arm's length. His coolness and disdain for their thinking was never concealed; and the feud between Rockefeller and Party regulars across the nation had all the bitterness of an intensely emotional family quarrel.

In New York this bitterness had a special quality of acrimony. The Republican Party of that state had been for years almost a dependency of the Rockefeller family, like the Rockefeller Foundation or the Rockefeller University. For a decade the family and its friends had picked up every deficit of the statewide Republican Party in every campaign; and, on occasion, Nelson Rockefeller could pull out of his inside pocket a little folded paper, typed in blue, which reminded him precisely of the total the Party had cost the family over the years, a very large figure indeed. Upstate New York Republicans, as primitive in many ways as rural Ohio Republicans, resented the liberal Rockefeller programs and the Rockefeller style—but the state Party depended on his generosity, and his discipline over its votes in the legislature was severe. With the larger men of the state Party—Senator Jacob Javits and Mayor John Lindsay—Rockefeller maintained relations that ran from cordial to cool; they, too, though agreeing with his programs, smarted under his splendid and innocent assumption that in New York he was sole master.

In the Empire State, Nelson Rockefeller was beholden to no one; no crevice of weakness or obligation could be found by lobbyists, little politicians or important industrialists to exert pressure on him. Once a hugely self-important, enormously wealthy, lavishly generous contributor to the Republican Party visited him in New York. Scion of a great whiskey-and-spirits empire, the young man wanted Rockefeller to reduce New York State's liquor taxes, among the highest in the nation. When refused, the young man flippantly said, "Well, I'll just have to go up to Albany and buy up the legislature myself." Cold-white with anger, Rockefeller rose from his desk and said, "Now I must ask you to leave this room."

Rockefeller had always wanted to be President—ever since his service with Eisenhower's administration in 1953. But, trapped in Washington at too low a level, frustrated by Eisenhower's passive concept of administration, constantly at odds with John Foster Dulles' diplomacy, he became convinced that the only true authority in politics comes from the people in direct elections. Thus, brushing aside all lesser New York politicians, he came home to run in 1958 for Governor and won; he stumbled through an amateurish effort to wrest the Republican Presidential nomination in 1960 from Richard Nixon, then set his sights on 1964. The intervening years were harsh; a beloved son was lost in New Guinea in 1961; the next year his thirty-two-year-old marriage dissolved. He was re-elected in 1962 as Governor and then remarried.[1] But, sweet as the new marriage was, it was to frustrate his life's ambition. Branded a wife-stealer by the old moralists in his campaign against Barry Goldwater, he and his new wife were openly mocked in public; and the Party was split in the greatest electoral disaster of the twentieth century. Deserted by most of the Republican leadership in New York State early in 1966, Rockefeller fought a furious uphill battle for re-election, won it by the substantial margin of 392,263, and then rested.

All through 1967 and into 1968 the dominant question of Republican politics was what this man would do next. Those who dared pinion the lordly Governor with a hard question received no answer. To those he trusted most, at the end of a conversation, he would growl, "Let them come to me. I'm here. They know my record." But the Party was unwilling to come. And he was unwilling to seek.

Rockefeller, after his re-election in 1966, had come to peace with himself. He might, alone at night, toy in the imagination of dreams with a fictional Nelson Rockefeller, magisterial President of the United States, whose knowledge of affairs at home and abroad untied the complexities of the twentieth century. But by day he was Governor of New York, enthralled by the problems of his home state, self-fulfillment satisfied so long as the voters of New York went on voting for him. To touch the night dream would be to shatter it; to reach for it would be to stimulate the venom of the scores of thousands in the Party structure who would never forgive him for destroying Barry Goldwater. Even more im-

[1] See *The Making of the President—1964,* p. 80.

portant: in his own home he was now content. His new wife and their two little boys had given a warmth to living that he was reluctant to forsake. In ten years, counting primaries and bond issues, he had fought nine exhausting campaigns; he did not want to drag himself through such combat again, or expose his wife to the humiliation and abuse of 1964.

Pressed over and over again by reporters about Rockefeller's thinking, his witty and devoted press secretary, Leslie Slote, found a formula that satisfied everyone. Rockefeller, said Slote, was not a *political* candidate. He was an *existentialist* candidate. He could not possibly become a real candidate by trying to be one, for that would wreck the Party again. He could *become* a candidate only by *not* trying to be a candidate. And since he did not want to try, the best posture was the existential posture, the most natural personal posture: to do nothing.

In politics, this translated into very simple terms: let George do it. (See Chapter Two.) George Romney was the best man Rockefeller knew for the Presidency, after himself. Rockefeller respected Nixon as a formidable political quantity; but as a personality who might sit in the White House—the idea seemed like a bad joke to the master of the Empire State. Romney, however, was, like himself, governor of a great industrial state, sensitive to civil rights, a good executive. If Romney was weak on foreign affairs or in his speeches, that could be remedied. Rockefeller could supply speech-writers and research; Rockefeller could release his all-purpose foreign-policy expert, Henry Kissinger, for a full-day briefing of the Michigan Governor. George would make the run. There was no doubt about the sincerity of Rockefeller's daytime support of Romney, no matter what the night dreams may have whispered to him. Long after the Romney campaign began to lose altitude in mid-1967, when other younger men like Percy, Lindsay or Hatfield might have challenged for the prize of nomination, Rockefeller's intransigent support of George Romney paralyzed all other potential progressive candidates: nor did they dare to gather together to wrest from him leadership of the liberal wing of the Party. Even outside formal Party circles, Rockefeller worked for Romney as blocking guard. Up until January, 1968, he was still playing the role. In Boston, on Saturday, February 3rd, retired Lieutenant General James M. Gavin had gathered a planning session to see whether there was enough substance to the boomlet for his candidacy to warrant entering the New Hampshire primary against both Romney and Nixon. But Rockefeller, learning of the meeting, had his political deputy George Hinman call Boston to scotch the plan in embryo. He would not tolerate it. George Romney was *the* standard-bearer of the cause.

Though Rockefeller, honoring his commitment, might persist in support of Romney to the bitter end, it was impossible for the press or other politicians to take this commitment seriously. As December gave way to January, and January, in turn, wore on to February, it became obvious that if the progressive Republicans were to frustrate Nixon's purpose, they must seek another leader than Romney. And who else could it be but Rockefeller? From the turn of the year on, this was the overriding question within the Republican Party.

By mid-February, pressure was mangling New York's Governor. In a final effort to pump enthusiasm—and money—into the Romney campaign, Rockefeller had flown to Detroit to address a fund-raising luncheon. There, on the weekend of February 24th, the press caught him: Was he himself a candidate? they demanded. "I am not a candidate," he replied. "I'm supporting Governor Romney and I think he's the best man." But would he accept a draft? they persisted; and, curtly answering yes, Rockefeller flew back to New York, leaving behind a blazon of national headlines that were deeply to embitter George Romney. In New York more bad news was waiting. That Sunday afternoon Leonard Hall, Romney's campaign manager, arrived in the Rockefeller suite to gather with William Scranton, a onetime candidate himself, and George Hinman, New York's GOP National Committeeman. To them, Hall reported the results of the last secret poll Rockefeller had financed for Romney in New Hampshire—still no change; Romney, two weeks before the primary, was at the short end of a six-to-one tally, and doomed. Unless someone moved at once, the nomination would be Nixon's. What to do? Scranton, having learned from his own tempestuous experience in 1964 that to wait is to lose, counseled immediate mobilization of all governors. Hinman counseled waiting. Rockefeller could not make up his mind—it was days too early to pull the rug out from under George Romney.

Three days later, pressed by the inevitable, Romney withdrew from the race on his own. But the mad month of March made Rockefeller's decision no easier. Half the dilemma lay in his own mind—the other half in the Party that was his patrimony. In his mind it ran as in Macbeth's mind, he would be king, but would not strike the blow. Among his friends in the Party, counsel was similarly schizophrenic. The withdrawal of George Romney had shaken liberal Republican leadership from coast to coast. All felt Rockefeller *must* run—but they split on the question of how. Should he take the primary route and risk tearing the Party apart as he had in 1964? Or should he stand available above the battle and wait for the Party to come to him? Two days before the New Hampshire primary a full cross-section of the important men who led the progressive wing of the Republican Party gathered in the Rockefeller apartment on a rainy Sunday—seven governors, three former Republican National Committee chairmen, five Congressmen, Mayor John Lindsay, and three United States Senators—to discuss the problem. Two days later a full report on the secret session from one of the participants was in the hands of Rockefeller's downstairs neighbor, Richard M. Nixon. And Nixon summarized it well—they had come expecting Rockefeller to tell *them* what to do; he had sat there as if expecting them to tell *him* what to do. So nothing had happened, no decision had been taken.

The pressure built steadily, but to no clear conclusion. Having given up the Presidency in heart and mind, but not in yearning, Rockefeller had long since liquidated the first-class staff that had captained his 1964 campaign. There remained now only George Hinman, wise but tired; a new press secretary, Leslie Slote, quick and bright but inexperienced in national politics; and Robert Douglass, a young man of extraordinary ability but totally immersed in state politics in Albany. Rockefeller turned in stress to the one man he trusted most outside his own family, Emmet John Hughes, columnist and historian, and another ten days of indecision followed the New Hampshire primary as Rockefeller and Hughes, together, reviewed the pros and cons.

Hughes was of the opinion that Rockefeller should not run at all. There were the subjective factors: Rockefeller was unprepared in spirit or position to run—he had no appetite for campaigning, was engrossed in his state programs, and had no staff. Above all, on the dominant issue of the moment, Vietnam, he had neither public nor private posture. More importantly, for Rockefeller as for Kennedy, tactical decision hinged on primary contests. Rockefeller could not enter only the single Oregon primary, which he might win; he would have to enter *both* the Nebraska *and* the Oregon primaries; and the Nixon staff had made sure that if Rockefeller declared for the Oregon primary, Nebraska's attorney general, as was his legal authority, would list Rockefeller, willy-nilly, in the Nebraska contest, where he would be utterly annihilated. If ever the nation and Party were to turn to Rockefeller, concluded Hughes, it would turn simply because he was available, needed, and wanted—the polls and public opinion would decide his fortunes, not the primaries.

Thus the first decision—and major irrecoverable blunder. In hindsight one can see that Rockefeller was challenging the entire structure of his Party—as were McCarthy and Kennedy on the other side; his resources were greater than those of the two Democrats, certainly in statehouse support if not in troops. But structures do not yield except under pressure. In politics, one challenges establishments in primaries, not elections. John F. Kennedy had done so in 1960, McCarthy was doing so in 1968, Rockefeller himself had made a near thing of it in 1964. "He either fears his fate too much, or his deserts are small, that dares not put it to the touch, to gain or lose it all," ran the old rhyme. Rockefeller neither feared fate, nor were his deserts small; yet he dared not put it to the touch.

A smaller man in politics than Rockefeller would have perished completely after his withdrawal press conference on March 21st. In the crowded West Ballroom of the New York Hilton Hotel, some 300 newsmen from all over the country had convened to hear the statement which, *The New York Times* had assured in a front-page story two days before, would be a declaration of candidacy. Instead, flatly, Nelson Rockefeller declared: "I have decided today to reiterate unequivocally that I am not a candidate campaigning directly or indirectly for the Presidency of the United States." He seemed cheerful, relieved, entirely happy about the decision, leaving the door open only by the narrowest crack to future reconsideration. Rephrasing Rockefeller's prior statement, a reporter queried, "You said you would be willing to accept the true and, I think, genuine draft of the Convention. . . . What possible circumstances would cause you to accept the draft?" "I suppose it would have to be the vote of the majority of the delegates," answered the Governor. All across the country, thousands of Rockefeller well-wishers, hundreds of politicians had been waiting to hear the trumpet call to battle; the month-long public indecision had to end somewhere, somehow. Now it ended. Finish.

Everywhere, smaller politicians hastened to make their peace with the local or national Nixon organization. But among these, hurt, injured and confused, the most important was certainly Governor Spiro T. Agnew of Maryland—long the chief Rockefeller champion among governors, organizer of the Draft Rockefeller movement. So certain had been Governor Agnew of Governor Rockefeller's positive intentions that he had wheeled into his office a television set and invited capitol newsmen and several friends to watch the speech and kickoff of the Rockefeller campaign in which he would play so large a role. Unwarned of the reversal, Agnew was humiliated as ignorant, too unimportant to be taken into the know. Like scores of others, Agnew was never to come back to Rockefeller; his orientation to Richard Nixon began at that moment.

March continued in its upheavals. There had already been, of course, the McCarthy upheaval in New Hampshire, the shivering of the dollar in the spring, the declaration of Robert Kennedy—all before Rockefeller removed his name from consideration. Almost immediately there were to follow more important events—the renunciation of Lyndon Johnson, the Wisconsin primary, and the assassination of Martin Luther King with its aftermath of riot and bloodshed.

Nelson Rockefeller is a man to be taken seriously; he had always, over and over, discussed his relation to his Party with utmost frankness

—his Republican brethren, he said, would never turn to him for the Presidency except in a national crisis. Now, within days of his withdrawal, the national crisis had burst in the streets, on the screens of television for all to see.

Moreover, another seductive development had come to pass—almost within hours of his March 21st withdrawal. The social-financial-industrial elite of the Republican Party had always regarded Rockefeller as Democrats of the same class had regarded Franklin D. Roosevelt —as a traitor to his class. Now, in the aftermath of his renunciation, almost overnight, they switched. Nelson, they had assumed, was wound up like a toy and would always run for the Presidency; this time he had let them down by *not* running. Their pressure built: Mr. John Hay Whitney of the Whitney fortune felt he must run; so did Mr. Walter Thayer; so did Mr. J. Irwin Miller of Indiana, of Cummins Engines and a Yale trustee; so did young Stewart Mott of the Mott fortune in Michigan. And so did thousands and thousands of others in a new authentic Draft Rockefeller movement which sprang up, under their leadership, within days.

National crisis called; old friendships urged; even Rockefeller's own brother David, in other years a family resistant to Nelson's political ambitions had switched. David, too, felt he must run.

By the end of April the Draft Rockefeller leaders had presented to Rockefeller an ultimatum. At a meeting on April 23rd, at Jock Whitney's Whitney Communications Corporation, they demanded of Emmet Hughes, as Rockefeller's spokesman, a decision: either Hughes must persuade Nelson Rockefeller to reverse and announce candidacy immediately, or they would all give up and dissolve their citizen activities. That night, Messrs. Emmet Hughes and J. Irwin Miller dined with Nelson and Happy Rockefeller; they presented their case; Mrs. Rockefeller agreed. And Mr. Rockefeller, almost casually, agreed, too.

On Tuesday morning, April 30th, from Albany, on national television, Nelson Rockefeller announced that he was indeed, after reconsideration, a candidate. "Today I announce my active candidacy for the nomination by the Republican Party," he said, and went on to give his reasons for his change of heart: "First, the dramatic and unprecedented events of the past weeks. . . . Second . . . to comment from the sidelines is not an effective way to present the alternatives. . . . Third . . . to assure that the key issues are fully explored. . . . Fourth, I am deeply disturbed by the course of events, the growing unrest and anxiety. . . . For these reasons I seek the nomination."

That same day Massachusetts Republicans, whose suburban ladies were presumably tuned in to the morning announcement and TV press conference, and also exposed to the lovely profile of the candidate's smiling wife, went to the polls. In a write-in upheaval that repudiated

Governor John Volpe's state leadership, they gave Nelson Rockefeller all of Massachusetts' thirty-four delegates on the first ballot—and he was off.

Then nothing happened.

A Presidential candidacy is too great to be organized overnight; only one in modern political history has ever succeeded—the candidacy of Adlai Stevenson in 1952, a magic moment of a magic man. There is no *rule* that a campaign cannot succeed in a three-month effort, and if a party is deadlocked, as were Republicans in 1940, skill, luck, money and media may deliver the prize to a man like Wendell Willkie. But the odds are against it.

The Rockefeller candidacy of 1968 began late; its staff, starting on May 1st, had to be organized from scratch; the public image of its candidate was one of vacillation; above all, the attention of the press and the media was elsewhere. All through the month of May the Oregon and California campaigns unrolled on the West Coast, where Robert F. Kennedy and Eugene McCarthy dueled on the slope of the Pacific to the attention of the more important members of the national press and the preoccupation of television. Through the month of May only junior reporters and agency men accompanied Nelson Rockefeller, and national indifference frustrated their writing, while editors tightened their dispatches. It was as if Nelson Rockefeller had become the rich man's Harold Stassen.

On June 5th, Robert F. Kennedy was assassinated.

Within a week a complete change in tone and quality had come about in the Rockefeller campaign, a change one could not measure or precisely define; but it was there to see—and it concerned Robert Kennedy.

There had always been a coefficient of politics between the campaigns of Robert F. Kennedy and Nelson Rockefeller. The sound of cornets with which Kennedy had launched his campaign in mid-March had, in a subtle way, affected the earlier decision of Rockefeller's withdrawal. Since Kennedy had then pre-empted the crusade that Rockefeller hoped to lead, and since Rockefeller could not outdo Kennedy in the rhetoric of 1968, the contrast had seriously influenced his earlier negative decision in March. That decision of Rockefeller's had, as we have seen, been the most reasonable, yet wrong, decision in the politics of the year. But there should always be a touch of unreason—not too much—in a great leader. A great leader should be able to persuade his people to ignore the rules of the game. Churchill had done so with the British in 1940, persuading them against reason to resist the Nazis. Ben-Gurion had done so with the Israelis at the birth of that nation in 1948 when, told that the existence of Israel was against all the laws of economics, he replied, "So—all right, we'll repeal the laws of economics."

Once one joined Rockefeller on his June and July excursions around the country, one could see that he had similarly repealed the laws of partisanship. Or else the assassination had done so. For, as I joined him, still mourning from the Kennedy campaign, I felt at home again— the gaiety and zest of the campaign were the same. The crowds were the same. The message was the same. The hunger for a hero was the same.

It was not so much the transfer of personal allegiances; one could note, of course, with some astonishment, that Tom and Joan Braden, the California publishers, who only a few weeks earlier had headed up the Kennedy Citizens drive in California, were now enlisted in the Rockefeller Citizens drive across the country; other important names had also switched. But more important were the ordinary people who came out to greet Rockefeller—those who yearned for a change. The same young people followed Rockefeller as had followed Kennedy in throngs as he traveled; the same heavy admixture of Negroes who wanted a champion made his rallies come alive.[2] The signs were the same as those that had greeted Kennedy: "ROCKY IS ZAP," "GO-GO-GO WITH ROCKY," "ROCK-ROCK-ROCK WITH ROCKY." And the crowds responded to all of Rocky's speeches with the same emotional undertones as the Kennedy crowds.

The candidate was at home with such crowds as, day by day, all through June and July, his private airliner carried him around the country. I have followed Nelson Rockefeller for more years now in politics than any other living figure except Hubert Humphrey, and it was interesting to see how much had flaked off on the original starchy executive from his adventures in New York politics. There had descended on him a sediment of phrase from his experience with the friendly Jews of New York: the habit of answering a question with a question, or closing a statement with a question (e.g., after denunciation of the Democrats, the closing remark: "This is a way to run a government?"). There had come to him a way of addressing an all-Negro audience which only long contact could have taught. He would chant about schools, equality and opportunity. The audience would chant back, "That's right!" Rockefeller would reply, "That's right, man, that's right." They would chant again, and he would close it by

[2] Rockefeller seemed to draw a larger share, although still tiny, of Oriental Americans into his audiences. 1968 was the first year that this correspondent noticed young Japanese Americans and Chinese Americans both in crowds and in inconspicuous positions of responsibility in political campaigns. The last of the minorities to enlist in American politics, they were heavily for Bobby Kennedy in California, heavily for Nelson Rockefeller across the country.

ascending into dialect, "Yeah, tha'ss right, tha'ss right." They would snatch his cufflinks, his spectacles, his papers from him; he enjoyed it; crowds would pound on the windows of his bus, and he would pound back. But within reason. Once, after waving and waving for minutes in a stalled bus, he snapped at the driver, "Driver—get going. There's a limit to how long I can wave at these people and they can wave back."

Outdoors, Nelson Rockefeller was a free creature. Richard Dougherty of the *Los Angeles Times,* compared him to an old-fashioned fictional British Duke who thought no one loved him for himself alone. But with the press and in campaigning, Rockefeller found love and affection. When the press celebrated his sixtieth birthday while flying from California to St. Louis, decorating the plane with colored ribbons and serving egg-rolls from San Francisco's Chinatown, he was touched. Genuinely fond of him, the accompanying press collaborated on a painting to be given to him as a birthday gift—and when Leslie Slote presented it, said Dougherty, it was probably the first time in his life that anyone outside his immediate family had thought to give Nelson Rockefeller a birthday present simply because they liked him.

He had the crowds, no doubt. If he could get his grip on the Party's instruments of nomination and then appeal to these overwhelmingly Democratic crowds, he would win. But to get through to the nomination meant he needed Republican delegates; and that was the purpose of his transcontinental exertions. For three months he traveled, 66,200 miles, addressing Republican delegates in forty-five states, trying to prove that he was, after all, a real Republican.

Indoors, he was another Rockefeller. Somehow, good glands, clean life and magnificent genetic inheritance made him capable of any exertion during his eighteen-hour days. Thus, outdoors he could be the troubadour and fugleman of new politics, and indoors, by a switch of personality, become a neat Republican executive in command of all figures, budgets, programs and managerial know-how. Talking indoors to Republican delegate clusters, he was low-key. Figures rolled from his tongue. He would denounce government spending, demonstrate the importance of local government, shimmer budgetary and financing realities over his fingers like a Benares merchant ruffling Cashmere shawls. Indoors, he meant to prove to delegates that change could be managed by good cost-accounting procedures. He was at his most impressive in such closed sessions with delegates. At the end of such a Rockefeller performance in Nashville, Tennessee, I eavesdropped on the conversation of several delegates who were already locked up for Nixon, but who had listened attentively. One said, "I guess he accomplished what he came here to do; he came here to take the horns off Nelson Rockefeller, and I guess he did. But he didn't move anybody." Another said, "Well, he sure moved me, he isn't half as liberal as I thought." And the other said, "I guess so. He didn't sound as liberal as I thought either." Then they drifted away. R. W. Apple, Jr., of *The New York Times,* summed up the Tennessee meeting that night as he might have summed up any other of the meetings in which Rockefeller was attempting to sway the delegates long since chosen to the Republican Party's convention: "Nelson Rockefeller arrived in Tennessee with twenty-eight delegates sewed up for Richard Nixon, and he left with twenty-eight delegates sewed up for Nixon."

There was always a real hope under the gaiety of the last phases of the Rockefeller campaign. The adventure would have seemed a preposterous exercise in unreality unless one thoroughly knew the planning. Rockefeller was seeking not convention commitments, but second-choice votes. If his planning and his home figures on Eastern delegates were correct, he would have only 300 or 400 votes. Only if Ronald Reagan, of California, were also going to break into the contest could those 300 or 400 Eastern votes be enough to deprive Nixon of the nomination and make the Republican convention a free-for-all.

To outsiders the thought might seem fantasy; but there was substance to it. On the weekend of July 4th, Rockefeller's chief surrogate, Emmet Hughes, had visited Ronald Reagan at his home in Palisades Park in Los Angeles and established secretly the one certainty that was necessary to give the Rockefeller campaign validity. One of the Secret Service men attached to Rockefeller had, only a few days before, been transferred to guard Reagan; he gaped at Hughes' secret arrival. Hughes and Reagan spent an hour and a half together. Politics were politics. Hughes and Reagan made no deal; Reagan assured Hughes, who would impart the message to Rockefeller, that he, Reagan, was in this race for keeps. Rockefeller could rely on that. Beyond that—no commitments. If both Rockefeller and Reagan did their best, they would meet after Nixon's destruction in Miami and clash for the soul of Party and country. It was Miami that would test their linked but rival dreams.

Miami Beach rose like a mirage beyond the waters—the causeway crossed a blue lagoon, and there against the skyline and the sea shimmered an alabaster ridge of dreams.

One came prepared to loathe it—yet one could not. It was a city of no history, and no triumphs, its only heroes such folk-celebrities as Jackie Gleason, Arthur Godfrey and Walter Winchell. But dreams had built it—from the first New Jersey land-promoters who had dredged the mangrove swamps to fill in the desolate sandbar, from the enterprisers who planned to make of it coconut plantations or avocado ranches, to the Jewish entrepreneurs whose imagination, in the years since World War II, had raised this profile of glistening hotels that ran as far as the eye could see, north from the causeway along the ocean front.

Gaudy and gleaming, the hotels cut their silhouette against the sky, to absorb and disgorge each year some 2,500,000 visitors come to take the sun, visit the night clubs, look at the girls, flock to the islands for the gambling, laze and dream. The Beach had swollen year by year with people come to dream: land-speculators wiped out by interest rates or hurricanes and replaced by other land-speculators; businessmen pausing to catch breath between schemes and scheme again, on the phone to back home at all hours; beauties and hustlers dreaming of whose eye their forms might catch; and, in the side streets, in the rooming houses and one-story flats, the old folks, on garment-industry pensions from New York or Social Security, dreaming of what perhaps it might have been if they had begun life, not ended it, here.

For all dreamers, Miami held indulgence. Indulgence was its business—not the sedate indulgences of Palm Beach to the north, where the old established money and the descended fortunes came to rest, but fleshy indulgence for men on the make, and the new money. Massage, and sun, and surf, and girls, and room service faster than anywhere else in America; and food extravagantly expensive but of solid excellence, food for any taste from the best bagels and lox, the best pizza and fettucini, to borscht or minestrone or French onion soup, to the best fish and the best steaks, done American, Parisian or Roman. Here was a place where one was expected to sleep late, breakfast at noon, swim in the afternoon, wait for the exquisite twilight when the diamond glitter on both sides of the bay underlit the dusk clouds, and then indulge one's self again, and go to sleep dreaming. The indulgence of Miami Beach was a swaddling from the world—from crime in the streets, from thought of war in Vietnam, from the note coming due, from the tangle of decision in the North and in the cities. Here was a place designed to kiss away reality and seduce its visitors into believing that things might be as they dreamed that things should be. The Republican convention of 1968 was the first national convention Miami Beach had ever managed to lure—but it treated it as it treated all other conventions, planning to wrap it in its languor and lazy pleasures, soothing away care and turmoil.

One comes to any convention with an anticipatory sense of excitement; there is a game to be played, good or bad. One has a scoring card of delegates; when their will is frozen on balloting night, the nation has a Presidential nominee. In a traditional convention city like Chicago or San Francisco, where hotels lie close-packed in the central city, one stalks the delegates or their leaders from hotel to hotel, lobby to lobby, committee meeting to committee meeting, caucus to caucus, the zest of hunt intensified by the compression and congestion of the big city.

But Miami Beach sprawls. From Bal Harbor in the north to "Bagel" beach in the south, the 2,666 delegates and alternates stretched over almost ten miles of hotels, excitement dissipated by their scatteration. Most of them new, uncertain of their role, amateurs in the practice of convention politics, the delegates let the climate of the Beach absorb and enwrap them. Stuffed with food, happy with drink, stroked by the sun, relaxed beside the turquoise swimming pools, cosseted by their hotels, no call of revolt or resentment could stab them, and within hours of their arrival, languor settled over them. One could learn little from talking to them, for they could repeat only what the radio and television networks were telling. Decision and direction lay far beyond them.

It was easier to sort out the convention by moving stage by stage, north to south, where the nerve ends of the striving candidates' efforts knotted at the headquarters hotels; and as one did so, one traced one's way from dream to reality.

Farthest north of all the major candidates' hotels was the Americana —gaudy with theatrical color, its lobby encircling an exploding cone of tropical plants. This was base for the New York delegation and Nelson Rockefeller. Here a political mirage beckoned attention far beyond the limits of Miami to the nation itself. All through the year, from January on, Nelson Rockefeller had outpolled all other Republicans—Romney, Reagan, Nixon himself. Rockefeller's strength lay outside the convention, outside the Party, in that broad and shifting mass of independents and shallow-anchored Democrats he had so consistently drawn to his support in his home state. If the party *did* want a winner, then Nelson Rockefeller was its surest winner—his job was to persuade the delegates that the mirage was real, that the surest guarantee of victory in November was the Rockefeller magic.

This theme Rockefeller had been pressing now for weeks, with scorching intensity, on all the delegations he had met in the forty-five-state swing of his belated drive. To most observers, the drive had seemed to have a growing effect until the eve of convention—and then, in Miami, triumphantly Herbert Klein, Mr. Nixon's chief spokesman, had spiked it. With a smile broad as summer itself, Klein had broken the results of the last Gallup poll on TV just one week before convention—Nixon *ahead* of Rockefeller, against either Humphrey or McCarthy, by two to five percentage points. It mattered little that two days later the Rockefeller staff could pre-leak the Harris poll, which contradicted the Gallup poll; or would flood the convention with its own privately commissioned Crossley poll, which showed that in the key industrial states, where the electoral vote was concentrated, Rockefeller decisively outran Nixon. The Rockefeller mirage had been ruptured.

Thus, as the day of convention opening approached, the Rockefeller staff fell back on the arithmetic of the convention itself. Here persuasion was even harder. The arithmetic ordained that 667 votes would nominate a candidate. But the news agencies, news magazines and television were already drenching the convention with numbers. And the numbers, though they fluctuated, all fell into a familiar bracket—Nixon had 657 votes, said CBS; had 623 votes, said ABC; had 619 votes, said *The New York Times*. For the Rockefeller staff the critical figure was 600. If Nixon could be brought below 600 on the first ballot, if only the convention could be forced to a second ballot, if the delegates could be compelled to face real choice—then there might be a chance.

One examined the dream and its strategy as the young Rockefeller men war-gamed their plans. They held for sure, or in the name of various favorite sons, the industrial Northeast. From Connecticut, Massachusetts and New York through Pennsylvania, Ohio and Michigan, their power base was solid. Once, years ago, the financial masters of this power base could crush any rival force in the Republican Party; but in 1968 that system of politics was long dead; even the Northeast power base was held now not by force but by political appeal. Could the appeal expand?

The name of the game as seen by Rockefeller's lieutenants was "erosion"—one delegate here, three delegates there, a fourth delegate snared in another obscure state, and they might chip Nixon below the magic 600 on the first ballot. The most optimistic of their estimates, however, ran thus: On the first ballot, Nixon 541, Rockefeller 306, Reagan 267. On the second ballot, Rockefeller 430, Nixon 459, Reagan 318. On the third ballot, Rockefeller 481, Nixon 387, Reagan 336—and then, ran the dream, would come an interruption of balloting, a glorious night of politicking, a climactic facing of the Republican Party with its future. Would it go left with Rockefeller or right with Ronnie Reagan? Would it go South and racist, or build the Party's future in the North?

The Rockefeller dream, however, had a symbiotic relation with the Reagan campaign. All Rockefeller planning rested on an element beyond its own control—the personality, planning and performance of Ronald Reagan, Governor of California. Unless Reagan's men could deliver, on the floor in mass and in time, the 267 first-ballot votes predicted on the Rockefeller sheets, the plan lacked any substance.

So one journeyed south down Collins Avenue to the Deauville Hotel, headquarters of Ronald Reagan.

The Reagan campaign was oriented to another dream, a dream which rested on the new reality that Goldwater had first stripped bare in his 1964 campaign: the reality of the new South, which, with one quarter of the voting strength, is the most explosive and purposive bloc in any Republican convention. At some undefined time between 1960 and 1964 the Southern Republican party had come of age and sensed its power; it meant never to be ignored again in national politics. At any moment in 1967, had he chosen, Ronald Reagan might have captured this bloc of Southern delegates and deadlocked the nomination as Nelson Rockefeller now hoped. Graceful, witty, a thorough conservative but non-racist, Reagan might have given the American right the spokesman for which it has so long sought. But he had tarried on the way (see Chapter Two) and had been propelled back into action only after the assassination of Robert Kennedy, when the national emotion of shock and disorder had created a national audience for him again. Reagan's last-minute blitz had been concentrated since June in the South, where Richard Nixon's lieutenants had long preceded him. Reagan's convention operation was now geared entirely to the undoing of Nixon's work. If the Southern delegates could be ripped away from Richard Nixon, Strom Thurmond and John Tower, then indeed the Reagan-Rockefeller dreams might work—and Reagan and Rockefeller, having jointly disposed of Richard M. Nixon, would meet, each with one foot planted on Nixon's political carcass, and duel to the death for the delegates left in his estate. It would make a glorious scene; the volcanic furies of 1964's convention would be as nothing; the 1968 convention might, indeed, make history, as the twin genii of the Republican spirit clashed in *Walpurgisnacht*. But no one, on either the Rockefeller or the Reagan side, had thought that far ahead.

Instead, on entering the Deauville Hotel and ascending to Reagan's sixteenth-floor command center, one found a hush. Whatever had moved the furies of the Republican right in 1964 to throng and jostle in Barry Goldwater's anterooms in San Francisco had now been stilled. No rush, bustle, commotion or crusade went on here. Instead, here, as in the Rockefeller headquarters, there was only the desperate, agonizing, slow one-by-one counting of delegates, under the command of F. Clifton White, once king of the Goldwater machinery. White could be candid with this old friend, and his normally ebullient nature was gloomy. He had, with every artifice of cajolery, just snatched 16 North Carolina votes from Nixon. But this was not nearly enough. One hundred more votes in the South would make all the difference; and the 100 lay in four states— Georgia (30), Mississippi (20), Florida (34) and Louisiana (26). Without them, White could deliver only 170 or 180 votes to Reagan; with them, he might even surpass the Rockefeller anticipation of 267. "I've got to drag people across the line," said White, "but they've made these half-baked commitments to Nixon, and they wriggle and wriggle and they can't get off." All the lieutenants of White's Southern triumph in 1964— Tower, O'Donnell, Thurmond, Kleindienst—were now lined up against him, and they had been at work for Nixon for a long time. They held the pledges. White had just escorted former Louisiana State Chairman Charlton Lyons to the elevator, and was frustrated. "He's on the wire, I know he's on the wire," said White, "there were tears in his eyes when he said goodbye, he agrees with everything we say—but he can't get off his commitment to Nixon." White was now, in desperation, about to go to work again on the Florida delegation. Florida came early in the ballot, with 34 votes; if he chose, White could make a deal in the delegation to let it vote by the unit rule—all or nothing. He held pledges for Reagan from 11 or 12 delegates; but in the middle stood its state chairman, William Murfin, a druggist from Hobe Sound. How could one reach Murfin? asked White. "He drives me out of my cotton-picking mind. He won't go with us unless a majority in his delegation goes for us; we're three votes short of the majority and I've just got to drag three or four delegates across that line." The trumpets sounded here for Pickett's Charge; but the Southerners had had enough of gallant lost causes; they wanted winners.

Thus, with the Rockefeller dream dependent on the Reagan charge, and the Reagan breakthrough dependent on whatever "erosion" the Rockefeller guerrillas might contrive, the closest approach to reality one could find was in Nixon headquarters—and so one traveled south another mile and a half to the Hilton-Plaza Hotel, the newest of the Miami caravanseries, where, on its top four stories, was established the Nixon command.

Nixon's 200-room headquarters hummed with a different tone. The corridors were crowded, but no one lingered at the Coca-Cola coolers or coffee urns; these were people who knew their business and had been preparing for it for a full year. Blue lapel badges indicated the precise rank of the Nixon operatives. Each badge had an underline with four conspicuous boxes—if three were crossed off and only one clear, the bearer had access only to the fifteenth floor; if two were crossed off and two remained clear, he had access to fifteenth and sixteenth; if three squares were clear, then to fifteenth, sixteenth and seventeenth floors; and if all squares were cleared, he might pass freely to the penthouse floor, where were established the candidate's living quarters and the solarium command posts. New arrivals eyed each other's badges instantly, jealously measuring their own importance against a friend's by the number of crossed-off boxes.

From the command post in the cleared-out solarium rooms one had an instant overview of what a year's effort had created—and what Nelson Rockefeller's hasty three-month effort and Ronald Reagan's last-minute charge were trying to overtake. The first Nixon communications expedition had arrived in Miami to survey the scene eight months earlier in December. Experts had equipped the command with radios and telephones; web upon web of floor communications and interlinks, cross-channels and direct lines radiated and meshed both at the command wagon at the convention, and here in a seventy-two-line switchboard outside the solarium. Within the solarium, behind a dais, a huge blackboard ran across an entire wall, marked state by state, and day by day from August 1st to August 8th. In front of the dais, where convention-commander Richard Kleindienst would sit with his nine regional directors and staff, were seats for all fifty of the state captains; and every day, in the morning and afternoon closed sessions, each state chairman would report his delegate totals.

And the delegate totals, though they might fluctuate, with a splintering off here or a chip gained there, told the profile of Nixon's strength: Rockefeller held a clean lead over Nixon in only one region of the country—the industrial Northeast; but even here Nixon had recessive strength —in Pennsylvania, New Jersey, upper New England. In the South and Border states Nixon clearly held a commanding lead—more than 350 out of 394 votes, unless Reagan could raid them; and the Nixon lieutenants were confident that no such raid could penetrate the defense of grim Strom Thurmond. In the Midwest, two favorite sons—Rhodes of Ohio and Romney of Michigan—held out against the Nixon superiority; but with the exception of Minnesota and Iowa (split), from Indiana and Illinois right through to the Rocky Mountains, Nixon held all for another 200. Even in the Far West, where Reagan held California, Nixon outmatched his adversaries for another 130. All in all, though the precise totals of the Nixon boards were kept secret, he apparently held over 670 votes—a slim majority but a certain one.

Crisp, businesslike, clean-shirted, neatly barbered, Nixon lieutenants when they gathered looked like a meeting of a junior chamber of commerce. They bore rancor for no one. Rockefeller's command might glisten with famous names past and present, but that did not bother them— "We've got names out of the telephone book," said one. No such passion animated Nixonians as had stirred the Goldwater crusaders of 1964. Indeed, passion was the very emotion they sought to avoid—passion had ruined the Party in 1964, passion ravaged the nation in 1968. The entire Nixon campaign, through the primaries and down to election itself, hung on this thought—that the nation had had its fill of turbulence, bloodshed, killing, violence and adventure. Nixon was to phrase his theme best in his own inaugural in 1969; but, operationally, at headquarters they described their campaign as a "low-profile" campaign, with no promises to the nation beyond law-and-order, no commitment other than to do their best. It was impossible to make glamorous or romantic the figures involved; but it was impossible not to respect what they had done as an exercise in politics—they had caught the mood of their Party accurately, frozen the mood in the delegate count, and now stood watch over the convention to make sure that the hushed volcanoes of 1964 did not erupt once more.

So one journeyed south another three miles to the last stage of observation—the convention hall. The newly enlarged Miami hall is an excellent place for a political convention. Efficiently air-conditioned, spacious (it seats 17,000 people), well-lit, its critical feature is the shallow slope of seating. The most explosive conventions this correspondent has witnessed, in Chicago and San Francisco, took place in such auditoriums as the Stockyard Amphitheater or the Cow Palace where the high galleries, rising steeply to the roof, make the floor a pit for gladiators, compress the assembly into drama, invite spectators to clash, throw things, boo, yell, jeer, shriek. The Miami auditorium spreads the emotional charge thin—as if it were a saucer, not a cup.

There in the center of the saucer sat the delegates. Here and there splotches of color indicated various state delegations—Californians in orange ponchos with yellow tassels, Floridians in orange-juice-colored blazers, Ohioans with red-and-white sashes, Georgians in red derbies, Wyoming's men in cowboy hats, Hawaiians with flat, flowered hats and leis. But, overwhelmingly the color of the group was gray—not in hue or shading, but in feel and texture. Delegations from Pennsylvania, Massachusetts, New York could be recognized by the pattern of a more varied ethnic mix, profiles of Americans of Mediterranean descent, the dark of the few Negroes who stood out in the convention. But such minorities were lost in the clean white faces of middle America—lost among the solid businessmen in dark suits and horn-rimmed glasses, the neat-frocked wives, the intelligent and slightly aggressive chairladies of women's groups, the eager, intent faces of clean young lawyers, the drowsy, bored faces of Midwestern office-holders, county clerks, deputy sheriffs. It was difficult to describe them or characterize them, especially for the legions of foreign correspondents who had come, as usual, to make sport or find excitement in the antics of American politics. They sought a guiding intellectual generalization to cover the group. But it was not Wall Street that held the convention in its grasp, nor the military-industrial establishment, nor any Goldwater conspiracy. It was Main Street—and Main Street wanted Richard M. Nixon. Senator Jacob Javits of New York, watching them, said, "All these people here who support Nixon are as nice as they could be, but they don't begin to understand the problems of the cities, the urgings of the ghettos, the heat of the subways."

Tedium gripped the convention from the clack of the opening gavel, at ten in the morning of August 5th, 1968. Introducers introduced introducers who introduced other introducers; orators orated on the problems of the country and the problems of the city; youth addressed the convention, ladies addressed the convention, welcomers welcomed one and all; Dwight D. Eisenhower had tape-recorded a message; actor John Wayne gave an inspirational reading called "Why I Am Proud to Be an American"; choral groups sang, bands played; on and on the proceedings went, in ceremonies now weirdly obsolete, in pursuit of a cause no one could find.

From the convention hall, boredom spread all up and down the Beach. No convention in history had been as dull as this except, perhaps, Eisenhower's renomination in San Francisco in 1956. Delegates and newspapermen dozed in the sun by the pools, fell asleep, and awoke knowing they had missed nothing. Lassitude smothered every stirring—a pink elephant in the courtyard of the Fontainebleau Hotel drew almost as many of the curious as did the arrival of Reverend Ralph Abernathy at the head of the Poor People Campaign's mule-driven caravan. Not knowing what lay ahead in Chicago, men gossiped irritably about the security precautions of this Republican convention—the infra-red stampings on the back of one's hand to get in and out of the gates, the carbined state troopers patrolling the convention approach, the security helicopters coursing up and down the beach so low that the buzz interrupted conversation by the shore. Or one gossiped about restaurants and parties—and at restaurants one found Rockefeller men dining back to back with Nixon men, cordial, friendly, jovial, with none of the bitterness of other conventions. Boredom lay on the convention like a mattress.

It was not that the Nixon staff had planned the boredom. On the contrary, wistfully, they wished the nation would see their hero as a great romantic leader lifting it to new levels of calm, common sense and achievement. But the boredom served their purposes. For them to attack either Rockefeller or Reagan, even to counterattack the Rockefeller or Reagan assault, would be to admit there *was* a fight, and perhaps cause delegates to waver. We have, said one of the Nixon staff men, a country on the verge of a nervous breakdown; we don't want to add to it. Political gamesmanship urged them to turn to the public with placid, optimistic faces: every newspaper poll, every public delegate count gave them a commanding lead. They did not want to disturb the impression; and the resonance of the media exploration of delegate preference made an echo chamber of the convention's politics. CBS, for example, had by far the most elaborate, precise, and accurate delegate-counting operation of any of the great news institutions. So elaborate was its count, its daily, almost hourly checks on individual delegates, that, finally, in an illustration of the law of physics which says that an attempt to measure matter can change matter, the CBS count became a political factor in itself. In despair, one afternoon, F. Clifton White, of the Reagan leadership, told of an attempt to sway one delegate away from Nixon to his own champion. The delegate insisted he could not, he was committed. To whom are you committed? asked White. To CBS, said the delegate. Thus the unspoken Nixon tactic—quiet, precise, semi-military discipline and control within the solarium of the penthouse; and, outwardly, optimism and indifference, courtesy and dullness, the casual yawn, the easy repetition of UPI's or CBS's or ABC's or any great newspaper's delegate projection.

Thus, the Rockefeller and Reagan candidacies expired at Miami Beach. They flailed and tugged and tore at the mattress. It would not move. Had they succeeded and then come to final terrible confrontation with each other, the spectacle might have surpassed even that of Chicago a fortnight later. But, instinctively, the men and women from Main Street did not want that. They sought not drama, not resolution of issues, not adventure. They sought caution, quiet, and a winner. Richard Nixon was the One, the authentic expression of a sober Republican majority.

Rockefeller and Reagan were not so much destroyed as suffocated at Miami. On the evening of his defeat, Rockefeller, when asked why he thought he had lost, responded: "Did you ever see a Republican convention?"

No particular chronology of the Republican convention is necessary for the purposes of history. There remain, however, a few episodes that should be recorded for the significance of farewell, or possible greater significance for the future.

Vietnam created the first of the episodes. For Republicans as for Democrats, the Vietnam war lay like a curse on the future; and Republicans, like Democrats, were completely divided on its resolution. Unlike the Democrats, however, the Republicans were able to compose their differences in the quiet of committee room, and in several secret meetings, in a triumph of back-room negotiation over open contention.

The Foreign Policy and National Security Sub-Committee of the Republican Platform Committee, headed by Representative Glenard P. Lipscomb, had brought to Miami an original, semi-official draft of Vietnam policy. The draft boggled the mind; written in the liturgical rhetoric of the John Birch Society, somewhat more martial than the Goldwater position of 1964, it indicted the administration for failure, and declared, in effect, that the failure had come from too little escalation, too small an effort in Vietnam; it all but sounded the call for the march on Hanoi. There could be no doubt that it reflected accurately the sentiment of the majority of the Republican platform-drafters.

But the power lay not with the drafters, it lay with Messrs. Nixon and Rockefeller. Messrs. Romney and Javits likewise had strong convictions. After some initial friction, an alliance on the platform was quickly formed between the Rockefeller and Nixon forces—after all, it was they, not the ghost of Barry Goldwater, who would have to defend this platform if nominated. First the variances between the Romney and Rockefeller proposals were adjusted in quiet; then Mr. Javits, about to face one of the most vocal doves in the nation in his home-state-race for re-election as Senator, was permitted to insert a clear and vigorous call for peace negotiations. For a twenty-four-hour period it appeared that the Nixon forces in Miami wavered between appeasing their Southern and right-wing delegates and the reality of the outer world; a veiled threat was circulated by the Rockefeller staff that if the platform did *not* include an appeal for peace, Rockefeller would stump the nation against the party and its candidate whoever he might be. The threat turned out to be unnecessary. A telephone call from Miami to Montauk Point, Long Island, where Mr. Nixon was resting prior to departure for Miami, surprised his own staff members by Nixon's willingness, even eagerness, to accept a Vietnam plank that pointed the Party in the direction of negotiation rather than escalation. And thereafter all that was necessary was the pasting together of various paragraphs to appease all interested groups, and the cosmetizing of the whole as a unity program.

The final Vietnam Resolution of the Republican Party is a masterpiece of political carpentry. Its last draft still exists in typescript, in numbered sentences and paragraphs, highlighted by word and phrase to yield a little something for everyone. The first two paragraphs, marked with a "P" (for platform draft), came from the original Neanderthal text and denounced the administration for "breach of faith," scoring its failure, declaring that "it is time to realize that not every international conflict is susceptible of solution by American ground forces." The third paragraph consists of four numbered sentences, interlarding, as marked in the margin by an "R" or an "N," both Nixon and Rockefeller language. The fourth paragraph yielded outright to the Rockefeller forces, stressing that "the issue is not control of territory but the security and loyalty of the population." On paragraphs 5 and 6, Nixon, Rockefeller and the Neanderthals all agreed—denunciation of the administration's pacification program. And so through to the end of the draft, men scrupulously weighing and trading phrases of war and peace while their sons fought and died 10,000 miles away. Paragraph 7 is clearly marked as a Nixon paragraph: "To resolve our Vietnam dilemma, America requires new leadership. . . ." Paragraph 12 is marked as being included at the insistence of George Romney: "We pledge a program for peace in Vietnam . . . a positive program that will offer a fair and equitable settlement to all, based on the principle of self-determination." Paragraph 13 is marked as a Rockefeller paragraph, designed to absorb the thinking of and please Jacob Javits: ". . . We pledge to develop a clear and purposeful negotiating position." And then all factions, from far right to near left, agreed on the closing *diapason:* "Our pride in the nation's armed forces in Southeast Asia and elsewhere in the world is beyond expression. In all our history none have fought more bravely or more devotedly than our sons in this unwanted war in Vietnam. They deserve—and they and their loved ones have—our total support, our encouragement, and our prayers."

The brave men who died and fought in Vietnam—and 173 were killed in Vietnam in the week of the Republican convention—deserved clearer leadership and, perhaps, more noble eloquence than this. But the platform had made it possible for the Republican leadership, if elected, to adopt and pursue any course of negotiations to bring peace—and claim that the unified Party had adopted this platform without a single dissenting voice.

The balloting which began at exactly nineteen minutes past one on Thursday morning, August 8th, resulted in the victory of Richard M. Nixon by 692 votes to 277 for Nelson Rockefeller and 182 for Ronald

Reagan—with the rest scattered among favorite sons.

The totals now seem carved on tablets of stone, testimony to irre-sistible victory. Yet, buried within the figures are the same "ifs" that haunt every episode of the politics of 1968—for the final Nixon total sponges away half a dozen unstable pockets of will and pressures which, had they burst, might have brought the Republican convention to explo-sion. Though Barry Goldwater had won his nomination in 1964 by a clear margin of 228 votes, Richard M. Nixon won his by only 25 more than the necessary 667. If, for example, Florida with its 34 votes had been pulled by Clifton White across the line to Ronald Reagan, the Nixon margin would have evaporated in the first tenth of the ballot list. If Mr. Rockefeller had been more graceful in his handling of Spiro Agnew in the spring, Maryland's 18 Nixon votes would have been Rockefeller's for sure. If, as the balloting proceeded, these switches had happened, the 18 New Jersey last-minute floor-breakaways to Nixon might have remained in shelter, voting for their favorite son, Clifford Case. And if so, certainly Pennsylvania's 22 breakaways to Nixon would have clung to their safety under Shafer's stand-in for Rockefeller. One can go on down the ballot and easily find the slippages which might have reduced Richard M. Nixon's total by 100 votes and thrown the convention into chaos.

But it never happened. Never were the Nixon lieutenants inwardly as confident as they skillfully made out; indeed, as balloting started, the final absolute hard count of their floor leader, Rogers Morton, read 666 votes—one short of a majority; and Mr. Reagan was just outside the con-vention hall, beseeching the Mississippi delegates in his campaign trailer to cast their 20 votes where their heart told them, not where their commit-ments to Nixon bound them. Skillfully, shrewdly, with the finest political *savoir-faire* and managerial talents, they made the apparent victory of Richard M. Nixon, celebrated in press and on TV, a reality that history confirmed.

It was at 5:04 that the climax began, as Chairman Gerald Ford of Michigan brought the convention to order for the purpose of placing names in nomination and a Southern voice responded, "Mr. Chairman, for the purpose of stating the Alabama position . . ."

Then followed dreariness. Hour after hour, with mechanical inflex-ibility and baroque irrelevance, for nine long hours the Republican con-vention proceeded with the ancient rituals of nominating a President of the United States, as tacticians, political freaks and publicity-hungry poli-ticians abused the patience of delegates and national audience alike with speeches, demonstrations, seconding speeches, more speeches, more demonstrations. Outside in the dark night, the Negroes of Miami rioted, and television reported that seventy policemen armed with shotguns were moving into the combat area. In those rites of violence which had, alas, become too familiar, four people were to die that night, senselessly as in all riots. But in the hall, six miles away, the names of nominees went on and on: Reagan of California, Hickel of Alaska, Rockefeller of Arkansas, Romney of Michigan, Carlson of Kansas, Fong of Hawaii, Rockefeller of New York, Case of New Jersey, Richard M. Nixon, Rhodes of Ohio, Stassen of Erehwon, Thurmond of South Carolina, twelve in all.

After eye and ear had taken all the beating possible, this correspondent made his way to the Rockefeller suite at the Americana Hotel to await the outcome of the balloting, and the unrolling of the scroll of ifs. It is difficult always to be with an old friend in defeat, but the memory lingers over fragments that are more than personal. Those in the room, all Rockefeller friends, were a tiny cross-section of what there is of an American elite: former Ambassador to London Winthrop Aldrich; Brooke (Mrs. Vincent) Astor; Mary (Mrs. William) Scranton; Mr. and Mrs. Maurice Moore of New York's great law firm Cravath, Swaine and Moore, so intimately cross-connected with the publications of Time Inc.; publisher Gardner Cowles of *Look* Magazine; industrialist J. Irwin Miller of Cummins Engines; Mr. and Mrs. Thomas Braden of California; Professor Henry Kissinger of Harvard; writer Emmet Hughes; and three Rockefeller brothers—Nelson, David and Laurance (a fourth, Winthrop, was on the convention floor). No less than three were past or present members of the Harvard Board of Overseers, who dutifully broke into applause for a fourth Harvard Overseer, Douglas Dillon, when he appeared on television to nominate Clifford Case of New Jersey as part of the strategy of the Rockefeller holding action. Thirty years ago men such as these controlled the Republican Party, could compel Midwestern and Far Western delegates to do their bidding, force the nomination of Wendell Willkie against the will of the primitives. But American politics had matured beyond their control, and this convention was beyond them. There was, one recognized, no Establishment. Or, if there was, the junior Jaycees of the Nixon staff were at least as potent in America today as any other establishment. One watched the final stages of the Rockefeller operation as the hour of balloting drew close, and one recognized the warmth and closeness of the brothers as well as the virility that had made and kept the family fortune a force in being. None of the three Rockefellers was in the room as an idle spectator; minute by minute, hour by hour, they were at the telephones, calling, exhorting, beseeching across the floor of the convention from Maine to New Mexico for the last one, two, three delegates that might be swayed. The family vitality still ran strong; one caught the echo of the past in the crisp voice of David Rockefeller talking on the phone to a wavering delegate: "The time is *now*."

Of all in the room, the least grim was candidate Nelson Rockefeller himself—going and coming from the telephone alerts of his command and control centers, then returning to play host, rearranging chairs for his company, filling their drinks, making sure they were comfortable.

Shirt-sleeved, burly and relaxed, he circulated among them, joked, then settled down as the count began. It was, for the Rockefellers, over within five minutes—at Florida. "Oh-oh, there it goes," said one of his staff command as the Florida vote went to Nixon, and none in the room commented. Rockefeller joined his wife on the sofa and she put her arm about him in comfort; he patted her knee gently in response; and the crusade was over except for the telephone call to Nixon as the balloting came to a close. "Dick," said Rockefeller, "I want to congratulate you. . . . I gave you a hard run there. . . . Your strategy was perfect, you handled it perfectly. . . . Ronnie didn't do as well as I thought, I was counting on him for a little more muscle. . . . I'm going to Maine, that's where I was born. . . . Who're you going to take as Vice-President. . . . Too many? . . . Oh, listen . . . I followed the opposite course, you had everybody in there, I had nobody, you're smart, that's best. . . . Give our best to Pat, tell her that she and your children looked lovely on TV. . . . Congratulations and take care. . . . It's a thrill talking to you. . . ."

And then Rockefeller was serene. A farewell press conference, ending with one of those rare rounds of applause that the press gives a candidate it cherishes, and he was out of it. It was up to Nixon.

The next twelve hours were, for Mr. Nixon, to be anything but serene.

Every candidate arrives at a convention almost certain of whom he seeks as his Vice-Presidential running-mate; it will be the first important decision he makes in national leadership. And then, in the excitement of the convention, as the jagged realities of politics make themselves felt in the pull-and-shove of contending forces, his pre-planning comes unstuck. Always, in every convention—from Roosevelt's in 1932, through Eisenhower's in 1952, through Kennedy's in 1960—the contender suddenly sees all things differently from the moment the balloting ends, when now he must make a real, not a putative, choice.

It is difficult to trace the process of the choice of Vice-President Agnew, for the choice of a Vice-President is settled in the mind of one man alone; the decision is as intimate, and forever thereafter as private, as the decision of marriage. Choice had been going on in Mr. Nixon's mind for many weeks before the convention. His staff had sorted out the same dozen well-known names into what some of them called "liberals," "conservatives" and "political eunuchs." Nixon had, in his usual way, tested his thinking on all his close associates. He had queried them over and over again on their preferences; he had floated Spiro Agnew's name several times in such discussions—but staff enthusiasm for Agnew was as close to zero as was reasonably measurable. Nixon had been under pressure from the Congressional wing of the Republican Party for weeks to choose John Lindsay, Mayor of New York; indeed, Congressman Bob Wilson of San Diego had polled House Republicans for Nixon to find Lindsay a three-to-one choice among his former colleagues. Yet Nixon himself preferred, above all others, Robert Finch of California. Finch was to him a younger brother, closer, more trusted, conspicuously more able and more visionary than any other man he had known over the years. He had telephoned Finch with a hard offer several weeks before the convention. But Finch would not—he felt he simply was not yet ready to carry, as he put it, "the other end of the stick" in a campaign so important as the Presidency. Finch suggested scholar John Gardner— a man whose intellectual credentials would lift the ticket entirely out of ordinary political dimension. Nixon toyed with the idea of adding such a name to the ticket, then tentatively substituted that of Franklin Murphy, former Chancellor of UCLA, as his preference in the world of thinkers. All these, and other conspicuous names, revolved around and around in Nixon's reflections for weeks; but the private polls he secretly commissioned to test names were of little help; none of the conspicuous names could add or detract more than a point or two from the test percentages resulting when Nixon's name was offered alone. And Agnew's name was not even on the polling list.

Nixon had settled in thus, in Penthouse B of the Hilton-Plaza, at seven o'clock on Wednesday evening, having finished a cheese omelet, milk and ice cream, to watch the nominations, sipping Seven-Up. Now candidates, being human, find particular brilliance in men who discover their own hidden virtues. Rockefeller had thus thought that Shafer's speech nominating Rockefeller was the best of the evening. Nixon, similarly, thought that Agnew's speech nominating Nixon was the best. Nixon was enormously impressed by the man with the square-cut jaw, the athletic frame, the command presence on the screen; he had met Agnew only four months before for the first time, had seen him three or four times since, but he felt Agnew had "authority," was "solid." He questioned all in the room—his personal staff—and they, like their chief, had enjoyed Agnew's speech immensely. At about eleven Nixon went for a half-hour drive around Miami. Briefly, he told two pool reporters that he wanted as his Vice-President a man he could trust, who could work with him for four years, and who understood the cities. He, Nixon, could handle foreign affairs. He returned to watch the balloting on television, keeping track of the votes on a score sheet, quite calm, and when Wisconsin's Governor Knowles announced that state's vote to give him his majority, Nixon cheerily said, "I'm glad Knowles did it."

Then it was time to choose a Vice-President. Midway through the balloting, floor pages had begun to deliver notes to selected Republican dignitaries at the convention. "I would appreciate it," read the typewritten slips, "if you could meet with me tonight in my room in the

Hilton-Plaza as soon as possible after the end of the balloting. Arrangements to escort you to my room will be handled by Mr. Hamilton at the reception desk on the 15th floor of the Hilton-Plaza. So as to avoid any possible confusion, please bring this memorandum with you. (signed) Dick." Now, from the jostle of the convention, the Republican leaders were making their way to their new maximum leader, for the ritual of conferring on the ticket's running-mate.

While he waited for the floor leaders to arrive, Mr. Nixon took a first sampling of opinion from the twenty-four men of his operational staff in the solarium. There were few new Vice-Presidential names to be added to the ones so long and so often discussed. There were the liberals—Lindsay, Percy, Hatfield. There were the conservatives—Reagan above all others, then John Tower and George Bush of Texas, Howard Baker of Tennessee. And, finally, the political eunuchs: Volpe and Agnew. The conference was not an elimination process—the forty-five-minute meeting was too short, the number of people too many. But Volpe and Agnew survived the discussion well.

The staff meeting broke up as Mr. Nixon took the congratulatory telephone call from Hubert Humphrey, and then he convened with the leaders who had come from the convention to his gold-and-white-brocaded Penthouse Suite. It was a jovial meeting, as the leaders treated themselves to well-earned bourbon and Scotch and considered their advice. Rhodes of Ohio and Brownell of New York were for Lindsay; but the others at the gathering were overwhelmingly conservative. Barry Goldwater declared he could under no circumstances accept Lindsay; Thurmond would not have Lindsay; neither would the lesser conservatives. Lindsay was out.[3] Ronald Reagan—the other "glamor boy," in Nixon's private phrase—was also out. Several Northerners observed that the North and the industrial states could not accept Ronald Reagan (Strom Thurmond's favorite) any more than the South could accept Lindsay. Robert Finch observed that Reagan simply would not accept the offer. The Reverend Billy Graham observed that, whoever it was, it should be a man of high morals. The long night meeting of weary men got nowhere. There was something decisive to be said against everyone—except Agnew and Volpe. Between four and five in the morning, the meeting broke up in indecision, all having waited for Mr. Nixon's decision, while he waited on their advice.

---

[3] Lindsay had probably already eliminated himself the previous day. Fearful of being mousetrapped by Congressional pressure to accept second place, he had sent, through an intermediary friend, a message of awesome sternness to Mr. Nixon. If the Party compelled him to run, if a Party duty were made of it—then he would. But he wanted Mr. Nixon to know that if he were so chosen, he would, as Vice-President, feel himself free to speak out on issues, either on foreign affairs or urban affairs, whenever he disagreed with the President and make his opposition known. If I were Nixon, said Lindsay, I wouldn't dream of accepting my offer.

At 6:30, Mr. Nixon went to bed and rose at 8:30 to descend to the Jackie-of-Hearts Room (so named for Miami's favorite adopted son, Jackie Gleason). Nixon had promised he would announce to the nation the name of its new Vice-President at about eleven in the morning, but he was no nearer decision than ever. The nine-o'clock session in the Jackie-of-Hearts Room was, in effect, a rump session of eleven elders who had not been able to make the all-night session in the Penthouse Suite. Relatively rested and refreshed, these gentlemen, full of vigor, gave one another a hard time, beginning all over again with the same list of names that Mr. Nixon had heard chewed over twice before since his nomination. Again the record turned, the same tune was heard, and the needle stuck: The Southerners in the group absolutely refused to consider Lindsay—or Percy, or Romney, or Hatfield. The Northerners, who wanted Lindsay, absolutely refused to consider Reagan or Tower. The meeting took on the quality of a nominating committee at a boys' club. Wilson of California, having given up on Lindsay, suggested Congressman Gerald Ford—because Ford was in the room. Senator Everett Dirksen suggested Senator Howard Baker of Tennessee—his son-in-law. Senator George Murphy suddenly, out of nowhere, suggested Robert Finch again—because Finch was in the room. Since at this time such meetings were rapidly getting non-productive, Mr. Nixon finally withdrew. Summoning his own uppermost inner circle together, he retreated to the Penthouse Suite again, whither a dozen Seven-Ups, a dozen Coca-Colas and two buckets of ice were quickly sent.

The final meeting on the Vice-Presidency of the United States is the most obscure of all four meetings on the road to selection. By now even the Nixon staff was confused, and various responsibles sent various messages to the Secret Service of the United States, with or without authority. In the morning the Secret Service was detailed to stand guard over four probables: Messrs. Hatfield, Lindsay, Reagan and Percy. Shortly thereafter the Secret Service was told to drop Hatfield and add John Volpe of Massachusetts. Shortly before noon it was told to add Spiro Agnew of Maryland. Whether these instructions had any relevance to the meeting or discussion in the Nixon Suite, one does not know. The next President gathered with six of his closest for the final decision: Robert Finch, H. R. Haldeman, John Mitchell, John Tower, Robert Ellsworth, Rogers Morton. By now all had been eliminated by the crossfire at the previous meetings except for the two political neutrals, Agnew and Volpe—plus Robert Finch. Finch left the room when they discussed his name. In such a matching, there was no contest—with only two negatives those in the room voted that Robert Finch should run as Vice-President. Mr. Nixon emerged to give the message to Mr. Finch—that the group wanted him, that he himself wanted to have him.

Mr. Finch's instant thinking is unavailable. Friends describe him as appalled; the world waited for Nixon's decision, press and TV clamored for the name of the Vice-President. All this should have been settled hours ago. The choice of his name, Finch now said, would smack of nepotism. Finch felt he could be a better friend and adviser than a running-mate to the old companion who now offered him partnership. The upshot: Finch refused. When the final meeting resumed after its brief interruption, there were only two contenders left—Messrs. Agnew and Volpe. Of whom, Agnew was the more impressive. And at 12:30, Richard Nixon decided on the most important political appointment in America: Spiro T. Agnew for Vice-President. Robert Ellsworth was dispatched to deliver regrets to Governor John Volpe on the telephone; simultaneously Rogers Morton was telephoning Governor Agnew with the good news; and Mr. Nixon was descending to face the television cameras and announce his running-mate.

There remained now nothing but the afternoon ceremonies and the acceptance speech. The acceptance speech at any convention is, along with the balloting, a moment that merits attention. In his speech, a candidate must genuinely express himself, and himself alone, no matter how many other hands help him on his draft. Thus the galleries were full, red-white-and-blue bunting stretched everywhere, the delegates on the floor waving red-and-white Nixon placards, blue-and-white Agnew placards, the ceiling nets, bulging with orange balloons, swaying and ready to burst, as the convention awaited the voice of its leader.

Mr. Nixon, in public as in private, has several styles of speech. In private, he can be either crisp, precise and orderly, or, when the mood takes him, a relaxed, tangential, imaginative rambler. Two separate styles likewise mark him in public. Normally, at unprepared stump rallies or in public question and answer, his prose runs to the meat-and-potatoes, regular-fellow, let's-all-get-on-the-team-together style. Or it can be, occasionally, another style—a powerful system of straightforward declarative sentences which reach their eloquence by simplicity and force, as in the genuine heights of his inaugural address. It is the first or regular-fellow style that so offends the ears of the intellectual and literary elite. Even were Nixon to read the Lord's Prayer or a Shakespearian sonnet, this elite has been so conditioned to resentment of his style that they would put their fingers in their ears. No version of English, no French, Italian, European or foreign-flavored use of the language is so offensive to the taste-masters of American rhetoric as the humdrum use of the mother tongue in the Main Street or Midwest style. Nixon's acceptance speech was a composite of both his public styles, and was to be delivered with fervor.

He had been working hard on this speech: he had sequestered himself the week before the convention at Montauk Point, Long Island, for the task. He had scratched outline after outline on his yellow pads, read and reread his notes, then drafted, dictated, polished. He was moody, for he meant it to say exactly what he meant; he had paced the ocean shore as he thought about his speech—the sound of waves always soothes Richard Nixon—and one evening, walking in the fog along the beach, thinking about it, he had lost himself, to the consternation of his Secret Service men. But now he was ready.

One bent forward to hear him, and as he began, for a long terrible moment of introduction, one thought that Mr. Nixon was going to run as the regular-fellow.

"I have news for you. This time there's a difference—this time we're going to win. . . for a number of reasons. First a personal one. General Eisenhower, as you know, lies critically ill in the Walter Reed Hospital tonight. I have talked, however, with Mrs. Eisenhower on the telephone. She tells me . . . there is nothing that he lives more for, and there is nothing that would lift him more than to win in November. And I say, let's win this one for Ike."

The audience cheered, the press gallery groaned. It *was* regular-fellow at the stump.

Then, abruptly, he went into his written draft, and the quality was different. He had a message, his speech had themes; he was framing his purpose and direction, using and weaving together all the lines that had touched the nerves of his audiences on the long primary trail from New Hampshire to Oregon. The speech was not new; those who had followed him could transmit, at the end of every tenth sentence, the tested punch-line. What was new was context and frame. He was saying exactly what he thought: it was to be the campaign of a conservative, but not the radical conservatism of Barry Goldwater driving from the Party all those who disagreed; it was a centrist conservatism, inviting both extremes to a unifying moderation.

Unity, thus, was the first theme:

"A party that can unite itself will unite America. . . . As we look at America, we see cities enveloped in smoke and flame. We hear sirens in the night. . . . Did we come all this way for this? Did American boys die in Normandy and Korea and in Valley Forge for this?

"Listen to the answers to these questions.

"It is another voice, it is a quiet voice in the tumult of the shouting. It is the voice of the great majority of Americans, the forgotten Americans, the non-shouters, the non-demonstrators. . . . They work in American factories, they run American businesses. They serve in government; they provide most of the soldiers who die to keep it free. They give drive to the spirit of America. They give lift to the American dream. . . ."

From there, Mr. Nixon reverted to the tested themes of the primaries: "When the strongest nation in the world can be tied down for four years in a war in Vietnam with no end in sight," etc., and on to the listing of the catastrophes of the American condition, until, using again his primary line, "It's time for new leadership for the United States of America," he continued: "There is only one answer to such a record of failure, and that is the complete housecleaning of those responsible for the failures and that record."

Then, to his pledges of leadership.

In foreign affairs, a neat balancing of old patriotism with peace and reconciliation: "I pledge to you tonight that the first priority foreign policy objective of our next administration will be to bring an honorable end to the Vietnam War.

". . . To the leaders of the Communist world we say, after an era of confrontations, the time has come for an era of negotiation. . . . We extend the hand of friendship to all people. To the Russian people. To the Chinese people.[4] To all people in the world. And we shall work toward the goal of an open world, open sky, open cities, open hearts, open minds. . . ."

He lamented the low esteem into which America had fallen abroad. "For five years hardly a day has gone by when we haven't read or heard a report of the American flag being spit on, and our embassy being stoned, a library being burned, or an ambassador being insulted," and then he bridged over to his main domestic theme,

"If we are to restore prestige and respect for America abroad, the place to begin is at home, in the United States of America. . . . Our founders recognized that the first requisite of progress is order. Now there is no quarrel between progress and order because neither can exist without the other. So let us have order in America . . . and tonight it's time for some honest talk about the problem of order."

Law-and-order caught the mood of the convention; Vietnam and foreign policy had confused them, as it did all Americans. Now, for law-and-order, they stamped and cheered as Richard Nixon promised a new Attorney General, a new Department of Justice which would make war on organized crime, loan sharks, numbers racketeers, pill-peddlers, narcotics-peddlers, for "let this message come through clear from what I say tonight. . . . Time is running out for the merchants of crime and corruption. . . . The wave of crime is not going to be the wave of the future in the United States."

Having established order clearly as his first priority of policy, he

---

[4] The platform had, as a sop to its Neanderthal wing, declared on China that "improved relations with Communist nations can come only when they cease to endanger other states by force or threat. Under existing conditions we cannot favor recognition of Communist China or its admission to the United Nations." But Mr. Nixon felt, as every candidate does, that a President had a free hand to choose what part of the platform would bind him and what not.

balanced quickly with the theme of progress. Not progress by a deluge of government programs ("I say it's time to quit pouring billions of dollars into programs that have failed in the United States of America"), but progress that would enlist, along with the government, "the greatest engine of progress ever developed in the history of man—American private enterprise. . . . With progress must come the building of bridges," bridges to human dignity across that gulf that separates black America from white America. Then, pointing the matter more sharply, he said:

"Tonight I see the face of a child. He lives in a great city. He's black or he's white, he's Mexican, Italian, Polish. None of that matters. What matters is he's an American child. That child in that great city is more important than any politician's promise. . . . He sleeps the sleep of a child, and he dreams the dreams of a child. And yet when he awakens, he awakens to a living nightmare of poverty, neglect and despair. He fails in school, he ends up on welfare. For him the American system is one that feeds his stomach and starves his soul. It breaks his heart. And in the end it may take his life on some distant battlefield. . . .

"To millions of children in this rich land this is their prospect, but this is only part of what I see in America tonight.

"I see another child tonight. He hears a train go by. At night he dreams of faraway places where he'd like to go. It seems like an impossible dream. But he is helped on his journey through life. A father who had to go to work before he finished the sixth grade sacrificed everything he had so that his sons could go to college. A gentle Quaker mother with a passionate concern for peace, quietly wept when he went to war but she understood why he had to go. A great teacher, a remarkable football coach, an inspirational minister encouraged him on his way. A courageous wife and loyal children stood by him in victory and also in defeat. And in his chosen profession of politics, first there were scores, then hundreds, then thousands, and then finally millions who worked for his success.

"And tonight he stands before you, nominated for President of the United States of America."

CHAPTER NINE

THE CHICAGO CONVENTION: THE FURIES IN THE STREET

"Extremism in the defense of liberty is no vice; moderation in the pursuit of justice is no virtue"—a theme first advanced by Barry Goldwater at the Republican convention of 1964 and adopted as their own, at the Democratic convention of 1968, by the rioters and the police who responded to them

CHICAGO of 1968 will pass into history as far more than the site of the Democratic convention. The great city by the lake has always been America's favorite political gathering place—Abraham Lincoln, Franklin D. Roosevelt, Dwight D. Eisenhower were all first named here. So, too, were Ulysses S. Grant, Grover Cleveland, Adlai Stevenson and Richard M. Nixon.

But in 1968 the name Chicago won a significance far beyond date and place. It became the title of an episode, like Waterloo, or Versailles, or Munich. At Chicago, for the first time, the most delicate process of American politics was ruptured by violence, the selection of Presidents stained with blood. 1968, throughout, was a year in which the ghosts of America's past returned to haunt the present; but at Chicago the goblins of America's future first appeared to haunt tomorrow.

Drama was the mood of the year; Chicago was its high point; and thus, perhaps, it is best to begin the story as if one were approaching a passage of theater.

First then, the stage setting, the city itself:

Chicago, second city of the land, population 3,480,000, sprawls twenty-three miles along the southwest rim of Lake Michigan, its shore fringed by beauty. More than sixty years ago, city-planner Daniel Hudson Burnham declared this to be a city that should "dream no little dreams," and persuaded the city fathers to reserve the entire lake front for green and parks. Today there rises along the shore, a clifflike ridge of great buildings, extravagantly designed apartment towers, imposing hotels, glistening luxury shops, all looking down on gardens, flowers and trees to present to visitors one of the most majestic façades of any city in the world. Culture has passed through this town, flirted with the city, touching it in the past with poetry, leaving behind a great art museum, a great university, two great newspapers. But the city's image was caught best and forever by its poet laureate, Carl Sandburg, who put the gloss on Chicago—"Hog Butcher for the World, Tool Maker, Stacker of Wheat, Player with Railroads and the Nation's Freight Handler; Stormy, husky, brawling, City of the Big Shoulders." For Chicago is a working-man's city—like Detroit, or Brooklyn, or Pittsburgh, only larger and more powerful. New York may be Cosmopolis; Chicago is what America is all about.

Chicago is industry—people who make things, get things done. Sandburg's Chicago is, of course, dead: though the stockyards still stank of death and offal in the summer of 1968, the meat industry is moving away and hog-butchering declines. Railways shrivel in Chicago as they do everywhere in America; wheat and corn move from the great plains to the outer world by more convenient lake outlets. But the essence of what Sandburg caught is still there: muscle. From the new towers one can look south through the smog over the greatest steel-making complex in the world—from South Chicago through Gary, the great mills pour more steel (25,000,000 tons annually) than the Ruhr of Germany, than the British Midlands, than all of France. Chicago beats and twists this steel into tractors, trucks, freight cars, heavy equipment. And Chicago does far more than process brute metal. In the stadium of the University of Chicago is a plaque that notes that here the first continued fission of the atom was achieved—and an enormous electronics industry now employs scores of thousands; so does the printing industry; so do food industries; so do the wholesale and banking establishments. No one who wants work in Chicago is unemployed. But it is a hard-knuckled city, a union town, friendly if one knows how to make friends, uptight to strangers.

Chicago sorts itself out neatly on a map. Behind Burnham's magnificent lake front the beauty quickly crumbles into endless stretches of one-family or two-family homes of working people, their factories and shops dreary concrete patches among undistinguished wood-frame or red-brick huddles. North of the Chicago River—which bisects the town— and in a great swath to the west live those called by sociologists the "ethnics"—Germans, Poles, Italians, Irish, Jews of the working class. In the suburbs, and chiefly to the north, live the white Protestant middle class and those of the "ethnics" who seep upward toward the sun, the light, green lawns and good schools. South of the river and the Loop is the Black Belt, the greatest internal political pressure source, where the blacks of Chicago have grown by nature and migration to 30 percent of the city's population (up from 14 percent in 1950).

Somehow all these people within their communities have managed over the decades not only to live peacefully together but also, in the past thirteen years, to thrive with an exuberant vitality which is their pride. And of all of the proud of Chicago, no one is more proud than Richard J. Daley, their mayor, who, in 1968, ached to have the Democratic Party meet in his city.

Daley was not alone in claiming the convention of the Party for his city; others, too, sought the honor; and an examination of the rival claims exposes various faces of the political realities of the year:

§ Houston, for example, was a major contender. It boasted that its new Astrodome was far and away the best convention hall in the nation. This, of course, was true—but Houston was a Southern city in the process of transition, and it was certain that Negro delegates and dignitaries would not be comfortable there. Thus, Houston—out.

§ Philadelphia had a good claim on the convention and advanced it firmly enough to sway most of the nine men on the site-selection committee. Philadelphia was a Democratic stronghold in a swing state, had a good convention hall, was convenient to such centers as Washington, New York, Chicago.

The decisive factor running against Philadelphia was another reflection of changing reality. Its hotel facilities could not possibly meet the bloated needs of a modern Democratic convention. The number of delegates and onlookers[1] had so swollen since 1960 that by 1968 the convention planners knew they needed at least 6,500 good hotel rooms for the 3,000 delegates and equivalent number of alternates required officially to come. Beyond that, the spectacle required 7,500 first-class hotel rooms for the press and media, whose appetite had so enormously grown in the past decade.[2] Beyond that, again, there would be Governors, Senators, diplomats, dignitaries and guests, with their staffs, plus hundreds of convention personnel. All in all, no less than 20,000 good hotel rooms

---

[1] The swollen rolls of the Democratic national convention are a reflection of one of the rare lapses of good judgment of John F. Kennedy. Eleven days before he died, he accepted the suggestion of his advisers that the number of delegates to a Democratic convention be roughly doubled by a complicated formula intended to reduce the influence of Southerners in choosing a Democratic nominee. The multiplication of delegates since that decision has reduced the representative influence of each individual, and converted the Democratic conventions of 1964 and 1968 to potential mob gatherings.

[2] The two largest networks, CBS and NBC, are bound by union contracts to provide "first-class" lodgings for all their engineers, electricians, mechanics, of the same quality as go to Messrs. Cronkite, Sevareid, Huntley and Brinkley. Each of these two networks demanded 750 rooms for their personnel.

were, and are, needed for a Democratic convention, and Philadelphia could not guarantee them. So, Philadelphia—out.

§ Miami was the major rival of Chicago for the Democratic convention. It had, as we have seen, a fine convention hall and more than adequate hotel space. Moreover, press and TV favored it—the Republican convention would end on August 8th, the Democratic convention would start on August 26th, and why not, they argued, save the millions of dollars in electronic installations, the wear-and-tear on nerves and energies, that would be required to move from one city to another? Miami had bid $800,000 to defray the Party's convention costs, Chicago had topped that with $900,000, but the slim margin of bidding was an irrelevancy.

What was critical to the Democratic Party was the matter of security. If street trouble broke in Miami, the Democratic convention would have to appeal for protection to the Florida National Guard, which was at the command of that erratic Republican, Governor Claude Kirk. And anywhere else the Democratic chieftains looked in the North or West for any other adequate convention site, they could identify only New York (whose National Guard was commanded by Republican Rockefeller) or California (Republican Ronald Reagan) or Pennsylvania (Republican Raymond Shafer)—except for Illinois. In Illinois, Democratic Mayor Daley commanded the police, Democratic Governor Sam Shapiro commanded the National Guard. In terms of security and politics, Illinois was best.

But decision was Lyndon Johnson's alone. Lyndon Johnson had learned a President's prerogative in staging conventions of his party in 1964. Flying back from the Atlantic City convention of that year with Democratic National Chairman John Bailey, he had grumbled about the choice. He, the President, had been given the best hotel suite in the town, and it was still second-rate. Who, demanded the President of Bailey, had chosen Atlantic City? Bailey excused himself—it was President John F. Kennedy who had chosen the place, not he, Bailey. Thus Johnson took it on himself to decide the place of the next convention, notwithstanding the site committee's fears of violence. Johnson chose Chicago for traditional reasons as well as new reasons: it was central, it was generous in its bidding, it guaranteed security. Above all, because Johnson liked Daley, and Daley wanted it. No Democratic convention had been held in Chicago since 1956, the first year of Daley's mayoralty, and Daley yearned to show the world how wonderful his Chicago had become.

Next, the preparation of the stage.

The stage-handlers who prepared the setting were men of two different kinds: the security forces and the television forces.

For the security forces, the safeguarding of the convention, within and without, was the overriding factor. Politics concerned them but little. By midsummer, thus, they had dressed the scene as never before in American politics: 11,900 Chicago police were prepared for twelve-hour duty throughout the emergency—with battle plans, bivouacs, command posts and mobile tactical forces all plotted on charts. Cook County's 300-man riot squad was on the alert. Five Chicago school-houses had been prepared to sleep up to 7,500 men of the Illinois National Guard, providing five 800-man battalions, of three rifle companies each, at street-readiness. From Washington, a thousand FBI and Secret Service agents were being deployed. Far away, at bases in Oklahoma, Colorado and Texas, the U.S. Army had detailed 7,500 regular army troops for emplanement on call to the convention city. And Convention Hall, at the stockyards, was a fortress—a one-square-mile security area had been proclaimed all around it; chain-link fences topped with three strands of barbed wire ringed the amphitheater itself; manhole covers on the approaches to the stockyards had been sealed against hidden bomb-throwers; 200 firemen stood by to frustrate bomb-throwers and arsonists if any *did* filter through security; and a catwalk, ninety-five feet above the floor of the convention, had been built for Secret Service and police to survey the gathering below with binoculars, walkie-talkies and rifles.

The background these stage-setters had made by the middle of August was unique in American political experience—and the mood was compounded by the condition of the city and America in the hot summer of 1968. Air transportation had finally snarled itself into the long-predicted breakdown of sky traffic over Eastern America. Planes might be delayed for hours leaving New York or Washington, and even longer in the traffic circling above O'Hare field waiting for a landing slot in Chicago. When one alighted at O'Hare, one found Chicago suffering from a taxi strike—and how would one get to one's hotel? When one got to one's hotel, one found there was a telephone strike—no private lines or switchboards had been installed for those who expected them; and how could one get through the overcrowded switchboards of the hotel to pass messages?

On no group did these frustrations weigh more heavily than on the second group of stage-setters—the television men. Their mood, their spirit was to color almost all that America, including the arriving delegates, would see of the grand gathering. And the mood of the television men was bitter to begin with—for they were artists, in an art as esoteric as that of a commander-at-his-bridge of an aircraft carrier of the U.S. Navy in battle, and they were not to be permitted to practice it. Their art was that of live television, and the nation had come to take their art for granted, had accepted the easy indulgence of immediacy, the sense that the viewer was there on the spot seeing what was happening while it happened. Underlying the art, however, were an immense technology and the even more imposing skills of the few men who could manipulate it. At Miami, CBS and NBC each had more than thirty television crews posted at remotes all over the city, linked by telephonic land lines, all in instant communication with each other and their central controls. From these central controls, approximately $40,000,000 of equipment had permitted the master directors to flick switches, deploy more than sixty live cameras, and make of a whole week of political proceedings a single continuum of action and place. The unrecognized men who direct these great apparati—Wussler, Diamond, Leonard, Manning and Hewitt of CBS or Murray, Frank, Northshield, and Frankel of NBC—can be appreciated only by other technicians or their executive superiors; but they are fiercely proud of their craftsmanship, even more fiercely competitive with each other, and bestride their own little world like barons of the realm. They had come to Chicago to give the nation what the nation expected of them—the illusion of being there, right there, when it happened.

Except that they were trapped. Their fantastic equipment for instant communication had been rendered half useless because the striking telephone workers of Chicago would permit no installation of lines except at Convention Hall itself; and every other union in the union town jealously protected their craft-brothers against scabs. Giving up their hope of instantaneous visual transmission of action as it happened by live remotes, the television men fell back on old-fashioned cameras with old-fashioned film or cumbersome video tape. But to get such film or tape on the air, it would first be necessary to speed it by courier to the only two transmission centers available to each network—their downtown Chicago affiliates or, more importantly, the broadcast facilities from Convention Hall, permitted to function only by special dispensation of the telephone union. This shipping of film or tape would interpose a delay in showing action while it was happening; to this would be added the time needed to develop film or process tape, and cut it for showing at the two transmission points. The delay would, later, have a vital effect in blurring political judgment at the convention. But as they approached the convention, the television men expected not only some minimal cooperation from the city of Chicago to compensate for their plight, but, hopefully, perhaps some extra effort at help reflecting the magnitude of events. Instead, they received none. Mayor Daley's police would not let their trucks park near hotels; cameramen were forbidden to occupy sidewalks; courier cars overspeeding to deliver film to transmission points were to be arrested. The networks toyed with the idea of flying film by helicopter over traffic to the transmission point at the convention: that, too, was forbidden; the United States government had placed an inviolable canopy over the convention site; no planes or helicopters were permitted to overfly.

Thus the preparation of the set: security entirely in the hands of police and military, suspicious of all; Daley in control of the streets; and the television men, in control of the imagination of the nation, vexed and harassed. Nor could Daley, a primitive man, see any reason why he should tell his cops to pamper the men who would paint his and their portrait in full color across the nation.

Enter, now, the long parade of *dramatis personae:*

§1 First, Mayor Richard J. Daley of Chicago, sixty-six, the best old-fashioned mayor of the country. Since he was cast as the Villain of Chicago, let the defense speak first:

Elected mayor of Chicago for the first time in 1955 by a plurality of 126,667 votes (his license plate still bears the number 708,222, which was his total in that election), re-elected in 1959, again in 1963, again in 1967 (by the splendid majority of 519,696), he was, if any man ever was, the choice of the people of his city. Son of a sheet-metal worker, in-tuitively linked with the unspoken culture of white workingmen, he had clawed and clambered his way up through the Cook County machine to its summit, remaining modest in all habits except pride.

And he had served his city well. When Dick Daley first became mayor of the moribund city of Chicago in 1955, not a major new build-ing had been built in its downtown central city since the Marshall Field building of 1932. In the years since 1955, downtown Chicago, like a giant waking from sleep, had exploded in a building boom of glistening towers, minarets, monuments. The corrupt police force had been purged; public housing had been built on a scale matching New York, Boston or New Haven; its poverty program, under Dr. Deton Brooks, its black admin-istrator, was one of the more imaginative in the country; black political leaders of the South Side had been so thoroughly accepted as equals in the Cook County machine that the word integration was a superfluity; professors of the University of Chicago advised the mayor; the news-papers respected him; the unions considered him their man; business leaders praised him. Said David M. Kennedy in 1968, then chairman of a Chicago bank, now Secretary of the Treasury: "I don't think there is a mayor anywhere who is doing more for his city in an intelligent, forth-right, objective way than Mayor Daley."

In politics, however, Daley is an Iron Buddha. No one knows his thinking until he speaks. Few knew that Daley, attacked by the peace mobilizers of the streets, had been for months one of the most convinced doves in the nation. Nor did politicians know more of his inner think-ing on other matters. Down to the very opening of the convention no one knew for sure which candidate Dick Daley was going to back. With his support for Humphrey, the convention would become a ritual formal-ity; without it, the convention might come apart. All expected him to be with Humphrey; but his silence reminded politicians of old-time Boss Richard Croker of New York. Once, at one of Tammany's boisterous Fourth of July parties, when everyone else broke into voice singing "The Star-Spangled Banner," an associate noticed that Boss Croker was not singing, and asked why. "He doesn't want to commit himself," growled a crony. Nor did Daley want to commit himself even on the eve of convention.

Of one thing only, everyone was sure—that when Daley committed, the entire Illinois delegation of 118 votes would be committed, too. At Miami, where "erosion" was the watchword, delegates had been sought at retail, one by one. In Chicago they came in wholesale packages, by states; and of the wholesalers, Daley was the most important. "If," said Martin Plissner, CBS delegate analyst, "Daley instructs the Illinois delegates to vote for Ho Chi Minh, all but twenty votes will go to Ho Chi Minh without a question."

For Daley believes in authority—rigid, inflexible, unquestionable authority. In Chicago his authority approaches autocracy. He controls the police (his orders to the police after the April, 1968, riots had been to "shoot to kill"); until March, 1968, the Illinois National Guard commander was a Trustee of his Chicago Sanitary District; Daley's appointee was the United States Attorney for Cook County; his man controlled the parks; his appointee was governor; his former law partner sat on the U.S. District Court. Add to this profile of power several other personal qualities—a hubris, or overweening pride and arrogance; a totally graceless use of the English language; an unfortunately rough-hewn face which, in anger, with the underlip shot out, looks like a turtle's swollen with rage—and one has a man whose symbolism overshadows his great achievements. Chicago was to enlarge this symbolism nationwide.

§2 Offstage now, another symbolic character:

David Dellinger, fifty-three, of New York was as far from the world and experience of Richard Daley as imagination could stretch. A Phi Beta Kappa from Yale (class of '36), descended on his distaff side through the Daughters of the American Revolution, an Oxford postgraduate, a round-faced, soft-spoken character, he appeared almost a man of the cloth except for the cigars he smoked. But David Dellinger was also the "Uncle Ho" of the American peace movement, chairman of the National Mobilization Committee to End the War in Vietnam.

Talking to Dellinger was, on first meeting, like a tour through the world of innocence. Dellinger believed that government must be returned to "the people." He had visited Communist Hanoi several times and found its system of government admirable; he gently affirmed that the people in every province, every county of North Vietnam discussed their problems and controlled their own lives. He hated war and authority—

had refused to register for the draft in 1940 (and served a year and a day in jail); had refused to report for induction later (and served two more years in jail); had undergone other arrests. By 1968 he had become the father figure of the 100-odd groups of resisters and protesters of the Vietnam war across the country—and also an extremely able street tactician and organizer.

By the fall of 1967, after the success of his October demonstration at the Pentagon, Dellinger was ready, to consider disruption of the Democratic convention at Chicago, to show the American people what a mockery their political system was. It would be the grandest of confrontations yet. A first meeting of his 100-man Mobilization Steering Committee in December authorized him to call a conference to discuss planning. On January 27th, in a New York apartment, twenty-five people gathered to draw up strategy, a bit disconcerted that they could not entice black militants to make common cause. In late March, in Chicago, followed another clandestine meeting of the tacticians of the movement to lay precise plans: radio communications, street communications, mobilization posts would be established across the city. But Dellinger insisted they did not seek violence. I asked him during this planning period what would happen, though, if the demonstrations themselves provoked violence. The gentle man was thoroughly perplexed and answered: "I don't know until history unfolds; I oppose violence; where my confusion is—is what about the victim against whom the police use violence, has he got the right to use violence to defend himself?"

§3 Enter next a new political face, George McGovern, forty-six, United States Senator from South Dakota, who had announced his candidacy for the Democratic nomination on August 10th, 1968, only two weeks before the convention.

McGovern—like Humphrey and McCarthy—was a onetime professor (of history and political science), a leader in the academic perpetration of American politics so conspicuous over the past decade. Young, charming, gay, father of five, deeply opposed to the bombing of North Vietnam, he had called the bombings "a policy of madness" as early as spring of 1967. His old friendship with Hubert Humphrey led him to believe that he could be the bridge over which Humphrey might pass to reconciliation with the peace groups. A man of great kindness, his wit had a refreshing candor. When asked what separated his candidacy from that of Eugene McCarthy, he said, "Well—Gene really doesn't want to be President, and I do."

By August and his arrival in Chicago, McGovern had become, however, the gathering point for 300-odd leaderless Kennedy delegates, camping uneasily about him while waiting for the chief offstage actor, Senator Edward Kennedy, to make his move. McGovern's heart had belonged to Robert F. Kennedy all through the spring months; were

Edward Kennedy to announce his availability, the McGovern candidacy would evaporate overnight. And from McGovern's headquarters at the Blackstone Hotel one could see the fallout and confusion that the assassination had spread among the leaders of the Kennedy movement. McGovern's two chief lieutenants at Chicago were Pierre Salinger and Frank Mankiewicz, both of the high Kennedy staff. And across the street at the Conrad Hilton one could find the rest of the Kennedy staff fragmented and divided. Lawrence O'Brien had joined Humphrey and, from the twenty-fourth floor, was in command of all Humphrey's convention operations. Nine floors below, Richard Goodwin and Pat Lucey had joined the McCarthy command. Elsewhere were Kenneth O'Donnell and Ted Sorensen, uncommitted to any announced candidates, on stand-by awaiting word of Edward Kennedy's intentions. Arthur Schlesinger, the Kennedy historian, arrived wearing a McGovern button, stayed two days, and then on Tuesday morning, the day after the convention opening, flew off to Japan—the sense of impending disaster was too clear to him.

§4 Follows Eugene McCarthy.

The most enigmatic man in the politics of 1968 was never more enigmatic than in the weeks preceding the convention.

Eugene McCarthy had, in 1968, created a cause. He did not control the cause, nor could he organize it, but he had crystallized it. He, too, like Humphrey and Nixon, had been in politics for some twenty years; uninterested, however, in political mechanics, he bore no luggage of commitments with him from these long years; no man held any claim on his loyalties, nor he on any other man. But in 1968 he had brought with him, into the arena of protest and politics, thousands of young people who would, forever after, insist on being part of politics. To these alone he gave commitment. But it was the commitment of a martyr, taking comfort from the future, not the present, much as Latimer at the stake in 1555, about to be burned for his faith, had offered comfort to his fellow martyr, Ridley: "Be of good comfort, Master Ridley, and play the man—we shall this day light such a candle by God's grace in England as I trust shall never be put out."

The death of Robert F. Kennedy had propelled McCarthy to center stage as the only real alternative to Hubert Humphrey for the Democratic candidacy. Politically a new crest of popularity had carried McCarthy forward since June. A massive shift of loyalties had swept toward him, by every polling index, huge blocs of Kennedy's Negro and minority votes. He had scored astoundingly well in the New York Democratic primaries two weeks after Kennedy's death, snaring at least 52 of the 123 elective delegates of that state. His pulling power was obviously huge—his coattails had dragged in Paul O'Dwyer, one of the more meager political figures in the Empire State, to New York's Democratic

Senatorial nomination. Through June and July, crowds surged by the tens of thousands to hear McCarthy speak wherever he went; in state after state he outran Humphrey in the polls, showing particular strength among independents and Republicans; money poured into his campaign coffers.

Yet the candidate seemed uncomfortable in his growing prominence—and as the convention approached, his behavior grew more and more erratic. He mused publicly about going to Paris to examine the peace negotiations there, a breach of political tradition dangerous not only to himself but to American diplomacy. He dropped that thought. Then, when the Russians invaded Czechoslovakia, he casually dismissed the invasion as an episode scarcely to be considered "a major world crisis." It was rumored that several Southern delegations planned to reverse the usual liberal demand for a "loyalty" oath from the South, and insist that McCarthy's Northern delegates equally pledge loyalty to the convention's ultimate nominee. When so informed, McCarthy threatened to pull out of the convention entirely and hold his own rump convention. But his staff dissuaded him from that.

Whether or not McCarthy ultimately might have wrested the nomination from Hubert Humphrey is another of the "ifs" of 1968; it was probably never in the cards. As he approached convention day, however, McCarthy's delegates numbered well over 500; this number might, by alliance with the Kennedy and McGovern delegates, reach 900, and might, given a rupture between Humphrey and the Southern delegates, conceivably be pressed to a majority. But his organization reflected in no way any hard practical intent to make this faint possibility real.

Between the masses whom McCarthy aroused and the practical, tactical dispositions needed to grab the nomination, one could detect no genuine over-all command. Blair Clark was still officially at the top, trying to pull together an organization whose separate parts no one could dominate except the candidate himself. But the candidate did not choose to dominate. He was bored by conferences and strategies. Richard Goodwin was thus primarily responsible for the McCarthy task forces on the platform, chief among them the development of a Vietnam policy; simultaneously he acted as chief liaison with the Kennedy forces and had freewheeling rights to make contact with various delegate brokers, North and South. Student control and direction lay with Sam Brown. Stephen Mitchell, Adlai Stevenson's old campaign manager, was independently trying to shake the Rules and Credentials committees to open floor fights. And Pat Lucey of Wisconsin, a Kennedy loyalist who had enlisted with McCarthy only a few weeks earlier, had begun to organize the delegate-control operation only eleven days before the convention began. Reviewing his new companions, Lucey observed one day, "I never in all my life was in any operation in which so many people hated each other." [3]

On one matter of organization, however, McCarthy had taken precise and foresighted decision. He did not want *his* students, *his* innocents, *his* children to be wrapped up in the demonstrations and coming confrontation that David Dellinger and his street tacticians were planning for the convention. McCarthy youngsters swarmed up the curving stairs of the first floor of the Conrad Hilton Hotel, the bushy-haired and the mini-skirted, the blond and the bespectacled, the barefoot and the preppy-trim; they were there with their blue-on-blue buttons, their flower-petaled insignia, their guitars and their song; to these, above all, Eugene McCarthy gave pure loyalty. He did not want them conscripted by emotional appeal and organized to charge by those who planned to use their bodies for confrontation. McCarthy had vetoed plans of men like Allard Lowenstein to bring hundreds of thousands of them to Chicago, knowing that blood would be on his head if he permitted it. Instead, he instructed all McCarthy headquarters across the country to keep his students at home. He had further conferred on Sam Brown broad authority over those McCarthy students who would come anyway—liaison with city authorities to keep McCarthy students out of trouble, responsibility for whatever inventions of imagination could be worked out to absorb the energies of those who came. From a store-front headquarters on Wabash Avenue, Brown directed an effort to keep students engaged in such causes as picketing local A & P's to protest sale of California grapes, warily keeping an eye on the leaders of radical action trying to draw McCarthy students off to more violent street projects.

For McCarthy, the cause was quite clear: to end the war in Vietnam and change the frame of American politics. Both these purposes came together in the phrase that covered his Chicago strategy: "the open convention." This convention, ran the McCarthy theme, was packed, controlled by machines. The leading candidate, Hubert Humphrey, was a stand-in for Lyndon Johnson, a war candidate. But the Democratic Party had the right to insist on an open debate of issues. This was the broad thought; and McCarthy's lieutenants had been off and abroad like guerrilla bands about the convention city for a week

[3] Of the chaos of the McCarthy campaign, many anecdotes can be told. One will do. Early in July the Senator's staff had commissioned a number of state-by-state polls, at $6,000 each, in order to impress wavering delegates with McCarthy's enormous potential among Republicans and independents. Seven of these secret polls were entrusted to public-opinion analyst Oliver Quayle, who was given the addresses and a hard deadline by which and to which to mail the polls. Quayle met deadline, shipped off the polls Special Delivery to the given addresses and received his check with no comment. Only later, in October, did the Post Office return two of the still-sealed envelopes to him as "undeliverable." The address was nonexistent; and no one on the McCarthy staff had bothered to check back to find out what had happened to the information they had so urgently needed and for which $12,000 had been spent.

before McCarthy himself arrived, overlapping, interweaving, pleading in any ear or with any delegation they could reach for the "open" discussion of issues in an "open" convention.

Senator McCarthy arrived in Chicago, from Washington, on Sunday, August 25th, in his chartered airliner, with a full complement of television crews, twelve members of the press and his devoted staff. No politicians accompanied him on the journey. In his first-class compartment Mr. McCarthy had with him Robert Lowell the poet, William Styron the novelist, Shana Alexander the essayist, and three European correspondents whose favorite he had always been. Senator McCarthy was in a discursive mood and talked of several matters: first, his students, for he loved the youngsters who had followed him across the country and whom he had brought, in so many cases, to adulthood. He was worried about their future. He talked also of the Czechoslovakia crisis, which he had so awkwardly dismissed four days before. He was quite moody and historical. As a Catholic, he felt the faith sometimes did better in a land controlled by Communism than in a land controlled by the Church establishment; Catholics respond best to their religion, he thought, under pressure. And then a reversion to Robert Kennedy; why had the Kennedys always expected him, McCarthy, to support them after he, McCarthy, had lost, but never offered to support him if they lost? And, finally, the Presidency itself. Someone asked him if he thought he could get it; and he replied, "Who would want the job?"

§5   Last, but chief, among the characters to be presented: the Vice-President of the United States, Hubert Horatio Humphrey, fifty-seven, scarred and embittered by four years of servitude to Lyndon Johnson and by the desertion of his old liberal friends.

Humphrey had prepared for this convention as if he were reacting against all those who had so long charged him with idealism, eloquence, humanity and softness, as if the convention were an exercise in old-fashioned politics. He planned in 1968 to play this game tough. Thus, so long as Kennedy seemed his chief rival, he had deputized his ablest assistant, William Connell, to prepare for the convention as if to prove to the Kennedys that he could outsmart them at any turning or corner of back-room politics. Connell's eight-foot-long shelf of black books in Washington's Executive Office Building, breaking each state down by region, by city, by county, by power-brokers, by union-control, by delegates, had become the finest political encyclopedia of the Democratic Party in 1968. By the week of the convention, Connell and Lawrence O'Brien, who after the death of Robert Kennedy had become chief of staff of Humphrey's convention command, could reasonably count on between 1,400 and 1,500 delegates where 1,312 were needed to nominate—if only all held still.

The Humphrey delegates were the old structured vote. Humphrey had entered no primaries, which he later regretted; but the AFL/CIO structures had delivered to him almost all of Pennsylvania, Maryland, Michigan and Ohio; Democratic governors and mayors, who had found Humphrey the man in the Johnson administration most sensitive to their problems, could deliver hundreds more delegates from New Jersey to Washington. The one possibly unstable element in the Humphrey coalition was the South, with its 527 votes. The South would be firm in support of Johnson and the war and, by derivation, of Humphrey, the administration man; but if Humphrey yielded too much to Northern liberals either on the conduct of the war or the rules of the convention, Southern loyalties might prove shallow. All in all, the mechanics of Humphrey delegate control had been well and competently handled.

What the Humphrey campaign lacked was theme—and it was to lack theme until the final weeks of the campaign. Fire, flash, humor, high purpose had always been the style of a Humphrey campaign—now they were absent. His operational staff was first-class; but the words, phrases, speeches sounded old, tired, a high-decibel mumble. His research staff was headed by that sober economist Robert Nathan, who had won his first fame under Roosevelt in World War II; but younger thinkers, even on Humphrey's own staff, styled Nathan "the Theda Bara of the Intellectual Set."

Usually, in a Humphrey campaign, one did not have to ask deputies about theme; it gushed from the lips of the candidate himself. But now, somehow, Humphrey was locked in layer upon layer of reservation and personal problems. He had been more deeply and emotionally shocked by the death of Robert F. Kennedy than any other candidate, and had gone into retreat for almost two weeks. An early wave of the Hong Kong flu had kept him ailing for two weeks in July. He had not too little but too much staff, and his kind heart was never stern enough to organize them all, efficiently, under one master until just before the convention; he could not bring himself to scold, dismiss or remove old friends whose conflicting and overlapping duties called out for strict control. Thus, irritable and harrassed, the Hubert Humphrey who had launched his campaign with a call for "the politics of joy" on April 27th arrived in Chicago on August 25th morose and, except on TV, almost unsmiling.

He had reason to be unsmiling. Pinioned in his official role of Vice-President, he must suffer the denunciation of all his old friends for the war, as if his old record of twenty years' service to the liberal cause had been sponged away by the rewriting of history. And though his trap had many chambers, there were no exits.

His old friends challenged him to repudiate Lyndon Johnson. But he had served with Lyndon Johnson for four years, was still Lyndon

Johnson's Vice-President; despite whatever humiliation Humphrey had undergone, friendship still bound them, as did the high policy of the administration of which he was still a member. "Nothing," said Connell, "would bring the real peaceniks back to our side unless Hubert urinated on a portrait of Lyndon Johnson in Times Square before television—and then they'd say to him, why didn't you do it before?"

The problem of separating Humphrey's image from Johnson's was always uppermost in the minds of the Humphrey planners, even those who had worked for Johnson. But the separation of image required more than just phrases—it required that Humphrey establish a position of his own on Vietnam. Humphrey had been prepared, under much urging, to do just that before the convention; but a visit to Johnson at his Texas ranch two and a half weeks before the convention had restrained him. In highest official secrecy, Johnson had told his Vice-President of an imminent breakthrough in the Paris negotiations, a breakthrough that would be threatened if the Vice-President of the United States spoke out publicly at home. So Humphrey had desisted and must, at Chicago, mastermind some sort of Vietnam plank which would at once appease his old liberal, peace-minded friends, yet not upset Lyndon Johnson.

Lyndon Johnson's motives haunted the Humphrey leadership. No one could guess what was on Johnson's mind. Humphrey staffers recall seeing their chief look moodily out of his Executive Office Building windows toward the White House day after day in early August, wondering what Johnson was really up to. Whisper, rumor, mutterings had it that Johnson was reconsidering his renunciation. Whether there was any substance to such rumor we shall examine later (see footnote, page 279). But at Chicago, control of the convention traced directly back to the President, not to the leading candidate. Johnson not only controlled the critical Southern delegations. Through men of his choice, he controlled the speakers' podium, with all the buttons permitting speech from the floor. Security was controlled by Johnson. Even tickets were controlled by Johnson's man, John Criswell; and—final humiliation—Humphrey's son-in-law, Bruce Solomonson, had to line up with the crowd of favor-seekers outside Criswell's office every morning to plead for extra tickets to seat the Vice-President's own family in the convention galleries. What Johnson did not control, it should be added, Mayor Daley of Chicago controlled. Humphrey could, and did, write to Mayor Daley wisely urging that the demonstrators moving on Chicago be given permits to demonstrate and halls to convene; but Daley did not bother to answer him. And Daley controlled the local police. Should events get out of hand—in the streets, on the floor, at the podium—there was no crevice of control anywhere that Humphrey could call his own.

Endurance, then, became the principal Humphrey policy at the convention. Let the demonstrators rumble, let Johnson mutter, let Daley run the city, let McCarthy and McGovern threaten—if all of the O'Brien-Connell delegate planning worked, if only the South and the old structures held together for Humphrey for a few more days, he, Hubert Horatio Humphrey, would be the Democratic nominee for President, free at last to be his own man. Then it would be only between himself and Richard M. Nixon; and Humphrey was convinced that, no matter what any poll said, he could take Richard M. Nixon. The convention was an indignity and a burden to be borne for only a few more days. So, Humphrey.

§ There remains then only the chorus to the drama—the delegates, all 6,511 of them to be squeezed onto a floor that normally held only 4,850, delegates arriving by bus, auto and airplane, delegates finding themselves isolated by lack of telephones, delegates arriving to be told that there were no seats in the galleries for their wives, delegates whose hearts belonged to Robert Kennedy and found no balm in Gilead. Confused and uncertain, they milled about. Normally, the two largest delegations—California (174) and New York (190)—set the convention tone. But the majority of these had belonged to Robert Kennedy, and, as the two largest blocs at the convention, they now found themselves orphaned, with no political home from which to operate. Upon them, also, was heaped humiliation—they had been separated by the Johnson design of the convention and given the furthest rear seats of the convention floor, separated from each other as far as physically possible. Sensing themselves abused, they were to become pockets of bitterness.

By and large, the majority of the delegates were the kind of men and women who had always come to American conventions—middle-aged, established in their parties, their unions, in civic responsibility, in high office. For such people, conventions have always been part carnival, part family reunion, part business. But among them was an entirely new leaven, the delegates of the new mood of 1968, for whom the convention was not only business, but crusade. The men of the new politics grouped largely under the McCarthy banner; but they spread through most of the Northern and Western delegations pledged to Kennedy, or McGovern, or nobody but their conscience. Clergymen numbered twenty-six, a record. College professors were as numerous as farmers or labor leaders. (Wisconsin's McCarthy delegation, for example, counted nine professors and, for the first time in that state's history, *no* farmers.) The insurgents had come to Chicago to bring an end to old politics; they were crusaders playing a new convention game called St. George and the Dragon; and the Dragon was Hubert Humphrey.

*   *   *

The game had begun a week before the formal opening of the convention when the three preparatory committees, of 110 delegates each—on Rules, Credentials and Platform—had gathered to examine the disputes that might come before the full convention, and make recommendation on their resolution. In each of these committees the McCarthy strategists meant to open issues so sharply between themselves and their rivals as to make clear to the convention, to the nation and to the Chicago street audience just how mechanically, how wickedly, how ruthlessly a small band of machine bosses controlled the Party at home and forced it forward in war abroad.

In the Rules Committee the Humphrey forces deftly met the challenge, parried, then absorbed it. The McCarthy men claimed the convention was boss-controlled—delegates brokered wholesale by the unit rule. The unit rule, was, of course, no Humphrey invention, nor any man's invention. Traditionally, small states bind all their convention delegates to vote as a unit, thus maximizing their influence at a national convention. For a small state to split its vote is to splinter what little strength it has. But a unit has to be controlled by a leader—thus unit rule, in the new dialogue, was synonymous with boss control. Was it now considered unpopular? Well, then, said the Humphrey people—let it be abolished. At this 1968 convention, recommended the committee, all delegation unit rules should be forbidden; and in 1972 unit rules should be further outlawed at every level of the multi-tiered caucus-and-local-convention selection process, down to the grassroots. Together, McCarthy and Humphrey forces would urge this change on the convention next week, and debate it against the Southerners who opposed and whoever else dared take their side.

In the Credentials Committee, more important deliberation went on. McCarthy tacticians had placed on the agenda of the Credentials Committee challenges to the legitimacy of delegations from no less than fifteen states. So, starting with the hearings on Mississippi on Monday, and ending with hearings on Michigan and Indiana on the Friday before the convention, all day long, every day, in the International Room of the Conrad Hilton, the Credentials Committee heard the cases and sat in judgment on American politics from Connecticut and Pennsylvania in the East to Texas and Washington in the West.[4]

The Credentials Committee hearings might have degenerated into a succession of brawls. Fortunately, the Party's National Committee had chosen as its chairman Governor Richard Hughes of New Jersey,

---

[4] Chief researcher and theoretician of the McCarthy challenges was a gifted young Yale Law School student, Geoffrey Cowan. *The Democratic Choice,* the handbook of the insurgents in their challenge to the governing hierarchs of the Party, was chiefly authored by the twenty-six-year-old Cowan. It is the best quick study of delegate-selection processes in America that I know.

and they could have made no better choice. Hughes, a man of the old politics, a stern commitment man on the war, was a judge by profession and instinct, a man of absolute fairness whose honor insisted on review of facts. As, under his gavel, the long procession of witnesses gave their testimony, one was slowly overwhelmed by a sense of the grotesquely obsolete. More than 600 delegates to this convention had been chosen by processes begun over two years before. In three states, one man alone could appoint all, or most, of the delegates to a national convention. In Georgia, the Party rules let the governor appoint the state chairmen, who then, with the governor's approval, appointed all the names on the slate. In other states, many or all delegates were appointed by the Party's executive committee, whose members were themselves chosen by processes incomprehensible to any but seasoned full-time politicians. In yet other states, delegates were chosen by unofficial caucuses meeting at obscure halls, schools or private homes where extremists and activists, proclaiming themselves Republicans or Democrats, could raid and dominate the grassroots selection process in either party. From Laredo, Texas, to Meriden, Connecticut, the Credentials Committee went around the nation, hauling up the roots of politics, shaking them before the TV cameras and the nation.

Where the clear issue of race could be defined in the jiggering of delegations, Hughes, with a combined Humphrey-McCarthy majority behind him, could act. The convention of 1964 had forbidden racial discrimination in the selection process; under this authority, the Credentials Committee could recommend the barring of the regular Mississippi delegation and the splitting of the Georgia vote, half to the regulars, half to the McCarthy insurgents.

Almost every other challenge was, however, a plea demanding a judgment by principles no man had ever defined; was a party a private institution, a gathering of like-minded club men entitled to make their own rules state by state? Or was it a public institution, to be governed by rules that bound all alike? Exactly how should a party go about selecting its national leader before offering him to all the people as candidate for President in the ultimate open election? Deftly, again, Hughes steered the committee away from chaos. Half a dozen disputes would go to the floor for a test of muscle. But, more importantly, the committee would recommend to the Democratic National Committee a new approach—that it set up a new group to re-examine the entire delegate-selection process, re-structure it on new principles, and make ready a convention of new shape before the call of 1972. It is so easy now, looking back at the convention through the screen of later turmoil, to remember only violence that it is important to recall how large were such real achievements as those achieved in both Rules and Credentials committees, how fundamentally their changes would alter by 1972 the nature of Democratic conventions.

Yet it was the third committee, the Platform Committee, that attracted the most attention, that generated the great excitement which would enfever the coming days. And of the Platform Committee's many subcommittees, none was more important than the foreign-policy subcommittee, for the foreign-policy subcommittee was to debate the Vietnam war and recommend to the governing party of the nation what its course should be. By the time the Democrats gathered in Chicago, 27,000 Americans had been killed in a war the Democratic Party had accepted; and during the week of its convention 408 more were to die.

One cannot follow all the ins and outs of the debate on Vietnam, yet one must fix its quality. Never before had a party gathering attempted so violently to intrude itself in state policy while its party leaders were fighting a war. Men who had once sat around the table with John F. Kennedy to outface the Russians in the Cuban missile crisis, now, without credentials, darted about like lobbyists seeking a crevice of influence on decision. In Paris a negotiating team headed by two of America's most distinguished Democrats sought to bargain their way out of the war, yet found their political entrails at home bared by their own Party for the enemy's scrutiny. In hotel rooms and press conferences, old friends clashed, sabotaged, compromised and sought to disembowel each other. And over all of them, just as at the Republican convention, hung the fog of ignorance—men who had never slept a night in an Asian village or learned a word of any Asian tongue, devoid of any learning in the realities of Asian power, fought over the semantics of traditional Western diplomacy, spinning a web of words to net peace from the Communists of Vietnam.

Factions formed, broke, re-knit, fell apart again, as gradually one could discern the same strains in each of the two rival and contending camps. Somewhere vaguely down the middle of every American conscience ran a dividing line of devotion, loyalty and morality: does one continue to fight a cruel and bloody war simply because honor is at stake? or does one quit and accept America's first surrender simply because the nation is tired? From this blurred center-line, the spectrum on either side of commitment or withdrawal runs to the extremes. Close to this center-line are those who wish to build a bridge to each other across the difference; and to right or left of them are those who wish to dig a moat along the difference and force the nation to sharp choice.

So ran the divisions at Chicago, too—the peace forces split between bridge-builders and moat-diggers, the war forces similarly split. Under the pressure and power of Lyndon Johnson, the Humphrey forces were nailed, finally, to support of the war. Under the pressure of the streets and the students, the peace forces, led by Richard Goodwin, accepted the sharpest alternative across the moat—the language of Goodwin now challenging every thesis of the President whose voice he once had been.

By Sunday evening just before the convention, after a week of turbulence, the Platform Committee knew that it would have to present to the convention a floor fight that would far overshadow in passion those presented by the Rules and Credentials committees. For the floor fight, as it shaped up in the majority (Humphrey) and minority (McCarthy-Goodwin) planks on Vietnam, reflected the critical issue that had divided the Democratic Party, indoors and outdoors, for a full year.

The majority plank stated bluntly: "We reject as unacceptable a unilateral withdrawal." It went on to proclaim: "We strongly support the Paris talks and applaud the initiative of President Johnson which brought North Vietnam to the peace table." Its program stipulated: "Stop all bombing of North Vietnam," but (a great but) only "when the action would not endanger the lives of our troops; this action should take into account the response from Hanoi."

The minority plank, on the other hand, demanded "an unconditional end to all bombings in North Vietnam"; second, the negotiation of a "mutual withdrawal of all United States forces and all North Vietnamese troops from South Vietnam . . . over a relatively short period of time." Third, "we will encourage our South Vietnamese allies to negotiate a political reconciliation with the National Liberation Front looking toward a government which is broadly representative of these and all elements in South Vietnamese society."

The issue was quite clear, late Sunday evening before the convention, reduced to the clarity it had required eight months to reach. On the one side: a forthright renunciation of America's commitment to a nearly hopeless war, withdrawal, a diversion of America's resources to its home problems, and the abandonment of South Vietnam to work out whatever government it could in a society whose people we had reduced to ruins and beggary. On the other side: an open-end commitment to go on with the war until the enemy should also tire and then meet us to discuss a real peace—at whatever cost it might further require in blood and money. Representative or unrepresentative, democratic or undemocratic, no such elected body of men in convention had ever presented their people, in the middle of a great war, with all the world watching, so clear a choice—or alternatives so unpalatable.

By the time the Democratic convention assembled, thus, at 7:31 on Monday evening, August 26th, and soul-singer Aretha Franklin belted out "The Star-Spangled Banner" in a syncopated rock version that sounded more like a yodel than the national anthem, it was obvious that this promised to be one of the most unusual conventions in

American political history. Walter Ridder of the Ridder Publications found an apt metaphor. It all reminded him of the *Lusitania*—the ship had been struck by twin torpedoes (the war and the race issue). The captain had fled the bridge, but the first mate was telling everyone it was going to be all right. The turbines still turned, smoke belched from the stacks, but water was flooding the hold. The 6,000 delegates and alternates aboard did not yet know what was happening and scurried about to find out; and all the while the ship was sinking steadily, inexorably, into the water.

No linear account can give a correct description of what followed at Chicago—all too many events were happening at once; too many forces were present; the environment of television which dominated the convention was itself, as we have seen, unsettled; and no single person had complete understanding of all that was happening while it was happening.

But we can fix as a starting point the problems of Hubert Humphrey, who hoped to be President, staggering about, buffeted by events, trying to find his stance, his proper posture. He was Vice-President of the United States, cursed with responsibility of state. He was also a politician, with needs entirely different from those of the Vice-President of the United States. He was, and is, a very human and emotional man. And in the wings were two offstage personalities, Lyndon Johnson and Edward Kennedy, whose purposes he could not understand. As events ricocheted one off the other, Humphrey had to absorb, personally, the impact of each, then adjust his position, then watch all others readjust to draw bead on him again.

The most important train of events was part of the grand history and secret diplomacy of 1968, and this train of events had begun far away, overseas. For weeks before the convention, an unwritten and unpublished script had governed the high diplomacy of America, a script which Lyndon Johnson hoped would end his Presidency with an outburst of doves, a flourish of trumpets, an end to war in Vietnam and peace on earth. All through July and August, American diplomats had been preparing for a summit conference of their President with Premier Kosygin of Russia. Nothing had so raised the prestige of President Johnson in the years of the war in Vietnam as his meeting in June, 1967, with Soviet Premier Kosygin at Glassboro, New Jersey. Another summit, he felt, might do even better. In August, therefore, the key machinery at the White House and at State was readying another conference. By Tuesday, August 20th, Assistant Secretary of State William Bundy had finished drafting a secret diplomatic note to be sent to all America's major allies abroad informing them of the approaching summit and its purpose; George Christian, the President's press secretary, was on stand-by to inform the nation. The precise plans for this summit meeting are still obscure, and belong to the history of diplomacy; but for Lyndon Johnson it meant the most dramatic conceivable demonstration of his good-will and, if lucky, of his world achievement. From a successful summit in Europe, a quick flight would bring him as peacemaker to a cheering convention in Chicago—and then, who could guess what might happen?

On Tuesday evening these plans ruptured. The Soviet Army, in a wanton, brutal and superbly executed plan, invaded and occupied the free state of Czechoslovakia. American Intelligence still cannot closely reconstruct the summer's events in the Soviet Union—rioting, disorder and military suppression in the Ukraine; the conflicting pressures within the Soviet government; the final seizure of the initiative by the Red Army and the invasion of Czechoslovakia to cauterize the infection of dissent. In Russia, as at home, apparently the instruments had overborne political leadership and begun to make policy on their own.

The shock of the invasion; the possibility of a major international crisis; the instant shadow of a new and more terrible war now overhung everyone. Most unsettled, however, was Hubert Humphrey. He had been for several months quite aware of the quality of Johnson's casual and contemptuous remarks about him to visitors. To one newsman the President, when asked to comment about Humphrey, had curtly remarked, "He cries too much"; when the newsman pressed further, the President had only repeated, "That's it—he cries too much." In July the President had expanded on such criticism to another friend: "Hubert's just too old-fashioned, he looks like, he talks like he belongs to the past." The President in this conversation observed that Hubert kept talking like he was out of the New Deal, only about pocketbook issues; that he didn't understand the changes going on in the country.

Now, on the night of the Soviet invasion, the President had summoned the National Security Council to discuss the situation. Then he had detained Humphrey for a "Dutch Uncle" talk, a stern face-to-face lecture which rambled on about Humphrey's inadequacy as Presidential timber, charged him with being too soft on foreign policy, with leaning over backward to placate Eugene McCarthy's doves, and accused him of stretching the patriotism of John Connally and the Southern delegates to the limit.

Thus, privately unsure of himself, not knowing whether the President was about to repudiate him even before the convention began, Humphrey had flown to Minnesota for the weekend. He arrived in Chicago on Sunday afternoon, to be greeted by a bagpipe band and to walk a private tight-rope all through Sunday and Monday. On the one hand, he *must* somehow placate the Northern liberals who required, minimally, that he support the abolition of the unit rule; Humphrey's staff had, indeed, already supported abolition of the unit rule before his arrival, thereby breaking a pledge he had given John Connally. Southern delegates, enraged, openly talked of breaking away and running Lyndon Johnson on their own. Thus, on the other hand, Humphrey was required to mollify the incipient Southern revolt by following Johnson's lead on the Vietnam war, accepting language in the Vietnam plank harsher than his heart desired. It was a most delicate balancing act, absorbing all the thinking he could give as, for thirty-six hours after arrival, he bounced around from television interview to television interview (to shore up public support) and from state caucus to state caucus (to shore up delegate support).[5]

[5] A fascinating story that requires later investigation is whether or not there was, indeed, momentarily in that week before the convention a rustling of indecision in Lyndon Johnson's mind—a recantation of his March renunciation. Johnson's summer conversations with so many visitors in derogation of Humphrey caused many in Humphrey's camp to believe that the President did intend to run again. A successful summit conference with Kosygin might well have incubated a genuine draft for Johnson on the floor. But that is one of the lost "ifs" of 1968. A few facts do emerge from the confusion of the five days between the invasion of Czechoslovakia and the end of the Johnson boomlet, if there was one. There was the disturbance in mind of several of Humphrey's closest associates, provoked particularly by the sudden coolness of Richard Daley to the Humphrey candidacy. There were the conversations and probes of the White House staff, who were quoted as saying that "Hubert's been destroyed by the Czechoslovakia thing"; and, again, the White House's private, quick dissemination of the hopelessness of the Humphrey campaign as reported in polls from Oklahoma, Tennessee, Kentucky, North Carolina which indicated Humphrey would run third behind George Wallace; and reports from the White House staff of mounting pressure on the President, from Southern governors, to run again.

Humphrey himself was so disturbed by such reports that on Saturday evening before the convention he telephoned a New York friend from Minnesota to find out what the politically well-connected friend could tell him. The friend remembers Humphrey in this conversation as being as wounded, hurt and baffled as a child who had just been beaten. Was the boss going to dump him? Humphrey wanted to know. He admitted that the conversation on Tuesday night after the National Security Council meeting had been rough; but he could not get the feeling from that conversation that Johnson was going to run himself. "I can't believe it," repeated Humphrey, "I can't believe it." Not even after the election would Humphrey confirm or deny whether he felt himself under pressure of an imminent Johnson sell-out. "I prefer to take the President at his word," he said long later. "I trust him. I go on faith."

If there was a Johnson boom, it died on Monday evening on the first night of the convention. There had for weeks lingered in Johnson's recollection the fact that in the last trial run of the Harris poll before the Miami convention, he, Johnson, had outrun Richard M. Nixon. Now, in the last weekend before the Chicago convention, Harris had just completed another poll, testing Nixon against Johnson, Humphrey and McCarthy. Under contract to the *Washington Post,* Harris could not release the results until they were on the desk of that paper and moving over its syndicate wires early Monday evening. Humphrey, McCarthy and Johnson staffs all pressed for the results. In the war of nerves, McCarthy men had floated a rumor, picked up by the press, that the Harris poll would show Humphrey running more than 20 points behind Nixon. Badgered by the staffs of all three candidates over the weekend, Harris stoutly refused to pre-leak his results until they were in the office of the *Washington Post.* On Monday afternoon Marvin Watson, Johnson's

Under assault, thus, from his Southern flank and the candidacy, real or imagined, of Lyndon Johnson, Humphrey found himself, simultaneously, confronted on the other flank with another boom, real or imagined, for Edward Moore Kennedy.

The Kennedy boom had begun on Sunday afternoon just as the Johnson boom among Southern delegates was reaching its crest.

And we must see Sunday, August 25th, as a day of general confusion: press conferences are rocketing and counter-rocketing so fast that no one person can follow them all; all three major candidates follow one another on the national television Sunday forum shows; the Platform Committee, exhausted, is now trying to hammer together all the promises made by all its subcommittees and members into some minimally reasonable blueprint of the future; the Vietnam plank is being fought over, in and out of committees; thousands of regular army troops are deplaning in Chicago from Fort Hood, Texas. Also from Texas are arriving delegates and alternates to the convention to find that the Conrad Hilton, where they have made their reservations, is short 120 rooms. Yippies are aprowl in northern Chicago; the police are rounding up the black leaders of the Blackstone Rangers, most of whom have fled town; parties are awash with fine liquor, where tables tantalize with fine food at half a dozen private clubs and lake-tower apartments; police check guests at such parties against invitation lists, with a security as tight as convention security itself. And as eminent publishers, Democratic leaders, ordinary delegates and Chicago's local eminences circulate from party to party, two rumors sweep the parties, the lobbies, the caucuses:

First, that Stephen Smith has arrived—Smith, the cool, levelheaded, grieving brother-in-law of both dead Kennedys, Robert Kennedy's campaign manager, the only authorized spokesman for the Kennedy family is in Chicago. Second, the Illinois delegation has cau-

---

personal representative, left a message that "Austin" wanted to reach Harris. Unable to refuse to call back the President of the United States, Harris delayed until nine P.M. Monday, when the White House switchboard put him through to the President's ranch in Texas. Harris recounted his results, which showed Humphrey, McCarthy *and* Johnson all alike running behind Nixon by 6 percentage points. At the other end of the phone came an expression of disappointment approaching shock. Harris was asked what would be the reaction to a personal Presidential visit to the convention to attend the sixtieth birthday party which Dick Daley was planning for Johnson; Harris replied that he felt the President might be booed; and the conversation ended with an expression of the President's total incredulity.

However it was, it was obvious that the polls would report publicly the next day that Johnson was no stronger a candidate against Nixon than Humphrey; and whatever plan, or boom, there had been for Johnson among Southern and Border states ended as word of the poll spread. By midnight on Monday the Southern governors, with all their votes, were falling into line again for the Vice-President against the peace candidates; and by late Tuesday evening, the next day, Humphrey's nomination was sure.

cused, and Daley, presumably in the bag for Humphrey, has now refused to commit his votes. He plans to hold off for forty-eight hours "to see if something develops." Next Daley confers with Jesse Unruh, leader of the 174-man California delegation pledged to Kennedy, and Unruh refuses all comment.

What is happening?

By Monday morning what is happening is a Kennedy boom, leaderless, incohesive, a strange, insubstantial, yet inescapably romantic combination among peace delegates and hardened politicians alike. The polls of the weekend (real or imagined), the polls continuing day by day around the country, tell the leaders Humphrey cannot win. Old-fashioned politicians cannot forgive Eugene McCarthy for his spring campaign; the name of Edward Kennedy thus becomes an escape hatch from dilemma. Unauthorized, former Ohio Governor DiSalle announces he, personally, will put Edward Moore Kennedy's name in nomination on the floor; a Kennedy volunteer headquarters opens at the Sherman House Hotel; and the Hilton Hotel, by Monday afternoon, is speckled with Kennedy button-wearers. A flimsy yellow cardboard, hand-scrawled, makes its first appearance: GET READY FOR KENNEDY IN 68. Another follows: '72 IS TOO LATE, 68 IS THE DATE—DRAFT TEDDY KENNEDY; and others, and still others.

The convention's first session on Monday evening speeds up the tempo, for the first session degenerates almost immediately into a brawl. Southerners are furious at Humphrey's "sell-out" on the unit rule; liberals are ready to do battle right there on the floor wherever racism, real or imaginary, can be detected in Southern delegations. There is no control except that of sterile rules, of Secret Service, of armed guards, of the sergeant at arms. Delegates scuffle among themselves to reach their state microphones, then find their microphones refused recognition from the podium in the growing turmoil. It is hot; the hot-dogs of the convention stands are almost inedible; the food-vendors have been instructed not to put ice into cold drinks lest gallery or delegates throw their ice cubes at one another; radios and television sets tell the delegates that now the Negro bus drivers of Chicago are on strike, too; they learn that there is a riot of Yippies against police in northern Chicago; at 2:43 on Tuesday morning, still arguing about which Georgians should be seated, the convention's first session is adjourned in exhaustion.

Tuesday, things get worse. Now everyone is holding press conferences, and a portable card-catalogue would be necessary to file the conflicting claims. Self-winding Kennedy spokesmen—old friends, old associates, great names, influence-seekers, leverage-seekers—begin to sound off in delegation after delegation, like a system of organ pipes hammered by a demonic player, testing every stop in the range from

vox humana to *vox coelistis*. The Southern Christian Leadership Conference marches its poverty-stricken Poor People's demonstrators
through the lobbies of the convention city in the midst of the turmoil,
and the black people are all for Kennedy, any Kennedy. So, too, are
now most of the McCarthy people. McCarthy, in a moment of historic
detachment, several days earlier had privately told Publisher John
Knight that his chances for the nomination were zero. Publisher Knight's
papers now print this interview on Tuesday; the McCarthy delegates
feel as orphaned as the Kennedy delegates had felt a week earlier.

By Tuesday evening, when the convention convenes again at 6:03,
TV has found in the Kennedy boom the jugular it has been seeking in
the convention story. The canvas of action has, up to now, been so
broad, the technicalities of debate on rules and credentials so esoteric,
the outside events so bizarre, that it has been difficult for network
directors in their control booths to give the story the narrative unity
and clean clash any work of art demands. Now, a sudden romantic
unity is given by the surge to Teddy Kennedy, the prince returning to
claim his inheritance, his people on the floor rising to reclaim honor
from chaos and squalor. Across the floor, flogged on by their directors
in control booths, speed the reporters of the great networks in competitive and artistic rivalry to make the story clear.[6]

The story of the Kennedy boom, as it crests now, between ten and

---

[6] It has always seemed to me unfair to criticize the floor reporters of television
for behavior forced on them by the commercial competition of their networks. To
report a convention from the floor, the networks choose their best political correspondents—and men like Wallace and Rather of CBS, Vanocur and Chancellor of
NBC are men of extraordinary ability. They bring to the floor of a convention more
knowledge, more political savvy, more experience in more conventions than 95
percent of the delegates who sit there. Turned loose in the compact space of the
convention floor, with dozens of Governors and Senators, scores of Congressmen,
political bosses, old contacts and political freshmen, they are as happy as dogs in
a meat market. No one can escape their cameras and microphones; nor do many
delegates want to escape a televised interview, for a moment of national exposure
makes them large at home; a well-chosen phrase, the first statement of a position,
a challenge, a decision may make them national characters, quoted and requoted
within the hour. The delegates locked on their floor, and, at Chicago, pinioned in
place by rigid police controls, could scarcely ever know what was happening in
their midst except as they gathered it through radio and television, which assembled
fragments from their galloping electronic horsemen and re-broadcast them back
directly to the floor below. Delegates thus lived in an echo chamber; and so, as a
matter of fact, did the reporters themselves. Floor reporters are turned loose on
a chase, and the director in the control room calls the course, the story-line they
must chase. On the convention floor someone can always be found to say anything,
and it remains only for good direction to put the fragments together in dramatic
form. Neither delegates nor reporters can be blamed; only the mechanism and its
programming, which calls for competitive and rival drama to hold audience. If the
script that night had called for the discovery and dissemination of a Southern revolt,
or the candidacy of Lester Maddox, the reporters could have delivered that to the
nation, too—all carved out of truth, from the lips of authentic and honest men on
the floor.

eleven on Tuesday evening, before the eyes of the nation is, however, not that way at all. Nor has it been so, for hours.

Reconstruction tells the reality differently from the visual drama, and reality begins with Edward Moore Kennedy himself. Anguished and brooding, numbed by love, hurt and shock, grieving for his murdered brother, he had earlier given friends days of concern that he might abandon politics altogether and retreat into some inner silence. He had broken his silence the week before the convention, with a televised address from Massachusetts, a clear call for negotiations in Vietnam. But persistently, from Chicago back to Massachusetts went political reports that in the atmosphere of the convention city a Kennedy draft was conceivable. A first and secret trip to Chicago, Friday before the convention, of Kennedy's brother-in-law Stephen Smith confirmed the report that a draft, though unlikely, was being gossiped about. Saturday, Mayor Daley called Teddy Kennedy in Hyannis Port to urge him to announce his availability for a draft. Kennedy would not. To announce availability, Kennedy knew, would imprison him—if the nomination for President did not come to him spontaneously, he would then be forced to accept the Vice-Presidency; and to organize a positive coup for the nomination aroused in his then somber spirit no enthusiasm at all.

By Sunday, Smith was back in Chicago, again in contact with Daley. Daley, as we have seen, had decided on Sunday not to commit the Illinois votes. Daley always counts: if the South withdrew from Humphrey with its 527 votes, as seemed possible Sunday evening, if the McCarthy and McGovern forces held firm and then joined Kennedy, then he, Daley, with a few of his old allies, might all together count enough votes to deny Humphrey the nomination—and then they would see who came out on top. This draft-Ted-Kennedy coalition always amused those close to the operation by its piquant unlikelihood; it would require a combination of Eugene McCarthy of the new politics *and* Richard Daley of the old politics to unite as partners behind the last scion of the clan; a McCarthy-Daley combination would have been a thing of wonder to behold. In all this, with impeccable correctness, braced by the clarity which distance gave him, Edward Kennedy behaved well and wisely. Only if an authentic, unquestionably spontaneous, self-obvious draft developed from the convention floor, calling on him, coming to him, would he accept the nomination as duty; but he would not in any way, by indirection or by intermediary, incubate the draft himself. There is a rule in politics that unless one has the taste of power in one's mouth, one cannot ever bite on it; and the taste of power in the mouth of the last sorrowing Kennedy, so soon after his brother's death, had been fouled.

If a moment of nearness to a real Kennedy candidacy came, it came and passed in a five-minute period some time about 4:30 on Tuesday afternoon of the convention. Stephen Smith had been invited by Richard Goodwin to consult with Senator Eugene McCarthy in his suite at the Hilton. There, McCarthy asked Smith what Teddy was going to do. Smith responded that Kennedy was not a candidate—that he himself had come at McCarthy's invitation, to listen to what McCarthy had to say, and would report back to Kennedy in Massachusetts. Ambiguously, his generosity snarled by his reservations, McCarthy said he would like to see his own name go into nomination; but at some point in the balloting, he would stand on the floor, withdraw his name, and urge his people to support Edward Moore Kennedy. Yet he, McCarthy, would not nominate Edward Kennedy. Then McCarthy continued, gratuitously adding, "While I'm willing to do this for Teddy, I never could have done it for Bobby." Smith's emotions still flare with anger as he recalls the remark. (Later, when a news magazine said that his eyes were full of tears at the offer, Smith reportedly corrected the account, saying that those weren't tears in his eyes, "it was all the spit in them.")

Smith left, remarking only that he would inform Kennedy in Massachusetts of the conversation, and would keep in touch. McCarthy's couching of the suggestion had left him negative; Edward Kennedy, in Massachusetts, was equally negative in reaction; and Daley of Chicago, to whom Smith reported the conversation, commented earthily on the insubstantiality of the offer. That same afternoon, moreover, the Kennedy boom was incubating its own counterforce. The Southerners, who had been voicing their resentment against Humphrey, now saw in Humphrey someone much more acceptable than another Kennedy. Lyndon Johnson too, on this Tuesday, was on the telephone to his deputy, Marvin Watson, urging Watson to flog the Southern governors into line for Humphrey in order to stop Kennedy. By late afternoon the Southern breakaway from Humphrey had collapsed. Southern leaders prepared to bolster him in his fight for the majority report on Vietnam against the McCarthy peace plank—or, if necessary, against Edward Kennedy. By evening the Humphrey delegate count had shot up to over 1,500; and the Kennedy boom was over.

So we return to the convention floor on Tuesday night; the Kennedy candidacy has ended, unknown to most, hours before. But on the floor it is reaching its peak before the nation's viewing audience and the delegates alike. By now the convention is approaching one of its madder moments. The New York and California delegations, hitherto paralyzed and without cause or leadership, now are convinced they have their own candidate in Edward Moore Kennedy, and they charge about caucus rooms and corridors buttonholing support for Kennedy from other states. The television networks are now furious—Dan Rather, one of those few television stars loved even by other stars, a reporter whose high competence is matched by his good manners and ever-gentleness, has been slugged and beaten to the floor by a security agent. The television networks will avenge him by spending their wrath on every security agent, every policeman, from now to the end of the convention. Debate goes on and on, as the interminable credentials challenges are unrolled and voted on on the floor; Negro delegates from the North rise and stalk out in disgust at the way the voting goes on the Alabama delegation; a brawl breaks out between some of the rival Georgia delegates. By eleven in the evening the convention has come to discuss the Rules Committee recommendations, and the great Vietnam debate is scheduled for still later that night. Fantasies sweep the convention, and the delegates entertain a motion that young Democratic leaders from each state should be officially seated on the National Committee, as if youth were a corporate body, apart and segregated from older Democrats. The motion is narrowly defeated. New York starts a spontaneous demonstration, waving WE WANT KENNEDY banners. The gavel raps and raps; a roll-call is held on the unit rule, and the unit rule is forever abolished. UPI reports tear gas is being used to disperse demonstrators downtown. It is now past midnight and the convention approaches discussion of the platform. Radio and television report more riots and police clashes at Lincoln Park. Platform Committee Chairman Boggs wants to read the Vietnam plank. Three or four delegations interrupt and clamor for recognition. The peace delegates yell that it is now after one in the morning, and that the whole procedure is a plot to bury debate on Vietnam in the dark after the nation has gone to bed, when no one is listening. Brawls. Scuffles. Loud, rhythmic clapping from the rear of the hall. Rhythmic chanting, "Let's Go Home, Let's Go Home." Chairman Albert insists he can't adjourn the convention; he calls on the sergeant-at-arms to maintain order; delegates yell back, No, No, No. It is impossible to continue. At 1:17 on the morning of Wednesday, August 28th, the television cameras get what they have been waiting for—a long shot with a zoom lens, directly on the face of Richard Daley. They have him for a glorious instant of self-caricature, his jaw thrust out, his underlip full, his face furious, his finger giving the slash-signal cutting across his throat, the director's sign to cut and end. Chairman Albert catches the signal, recognizes Daley, Daley calls out, "Mr. Chairman, I move to adjourn until twelve o'clock tomorrow." Albert calls for ayes and nos, the ayes have it, the convention closes its second session at 1:17 on the morning of Wednesday, seven hours after it has begun—with the debate on Vietnam *and* the nominations *and* the balloting still to take place.

A contagion of madness, a sense of helplessness, a sickening loss of control denying order and identity to all, had been spreading by television and media for days prior to the climax of Wednesday. Thus, by the night of Tuesday/Wednesday, life in the streets of downtown Chicago had acquired a rhythm of its own. One must not ignore the fact that over 99 percent of the area of Chicago, its citizens slept peacefully and went to work tranquilly, hampered only by the bus strike and the telephone strike. But, politically, the contagion had begun to flush and agitate downtown Chicago with high fever.

One must look briefly at the street environment of downtown Chicago in the week of the convention, for as America goes on to learn more about mobs and street control, it will have to learn to separate out the manipulators from the manipulated in crowd masses. In Chicago for the first time, all the elements of American crowd dynamics were available. They were the following:

§ First, the Negroes. Over the previous three years they had proven the most violent of crowd masses. But in Chicago, blacks had been neutralized by the vigorous political roots of the Daley machine; by strict police control; by the absence of a real sense of black injustice; and, above all, by Negro disaffection from the elitist white radicals. In Chicago, fortunately, the blacks decided to stand off and, quite sensibly, let the white radicals do their own thing.

§ There were, as always, the curious—the gawkers, the souvenir-hunters, the peerers, the simple-minded who always want to be there where it is happening; who want to be able to yell, "I seen it, I seen it, I seen it myself."

§ Then there were the crazies. The crazies sprout everywhere in today's world, but in America one of their covering titles is "Yippies" (for Youth International Party). The Yippies are a giant put-on, a visual pun, a strolling farce of lost and forlorn people seeking identity who wear beards, or stovepipe hats, or Australian bandoliers, or walk barefoot carrying their belongings on their back, or sleep in the open rain. They are a sad people, and when one examines the seasonal clusters where they come to roost, in Cambridge or San Francisco or New York, tears come to the eyes at their diseases (mainly venereal), their health (decayed from malnutrition and drugs) and the disturbances, rarely dangerous, of their minds. The crazies have resigned from the corporate society of America, but nurse a manic wit for mocking society which intrigues the media. The crazies—who are not stupid, only crazy—have learned the power of the mimeograph machine to rouse press attention, to entice television coverage to their happenings.

Only three kinds of people take the crazies seriously—the police; television; and those calculating organizers who can manipulate them as a skirmish line into the forefront of confrontation, to be pulped and bloodied by the cops, as Turkish generals used *fantassins* in peek-a-boo pants to meet the first rush of the enemy.

To Chicago the crazies had come, not to make trouble but to make fun and stage a "Festival of Life."

§ There are then, next, in most American mobs, the innocents. These are people whose morality urges them to stand witness for a cause, to prove their manhood and conscience by exposing their bodies to brutality and beating.

In Chicago, most of the innocents were those who, ignoring McCarthy's directives, came there because they felt McCarthy spoke for the cause of peace and that they must protect both the man and the cause.

§ There are, last, always in any mob and the most critical part of it, those who seek to control, to move, to marshal and mobilize it—to fuse it under their own direction and conscript the innocents, gawkers and crazies alike into an unthinking mass of bodies whose emotions, once captured, will make them the unwitting instruments of a few. It is necessary for any control group to have, at once, a cause and an adversary.

In Chicago the control group was David Dellinger's National Mobilization Committee to End the War in Vietnam. The cause, peace. And the adversary, the police of Chicago, who played the role of adversary in a manner no earlier anticipation of expected stupidity could have forecast. The Mobilization sought confrontation; bloodshed would serve their purpose; the Chicago police gave it to them. Only philosophers can apportion guilt between them; in this reporter's judgment, both were equally guilty.

The Mobilizers had not done too well preparing for their Chicago confrontation. Their staff was thin—David Dellinger, father figure of the Resistance; and two veteran "student" deputies, Tom Hayden and Rennie Davis. No great response had followed their spring call to the nation; they had called for half a million peace demonstrators; had then hopefully expected 100,000 peace demonstrators; had been forced to realize that there would be at most 20,000 to 30,000 people who would come to Chicago to witness for peace; and most of these would be young McCarthy people whose own student leaders were prepared to frustrate the Dellinger-Hayden-Davis command. Nor were there to be, as once planned by the Mobilization, 100 mobile command posts for the great demonstration-confrontation; they were able to man Chicago with only an estimated forty mobile command posts. As they approached the convention, they were reduced only to their skills in street fighting and whatever opportunity the blunders of the Chicago police might provide to recruit more bodies. The climate of the streets and of the media would be determinant.

Thus, while television spread the story of the struggle over the rival peace planks of the Democratic factions, the climate of the streets had begun to change as early as Friday, August 23rd.

It began to change first in jest. The crazies had decided they would nominate a pig for President; the pig had a name, "Pigasus"; the crazies had scheduled Pigasus' introduction to the public for Friday at the new Chicago Civic Center, where, to the west, rises the gargoyle-faced City Hall in which Mayor Daley has his office. Embellishing this open plaza rises a stunning metallic sculpture by Picasso. Thus, in Picasso Plaza the crazies introduced Pigasus to the press and cameras, and in frolic glee watched the Chicago police actually arrest Pigasus. The crazies announced they would now nominate Mrs. Pig, a sow, and send greased-pig delegates scampering over the convention floor.

A sense of humor is not noted among police anywhere in the world. The Chicago police, taking their lead from Mayor Daley, are particularly devoid of humor. They had been made to look like clowns; now they would enforce the law. A still obscure, unwritten understanding seems to have existed between demonstrators and Chicago police by which those who chose to spend the night sleeping on the grass of Grant Park, beneath the windows of the Hilton, would be inviolate. But those who chose to sleep or carouse in Lincoln Park, three miles north of Grant Park and the Hilton nerve center, would be forbidden. It was the quite reasonable observation of the Chicago municipality that, since Chicago's citizens are forbidden to sleep in public parks at night, strangers from afar should obey similar rules.

Except that the rules, the procedural rules, are the first and most fragile target of all political demonstrators. The more arbitrary the rule, the more fragile.

Thus, as early as Thursday before the convention, the Mobilization, using the crazies as puppets, had objected to being cleaned out of Lincoln Park; an Indian "Yippie" fired a shot, the police fired back, the Indian was killed—the first (and only) fatality of the violence in Chicago.

Sunday evening, in another police attempt to clean out Lincoln Park at night, a much bloodier fracas broke out, with a good thousand participants. That night the police managed to arrest Tom Hayden, the youthful Lin Piao of the American guerrilla movement. Monday followed, with demonstrations for the release of Hayden (who at four in the afternoon was indeed released by police and whose shadowy role was never thereafter clear again). Monday evening the police, again returning to the fray, made a sweep of Lincoln Park, and by now the crowds there had increased—the innocents, the curious, the gawkers had joined the crazies and the Mobilizers. The police chased all from the park, and pursued them through the narrow streets of Chicago's Old Town, clubbing and tear-gassing resisters, onlookers, diners-out alike in what has since been described as a "police riot."

By Tuesday, street events had enlarged to another dimension. From the convention itself radiated chaos and contention. Was Teddy Kennedy running? Was the peace plank to be steamrollered? Was McCarthy to be expunged? Early on Saturday, David Dellinger had announced that he would, on Wednesday, march his Mobilization to End the War protesters down the streets of Chicago, south on Michigan Avenue, to the convention area. The announcement had made little impression. The Mobilizers had been negotiating with city authorities for weeks; the area chosen for their demonstration required that the city turn over to them private property of private people who did not *want* a demonstration on *their* property. The authorities had, thus, refused after three days of negotiations to give the Mobilizers any demonstration or march permit at all, and so, on Tuesday, Mr. Dellinger at a press conference announced that his Mobilizers and any others who cared to join would march anyway, on Wednesday evening.

By Tuesday night, convention, media, police, authorities, innocents were all adrift. And as the convention came out of control on the floor and television spread an authentic feel of its dislocation, the police in the evening moved on the campers at Lincoln Park, driving once again the forlorn, the crazy and the calculating from Lincoln Park to sanctuary at Grant Park.

Thus, late Tuesday night the rioters had taken shelter in Grant Park, where, under the beige cliff of the Conrad Hilton, watched by the protective eye of national television, they filled the night sky with their chanting, "Sieg Heil, Sieg Heil, Sieg Heil," or "Stop The War, Stop The War, Stop The War," rising in chorus until after three in the morning below the windows of Hubert Humphrey and Eugene Mc-Carthy.

For months later, Democrats of conscience and good-will would stab each other with the question: Why didn't Hubert do anything? Why didn't Hubert stop it? After Tuesday, shouldn't he have known what was coming? What was he doing Wednesday, anyway?

Answers to most of these questions are impossible. No yes-or-no, cease-and-desist decision was ever brought to Hubert Humphrey. Initiative, attack and assault lay with the command of the Mobilization Committee; the police response was to come far below from men whom Humphrey could not control. And Hubert Humphrey, on the twenty-fifth floor of the Hilton, was to be absorbed and preoccupied with the infinitely complex details of candidacy and nomination which would lead, he hoped, to the happiest day of his life.

The only answers come from following Hubert Humphrey and the rioters through Wednesday, their day of climax.

* * *

Humphrey had been up quite late on Tuesday evening, an emotional night—he had gone to the wedding-anniversary party of his son, Robert, and had grieved that it was one year to the day since the death of his cherished brother Ralph. He had come back to his suite with a few aides and discussed his last two unresolved questions: who should nominate him? and whom should he choose as Vice-President? Then, sometime after one in the morning, he had gone to sleep.

The next day, Wednesday, with the nomination almost certainly his, should have been a day of rest, reflection and some privacy, as it had been for Richard M. Nixon at Miami. But somehow Humphrey had let himself be scheduled into a torrent of time-wasting, mind-consuming appointments. His first appointment was breakfast with Mayor Daley, shortly after eight. Daley now pledged Humphrey complete support, but it was already unnecessary; while they ate, Teddy Kennedy telephoned from Massachusetts to assure Humphrey that he was out, out, out of it. Humphrey went on to a second breakfast with Governor John McKeithen of Louisiana, who also pledged his undying support and loyalty (McKeithen was to repudiate Humphrey several weeks later) and assured him that all the Southern favorites had withdrawn. A full staff conference followed, and it was decided that Mayor Joseph Alioto of San Francisco would nominate him. But someone had pledged in Humphrey's name that he would address the Connecticut caucus, so now he must hastily run out and do that; someone else had pledged that he would speak to the Washington caucus, and he must rush out and seek that delegation also—vainly, as it turned out, for Washington was caucusing at the amphitheater, and Humphrey's staff had misdirected him to a downtown hotel.

When Humphrey returned from that, late, the calendar of his day was already full. Humphrey had no Kenneth O'Donnell or H. R. Haldeman, no single person who had complete control of his body, movement, time and appointments. Everyone on Humphrey's staff loved him; he loved them too; all had a piece of the action; and the candidate, with his boundless energies, seemed able to support all their impositions, including that of this friendly correspondent.

One must grasp the scene, as if stage-designed for bedroom comedy. The scene is Room 2525A of the Conrad Hilton, looking out over the lake front; the blue waters of the lake and sunny skies beyond are dotted with the distant, peaceful craft of summer sailors; the room is tastefully decorated with red flowers. There is a huge living room, with a dining alcove and an adjoining bar; there is a conference room; and there are two rear bedrooms. In and out of all these lairs dart people— friends, advisers, speech-writers, hoping to catch the candidate in an unguarded moment for just that one critical word of advice, just that one urgent message. The Secret Service down the corridor tries to filter out the well-wishers, but Humphrey has so many truly intimate friends that the guards can do no more than cut the flood to an unmanageable stream. All about, in every room, are television sets, with reports from the networks coming in constantly. No one can escape television; in Humphrey's living room are two flanking color sets, dominating the scene; Humphrey does not drink all day long; but others are helping themselves liberally at the bar. And thus one must see, from midday on, the scene in the candidate's room with a split vision—there are the visitors, the problems, the decisions in the room, but there also, on television, is the convention, the great debate on Vietnam all afternoon, to be followed by the nomination in the evening. Staff communications are restricted because of the telephone strike; there are only two telephones in the suite, both of which must call through the crowded Hilton hotel switchboard that has now all but broken down. There is also a Secret Service security telephone, the privilege of the Vice-President; but with absolute scruple the candidate will not use it, for it would give him a partisan political advantage over his rival, Eugene McCarthy.

First up when Humphrey settles into his suite are baseball's Jackie Robinson and Elgin Baylor, basketball star of the Los Angeles Lakers, who have been waiting for over an hour. Someone has persuaded Humphrey that he must eat with these two distinguished black athletes, and have pictures taken lunching with blacks—to contrast with the Strom Thurmond, Southern-racist legend the Democrats hope to affix to Richard Nixon. It is 1:40 when lunch begins an hour late—a lunch of cheese sandwiches. (Over the thirteen years that I have been following Humphrey, I have never known any candidate who turns more to cheese as a natural provender in crisis.) Humphrey eats with the two black athletes; in the conference room, four speech-writers are now frantically putting together a final draft of his acceptance speech: Ted VanDyk and John Stewart of his own staff, Gus Tyler of the ILGWU and Jack Valenti, one of Lyndon Johnson's favorite wordsmiths. They are also, simultaneously, doing a rush job on Alioto's nominating speech. On television, the great debate on Vietnam has begun. At the lunch table, Humphrey's attention is distracted. He is watching a succession of three who once were friends, now his adversaries on TV—O'Dwyer, O'Donnell, Goodwin—and, simultaneously, being gracious to his black guests. To Robinson and Baylor he is saying, "Nixon made a calculated decision, this law-and-order issue is subdued racism, they made it an issue and we're going to challenge them. . . . This is the most important day of my life, and I'm not going to stop now, I'm going to say what I think. . . . For some things you got to pay too high a price in life, and I'm not going to pay the price of silence for what I believe in. . . ." Meanwhile, in the conference room, the draft of the Alioto speech is finished, and Humphrey hastily scans it, goes back to conversation. His old Minnesota sidekick and favorite, onetime Governor of Minnesota, Karl Rolvaag, now the Ambassador to Iceland, strides in. A wave to Rolvaag. A phrase floats from his conversation: . . . "I talked to Rockefeller on the phone and told him we needed a coalition government. . . ." The lunch conversation is interrupted again and again. At 2:05, Mayor Joseph Alioto of San Francisco comes in to be photographed with the Vice-President. Congressman Clement Zablocki is on television, defending the Humphrey plank on Vietnam. Humphrey's attention is now split three ways. Photographers come in to catch the Vice-President's smile frozen in a picture with Alioto, in another picture with Robinson and Baylor.

At 2:10 the lunch is over, and when the photographers leave, Humphrey's smile vanishes. One looks again at the old friend: the face is ruddy, but it is drawn and thin; the old musical voice sounds reedy; and the lines of the past week's tension have carved his normally sharp features into deep gashes; he is no longer the boy orator, the apostle of kindness and joy and wonder, but a wound-up man, whose jowls should normally have fleshed out at this age, but now, pendulous, accentuate by their thin folds his gaunt aspect.

There is a fleeting five minutes of privacy before the next visitation occurs, and all through the day, in such moments, Humphrey will turn toward the television sets and, pointing his finger in debater's style, denounce them. "We're going to win," he snaps at the television sets, "we have to. But that instrument there—if that instrument would stop playing up the kooks and rioters, they put them on only when the cops are fighting with them; that instrument just recruits trouble." All day this debate with the unhearing television set will go on as Hubert Humphrey realizes that slowly, mercilessly, in the television drama that features Richard Daley as chief villain, he, Humphrey, is being cast as the insensitive creature of the old bosses, the candidate of the cops against the young and peace-loving.

The moment of privacy is over. Senator Magnuson and former Governor Rosellini of Washington come in. A minute later Humphrey's wife, Muriel, and daughter, Nancy, come in; but his family, recognizing his pressures, withdraws quickly. At 2:15, William Connell abstracts him from the living room for a private talk on nominating tactics and seconding speeches, while Magnuson and Rosellini wait. Humphrey emerges from one of the bedrooms, talks briefly with the two Washingtonians, and, when they leave, turns up TV again and is infuriated by the visage of Sander Vanocur of NBC. "It's an outrage, it's an outrage," he snaps, "what they did last night with that Kennedy thing. It wasn't a Kennedy boom, it was a Vanocur boom."

At 2:40 the room is momentarily clear again, although the speech-drafters are continuing in the conference room, and a few silent friends are ducking from Humphrey's view in the bar. At this point he sits down with the two most serious people of the day—Lawrence O'Brien, chief of convention management, and William Connell, his personal assistant. Now there is a pause for serious business; they all take off their jackets, and Humphrey, in his blue shirt-sleeves, gives his fine mind to the substantive problems of the day for the first time. They are talking of the Vice-Presidency, and it seems that there are five main choices: Muskie, Harris, Alioto, Hughes and Shriver. Shriver has become important only in the last few hours, since breakfast with Daley; Daley likes Shriver, a Catholic, a Midwesterner, a Kennedy brother-in-law. They are interrupted by the little problem of getting Alioto onto the floor to nominate Humphrey. Connell is detailed to reach Jesse Unruh, boss of the California delegation, through the impossible telephone system, to see if Unruh will yield a delegate's place to Alioto to permit the nomination. All the while the three serious men are considering Vice-Presidents, policy details, image—and simultaneously the television sets are assailing them with convention debate about the ongoing war where American men are dying. O'Brien wants the acceptance speech to be the kick-off of the campaign—a springboard from which Humphrey will flip out, double-twist, and splash into the election as his own man. A yelp comes as Humphrey reads the speech draft before them: "What I need are literate speech-writers!"

The television sets drone on as Vietnam continues to be debated on the open floor. A snatch of the Sorensen speech disturbs the Vice-President to the point of bitterness, for Sorensen's is the best defense of the minority peace resolution. Senator Wayne Morse comes on TV a bit later, and Morse makes Humphrey sad—Humphrey likes Morse, they have been allies for years, except on this issue. Within this room of many lenses, many impacts, Humphrey's attention must leap from action to decision, to program, to plan, to television. Others are waiting in the room with great problems as, at 3:55, the debate ends and the convention prepares to vote on Vietnam.

Now Humphrey wants the room tidied; he is a man of immaculate personal habits, is offended by dirt. Ashtrays full of butts, half-empty drink glasses, matches on the floor must all be cleared, and he sets about it himself. There is no time to collect himself before he must meet with two correspondents who have agreed to merge their interview—Hays Gorey of *Time,* Susanna McBee of *Life.* A presentiment has told Humphrey's staff that he will lose the battle for TV support, and now with *Time* preparing a cover story on him and *Life* preparing to feature him, the staff knows he needs balancing magazine support. It is an extravagantly frank interview, of which only fragments will later appear in the magazines.

The interview becomes jagged as television shows the states about to begin their balloting on the purpose of sacrifice of American life in Vietnam. As the balloting ends (1,567¾ for the Humphrey-Johnson resolution as against 1,041¼ for the McCarthy-Goodwin resolution), there is again the split image. On screen, the huge California delegation is singing "We Shall Overcome," and the even larger New York delegation, also singing "We Shall Overcome," is standing on its chairs and pinning black armbands for mourning on their sleeves. And Humphrey is simultaneously trying to explain to the *Time-Life* interviewers his position. Johnson wanted the word "reciprocity" in the resolution in return for a bombing halt. He, Humphrey, had prevailed; his words had been "restraint" and "reasonable response." He insists he has been misinterpreted, that he has been made to appear a hard man. " 'Hubert hardens his line,' say the papers," he cantillated, "but how can they say I'm hardening my line, when all I'm saying is that you shouldn't sell anybody out?"

The "peace plank" is defeated; the convention recesses at 5 o'clock and is summoned to convene again at 6:30 for the purpose of nominating a President. Ten minutes later Humphrey brings the interview to an end, because the tide of old friends, advisers, waiting seekers outside is too much. This day Humphrey is not in command either of himself, the convention or anything. The television goes on: an announcement comes that at last, late, the negotiation committee of the communications workers has decided to recommend an end to the telephone strike. Meanwhile a Pennsylvania group comes in to chat with Humphrey; Pennsylvania has always been one of his political strongholds, and so he must see Pittsburgh Mayor Barr and former Mayor of Philadelphia Richardson Dilworth, former Governor George Leader; then others follow, and others, and others. By 7 o'clock the room is full of people, gathering to join the candidate in watching the balloting on his nomination; dinners are being ordered; old friends throng.

And then, faintly, ever so faintly, comes the smell of tear gas—a slight itching of the eyes, an annoying invitation to cough or sneeze unwillingly. Tear gas is the most useful instrument of street control, the gentlest touch of savagery restrained—but it is unpleasant and frightens one. Now the intake shafts of the Hilton's air-conditioning are sucking tear gas up to Suite 2525A.

The Vice-President, under total harassment all day, has about this time announced that he will take a shower, change into some clean clothes, and thus escape from the pressure of his friends to do those necessary things as well as convene briefly with his writers on the next draft of his acceptance speech. Thus, at about 7, this reporter decides to leave the Vice-President's suite, seek out his own wife for dinner at the

Blackstone Hotel across the street—and find out what the tear gas means.

Down in the lobby of the Conrad Hilton Hotel, a throng, black and white, were sneezing and crying, handkerchiefs to their noses. No one knew what was happening. Directly across the street was Grant Park. It was now the moment of summer dusk, which cast the demonstrators as ghostly figures, beards dangling and hair streaming, moving shadows between the trees. The National Guard was there in force, as well as the police, but one could not at the moment make sense of what was happening as one could later, in reconstruction.

In reconstruction it appears that the drifters, students, curious and unattached who had taken refuge from the violence of Tuesday night in Grant Park had grown restive during Wednesday. They had wandered vaguely through the green gardens that lie between Michigan Avenue and the lake front, tearing down the American flag at one point. One must imagine what happens in a mob, for a mob is an animal without frontal lobes of decision; it resembles a school of fish that sways by instinct, all together as one organism.

People chivvied by the police had milled about the lake front all afternoon, like particles; and had learned by radio and TV that the forces of peace in Vietnam were being overwhelmed by the bosses and mechanisms of Hubert Humphrey. In this aimless ambulation, their first clash with the police and National Guard had come at about 6:30 in the evening, a few blocks north of the Hilton Hotel, probably at the intersection of Michigan Avenue and Congress Street. The National Guard is one of the most useful institutions of American society; it varies in quality from state to state, but whatever they are and wherever they are, they are us: civilians in uniform, with a tendency to be rattled in combat until blooded by experience. At about 6:30, thus, at the corner of Congress and Michigan, a National Guard officer had given the orders to fire off tear-gas grenades because, said he later, "the safety of my own men was threatened." It was this tear gas, borne by the wind south and west, which forty-five minutes later was suffusing the ground floor of the Hilton and being sucked up the air shaft to Hubert Humphrey's suite.

I walked quite unimpeded and unchallenged by the swarming police across the street to the Blackstone Hotel.

One must see this next scene as in a cut-away arena. There is the lake front with its green apron in front, set off from the city by the border of Michigan Avenue, running north-south. Rising above the avenue in imperial height is the Conrad Hilton, from which, on the nineteenth floor, the suite of Mr. Nixon's unannounced observation post looks out; on the twenty-third, the huge McCarthy suite looks out; on the twenty-fifth floor, Mr. Humphrey's Suite 2525A. All these suites offer magnificent views of the action, but they are too high for voices to reach them. Directly north of the Hilton on Michigan Avenue, across Balbo Drive, is the Blackstone Hotel, another folklore favorite of American political history. Here is installed much Secret Service. The Daley hospitality suite is on the fifth floor, although Mayor Daley at the moment is at the convention. On the fourth floor is the spacious suite of candidate George McGovern; and on the third floor, with a fine view of Michigan Avenue and the lake front, as well as in excellent hearing range, is the suite of this correspondent. This last detail is the most inconsequential, but offered only as the witness presents his credentials.

By 7:30, from the window ledge of Room 307, one can see the following array on the green carpet of Grant Park: A bridge passes over the concealed and sunken railroad tracks in Grant Park and connects Lake Shore Drive in the distance with Balbo Drive, just under my window. Dusk has now closed and in the dark, fitfully illuminated by television or other unidentified lights, one sees that this bridge has been closed off by white-and-blue police vans. Beyond the vans, in the distance, stands a picket line of policemen in azure-blue helmets, milk-blue shirts, dark-blue trousers. Beyond them are the sturdy olive-drab ranks of the Illinois National Guard of the United States Army and their jeeps. This array is supposed to bar the Blackstone-Hilton complex from direct assault by the drifting crowds thrusting toward Balbo from Grant Park and the lake front.

But the assault would not come from the lake front. It would come from the north, down Michigan Avenue to the intersection of Balbo, where it must face another triple-ranked police formation, lined up quietly in various shades of blue, their billy-clubs held at rest across their thighs, to stop the Mobilization's announced intention of marching south all the way to the convention, six miles away. One cannot quarrel tactically with this deployment. Perhaps the file of demonstrators should have been halted earlier up the road. But, certainly, a responsible police official, mindful of the assassination of Robert Kennedy and Martin Luther King, of youthful violation and destruction of campus offices, would have decided that, at all costs, the Hilton Hotel, where Hubert Humphrey, the Vice-President, and Eugene McCarthy, contender, rested, must be kept safe from the surge of a mob that might tear up the hotel and its suites in confrontation. Police work is different from judicial work; police must stop a disaster before it happens; they are touchy, edgy and prone to slug before inquiry; judicial investigation inquires only after the fact.

However it was, by 7:30 the surge is apparent directly beneath my window. Whoever has joined in the march has now given up any control of his own movements. There is no independent command of the innocents who, out of love of peace, have fallen into line to make protest. The command authority, the guiding presence for them all are the anonymous hidden squawk boxes of the Mobilization, wherever they are stationed. The Mobilization dominates the sound of the street.

In conventional American politics this is a small crowd. It would make a poor rally for a major candidate—the experienced eye sweeps over what is below and guesses that there may be between 2,000 and 3,000 people. It is also a mixed crowd. Somehow the Poor People's Campaign has secured a permit to march on Michigan Avenue, and a small black contingent with its mule-drawn wagons is caught in the crowd. Over the yellow canvas canopies of the wagons is painted the slogan JOBS AND FOOD FOR ALL. The mules are restive in the crowd, and the police, always more tolerant of animals than of human beings, let them through; then they close their ranks.

It is now, practically, an all-white crowd. But they have become only "bodies" under the control of the squawk boxes and slogans of the Mobilization and its allies. They are being herded to a confrontation by an unknown command which few, willingly, would have accepted—like cattle down the abattoir chutes of the Chicago stockyards.

The squawk boxes give the chants and the slogans, and the mob beneath the window picks up the chants from the squawk boxes. They yell to the cops, "Hey, Hey, Go Away, Hey, Hey, Go Away." The triple tier of cops on Michigan will not go away. The mob picks up another chant: "Peace Now, Peace Now, Peace Now." The forefringe of marchers approaches the police at the intersection of Balbo and Michigan. The cops will not budge, and the procession stops. From behind, in the rear ranks of the crowd, whose fore ranks are being shoved up directly against the police, comes a chant of anonymous, organized voices, "What's Holding Us Up, Let's Go, Let's Go! What's Holding Us Up, Let's Go, Let's Go!" It is all reminiscent of Horatius at the bridge— while those in back called forward, and those in front called back. There is to be observed from the third-floor window, the shove and sway, the surge and oscillation as contrary emotions move the packed bodies. More chants, picked up from the squawk boxes, "Stay on Michigan, Stay on Michigan," "Stop the War, Stop the War." One looks down on the swaying mass: the red flags of revolution; the black flags of the anarchists; Viet Cong flags; red-and-blue banners; Omega banners; no American flags. In the immobile, tightly crowded pack, the soft flesh of those up directly against the police does not move. Toilet paper is coming down from the windows of the hotels that shape the scene; wads of documents, bundled up, are being tossed on police below from protest-sympathizers in hotel windows above; one hears the sound of bottles splintering below. The police are under attack—not from the marchers, but from the dark above. And at this point, which is about 7:55 in my notes, I read that the demonstrators are now chanting: "Fuck You, LBJ, Fuck You, LBJ, Fuck You, LBJ."

Ten minutes later, I find that my notes read, at 8:05, "The Democrats are finished." For what happened in those ten minutes, given its dramatic dimension by television, was to be totally inexpungeable in memory.

For, simultaneously with, or only seconds after, the chant of "Fuck You, LBJ," my notes become almost illegible with excitement:

Slam! Like a fist jolting, like a piston exploding from its chamber, comes a hurtling column of police from off Balbo into the intersection, and all things happen too fast: first the charge as the police wedge cleaves through the mob; then screams, whistles, confusion, people running off into Grant Park, across the bridges, into hotel lobbies. And as the scene clears, there are little knots in the open clearing—police clubbing youngsters, police dragging youngsters, police rushing them by the elbows, their heels dragging, to patrol wagons, prodding recalcitrants who refuse to enter quietly. It is a scene from a movie of the Russian revolution—the vast fan of people on the outskirts of the mob, running away, dispersing through the park like a flutter of leaves in the wind, caught under the park lights, police chasing them, some running north, others south.

There is a pause as the police hold the center of the intersection now; as bottles clank on them, they surge again, and the crowd surges away, and one can see the crowd reforming 100 feet north of the Blackstone on Michigan Avenue. Gas grenades explode below; the police lift a yellow barricade that has been overturned, and, carrying it like a battering ram, they rush the crowd again. Trash barrels are being hurled and thrown into the square, and they rattle across the street. There are splotches of blood down below, and a vast rolling "Boo, Boo, Boo" rises in sound from the crowd to the hotel windows above.

The first melee lasts ten minutes, until 8:05, and there is a pause. The squawk boxes are in command again: "Cool it now, lots of people are getting hurt. . . . Cool it, cool it. . . . We have a medical center on the north side of the street. We have a medical center on the south side of the street. . . . Don't throw things, please, don't throw things."

At 8:10, more police reinforcements arrive; one group advances slowly in a triangle formation, point toward the bridge crossing in the park, moving people across the bridge; another triangle formation advances under good control up Michigan and the crowd falls back half a block. Then those in the front rank of the crowd kneel, with arms folded across their breasts. They take up a song, "America the Beautiful." Those behind begin to chant, "Peace Now, Peace Now." Two patrol wagons roll up behind; bottles and paper bundles are being thrown at the police. Several police advance on the ranks of the kneeling and they are talking; one cannot hear what is being said. Then violence bursts again. The police seize two demonstrators. They resist. A commotion explodes in the front rank; one sees the clubs coming down; two demonstrators are being dragged to the patrol wagon; one falls; he is dragged by his heels to the wagon, his head bumping on the ground. A neat, smartly tailored lady is enraged, she dashes from the sidewalk, her arms flailing at the police dragging the demonstrator; the police grab her by the elbows, she is being dragged into the patrol wagon. There is much blood now—police blood and demonstrators' blood. The mob is yelling "Sieg Heil, Sieg Heil, Sieg Heil." The chant changes occasionally to "The Whole World is Watching, The Whole World is Watching, The Whole World is Watching." By 8:30 the violence on Michigan has cooled, and my notes record no more episodes.[7]

The Whole World was indeed watching. But watching through the eyes of film and television.[8] The genius of cinema, its magic control of emotion, comes through the ability it gives its masters to extend the emotion: to freeze on the close-up and expand the impact of anguish or blood to fill an entire screen; or to split and shift camera views to stretch one minute into five minutes by cross-cutting between fragments of film shot at different angles; or to establish visual sequences in such order as the directorial mind conceives as the most emotionally powerful.

This, now, was about to happen.

For, although the peak of the violence had passed by 8:30, the cameras of the nation—cut off, as we have seen, by Daley's police and the telephone strike from instantaneous television display—were now being emptied of film or tape, rushed to the convention hall, where they must be developed, then viewed, then edited, and finally—an hour or an hour and a half later—spread by Telstar across the oceans, by microwave across the country, and by little portable TV sets to the delegates on the floor in the midst of their nomination of a President. This delayed inter-cutting of the first developed film of bloodshed with the current pro-

---

[7] Riot was not, of course, confined that evening to the corner of Balbo and Michigan, which is where the media caught the apex of the confrontation. Minor riots took place all up and down Wabash Avenue from 14th Street to Jackson and in many back blocks. As the demonstrators dissolved in clusters, police squads chased them, some with good political and technical efficiency, some with unrestrained combat venom. Demonstrators were chased into hotel lobbies; plate-glass windows were broken; innocents and bystanders were hurt. No one person could be everywhere; the fragments of the story are still being assembled; an excellent early reconstruction of the great confrontation by Raymond R. Coffey can be found in the *Chicago Daily News* of Saturday, September 7th, 1968; until a final study is made of the great riot, his account stands as the best I have seen.

[8] Far and away the best study of television in political action in 1968 was Thomas Whiteside's account in the Winter 1969 issue of the *Columbia Journalism Review,* entitled "Corridor of Mirrors: The Television Editorial Process, Chicago."

ceedings on the floor of the convention and Daley's face created the most striking and false political picture of 1968—the nomination of a man for the American Presidency by the brutality and violence of merciless police.

The Chicago police had been provoked as no other police force had been provoked; but they had reacted exactly as Messrs. Dellinger, Hayden and Davis should have known they might—with brute and unrestrained force. If the Chicago police won the battle of the streets, the Mobilization, exactly as it planned, won the greater victory—that of public opinion. Like the American Army in Vietnam, fighting the Viet Cong, the police had never been instructed in the nature of political or guerrilla warfare, whose purpose always is to convert neutrals into allies by provoking the indiscriminate retaliatory violence of superior forces. I find it difficult to criticize, morally or technically, the strategy and disposition of the Chicago police on Wednesday night. They were charged with defending the headquarters hotel of the Democratic Party, and the suites and lives of the two remaining major Democratic candidates for the Presidency in a year of assassinations. Yet politically, on the stage of the watching world, they brought disaster on all they were charged to defend. Of their actions on Wednesday evening it can be said, as Talleyrand said, *"C'est pire qu'une crime—c'est une faute"* (It is worse than a crime—it is a blunder). And later on Thursday the police were to pass from blunder to berserk unreason.

Of those watching from the hotel arena tier, perhaps the coolest of the observers was Eugene McCarthy, two floors below Hubert Humphrey.[9] At about 7:30, McCarthy had been sipping a drink, in philosophic mood, when Walter Ridder, standing by the floor-to-ceiling windows, saw police cordons drawing up on Michigan Avenue and called, "Good God, what's happening down there?" McCarthy joined the Ridders to watch the riot through the sealed windows. It appeared to McCarthy, cool and scholarly from the heights, that it was to be a holocaust, like Cannae. The demonstrators, he said, were about to be trapped in Hannibal's double-envelopment movement—there, he pointed out, on Michigan Avenue was the main body, the police. But, he said, if you look closely, back there in the trees and toward Lake Shore Drive, you have the National Guard. When the battle gets rough, the National Guard will move out, around the flanks of the battlers, in a classic double-envelopment movement. He watched, shocked and grieving, as the maneuver took place, then compared it to a surrealistic dance, "a ballet of purgatory."

From the height of the McCarthy floor and Suite 2320, the battle

---

[9] For the account of Senator McCarthy's reaction, I am in debt to Marie and Walter Ridder, whose unpublished reporting of that night has so graciously been made available to me.

was a distant one, until, shortly after its conclusion, the McCarthy youngsters began to bring back the wounded to the McCarthy operational floor, the fifteenth. Then, slowly, McCarthy's detachment changed to outrage as the blood and gore of the hurt sank in on him, and to fury as the minions of the Hilton Hotel protested the tearing up of sheets and pillowcases to bandage the wounded.

Alone thus among the large men of the convention he decided to give care and shelter to the casualties and busied himself with them for some time, ignoring his own nomination and the balloting on television, torn by perplexity: whether he himself should descend to the street scene and try to stop the action, or stay in his hotel. No other decision except the correct one came: the young people he had drawn to politics were being beaten; but street agitators had captured them from him; to go down now would be to lend his name and his cause to those who sought to provoke the violence. He had been persistent in dissuading his young people from the demonstration; to go down now would make it appear that *his* people were the ring-leaders. "If I go down, I claim them; and they're not mine; I don't want any confusion here," someone heard him say. And thus, to the end of the evening of his defeat, melancholy and somber, denying bitterness even for Hubert Humphrey: "It's no use being bitter about Hubert, he's too dumb to understand bitterness."

Two flights up, however, on the twenty-fifth floor, in the Humphrey suite, all was bitterness.

I had made my way back to the Humphrey suite by about ten minutes past nine. The Vice-President had changed into a clean suit and a starched white shirt. Nominations had just begun on television. I inquired whether Humphrey was aware of what had been happening. Only barely, it seemed. He had spent the two hours of crisis eating with his staff, finally getting down to work on another draft of his acceptance speech. He had showered; had been rubbed down; had, briefly, been urged to look out the windows down below, but had been too busy to spend more than a few minutes peering out and down so far away; he had watched in a quiet interlude sometime after the first charge, when the demonstrators had been driven several blocks north toward Congress Street. He had heard about the riots from his staff, but had seen none of the bloodshed; and television had not yet aired the scenes.

Yet he knew he had been punished. Like a tormented beast, he could not tell what and who was plaguing him. "The interesting thing about all this," he was saying, stunned, when I came in, "is that if anybody could qualify for the title of hawk, it would be Nixon, but he's never been picketed, only me."

Slowly, his anger grew as he watched the television sets and what was to be the penultimate climax on his way to the Presidency, a milestone in the career of the "politics of joy." Alioto rose on screen to nominate him; back and forth the cameras swung from Alioto to pudgy, cigar-smoking politicians, to Daley, with his undershot, angry jaw, painting visually without words the nomination of the Warrior of Joy as a puppet of the old machines. Carl Stokes, the black mayor of Cleveland, was next—to second Humphrey's nomination—and then, at 9:55, NBC's film of the bloodshed had finally been edited, and Stokes was wiped from the nation's vision to show the violence in living color.

The Humphrey staff is furious—Stokes is their signature on the Humphrey civil-rights commitment; and Stokes' dark face is being wiped from the nation's view to show blood—Hubert Humphrey being nominated in a sea of blood.

It goes on like this for two hours; the room fills with people; photographers come and go to get their portraits of Humphrey on the evening of victory. The candidate's smile lights up when they shoot; when they leave, his face freezes again. The conversation in the room is subdued; his friends leave the candidate alone, and he sits there, grim, his forefinger touching his nose, more embittered minute by minute at what television shows. "I'm going to be President someday," he admonishes the television set, furious, "I'm going to appoint the FCC—we're going to look into all this!" But the sets do not respond.

Over their portable TV sets, the delegates are also seeing for the first time what has happened over an hour ago. They think, quite reasonably, that Chicago is running in blood, at the very moment of their proceedings. Allard Lowenstein rises to demand the convention adjourn; no business should be transacted here while "people's rights are being abused on the streets, maced and beaten unconscious." Frank Mankiewicz of Robert Kennedy's staff talks on screen about the streets of Chicago "flowing with blood." At one point a misunderstood television film clip of earlier violence indicates the rioting is breaking out fresh. Yells seem to come from beneath the window, and Humphrey asks, "Is something happening out there again?" Someone rushes to the window, looks out, finds that all is quiet on the street, the National Guard in control, and reports back to calm him. Television reports that a movement is growing on the convention floor for peace delegates to leave the proceedings and hold a rump convention elsewhere; buses are ready to take them to the Drake Hotel. An old Humphrey friend, Abraham Ribicoff, occupies screen attention as he denounces Daley and the Gestapo of the streets of Chicago.

Finally, at 11:19, the roll-call of the voting by states for a Democratic nominee begins, and Humphrey settles into his easy chair, with a pad of stationery marked "Office of the Vice-President of the United States"; with a black felt pen, he prepares to mark off the count against his staff's predictions. By now the room is a-throng and a-bustle with television cameras, politicians, friends, selected newsmen, and Humphrey's melancholy is coated by a mechanical smile, a public joviality, as he plays the role of victorious candidate. He is a poor actor, and the artificial happiness he displays at anticipated victory embarrasses friends and staff, who know his heart aches. He leans forward, marking the score, with exaggerated flourish and exaggerated remark as the count begins. He has 23 from Alabama (out of 32), 17 from Alaska (out of 22), 30 out of 33 from Arkansas—and the solid South with him all down the line. At Pennsylvania, he will have it, and he leans forward for the photographers again, pulling his dark suit down to smoothness.

At Pennsylvania he gets 103¾ votes for 1,317½ total, and the nomination is his. "I feel like really jumping," he says, and Orville Freeman, his old friend and Secretary of Agriculture, jumps up and down as if they were both boys again, starting in Minnesota politics twenty years before, with all the future fresh and beckoning to them. Mrs. Humphrey appears on television and Humphrey says, "I wish Momma were really here. Look at how pretty she really is. I'm going to give her a big kiss," and he leaps from his chair and lets the photographers have a snap of the Vice-President kissing the television screen. Then he is called to the security phone; two calls have arrived simultaneously—one from Lyndon Johnson, with congratulations, the other from Richard Nixon. Humphrey takes Johnson's first. Then Nixon's.

Thus, at 11:47, Wednesday evening, August 28th, Hubert Horatio Humphrey is nominated by the world's oldest political party, the governing agent of the United States, to be its President. National Guardsmen with movable barbed-wire barricades are installed beneath his windows. From the convention there sets out a candlelight parade of peace delegates to convene till early morning and consult on the formation of a new party. On the fifteenth floor of the hotel, aching and wounded children cry and hold their hurts. But the Vice-President of the United States cannot show his hurt in public.

Later, he remembered how much it ached, the night he smiled and kissed the screen and played the role of victor. "I was a victim of that convention," he said after the election, "as much as a man getting the Hong Kong flu. I felt when we left that convention we were in an impossible situation. I could've beaten the Republicans any time—but it's difficult to take on the Republicans and fight a guerrilla war in your own party at the same time. Chicago was a catastrophe. My wife and I went home heart-broken, battered and beaten. I told her I felt just like we had been in a shipwreck."

Three last episodes remained to complete the tale of the Chicago convention—in one of which Humphrey was to score well, in the second of which he performed as well as he could, on the third of which he was finally, blamelessly, irrevocably, to be hanged.

Of these, the choice of Vice-President came first, and here Humphrey, intuitively, made his best score of the convention. After the final party-goers had left Suite 2525A, shortly after one in the morning of Thursday, there followed the first of the parade of those who, ritually, could claim a voice in the choice of the next Vice-President. In Humphrey's mind, the three chief contenders for his running-mate had for weeks been Senator Harris of Oklahoma, Senator Muskie of Maine, and Governor Richard Hughes of New Jersey. But the first of the claimants for participation in his choice came at about 1:30 in the morning—a delegation of Southern governors led by John Connally of Texas. When they had left after an hour, Hughes' name had been eliminated; some consolation had to be given to the Southerners for their defeats on unit rule and credentials, and Hughes was the sacrifice. Southern Republicans had vetoed Lindsay at Miami; Southern Democrats now vetoed Hughes at Chicago; Southern vetoes run strong. In a twenty-minute meeting with Hughes immediately after the departure of the Southerners, the Vice-President broke the news to New Jersey's Governor, a great gentleman who took it well.

By three in the morning Humphrey was finally alone again with his two closest aides—Connell and Ted VanDyk—and as he lay on his rubdown table, head hanging down, his vertebrae being cracked, they discussed a glamorous added starter whom John Connally had suggested—Ambassador Cyrus Vance, once Deputy Secretary of Defense, at that moment negotiating with the Viet Cong in Paris. As the suggestion of John Gardner had been for Richard Nixon, so the suggestion of Cyrus Vance was for Humphrey—an intriguing opportunity to add a non-political dimension to the ticket. When, at four in the morning, after twenty-one hours of unbroken tension, Humphrey finally fell asleep, there were, as Connell described them, only three candidates in his mind—Harris for youth, Vance for class, and Ed Muskie, solid, sound, dependable and middle-road.

By morning Vance had evaporated from consideration, and as Humphrey polled Congressmen, mayors, advisers and old friends, the choice narrowed once more to Muskie and Harris. Harris was young —thirty-seven—eloquent, hard-working, a driver, and highest in Humphrey's personal affection. No one disliked Harris. But all pointed out that a youthful thirty-seven-year-old with no experience in international affairs was scarcely ready to serve if tragedy or accident called for a new President in the next few years. As for Muskie: Ed Muskie was a man with no enemies; quiet, sober, a Senate professional, a man of low-key humor. As Humphrey later told another of his protégés, Senator Walter Mondale, "When it came down to making a choice between Harris and Muskie, I went for the quiet man. I know I talk too much, and I wanted someone who makes for a contrast in styles. Two Hubert Humphreys might be one too many." Thus, at four in the afternoon, with both the final contenders in separate rooms of the big suite, Humphrey made his decision; he broke the news first to Harris, brought Harris into Muskie's room and told Muskie: "Shake hands with the man who's going to nominate you"—then descended, at 4:34, to his press conference.

There was, next, Humphrey's acceptance speech, which now he had time to reconsider in the first hours of quiet thought in a week. After its days of turbulence and excitement, no speech could have pulled the Democratic convention together except a masterpiece devoting itself entirely to the meaning, the events and the historic perspectives of the convention itself.

But the old Hubert Humphrey who might have done just that was now too tired to reflect and still felt only vaguely the terrible disturbance in the ranks on the floor. Out of his original speech, in which were embedded phrases, thoughts and drafts from Norman Cousins and Jack Valenti, from Bill Moyers and Ted VanDyk, from half a dozen other friends, Humphrey now tried to refashion something of his own. A man of more native eloquence than any of his advisers, Humphrey might, had he had time, have created the required masterpiece. But he had no time, and thus the convention was treated to a standard political oration of the kind of prose which, in Chicago, on the night of August 29th, 1968, had been rendered archaic by the events of the previous twenty-four hours.

Much of the convention was in anger when Humphrey began, anyway. The Blackstone, the Hilton, the Sherman, from which so many delegates had come, still stank of vomit, mace and stink bombs. On the route to Convention Hall, Daley's precinct captains had marshaled clusters of people, some numbering in hundreds, denouncing television, holding up signs, WE LOVE OUR CITY, WE LOVE OUR MAYOR, WE LOVE OUR POLICE, TOO. Somehow, also, in a convention hall where scarce tickets had been a matter of fist-fights, Daley's lieutenants had managed to get their hands on hundreds, and both press and audience galleries were packed with Daley's partisans holding banners saying WE LOVE MAYOR DALEY, bursting into chants, "We Want Daley, We Want Daley." Delegates on the floor were in fury at the gallery-packing; silence descended only when the memorial film for Robert F. Kennedy was run off in the darkened hall, to be followed by mass singing of "Glory, Glory Hallelujah," which ran on and on, over the furious gavel of the chairman, until it ran out of steam on its own. Finally, two hours later, Hubert Humphrey rose to speak.

He began with a short reference to the violence that lay uppermost in everyone's mind: ". . . one cannot help but reflect the deep sadness that we feel over the troubles and the violence which have erupted, regrettably and tragically, in the streets of this great city, and for the personal injuries which have occurred. Surely we have now learned the lesson that violence breeds counterviolence and it cannot be condoned, whatever the sources." Then he tried to poultice it by quoting St. Francis of Assisi.

"Listen to this immortal saint: 'Where there is hatred, let me know love. Where there is injury, pardon. Where there is doubt, faith. Where there is despair, hope. Where there is darkness, light.' "

Thence to a solid review of the convention's work, falling on unhearing ears:

"This week our party has debated the great issues before America in this very hall. . . . We have heard hard and sometimes bitter debate. But I submit that this is the debate and this is the work of a free people, the work of an open convention.

". . . in the space of but a week this convention has literally made the foundations of a new Democratic party structure in America. From precinct level to the floor of this convention, we have revolutionized our rules and procedures, and that revolution is in the proud tradition of Franklin Roosevelt"—cheers!

". . . and Harry Truman"—cheers!

". . . and Adlai Stevenson"—cheers!

". . . and John F. Kennedy"—cheers!

Then with great courage, Humphrey went on:

". . . and Lyndon Johnson."

It was the first time in this correspondent's attention that the name of Lyndon Johnson, sitting President and chieftain of his party, had been mentioned since John Bailey had dropped the name on opening night; the hall rocked back and forth with challenging cheers and boos. With stout courage, Humphrey continued above the sound, accepting the defiance:

"I truly believe that history will surely record the greatness of his contribution to the people of this land, and tonight to you, Mr. President, I say thank you. Thank you, Mr. President."

Of the three great issues he saw before the nation, Humphrey spoke first of Vietnam. The purpose of the speech, as originally conceived, had been to set Humphrey out on his own, separate from Lyndon Johnson in image; but events of the past week had cemented them together. Words could not detach him, though he tried.

". . . if there is any one lesson that we should have learned, it is that the policies of tomorrow need not be limited by the policies of yesterday. My fellow Americans, if it becomes my high honor to serve as President . . . I shall apply that lesson to the search for peace in Vietnam as well as to all other areas of national policy."

The second issue he saw was, as realistically it had to be in America of 1968, "peace at home." "We do not want a police state, but we need a state of law and order, and neither mob violence nor police brutality have any place in America. And I pledge to use every resource that is available to the Presidency, every resource available to the President, to end once and for all the fear that is in our cities."

The third issue was unity—national unity and party unity.

On national unity:

"I take my stand—we are and we must be one nation, united by liberty and justice for all, one nation under God, with liberty and justice for all. This is our America. . . . Winning the Presidency, for me, is not worth the price of silence or evasion on the issue of human rights. . . . I choose not simply to run for President. I seek to lead a great nation. . . ."

On party unity:

"To my friends Gene McCarthy and George McGovern . . . to these two good Americans: I ask your help for America, and I ask you to help me in this difficult campaign that lies ahead. And now I appeal, I appeal to those thousands—yea, millions of young Americans to join us. . . . Never were you needed so much, and never could you do so much if you want to help now. . . ."

Thus, to the peroration:

"I say to America: Put aside recrimination and dissension. Turn away from violence and hatred. Believe—believe in what America can do, and believe in what America can be, and . . . with the help of that vast, unfrightened, dedicated, faithful majority of Americans, I say to this great convention tonight, and to this great nation of ours, I am ready to lead our country!"

Whatever hope there was in this last exercise in tired words rested on the belief that words can soothe, that words can heal, that words carry a message.

But within the next twelve hours, in the dark night, this hope was to be blasted by the Chicago police; their minds had tuned out all messages. In democracies, police must be, above all, instruments of policy. One can thus make a strong brief in defense of the conduct of the Chicago police—and this reporter will support such a brief— through the first three days of convention violence. High policy required that the nerve centers of the convention be defended; and the police, however tactically in error or in blunder politically, had enforced policy as crude instruments. But on the dark dawn of Friday the police instruments acted on their own, with no policy or moral authority but their own. For this, Hubert Humphrey, Richard J. Daley, the Cook County machine were to pay the price, as do all in authority under whom the instruments of government go wild.

The convention was over by 12:10 A.M., Friday, August 30th. Humphrey, still encumbered by the drapery of his friends and lovers, soothed by affection, had gone off to a party, then returned to the sleep he needed so badly at two in the morning. McCarthy had also gone to sleep. The correspondents, having filed their dispatches, had also given up making sense of the Democratic convention. But the momentum of emotion, the unwinding of tension had kept many still adrift in the city through the night, wandering from place to place, seeking companionship as people always do at the end of a political campaign when comrades who will not soon see each other say farewell.

On the fifteenth floor of the Conrad Hilton a number of McCarthy students still lingered. The fifteenth was the operational floor of the McCarthy enterprise; the twenty-third, the command floor. It was difficult for these young people quickly to disperse, they who had known each other from New Hampshire to California, and become almost kin. In one of the windowless corridors a number of boys and girls sat or stood, singing folk songs to the accompaniment of a guitar. Down the corridor, others were already asleep in their rooms; a few had gathered in the later famous Suite 1505A and 1505B. In the square well of the fifteenth-floor lobby, where the elevators open, a few others still reminisced, and one foursome played bridge. They had lost a campaign, but had changed American history, and they warmed themselves now with friendship.

Down below, the National Guard and the Chicago police still patrolled the approaches to the Hilton. At some time before dawn, it appears, something was thrown from a window, or perhaps several things. One witness who had been looking out from the nineteenth floor later said that whatever was thrown was being thrown from the eighteenth floor. Police and National Guard insisted that what was thrown was being thrown from the fifteenth floor, Corner Suite 1505A and 1506A. The first verbal and immediate charge was that fish were thrown—sardines or herrings, but unspecified whether in the can or not. Later versions said that beer cans were thrown; still later it was that ashtrays were thrown. Later elaborations of the official police version made it sound as if a fusillade of missiles were coming down from the front of the Hilton—ball bearings, cocktail glasses, a coffee pot, ice cubes. Several sets of facts are, however, clear:

§ First, there is no evidence whatsoever that the McCarthy students had themselves been throwing anything. At about 4:30 in the morning, a police warning had come to them that something was being thrown from the windows of Suite 1506A. They had then closed and locked the windows of that suite. Checking and re-checking later, I could find no witnesses who had seen or known of anything being thrown from that floor. Moreover, these students had campaigned from New Hampshire to California without violating a single law, or getting as much as a traffic ticket; and for them, that night, their war was over.

§ Second the police and the National Guard *were* indeed being pelted from somewhere in the Hilton Hotel, and they had caused the awnings of the hotel on Michigan Avenue to be lowered to protect them. But they had now been hit often enough by missiles, denounced often enough over the air, to have reached a rage blinding them to tactical or legal procedure. Now they would get somebody—anybody. And in their parochial political understanding, McCarthy was the name of the enemy.

They had, thus, without writ or warrant, charged into the hotel at just about five in the morning, taken an elevator, and, berserk, without any attempt to discriminate, begun to raid. Richard Goodwin had casually come back to the hotel at this time, and, ascending to his twenty-third-floor room, he decided to get off the elevator on the fifteenth floor to say goodbye to the youngsters he had known so well. When he stepped off the elevator, the first wave of police was already in the corridors—screaming and crying rang through the fifteenth-floor lobby. Police were breaking open rooms, hustling girls to pack their bags and get out. While Goodwin stood there, another elevator opened and another squad of police charged out; and yet another, with six or seven armed National Guardsmen. As the police charged the bridge-players with clubs swinging, one boy lifted the table to defend himself, and a billy club splintered over his shoulder, breaking it. Goodwin still has the splintered police club. Goodwin remembers his own paralysis—he had, after all, been adviser to two Presidents, drafted messages on war and peace, had himself composed the words that told American youth they were to be sent to war in Vietnam. Yet when the police lifted their clubs to beat him, and then desisted, it was not because they recognized any past authority—only because he was beardless, wore a business suit, and looked older. Seeing the youngsters being dragged physically into the elevators by the police, Goodwin caught another elevator and hastened down to the lobby to see if he could stop the round-up before they were hustled off by the police to jail.

"Help us, Mr. Goodwin, help us!" was the first cry that came to him as he reached the lobby—and there he saw the little knot of students, surrounded by police, the girls crying and hysterical, several boys bleeding. They were teen-agers who had first ventured into politics eight months before and only now were tasting its raw and underlying violence.[10] Goodwin, assuming authority, told them to squat on the floor. The police ringed the sitters. Goodwin told the police that both Senator McCarthy and the Vice-President himself were on the way down to the lobby to take command. This stilled the police momentarily. Loudly, Goodwin gave directions to the youngsters, dispatched one or two to telephone the press and television, made known to the police that television was coming to witness this; and several of the police began to drift away. Surreptitiously, Goodwin told another student to telephone immediately to the McCarthy and Humphrey suites and ask both men to come at once—the candidates, with their Secret Service guards, might quench the violence and save the youngsters. While he gave instructions, Goodwin continued to try to calm the police and the students. One student glared at the ringing police and may, so Goodwin remembers, have cursed one of them. The policeman lunged with his club and began to beat the student. Two teen-age girls, hysterical, threw themselves between the body and the club to protect their friend; two other policemen hauled the clubber off the body.

The police, apparently under no command, had begun to melt away as they heard television was coming and so there were no more than nine or ten left when Eugene McCarthy, accompanied by his Secret Service guard, descended from the elevator. McCarthy, athlete and poet, offered a command presence. He had been up very early, at five, preparing to take one of his morning strolls, a Minnesota farm boy's habit, when Goodwin's message had reached him, and he had come at once. Hubert Humphrey had been asleep; Goodwin's message had roused only the Vice-President's press secretary; Norman Sherman, whose devotion insisted he protect his candidate from intrusion. Humphrey was now, finally, sleeping the sleep he had needed so long, and Sherman would not rouse him.

Thus, it was McCarthy alone, very cool, at his absolute best, who faced the police and demanded to know who was in charge. There was no answer. "Just what I thought," said McCarthy, "nobody's in charge." Then, very quietly, he told his children to rise, to go back up by the elevators to their rooms in twos and threes; and no police dared follow them. McCarthy's Secret Service guards gave him their advice: if he left town as scheduled early in the morning, the police, they felt, would raid and haul off to jail all the students left behind. McCarthy, thus, postponed his flight from Chicago from early morning to late afternoon, as his staff, the rest of Friday, collected money, bought airplane tickets, and evacuated the students from Chicago.

Of the various questions that still plague Democrats, two at least have easy answers.

§ Why did Hubert Humphrey not *do* something about the police

[10] The police report officially styles the lobby group a "threatened sit-in" and says: "Many of them were carrying on in a loud and emotional manner."

at Chicago? The answer: Neither on Wednesday, Thursday nor on Friday at dawn did Humphrey have any idea, truly, of what was happening in Chicago streets—he was too busy at another, older level of American politics.

§ And why did Eugene McCarthy not come out in support of Humphrey in the later election until so much too late? The answer: A man of McCarthy's morality could not accept the sight of blood that Friday dawn at the Hilton, the beating of *his* own students, and then go on to support a ticket which had not condemned this brutality. It would, he felt, be breaking faith with those he had called to follow him.

These questions were simple, so were the answers.

More important in retrospect was the question of the function and future of political conventions in the American political process.

American conventions are a political phenomenon which most foreigners and many Americans fail to understand—for it is uniquely and particularly American, drawn from no handbook of political theory, designed by no master philosopher. Conventions were nowhere envisaged by the Constitution writers of America—for they could not foresee the growth of America as a nation, its geographical sprawl, its vast diversity, its slow absorption of so many new social and ethnic groups. It was not until 1831 that the present convention system evolved, a happy offbeat accident, an invention devised by the Anti-Freemasons. What has preserved it over the years is that it has worked so well, providing the nation along with such nonentities as Harding, Landon, Cox and Davis such names as Roosevelt (Theodore), Wilson, Roosevelt (F.D.R.), Truman, Willkie, Eisenhower, Stevenson, Kennedy and Nixon. No other nation in this century has had so long a stretch of superior choices, nor such talent to choose from.

The convention does not stand by itself as an isolated event in a year. The convention is the final flexible coupling in a year-long adventure of many men, in many states, whereby the fixed, parochial preferences of each state are finally bargained out on one site, at one time. Its vital values are best illuminated by a glance at its most widely discussed alternative, the national primary. The national primary in America could only be a disaster, requiring sums of money for media, travel and promotion equivalent to the cost of a general election. None but the best-financed could contend, and the best media techniques would determine the winner. And appeal, within each party, would be made to the extremes within the party, thus tending to present the nation suddenly with two candidates in the general election sharply at clash, neither reflecting the broad center spectrum of American opinion.

The conventions as they stand today, however, come at the end of a long education process. The primaries stretch over months, with a rhythm of their own, each one exposing a bit more of a candidate's personality, judgment, behavior and style. A man like Eugene McCarthy, so pitifully underfinanced at the beginning of 1968, was able, in the present system, to assemble his troops for action, and month by month earn audience and attention. A man like John F. Kennedy, so burdened by religious intolerance and prejudice at the beginning of 1960, could demonstrate his ability, state by state, to call to men above prejudice. A man like Richard Nixon, repudiated and abandoned by all political wise-men, could prove in the primaries of 1968 the resilience of his nature, the depth of his forgotten appeal. The conventions cap this process of public education, root the choice of leader in the earth of differing communities, beneath the manipulation of the media-masters or of political bosses.

What lies at fault in the convention system was amply demonstrated in Chicago. It is not so much that delegates in some states are clandestinely or mechanically selected. It is that no over-all governing principle determines the frame in which delegates are selected. Such principles must, of course, be established—broad national principles which require consultation and choice by ordinary voters at official polls; principles which eliminate race discrimination at these polls; principles that require consultation of the voters in the year of the election; principles which sharply restrict, but need not necessarily eliminate altogether, the number of delegates appointed by party leadership or state committees in recognition of past service or civil eminence. But if such reforms are essential, it is essential also to recognize that no one rigid pattern can be imposed on all the states of the Union. Within the principles as agreed on, states must be free to choose the dates of their election of delegates, the manner of their election (by district or at large), the legal mandates placed on them.

Other reforms, too, are necessary—in the case of the Democrats, certainly, a cutback on the enormous numbers of delegates that now bloat their rolls to shepherded mobs. In the case of both parties, an extension, perhaps, of their sessions to permit deliberation as required by issues, not as required by the media; and, above all, some control of the environment of communications. To permit American conventions to become, as they have become, a quarry for dramatic fragments by competitive television networks is to let camera values control the atmosphere of politics. The networks perform their ceremonial function best in American history when they pool their coverage, as at great events in Washington or in space launchings. To restrict the reporting of a convention to a pool coverage controlled by the networks as a combine, to give them let for competitive rivalry only in the sharpness of their off-scene commentary is in no way a restriction of freedom of the press. And it purges the process of convention of the frenzy of rival drama, reduces it to the sober, serious business it really is: the choice of a man for President.

Reforms are generally spoken of in terms of the past—reflecting the need of discarding what is outworn by time and replacing it with what the present demands. Reforms must, however, anticipate tomorrow. And in the tomorrow of American politics, whatever reforms of the convention process are considered, the reform and improvement of its security precautions are inescapable. Marauders are now loose on the American scene. Of all the fragile institutions of American politics, the convention itself is the most delicate. Its firm protection from raiders of the street is essential; yet the free gathering of petitioners, protesters, appealants, lobbyists that give a convention its dimension of discussion is also necessary. Such decisions, Chicago demonstrated, can no longer be left in the hands of local politicians or street police. Wherever any convention gathers, no matter in what city, security policy and its direct control must be in the hands of the convention itself; and any city unwilling to accept such a sharing of responsibility should be excluded from consideration as site.

No civilization since time began has ever devised a perfect system for the choosing of its leaders; all have ultimately collapsed either because the success of the system undermined its virtues, or failure of the system exposed its people to disaster. America stands in no such imminent peril today; yet the essential ingredient of the system, faith in itself and its leaders, is challenged. It would be senseless not to sanitize and improve American choice of leadership by convention to strengthen the faith. But it would be frivolous to throw away a system that has worked so well until now, before a better proposal for choice of leader has been suggested.

PART
THREE

INTERPASSAGE

THE great conventions are always a turning point in a Presidential year. It may be, however, that in 1968 they marked a turning point in the nature of American politics.

Up to conventions, normally, candidates pursue their quest with a classic logic to guide them—by the solicitation of known leaders and brokers of influence, by the accumulation of blocs of delegates, by the conquest of select primaries. The art of persuasion, which has been the essence of American politics, can concentrate at the conventions on known, definable, responsible or susceptible individuals. Beyond conventions, however, the art of persuasion must grope in the mystery of an indefinable public, where a myriad-million voters must be stirred, measured, and propelled to vote by tools and means entirely different from those that govern the approach to the conventions.

The storm-swept year had already proven itself unique in this century of American politics by its quality of violence before Chicago. Chicago froze the quality of violence in memory, caught it in images, shook all the considerations that had hitherto governed the politics of conventions. If a convention were not to be, as it always had been, a forum of negotiation and compromise, but became instead the scene of a television happening where a few could mobilize an event to coerce the many, what did the future hold?

Just as important were the questions that rose from the politics that followed the conventions of 1968. For if, on the one hand, the growing violence threatened old ways of public decision, so, on the other hand, did the growing mastery of media by new professionals challenge another pattern of American politics.

It is most useful, perhaps, to look at the broad scene of America in the fall of 1968 through the eyes of one of the sub-sects of the professionals, the public-opinion analysts. Never before in American history did analysts and pollsters hold such sway over action—not only at the

Presidential level, but at Congressional, Senatorial and Gubernatorial levels. More money was spent, more decisions affected by polls than ever before; and never did the polls achieve greater precision or change more greatly the environment they were supposed to measure.

Polling has been part of American politics since Mark Hanna directed William McKinley's campaign of 1896 and was able to predict, from the reports of his doorbell-ringers in the Midwest, that his candidate was riding to a sweep. Polling has moved through various phases in the last half century, through the debacle of the *Literary Digest* poll of 1936 (which predicted Landon over Roosevelt), through the debacle of 1948 (which predicted Dewey over Truman) to its present status as one of the more refined and reliable social sciences; and its view of the electorate is at once the most illuminating we have, and the most frightening.

Many scholarly disciplines contributed to the present remarkable acuity of public-opinion sampling. The Viennese school of social scientists with their probes of formation of social attitudes; the market research of advertising agencies in America, beginning with their sampling of coffee and soap markets in the twenties; the governmental and census sampling techniques during and after the war, carried to doctrinal clarity by Dr. Rensis Likert of the University of Michigan; the ecological analyses of V. O. Key, dissecting political behavior by voting cuts—all these have combined to create the present system of opinion analysis, mass sampling based on the probability theory, with Americans regarded as whirling, interlocking constellations of particles, impinging one on the other, colliding, flaking off, changing orbit.

A good national poll regards America as a universe of 120,000,000 adults from which a sample of no more than 1,500 or 1,600 individuals can give results with only 2 or 3 percent margin of error. Voters are clustered theoretically in groups of five, each five representing 400,000 voters. Three hundred polling points—one for each cluster of five—are then picked at random among the 3,130 counties of the United States; the pollster starts with a first polling point in the largest United States county, geographically measures off a unit of 400,000 voters, sets up another polling point, measures off another unit of 400,000, until the country is speckled with clusters. And then, miraculously, if the model and the screen have been soundly designed, this accidental pattern reflects almost precisely the demographic reality of America, all its key groups and inner interlocking communities caught in the web.

This newsreel of American preferences—for a poll, to be understood, must be seen not as a snapshot but as a film—is the basic tool of all other professionals. Speeches are adjusted to what the polls say; travels are gauged and planned by them; computerized mailings flood out to specific-interest groups identified by opinion-analysis; campaign spending—as well fund-raising—depends on the profile that the polls define. Above all, television programming rests on what opinion-sampling and market research report. Experts gauge and measure audiences by millions of viewers and thousands of dollars—pin-pricking specific groups by thirty-second, sixty-second, five-minute "spots." 1968, it should be noted in passing, was the year of the "spots"—the earlier 1960 and 1964 tradition of half-hour exposures of a candidate-with-a-message was ignored until the final week of the campaign; one minute on Monday evening's "Laugh-In" ($56,000) or one minute on the Olympics, the World Series, or the weekend football games ($60,000 to $70,000) was judged more important in reaching the mass mind, and stirring it, than any considered address of either candidate.

The fall of 1968, when Richard Nixon and Hubert Humphrey fought it out for the Presidency, was full, thus, of the sound of an ominous future. The revolt in the streets was an attempt of the alienated to express their desire for identity, an attempt to control their environment by protest. The strategy of the candidates was an attempt to comprehend and sway the voters as if they were digits, whose quality could best be profiled in percentages. At the bottom, American politics surged with new passion; at the top, American politics was directed with detached precision by new professionals of opinion-analysis. In between were caught the Americans of the middle.

The new arts of violence and the new arts of opinion-manipulation were of vital significance in the campaign of 1968 and will be more so in years to come. But the reader will learn little about them in the chapters that follow. The chapters that follow are written from a political philosophy which holds that politics is still simply communication and response between the leaders and the led; and that the fall of 1968 could, conceivably, be the last in which an election in America is best understood by trying to understand what the leaders sought to do and tell the people.

CHAPTER TEN

SEPTEMBER: NEW SHAPE
IN THE DARKNESS

Among the estimated 89,000,000 Americans watching the Democratic National Convention at its peak on television on Wednesday, August 28th, 1968, was Richard M. Nixon, at Key Biscayne, Florida.

Though his working life has been passed chiefly on the far shores of the continent, close by the Pacific and the Atlantic, some emotion always brings Richard Nixon back to the Caribbean waters off Key Biscayne, and Florida. Here he had begun the original planning for his 1960 campaign; here, to Florida, he had returned to sun his hurts after his defeat in 1960 by John F. Kennedy, and again after his defeat by Pat Brown in California in 1962; and then, again and again, in 1968, for the conferences and planning which framed his Presidential campaign. Here, at Miami Beach, he had finally captured the Republican nomination; had only briefly forsaken Florida to airlift his entire staff and campaign organization to Mission Bay, California, for a fruitful week of strategic planning by the Pacific; and then flown back to Florida, via New York.

Now, at Key Biscayne, while the Democrats held center-stage with their convention in Chicago, he meant to pass the days with his favorite play-companion, Bebe Rebozo, and two personal aides until it would be time to compete for national attention again. On Thursday before the Democratic convention he had sailed off to Walker Cay to fish, then come back to the mainland on Saturday night to learn what was happening in Chicago from Haldeman and Chapin, who were manning the phones waiting to hear from the Nixon observation post in Illinois. Nixon had gone houseboating with Rebozo on Sunday, and then on Monday and Tuesday was off again to sea, visiting another tiny offshore cay.

He had thus seen nothing of the Democratic convention when he returned, surfeited with rest and sun, to Key Biscayne on the Wednesday morning of its climax. Impatient, Nixon was insistent on returning to New York and going to work at headquarters. Haldeman restrained him, for he had been watching television; Haldeman felt that Nixon was gaining so much by the spectacle in Chicago that to interfere with the nation's attention by putting Nixon back into competition for the public eye would be a mistake. It was Napoleon's old maxim: "Never interfere with the enemy when he is in the process of destroying himself."

Nixon had thus been detained, by wise counsel, to watch the witch's carnival of Wednesday evening in his villa at the Key Biscayne Hotel; and, says Haldeman, "slowly we got horrified; you began to wonder what the Hell was going on." Gradually, as Pat Buchanan reported in by phone from the Conrad Hilton Hotel, and TV illustrated the reports with color and blood, the feeling came over the group, says Haldeman, "My God . . . this is really going to be bad, they're on both sides of a losing game, and neither side can win." Nixon's view was different from Haldeman's— he felt that a man of Humphrey's oratorical talent and general ability would be able somehow to pull his party out of its self-destruction. Haldeman felt not.

Nixon made his courtesy telephone call to Humphrey immediately after Pennsylvania's votes gave Humphrey the nomination. (See Chapter Nine.) From what report we have of the conversation, it went something like this: Dick observed that Hubert was one up on him—he'd gone over the top on the roll call earlier than Dick had. One of them observed that they were both fortunate in having such fine wives and families. The other agreed. They joked about the Vice-Presidency, and Dick, understandingly, let the conversation end by saying he ought to hang up because he knew what Hubert must be going through tonight—first, picking a Vice-President, then working on his speech. Hubert replied only that he had a lot worse problems on his hands than Dick had had, which was true; and the conversation closed.

It was the dialogue of two small-town boys, incomprehensible anywhere but in America; and the rest of the Presidential campaign would also be incomprehensible if one did not realize how deep under their common idiom ran their cleavages, all the way back to the cleavages of those small towns in which they had grown. Though both men could now discourse with great experience and much data about budgets, missiles, space shots, legislation and foreign affairs, the set of their minds, in discussing differences over such matters, had been shaped in Whittier, Southern California, and Doland, South Dakota.

One should linger over the two candidates and the quality they share. Biographies of Nixon and Humphrey give full details of their childhood and growth. But of each one's experience, a few fragments must be recalled for the useful, prismatic distortion they give of two exceedingly complicated men. For even in such villages as Whittier and Doland there were those whom life greeted with bitterness and those whom life greeted with gaiety. The two men came of these different molds, each lighted from childhood with a different view of the world as seen from the early-century villages of America as they prepared for the change.

Life greeted Nixon with hardship. Whittier is now being digested by the process that social scientists call urbanization; the over-spill of the great Los Angeles metropolis is erasing its identity; the palm trees still sway over the streets, but the orange groves are being bulldozed out by real-estate developers, and its quality as a Quaker settlement is now almost totally gone. But in this town, with its quaint Midwestern manners, Richard M. Nixon had grown up from the age of ten with life seemingly set against him. In 1955, when Nixon was Vice-President, I drove to Whittier to search out his childhood and found a gentle old lady who had been one of his high-school teachers in Whittier. She was disturbed by what Dick was saying as Vice-President—he was then, in 1955, at his ferocious, partisan peak. But she tried to explain him. Dick had always wanted to be on the football team, she said. But he couldn't, because he couldn't stay long enough after school for practice—he was one of the "poor boys," who had to go home to East Whittier by school bus early in the afternoon. He had to work in the family store. He came of a good Quaker family—only . . . Only what? Well, his mother, Mrs. Nixon was a saint, a real saint, "sweet, conscientious, kindly, pleasant." But his father was so nervous and irascible; when Mr. Nixon yelled, in those loud arguments he was always having, everyone could hear it. Yet she liked Dick. He was interested in the Constitution, she remembered, and won a prize from the *Los Angeles Times* for an oration he made on it. He was a good debater, too, she recalled, "a good collector of facts, but not brilliant," a boy with a good vocabulary, but "glib" and "adroit."

Other stories of Nixon's boyhood are kinder to his father, for they express the pressure of poverty on the father and the son. Frank Nixon had been a Columbus, Ohio, streetcar conductor; he had migrated to Southern California and there married Hannah Milhous. The father's life was hard; he had tried farming (a lemon ranch) and failed; had opened a grocery store and service station; money was tight; Nixon remembers one Fourth of July when his family was the only one in the neighborhood that could afford no firecrackers for its children. One recaptures the tension of the father: scrabbling for a living; one child (Arthur) dying early of tubercular meningitis; another child so sick of tuberculosis that Hannah, the mother, must go to Arizona with him for two years to try (and fail) to save his life, while the father cooked for the other children alone in the evening; the family close-knit but squeezed by poverty. The pressure on the boy must have been immense—a good student, hard-forced, no help on the way up, having to make it on his own. A scholarship took him from Whittier College, where he had been class president, to Duke

University Law School, and there, intensely competitive, pugnacious and wistful, sensitive to slight, he scored as a leader, graduating with honors. A short-lived business enterprise in Whittier after law school ended in failure (as had Harry Truman's haberdashery shop); Dick Nixon had had been ahead of his time; he had foreseen there would be a market for orange juice in America someday and had tried to package orange juice before instant refrigeration, dehydration or distribution was ready for store-bought orange juice. Nixon's orange juice soured; the venture failed. Had the venture succeeded, the nation might now be drinking "Nixon's Orange Juice," Nixon would by now have passed through and far beyond the presidency of the Whittier Chamber of Commerce, perhaps by now have become a captain of industry, a major contributor to political campaigns, a Regent of the University of California. Life set him on another course of experience in politics and learning. Yet the cast of the mind remained that of the small town; the faith remained that hard work, diligence, competition and luck would give reward.

Life greeted Hubert Humphrey, on the other hand, with joy. Doland, South Dakota, population 481, was probably poorer as a town than Whittier, Southern California, when the two boys were growing up. Nixon's father had been a grocer—Humphrey's father was a druggist. In Nixon's family, Hannah Nixon, although frail and quiet, was dominant; in Humphrey's family, Hubert senior was the master. Not only that— exuberant, boisterous, imaginative, an authentic village romantic, Dad Humphrey believed that all things were possible. Humphrey loves to recount[1] how his father used the drugstore money to stock up with operatic records; how his father once, deciding on the spur of the moment that he wanted to hear great music, got into his old car and set out directly in the night for New York to hear the Metropolitan Opera perform. Humphrey's father was of the village elite—and also the village radical, the pump intellectual, the book-reader, the provoker of thought, the daring local political leader who came out for that Catholic Alfred E. Smith when few in Protestant South Dakota dared whisper the name. On Sundays the village learned would gather at the Humphrey house to join Humphrey's father in listening to the various divines who occupied the Sunday air-waves, and then discuss their sermons.

When one hears Humphrey discussing his boyhood in South Dakota, the scene is all lit with sun; and the shadows, dappling the sunlit highs, make the joy of life sharper. As the Depression grew, the shadows grew; the family was forced to leave Doland (as so many others have left since) and open another drugstore in Huron, South Dakota; Hubert Jr. was forced to leave the University of Minnesota, work in the family drugstore, study pharmacy; only six years later could he get back to university life

---

[1] See *The Making of the President—1964*, pp. 311–13.

again. But the years of poverty left no psychic scars on Humphrey; the personality had been shaped before he left Doland—one of happiness, unrestrained sweetness, and a nostalgia for the talk of his father's home. The talk of Hubert Humphrey still echoes more naturally with Biblical rhythms than that of any other American politician; the cadences of the King James Bible sound over and over again with the natural, unfeigned swing of someone who has read passages aloud and memorized them in Sunday school. Had the Depression not squeezed the Humphrey family out of Doland, Hubert Humphrey might have become Doland's Congregational minister, later a large and liberal churchman; or the principal of the high school, later a university president. But life was to set him, too, on another course—and the cast of his mind was also, always, to be small-town American; only different from Richard Nixon's. Nixon's wished to have things clear-cut; Humphrey's wished to experiment. One was an evangelist; the other felt that life must be mastered. Both are civic minded—one would have raised money for the missionaries, the other for the high-school football team. One might have been the school's athletic coach, the other might have been the English teacher. Both, had they lived in the same town, might have been Scoutmasters; but their Scout troops would have been rivals.

By 1968 both of these small-town boys had learned a great deal; it would have been good to witness a clean-cut clash between the two; but another small-town boy, George Wallace, was to intervene and blur that clash. Yet with what they had learned, Richard Nixon and Hubert Humphrey set out on the first round of their contest.

In September, 1968, it was Nixon off, first, to a fast start in the week after Labor Day—with every wind in his sails, the polls granting him an apparently insurmountable lead over Humphrey, crowds roaring to greet him wherever he touched down. In Chicago, a week after the battle of Michigan Avenue, 400,000 thronged the streets—without stink bombs, bottle-throwing, tear gas or coercion, as if applauding by their presence the quiet alternative to the Democratic violence. A quarter of a million greeted him the next day in San Francisco, 30,000 in Houston, and in White Plains, New York, Governor Nelson Rockefeller and Senator Jacob Javits joined him on the platform in harmony in what they claimed to be the largest rally in Westchester County's history.

One saw Richard Nixon best, however, not at such monster rallies as Chicago's, or at later climactic rallies in New York's Madison Square Garden, but in the small towns where he spoke freely and unprepared, from "the speech." "The speech" had been evolving from early primaries in winter to September, yet it remained the same speech, for it was the same man, and he would remain so with the same message from January, 1968, to the inaugural in January, 1969. Out there, in the sun, as one listened to the man in the open, one heard a 1968 Nixon quite different from the 1960 Nixon. The snarl and self-pity which had coated his campaigning of 1960 were gone; the years had mellowed him; what was left was genuine and authentic, true to the inner man. And the message, though the same as in 1960, was reaching an audience living in a country that violence, discontent, adventure and war had changed.

In the sun, say, at Park Center, in Charlotte, North Carolina—or any other medium-sized town—one saw him as natural. The pretty blond-haired girls down front, the bunting on the platform, the handsome, sturdy, always-middle-class audience stretching away to the edge of the park, the balloons festooned everywhere gave that sense of a solid, healthy America which television disdains to capture. After the introductions, the courtesies, the bobs to the dignitaries would come the message, a reprise of his Miami acceptance theme:

> . . . something is happening. We are going to win in November all over America. . . . We are going to win first because across this country a big team has been assembled, all working together, not just for a party, but for a victory that will be bigger than a party, a victory that will bring to our ranks Democrats, Independents . . . and a team . . . that can unite itself will unite America and that is what we are going to do with your help.
>
> . . . a new voice is being heard across America. It is different from the old voices, the voices of hatred, the voices of dissension, the voices of riot and revolution. What is happening is that the Forgotten Americans, those who did not indulge in violence, those who did not break the law, people who pay their taxes and go to work, people who send their children to school, who go to their churches, people who are not haters, people who love this country, and because they love this country are angry about what has happened to America, the Forgotten Americans, I call them . . . they cover all spectrums, they are laborers and they are managers, and they are white people and they are black people . . . who cry out . . . "that is enough, let's get some new leadership."

It was a Republican voice, a voice as old, almost as the founding of the Party; but it reflected the changing world.

> . . . I say to you that when the strongest nation in this world can be tied down in a war in Vietnam for four years with no end in sight, when the richest nation in the world cannot even manage its own economy, when a nation with the greatest tra-

dition for respect for law and rule of law is torn apart by un-precedented lawlessness . . .

One might notice the elocutionary flourishes and gestures of Whit-tier, California.

> . . . when respect for the United States of America falls
> so low [*here the speaker crouches, and points to the ground*]
> that a fourth-rate military power like North Korea will seize an
> American Naval vessel on the high seas, and when the time
> comes [*here the speaker raises his forefinger to the sky and
> shakes it warningly*] for the first time in our history that the
> President of the United States cannot travel abroad or to any
> major city in this country without fear of a hostile demonstra-
> tion, then the time has come [*here both arms are thrown up,
> wide-spread, like a revival preacher at his climax*] for new lead-
> ership for America! [*Cheers.*]

However much unchanged were the gestures or the phrases, Nixon
was touching a reality that had not been there in 1960; both he and the
nation had changed in their perceptions.

Anticipating his first swing through the South, most reporters had
expected to find Nixon in such a state as North Carolina unveiling for
the first time the Southern—or racist—strategy imputed to him by Democrats. The *Charlotte Observer*'s young political reporter, Paul Jablow,
summarized it best:

"If his speech here Wednesday was any indication," wrote Jablow,
"Richard M. Nixon's 'Southern Strategy' is that Southerners are 'just
folks' like everybody else. It was a speech from Norman Rockwell,
Reader's Digest, and the lighter side of Sinclair Lewis. It crossed no
Mason-Dixon lines of the mind and it certainly didn't try to out-Wallace
George Wallace. . . . He was speaking to the 45-year-old man with the
mortgage, the housewife taking a job so the last child can go to college,
and all the non-violent fed-up. Besides, it wasn't his people who jumped
all over Clean Gene McCarthy. Nixon's paradise is not one achieved
without sacrifice. But it is the sacrifice for the kids, for the house in the
suburbs, of good old All-American hard work, not the sacrifice of tax
money for more federal programs or of old attitudes. . . . This was
Nixon's first foray into the South, and it was supposed to give some indication of how he would make special efforts to woo the region's voters.
But it could have been given in Bayonne, New Jersey, Des Moines, Iowa,
Houston, Texas, or even Sinclair Lewis' old town of Sauk Center, Minnesota. And if all this isn't enough to make Hubert Humphrey worry, then
worry he should."

* * *

If there was a confidence, vigor, and new self-restraint in Nixon-on-the-stump of 1968, the Nixon-at-work in 1968 was even more greatly changed. Few campaigns had been more badly mismanaged than the Nixon campaign of 1960, with its overlapping and conflicting authorities, its details snatching at, then absorbing, the candidate's time, its bottlenecks choking every access to his decision at every stage. The new campaign of 1968 reflected much that Nixon had learned since 1960, a capacity for growth undeniable.

The quality of the new campaign was apparent as soon as one entered the planes of the flying party. In 1960, correspondents had been treated like outcasts and vagabonds, and their growing resentment had been the filter of bitterness through which the nation saw Nixon. So important, however, were press relations in the campaign of 1968 that detailed planning and physical re-designing of planes for the campaign tour had begun three weeks before Nixon's nomination, and entrusted to one of Nixon's uppermost-level aides, John Ehrlichman.[2] Ehrlichman, believing that "plane time is working time" for press as well as staff, had ordered that both the press plane (the *Julie*) and the staff plane (the *Tricia*) be outfitted with first-class seats, first-class configurations, first-class communications. Clean-cut and enthusiastic, in this, his first campaign, Ronald Ziegler had learned, as press officer, how to meet all the press's professional needs. There was a new availability in the Nixon staff; one could talk at any time to Charles McWhorter, a jovial walking encyclopedia of American voting patterns and in-state differences; to Robert Ellsworth, political strategist; to Haldeman or to Chapin about the candidate's mood, moves and plans; and all responded with easy courtesy. In 1960, correspondents left Nixon to join the Kennedy tour with a sense of returning home from the enemy camp; in 1968, one left the Nixon tour to join the Humphrey tour as if leaving a well-ordered and comfortable mansion for a gypsy encampment.

Control radiated from the staff plane. Two open-circuit ground-to-air phones; seven internal phone circuits; six ground-to-ground press phones and four for staff, hooked up instantly where the plane alighted; a radio-receiving Xerox machine; an airborne teletype, receiving or sending at 100 words a minute; fifteen walkie-talkie machines with air-to-air or air-to-ground radii of five miles—all combined to create a web of invisible communication, about the plane, whether in flight or at rest, that made every input from New York headquarters or around the country instantly available, made question and answers a matter of minutes.

The campaign peaked here in the compartments of the *Tricia*. No more important man in the campaign operated than Bob Haldeman, who

[2] Ehrlichman is now Counsel to the President in the White House.

sat in staff territory just outside the Nixon compartment, and who regarded his candidate much as Sol Hurok regards his operatic stars. No piece of paper passed forward, no visitor entered except by Haldeman's judgment of the best use of the candidate's time. Constantly on call were the cluster of speech-writers, organized under James Keogh, on leave as Executive Editor of *Time* Magazine, as if for daily, rather than weekly, story conferences: Price and Buchanan, of course, now, as at the beginning, balancing Price's liberal bent with Buchanan's conservatism; Martin Anderson, a Columbia professor, a generalist; and William Safire, an all-purpose talent ready with longer historical speeches as well as the one-line snappers which Nixon so enjoyed, and which were Safire's literary hobby; and beyond these lay the staff at headquarters in New York, feeding research, data, information, daily news analyses over Xerox and teletypes to the plane around the clock.

At the headquarters in New York, which the plane controlled, the change in organization was similarly apparent.

An American Presidential campaign organizes armies of volunteers, millions of citizens who can be persuaded either that the fate of the Republic rests on their efforts or that they can, during a campaign, make the fix or connection essential to their ambition in the next administration. But at the top, campaign organization requires managerial talent which can divide, then efficiently supervise, responsible men in responsible functions. These functions, in any campaign, from Congressional or mayoralty race to the Presidency, are classic and imposed by the quality of modern America: first, money to pay for the entire exercise, because money, as Jesse Unruh is so fond of saying, is "the mother's milk of politics." Next—not necessarily in order of importance—a troop organizer to mobilize and use volunteers successfully; next, a press director to service and massage the press; next, a media staff to buy, manipulate, produce or provoke the essential TV time to spread the message; next, and critical for history, a research-and-issues staff to provide the candidate with the raw data of information for his reflection; lastly, a logistics group to move the candidate and his supporting cast of luminaries and featured players around the country on schedules that superior direction indicates.

It was, in 1968, as if some blueprinted table of organization had now translated, precisely, all these classic functions into personnel and offices. It was as if, as is probably true, Richard M. Nixon with his bent for pragmatic, managerial analysis had reviewed his campaign of 1960, discarded the obsolete model, then re-designed a managerial structure fitted exactly to the function, the times of 1968, and tailored to his personality.

Three sets of offices—with a headquarters staff of no more than 200 —stretched along Park Avenue in New York between 54th and 57th Streets, close enough for luncheons, drinks, caucuses and errands, and all of them close enough to Nixon's own apartment on 62nd Street for personnel to be summoned there for direct talk whenever the campaign brought him back to New York.

Finances came first on the walk up Park Avenue, and on the corner of 54th, on the sixth floor, onetime Los Angeles banker, onetime Eisenhower budget chief, long-time Nixon loyalist Maurice Stans (now Secretary of Commerce) presided over the nursing of "mother's milk." Stans could explain what he was doing and what was happening more clearly than any finance chairman of any other national campaign—and the calm in his offices contrasted bizarrely with the aching woes of his desperate counterpart, Robert Short, Humphrey's finance chairman, in Washington. Stans knew exactly what had been spent, what was going to be spent, where the money had come from and where the rest of the money would be coming from. He had raised and spent $8,000,000 for the Nixon effort up until nomination; he would raise and spend $20,-000,000 more to finance the election. It was all programmed: there was the root-Republican money, the hate-Johnson money, the smart money, the little money; and then there was the big, big money from the large, classic contributors, nursed out of them personally by regional chiefs who spread over a geographical and ideological spectrum from arch-reactionary Henry Salvatori in California to liberal Max Fisher in Detroit. Plus the new money. The country was prosperous; in the five years of the denounced Johnson administration so many new people had grown rich that they could now afford to give more money, from the strangest places, from unrecognized wealth in a freshet of non-deductible contributions; more than half the contributors of $5,000 or over were new names since 1964. So serene was Stans that he felt he need promise nothing in return for money—no ambassadorships, no deals, no privileges, no Cabinet posts, no appointments. And he knew where the campaign would spend the money; ten million on the media, two million on citizen organization, two million on the logistics of campaign travel, the rest on extras.

Money seemed no worry in Stans' offices; nor did one find any concern in the other staff offices up the avenue. At 450 Park Avenue, research ran efficiently under a chief for domestic policy, Alan Greenspan, and a chief for foreign policy, Richard Allen. Communications policy ran smoothly under Herb Klein, now elected overseer for the long view, reporting directly to the traveling candidate the shape of press reaction and the management of future reactions. Volunteer organization and direction lay in Washington, where Richard Kleindienst and Thomas Evans had been inserted into the Republican National Committee and were smoothing out the quadrennial problem in partnership between citizen volunteers and Party regulars across the country.

All came to a head at 445 Park Avenue, where, on the third floor, John Mitchell, with deputies Flanigan and Garment, reviewed all operations in a daily morning meeting of division chiefs, which expanded on Wednesdays to include the national Republican chieftains flying in from Washington. From the bull-pen of 445 Park Avenue, a staff of seven men, under John Whitaker, a onetime geologist, coordinated a field staff of ninety advance men, preparing, controlling and scheduling the movements not only of Nixon and Agnew, but of half a dozen star "surrogate" speakers.

And between 445 Park Avenue and the candidate, wherever he might be, the web of electronics and communication meshed organization, media, movement and personality into a strategy with clear design that would net, on election day, November 5th, 1968, the 270 of the 538 electoral votes necessary to elect a President of the United States.

The strategy began with the so-called "battleground states," and the strategy is best recognized by contrast with the strategy of 1960. In 1960, Nixon's neat organizational mind had generated a paper pattern that degenerated into a gimmick—he wished in 1960 to be the first national candidate to campaign in every single one of the fifty states, an absurd waste of energy and time. In 1968, however, the strategy began by elimination. "We couldn't lose Arizona," said Peter Flanigan, "unless Nixon committed rape in public on the statehouse stairs in Phoenix." Similarly with the farm states and certain Rocky Mountain states—they were solid for Nixon, no point in wasting battle effort there. On the other end of the spectrum were states like Massachusetts—it was impossible, Nixon's private polls said, for him to carry Massachusetts unless, inconceivably, Cardinal Cushing, President Pusey of Harvard, and the Boston City Council all publicly endorsed him; and even then it would be chancy.

There remained, then, a number of major states and several Border states where the race would be won or lost. The big ones were obvious: New York, 43 electoral votes; Pennsylvania, 29; New Jersey, 17; Ohio, 26; Michigan, 21; Illinois, 26; Wisconsin, 12; Missouri, 12; Texas, 25; California, 40. Each of these states was a separate problem, and a chief analyst, Kevin Phillips, a young psephologist, was responsible for feeding the candidate, the regional media experts, the state organizations with precise ethnic breakdowns, historical breakdowns, breakaway patterns in past voting habits for each of these major states. If the election was to be a sweep—and in early September, at Nixon headquarters, no one questioned that it would be a sweep—all of these states, including even New York, would fall to the Republicans for a bouncing 251 all by themselves. But if it was to be a close race, which seemed then unlikely, there was a built-in insurance policy in the "peripheral strategy."

The peripheral strategy locked into the counter-Wallace strategy. It was a strategy of containment.

There was George Wallace, in September, with 20 percent of the popular vote in the public polls—and apparently rising. What to do about

Wallace? Nixon had laid it down, at the Mission Bay gathering, that none of his people, North or South, were to out-Wallace Wallace. He insisted, as he was to insist to the end of the campaign, that he would not divide the country; he wanted a campaign that would unify a nation so he could govern it. To compete with Wallace in the South on any civilized level was impossible—thus, states like Alabama, Mississippi, Louisiana and several others were scratched as targets, as were, at the other end of the spectrum, Massachusetts and Rhode Island. Instead, Nixon would challenge Wallace in the peripheral states—Florida, North Carolina, Virginia, Tennessee, South Carolina. In these states Humphrey could not win by any stretch of the imagination; the contest was between Nixon and Wallace; and by insisting that a vote for Wallace was a wasted vote, a *de facto* vote for integrationist Humphrey, the Nixon candidacy might come out ahead in a three-way split. At the beginning, no conflict was seen between "peripheral" and "battleground" strategies; they locked one onto the other; they amplified each other. "It's conceivable," said Phillips at one point, "that you could see something bigger than Johnson's victory in 1964, that we could carry everything but only four states—Massachusetts, Rhode Island, Alabama and Mississippi." It was only later that the trap within this strategy became evident—for, to enlarge his base in the Northern industrial states, Nixon would have to reach across from the rock-solid Republican base there, across center, to the independents, the disenchanted Democrats, to the ghettos. But to do that would be to shake the peripheral strategy in the new South. And to hold to the course he had set for the peripheral strategy limited his call in the North.

The course Nixon had set himself was quite clear, and he had voiced it nationwide in his Miami acceptance: Peace Abroad, Peace At Home, an end to adventure; and unity, unity in the Party, unity in the nation. Let the nation choose, classically, between the ins and the outs, between the record of the administration and the alternative he proposed. Tactically, there would be no debates with Hubert Humphrey, as there had been with John F. Kennedy in 1960; there would be no discussion of Vietnam in public while the Paris negotiations were going on—he would not bind himself to any course that might hobble him in diplomacy once elected. It was, everyone agreed, the strategy of caution and safety. But it was to become, as the campaign wore on to its final drama, a strategy of utmost daring—a gamble that freedom from any commitment on the part of the incoming President was worth the risk of not becoming President at all.

Yet it all seemed so safe and smooth in early September. Never, in any campaign, had any candidate had so precise and sober measurements of public opinion. Though Kennedy had begun the insertion of opinion-analysis into tactical decision with the Harris operation of 1960, Nixon carried the practice into the campaign of 1968 with an advance of new magnitude. Opinion Research Corporation of Princeton had been retained to construct a longitudinal design of the electorate in fourteen "battleground" areas. Thirteen of the fourteen areas were key Eastern or Midwestern states (plus California and Texas), and the fourteenth was a conglomerate "area" of four Southern or Border states clustered as one battleground. An original July study of 1,000 voters (by one-hour depth interviews) in each of these areas had created a benchmark for departure. Three subsequent interviews of each respondent, continuing into October, had followed their ups-and-downs of emotion. Computer print-outs in Princeton spat out their folds in mounds twelve feet high, analyzing and cross-analyzing again the reactions. Presiding over this entire operation was a professor of political science of Indiana University, Dean David Derge (also vice-president of the university), a man of cool, detached scholarship. Derge, who described himself as the "interface" between the digits and the meaning, interpreted the results for Mitchell's headquarters, whence to the Nixon plane. Derge considered not only his own operation but the entire staff as "if organized by the Harvard Business School." Starting in September, "rolling waves" of a scientifically designed cross-section lifted out a 250 sample each day to test shifts and currents of opinion. But even Derge, a shrewd analyst, could not tell in September what late October held. He was worried, however, by the Wallace vote—then still rising. A Wallace voter, said Derge, is a defector; no one loves George Wallace; no loyalties run deep for him; the Wallace vote could go up from its September 20 percent to as high, perhaps, as 26 or 27 percent—or, again, drop off by a third. Women, Derge said, feared George Wallace. His vote was basically masculine—the tough kid on the block who'd grown up to be a tough guy, the "kind of guy the Tuesday night bowling league might choose to represent them with a group of unfriendlies." But apart from the Wallace question—a big "apart"—Derge was certain, as was everyone else, that the Nixon sweep was riding.

Thus, in complete serenity, the Nixon campaign moved through September. There had indeed come to be a new Nixon. This one was a competent, able manager; this one had now subordinated the instruments, apparently, to his purpose. Gone were the old pugnacity, the old sock-and-slash style, the old tendency to buckle under strain; it was a firmer, wiser, thoroughly mature man who was now in command. He would yield from his unity line neither to his right nor his left; and when there peeped out from under the new Nixon the old Whittier boy, the bitterness of sad reminiscence that had lingered into 1960 was now clothed in self-mocking excursion into times past, as at his extraordinary lunch at Antoine's in New Orleans.

He had spoken that day at the American Legion convention—his sixth such appearance over the years before the convention, he pointed out—and then, in his unhurried schedule, decided to stop and lunch at

Antoine's, New Orleans' most famous restaurant. Sweepingly, he had invited all the accompanying press to join him there with staff and grandees of the Louisiana Republican Party. Nixon was enjoying himself and he rose toward the end of the meal to talk off-the-record. Nostalgia carried him back to the first time he had been to Antoine's, and, full of good food, we all relaxed to hear a Nixon ramble, going backward and forward from the same point of time past. No one took notes; but the pleasant interlude clings to my memory and went something like this:

"When Pat and I first got married—when was that, Pat?"—with a laugh—"oh yes, 1940, we went to Mexico. That was just after I graduated from Duke and I went from Duke up to Lansing, I still remember that bus ride, and I bought a car with her money—she had the money—a 1939 Oldsmobile, and I drove it back all the way across the country, and then we split the cost of our honeymoon, and went to Mexico for two weeks. Sometimes we drove all night to save the cost of a hotel, and I think we saw every temple, every church in old Mexico and it all cost us only $178. Well, then a year later we decided to take a vacation, because I think you should take a vacation when you're young, even if you have to borrow for it, we saw too many old folks tottering around in Mexico and decided not to wait that long. Well, we took a United Fruit boat— no, I should say ship, I'm a Navy man—for a two-week trip from California through the Canal to New Orleans. We had the worst cabin in the boat, it was the *Ulua*—our cabin was right down there in the hold with the sound of engines and the smells. So when we came to New Orleans, we decided to eat one meal in a good restaurant. We came to Antoine's and we ordered one Oysters Rockefeller for the two of us, and one pompano-in-a-bag. That's the same pompano you fellows had today, only more elegant. And I just want to remind you fellows—you had lobster dinner in Mission Bay, you're getting pompano here today—next week in Santa Barbara you get hot dogs!"

The old Nixon could not have spoken that way. After which he led the press for a tour of Antoine's famous curiosa, insisted we spell the last name of the proprietor right in our dispatches (Mr. Alciatore), praised the California wines in Antoine's wine cellar, even had a word of praise for New York champagne ("it's very good for christening ships"), and was off again, on schedule.

Everything seemed to be running on schedule as we took off on the next leg of the schedule and I joined my old friend Raymond Price, the shy and quiet philosopher of the operation. Price and I played a guessing game, and his estimate of the outcome was lower than anyone else's on the Nixon staff. Price figured that a Nixon/Humphrey/Wallace break of 48/41/11 would be good enough for a real win. Humphrey, he reminded me, was a damned smart operator—Humphrey worried Price. What could lose it for you? I asked. And Price said: Four things—a critical error on our part; a truce in Vietnam; a meeting of LBJ with the Russians; and the inherent loyalty of the Democrats to their Party.

Price had good reason to be worried; but his worries seemed almost fanciful as one transferred to the sad gypsy carnival of the first stage of the Humphrey campaign.

Hubert Humphrey had begun his campaign, stunned and punch-drunk from Chicago's events. The torment and strain of the days prior to and during the Democratic convention had left him a case of battle fatigue. Had any superior restraining hand been able to govern him, it would have insisted that he sit still for at least a week at his farm in Waverly, Minnesota, to catch his breath and collect his thoughts.

But no such restraining hand existed—and time pressed, with only eight weeks left to election day.

Thus, with every nerve quivering with indignation, no rest, no strategy and little plan, Humphrey squirted forth on the campaign trail in an opening performance almost magnificently erratic. He had flown directly from Chicago to his Minnesota home on Friday evening after the convention and slept late on Saturday. Then, in his first public statement of the campaign, he denounced the riots in Chicago as being "planned" and "premeditated," and gone on to defend Mayor Daley, saying it was time to "quit pretending that Mayor Daley did something that was wrong." A day later he flew into New York to review its annual Labor Day parade, and taped several interview shows, backtracking, insisting he did not "condone the beating of those people with clubs," and stating that some Chicago police had "overreacted." From New York he flew back Monday evening to Waverly with Lawrence O'Brien, who was desperately trying to improvise a campaign plan, flew back to Washington for a day, flew back to Waverly for two days, then again back to Washington for the weekend, and then "formally" launched his campaign on Monday, September 9th—at which point everything got worse.

The "formal" opening of the campaign had been planned as the classic jet-borne sweep across the continent—Philadelphia to Denver to Los Angeles in a single day—to be followed by another more leisurely back-swing through Texas and the Midwest to the East Coast. And as Humphrey followed this schedule, he trailed back and forth across the continent a shawl of total confusion and contradiction.

The transcontinental trail of gaffes began in Philadelphia. A disappointing rally in downtown Philadelphia had drawn a crowd of only 10,000 people, salted with hostile demonstrators, in stark contrast to the staggering 400,000 that Richard Nixon had just drawn in Chicago, at the kickoff of the Republican campaign only a few days earlier. In Philadelphia, reporters had pressed him with questions, and the Vice-President of the United States, speaking off-the-cuff, remarked that he thought "negotiations or no negotiations, we could start to remove some of the American forces [from Vietnam] in early 1969 or late 1968." No sooner had the news wires carried this remark to Washington than Secretary of State Dean Rusk flatly repudiated it.

From Philadelphia to Denver; and in Denver, Humphrey assured a largely student audience that the minority plank on Vietnam at the convention was so "mildly different" from his own position that he could easily have run on it. No sooner aboard his plane, however, and quizzed once again by reporters, than he must backtrack. He had not realized that the minority plank, over which such furious debate had raged, had called for an unconditional halt in bombing; he reiterated his own conviction that bombing should stop only if it could be done without endangering American troops and if the proposal brought a reasonable response from Hanoi.

The next day headlined Lyndon Johnson's speech to the American Legion convention in which the President himself specifically and publicly parted from his Vice-President in proclaiming that "no one" could predict when American troops would be coming back from Vietnam. Questioned at Houston about the difference of opinion between the two highest officials of the nation, Humphrey brandished a copy of the *Houston Post* which headlined: MARINE REGIMENT HEADS HOME FROM VIET WAR, to prove his point. Descending from the platform, he learned that the story indicated no reduction in American troops in Vietnam at all; the returning regiment had already been replaced by an equivalent 4,500 men in July. He was, as he tried to untangle himself, R. W. Apple wrote, like "a man with his fingers stuck in taffy," and by week's end one could only ask whether the President and his administration were, indeed, undermining their candidate in public; and whether Hubert Humphrey knew at all what he was talking about.

From this sequence of blunders, Humphrey returned for two days of Washington conferences, to listen to reports of the situation at headquarters which O'Brien was still trying to pull together. No more gloomy report has ever been given a candidate than that of the candid O'Brien; and, further depressed, Humphrey took off on the next week's flight. By now, with the full echo of the convention resounding from around the country, he understood that his absolute first priority must be to reunite his own fractured Party if he were to have any chance at all. And thus, in another symbolic flight, Humphrey scheduled himself to touch bases, in a unity swing, that would carry him from a rally with Teddy Kennedy in downtown Boston, to a rally with George McGovern in South Dakota, to a rally with Adlai Stevenson, Jr., in Springfield, Illinois, thus underlining the quality of his candidacy with three billboard liberal names in a single day.

In Boston, the evil of the streets rose to greet him, and for the first time I began to understand what Chicago had done to the man, and how completely changed was the mood of America from campaigns of other years. The Vice-President of the United States had come to state his case; the Senator from Massachusetts stood there to greet him. Ten thousand people had gathered at noon at the crossing of Boston's Washington and Summer Streets, in the old garment and leather district, to hear him. And a few hundred students had gathered to deprive the candidate of his right of free speech, the audience of its right to listen. Every conviction I had ever held on the unrestrained right of dissent was now to be tested.

For these were not ordinary hecklers; they had come in buses, marshaled and mobilized, and stationed themselves early. Their banners waved for the TV cameras—COPS PLUS DEMOCRATS EQUAL PIGS; MAYOR DALEY FOR HEART DONOR; PEACE NOW; DON'T HUMP ON ME; STOP THE BOMBING—but the banners did not bother me. Nor their flags—the black flags of the anarchists, SDS banners, Viet Cong banners. Nor the filth and obscenity of their shouting. It was the precise, rhythmic, organized cadence of their effort to break up Humphrey's public discourse. Humphrey would speak, and the organized students would shout "Sell-Out, Sell-Out, Sell-Out!" The platform microphone would be turned up full force and they would chant "Bull Shit, Bull Shit, Bull Shit!" Humphrey, contending with them, angry, would raise his voice to a shriek, and the marshal of their disruption would give the signal. The marshal, a swarthy youth with deep down-turned mustache, rode piggy-back on the shoulders of another student, dressed in green sweater, a white handkerchief on his forearm, and as Humphrey, in occasional pauses, would try to make a point, the marshal would bring his arm down and his mob would yell, "Shame, Shame, Shame, Shame," and then "Bull Shit, Bull Shit, Bull Shit," or "Sell-Out, Sell-Out, Sell-Out." Hate contorted the faces of the young; at one point, through the mob came hurtling a placard whose stick hit CBS correspondent David Schoumacher in the forehead, narrowly missing his eye; one had no doubt that, had there been no police on stand-by, they would have rushed the platform and, indeed, done physical violence to those who resisted. There, at the roped-off center of the rally, one knew in one's own heart that, had it come to violence, had the student mob rushed, one would have struck back with equal violence as had Mayor Daley's cops in Chicago. One knew that whatever it was Humphrey had had to say to a larger nation, the larger audience, would be erased this night on television, and only violence, inviting further violence across the nation, would be shown on the ninety-second clips of the networks.

The press and television would, indeed, report Humphrey as a victim of the marauders; but the nation is hardly inclined to elect a victim as President. Thus, riding on with Humphrey from Boston to the Midwest, listening to a bitter and grief-stricken Vice-President reduced to discussing the street tactics of confrontation, the microphone pitches required to drown out organized chantings, the relative merits of indoor and outdoor meetings, the somber future of American political campaigning if the marauders persisted in their action—listening to this, I felt his cause hopeless.

Nor was there any reason for a brighter view when I left his plane and returned, several days later, to Washington to examine the development and structure of the campaign organization.

There, in Democratic National Committee Headquarters in Washington, D.C., the sixth-floor command suites had become a Crossroads of Lamentation. Only the cycle of American politics could have reduced the party which had engineered the stupendous victory of 1964 to this desolate estate just four years later.

Even given the rending of Chicago, the cleavages of the Vietnam war, the violence of the streets, the pressures of the turbulent year, one could not believe that a major Presidential effort would appear so completely pathetic.

It had been obvious from the death of Robert F. Kennedy on, from June 7th, 1968, that Hubert Humphrey was the leading candidate for the Democratic nomination. Already, at the end of May, Richard M. Nixon had peeled away from his staff a forward echelon to plan beyond the convention to the electoral campaign itself. (See Chapter Five.) But Humphrey had not. It was not that Humphrey's veterans were unaware that there must be an election plan as well as a convention plan; it seemed that no one man had been responsible for preparing such a plan, or, rather, that too many had been responsible. Too many men spoke for, and to, Hubert Humphrey. William Connell and his staff group were closest to the Vice-President; but they had not been responsible for post-convention planning. The United Democrats for Humphrey, under its rival co-chairmen, Senators Mondale and Harris, had been most effective in rounding up delegates for the convention itself; but neither Mondale nor Harris had had full authority to think beyond the convention. Secretary of Agriculture Orville Freeman had realized that there must be a campaign plan and had, indeed, composed a good one in a fat black notebook. But whether the Freeman plan had ever come to Humphrey's attention no one could tell; at any rate, the Freeman plan now rested somewhere in the compartments of the campaign, a document for future archivists rather than an operational timetable.

Lawrence O'Brien had been announced as convention manager for Humphrey on July 27th. But *he* had not been responsible for post-convention planning. A man of rigid honesty, O'Brien had lived too long, lean, and stretched in purse on a government salary; a generous book contract for his memoirs waited for him, and six-figure salaries beckoned him from private industry as soon as he should leave government. O'Brien had agreed to serve as Humphrey's convention manager only down to and through the convention—it being clearly understood *his* responsibility ended the day the convention was over, when he would depart politics to earn some real money for his family. It was only in the last few days of the convention that O'Brien had realized that there was no plan at all for the general campaign which would follow the convention and deputized his former partner, Joseph Napolitan, a professional campaign manager, to draw one up. I remember strolling into Napolitan's suite in Chicago on the Tuesday before the Wednesday nominating ballot and finding Napolitan, in shirt sleeves, furiously banging away at a typewriter. The normally affable and friendly Napolitan had no time at all to talk. "I'm writing the campaign plan," he said. "Do you know there isn't *any* campaign plan? I have to get this ready by tomorrow!"

Then had followed nomination day, the balloting, and the disaster in the streets and on television. Thursday (see Chapter Nine) Humphrey had been busy with the choice of Vice-President and the rewriting of his speech; and then, finally, at three o'clock in the morning of Friday, he had summoned O'Brien again to his suite and poured out his emotions: he was desperate; he had neither campaign plan nor campaign manager; he had to face the Democratic National Committee that day and announce to them his choice of new National Chairman. "Larry," said Humphrey, "I've just got to have you." And O'Brien consented.

Thus, with two days off for Labor Day weekend and recuperation, O'Brien and his personal staff, Joseph Napolitan and Ira Kapenstein, joined the Humphrey plane in New York on Labor Day and flew back to the Humphrey homestead. En route, Napolitan typed a three-page media plan, for at this point there was none, handed it to O'Brien, who handed it to Humphrey, who marked it "O.K., HHH—go."

In the guest cabin at Humphrey's homestead that night, September 2nd, O'Brien, Napolitan and Kapenstein sat down with scrawl pads to rough out the campaign plan; the next day they were joined by that hard-headed citizen Orville Freeman, who informed them, bluntly, that though Humphrey was scheduled to start the campaign the next week in Philadelphia, there was still no schedule, no advance men, no money in the bank. Jointly and mournfully, cruelly but correctly, the new campaign management therefore decided to cut Hubert Humphrey off for the next ten days, to let him "fly by the seat of his pants" while they tried to build an organization under him or, at least, pull together the various parts of organization already existent in Washington.

By Thursday morning, when O'Brien arrived in Washington to take his desk at the Democratic National Committee, there were then less than eight weeks to go before the election. In 1960, seven full weeks of planning time had elapsed from the Democratic National Convention in July to the beginning of John F. Kennedy's campaign in September. In 1968, no such interlude of time gave breathing space. Poverty had forced the

Democratic National Committee to begin the firing of personnel before O'Brien arrived; there was the simple matter of housekeeping, as various headquarters in Washington required consolidation and desk space. There was no money—for example, no one could pay for a band to greet the Humphrey campaign at Los Angeles on the coming Monday and someone had to be found instantly to write a personal check for the band. There was no advertising agency. And across the country, the shattered fragments of the Democratic Party, stunned by the convention, stalked each other, faction by faction, state by state. No organization except the old regulars in New York; in Texas, no state chairman, and Party leaders sitting on their hands; in California, guerrilla warfare among the state's Party chieftains; and across the country, no over-all control of national campaign either by region or state.

There is a push-pull, or "resonance," effect in politics; the better things go, the better things go; and the worse things go, then the worse things go. But money is a good starting point to observe the resonance. Without money, one cannot finance either the logistics of a campaign or television and media time; without television commercial time or the creative provocation of positive television coverage, one cannot affect public opinion; public opinion is reflected in public-opinion polls; and if the public-opinion polls show a candidate losing, then his sources of money dry up—who wants to bet on a loser?—and the shrinkage of money reflects itself in a shrinkage of television exposure, and the resonance effect amplifies.

The oscillating effect could be seen naked in the three adjacent offices of Messrs. O'Brien, Napolitan and Robert Short on the sixth floor of the Democratic National Committee headquarters at any time in the month of September, as the polls showed Hubert Humphrey variously fifteen (in the Gallup poll) or eight (in the Harris poll) points behind Richard M. Nixon. First there was the office of Robert Short of Minnesota—the new finance chairman, an old friend of Hubert Humphrey, a clean, vigorous, normally optimistic man. There simply was no money. Short had arrived in his office, after convention, to find that $4,000,000 had been spent, wildly, on the Humphrey effort before convention—but there were no records of where it had come from or how it had been spent. Only now there was none left—the National Committee had a deficit, the Humphrey campaign organization had a deficit. Short was raising $1,000,000 by borrowing—an intricate legal matter, given the laws of political financing. But the hate-Kennedy money which had financed Humphrey until Kennedy's death had dried up; the hate-Johnson money which had financed Eugene McCarthy had also dried up; there was no Texas money, as there usually is in a Democratic campaign; there was no "smart" money from the great corporations and operators who usually bet on both sides, if both sides have a chance. There was only the old "love-Hubert" money, chiefly out of New York and Minnesota, and that had been used up or was not enough. Short, optimistic as always, was putting together an entirely new network of money-raisers—he was going to get, he swore, $2,000,000 for television money for the last two weeks of the campaign, no matter what happened, so that in the last fortnight Humphrey could match Nixon dollar for dollar in television and radio time.

Short's problem made Napolitan's problem more complicated. Napolitan was in charge of media. Napolitan felt, as turned out to be correct, that the public polls—except for Harris—were off-base. He felt that with proper media time, with proper regional and network spots and exposures, they could get the Humphrey message across. But data was lacking to go on. On Labor Day weekend the Committee had commissioned five separate public-opinion analysts to do polls in seventeen separate states. Of these, at the end of September, two analysts were still holding out. They had completed their findings, but would not deliver until paid. It is an axiom of politics, binding on button-makers, printing firms, television stations and pollsters that one cannot collect a debt from a loser in a political campaign. One pollster, holding results absolutely essential to the programming of the campaign, insisted that not until the certified check of $10,000 was in his hands would he deliver his results to the Humphrey campaign. Napolitan could not, thus, schedule television or media strategy to woo the public until he knew which kind of public where would be receptive to which message and how. Even that was academic, from Napolitan's point of view. On Labor Day, frantic telephone calls had gone out to advertising agencies and television producers to set them in motion producing documentaries, spots and newspaper advertisements to spread Hubert Humphrey's message. They had worked overtime, and by the end of September their first product had begun to arrive at the Democratic National Committee. "We have beautiful ads," said Napolitan, showing me his proofs; "all we need is a million dollars to buy space to publish them." I hastened to go, for this was the kind of threadbare political poverty to which only the old Richard M. Nixon of Whittier, California, could have given eloquence. "Wait," said Napolitan, inserting a spool in a tape-recorder, "I want you to hear our radio spots. They're wonderful. This is your only chance to hear them— we'll never get enough money to put them on air."

This, then, was the state of the campaign in the first month of the Democrats' attempt to retain the Presidency. By the end of the month, something, of course, had been pulled together. Schedulers, advance men, regional and state-by-state chairmen were in place. The various pre-convention parts of the Humphrey organization had been tied in a framework, and Orville Freeman's daily organizational sessions were linked to thrice-weekly strategy sessions in O'Brien's office; but over all loomed the single greatest problem still unsolved. Ira Kapenstein, O'Brien's deputy, put it thus: "All the foul-ups in scheduling, all the fluffs in his speeches, all that doesn't mean anything. There's one hard decision we've got to make. He's got to bite on the nail. He's got to be his own man, he's got to break with LBJ, and he's got to break on the Vietnam issue. Unless he breaks on the issue and becomes his own man, then he can't be President, and maybe he doesn't deserve to be President."

All this was the continuing agony of Humphrey in the month of September. Booed and jeered; written off by press, columnists and polls; uncertain in his own conscience whether he could morally ask contributions for further funds, he must go on. Later he said, "I called Bob Short at the beginning of October and I told him to give me just a few more days—if there wasn't any progress, I'd not ask him to lift the phone and ask anyone else for a single cent. But I made up my mind, even if I had to hire a station wagon, Muriel and I would go out across the country and say what we thought and carry the message."

Yet listening to the message was unrewarding. One gave Humphrey credit for gallantry in action, under public humiliation that no major candidate had ever known, worse even than that of Barry Goldwater. And one acknowledged, listening to his trumpeting voice, that the man was still, as ever, the greatest master of quick wit and stump oratory of American politics. But how would he get out of the trap?

The lack of money, the booing and jeering, the split in the Party, the discounting of his chances by the press—these were only the visible bars on the cage. But the cage was more real than that.

It was one of history, of conscience, of responsibility. First, there was Vietnam. In the highest possible sense, Vietnam was a matter of conscience for candidate Hubert Humphrey. He was Vice-President of a nation at war; half a million American men fought in Vietnam—28,000 had died. He owed them a loyalty—to give their sacrifice meaning. On this he could not, *would* not, run out. Knowing the intricate, persistent, unremitting effort of the American government to win peace by negotiation, he could not accept the thought that any magic formula would bring peace. Richard M. Nixon could, wisely, be silent on the issue. But Humphrey, as Vice-President, could not attack his own administration— nor did he dare defend the issue before the electorate and his divided Party. Thus, a man of peace committed to a war, Humphrey waffled and wobbled.

Humphrey had no central theme that one could discern. He had begun in spring with a strangely inappropriate paean to the joy and happiness of American politics. His close friends attempted to explain there really was a master theme within the speech—that he was urging America to face up to its terrible problems not with despair, but with courage and hope. Yet if this was the message, it was buried so deep in his opening remarks that it would have required a mine-detector to make it clear. By September even that theme had vanished in the cascade of positions and papers that his research staff worked out for him—positions on Medicare, schools, housing, farm programs, urban renewal, law-and-order. A similar cascade came from the Nixon camp. No one read either; but Humphrey's was overwhelming. For a while, to amuse myself, I kept count of the cumulative "points" in the rival programs. But when Humphrey put together a ten-point program for farms, with an eight-point program for education, with a five-point program for improving Social Security, and continued with an eighty-four-point program for law-and-order, I gave up, yielding the point count to Humphrey and the election to Nixon.

With no theme, there remained only tactics—of which the chief was to goad Nixon into anger or blunder, and force him to debate publicly. The shafts of Humphrey wit were never brighter—Nixon was "Trickle Down Dick"; Nixon was "Fearless Fosdick"; Nixon was "Sir Richard the Unready." Nixon's "firm positions would make an ad for Jello look like concrete." Nixon was "the sort of fellow that says I love my wife, but I am not going to give her any money." "Where do you stand, Mr. Nixon, where do you stand?" Humphrey would chant from every stump, needling him, teasing him, challenging him to debate. "Mr. Nixon, where do you stand on higher education? Mr. Nixon, where do you stand on expanded Medicare? Mr. Nixon, where do you stand on the wheat program? Where do you stand on Justice Fortas? Where do you stand, where do you stand?"—and then, shaking his head after calling out to the skies, "I must say he is elusive. He's the fastest-moving target I've seen since a bevy of doves and quail went out of the field."

With this tactic, however, went only the vaguest kind of strategy—for the strategy of the Democrats, from beginning to end, was to recapture the Democrats. If the great and ancient Party could be pulled together again, if the solid base which for a generation has fluctuated at 50 percent of the nation could be brought back to its old loyalties, then Humphrey might have a chance. Thus from Humphrey's lips constantly flowed the old litany of the triumphs of the past of the Party; romantically, eloquently, passionately, he extolled its past achievements and promised more to come. Whether audiences liked it or not, whether the nation wanted it or not, Hubert Humphrey would not retreat an inch from the grand tradition of old reform, or from the grand assumptions that underlay the Party. Within earshot, Humphrey could still make the blood race, the heart beat faster; but earshot was limited range, and no television or media time could spread the emotion. In good form, even deep in the Border states, at a place like Louisville, Kentucky, where no particular love or concern is held for black Americans, he could lift the evangelist's voice and declaim for the rights of black and white Americans alike: "I didn't sell my soul for this nomination," he concluded, referring to the supposed Nixon-Thurmond deal, and his voice quivered, "I stand on human equality, on equality of opportunity for every American, regardless of race, color, or creed. Stand up, I tell you, stand up for human rights, *stand up,* STAND UP"—and the entire audience, carried away by his concern, rose and gave him a standing ovation.

But it was precisely on the issue of human rights that the old Party was splitting. All through September, as Hubert Humphrey's share of the national vote seemed to nudge a bottom of 28, 29, 30 percent of the electorate, there could be no doubt that millions upon millions of Democrats had forsaken the Party of their fathers and gone elsewhere.

And there was no doubt where they had gone: to George Wallace—another small-town boy, from Clio, Alabama.

The Governor of Alabama, with the over-cropping black eyebrows, had first appeared on the national scene, a little chipmunk-faced man, standing before national television cameras, overtowered by Deputy Attorney General Nicholas de B. Katzenbach, in the door of Foster Hall of the University of Alabama on a hot day in June, 1963, defying the government of the United States on the issue of integration and the admission of Negroes to the university.

The episodes of the day—and George Wallace's final, formal submission to the United States Army that afternoon—marked the take-off point of a small-town politician about to become a national figure. But the small-town boy from Clio, Alabama, came of a background quite different from those of the small-town boys from Whittier and Doland.

Clio, Alabama, a seedy, mournful village, a depot of the Central of Georgia railway line, is the county seat of Barbour County in the cotton-chopping southeast corner of Alabama. There is little to do in such villages, except talk about crops, Negroes or politics. And there are only a few ways out of such horizons of poverty, of which the most alluring is the way of politics. George Wallace, son of an unsuccessful farmer, was cast for politics from the day he passed adolescence. A scrapper (he was Golden Gloves bantamweight champion of Alabama, weight ninety-five pounds, in his senior year in high school), a good student, politics took him young—he was president of his high-school senior class, a debater like Richard Nixon, occasionally a page in the state legislature at Montgomery.[3]

The University of Alabama, through which Wallace worked his way,

[3] For three fuller accounts of George Wallace, see: Marshall Frady's *Wallace,* published by World; Bill Jones' *The Wallace Story,* Viewpoint Publications, Montgomery, Alabama; and a remarkable study by James Jackson Kilpatrick, *"What Makes Wallace Run,"* in the *National Review* of April 18th, 1967.

left no apparent sheen of culture, learning or history on the Wallace personality, except for an exaggeration of his appetite to get into politics. He graduated in law in 1942, but the war interrupted his career. Enlisting in the Air Force, Wallace became a flight mechanic on the B29's that bombed Japan from the Mariana Islands, a harrowing experience from which he emerged with an honorable discharge and a 10 percent "nervous disability" allowance. From the war, it was directly back to politics for George Walace, hand-shaking his way through chickenyards, school buses, barbershops, corner drugstores to election to the Alabama legislature in 1946. And from then on, with a passion equaled only by some natives of West Virginia and South Boston, politics was his life. A fellow politician in Alabama later observed, "George can out-politick any man all day long. When I'm through politicking I like to go home, I like my likker, I like my woman. George just goes on politicking right through the day."

Six years in the state legislature gave him the platform from which he could climb to circuit judge in 1952. By 1958 his ambition had propelled him into the race for the governorship, where, to his own astonishment, he found himself outflanked on the right by a racist named Patterson. Losing, Wallace announced to a few friends, according to chronicler Marshall Frady, "John Patterson out-niggahed me. And boys, I'm not goin' to be out-niggahed again." Running again in 1962 for governor, no one could "out-niggah" George Wallace. Elected, he announced his platform in his inaugural address: "I draw the line in the dust and toss the gauntlet before the feet of tyranny, and I say, 'Segregation now . . . segregation tomorrow . . . and segregation forever.' "

With this, at his inauguration in 1963, George Wallace had indeed tossed down the gauntlet—not before a tyranny, but before the administration and person of John F. Kennedy, trying to move America to a conciliation of races.

The new Governor of Alabama might, but for one fact, have gone down as a major figure in the new South. Heavy appropriations for more schools (fourteen new junior colleges authorized), more hospitals, mental institutions, nursing homes and clinics, free textbooks, increased social-security benefits for state employees, the largest road-building program in Alabama's history were his achievements. They might have marked him as one of the South's outstanding progressive governors. But the one fact dominated all—George Wallace was an unabashed racist.

In a period when the term "racist" is so carelessly flicked about, the word must be used precisely. And, in all precision, George Wallace was and is a racist.

George Wallace believed, and believes now, that black people are biologically and genetically an inferior species of the human race. He believes that segregation best preserves the values of both black and white races. There is no legal or theoretical blueprint of "apartheid" in his mind; the old traditions are good enough for him. For him, Negroes have a particular way of life with which whites should not interfere; nor should whites permit Negroes to interfere with their ways of life. Wallace, like so many Southerners, feels that Negroes kill, wound, slash, steal and couple with animal abandon that sets them off from the "Anglo-Saxon tradition." Yet, although regarding Negroes as part-animal, part-human, Wallace disclaims "hate." "You must be careful," said a Southern reporter, "to make clear that Wallace isn't a hater. He doesn't hate Negroes. He's a segregationist, not a lyncher." Wallace is infuriated by the epithet of Nazi or Fascist hurled at him in the North. If George Wallace hates anything, it is not Negroes—it is the Federal government of the United States and its "pointy-head" advisers, the "intellectual morons," the "guideline writers" of Washington who try to upset the natural relation of races and force Negroes and whites to live together in unnatural mixing.

George Wallace might in other times have ruled as Governor of Alabama and then occupied only his proper place in the baroque Hall of Fame of Southern politics along with Cotton Ed Smith, Theodore Bilbo and the great Huey "Every-Man-a-King" Long. But the confrontation in the courtyard of the University of Alabama in June, 1963, occurred at a time when the Federal government's indifference to prejudice was changing, and the mass media were entering on their present dramatic dominance of American life. Overnight, George Wallace was a national figure. He had rung an echo in a new embittered stratum of Americans that spread nationwide. Invitations to speak poured in, national audiences waited for him. Wallace chose, chiefly, to speak at Northern colleges; the very sharpness of emotions he aroused amplified his voice. Students, bearing peace placards, would beat him over the head; they would rock his car, trying to overturn it; and the publicity spread his message. Entering three Democratic primaries in 1964, Wallace scored 266,136 votes (33.9 percent) in Wisconsin, 172,646 (29.9 percent) in Indiana, and an astonishing 214,849 (42.7 percent) in Maryland. The Wallace campaign of 1964 was washed out, first, by Lyndon Johnson's overwhelming presence that year, and, second, by Wallace's decision to let Barry Goldwater be champion of segregation south of the Mason-Dixon Line. But what remained was a skill, a residual know-how of national campaigning, a feline feel for the contours of national politics that was to make him a major force in the Presidential campaign of 1968.

As early as 1967, few men acquainted with Southern politics could be unaware that George Wallace, having installed his wife, Lurleen, as his gubernatorial successor, was going to make a second, larger try in 1968. As early as spring of that year, some political dowser's rod had made quite clear to George Wallace where millions of people itched, and could be scratched. To James Jackson Kilpatrick, in an outgoing interview, Wallace said, "What are the issues going to be in 1968? . . . Schools, that'll be one thing. By the fall of 1968, the people of Cleveland and Chicago and Gary and St. Louis will be so god-damned sick and tired of Federal interference in their local schools, they'll be ready to vote for Wallace by the thousands. The people don't like this triflin' with their children, tellin' 'em which teachers to have to teach in which schools, and bussing little boys and girls half across a city just to achieve 'the proper racial mix.' . . . I'll give you another big one for 1968: law and order. Crime in the Streets. The people are going to be fed up with the sissy attitude of Lyndon Johnson and all the intellectual morons and theoreticians he has around him. They're fed up with a Supreme Court that . . . it's a sorry, lousy, no-account outfit. . . . Housing? Sure, that'll be an issue . . . any time the Federal government lays down the law for people . . . fixing the terms and conditions on which they can sell their own homes. . . . Folks won't stand for it. And there's nothing about the sale of private housing in the Constitution either. . . . Vietnam? Yeah . . . well, I think we've got to pour it on. We've got to win this war. . . ."

Most Northern writers are inclined to look on Southern politicians in the comic tradition of Senator Claghorn, at once hilariously funny and mysteriously menacing.

But the Wallace campaign, as it took off in the fall of 1967, was neither comic nor mysterious—it was open, smart, and thoroughly ignored.

At the level of practical politics, the enormous problem before the Wallace staff was simply to get him on the ballot. The laws of every state of the Union reflect the unspoken Anglo-American tradition that voters in a free country can have only one effective choice—between a majority and a minority party. To create a third party in America, one must mount a transcontinental assault on habit, tradition, emotion and, above all, fifty different election laws. To field a new party in New York, for example, a group must have at least 12,000 valid voting signatures, of which at least fifty must come from each of New York's sixty-two counties—which is easy in big cities, but in counties of less than 4,000 population nearly impossible. In West Virginia, the voting registrant and the registered voter must record the signature of voter in the "magisterial district" where both live—if only one can find out what and where is a "magisterial district." In Nebraska, a third party is recognized only if it holds a convention. In California, even more difficult laws require 66,059 registered signatures from all across the state to form a new party. The skills, the legal knowledge, the dedication required for the mounting of a nationwide presentation of a new party in America are almost impossibly demanding.

By the summer of 1968, however, the Wallace leadership had proved that its resources in talent, skill, energy and money ran far beyond anything anticipated from a group dismissed as red-neck hillbillies. Four young Southern lawyers (Sikes, twenty-eight, Fine, thirty-one, Turnipseed, thirty-two, DeCarlo, forty) had divided the country up into regions; by spring twenty to thirty young Alabama lawyers were researching the election laws of every state in the Union; and the machinery of the state of Alabama, controlled by George Wallace, was extruding and dispatching young Alabamans all across the country to organize the faithful. Greeted by stink bombs in some places, by plastic bags full of urine in other places (Dartmouth College), by brawls and gun threats in yet others, they found that the greater the violence against them, the more ready and numerous were their faithful of the underground to come out and work.[4]

There was always a grand sense of persecution among the Wallace workers, a nearly religious faith that everyone was against them but the people, and that the saving of white America from the pointy-heads was a cause greater than politics. By the summer of 1968, Wallace parties—usually styled the American Independence Party—were established in forty-nine of the fifty states of the Union, and in the fiftieth—Ohio—a Supreme Court suit was under way to force Ohio to give the new party a fair attempt to place itself on the ballot. When that suit was won in the fall, Wallace had qualified in all fifty states of the Union!

This huge effort had been regarded almost as a comic side-show all through the spring of 1968. From the middle of 1967 to the summer of 1968, no poll had shown him with more than 10 percent of the national vote, a figure alarming enough but stable.

Then, within days after the assassination of Robert F. Kennedy, the polling response to Wallace began to rise; and with the violence of the Chicago convention another jump in response was apparent. From 9 percent (April-May), Wallace moved to 16 percent (June), to 21 percent (mid-September), and by linear extrapolation would, if the trend continued unbroken, reach close to 30 percent by voting day! Thirty

[4] The quality of the underground faithful, as they surfaced, occasionally astounded even the anticipation of the Wallace field agents. Country-boy politicians, genial segregationists, they had little stomach for real violence. Thus, they were genuinely shocked to find that one of their Southern California headquarters had been infiltrated by a group called the Foothill Irregulars—which not only packed pistols at meetings but reportedly had a cannon located in the hills outside San Diego ready to fire when the Communists tried to take over that city. They found themselves occasionally under suspicion themselves. When Tom Turnipseed arrived in Montana to oversee the Wallace operation there, he found one of his local leaders had just been thrown out of the local John Birch Society as being too extreme a fanatic even for them. "I hadn't been in town two days," said Turnipseed, "before he was telling people that I was a Moscow-trained agent."

percent for George Wallace would bring absolute political disaster, for if Wallace reached that point, no candidate would have a majority of the Electoral College. And in a time of war, a leaderless America would wait for weeks, perhaps months, on the Electoral College or the politics of the House to produce a flawed and shadowed President.

So, one went to see what was happening. I joined the Wallace campaign in Chicago, four weeks after the Democratic convention. He was to come in at the airport, travel the Loop and speak in the working-class, all-white suburb of Cicero that day.

His plane was an old war-vintage DC4, chartered from some obscure company. Pistol-packing Alabama state troopers accompanied him. The coffee was stale, the cheese sandwiches were dry; no liquor was permitted aboard, root beer was considered a hard drink, Coca-Cola and orange juice were approved; and smoking was frowned upon. In the forward compartment, in an aisle seat, sat George Wallace—a man obviously nervous in flight, with perhaps some remembered carry-over from rocking and tumbling his B29s had taken during the war. A big gold ring glistened on his finger, and in repose his somber face glowered. Occasionally he would run a comb through his sleek glossy hair, halfway between chestnut and jet black; and his close-set eyes were shrunken into deep, dark hollows under the great eyebrows. He was a very little man, almost a frail man, above all a nervous man, his hands twitching when he spoke, shifting from pocket to pocket as he rose.

He led his country picnic through the streets of Chicago, and scores of thousands were there to greet him. The signs spoke the emotions he aroused: I WORKED TO BUY MY HOUSE, GEORGE, PROTECT OUR HOME. NEWS MEDIA UNFAIR. LAW AND WALLACE. WALLACE, DALEY AND THE POLICE. AMERICA—LOVE IT OR LEAVE IT. WALLACE REMEMBERS THE PUEBLO. HAVE OUR SCHOOLS BEEN SOLD TO THE GOVERNMENT? POLISH WANT WALLACE. ITALIAN POWER FOR WALLACE. WALLACE—FRIEND OF THE WORKING MAN. VOTERS RING THE BELL OF LIBERTY WITH WALLACE. GIVE AMERICA BACK TO THE PEOPLE, VOTE WALLACE. The procession proceeded through downtown Chicago, flanked on either side by loping groups that mixed Wallacites and anti-Wallacites alike. The students loping along, both white and black, chanted "Wallace is a Pig, Hey Hey, Wallace is a Pig, Hey Hey," and the Wallace people chanted "Go-Go Wallace, Go-Go Wallace," while the rest of Chicago strolled by on the crowded noon sidewalks pretending not to hear.

It was that evening, in Cicero, that one got the full flavor of the man and what he roused. Cicero is a solidly working-class suburb. Once the base of Scarface Al Capone (population 69,130 according to the 1960 census and almost entirely white), Cicero is afraid, as are other still-white working-class neighborhoods, of the black over-spill from the central ghettos. In Cicero, Wallace was appealing to the solid under-lay of his Northern constituency. He had brought with him several Southern labor leaders, introduced them one after the other, identified himself immediately as the friend of the workingman, and identified their enemies— the pointy-heads, the long-hairs, the anarchists, the bureaucrats, the intellectuals: ". . . an' some of these newspaper editors, that look down their nose at every workingman in Cicero, on every workingman in the United States and calls them a group of red-necks or a group of punks because we want to defend America . . . and when we're talking about domestic institutions we're talking about schools, we're talking about hospitals, we're talking about the seniority of a workingman in his labor union, we're talking about ownership of property, that's what we're talking about. I want to say this about the school system of Alabama and Illinois, we don't have any recommendations to make in Illinois about what kind of schools you ought to have in Cicero. You people are intelligent enough in this city and this state to determine yourselves what's in the interest of your child, where he should go to school. And we don't need guidelines to tell us, and we don't need half a billion dollars being spent on bureaucrats in Washington of your hard-earned tax money to check every school system, every hospital, every seniority list of a labor union. An now after the election they're going to check even on the sale of your own property. . . . One of the first things I'm going to ask the Congress to do is to repeal this law about the sale of your own property and let them know that a man's home is still his castle. . . ."

And on, and on: about law-and-order; about the militants and activists and Communists and the beards, and how he was going to plow them under the courthouse, and how when he got to be President, if they lay in his way, he'd just run over them. And how you couldn't walk safe at night in the big cities of the country. And how it was time for us to stop worrying about what Ghana and Guinea and Nigeria thought about us, they should start thinking about what we thought about them.

As he spoke, the Cicero crowd rocked with him. He was saying what was on their minds, saying it like it is, saying it the way they said it to each other in the bars. And, so shortly after the Boston brutality of the left toward Humphrey, one could not but reflect on the counter-brutality that Wallace roused on the right. The left would not let Humphrey have his say. The right would not permit silent dissent at their meeting. While Wallace spoke, violence sputtered on the fringe of his Cicero crowd. A youth carrying a McCarthy placard found himself assailed; the attackers kicked his ankles; a fat middle-aged blonde woman pushed through the crowd and screamed, "Shoot 'em, kill 'em!" The youth carried a sign saying, DON'T LET WALLACE MAKE THIS A POLICE STATE. The fat woman clawed his face, slapped it. The crowd, approving her, yelled, "You nigger-loving homosexual!" "Take a bath, you dope addict!" An apparently Jewish reporter was taking notes, and several yelled, "Hey, you Hebe, you Jew bastard—how you doing, Moishe, you writing backwards?" As at Boston, it was an entirely new experience to me in campaigning. If the streets and the violence of the streets were to dominate American political campaigns, would we be forced then to fall back into the cold, manipulated world of the television media, from whose safe and sterile studio enclosures candidates would speak to people?

I was to continue to travel with Wallace through the industrial towns of Michigan the next day, but there was no more to be learned in traveling with Wallace for days than for hours—one could report only the fluctuation in depth and intensity of heckling or cheers he roused. His message was absolutely simple, short and clear. He was telling the people that their government had sold them out. Alienation is one of the more fashionable words in current American politics. It is the negative of the old words, the old faith that America was a community, and that government served the community. Alienation is disillusion—the sense that government no longer serves the interests of the people, with the derivative that government must be seized and compelled to work, or government must be ignored and overthrown. The year had begun politically when the best of the students had trooped off for Eugene McCarthy, moderately alienated but still hopeful that somehow government could be made to work. They had been succeeded by the thoroughly alienated student-mobilizers of Chicago, who believed it should all be brought down. Now, here in September was yet another alienated group—the young working people of the industrial cities. They had seen the students, the middle-class young, their social "betters" rioting and blood-letting on television. Now they were being given a cause of their own. They had lived in the industrial cities ignored, unheard, unlistened to, their problems and aches unacknowledged by government or media; they had listened to learned commentators and found few spokesmen for what bothered them. Now they listened to George Wallace, because no one else seemed to speak their language.

There was little strategy in the Wallace campaign, no larger understanding of the resources he might have mobilized from this group of alienated. The Wallace campaign, as it developed, made decent people ashamed to stand with George Wallace; it degraded their sense of themselves as Americans because it gave them no other cause but hate. As tacticians, the Wallace leaders were conspicuously more able than any other minority-party leaders had been in a generation. As country-boy politicians and shrewd lawyers, they had proved their abilities by establishing a new party in fifty states. But they could not go beyond that to understanding of spirit. They could add and subtract, and one could reconstruct their planning only by following their figures.

The Wallace strategy at its peak rested on the hope that with luck Wallace could carry seventeen states (eleven of the old South, and Border states running as far north as Delaware and Missouri) for a total of no less than 177 electoral votes. With 177 Wallace votes, there would be no majority either for Nixon or Humphrey and the election would go to the House of Representatives. It was not that George Wallace wanted to bargain either in the House or the Electoral College. He had proclaimed that there was not "a dime's worth of difference" between the two major parties. His plan was simply to let the Federal government linger in electoral paralysis until a President had been chosen in the back rooms. His chief thinker, Bill Jones, said, "We aren't going to be caught supporting either one of them. We got to be free to attack both of them."

If, as they hoped at their September peak, Wallace did carry seventeen states, then, they felt, a longer-range perspective would open to them. His victories would so terrify local politicians everywhere that in 1970 scores of Congressmen, perhaps more than a hundred, would run in alliance with George Wallace's American Independence Party. With such a Congressional base, all perspectives would change. This dream, as it turned out, was shattered in October. But in September it seemed possible, and thus American politics was thrown thoroughly off-course. Wallace, it was obvious, would take conservative votes from Nixon in the South and working-class votes from Humphrey in the North. If Wallace grew in strength, the election would go to the House. If he shriveled in strength, Humphrey might have a faint chance. If he stayed put in the tug on loyalties, it was Nixon by a landslide.

Yet nothing in 1968 stayed put for more than a month; and in October, events were to reduce George Wallace from a menace to an annoyance, and make of what seemed a sure-thing for Nixon the cliff-hanger that was appropriate to the year.

CHAPTER ELEVEN

OCTOBER: ALL PASSION SPENT

NORMALLY, in a Presidential year, the American autumn rises through crescendo to the roaring climax of late October. Crowds swell in the cities to the hundreds of thousands, schoolchildren line the streets of small towns with peppermint-striped flags, good friends, in anger, stop talking to each other, and the drunks brawl over their rival champions.

But in 1968 it was entirely otherwise. It was as if, all passion spent, an enormous indifference overtook the American people. It may be that new custom was slowly persuading American citizens to absorb politics over television in their homes; or it may be that, emotionally worn out by the events of the year, Americans pondered their preferences in private. But in 1968 no campaign songs echoed in any man's memories; it was a year when the pollsters reported ever increasing difficulty in interviewing citizens, who refused to talk politics; and when a national public-opinion survey brought back the news that 43 percent of all those polled said that, in their hearts, they preferred somebody else to the candidates offered them.

October 1968 offered, then, not a crescendo—but a diminuendo, a turning-back to habit, as old political patterns that had seemed a few weeks earlier to be utterly torn, slowly, instinctively reasserted themselves. Travel with the candidates in October, 1968, left few memories; no excitement surged to overcome weariness; what genuine interest one could develop, apart from the ultimate choice of President, was in how far, how fast, the natural counter-set of old loyalties would run. Americans were, in the end, to choose Nixon and the calm he offered the nation, opting for the orderliness which lay at the root of his personality and theme—but not until the natural drift of millions of Americans back to old standards had all but erased Nixon's September lead. And in tracing this counter-set, one cannot but return to Hubert Humphrey, for the month of October belonged to him.

* * *

September, for all Democrats, had been a month to be forgotten. From the day of their convention down to October 24th, their destitute National Committee had been unable to find the money to schedule even a single advertising spot on national radio or television for their candidate. Humphrey's voice, as he reeled around the country, might coin any phrase, reach any level of eloquence—but its chant carried no further than earshot in September. As he traveled, Party leaders fled him, as Republican Party leaders had fled Barry Goldwater in 1964, as if he were bearer of contagion. On his first trip to Texas, Governor John Connally had been too busy to greet him on arrival; in California, he had stumped the first week abandoned by Party leadership; in Connecticut, his old friend Senator Abraham Ribicoff kept a sanitary distance between himself and his Party's standard-bearer; in New York, the "reform" Democratic clubs seriously debated whether to "disendorse" him.

The month slowly, sickeningly for Humphrey, worsened as it approached its end. On September 27th, Humphrey received a forthcoming Gallup poll reporting Nixon fifteen points ahead of the Vice-President, by 43/28. And George Wallace, with 21, ran only seven points behind Humphrey himself! With this news, Humphrey flew on to Portland, Oregon, to face crowds, listless and apathetic, as small as several hundred. That night, outside his hotel, circled the protesters chanting, "Stop the War, Stop the War!" And with bitterness in his heart, Humphrey arrived in Seattle, Washington, on Saturday, September 28th, for another of those confrontations that had been lacerating him since Boston.

High in a corner of the Seattle Center Arena's balcony, to the right and rear the rowdies had gathered early, and a bloc of some 200 students, led by a tough with a bullhorn, were already roughing up the meeting by the time Humphrey arrived. "Fascist, Fascist!" they called the Vice-President. As he attempted first to conciliate them, then to argue with them, then to give the bullhorn man a time to speak, the meeting dissolved into chaos until, as their leader gave the signal and the gallery mob began the chant "Dump the Hump, Dump the Hump," the Secret Service decided it had gone far enough. Unceremoniously, Secret Service and policemen began to drag the marauders from the gallery and Humphrey was left to finish his speech, unreported and lost to the record.

In Humphrey's own memory, the night at Seattle was the turning point of his campaign. He had been badgered enough; he had been badgered by his Party, by the press, by rowdies; and now, returning to his hotel room, was being badgered further by a long-delayed text of a new position on Vietnam written by his staff. His mood swung that evening from deep melancholy to intense bitterness; alone in the room with his staff, he declared that the election of Richard Nixon would be a tragedy; mourned that the entire social fabric of the country was being rent; and concluded that somehow he must break through to be himself, if there were to be any hope of reviving the campaign.

The next day, Sunday, he flew to Salt Lake City and that evening, after the local politicians and well-wishers had been cleared from his room, sat down to consider Vietnam once more with his intimates: his staff members, Connell, VanDyk, Sherman, Welch; his favorite young Senator, Fred Harris; and Lawrence O'Brien and James Rowe, who had flown west to Salt Lake City for the late-night conference on Vietnam. On the side of the doves were O'Brien and Harris; supporting the commitment in Asia were Rowe and Connell. The doves felt the Party could not be unified and turned about unless Humphrey came out, flatly, for a bombing halt and peace. On the other side, Rowe led the insistence that nothing must be done to destroy the position of the American negotiators in Paris. All night, until almost four o'clock in the morning, they argued. "Everybody had his own point of view," recalled Humphrey, "everything we talked about, somebody said that will irritate the President, or that will irritate Teddy Kennedy, or that will irritate the McCarthy people, until I said to them, 'I don't care who it pleases, I'm going to write this speech the way I want it, and if people don't like the speech, that's the way it's going to be.' " And thus, until five in the morning of Sunday, Humphrey dictated the draft of what he proposed to say.

He began the next day, Monday, at a breakfast with Utah Democrats in Salt Lake City and told them, "If the elections were held today, we wouldn't have a prayer. You know it and I know it." Then he went to work once more on his Vietnam speech. By this time George Ball, having resigned as Johnson's Ambassador to the United Nations the week before to enlist with Humphrey, had arrived from Washington. In Washington Ball had dined the night before with Averell Harriman, America's chief negotiator in Paris. Bearing Harriman's wisdom, Ball went to work once more on the critical passage of the speech, the problem the same as ever: how to signal a *desire* to end the bombing, an *intent* to end the bombing, yet simultaneously not yield entirely to the enemy in the first stage of negotiation.

Not until mid-afternoon was the final draft ready. The Democratic National Committee had barely scraped together the necessary $100,000 for the first nationwide telecast it could finance for its candidate; and that night, September 30th, from Salt Lake City, Hubert Humphrey was to appear nationwide on television for the first time since his acceptance speech, the lectern stripped of his official Vice-Presidential seal and flag, Humphrey speaking not for Lyndon Johnson and the administration but for his own candidacy.

The famous Salt Lake City speech will go down in history as no great document of diplomacy. It was flawed, as every American speech on Vietnam has been flawed, by the American assumption that we were dealing with a reasonable Western enemy. But as a document in Humphrey's recapture of initiative, it was critical. Semantically, the variations of Humphrey's speech from previously announced administration and platform positions were so slight that one had to listen closely to the emphasis and style of Humphrey's personal delivery to detect them. Up until Salt Lake City, the position of the Democrats had been that any bombing halt in Vietnam must be coupled with reciprocity on the part of the enemy. Now, in a three point program, Humphrey declared that he would risk a complete bombing halt in the interests of peace, and then see what response might develop, reserving the right to resume bombing if no such response was clear.[1]

The change in phrasing of the American position had been small— of minor diplomatic import, of somewhat larger political importance, of greatest importance in the candidate's own esteem of himself. For years he had waited for the President's call, the President's instructions. Now, fifteen minutes before air time, with the final text of the speech already released to the press, the Vice-President initiated a call to the President to tell him what he was about to do. "I don't think this is going to impair your hand," said Humphrey to Johnson, "and it doesn't go as far as some people would like, but it goes a bit further than you would like." The President wanted to know how far Humphrey had actually gone, and Humphrey read the key passages from the text. The President wanted to know whether the proposed bombing halt was unconditional, and the Vice-President said the statement spoke for itself, urging the President to tune in the broadcast that was about to begin. "I'll listen," said the President, hanging up.

If the campaign of Hubert Humphrey could have been described, up to this point, as a campaign in search of a miracle, then the Salt Lake City speech was certainly no miracle.

Yet it was a turning point. Said Lawrence O'Brien, "The most important thing about the speech was the effect on Humphrey himself.

---

[1] "As President," said Humphrey, "I would stop the bombing of North Vietnam as an acceptable risk for peace because I believe it could lead to success in the negotiations and thereby shorten the war. This would be the best protection of our troops. In weighing that risk, and before taking action, I would place key importance on evidence of Communist willingness to restore the demilitarized zone between North and South Vietnam. Now if the government of North Vietnam were to show bad faith, I would reserve the right to resume the bombing. . . . Secondly, I would take the risk that the South Vietnamese would meet the responsibilities they say they are now ready to assume in their own self-defense; I would move, in other words, towards de-Americanization of the war. . . . Third, I would propose once more an immediate cease-fire, with United Nations or other international supervision, and supervised withdrawal of all foreign forces from South Vietnam."

He felt good about it, he was his own man." Equally important was the effect of the speech on the reporting of his campaign; Humphrey had, for so many weeks, been cast in the role of victim, that his first turnabout in role gave a major new twist to the melancholy reportage that had been cut to fit him. Most importantly of all: the speech had come at the proper time. A month had gone by since Chicago; blood feuds were cooling, passion abating; and millions of Democrats and hundreds of leaders were realizing that no other political home existed for them but Hubert Humphrey.

The upturn in the Humphrey campaign came episodically, slowly, then faster, then on a broad continental front. From Salt Lake City, Humphrey flew on to stump the Border states, and in Nashville, with relief, Humphrey could see student signs waving, THANK YOU MR. HUMPHREY; IF YOU MEAN IT, WE'RE WITH YOU; STOP THE WAR—HUMPHREY WE TRUST YOU—and no hecklers. As there were no hecklers in Boston a week later, where a group of Harvard students came out to greet him. As there were to be, by some mysterious alchemy of communication, few or no hecklers for the rest of the campaign.

Within forty-eight hours, more solid response began to come—the first flow of letters to the Democratic National Committee on Wednesday morning; swelling to 3,000 by afternoon; to 5,000 by Thursday. And these were letters bearing money in $5, $10 or $20 checks—money which a week later totaled over $250,000. Someone at Democratic headquarters had had the foresight to superimpose on the last minute of the Humphrey telecast an appeal for funds—and the appeal was to bring in two and a half times as much as the $100,000 the broadcast had cost. By October 10th, the first $1,000,000 had been contributed to the Humphrey campaign, and gradually the oscillation of money/public-opinion-polls impact began to reverse itself.

The Salt Lake City speech also gave Eugene McCarthy's supporters—if not McCarthy himself—a face-saving way to come home to their Party. On October 2nd, two days after the speech, it was reported that the McCarthy organization in Maryland was supporting Hubert Humphrey; the next day several New York reform clubs and the Student Leaders for McCarthy announced they, too, were coming back to the Party. On October 5th the Americans for Democratic Action, which Humphrey himself had helped found in 1947, announced that it, too, was coming home, and endorsed Humphrey by a vote of 71 to 16 of its executive board. Also that week ten Democratic Congressmen, hitherto McCarthy supporters, announced that they were publicly supporting their Party's nominee for the Presidency. The Dutch were reconquering Holland.

By mid-October the turn in Humphrey's fortunes was publicly apparent, as first the Harris poll reported that Humphrey had closed to within five points of Nixon (40/35) and then, more slowly, two Gallup polls narrowed the gap from the 15 points at the end of September to 12 points (43/31) by October 12th, to 8 points (44/36) by October 21st. With such signals, the Party leadership also began to close in support. By October 18th, John Connally of Texas was in line again—publicly promising all aid to his candidate and stumping Texas with him a week later; the next day, Abraham Ribicoff of Connecticut was also back in camp. And by the end of October, with the polls steadily closing, with columnists and commentators rousing themselves and the nation to the possibility of a close race, the money was coming in, too—of which, finally, $2,000,000 could be earmarked for television to let Humphrey and the Democrats match Richard Nixon and the Republicans, hour for hour, exposure for exposure in the last two weeks of the campaign.[2]

By the last ten days in October, the Humphrey campaign was rolling. One could not assemble Democratic veterans of such talent and experience as finally rallied to the Humphrey flag without producing combustion. Speech and research material now, finally, began to flow to the traveling campaign plane; sixty-three regional and state coordinators now reported each morning to O'Brien's headquarters in Washington; the dreary pattern of their reports were changing too. At the beginning of the month, no commentator had given Humphrey, for sure, more than 28 electoral votes; now, in the industrial East, came the first turn up. The *Boston Globe* reported in its poll that Massachusetts was in the bag for Humphrey; in Michigan, the *Detroit News* reported Humphrey neck and neck; in New York, the *Daily News* poll, opening in mid-October with a four-point Nixon lead, was within ten

[2] The problem of money still so haunts the veterans of the Humphrey campaign that their bitterness is worth underlining. "We could have won, and we should have won," Humphrey tells old friends who call these days. He will list the reasons for failure—the disaster of television coverage in Chicago, the rift with the McCarthy wing of the Party, the lack of a campaign plan. And then he will come down on money. "It's not the amount of money you get, it's when you get it," he says, for without sure money there can be no plan for media production or for programming. In the final week of the campaign, with $500,000 of sudden extra money for television, the Humphrey campaign managers found themselves literally unable to buy television time in California—all the time available for politics had been bought up by local and state candidates previously. "We finally got about five or six million dollars, all in all," recalls campaign manager O'Brien now; "if we'd finally gotten ten million dollars, we could have licked Nixon. And that scares me. The old tradition of sleeves-rolled-up volunteers may work in the primaries; but in a campaign there has to be more and more reliance on the fat cats who put up the money for the media, not on the volunteers. The impact of the media," continues O'Brien, "is the Democratic Party's major problem in the future, just the fantastic cost of the media. If we hadn't been able to match Nixon dollar for dollar in the last two weeks, this would have been the debacle everyone predicted. If you figure that by setting up a twenty-five-million-dollar media budget, and making a game of who gets the best time slots and who hires the most creative media talent— and if you elect a President that way, what the Hell's the country coming to?"

days reporting a shift to a four-point Humphrey lead. Pennsylvania was closing; so, too, was the state of Washington.

The quality of the campaign was now tauter, quicker, sharper, as the candidate, freed from hecklers and the drag of Vietnam, went to his natural rhythm and style, which was to attack, to challenge, to probe; and lustily he flailed at both opponents, drawing his own profile by contradiction, solidifying his Democrats by describing their alternatives.

Did they really want Wallace? he would ask of union men. To vote for Wallace was to vote for bloodshed, riot and hate—could they cast their votes for a racist? What was Wallace's record with the working people—how had union men fared in Alabama? What state had the highest murder rate in the nation? Alabama! What state had the highest sales tax in the nation? Alabama! Could anyone seriously entrust world peace to George Wallace and his running-mate, General Curtis LeMay, "the bombsy twins"?

Alternately, and with greater deftness, Humphrey would flail at Nixon—and the momentum of the last two weeks ran with him. The nation had heard all Nixon had had to say since early February, and now even the TV networks had difficulty finding novelties in his speeches. Debate, Humphrey demanded of Nixon, debate now! Richard the Chicken-Hearted became, variously, Richard the Silent, Richard the Worried, Richard the Last. Humphrey's speeches now were full of what he called, in homely fashion, "arousements." Thus:

"What has Richard Nixon ever done for old folks?"—"Nothing."
"What has Richard Nixon ever done for schools?"—"Nothing."
"What has Richard Nixon ever done for workingmen."—"Nothing."
"So what are you going to do for Richard Nixon?"—"Nothing!"

The organization in Washington was now on line, searching, researching, every crevice of a Nixon speech or statement for an attack opening. An injudicious Nixon campaign letter promising a relaxation of securities regulations became in Humphrey's counterattack a sell-out to Wall Street. An imprudent Nixon speech on October 24th raising, as Kennedy had done in 1960, the specter of a national security gap *vis-à-vis* the Russians was the springboard, overnight, for a slashing full-week attack by Humphrey on Nixon for toying with national security, undermining the confidence of America and its allies, for base partisan purposes.

An over-all theme now ran through the Humphrey campaign: the theme of Trust. Whom Can You Trust? Humphrey, Nixon or Wallace? The theme had come to Humphrey early in October, after the upturn, at a meeting and press conference in New York which he had shared with his running-mate, Senator Edmund Muskie. Muskie had proven himself an almost immeasurable asset to the campaign, an asset amplified and made greater each time the Republican opposite number, Spiro Agnew, caught the headlines in contrast. Muskie, a low-key, extraordinarily effective speaker in the New England style, had made trust—trust of people for government, trust of black for white and white for black, trust of Americans in Americans—his keynote. When, finally on the upturn in early October, Humphrey had absorbed the full value of his running-mate, he made the theme his own—and Humphrey could make it sing. Humphrey, in good voice, can make almost anything sing; and the proper time of day to hear him was always late in the evening—he would start the day sleepy-eyed and testy, build through five, six, seven, eight meetings, and then sometime between nine and eleven in the evening reach his peak.

He had begun, for example, on Friday, October 25th, in Los Angeles with an early-morning staff conference on Nixon's nuclear position, made a television appearance to denounce it (so as to catch the evening television shows), visited the Farmers' Market and been served lox-on-bagel for local television, addressed a suspicious student audience in San Jose State College, held a televised seminar with a group of California scientists, flown on to Las Vegas for an airport speech, and at Las Vegas, with two more speeches yet to go, as the sun set and the planes droned overhead, delivered himself of oratory which will serve as well as any to give the tone of the final Humphrey campaign:

> What is the question that is before the American people right now? Who can you trust? Listen to that precious word— who can you trust to lead this country in the next four years? ["Humphrey, Humphrey!"] Thank you, friends, I hope you will tell everybody. Who can you trust with the security of this nation and to win the peace that all of us want? ["Humphrey, Humphrey!"] And who can you trust to hold this wonderful country of ours together as one people and one nation, and who can lead this country forward?
>
> Now, our Republican friends have fought every piece of social legislation that has benefited this country, they have fought against social security, they have been against all forms of Federal aid to education, they have been against Medicare for our senior citizens. They have been against minimum wages. They have been against these great developments that have been so vital to the West, the great dams, the water conservation and the public power projects. You just name it, and I'll guarantee you that you will have found a majority of them in Congress against it. . . .
>
> The Democrats have been responsible for every piece of constructive legislation that has passed in these last thirty-five

years, and the Democrats have been responsible for all the legislation that has opened and developed this West in the last
thirty-five years. And anybody that lives out here ought to remember it and keep in mind the Democratic Party. . . .

When did you start to get so progressive, Mr. Nixon? All
your life you stood there and resisted and fought. You called
my party the party of treason—and he did. He fought Harry
Truman. He fought Roosevelt. He fought Kennedy and Stevenson. He fought Lyndon Johnson. And he fought me. And
I am going to lick him in this election. . . . Mr. Republican
is saying he's a friend of the workingman. Now that's news
for you, I'll guarantee you that—if he is a friend of the workingman, Scrooge is Santa Claus. . . .

When the Nixon Republicans were running this country in
the 1950's, they increased unemployment by two million, they
plunged the country into three profit-killing, job-killing depressions. And he says he is a friend of the workingman? I
want to tell you folks, better to have poison ivy any day.
. . . People need jobs, people have mortgages, they have
debts to pay, people want to send their sons and daughters
to college . . . and a man [Nixon] says he thinks that America could stand a little higher rate of unemployment. . . .

We have heard from several Nixons . . . kind of interesting. . . . We have the confident Nixon, vacationing in Florida's sunshine, taking the American people for granted. . . .
We have the statesman Nixon, who is above the battle for
peace—just cannot comment on anything; it's just something
he ought not to say anything about, way above it all. . . .
We have the liberal Nixon who . . . ended up when the
chips were down whistling Dixie by yielding to Strom Thurmond. . . . Then we have the Southern Nixon, basking under the magnolia blossoms, you know, reading the crime news
from the daily newspapers to the Southern audiences. And
then we have Sheriff Nixon. And then we have Professor
Nixon. And so on and so on. Mr. Agnew says that if you
have seen one slum, you have seen them all. Well, it was Mr.
Nixon's decision to choose Mr. Agnew, and if you have seen
one of Nixon's decisions, you have seen them all. . . .

The next President must hold this country together. . . .
He must help this nation find its conscience. . . . He must
create a society where dissent can be heard, where the poor
are helped, where the young are proud to be Americans.
. . . He must enforce the laws and he must ensure order.
. . . The next President must do everything he can to end.

the mad escalation of the nuclear arms race. . . . He must ensure the security of this nation even as we push forward step by step to a safer and saner world, a world which cannot be destroyed by one rash, erratic act, or one error in judgment . . . and these are the things I intend to do when you elect me your President. . . .

In memory, the mind's eye pulls back from such a scene, and the echo of Humphrey's voice, like a camera slowly withdrawing from a close-up, drawing back and back, to show the setting, then the larger scene, then the whole platform of the nation.

The Las Vegas speech had been good, as were the other terminal speeches—all there, all the themes: Trust. The Republican record. The Democratic record. Jobs. Peace. Harmony. It was warm in Las Vegas, and the audience had been dressed in sports shirts or summer dresses —but it was a middle-aged audience, a family audience, and the students few. It was a proper audience, laughing when Humphrey wanted them to laugh, being entertained and stirred and, above all, confirmed in what they wanted to believe. But, on departing, memory said that something was lacking—the wildness of enthusiasm that one remembered of other campaigns, the shriekings, the squealings, the jumpings, the mad roar of American politics when it is wild. And as the plane pulled up, and one passed over the twinkling paths of Las Vegas, the arteries of the pleasure capital of the West, they linked to all the other scenes one had seen across the country with the candidates: the nation bursting with an overburst of prosperity—the new schools, the new plazas, the new clearings for urban development, the great new auditoria and halls of a nation that had mounted crest after crest of prosperity and achievement in eight Democratic years. Humphrey had been part of this. But the mind drew away to other rallies—in downtown Los Angeles, the blacks and the old people and the workers, and Humphrey shrieking, his words bouncing from the walls, "I need your help, I need your help!" and people nodding. Or in New York at the garment center, in the last week, a huge crowd, five blocks of working-men and women standing shoulder to shoulder—but no wildness, no response to call, only the dutiful assent, the acknowledgment of faith. And everywhere, in every city, in every square, police and security agents posted on the rims of rooftops, with rifles and binoculars, blue gargoyles searching out hidden evil below, scenery entirely new to America. And never ever, in those last few weeks, that screaming passion which one remembered of the campaign of 1960, in both Kennedy and Nixon crowds, or the unbelievable swellings of Americans Lyndon Johnson gathered in 1964 when he was all hope and promise.

In those last few weeks, one could be seduced into comparing the

Humphrey campaign of 1968 with the Truman campaign of 1948. There was some substance to the comparison—but the analogy lay not in the crowds, which, though they grew, never reached the shouting coda of the "Give 'em Hell, Harry" climax of the earlier campaign. The analogy lay in the spectacle of a man who insisted on being true to himself, the personality emerging from under the carapace of scar tissue, preaching the faith by which he had lived and by which he sought to govern. The faith was the same faith as that of Harry Truman, the faith of the perfect liberal; what spoiled the analogy was that the country to which it was preached had so much changed. The nation had heard this faith for twenty years, had accepted it, applied it, grown prosperous under it and, in 1964, given it its final mandate in an expression of trust unparalleled.

But now, in 1968, the perfect faith had become a sterile orthodoxy —and an orthodoxy questioned. All those triumphs of the past of which Humphrey boasted had indeed given the nation fatter payrolls, better schools, longer vacations, more homes, finer hospitals, satellites in orbit, highways and dams across the land. But the faith had also brought unending war abroad, riot and disorder at home, and the streets were unsafe to walk. In 1948 and in 1964 the Democratic candidates, believing in their faith as a holy cause, had sought and received a national mandate, expanding the base of the Democratic Party to an overwhelming national majority. But Humphrey's crusade was not an attempt to expand his base—his crusade was simply to bring the Democrats back to their own church.

There was no perspective at any time of a national mandate in the planning of the Humphrey campaign. The roaring landslide that had swept the Democrats to power in 1964 was now ancient history; the Democrats had lost the confidence of the nation, they were to be a minority; they had no hope of winning a majority either in the Electoral College or among the people. Their only hope was to regroup enough of the scattered loyalties of the old coalition to force the final choice of President into the House of Representatives—and that meant an effort, above all, to recapture the key element of the old coalition, the workingmen of the Northern cities whom George Wallace had, at the end of September, seemed about to capture.

There was always a symbiotic relationship between the Humphrey campaign and the Wallace campaign—for if Humphrey preached Trust, Wallace preached Distrust; when one gained, the other faltered; when one surged, the other diminished. The Humphrey surge of October was, thus, the counterpart of the Wallace diminuendo.

There were any number of ways to approach this strange relationship.

The cruelest way was to strip the euphemisms and get down to the naked issue of race and hate, which George Wallace had made his own—and then compare the impact of that issue on the two campaigns of 1964 and 1968. The 1964 triumph of Lyndon Johnson had come about by a majority of 61 percent to 38 percent. If one breaks these percentages down by the thrust of race, one comes up with the guess that of Johnson's 61 percent in 1964, 51 percent was delivered by white people—centrists, moderates, Democratic loyalists, disaffected Republicans—and 10 percent by blacks. Of the Goldwater total of 38 percent, one can, by subtraction, estimate that he received some 24 percent from conservative, nationalist, hereditary white Republicans—and 14 percent (the ultimate racist vote of George Wallace in 1968) from white racists who hate blacks. This gives the polarizing extremes in the nation—10 percent black votes, 14 percent white racist votes, leaving in the election of 1968 some 75 percent in the middle to be divided.

In 1968, Nixon conspicuously, conscientiously, calculatedly denied himself all racist votes, yielding them to Wallace. He started thus with a 24-percent white traditionalist Republican base inherited from Goldwater, and added to it immediately another 17 or 18 percent of moderate or centrist Republicans who four years earlier had deserted to Johnson. But Nixon was never from August to election day to go above a total of 45 percent of the American people. He could not expand his base.

Humphrey, on the other hand, entered on his October surge from a level which all political history insisted he must expand. At his September low of roughly 30 percent of the electorate, 10 percent, certainly, were black voters—which meant that he held appeal only to 20 percent of American white voters, less than half of those whom Richard M. Nixon held, in the broad center span of American decency. It was impossible to conceive that the great Democratic Party of the United States would rest at that low; and as the Democratic Party pulled itself together, and the media began to alert the nation to the dimensions of the Wallace appeal, the counter-set began.

The main stimulant of the counter-set came, of course, from the Humphrey campaign; its theme, as we have seen, was Trust; its voice Humphrey's; and its tactics quite simple: to split the loyalties and conscience of the angry white workingmen who waved Wallace banners, pasted Wallace labels on their lunchpails, covered bumpers with Wallace stickers. "Let's lay it on the line," said Humphrey in Detroit, "George Wallace's pitch is racism. If you want to feel damn mean and ornery, find some other way to do it, but don't sacrifice your country. George Wallace has been engaged in union-busting whenever he's had the chance . . . and any union man who votes for him is not a good union man."

Other forces, however, began to converge against Wallace as his September peaks spread alarm. The polls, with their figures, had alerted the national media to the potential in Wallace. The media, trying to document the Wallace campaign in words and pictures, began to spread the image of a man not mastering disorder in the nation, but provoking it where he went. The headlines of his rallies could no longer report the same unending speech against the "pointy-heads"; they read from early October on, at random, thus: TENNESSEE MOB BEATS BOY WHO SASSED WALLACE. WALLACE OFFICE TARGET FOR BOMB (California). HECKLERS THROW EGGS, APPLE CORE AT WALLACE IN OSHKOSH (Wisconsin). CLASHES MAR WALLACE RALLY IN DETROIT. WALLACE SHAKES UP THE GARDEN (New York). POLICE CLUB LEFTISTS AFTER WALLACE RALLY (Cleveland, Ohio). FIGHTS BREAK OUT AS HECKLERS DISRUPT WALLACE RALLY IN TEXAS.

Louis Harris, in a post-election analysis, gives a graphic picture of the cumulative effect of this reporting as media and press began to expose, in nature and detail, the Wallace phenomenon at the beginning of October.

Through spring and summer Wallace had cut, in the Harris polls, a profile on the American public mind that either major candidate might have envied. At his peak, in September, Harris found half of all those he polled praising George Wallace "for saying it the way it really is." Even more agreed that "liberals, intellectuals, and long-hairs have run the country for too long." Over 80 percent said the Alabaman had "the courage of his convictions." An almost unbelievable 53 percent agreed that "Wallace would handle law-and-order the way it ought to be handled, if elected President." Sentiments such as these had carried Wallace in successive polls from 9 percent (early May), to 11, to 14, to 16, to 18, to 21 percent.

Now, at the end of September, as every alarm bell rang and every whistle blew, it was as if some unseen voice had called "About face." The number who thought Wallace was the best man for law-and-order began to shrink in the Harris poll from its high of 53 percent to 43, to 33, to 24, to 21. As media made clear the cold Wallace message, stripping "folksiness" from him, those who could not accept the label "racist" for themselves grew—and voters who thought Wallace a "racist" rose from 40 to 51 to 59 to 67 percent; in harmony, those who thought of him as an "extremist" rose from 51 to 56 to 62 to 69. Conversely, from his September high, Wallace began to drop—from 21 to 18 to 16 to 13.

But an even more formidable force than public opinion was coming to bear on the Wallace movement in October: the power of organized labor. Labor's support and labor's money had been essential to every Democratic national campaign since 1936—but never did those who lead labor perform more effectively, more skillfully, with greater impact, than in 1968. In the near-miracle of the Humphrey comeback in October, no single factor was more important than the army of organized labor, roused to the greatest political exertion of its history.

In a sense, the challenge of Wallace had been a challenge to the leadership of labor itself. Their own membership polls had, as early as midsummer, shown Wallace picking up 25 percent of the labor vote in Pennsylvania, 32 percent in Connecticut, in Maryland even higher. By September, in Flint, Michigan, at the large Buick plant there, a poll of the 8,000 autoworkers in Local 599 showed Wallace outstripping both other candidates with 49 percent of the total; in Norfolk, Virginia, the Wallace challenge within the union was the springboard in an attempt to overthrow the local's internal leadership; in Pennsylvania, in Baltimore, in Gary, steelworkers were breaking to Wallace. Totally dismayed by the early confusion in Humphrey's headquarters in Washington, the AFL/CIO leadership considered its support of the Democrat and its drive against Wallace almost a mission of its own. "We had to do what we did," said Lane Kirkland, executive assistant of the AFL/CIO's president, "because the Party was bankrupt intellectually and financially. I reached the point where I said I'd never go into Democratic headquarters. I'd go in feeling good and come out feeling terrible. The only useful thing they did was television, in the last couple of weeks; and beyond that they didn't do a god-damned thing except cry."

Refusing to cry, the AFL/CIO set out immediately after the convention, therefore, for a classic exercise. The strategy was homely and time-honored: to register working people, then get them out to vote. But the results, effort and techniques were staggering. Volunteers card-punched names of union members across the country, by state, county and precinct. Computers in Washington digested names, spewed them out broken down by walking lists, arranged by street numbers; volunteers, trained by the Communications Workers Union, manned telephones; others rang doorbells. Appalled at the official Party's disarray, the AFL/CIO assumed responsibility for getting out the black vote—and set up special units, grinding out special literature and special appeals in thirty-one black communities across the nation. The dimension of the AFL/CIO effort, unprecedented in American history, can be caught only by its final summary figures: the ultimate registration, by labor's efforts, of 4.6 million voters; the printing and distribution of 55 million pamphlets and leaflets out of Washington and 60 million more from local unions; telephone banks in 638 localities, using 8,055 telephones, manned by 24,611 union men and women and their families; some 72,225 house-to-house canvassers; and, on election day, 94,457 volunteers serving as car-poolers, materials-distributors, baby-sitters, poll-watchers, telephoners.

Wherever an "unexpected" Humphrey surge developed, there, un-derbracing it, was the effort of COPE (the AFL/CIO's Committee on Political Education): in Pennsylvania, 492,000 voters were registered by COPE, 4,000 unionists were enlisted for house-to-house canvass detail; in Michigan, 690,000 voters were registered by COPE, and thirty phone banks with 275 telephones manned by 550 volunteers urged workingmen to vote Humphrey. One could trace labor's efforts all across the country: steel workers, packinghouse workers, auto workers in Illinois; auto workers, machinists and service trades in California; oil workers in Texas; garment workers, building trades and electricians in New York. (In New York, one of the afternoon rendezvous points of one group of union leafleters and canvassers was the front door of Nixon's headquarters on the corner of Park and 57th.) Though labor's expenditure of money was impressive—perhaps $10,000,000 for all political activity in 1968 —more impressive, more useful for Humphrey were the manpower and the message.

By late October, labor's effort had begun to ravage the Wallace base in the North. Wallace as a "friend of the workingman" was a phony, ran the theme of the 20,000,000 pieces of specifically anti-Wallace literature distributed—his state was sucking off union plants from the North to fill them with non-union workers in the South; Alabama's child-labor laws were a mockery of decency; his Alabama was one of only sixteen states in the union with no minimum-wage legislation; his state ranked forty-ninth in the union in welfare payments to dependent children; his highway patrol was a union-busting outfit. If you're a bus driver, said the literature, you'd make thirty bucks less a week in Birmingham than in a Northern city; if you were a carpenter, you'd make forty bucks less a week; if you were a schoolteacher, you'd make $2,000 to $4,000 less in Alabama's schools than in the North. Thus, as Hubert Humphrey appealed to the consciences of white work-ingmen in the public squares and on radio and TV, labor's leadership drove home the split in conscience Humphrey's eloquence had wedged open by more direct appeal. A workingman could choose to go with racist George Wallace—but to do so he must desert all other traditional loyalties and his own interests; or he could choose to go with Hubert Humphrey and swallow Humphrey's attitude to the blacks. The argu-ment began to tell on thousands; by the end of October even Flint's Local 599 had reversed itself and come out for Hubert Humphrey.

To the undoing of George Wallace, moreover, George Wallace himself contributed. Like Daley and Romney before him, George Wallace never understood the national press or national television; wiser counsel than the country boys who attended him might have polished or presented him better; wiser planning might have made his last six weeks' effort less of a circus. Constructive thought might have given him just a touch of that dignity which every American, no matter how primitive, seeks in a President. But if one must choose a turning-point blunder in the Wallace campaign, a final error-in-decision after which no recapture was possible, then, in my opinion, it was a blunder of Wallace's personal decision—Wallace's choice, as Vice-Presidential running-mate, of General Curtis LeMay.

LeMay, almost indefinably, ran counter to the quality of the Wallace campaign. There was essentially something of the enlisted man in George Wallace's personality; it was there in his discourse, in his attitudes, in his strange, needling irreverence for authority combined with the enlisted man's tongueless patriotism and antique nationalism. The crowds he drew reflected this quality—they were also, overwhelmingly, those of whom America makes enlisted men. In moving through the Wallace crowds at his rallies, a peculiar rending of emotion had always come to me—they were at once so familiar, and so dangerous. Their faces, their voices, their bearing were those of men I had known and loved twenty-five years before when I lived with and reported the armed forces of the United States during World War II. The fathers of these men had been the dog-faces, the marines, the seabees, the tank corps, the Willies and Joes who had broken the back of Nazis, Fascists and Japanese—they had been my people during the war, friendly and warm, yet enormously dangerous and willing to kill. Curtis LeMay did not belong to such Willies and Joes. I cannot remember ever hearing American GI's, during the great war, speak as home-front propagandists would have had them: full of hate for Fascism, or dying for Mom and apple pie. If they had energy left over for talk at night, or if the conversation got away from girls, grub and guns, their anger would be directed not at the enemy but at the brass. Certain generals were exempted from their irritation—notably men like Eisenhower, Bradley, Chennault. MacArthur amused them by his flamboyance. But most generals were hated—notably Patton and Curtis LeMay. Meeting Curtis LeMay, as I had in Asia, one could not but instantly respect him then, and later, in restrospect, recognize how great a debt the Republic-in-arms owed to him. But one could not love him; and the men of his command loathed the harsh, unsparing, iron discipline by which he made the United States Air Force the supreme instrument of annihilation it became in the skies of Japan.

It had seemed to me, in my observations of George Wallace and his rally audiences, that Wallace was, if anything, a GI candidate. His supporters were the gun-bearers of the United States Army, who come off the assembly lines of our factories, from off its farm tractors, from the men who erect steel, from the men who hump cargo across the wharves. And to these, as well as the policemen, the firemen, the taxi drivers, Wallace was talking. It seemed to me, therefore, from the third day of October, when George Wallace announced in Pittsburgh that he was choosing General Curtis LeMay as his running-mate, that he had misread his own constituency. It was not so much that Curtis LeMay was a political mute, or that he was a man whose harsh prose frightened everyone (he had boasted that the United States could, if it would, and probably should, "bomb the North Vietnamese back to the Stone Age") but that Curtis LeMay was, in the enlisted man's eye, of the essence of the military establishment; and the campaign of George Wallace was basically set as much against all establishments as was the McCarthy movement. LeMay could bring no strength or eloquence to the Wallace ticket; he could only shake the emotions of those who sought, in George Wallace, to upset the American structure that had let them down.

This is a purely personal view. There was so much else going against George Wallace—the Humphrey drive, the alarm of the media, the organization of labor. But from the first week in October and the choice of Curtis LeMay, every poll, every sampling, even the very spirit of the Wallace campaign appeared to change. Down he went, gurgling, first in the Harris poll, then in the Gallup poll, followed by every other index, until finally, on election day, his vote was set by Americans at 9.9 million. And the peril with which he had threatened the two-party system appeared, for the year 1968 at least, to have been smothered by the much-maligned electoral system ordained by the United States Constitution.

It would be unwise to leave the story of George Wallace there, in diminuendo in late October of 1968. For Wallace, as a voice, may have been a matter of dark comedy. But what the voice called up from the American spirit in 1968 may become part of a somber future which Americans prefer to ignore.

For over a century, all major third parties in America have risen from the left. Not since the Know-Nothings in the 1850's has there been a significant national eruption of the right. From the Green-Backers and Populists on, discontent with American life has expressed itself through those of new visions. Theodore Roosevelt's Bull Moose ticket in 1912 snared 27.4 percent of the national vote; Robert LaFollette's Progressives snared 16.6 percent of the vote in 1924. Most of their new thinking was absorbed and later programmed as law by the major parties of the United States. Parties of the right have always been negligible —Father Coughlin's right-wing candidate, William Lemke, managed in 1936 to gather less than 2 percent of the national vote, and Strom Thurmond in 1948, running as a sectional segregationist, won only infinitesimally more: 2.4 percent, or 1,169,000 Southern votes.

But George Wallace in 1968 was different. His vote, which was to reach 14 percent of the national total, was *not* a sectional vote. That part of it which was Southern could, of course, be easily identified in the Old South pattern of prejudice. But of his 9.9 million votes, only 5.8 million came from the South. No less than 4.1 million came from the Northern and Western states; and these were, overwhelmingly, white workingman votes. Despite all the influences of the media, all the pressure of their labor leaders, all the blunders and incompetence of the Wallace campaign, they had voted racist. In 1964 their disturbance of spirit had been absorbed in the Goldwater vote. But in 1968 their convictions stood out, by their presence in public squares, and by the vote totals in the precincts, stark, clear—and alienated.

What George Wallace demonstrated was that of all those alienated with the set of American government, perhaps the largest group were the white workingmen of America; and in so demonstrating, George Wallace uncovered a reality that will be of concern for years.

Abandoned by the liberal voices, and the intellectual sponsors who made the workingmen of America their wards in the 1930's, white workingmen find now, in the public dialogue of America, almost no expression of their problems. The whole rub of the past eight years in American experimentation has been a rub against the condition of the white workingmen.

The white workingmen—at least, the union men—have now all but conquered the conditions of their work. For most, their unions have made their hours in their working places the best part of the day—air-conditioned, clean, safe. At the plant, the condition of life is better controlled for American workingmen by their union leaders than in any other country of the world. But when they go home from work, they enter another world—the community of the neighborhood, of their kin, of their ethnic groups. And this home-community world is no longer under any control they can affect.

In the age of experiment, as social theorists press government on to ends yet untested, it is the white workingman whose sense of community is most abused. From the tree-shaded streets of suburbia, the white middle class can insulate itself—by zoning and money—from the stress and strain of experiment, from the fear of violence. The white workingman and the white poor feel defenseless against such experiments; and since the cutting edge of all such experiments is the clash of black and white, the experiments seem to subject them, as powerless test-tube material, to an intermingling of race for which nothing in their education has prepared them. It is their neighborhoods that must be broken up by public housing that will drive them out and install blacks; it is their children, not middle-class children, who must be bussed; it is the streets on which their old ladies walk to midnight mass that become dangerous because of purse-snatchers; it is they who must, in their lives, pay in daily worries for the guilt of white slavers centuries ago. The fathers of these workingmen had come from Europe a generation ago, or they themselves had fled the South. What they had earned —the fat paycheck, the house, the school, the quiet neighborhood—they had earned by playing the rules. Now, from Washington, for eight years, the rules had been undergoing change. But change not for the rich or the well-to-do or the comfortable—only for them, and for their communities.

It was from such people that George Wallace drew his vote— denouncing the experimental government of Washington and twinging the nerves of race hate at the same time. A wiser politician, a shrewder campaigner, might have made more of the resources of alienation. But for so poor a campaign to harvest so large a vote, diminished as it was from its high, was to present to the future and the next administration a problem of politics as explosive as the Negro revolt itself. But in October, 1968, Richard M. Nixon, who would head that administration, had no other choice but to ignore that future problem.

The changing temper of the campaign had become apparent to the Nixon staff from mid-October on—not as crisis, not as cause for panic, but as the shadow of something new and indiscernible approaching. While the public polls—normally published five days to a week after the actual dates of their sampling—still showed the Republicans comfortably ahead, Nixon's own sensitive polling apparatus had, from the first week of October, begun to pick up the same ominous turnings that in a few days would be obvious to all. Nixon insiders refused to call it "slippage" until much later; in early October it was still called "movement." And thus, for the sixth time since the beginning of the year, Nixon enplaned for his hideaway at Key Biscayne and summoned his staff to review matters.

Those matters that were tactical could easily be dispatched in the three-day session:

§ Nixon, the longest-surviving public figure in the contest of 1968, had now worn his themes and proposals bare; and from the press came the normal and insistent clamor, chronic to all editorialists, for more discussion of issues, more specifics, more clear programs. To meet this attack, Nixon and staff thus decided at Key Biscayne on a series of ten nighttime radio broadcasts in the next three weeks—serious, scholarly, thoughtful discourses on welfare, youth, education, arms, peace and those other holy subjects of American politics. These were to be assigned by James Keogh to the speech-writing and research staffs, to be written, edited, drawn up and taped for radio broadcast while the candidate, live, staged TV happenings about the country. In addition, two instant books were ordered (the first to be published in six days) giving *Nixon on the Issues* and *Nixon Speaks Out* to the nation.

§ Humphrey's goading of "Sir Richard the Chicken-Hearted" to debate had begun to grip public fancy, and the Nixon staff had to face that. It was decided that Nixon would now lash back at Humphrey—he had played above the battle until this point; but all agreed there could be no debate. Nixon was still far enough ahead in the polls not to *need* a debate; and the memory of the Kennedy-Nixon debates of 1960 still admonished them from the past.

§ Certain previously hoped-for states—like Michigan and New York—seemed to be weakening, and the schedule was revised to stress more heavily travel in the big seven states.

§ There was the Agnew problem. A doleful and candid report from Patrick Buchanan, just returned from traveling with the Agnew party, was heard by the candidate. Agnew had by now made a fool of himself—not so much out of malice or stupidity as, simply, by a coarseness of fiber, an insensitivity which he, as a second-generation American, might above all have been expected to eschew. Coarseness in low-level office is sometimes amusing, but coarseness at the head of the American government is almost, in itself, disqualification for leadership. Agnew himself would have bristled at being called "the Greek"; but he had called Polish-Americans "Polacks," called a Japanese correspondent "the fat Jap"; had blurted out, early in the campaign, that Humphrey was "soft on Communism"; had stated that "if you've seen one city slum, you've seen them all." The best Buchanan could report to Nixon was that Agnew might, with some training and some hard seat-of-the-pants application, eventually turn out to be a reliable Vice-President; but, for the moment, it was best to ice Agnew and keep him under wraps. Agnew could not compete with the dry, sensitive composure of Humphrey's choice, Muskie, who was being more warmly received about the country than his head of ticket. It was possible to launch an attack on Muskie's record, some in the Nixon camp thought; but if the charges remained unproven, the attack might kick back; and the idea was discarded.

§ The Nixon staff recognized an old and dangerous echo of the 1964 campaign—the Democratic attack on Goldwater's hostility to Social Security. Humphrey and the Democrats had begun to hammer away, within the frame of their "trust" theme, at Republican indifference to Social Security and Medicare. Nixon would, therefore, not only stress his support of the present Social Security system but promise a better one.

All these, however, were tactical decisions, easily made. But elections, unlike primaries or conventions, cannot be won, and are not decided, by tactics. Elections are between the people and the candidate, involving realities larger than those any single speech or any single gambit can alter. And reality had forced Richard M. Nixon into a trap. His own ultimate purpose and fundamental planning had constructed the trap—but now there was no way out.

Nixon would be President. He wished to be a great President, and great Presidents are those who govern. But no President would be able to govern Americans at all in 1969 whose way to the Presidency in 1968 had further embittered and divided an American people already far too embittered and divided. Thus, Nixon's conundrum: to enlarge his base by appeal to the Wallace voters of the racist right might swing to Nixon those key states where they held the balance vote and also, conceivably, give him a popular majority. But such an appeal to racism, open or covert, was entirely alien to his conscience; and it would also guarantee that when he came to power, he would be hated by the submerged black tenth of the nation, and no bridge of good-will could ever link them again to the Federal government so long as he led it. Blocked thus on the right, Nixon was equally blocked to his left. To enlarge his base to the left was impossible. Even Hubert Humphrey was finding it difficult to out-promise the actual, ongoing programs of Lyndon Johnson; to try to rival Humphrey in appeal to labor or left would be to shake away Nixon's own conservatives on the right side of center whom he must keep. Trapped thus in the center, Nixon must remain in the center, and in American politics the center is where men come to rest while romance calls them out to depart the center for activity on the extremes.

Even graver, as a reality, was the Vietnam war. Humphrey had now, in Salt Lake City, spoken out on the war. By the alchemy of politics, the Democrat who had been denounced by the peace-seekers in Chicago in August as a war-hawk was now emerging in October as the peace candidate himself. Several times Nixon had considered early in the year a major statement on Vietnam; his last effort to establish a Vietnam position had been written and edited and radio time had been booked for it on Saturday, March 30th, when announcement of Johnson's coming national broadcast of renunciation on the 31st caused Nixon to cancel his own. From then on, Nixon had been firm: he would not in any way express himself on Vietnam policy while negotiations were going on. He was urged by one or two members of staff, again and again in October, to speak on Vietnam, but he would not. There was a high content of small-town emotionalism, of old-fashioned patriotism in Nixon's attitude; but there was also a very shrewd executive attitude. He meant to be President; despite the "move-ment" in the voter preferences, it still seemed certain that he *would* be President; the executive mantle, with all its responsibilities, seemed about to enwrap him. Thus he would not bind himself now, for cam-paign purposes, in policies or positions that would tie his hands, and perhaps cost lives, once he did become President.

Tactics thus could be modulated to the needs of the campaign; but strategy could not; and strategy, therefore, as the group departed from Key Biscayne, was reduced to the ancient ballad of American elections:

the "ins" against the "outs," a choice of more of the same or something new, left undefined.

There was, as one resumed traveling with Nixon after the strategy session of Key Biscayne, little fresh that one could report. A new slogan replaced the worn-out NIXON'S THE ONE. Now the banners read THIS TIME VOTE LIKE YOUR WHOLE LIFE DEPENDED ON IT. The attack on Humphrey was punchier; Humphrey was an "adult delinquent," Humphrey was "the fastest, loosest tongue in the West." Humphrey had "his hand in your pocket." The "forgotten man" theme was downplayed; it was now, in a dozen different variations, simply "turn the rascals out."

The campaign moved smoothly, as always. The techniques of the advance men improved—from airport greetings at arrival, to the multiplicity of balloons, to internal communications, to the phalanxes of pretty Nixon girls with their slim legs and blond hair who were seated in rectangles, front-center, before the cameras to screen the few hecklers from national view. It was all smooth, pre-programmed, efficient. And yet, occasionally there would still come a day to remind that a Presidential contest remained a personal matter between a leader and his people.

Such a day was the one that closed at dusk in Deshler, Ohio, in late October. We had been traveling all day by train north from Cincinnati, through industrial Ohio toward Toledo. Whistle-stop campaigning in America has been obsolete since Harry Truman's campaign of 1948, but candidates still toss a salute to the past by a railway excursion now and then; and the rail journey through Ohio is classic. I had accompanied Nixon in 1960 over exactly the same route,[3] and was following him now both for comparison with the past and to see what effect the Key Biscayne strategy might have on his behavior.

The trip was obviously planned for TV coverage; by now the TV cameras had become tired of Mr. Nixon's normal procedure and required new happenings to enliven the audiences ("One thing we decided in Key Biscayne," said William Safire, "is that the campaign needed some excitement"). The trip would also, in accord with the Key Biscayne plan, step up the stress on the theme of law-and-order.

Yet there was more to it than that. All day we drummed along the railway tracks fringed by paradox. The factories spewed smoke, their parking lots were crowded, trucks carrying away cargo and product in unending stream. But wherever the train pulled to a halt in the old downtown centers, one could observe the boarding up of the railway stations, the decay of the central business districts which had grown up on the rails because they were arteries of life. The old downtown centers of community were husks that had been gutted by change. The people

[3] See The Making of the President—1960, pp. 300–302.

who gathered at the rallies were prosperous, well-dressed, sober, in robust health. But they were afraid, and whenever Nixon spoke of crime, they cheered ("When Richard Nixon got finished," wrote Jimmy Breslin, "there was a strangler's hand coming out of every cornfield in Ohio"). All day we journeyed through peaceful countryside spotted with the sycamores, wild oaks and hardwoods of the great valley. But all day the view from Mr. Nixon's rear observation car as it rattled north could be seen only through the silhouette of the three Secret Service agents standing shoulder to shoulder on the observation platform, searching the receding tracks and the beautiful land for snipers who might kill.

We came to Deshler, Ohio, a town of about 2,000, after dark, and Mr. Nixon emerged on the platform in a tan topcoat, shivering in the chill. Deshler is famous for its feed grains, its tomato-production and its seed corn. A huge grain elevator to which farmers bring shelled corn is its outstanding monument, and along the tracks, nubbles of red-gold-yellow-white kernels lay thick as pebbles, where trucks had spilled them; an Ohio reporter told me that the best pheasant-shooting in the neighborhood lay along the tracks because the pheasants grew fat here on spilled kernels. Deshler much more than Los Angeles, Key Biscayne or Manhattan is Nixon's spiritual country, and so in this, his eighth speech of the day (with two more to come), he could talk plain language. He did his crime passage, the media theme for the day ("I was looking at some figures that my staff had prepared for me on the forty-five-minute train ride from Lima up here [to Deshler]. . . . In forty-five minutes, just forty-five minutes . . . here is what happened in America. There was one murder, there were two rapes, there were forty-one forcible crimes . . . ,"etc.). Then, in a brief burst at the close, he tried to sum up his campaign: "I want you to remember, my friends, that at the moment when you vote, you are going to determine your future, your peace, peace at home, you are going to determine whether or not you are going to have real income or imaginary income. You are going to determine whether America again is respected in the world or whether it's not. You are going to determine whether America is to go forward with new leadership or whether we are going to be satisfied with leadership that has failed us, that has struck out on every count."

It was the standard speech, of course. But I was most taken by the fact that Nixon delivered so much of the talk with his eyes shut, lids closed either out of weariness or against the TV lights that shone in his face. He rocked back and forth as he spoke, like a revivalist. I could not help wondering what a Presidential candidate saw at night at the end of a campaign through closed eyes, in a railway depot, in a town of 2,000—or whether he saw anything. Only later did I realize that Richard Nixon really had been seeing. Later that evening he telephoned Finch in California, as he so often did, to assess the day. It had been a good tour, he told Finch, the crowds along the route had been better than 1960. But the people in the crowds were so much older than in 1960, said Nixon—the young people must be leaving the farms and small towns, they were going to the cities. He had noticed that. A lot of thinking had to be done about this after the election, he concluded. Deshler recurred to Nixon again, still later. Through his closed eyes that evening he had, apparently, seen a young girl somewhere in the crowd holding up a sign that few of the rest of us saw. BRING US TOGETHER, it read. It must have summarized what he had learned in a year of campaigning in America in 1968, for he was to recall it in his victory remarks the morning after his election, and then make it the theme of his inaugural and administration.

The Richard Nixon whom I had followed up the same tracks in 1960 had been a divider, one of the most intensely partisan, sharply competitive men in American politics. The Richard Nixon who traveled along the same tracks, through the same towns, in 1968 remembered most sharply of the year: BRING US TOGETHER, and had decided he would be a healer. Rather than divide, he would risk his election.

October is the melancholy month, and in 1968 it was particularly so. Of October in America in 1968, the most cheerful memory history may recall is that after a year and a half of hiatus, our astronauts ventured once more into space, testing Apollo 7 on the first real try for the moon—and after eleven days came back safely, ready for the final march.

But meanwhile, back on earth, matters went worse. In the country's greatest city, a high-minded but hasty experiment had brought New York to flirt with disaster by setting black against white in the schools; a million children were deprived of learning for weeks, and the sense of authority crumbled. It crumbled in city after city as the children went back to school and learned to hate each other. The war went on; each Thursday evening the accounting of death in Vietnam flashed on screen. Abroad, the world offered little more of the solace of reason. The Russians were armoring the Egyptians for another effort to exterminate the Israelis; Biafra was starving, but no one had the stomach to intervene in a quarrel of blacks against blacks so far away.

On October 14th the 90th Congress of the United States closed its work. The 90th Congress will not be remembered, as the bold 89th will be, for its creations. The 90th Congress had been buffeted by events, as were all other Americans, and its chief accomplishments had come in response to events. It had passed open-housing legislation—but only under the shock of Martin Luther King's assassination. It had imposed a 10-percent surtax on the Federal income tax—but only under the shock of the spring dollar crisis. It had passed legislation controlling the sale of guns by mail order—but only under the shock of the

assassination of Robert F. Kennedy. It had postponed deliberation on
the Nuclear Non-Proliferation Treaty—but only under the shock of
Russia's invasion of Czechoslovakia. It had indeed increased aid to
education, passed more consumer and conservation legislation—but
these measures were only the final winding down of the original great
impulses of the Johnson triumph of 1964; that mandate had run out.
The war in Vietnam had eroded the mandate; and now, in October, the
politics of the last fortnight of the campaign of 1968 were to be shaped
not by what America's Congress had done, or failed to do, but by events
far overseas in Vietnam.

As so often before in 1968—as in the month of March, or as at the
Chicago convention—events in the final weeks of October moved on so
many tracks at once that whatever way one chooses to sort them out
distorts the picture. Yet the war in Vietnam, which had opened the year
with the Tet offensive, was now to dominate and make total chaos of its
last two weeks; and it is with the story of the war, rather than with the
behavior or response of the candidates, that one must seek the thread
of clarity in the campaign.

The background of October's events had been shaped by the negotiations in Paris. There, by July, two able Americans—Averell Harriman, chief negotiator, and Cyrus Vance, his deputy—had identified
what they thought were the basic considerations rising from the long
summer deadlock.

For the North Vietnamese, obviously, the first priority was the
stopping of the bombing of their territory; to this priority they attached,
publicly, the phrase "unconditional." For the Americans, the first priority had come to be the involvement of the South Vietnamese government in negotiations, for if South Vietnam did not participate in
agreement, no agreement in Paris would be of the slightest value.
Further, the South Vietnamese could not be expected to participate
unless there was a guarantee of the safety of their cities from attack as
a counterpart for promising the North Vietnamese similar safety for
their cities from our bombs. But no written *quid pro quo* formula would
work, for North Vietnamese face-saving required the public term "unconditional," and the dilemma of formalities had to be solved before
one could even test the greater dilemmas of settlement in substance.

By September, therefore, under the influence of Harriman and
Vance, a working position had been accepted in Washington: We would
state our "intention" to stop bombing; we would simultaneously, but
secretly, make clear to the enemy our "expectation" of the counterpart.
But we would insist on no explicit "deal." America would also make
clear, secretly, that bombing of the north could resume if the enemy's

counterpart was not forthcoming. The entire thought was slippery. What was certain of the American position is certain only in terms of the American politics: the September position, decided on by Lyndon Johnson and his council at a moment in the campaign when Hubert Humphrey's cause seemed hopeless, had been decided not to advance the Democratic Party but in the highest interest of the United States.

The story thereafter becomes more a parable of the clash of cultures in the twentieth century, of systems awkwardly, blindly, groping toward each other, unable to speak each other's language but relying on feel. I am unable to reconstruct the story of October even remotely to my satisfaction; except that the few available facts, as I learn them, are part tragedy and part farce; and through the facts comes the central thrust of Soviet initiative.

Soviet initiative began the first week in October.

On the official track, at government level, Secretary of State Dean Rusk dined on Sunday, October 6th, with Andrei Gromyko, Soviet foreign minister, his adversary for over twenty years. Rusk explained America's position to Gromyko once more, expecting little; but, he told his State Department colleagues later, Gromyko was "particularly noncombative" that evening.

The next day, Monday, on an unofficial track, another key Russian diplomat secretly met with an influential American political figure in New York. The conversation was very general, except that the Russian made known to the American that Russia had deep problems of its own, both domestically and in foreign affairs with China; despite the rupture of the summer summit by the Czechoslovak invasion, Russia still sought rapprochement with America. On the matter of the war in Asia, Russia wanted it to come to an end. Russia, he said, now finally held the upper hand in Hanoi's Communist government over the pro-Chinese Communist elements. If America stopped the bombing of the north, Russia could guarantee that a positive response from Hanoi would be forthcoming. The American intermediary—who insists he remain unnamed—relayed the message to the White House the next day, Tuesday. The White House responded with the thought that any bombing halt must require, in addition to the guarantees of South Vietnamese participation in negotiation, a guarantee of the inviolability of the Demilitarized Zone; but a day later the White House called the New York figure and told him to drop out of the exchange; the White House preferred to keep these negotiations on an official level.

On October 11th, in Paris, came a breakthrough at the official level: a direct request from the North Vietnamese negotiators to the American negotiators—if the North Vietnamese accepted the American position that South Vietnam's government should participate in negotiations, would there be a clear and "unconditional" cessation of all bombings of the north? The thought tantalized the Americans; but could they trust the probe?

On the next day, the New York channel of Russian diplomacy guaranteed its New York contact that if America stopped bombing, the North Vietnamese would indeed make counterpart concessions. At this point, several former members of the Johnson administration, of high and impeccable record, were brought into the New York sequence of negotiations; and one of them was dispatched to meet with Dean Rusk and urge that the Russian initiative in New York be taken seriously. By October 15th the government of South Vietnam had been brought into the information circle; and its President, General Thieu, gave assent to a bombing halt, provided his government sat at the conference table and participated in settlement.

Russian diplomacy had been quite busy and imaginative in New York, picking such improbable places as the steps of St. Patrick's Cathedral, a midtown Chinese restaurant and an apartment at the United Nations Plaza as rendezvous for the passage of its unofficial messages. On October 16th, at the United Nations Plaza, this channel closed off; the agreement of General Thieu, whom the Russians considered an American puppet, was indication of official agreement on quick settlement of the war; and thereafter, for the next two weeks, negotiations proceeded at the official level.

Substantive matters discussed in the next two weeks managed to please all parties—security from bombing of North Vietnamese cities, security for South Vietnamese cities, acceptance by Hanoi of the unchallenged American statement that we would continue surveillance flights of North Vietnamese movements, protection of the Demilitarized Zone, an anticipated movement to suspension of all offensive military actions on both sides. To these agreements, Lyndon Johnson added his own personal request—that there be put on the calendar a summit meeting between Russian leaders and himself to discuss the ABM program and put an end to the nuclear rivalry. The Russians agreed to the summit meeting which Johnson had sought all year long. (Only later, after the election, was the meeting scrubbed. When Johnson raised the matter with President-Elect Nixon, Nixon refused to let a lame-duck President speak for the United States.)

Such negotiations involving so many capitals and so many factions in each capital could not long be kept secret. By October 26th, ten days before the election, enterprising newsmen had begun to pry out bits of the story—the first reports coming from Vientiane, the capital of Laos. By October 27th, on Sunday, American negotiators in Paris had worked out a clean understanding with the enemy: that the format of future negotiations would include both the South Vietnamese government and the insurrectionary National Liberation Front; that all bombing of North Vietnam would stop, with America reserving the right of reconnaissance flights over the north and, if attack on the South Vietnamese cities ensued, the right of retaliation. On the next day, October 28th, President Thieu of South Vietnam—but *not* the South Vietnamese government—assented.

By October 29th, Tuesday, the promised end of the war in Vietnam was beginning to leak from every news source around the world—Ottawa, London, Paris, Saigon, Washington, New York. Fume and smoke steamed from the secret negotiations, with all the enwrapping prelude to drama that comes as an Apollo spacecraft spews downblast before soaring off into orbit.

The climate of the moment is important to remember. The American people had been emotionally buffeted all through the year. The words of the two major candidates had become dull. And now, suddenly, pressing through the worn rhetoric of the campaign was the hard profile of a peace in Asia. For forty-eight hours of anticipation, the campaign faded to secondary importance, and then, on Thursday evening, October 31st, it was Lyndon Johnson's moment. Licking his lips, shorn of emotion, the departing President announced, "I have now ordered that all air, naval, and artillery bombardment of North Vietnam cease as of eight A.M. Washington time, Friday morning. I have reached this decision . . . in the belief that this action can lead to progress towards a peaceful settlement of the Vietnamese war. . . . What we now expect . . . are prompt, productive, serious and intensive negotiations in an atmosphere that is conducive to progress."

Neither of the two candidates—Nixon or Humphrey—who later that evening followed the President on television with their own paid broadcasts could compete for impact; and the next morning, Friday, the nation's press was dominated once more by Lyndon Johnson, for the first time since his renunciation, for the last time in his career. In the public blur of appreciation, in the mingling of politics and concern, commentators and editorialists made what attempt they could to clarify a fuzzy, obscure and unwritten agreement with the enemy, and all concluded that peace was near.

This conclusion lasted no more than twenty-four hours, for by Friday afternoon and Saturday morning, it had been succeeded by another headline: SAIGON OPPOSES PARIS TALK PLANS, SAYS IT CAN'T ATTEND NEXT WEEK, read the *New York Times* front page; and across the country bewilderment spread. If Saigon had not agreed to the agreement, there was no agreement, and who was befuddling whom? Never was climax to election presented to Americans in more blurred form with less time for consideration: Was there a peace agreement? Or was this just talk? Was the administration trying to bring an end to

The Making of the President—1968

war? Or was it trying to save Hubert Humphrey from defeat? And never was public confusion more justified, for the leaders of both parties and of the American government were equally confused.

For the Democrats, the governing party, it may be said that they had acted in good faith. When the American administration announced the bombing halt of Thursday night, it did so believing that it had the full assent of the South Vietnamese government. It had, however, only the assent of its president, General Nguyen van Thieu. And so solemnly had Thieu been admonished by the American government to keep the secrecy of the preceding weeks of negotiation that he had kept the details of agreement secret even from his cabinet, his national assembly, and his vice-president and rival, Nguyen Cao Ky. Faced with a revolt of his assembly as the news leaked, menaced by a *coup d'état* of his vice-president, Thieu reneged. On Friday, Saigon time (Saturday, American time), came his shattering statement, "The Government of South Vietnam deeply regrets not to be able to participate in the present exploratory talks."

There could be no doubt that someone had blundered; of such blunders great issues in politics can be made. But over the weekend of November 1st and 2nd, with the Presidency of the United States apparently at stake, both sides approached the blunder as if it were a political explosive. Given the proper twist, it could explode either way, and one must see the temptation of the Democrats to exploit hidden opportunity, the temptation of the Republicans to exploit public confusion.

There is no way of getting at the dilemma of both parties except by introducing, at this point, the completely extraneous name of a beautiful Oriental lady, Anna Chan Chennault, the Chinese widow of wartime hero General Claire Chennault. Mrs. Chennault, an American citizen since 1950, comes of a line that begins with Mei-ling Soong (Madame Chiang K'ai-shek) and runs through Madame Nhu (the Dragon Lady of South Vietnam)—a line of Oriental ladies of high purpose and authoritarian manners whose pieties and iron righteousness have frequently outrun their brains and acknowledged beauty. In the campaign of 1968, Mrs. Chennault, a lady of charm, energy and great name, had become chairman or co-chairman of several Nixon citizen committees, wearing honorific titles which were borne by many but which she took more seriously than most. In that circle of Oriental diplomacy in Washington once known as the China Lobby, Anna Chennault was hostess-queen. Having raised (by her own statement later) some $250,-000 for the Nixon campaign, she felt entitled to authority by her achievement. And, having learned of the October negotiations by gossip and rumor and press speculation, as did most Americans, she had undertaken most energetically to sabotage them. In contact with the Formosan, the South Korean and the South Vietnamese governments, she had begun early, by cable and telephone, to mobilize their resistance to the agreement—apparently implying, as she went, that she spoke for the Nixon campaign.

She had, however, neglected to take the most elementary precautions of an intriguer, and her communications with Asia had been tapped by the American government and brought directly to the perusal of President Johnson.

Although Johnson had been made aware of Mrs. Chennault's messages even before his announcement of the bombing halt, he had not taken them seriously. It was not until Saturday, with the announcement of eleven South Vietnamese senators in Saigon of their support of Richard M. Nixon(!) and the repudiation of the Paris agreement by President Thieu, that the President's wrath was lit. By Saturday he had accused Senator Everett Dirksen of a Republican plot to sabotage peace (which Dirksen, presumably, hastened to relay to Nixon headquarters); and by Sunday, Johnson was in direct and bitter telephonic contact with Richard Nixon in Los Angeles (see footnote, page 383).

What could have been made of an open charge that the Nixon leaders were saboteurs of the peace one cannot guess; how quickly it might, if aired, have brought the last forty-eight hours of the American campaign to squalor is a matter of speculation. But the good instinct of that small-town boy Hubert Humphrey prevailed. Fully informed of the sabotage of the negotiations and the recalcitrance of the Saigon government, Humphrey might have won the Presidency of the United States by making it the prime story of the last four days of the campaign. He was urged by several members of his staff to do so. And I know of no more essentially decent story in American politics than Humphrey's refusal to do so; his instinct was that Richard Nixon, personally, had no knowledge of Mrs. Chennault's activities; had no hand in them; and would have forbidden them had he known. Humphrey would not air the story.

For the sake of the record, I must add that in probing this episode during the weekend of its happening, this reporter's judgment was that Humphrey's decision was morally, if not tactically, correct. At the first report of Republican sabotage in Saigon, Nixon's headquarters had begun to investigate the story; had discovered Mrs. Chennault's activities; and was appalled. The fury and dismay at Nixon's headquarters when his aides discovered the report were so intense that they could not have been feigned simply for the benefit of this reporter. Their feeling on Monday morning before the election was, simply, that if they lost the election, Mrs. Chennault might have lost it for them. She had taken their name and authority in vain; if the Democrats now chose to air the story, no rebuttal of the Nixon camp would be convincing; and they were at the mercy of Humphrey's good-will.

*   *   *

The events that led to the bombing halt and the events of the final weekend have never yet been fully explained. But the shadows they cast as they were happening conditioned the public environment of American thinking. And as the shadows flickered and fell, Americans had to make judgment on them. On Friday morning, Americans were convinced that peace was at hand; on Saturday, Saigon's repudiation of peace upset them; by Sunday, no one knew what was happening, and every dial and index of public-opinion sampling was spinning.

Never did a campaign close more erratically than that of 1968. As late as October 21st, the Gallup poll had given Nixon an eight-point (44/36) lead over Humphrey. By the time Gallup completed his next poll, on Saturday, November 2nd, two days after Johnson's announcement of the bombing halt, an upheaval had taken place and Nixon led Humphrey by only two points, 42/40. And for the first time that year the Harris poll confirmed the Gallup poll with absolute precision, 42/40.

All across the country, other regional poll-masters were finding similar shifts of opinion—Fred Currier's Market Opinion Research was discovering a seven-point change in Michigan; a three-point shift to Humphrey in Ohio was moving that state to the doubtful column. In California, Nixon's ten-point lead of mid-October was melting, and the *Los Angeles Times* on Sunday, November 3rd, reported the gap narrowed to only a single point in its statewide poll.

I called Louis Harris that weekend for guidance in judgment, and Harris, answering the phone, was almost ecstatic in professional excitement, scholarly analysis and historical analogy. We had been friends through many strange campaigns, and he felt this was the wildest of all climaxes—it was more exciting than Kanawha County in West Virginia when, in the last weekend of the primary of 1960, Democrats flipped from Humphrey to Kennedy; more exciting than Southern California in May and June of 1964, when, in the last weekend of the primary, Republicans flipped from Rockefeller to Goldwater; more exciting than New York City in the last weekend of the mayoralty of 1965, when it flipped from Beame to Lindsay. But where, I asked, was the flip coming? It's the women, answered Harris, the women's vote is going out on Nixon, the bombing halt has gotten to them, the women are for peace. And Harris was continuing his polling over the weekend because under the impact of such events no poll could predict a trend for more than forty-eight hours. On Monday, Harris announced his last formal poll: Humphrey, finally, astoundingly, ahead over Nixon by 43 to 40!

There was little either candidate could do under such circumstances —both seeking to be President, both within finger-touch of it, neither willing to risk the peace which each must seek once elected, yet both compelled to appeal to emotions divorced from facts. For them, as for the people, the question was unresolved—were the month-long negotiations truly the last chapter in the Vietnam war? Or a delusion? What clear statement could be made by either candidate which events would not make foolish in another few days? [4]

Americans let the people choose their President; the assumption is that, given the facts of their condition and their problems, the American people will choose wisely. In the final days of the campaign of 1968 the American people were deprived of facts, not out of malice, but because events muddied the facts. Had peace become quite clear, as fact, in the last three days of the election of 1968, Hubert Humphrey would probably have won the election; he would have been a minority President, but the President nonetheless. Through the confusion of those last three days, however, it became apparent that the bombing halt, begun on Friday morning, would not end the killing of Americans in Asia; and the tide of opinion that had begun to flow to Hubert Humphrey began, at the end of the weekend, to flow back to Nixon. The opinion of the Nixon leadership is that, had the election been held on Saturday or Sunday, Nixon might have lost; had it been a week later than it actually was, their margin of victory might have run as high as 2,000,000 to 5,000,000 votes.

The Nixon polling operation, under David Derge, was an enormously sensitive one and, inside the house, severely straightforward. It had conducted a number of overnight checks, by its WATS panels, on various high episodes of the campaign and the instant reactions—reactions to the Salt Lake City speech of Hubert Humphrey, to Nixon's refusal to debate Humphrey, to Nixon's opposition to the naming of Abe Fortas as Chief Justice of the Supreme Court. Most disconcerting of the panels' reports, however, were their findings on the peace-and-war issue in the last days of the campaign. As Humphrey twisted his posture from that of the war candidate to that of the peace candidate, the Derge in-house estimates of Nixon's electoral vote shriveled. An early October forecast had been that Nixon would win the Presidency by 427 electoral votes; the estimate shrank in subsequent tallies from 389, to 358, to 321

---

[4] For Nixon, under the menace of the Anna Chennault episode, possibly about to be cast by Democrats as the great saboteur of peace, the question was the most pointed. He solved it by questioning not the President's politics, but his judgment. In elaboration of this theme, Finch was authorized to brief the press and charge that the President had been either irresponsible or premature in announcing a deal before "he had gotten all his ducks in a row." The President, hearing this statement, and understandably irritated since he felt it was Mrs. Chennault who had, on Nixon's instructions, fluttered the ducks in Saigon, brought the matter up in his telephone call to Nixon on Sunday in Los Angeles. After Nixon had mollified the President on major matters, Johnson inquired, "Who's this guy Fink you got?" "It's Finch, not Fink," replied Nixon. "What's he doing making statements like that without your knowledge?" "Well," said Nixon, as reported by those who overheard the conversation, "you know how it is, you had George Ball making statements in your administration." "George Ball isn't any longer with this administration."

votes. Within forty-eight hours of Johnson's bombing-halt statement of October 31st, the rolling panel of Derge's opinion survey had come up with the shocking prediction that Nixon would win the Presidency by only 270 votes—the minimal technical total necessary to win!

In the fluctuation of voters' moods, there are no certainties until election day itself.[5] The only certainty is that in the fall of 1968 neither candidate had any hope of becoming a clear majority President. Divided as Americans were in attitude on Vietnam, they were just as divided in their opinions of America at home. Whichever major candidate won was doomed to be President by the vote of a minority, obligated, to create once more an effective American majority.

The strange year 1968 thus approached its end not with the exultation, the clarities, the wildly shrieking throngs American elections used to produce.

It approached its end, for most Americans, on the tubes of television in 15,000,000 American homes. None of the synthetic contrivances of the candidates' producers could match what the tubes had already shown —the blood and war in Vietnam, the riots in American streets, the assassinations, the renunciation of a President. As the producers of the two candidates shelled and counter-shelled each other with five-minute spots, one-minute spots, twenty-second spots, the tube glazed the eye with its vivid colors. The heavy artillery was the effort of the media-men to give America the sense of the personality of the two candidates. Having been alerted by their vast polling operation to the facts known to all pollsters— above all, that the women's vote was shifting away from Nixon—the Nixon media-masters did better. All day Monday and Tuesday, on whatever time they could buy regionally or nationally, they ran their Nixon half-hour biography, starting in Whittier, sad, sweet, nostalgic, full of sentiment and mother love to reach the hearts of American women whom they might catch between dish-drying, house-cleaning, and the pick-up of children from school. They spread Nixon's message more effectively than did Humphrey's media-masters, who made a poorer showing of the biography of their champion. The Humphrey biographies, curiously, made Humphrey seem a man thrust forward only by issues; the Nixon biographies made Nixon seem a man of heart.

On Sunday one could sit and hear Richard Nixon for half an hour on *Meet the Press* (excellent), Hubert Humphrey on *Issues and Answers* (also excellent), Eugene McCarthy for half an hour (finally pledging

---

[5] This observation of Nixon's staff receives some slight corroboration from a survey taken by the Harris poll, on Monday, for scholarly reference purposes and destined not to be published. The last Monday survey in the Harris polling differed with his last published (Humphrey over Nixon, 43/40) survey. Nixon, in the pendulum swing of emotions, had swung marginally back into the lead again.

public support to Hubert Humphrey) and George Wallace accompanied by Curtis LeMay for half an hour. Television was constant at the end, and it all came to an end on Monday evening, November 4th, in a mind-whirling blur from two TV studios in Los Angeles, where the candidates sat sheltered from the rain, the cold, the jostle, the pound of human voices that used to mark the old ritual climax of American politics. It came to an end, gaudy with color, artificially packaged, as the two candidates mastered simultaneous telethons for maximum visual impact.

One could note, as did the estimated 48,000,000 Americans who watched these shows that evening, mostly minutiae. The set designers had done better by Mr. Humphrey than by Mr. Nixon. Mr. Nixon was sculptured in a contoured swivel-chair, all by himself, very tired, his brows beetling again as they had in 1960, artistically much too stark. Mr. Humphrey had been designed to swing free and easy, and could stroll with a wandering microphone, sometimes accompanied by Edmund Muskie, wherever he wished. But the Nixon designers had a more sensitive color-consultant. The Nixon girls were prettier than the Humphrey girls on the sets; the dresses in their ranks, as they answered the phones of the telethon, were all a-shimmer with scarlet, orange, lemon yellow and shell pink. Mrs. Nixon herself, in turquoise, glowed. It was easier to look at the Nixon colors than the Humphrey colors, although Humphrey's fluid rambling across the set was very good.

Visually, the final contest was a stand-off. Mr. Humphrey had more stars working with him, accepting the messages and questions at the rate, so they said, of 130,000 questions an hour. Mr. Humphrey had Frank Sinatra, Mercedes McCambridge, Abbe Lane, Inger Stevens and Paul Newman. But Mr. Nixon had Jackie Gleason for a moment. Mr. Humphrey, one noticed, ran ahead on points for identity. His high moment of identification came when the cameras switched to Massachusetts and one saw Lawrence O'Brien walking along the sands of Hyannis Port with Senator Edward Kennedy, the last remaining Kennedy; the wind off Cape Cod blew their jackets up behind them into swallowtails, the same billowing wind that one remembered from November 8th, 1960; and one gathered that the last remaining Kennedy felt that Humphrey was the best man for peace. Nixon counter-scored with the young and eager David Eisenhower, his about-to-be-son-in-law; a cowlick of youthful hair dipping over his unlined brow, David Eisenhower reported that his grandfather, Dwight D. Eisenhower, wanted Mr. Nixon elected.

Over all this came words and messages. Sometimes, flicking between sound tracks, you could be reasonably sure in the blur whose voice went with what image. That was Nixon, hammering away at the weekend crisis, punching the message that the cities in South Vietnam were still being shelled and bombed, that the Ho Chi Minh trail was still full of trucks rolling south with thousands of tons of supplies to kill our boys.

That had to be Nixon. Then, watching both, the voice could be switched to Hubert Humphrey and it was trust again, our great cities couldn't be rebuilt without trust; that had to be Humphrey. The timbre of their voices had, over many years, become absolutely clear to me, and so whichever one was on sound-track was known. But their messages in the final stages of the campaign had overlapped in the great center which they were about to divide by a few hairs' breadth: they were both for arms to Israel; they were both for Social Security and Medicare, bigger, better, finer Social Security and Medicare; they were both for harmony and reconciliation and brotherhood; and both of them thought it was a great country that could do better. Mr. Wallace, who had concluded his final half-hour broadcast before the two major telethons climaxed, would, of course, have repeated that there was not a "dime's worth of difference" between the two parties. But he had run out of money.

The next day, it would be up to Americans to decide.

CHAPTER TWELVE

THE ELECTION: PASSAGE
IN THE NIGHT

THE country lay broad and beautiful beneath Richard Nixon as he sped back. The weather, on Election Day, was fair and warm all through the West and lower Midwest; rain and showers overhung the northern plains and mountains from the Great Lakes to the Pacific Northwest, but no clouds obscured his line of flight until the plane penetrated the overcast above the Mid-Atlantic States. Beneath, as he flew, some 73,000,000 Americans were voting on their next President. He had sought their loyalties now for over a decade; politics had been his calling for over twenty years. For the past two years he had sown well, planned wisely, worked as intensely as he knew how. But now, at harvest time, he was unsure. Beneath lay a nation at war, and rent with hates, preparing for him a rendezvous with crisis darker than any President had faced since 1860, a nation perplexed, confused and never more uncertain of its own will and national leadership than in the last weekend of the contest.

Since the day in mid-October, at Kansas City, when President Johnson had telephoned him about Vietnam, Nixon had been concerned. The President had told all three candidates on October 16th of the secret talks that had begun in Paris on October 11th, and of the imminence of settlement; he had asked all three candidates to think of "what was best for their country" and drop Vietnam from public debate. Recalling these last two weeks shortly after the election, Nixon felt it was then that matters had really turned against him. Contrary to his staff, he felt the greatest issue of his strength had never been law-and-order. In his own mind the key issue was the war in Vietnam, the desire of Americans for peace. For months, until the October telephone call, he had been chanting, "I say that after four years of war in Asia, after 25,000 dead 200,000 casualties, America needs new leadership." But after the President's phone call, just as he had been about to peak the issue, he had felt he must drop the theme from his speeches. He had had to become more general in talking of foreign policy, had had to let the edge of his challenge to the Democrats and Hubert Humphrey be blunted. If peace were imminent, no one would forgive him if he disrupted peace for political advantage in a campaign. And then had come the bombing halt, the foretaste of peace, and the wild fluctuation of voters' preference reported in his private polls as well as the public polls.

Thereafter, Nixon had felt his lead shriveling day by day, down to Election Eve. Monday before election, he had intensified his effort. He had added to his schedule that day a mid-morning happening—a visit to a Nixon headquarters in Southern California—to catch attention in the evening papers and the evening television shows of California, where his margin was so swiftly crumbling. Originally, a single two-hour telethon had been scheduled for nationwide broadcast from Los Angeles; but over the weekend, as his crisis mounted, Nixon had added to that another two-hour telethon special for the West Coast. He had thus worked all day, Monday, finished his last telecast to Californians at eleven, and finally reached his bed at the Century Plaza Hotel in Los Angeles, at 1:25 in the morning—by which time Americans were already beginning to vote in the hills of New England.

He was up within six hours—at 7:20, by his log—telling his aide Dwight Chapin he had slept "pretty well." He breakfasted on hot oatmeal, orange juice, milk and coffee, and then spent almost an hour on the telephone—calling John Mitchell in New York, Norman Chandler of the *Los Angeles Times* locally, talking with Mrs. Dwight Eisenhower, Murray Chotiner, his brother, Ed, and Maurice Stans, and consulted at intervals with staff members Haldeman, Ehrlichman and Garment.

Then—to the campaign plane, which he boarded at 9:45, Pacific Coast Time. Nixon remembers an "Air Force One" sign someone had painted and an American flag pasted on the outside of the plane, and the balloons in the plane as he walked through. But he was moody and, once aboard the plane, aloft, and in privacy, he called the family forward—Mrs. Nixon, the two girls, and young David Eisenhower. He wanted to warn them against the agony they had gone through on election night in 1960. I've been pretty optimistic in public, he remembers telling them, but now I want to tell you what's really going to happen. If people in this country are still really concerned about peace, he said, we could win big. But if they've been reassured about peace and now they're concerned with their pocketbooks and welfare, we could lose. The family, he remembers, was shocked. Richard Nixon went on, explaining: the bombing pause could cost us, he said, three to five million votes. It won't hurt us so much in the South or Midwest, but it will hurt us in the East. And if that happened, he admonished them, he didn't want them to go through what had happened the night of the election of

1960. This time they'd done everything they could, all the extras they could, the extra two hours of telethon, the extra happening in Los Angeles. And if they hadn't made it, it was not that they had failed— it was that events had gone against them. Events changed votes, not stump speeches. Nixon insisted that no one must turn on television before nine o'clock in the evening in New York, for they'd only be torturing themselves with the early returns from the East. Wryly, President Nixon remembers that the two girls turned on their sets at 7:30, which proves that not even Presidents can control daughters. Then he presented his wife with her gifts—a diamond-and-pearl pin, earrings to match.

Having attended to first things first, he next summoned his writing staff—Price, Buchanan, Safire, Keogh—forward, to thank them and joke with them. They were all still embarrassed about a slip of the tongue on the second telethon of the evening when Nixon had used the phrase "now we get down to the nut-cutting." To his Eastern writers, Nixon explained the origin of the term "nut-cutting," told about his first political dinner of "sheep-fries" in Missouri, and promised them a dinner of "sheep-fries" if he were elected. He twitted his thinkers about the radio speeches of the last two weeks; on no other campaign documents had Nixon, personally, worked so hard; the speeches had absorbed his best thinking from Key Biscayne on; but now, he wondered, had that "intellectual stuff" really done any good? No one knew.

Other conferences followed on the plane. A thank-you-and-farewell meeting to the media group brought in by Garment and Shakespeare. A thank-you-and-review to the political staff on the plane, Klein, Ellsworth, McWhorter, Finch. A thank-you to the wives acompanying their husbands, telling them how splendidly their men had performed. But he was restless. An hour and a half out of Los Angeles, Ellsworth brought him the report that Philadelphia was voting exceptionally heavily. A bad omen. Shortly after, he was told that he would have to appear live on television on his arrival at Newark, and began to think about what he must say. He lunched on ground steak with Bebe Rebozo, tried to take a nap after lunch, using his coat as coverlet, but was up half an hour later, restless again, calling people forward. Yet, except for one hand-shaking tour through the plane shortly after take-off, he remained secluded in his lemon-gold personal compartment of the *Tricia*. The feel of his presence on the plane was subtly changing—it seemed, said Pat Buchanan, that we all were a good deal further from that front compartment than we ever had been in the campaign.

The mood on the plane was subdued—little gaiety, no exuberance. Nixon staff-men ranged in their guesses from the most apprehensive, Buchanan and Finch, to the most confident, Haldeman. (On Haldeman's private guess-sheet of what was happening beneath them, Haldeman had even tallied New York for Nixon; "that was a big one to miss," said Haldeman, ruefully, later.) Finch was pacing the aisles ("I couldn't keep from remembering our flight back from the Hotel Ambassador in Los Angeles after the election in 1960"). Haldeman had settled back, leafing through folders on transitions in the Presidency, studying how one staffs up to govern the United States. It was quiet on the plane, and remained so as dusk settled.

It was somewhere between Mississippi and Indiana that the dark began to fall—the checkerboards of the flat Midwestern plains all so neat and clean. "You could almost feel the mood changing," remembers Len Garment, "as the darkness came over the land. There was a TV set in the staff compartment, and they were starting to give accounts—from Kansas and New Hampshire, and places like that. It was like inviting people to a party and then waiting to see who would come. I felt like an observer for the first time in a year. Everything had been done, and now I had a front seat at a drama, and it was like watching a stage-setting when the lights go down. We knew there was this hemorrhage of votes, this dreadful phenomenon, like a strange disease, and how far would it go, would there be this exponential disaster facing us? And down below there was this twinkling of lights from the towns that were beginning to light up, like a stage-setting just before the action begins. It was all so moving and beautiful. And people in the plane, drawing apart in their thoughts, leafing through magazines and papers, doing their own thing. It was very quiet in the last hour." Someone else remembers Nixon looking down as the plane passed into dusk over Indiana, absolutely still, as "if by looking down and concentrating he could pull in more votes."

The plane landed at Newark at 6:15, and by the time Richard M. Nixon arrived at Suite 35H at the Waldorf Towers at 7:05, the vote had been coming in on the national networks for over an hour.

The national voting results normally develop their silhouette between seven and ten in the evening, slowly emerging from the first sloshing about of random figures just as the darks and highs of a photographic print emerge from the solutions in a darkroom. Wild and meaningless digits tumble over each other on computers and screens, and then begin to cling to ridges, depressions, and political landscapes that thrust up in the first faintly recognizable historical patterns.

The counting of election night, November 5th, 1968, began almost classically. There was Kansas coming in first, steady on for Nixon at 9,000 to 6,000 (Humphrey) to 1,200 (for Wallace). With 2 percent of the national total, at five minutes past seven it was Nixon in the lead 44 percent to 36 percent (Humphrey) to 19 percent (Wallace). By half past seven the electoral strategy was beginning to show—Nixon was pulling well ahead in Tennessee and Kentucky and the peripheral strategy was paying off; commentators guessed that if Tennessee and Kentucky were with Nixon, Florida and Virginia must almost certainly follow (as, later in the evening, they did). By eight o'clock the margins were beginning to narrow, with Nixon at 42 percent and Humphrey at 34 percent.

And then, as Connecticut's voting machines began to churn out their figures, it was apparent that the pollsters had been right in their measure of Humphrey's stormy recovery. At 8:20 the first blast-off from Connecticut, an Eastern state, had Humphrey at 8,053, Nixon at 3,378, and Wallace at 1,178. And from then on, as the computers of the News Election Service with their new programming and new techniques spewed out their totals, the mind could barely digest what was happening. In Ohio: Nixon ahead in count, but the computorial analyses insisting the race was too close to count. In Michigan: Humphrey off to an early lead, so fast, so strong, that before nine NBC had awarded him victory. In Missouri: Humphrey leading in vote count, but CBS calling the lead for Nixon. New York, in a cascade, overwhelmingly for Humphrey. By 9:15 the Nixon lead, at 11 percent of the total vote, had narrowed to 41 percent to 38 percent over Humphrey to 20 percent for George Wallace. By 10:10 the profile of Hubert Humphrey's strength matched Nixon's fully in electoral votes with Minnesota, Michigan, Rhode Island, Maine, Massachusetts, New York, West Virginia, Connecticut and Washington, D.C., all solidly bagged and Pennsylvania leaning to him for 143 for the Democrat against 143 for the Republican; and at 10:20, with 29 percent of the national vote counted they were also exactly even in popular vote, with 41 percent for each and Wallace down to 18.

From eleven until midnight one could play fantasy. Humphrey was soon ahead by 42 percent to 41 percent of the vote counted—was this going to be the greatest upset in elections since 1948? Was it conceivable that Humphrey could win the popular vote, yet lose the electoral vote to Nixon? By midnight, however, this fantasy was fading and becoming nightmare. By midnight it was quite clear that Richard M. Nixon had won 202 electoral votes and possibly those of Maryland and Delaware also. George Wallace had won 45 electoral votes in five Southern states, and between them Nixon and Wallace held 247 sure electoral votes. It was inconceivable that Humphrey could win enough of the remaining states to overmatch this total in the Electoral College—and Richard M. Nixon was running, thus, not as he ran in 1960 to a photo-finish with a clear rival, but to a photo-finish against the structure, the history and the process of election as written in the Constitution, and the archaic Electoral College it ordained. Clearly and sharply, the Constitution had set up a Federal electoral system by which the American people might choose their leader directly—but not directly as a nation, directly only as citizens of individual communities, or states, which would then name the President of the whole. And at midnight, five major communities, or states, were so sharply divided that no one could tell where, or how, their combined 129 votes would go: California (40), Illinois (26), Missouri (12), Ohio (26), Texas (25). With the exception of Ohio, these were the same states that had haunted the election night of Richard M. Nixon eight years before when he had received the voting returns of the nation in the Royal Suite of the Hotel Ambassador in Los Angeles. This night he had absented himself from television and at midnight was analyzing on his yellow legal pads the reports from exactly the same states carried to him by his staff from his own surveillance net of the nation, masterminded from the thirty-fifth floor of the Waldorf Towers in New York.

Nixon, with the inflexible self-discipline he has developed over the last few years, had insisted that all television sets be turned off in Suite 35H that was to be his own on election night. The candidate who had rested his election strategy on television more than any of his rivals would not let it upset his thinking that night. He had sent out his dark blue suit to be pressed immediately on arrival, for he prefers to appear in blues on television, and the need of his appearance might be early. He had indulged himself in a hot, luxurious bath, the first departure from the habit of a quick shower in many weeks; and then had gone to nap, leaving instructions with Chapin that he was not to be disturbed by anyone until 8:30, and then only by Haldeman if Haldeman had information important enough to disturb him.

He could not nap, however, and emerged into the living room of the suite at 8:20 in an old rumpled suit, called for coffee and then said he wanted to be alone. He was alone for almost three hours, interrupted only by Haldeman bringing him fifteen-minute reports from the sprawl of the thirty-fifth floor, and Chapin bringing in coffee, cigars or an occasional staff visitor. In the suite adjacent to the candidate's was the TV monitoring room, staffed by men who would in a few months be the inner ring of the palace guard of the White House: Haldeman, as always, in command, and with Haldeman his own assistant, Laurence Higby; with them, Dwight Chapin; and John Ehrlichman, chamberlain of the campaign plane, whose performance in the previous two months had brought him to intimacy with and thus to the highest respect of the candidate. These guarded the access to the candidate, and monitored their television sets for the news the network computers fed. Down the hall was an operational room, where John Mitchell, Robert Finch and Murray Chotiner operated, in direct contact with Republican organizations all across the country by direct line. Reporting to Finch was a monitoring room below, to which were linked key-precinct reporters of Nixon's own staff in eighteen key states. In another suite was the Nixon family, David Eisenhower there with his betrothed. And in Suite 35A were the "think-staffers"—Safire, Buchanan, Price, Garment—sharing their space with visitors as an overflow hospitality suite.

By eleven o'clock it was obvious from the Haldeman-Ehrlichman reports of television, from the direct-wire and direct-contact reports, that Nixon's hastily pressed blue suit would not be needed by midnight. It was going to be a long night; and from eleven o'clock on, Nixon was in constant consultation. At eleven he summoned a conference of Finch, Mitchell, Haldeman and Chotiner to review the results that had come in. Finch, reporting the opinion of his key-state operators, was certain that Missouri would swing for Nixon. From eleven until almost two in the morning they weighed, again and again, just as did the public commentators, the same states:

§ *Texas.* O'Donnell of Texas had reported that Texas was in the bag on the basis of early returns. Yet it was not.

§ *Ohio.* The reports from Ohio, privately transmitted, were much better than television's reports, and Nixon felt he could score Ohio hard for the cause.

§ *Illinois.* Close.

§ *California.* Close.

On the phone, Nixon checked now and then around the country; added and subtracted figures from his pad. There seemed, by the report of those who talked to him, very little nervousness about him. But he was still unwilling to accept visitors from the outside world. Eminent personalities came and went in the hospitality suite; at half past midnight Nelson Rockefeller came to offer congratulations, but Nixon was not yet ready to accept them; somewhat later Senator Strom Thurmond and Senator Jacob Javits, an odd and mismatched pair who spanned the entire spectrum of the Republican Party, found themselves waiting together with the think-staff in Suite 35A; but they did not see the candidate. At one point Governor John Volpe made his appearance; and now and then members of the staff, led by Herbert Klein, went down to the public rooms of television to spread good cheer on the air. Governor Agnew called at one point, and Nixon said he would call him back.

It was at approximately 2:40 A.M. that Dwight Chapin brought the word down the corridor that Richard Nixon wanted to see the following: Messrs. Finch, Haldeman, Mitchell and Chotiner. All but Mitchell were survivors of Election Night, 1960. They waited in the living room of Suite 35H until, precisely at the stroke of three, Nixon emerged. Nixon sat on his couch and reviewed the totals available with his four friends and they could find no fault with Nixon's calculations: he would have, he felt for certain, California, Missouri and Ohio—and, thus, enough to make him President of the United States. It was time, therefore, for someone to go downstairs and announce the new President. Haldeman objected—while the result seemed clear to those in the room, he said, it was not clear to the nation at large watching television. To announce victory prematurely would make it seem as if Nixon were greedy for the prize, snatching for it. Reluctantly Nixon agreed and then, in a moment of mini-drama, made clear why the impulse had come to him. It was at precisely this time eight years before, he reminded those present, that he had descended the steps to the pressroom of the Hotel Ambassador in Los Angeles and there, at this hour, conceded victory to John F. Kennedy. His sense of history insisted that someone now punctuate the night with the sound of victory as he had punctuated that other night with the sound of defeat.

Nixon was alert now and confident. At 3:15 in the morning he finally returned Governor Agnew's call, saying, "Well, Ted, we've won." At 4:00 he called Nelson Rockefeller on Rockefeller's private bedroom line, waking Rockefeller from sleep, and thanked him for all his effort and help. Then he directed Chapin to round up any members of the staff still awake on the thirty-fifth floor and bring them in for an impromptu open house. They followed in, one by one—Finch, Mitchell, Haldeman, Klein, Price, Safire, Buchanan, Garment, Harlow, Rose Mary Woods and others. They remained for several hours, unwinding. Nixon smoked his fifth cigar of the evening, nursed a single beer for an hour, finally munched on sandwiches which had been brought up. The conversation rambled back and forth, each man remembering different things. Nixon asserted and reasserted his belief that he had made the right choice in Spiro Agnew for Vice-President—the man had capacity, brains, energy and quality. Someone quipped, "Well, we sure concealed that from the American people during the campaign." There was the problem of what to say in the morning acceptance before television, and Safire, recalling the night in Deshler, Ohio, brought back to Nixon's memory the sign of the young lady which had said, BRING US TOGETHER. Variously, Nixon quipped, gossiped and teased his staff, for there were no more campaign obligations, no more speeches or happenings the next day—except for the flight to Key Biscayne, which, now, he decided he would make as soon as Humphrey had conceded and he himself had acknowledged. Illinois was still hanging undecided on the television sets of the nation, and the indecision began to annoy Nixon; momentarily he swung into an executive mood, directing that everyone check on Illinois, that the *Chicago Tribune* be checked for news, that Mike Wallace be reached for CBS information, that the Nixon troops in Cook County be on the alert against a steal of ballots from the last few precincts in Chicago. Finally, at about eight o'clock, Haldeman urged him to get some sleep and ushered him to the bedroom. In the bedroom, before he went to sleep, Nixon's sense of history surfaced again—there they were, eight years later, still hanging on California and Illinois; and he asked Haldeman to make sure that everything possible was being done in both states to see that all the boxes were in, that nothing be let slip by this time.

By the time Nixon woke, at about nine o'clock, the election had jelled on television for the nation, as for political operators. Haldeman found Nixon, about nine, already awake, sleepy-eyed and in pajamas; now, for the first time, Nixon turned on the TV sets and watched the reports. ABC had already conceded him the election; as Haldeman and Nixon watched the screens, NBC also conceded; and Nixon, still in pajamas and bathrobe, walked down the hall to his daughters' bedroom to tell them, too. But they had already heard the news and Julie was ready to present to him the gift she had been secretly sewing for him for several weeks—the Presidential seal, done in crewel.

Though it was certain now that he was President, he decided to wait before any public appearance until the concession of defeat had come, as is tradition, from his rival in Minneapolis; and Humphrey's call was forthcoming at 11:30.

It had been a cruel day and night for Hubert Humphrey. As if by defiance of all political gravity, Humphrey had converted the downsweep of early autumn into a soaring upward streak that was to miss the rung of the magic trapeze by finger-short margins. He had finished his telethon in California late on Monday evening, partied at the home of a Beverly Hills friend, then flown home through the night to Minnesota, driving directly to the white frame township hall of Marysville to cast his vote, then disappearing from the public eye until shortly before midnight. He arrived then on the fourteenth floor of the Leamington Hotel to watch the returns on three television sets in a room crowded, as always, with friends and campaign aides.

There was a high passage of elation that greeted him when he arrived, an elation that had been building since almost ten o'clock, when the returns from Pennsylvania, Connecticut, Michigan, New York had outrun his staff's fondest expectations, when Ohio and Illinois as well as Texas and California still appeared in doubt. But by one o'clock in the morning he and his staff knew there would be no electoral victory. Their hopes now rested on the thrust of George Wallace. If Wallace could tie up enough electoral votes to deny Nixon an Electoral College majority, then the election must go to the House; and the House, by the election returns, was going Democratic. Whether or not to make a fight in the House, Humphrey's staff thought informally, would depend on the popular vote. They could not, they knew, win a majority of the electoral vote; but if they won the popular vote, by no matter how tiny a margin, and the electoral vote were indecisive, they would turn Washington upside down to elect Humphrey over Nixon in the House. By four in the morning, when Humphrey went to sleep, that prospect, too, was fading. And by the time he woke again—at about 8:30—it was clear to

Humphrey, a veteran of too many campaigns to misread tallies, that Nixon was President-Elect. Thus at about 10:30 Central Time (11:30 East Coast Time) he telephoned the President-Elect to offer congratulations and said he was about to descend to concede before the nation on television.

For Nixon, now, it was all over but cheers. In the early-morning wait he had decided to pack himself, family and staff off to Key Biscayne as soon as television was satisfied. Giving Humphrey clear leeway on the nation's air, he waited until 12:30 to appear in the ballroom of the Waldorf Astoria. Dressed in his dark-blue suit, a bit nervous, but smiling, he made the remarks that all winners of the Presidency make on such occasions—a compliment to his gallant adversary, thanks to his own workers across the country—spoke of his admiration for Lyndon Johnson and pledged to work with him through the transition, and then:

"One final thought . . . about this new administration. I saw many signs in this campaign. Some of them were not friendly and some were very friendly. But the one that touched me the most was one that I saw in Deshler, Ohio, at the end of a long day of whistle-stopping. A little town, I suppose five times the population was there in the dusk, almost impossible to see, but a teen-ager held up a sign, 'BRING US TOGETHER.' And that will be the great objective of this administration at the outset, to bring the American people together. . . ."

All American Presidents have held this high purpose close to heart. But none have had this purpose so challenged by the hard accounting that brought them victory. For the election returns of 1968 spoke of a nation divided against itself as never before.

On November 5th, 1968, 73,186,819 American citizens voted, choosing Richard Milhous Nixon President of the United States by 31,770,237 votes (or 43.40 percent of the total national vote) over Hubert Horatio Humphrey with 31,270,533 votes (or 42.72 percent) and George Wallace, with 9,906,141 votes (or 13.53 percent). All other minor-party candidates and freaks drew a total of 239,908 or 0.35 percent of the vote.[1]

The President's infinitesimal margin over the Democrat was 499,704 votes, barely four times as large as the 112,881 margin by which he had lost to John F. Kennedy eight years before. His total, however, was 2,338,345 millions less than he had drawn in his first try, despite the fact that the number of votes cast in the 1968 election was more than 4,000,000 higher than those cast in 1960.

What the tiny margin of victory concealed, however, was the fact of landslide—for the election of 1968 was the first landslide of its

---

[1] All the following figures, for the sake of conformity, are taken from the final official totals as published by the Associated Press. See Appendix.

kind in American history, a negative landslide. Americans turned against the whole set of Democratic policy and leadership of the previous four years—but could not make up their minds in which new direction they would move. Of the 43,000,000 Americans who voted for Lyndon Johnson and the Democrats in 1964, 28 percent, or 12,000,000, repudiated him, a repudiation greater than that suffered by any President except Herbert Hoover. But as they turned their backs on Johnson, Humphrey and the Democrats, and voiced their preference for a conservative alternative, they split their votes between a humane and centrist conservative and a menacing, racist conservative.

No more thoroughly blurred election has occurred in American history since that of 1876. The normal sweeps and surges of voting patterns that bring a President to the White House buttressed by his own House and Senate were totally absent. A nation torn in conscience, divided over war, embittered by race hatreds, presented with three, not the traditional two, candidates, voted in the various states as if each community had a puzzle of three major variables and a dozen local conditionings, each state trying to solve the puzzle in its own way. The number of those who split their ballots rose to 54 percent. Arkansas voted for racist, warlike George Wallace for President; for liberal Republican Winthrop Rockefeller as Governor; and for the peace-minded scholar Democrat William Fulbright as Senator. New York gave Hubert Humphrey 49.8 percent of its vote—a plurality over Nixon of 370,532 —but the Democrats lost control of the New York State Assembly. Pennsylvania turned out Democratic dove Senator Joseph Clark to give its Senatorial mandate to a youthful Republican, Richard Schweiker; but it gave its Presidential mandate to Hubert Humphrey and, in another spin, overturned the traditional Republican control of the Pennsylvania Assembly and gave it to the Democrats. In California and Iowa, Richard M. Nixon won handily—but Californians and Iowans both elected Democrats to the Senate the same day. Nationally, the Republicans added five governorships to their roll, bringing their roster of Republican governors to thirty-one—the highest since 1920.[2] (Every single major industrial state of North and West now has a Republican governor with the exception of two Democratic holdovers in New Jersey and Connecticut—yet Nixon carried only six of these major states in the election.) In the Senate, the Republicans added five to their total of seats, leaving them still a minority party of 43 as against 57 Democrats. In the House, the Republicans added only four seats, leaving them a minority of 192 against 243 Democrats. The House seemed more conservative in texture—but the Senate more liberal.

[2] The resignation, later, of Spiro T. Agnew to become Vice-President gave the Maryland Statehouse to a Democrat, thus reducing the Republican total to thirty governors—still their highest mark since 1952.

As if to underline their perplexity, the percentage of eligible Americans who voted dropped. In 1960 (Kennedy against Nixon) 63.8 percent of all eligible Americans voted; in 1964 (Johnson against Goldwater) 62.1 percent voted. In 1968, a year of wild excitement, when the voting percentage might have been expected to rise sharply, it dropped yet further—to 61 percent. The drop would be even sharper were it not for the fact that in the Southern states, where race was the cutting issue for both blacks and whites, the vote rose sharply. Of those fifteen states in the nation where the vote did rise, ten were Southern or Border states.

Psephologists will continue for years, as they are doing now, to break down the results of the 1968 elections by state, community and precinct.[3] But the gross and somber impact of the nearly tragic election of 1968 can best be seen by withdrawing from the months of the campaign and the day of voting, and projecting it against the past of American history.

In 1968 the American people repudiated the administration of Lyndon Johnson in one of the greatest somersaults of their political history. Only twice before have the Americans ever turned so completely against national leadership in any four-year period, and those repudiations followed, as did the 1968 upheaval, on cataclysmic events. In the 1928–1932 period the Depression exposed Herbert Hoover as a complete incompetent, and his total of 59 percent in 1928 fell to 41 percent in 1932. In the 1916–1920 swing, almost of equivalent magnitude, the American people expressed their dissatisfaction with a war that had come to no good end; but the nervous breakdown of Woodrow Wilson and his inability to campaign for his Party complicated that swing. Between 1964 and 1968, however, occurred a swing of mood so dramatic that the champion of 1964, Lyndon Johnson, did not even dare defend in the public places of 1968 the course which he had led the nation for four years. And never, not even in 1932, has any great American party's vote shrunk so dramatically.

When one adds the Wallace and Nixon votes together, their combined total of 56.9 percent to 42.7 percent for Humphrey is an historic turning-of-the-back on all the great promises and domestic experiments of one of the most visionary administrations ever to hold the helm in America. The vote was, to be sure, conditioned at every level by the unending war in Vietnam; but Americans were given no clear choice of direction in the war, either by Richard Nixon or by Hubert Humphrey. The net result was a blurred mandate for Richard M. Nixon rising chiefly

[3] Two excellent studies of election results in 1968 are *The Emerging Republican Party Majority* by Kevin P. Phillips (Arlington House, 1969), a novel study of electoral results by ethnic patterns and historical impulses; and *Lessons of Victory* by the Ripon Society (Dial Press, 1969), a liberal Republican analysis of the election's meaning.

from Americans' consideration of their condition at home. The mood was undeniably a swing to the right, an expression of a vague sentiment for a government oriented to caution and restraint. And the mood that underlay the election results provokes another observation on the unique moment in America. Never have its leading cultural media, its university thinkers, its influence-makers been more intrigued by experiment and change; but in no election have the mute masses more completely separated themselves from such leadership and thinking. Mr. Nixon's problem is to interpret what the silent people think, and govern the country against the grain of what its more important thinkers think.

The traditional refinement of the voting figures of the nation by region or ethnic bloc adds little to our close vision or analysis of the election except for its isolation of the Wallace phenomenon in all its dramatic and future portent. Geographically, however, the profile of the American vote in 1968 ran thus:

Richard M. Nixon swept thirty-two states with a total of 302 electoral votes—and those states stretch in a solid block, almost unbroken from the western slope of the Alleghenies straight through to the Pacific shore. Beyond the Mississippi, Hubert Humphrey won only four states—Texas, Minnesota, Washington and Hawaii. Humphrey's vote lay in the industrial quadrangle, the clotted urban East, those muscular, powerful states like New York, Pennsylvania, Massachusetts, Michigan, writhing in the torment of undefinable urban and racial crisis. Here, Humphrey carried nine more states plus Washington, D.C., which, with their total of 143 votes, brought his electoral total to 191.

The ethnic and socio-economic analyses of the vote seemed almost unimportant when contrasted with the primordial black/white split. The old Catholic/Protestant split, so significant as a cutting edge in defining the 1960 election, had faded since then. American Catholics of Italian, Irish, Polish ancestry gave slightly more of their vote to Richard Nixon than they had previously; so, too, marginally, did the Jews. But where one can split such ethnic votes they seem influenced chiefly by income levels—the poor and lower middle class voting overwhelmingly for Hubert Humphrey (except where race gave George Wallace the sheen of seduction) and the comfortable and well-to-do voting Republican.

In the social pattern there is to be recorded how well Hubert Humphrey did in various middle-class suburbs of the nation—notably in the suburban counties that fringe such cities as Boston, New York and Philadelphia. The education explosion of the past fifteen years has pumped out into suburbia, at least in the East, a new kind of people—college-educated administrators, teachers, scientists, civil servants, technicians, bureaucrats, corporate-enmeshed types who differ sharply from people of the same income levels a decade ago. An old rule of thumb, eroded by inflation, used to hold that anyone who earned over $10,000 a year was to be considered a Republican—either a businessman or a corporate employee at the executive level. But a new type of affluent American has grown up in the past fifteen years—an educated, technically trained elite whose members, though in many cases earning far more than the average private entrepreneur, vote differently. Sensitized by the influence media, protected from violence by the suburban belt, aware of a larger world abroad and a crescent scientific world a-borning, they vote as their conditioned intelligence tells them. The fall-off of the anticipated Nixon vote in Nassau County, in the suburbs of Philadelphia and in Boston was one of the striking sub-features of the election; only in California, in Orange and Los Angeles Counties, did the expected conservative suburban vote come through for Nixon in critical and thundering majorities.

Had there been a sharp definition of the two candidates' views on Vietnam, the war might have provided the great cutting edge of the election. But both candidates seemed engaged in variations of a fugue set by Lyndon Johnson. From beginning to end, Vietnam always rested in every poll, private, public or scholastic, as the number-one concern of the American people. Except that, on further refinement, no candidate could do anything with the information, for, once Americans had expressed this critical concern, they divided sharply as to how the Vietnam war might be solved. A candidate accepting surrender would have been destroyed; a candidate insisting on conquest at all cost would similarly have been destroyed. Thus both candidates passed on the issue of Vietnam, using it only to shade their self-portraits as men of independent thinking, deep patriotism and hidden concern.

In the absence of a clear-cut debate on Vietnam, the great issue of the election was race, or law-and-order, or, as it was never defined, the civil peace. Here George Wallace ruptured the pattern of American voting, whether permanently or not we do not yet know.

There are two ways of assessing the morbid phenomenon of the Wallace vote. One way is to look at the Wallace vote outside the Solid South, the other is to button down the historic trend-line in the Old South.

Outside the Solid South, George Wallace managed to accumulate no less than 4,100,000 votes. He did best in certain Rocky Mountain states (Nevada, 13.2 percent, and Idaho, 12.5 percent) and in several industrial Midwestern states (Ohio, 11.8 percent; Michigan, 10 percent; Indiana, 11.4 percent; Illinois, 8.5 percent). He fared poorly in New York (5.3 percent), in Massachusetts (3.7 percent), in California (6.8 percent). In two Middle Atlantic states, Pennsylvania and Maryland, he claimed, respectively, 8.1 percent and 14.5 percent. All in all, in no less than thirty states of the union George Wallace managed to disturb the balance of power; the two major candidates were able to win a clear majority victory in only twenty states. The amateur management of the final Wallace election campaign, the pressure of the media and influence-makers and labor unions, reduced the Wallace vote far below its true potential. Shrewd management of such voters in the future may make them far more significant.

More important is the trend-line in the Old South. The Old South is that region of the United States now in fullest revolt against the direction of the Federal government of the United States. Over the past twenty years—since the campaign of Strom Thurmond in 1948—at least five Southern states have shown that they will, under any leadership, at any opportunity, under any banner, vote against the directions which national Republicans and Democrats both share. Alabama, Mississippi, Louisiana are the core—they will vote, and have voted, against black people in any national election, for anyone, simian, unwashed or demagogic. To them, theoretically, should be added the state of South Carolina, held in line for Nixon in 1968 only by Strom Thurmond. Georgia, too, is now probably locked into the racist bloc.

For the Democrats, the problem the South poses is one of absolute peril. The old national Democratic Party—as distinct from the local or Congressional Democratic parties—has all but disappeared in the South. In the Old South, despite the rise in Southern voting, the Democratic share of the vote has shrunk to 31.1 percent. Of this 31.1 Democratic percentage, more than two-thirds, in the election of 1968, were probably Southern blacks. If the trend-line continues, the Democratic Party may disappear as a national party which can rouse loyalties in every section of the nation. If the Democrats shrink to a ghetto vote in the South, they could become a party dominated by Northern labor unions, big-city minority blocs, and ideologues who control the new campus proletariat. To this peril and its solution, the Democrats have yet to address themselves.

For the Republicans, the problem is one of equally difficult but more promising options. No one is more aware than President Nixon of the minority status of his Party, and the need to expand its base. In Nixon's own phraseology, Roosevelt "inherited" his grand coalition; he did not create it. The grand coalition coalesced about Roosevelt because the Republican Party had been blind to the changes in America. To create his own coalition, Nixon feels that positive action is required, and there are two prime areas of exploration—the first being the South, the second being the industrial cities of the East. It is in the South that the problem poses itself most acutely—for to create the lasting base in the South, the Wallace party must be reduced. The Wallace voters are people in transition, men who have deserted tradition because tradition runs against their animal instinct; yet they have found no home. To shame the Wallace voters for their racism, yet to meet their legitimate worries, is the prime prerequisite of expanding the Republican Party's Southern base. If the challenge is successfully met in the South, the base in the Northern cities will expand automatically, too. Yet this expansion of the Republican base depends not on tactics, but on how the new administration behaves on the grand scale of history, on whether it can match the Rooseveltian sweep and grandeur in the thirties.

For the nation, the structure of the Southern vote and its trend pose a problem of far greater magnitude. The new structure of the Southern vote offers a solid and permanent temptation to any extreme dissident to carry away an easy 45 electoral votes—and, in the future, perhaps as many as 90 votes—from the total of 538 in the Electoral College. The two major candidates, Republican and Democratic, would be condemned to divide the rest in what could become an unending series of contested elections.

Americans stand thus, for the first time in a century, in a new contemplation of their political personality. It is the choice of leaders that creates the personality of a political community; and if the way we choose our leaders is to be changed by the racial clash, so long buried in our history, then the debate over electoral reform and the choice of President is a debate that may alter the entire personality of American life.

A reporter who loves the American political process, acknowledging no greater wisdom than any other student, must occasionally abandon the reportorial role for reflection. And the highly personal reflections of this reporter, provoked to alarm as so many other Americans have been provoked by the elections of 1960 and 1968, refracts the national debate on electoral reform through the various prisms of his experience, here and abroad.

One begins with reflection on other political systems one has observed, and the way they choose leaders.

I begin in Asia twenty-five years ago, in Yenan, at a meeting of the cadres of the Chinese Communist Party in an unheated, draft-leaking, mud-chinked assembly hall where Mao Tse-tung spoke. There was no doubt, as Mao strode on stage in his brown Shensi woolens, who was master, always had been master, always would be master. As he entered the hall, the Central Committee members in the front seats all came to attention, smiling and fawning, and I remember Chou En-lai, now China's premier, pulling out his note-pad, conspicuously holding it high, to show Mao, the teacher-master, how attentive he, the pupil, was. There was no doubt then in 1944 that this leader was self-chosen; that authority was his alone; that no votes were ever taken in such an assemblage; that succession of leadership would pass at his will to whomever he chose; and that he would kill guiltlessly, as other Chinese tyrants had killed, because he alone held and understood the Mandate of Heaven. In the West, for centuries the same passage of authority by designation of tyrants was known as the Divine Right of Kings. Generally, over the millennia, East and West, leadership has always been passed on by such directed authority, without popular consent.

I remember the post-war experience of reporting in Western Europe, where people indeed did have a choice of expression for their leaders. In Western Europe, centuries of bloodshed and political experiment created what is accepted as the "parliamentary" system of choice. The people chose their parliamentary representatives, in their limited districts; a party bureaucracy harnessed these members under tight discipline; the bureaucracy slowly, over decades, extruded leadership figures from the ranks of members, and one could tell, years in advance, who would be the leader if the party came to power. The people had choice of party—but within their party they had little choice of leader. In post-war France, so many were the choices of party that two of the fundamental rights of free men were always constitutionally as clash. People have the right of free choice of party representatives; but they also have the right to be governed effectively and led in clear directions—and in France these two rights contradicted each other. With six major parties in the Assembly of the Fourth Republic, the loyalties of these parties' leaders to their voters and ideologies forced them constantly to fall out. When they fell out, leadership flickered so fast on the rostrum of the Palais Bourbon that no national decisions could, effectively, be made. Frenchmen had eyestrain watching the revolving characters. Thus came De Gaulle—a man who, whatever his faults, believed that people need government as much as they need air, water and food. De Gaulle came to power by a military *putsch;* he remained in power for eleven years because no other leadership could muster a majority against him; and fell, finally, when he chose to stake his career on a plebiscite of the "ins" against the undefined "outs."

The choice of the "ins" against the "outs" is of the essence of the American political system; translated from the vulgate into the discourse of political scientists, this system effectively offers the American people in a Presidential election a choice of two strong leaders responsive to popular will. Students whom I have talked to at rallies are commonly dismayed by the discourse of Presidential candidates. No matter what a candidate says at any rally, the common student complaint wherever I have gone is "He didn't say anything," or "He made a lot of promises, but he didn't say how" or "He didn't say anything specific about how he was going to end the war in Vietnam; he says he's for peace, but he didn't say how." The choice offered in an American election is never a choice of programs and specifics; it is simply a setting of direction, an attempt by two men to point the different ways they hope to go; in America, people vote not on program but on what they sense the inclination and direction of the candidates to be. Traditionally, therefore, this translates into "ins" against "outs," into the wonderful baroque language of the stump: "We point with pride to . . ." or "I say the time has come when we must stop . . ."

The Constitution of the United States did not set up the Presidential contest as this direct referendum between the "ins" and the "outs." American history imposed its own will on the intentions of the Constitution-writers. The Constitution, written by one of the most learned and scholarly groups of Americans ever assembled, set up the selection of President as something to be determined by wise men who had earned the trust of their local voters and who would meet, in an Electoral College, each in their own state, in sober discourse. Collectively, they would vote for the man they considered strong and wise enough to lead the nation. The man who received the highest vote would become President; the next highest recipient of electoral votes would become Vice-President; the selection would deliver the two best men in the country to lead.

But the system did not work that way. Within eight years of its adoption, it had miscarried and John Adams, as recipient of the largest number of electoral votes in 1796, was President, as a Federalist; and his rival, Thomas Jefferson, a Democratic-Republican, was adjudged second-best man and, thus, Vice-President. The stuttering of the system became more obvious four years later, when Jefferson himself became President—and his treacherous ally, Aaron Burr, attempted to snatch the electoral prize from him and wound up as Vice-President.

The Jefferson-Burr contest of 1800–1801 provoked the first great cry for reform, ultimately encased in the Constitution as its Twelfth Amendment. By then, however, a native and tenacious sense of politics in the increasing states had established the usefulness of what is now called the "unit rule." A small state could not expect to swing much voice in the choice of a President if it split its electors. By various devices, starting in the small states which attempted to maximize their electoral clout by unit voting, the custom and law became that whichever candidate carried a state, by however slim a margin, that candidate would also carry all the votes of the state. The custom was already binding political practice when, in 1804, the Twelfth Amendment was passed. But the Amendment-writers, ignoring this reality, limited themselves to an enormously complicated revision of the Constitution which left individual electors free in conscience to vote as they wished; and required that if they could not deliver a clear majority, then choice of

President would go to the House (each state voting as a unit for one among the three highest candidates) and choice of Vice-President would go to the Senate (each Senator voting between the two highest candidates).

The Twelfth Amendment to the American Constitution is probably the worst-worded, most legally complicated of all its provisions. But it was absorbed by the American people and encapsulated like a closed-over abscess as they went on to choose between the "ins" and the "outs," custom requiring electors to do their duty and vote for the candidate their state had chosen.

The amazing thing about the American electoral system, even with the built-in and unstable gimmickry of the Twelfth Amendment, is that it has worked so well. More than a century and a half has passed since the Twelfth Amendment was ratified. Under its provisions, a second election went to the House—in 1824, when John Quincy Adams was named President by the states voting in the House as single units. Twice since then the loser in the popular vote has won the majority of electoral votes and become President—in 1876 (Hayes over Tilden) and in 1888 (Harrison over Cleveland). But the American people accepted. There have been at least four close elections in this century—none requiring an appeal from the popular vote and Electoral College to the House. But the rate of uncertainty accelerates. Twice within the past decade, popular voting has brought the choice of President to the edge of chaos—Kennedy over Nixon by less than two-tenths of one percent, Nixon over Humphrey by seven-tenths of one percent. Both times the much-maligned Electoral College system saved us. But now the growth of the third party of the South threatens its ability to surmount the challenge of the coming decade; and a period of Constitutional emergency is upon us.

One must separate out principle from reality to appreciate the ongoing debate about reform of electoral laws for President.[4]

The key idea of the Constitution is Federalism—however much complicated by its Article Two and Amendment Twelve on the choice of President. The Constitution sets up, as principle, that the Americans should vote, in communities by states, as a federation.[5]

---

[4] The best study I have found on the laws and customs of American electoral choice is *The People's President,* by Neal R. Pierce (Simon and Schuster, New York, 1968).

[5] This principle has honorable and worthy antecedents. The longest-lasting free republic in the history of man, the Roman Republic, also voted by federal units. It was necessary for a consul to win the majority of units of thirty-five Roman tribes, just as an American President must win a majority of the electoral votes of the states. The Romans were as perplexed as we by the problem of direct voting. Their customs ordained that all voters must be physically present in the

The federal principle is a powerful one, perhaps sounder now in this Age of Experiment than when it was encoded in 1787. Where the Constitution errs, and dangerously errs, is in caging this principle within the entirely obsolete Electoral College. The electors of the College still legally choose the President, after the people have theoretically chosen the electors. In most states, however, the naming of electors is done in practice by party committees or party leaders to give lesser badges of honor to obscure party faithful; in most states, names of electors do not even appear on the ballot. In sixteen states the electors are fossilized, like flies in amber, by state laws that require them to vote for the candidate the people choose. They do not know each other, do not deliberate together, do not consider or discuss candidates. They are supposed to, and almost always do, vote for the candidate the people of their state have chosen. Yet the Supreme Court has held that they cannot legally be compelled to do so. And as passions rise, as the permanent third party of the South grows in strength, it seems ever more likely that these unknown relics of antiquity may attempt to exercise individual and selective judgment on their own. In 1960, fourteen electors from Alabama and Mississippi, and one from Oklahoma chose to cast their votes for Senator Harry F. Byrd of Virginia although he appeared nowhere on the ballot. In the closing days of the 1968 campaign a newspaper boomlet arose for Nelson Rockefeller as deadlock candidate if the electors could not achieve a majority. In all fact, the Electoral College, as at present frozen into the law of the land, is an anachronistic survival of a primitive past—as useless as a row of nipples on a boar hog.

The chief alternative proposal in present debate is that of direct election of the President by all the people of the United States, one

---

Ovile on the Campus Martius on that day in July when the consul was normally chosen. But since this system of direct voting would have given advantage to the four tribes who lived in Rome itself, and diminished the impact of citizens of other tribes who lived at a further distance or who had scattered from the Po Valley to Sicily in the growth of Roman power, direct voting took place under complicated rules, within the tribes, and each tribe had an equal vote. Thus, distant members could come into Rome for the vote and, voting in their tribes, would not be overwhelmed by the mob vote that urban politicians could call out. This system, of course, gave a violent advantage to conservative and well-to-do voters; ordinary farmers living far from Rome could not afford the time away from their summer labors in the field to come to Rome and cast their vote; nor could soldiers. The well-to-do, the elite, the *equitores* were those most able to make the journey to Rome for the great choice, and their vote, with rare exceptions, swung the elections to the *nobiles*. The convulsions of Rome, from the time of the Gracchi to the time of Caesar, hung, above all, on their effort to solve this constitutional problem—of how a government of free men, growing powerful in freedom, could govern a world empire and choose world leaders by their ancient customs. Ultimately, of course, they failed—but not before they had governed themselves for more than four hundred years, a considerable span. For the best studies of Roman voting, one should consult the works of that brilliant scholar, Lily Ross Taylor of Bryn Mawr. For a fanciful study of the problem, amusement may be found in *Caesar at the Rubicon,* an essay in melodrama by this writer.

man, one vote. This is a proposal favored by sitting-down political analysts. It rests on the generalized theory of the assembly-as-the-whole, or the principle that people, to exercise power, must exercise it absolutely directly.[6]

To approve the theory of assembly-of-the-whole as a way of electing Presidents of the United States is to be so unaware of present reality as to approach insanity.

There is, to begin with, the need to recognize that voting qualifications differ in every state. Four states permit citizens to vote under the age of 21—Georgia and Kentucky at 18, Alaska at 19, Hawaii at 20—the other forty-six do not. By altering its age laws to 18, or to 16, or to 14, any state can increase its proportion of the whole vote at will; it can also do so by altering its laws so as to include the large numbers of criminals, convicts, mentally incompetent now all variously excluded. Direct, national, one-man-one-vote elections would require a national election law establishing national qualifications and national registration in every one of the 3,130 counties of the United States.

But it requires more than that—it requires national surveillance of each of the approximately 167,000 voting precincts of the United States. And no national surveillance can work without the establishment of a national police system. Those who report elections know, alas, that the mores and morality of vote-counting vary from state to state. The votes of Minnesota, California, Wisconsin and half a dozen other states are as honorably collected and counted as votes anywhere in the world. There are other states in the Union where votes are bought, paid for and, in all too many cases, counted, manipulated and miscounted by thieves. The voting results of the valley counties of Texas are a scandal; so, too, are the voting results in scores of precincts of Illinois' Cook County; so, too, in ward after ward in West Virginia, in the hills of Tennessee and Kentucky, and in dozens of other pockets of rural or urban machine-controlled slums.

The present Federal system compartmentalizes voting in the United States by states; the votes of honest states are not balanced off or outbalanced by dishonest counting in other states; contagion of vote-stealing is limited. If all the 68,000,000 votes of 1960 and all the 73,000,-000 votes of 1968 had been cast in one great national pool, then the

[6] The antecedents of this theory are as ancient as the Roman roots of Federalism, yet quite contrary. The prehistoric Germans chose their leaders and went to war by assembling in the forests and deciding policies by the loudest yellings and clash of shields. The Gauls went the Germans one better, in a concept of assembly-of-the-whole which still intrigues me. When the Gallic tribes decided to go to war and the assembly had voted for it, muster was held immediately—every man raced home to get his spear and shield and then raced back to fall in line. And they raced very speedily; the last man to show up with arms after the call had passed was killed.

tiny margins of victory in both elections would have evaporated. Each candidate would, necessarily, have had to call for a recount, and recounts would have continued, nationwide, for months. Vote-stealers in a dozen states would have matched crafts on the level of history; and, so slim was the margin, we might yet be waiting for the final results of both elections. And no practical proposal has yet been made to establish either national qualifications, national registration or, above all, national surveillance of counting.

Another proposal—that of dividing the electoral vote of each state among the candidates in proportion to the popular vote within the state —is a proposal for retaining the receptacle of state-by-state voting, but for casting away its content. By this proposal, the electoral votes of each state would remain the same (the number of its Congressmen, plus two more for its Senators). But in each state the electoral vote would be divided to correspond with the percentages of the popular vote in that state.

This is a more substantial proposal than that of direct voting, but it has been debated, under various names and styles, for several decades in Congress.

There are two main objections to this system—one political, the other technical.

Politically, this system has been opposed chiefly by the spokesmen of the big cities and the minority ethnic groups, who likewise, and for similar reasons, oppose direct voting. The spokesmen of the cities and the ethnic blocs have always held that the structure of Congress is cast against them; Congress is dominated by traditionalists who control its committees, and, despite recent reforms, Congress is still weighted heavily in favor of rural areas. Such spokesmen insist that the traditional political counter-balance to Congress has been the President, as executive—he is elected by the states, in the largest of which huge electoral-vote blocs may be swung by the voting of local minorities. It is the Presidential, not the Congressional, elections that make the Mexican-American vote of Texas and California important, the Negro vote of Pennsylvania and Illinois important, the Jewish vote of New York important, the Italian vote of the New England states and New Jersey important. To abolish the winner-take-all system in the states is to eliminate the chief leverage the minorities feel they have in national politics. This argument is a difficult one to defend theoretically, or at any high-minded level; but, pragmatically, it reflects the nature of America.

A more important technical objection insists on hearing also—a technical objection raised to insistence by the development of the third party in the South. No one has yet defined, nor can anyone define, what is meant by "proportional splitting of a state's vote." Does one mean exact proportions? Should New York's 43 electoral votes have been split at 49.8 percent for Humphrey, Michigan's 21 electoral votes at 48.2 percent for Humphrey, Ohio's 26 votes at 45.2 percent for Nixon and so on? Most importantly—what, under this plan, would have been the distribution of George Wallace's percentages? The addition of his electors in Maryland, in the Carolinas, in Florida, in Michigan, in Indiana, might have been sufficient to throw the election to the House. And the mind boggles at what might have happened as the mathematicians decimalized the percentages of the election of 1960, which would have resulted in Kennedy over Nixon by 00.497 etc. over the 00.496 (almost) of the whole that America voted. How many digits would it have required to establish a President by digitalizing yet further the electoral votes of 1960 within the states to their ultimate percentages? Would it have given a clearer leadership to the American people than the solid, hard numbers of the old Electoral College which ran 303 for Kennedy to 219 for Nixon?

Yet a third system has been offered for consideration. It is the election of the President by electoral votes by Congressional district— one electoral vote for whoever carried the majority in each district, two votes (to reflect Senatorial presence) to be determined statewide. This is Federalism carried to extreme; the hard-core Congressional districts of the conservative South and the ethnic-minority blocs of the big cities would be given almost no incentive to vote; the results of such districts would be known years in advance by demographic calculation; and the swing districts of the suburbs with their own parochial needs would be the chief determinants of the choice of President.

One can find fault with any system of choice of leaders. For two thousand years—or longer, if one wants to go back to the Confucian initiative in Chinese thought—men have tried to find a perfect system of leadership. When Moses descended from Mount Sinai, the Hebrews asked of him, "Who placed you as officer and ruler over us?" and Moses had no answer. In Western history, church and academy, tyrant and politician, scholar and terrorist have all tried to answer this question in challenging or defending systems of government. None has had complete answers either. In the last century of American history, no less than 513 resolutions have been introduced into the Congress of the United States for revising our Presidential electoral laws; and none has been accepted because there are no perfect solutions to the problems of leadership—because the thrust of politics must always run in the direction of the preamble of the Constitution of the United States, which says "We, the people of the United States, in order to make a *more* perfect Union . . ." "More perfect," says the phrase, not "perfect." Perfection is impossible.

In this reporter's opinion, the American system of Presidential election has worked for almost two centuries; yet the challenge remains to make it "more perfect." No present proposal under debate offers a wiser or better system of choice than the Federal idea underlying the present way Americans choose Presidents. In any election, some must be losers, some must be winners—and the Federal system has worked, in the experience of this turbulent decade, better than any of the rival proposals would have worked, given the results of 1960 and 1968. What must be made "more perfect" in the system must be done to confront the challenges of the next generation—above all, the challenge of the racist minority which would divide, rather than draw together, the American people.

Nor are the steps to make the present system "more perfect" necessarily too difficult. In this reporter's opinion, the first requirement must be the elimination, by Constitutional amendment, of the entire Electoral College and the anonymous members who cast electoral votes. States, however, should continue to vote by state, giving or denying all their electoral votes to a single candidate, with no intermediary device of individual electors to permit escape from, or distortion of, their vote. If a third party manages to capture enough electoral votes—as is its right—to deny any candidate a clear majority of good, round, solid electoral votes, then, as the Constitution foresaw, the decision must go to a higher court of appeal. There is little reason that I can see to change the identity of the present Court of Appeal, which is the House of Representatives. But since, in such a case, the Federal idea of a vote by communities of states will have failed to prevail, the House should be released from its present Constitutional mandate to vote by state, unit by unit, one state, one vote. Congressmen, elected every two years, are the men closest to the swing of sentiment in American life; and they should be permitted to vote individually, one man, one vote, for the President (and his chosen running-mate, the Vice-President) until a majority has been reached among them. If, at some point to be determined, they cannot reach a majority, then, after a fixed limit of ballots, the man who earns the plurality of votes among them should be constitutionally accepted as President, and his running-mate as Vice-President. And then it is up to him to make history. We may face a future of minority Presidents—but it should be remembered that the greatest of American Presidents, Abraham Lincoln, was the President chosen by the most diminished minority vote that ever elected a President of this country. He had a clear idea of what he wanted to do, and the country responded. There is no escape from the fact that men make history, and clear leadership gives ordinary men their only choice in history. Which brings us back to Richard M. Nixon.

An elected President of the United States stands on a pinnacle from which the view is incomprehensible to all other men. He must look two ways from the crest of command. Before him is the forward slope of the future, and all the executive problems of this complex, changing society. Behind him is the backward slope of the past, the people who have chosen him, with all their prejudices and fixed, contending traditions.

The problems that face him on the forward slope are so complicated by figures, by substance, by foreign response, by secret intelligence, by choice of lieutenants, by anticipated granting of privilege, that nothing he can say in a quick press conference, a fireside chat or televised happening can make them clear. He must decide by executive decision alone how he will proceed across the forward slope.

But the prime requirement he has for solving the problems is that the people of America trust him. On the backward slope of the inherited past he must earn the confidence of the people struggling up after him to follow him. Lyndon Johnson was a man of utmost intelligence and of general good-will; yet he could not earn the trust of his people. Worse than that, he left behind a tradition of distrust in leadership, a repudiation of Presidential capacity unmatched, emotionally, since the repudiation of Herbert Hoover. The problems of leadership Johnson left behind to Richard Nixon are far greater, therefore, than those Eisenhower left behind to John F. Kennedy—in re-establishing the confidence of the people as well as in the complexity of the war abroad and racial clash at home. Richard Nixon must, at once, come to correct decision as he leads on the executive forward slope, and earn, on the backward slope where the people follow, the confidence of millions of Americans who no longer trust any government of the United States.

It is important, therefore, to have one last look at both the man and the problems he faces.

CHAPTER THIRTEEN

SEASON FOR SURVIVAL:
THE AMERICA OF
RICHARD M. NIXON

FROM the thirty-ninth floor of the Pierre Hotel, one could see the park sweeping away. More than a century ago, the city fathers of New York had accepted the dream of a great interior park for the future metropolis; and now the dream shaped life below.

It was December, 1968; winter had seared the grass to a tawny carpet, and the park was naked—the Mall, the Sheep Meadow, all the gardens bare, the pond frozen, the boats drawn up in winter stacks. But it was alive still. Parents drew bundled-up tots after them to the zoo. Skaters twirled on the ice, in red and green, blue and yellow, tiny dots of color, scarves streaming out behind them. The warm and sunny room was too far, too high, for anyone behind its closed glass to hear them laugh, or shout, or cry. But it was a good scene, and a dream older than a century had created it. Without this park, the expression of the dream, the city would be unlivable—if, indeed, it were still livable at all.

This had been his view for five years, as a private citizen whose apartment, two blocks north up the avenue, looked out on the same park. But now, for him as President, the enclosure of the pretty scene below would be a frontier of problems. North of the park rose the russet wall of Harlem, sheltering the ghetto—what dreams could penetrate there? Across the park rose the ocher cliffs of Central Park West, a façade beyond which stretched those streets through which none but the foolhardy dared walk at night. North and west, one could see the ridge of Morningside Heights, crested by the Cathedral and the buildings of Columbia, where, only this year, a great university had been all but ruined by the sickness of the times. South rose the spires of Manhattan, the command post of American industry—but rooted in traffic and congestion that all but strangled the city.

Richard Nixon would be leaving soon, but the memory would always be with him, of the city, and what a dream had done for it; and the need of other, newer dreams for the larger community of the nation. He had long since ceased to be a Californian; he had never, really, been a New Yorker; his home place, truly, was Washington. And so now Richard Nixon was preparing to go home.

He was easier now, as we talked, than he had been during the campaign. The wound-up tensions and weariness of the long adventure had been with him when I had first visited him after election in November. The strains were still evident then—the restless movements of his body; the self-interruptions of his own conversation; the darting rambles and tangents of talk, as he had let the thread of sequence snap, and strayed in self-indulgence to memories of the campaign, anecdotes about people, gossip and rumination about prospective appointees, fragments of books he had been reading. Now, in December, a new and different kind of pressure was building. Closed-circuit television, manned by the Secret Service, guarded all entry to the Presidential floor of the Hotel Pierre; in adjacent suites waited Governors, Senators, staff aides with memoranda and programs. He must next week appoint a Cabinet—and it was frustrating, he said; he was more interested in ideas than in personnel, only ideas wouldn't work unless you organized people to get them done. But he was unhurried, leisurely, almost as if relieved to escape for an hour from the pressures of Cabinet-making. He still scribbled self-reminders on the yellow legal pads; but as he draped his legs over the arm of his chair, the flow of his conversation now went smoothly as if, in exploring a question, he was exploring himself.

He was, he said, answering my question, trying to look ahead. And the problem was, he continued, that for all the first year the country would be reacting to problems already presented; priorities would be forced on us, not set by a long-range effort. And it was important to look ahead, to look beyond that first year.

Vietnam had become obsessive in American thinking, he believed. Neither the President nor the Secretary of State had been dealing adequately with other problems. Someday the war in Vietnam would be ended; he could make no prediction—six months, a year, two years, he could set no time limit even in his own mind. But when the war was over, there would still be the whole world waiting for attention.

The first of the problems was the Soviet Union and the United States. Not just the hard matters of offensive-defensive missile systems, or nuclear disarmament, or defusing the situation in the Middle East. But more than that: how do you set up a procedure on a carefully planned basis for a continuing dialogue? He wasn't talking about a "wishful peace," he said. The great powers of the past had never agreed on the kind of world they were going to have, and *a fortiori* between two powers with such different views of the world. But a continuing dialogue *could* affect the current areas of disagreement; it could avoid and anticipate other areas of disagreement.

Then, in lawyer fashion, he stipulated that "also imperative is the condition precedent." Which brought him to Europe. Europe was the condition precedent, and we had been neglecting it, neglecting the British, neglecting the French and, most of all, the Germans, for the problem of Germany was still the heart of the thing. That had to be solved; NATO had sprung from a complex of reasons, but one of them was simply the need of giving the Germans a secure homeland. This brought him to priorities. Europe was the first priority of attention; then the Middle East— that cried out for a long-range solution. And so did Latin America—another long-range solution needed there. Then the even more difficult problem of Africa—that was even longer-range in its perplexity; not a single African nation, he pointed out, had yet seen its government changed in an orderly election; so we had to go slow there, we could not let ourselves be alarmed by every *coup* in the Congo.

He paused to reflect, as if reviewing the first page of a first draft to see where he was going, and then he observed: if there's one thing I am, it's a "whole-worlder, not a half-worlder." So that if you were looking ahead as far as three or four years, there was the China problem—which was why Japan was developing its new sense of urgency, he felt. That's why it was important to have the Asian nations develop their own "collective security." The Asians weren't quite ready for that yet; he meant, he explained, they couldn't yet defend their own internal security; only when China realized that she couldn't overthrow all other Asian nations would the way be open for an eventual dialogue with the Chinese—just as the dialogue with the Soviet Union had begun only after the Soviets had realized that the Europeans were strong enough to protect themselves. He was looking forward, someday, to starting the dialogue with China—but that would come only with an Asia strong enough to stand beside us politically, economically, internally, when the Chinese sensed that their own best interests would be served best by concentrating on their own internal problems.

Just as our own interests would be best served by concentrating on our problems, it appeared. At this point, again reviewing his own thinking, he pointed out that he was talking about foreign policy first because it was the *only* thing you could start with. You couldn't do anything in America internally until you got that solved. He had been looking at the Defense Budget and "it was the most shocking thing, those damned figures." Unless we could find some means of de-escalating the arms race, unless we could do that, we simply couldn't save our own system, even our freedoms could be lost under the arms burden. He didn't have all the answers; disarmament conferences didn't work. You simply had to deal with it as a sequence of urgencies, and he and his Secretary of State would have to develop some programmatic sense of what could be done to unlock the situation.

Then, finally, we were on to his America. That, he said, was so much *harder* to put. What do I see? he asked of himself. Oh, he said, "I can see the United States years from now as the best-fed, the best-clothed, the best-housed nation in the world—but also the ugliest nation in the world." In a campaign, candidates say things differently. If you're a candidate, you say we've got to get out of Vietnam—right. You say we've got to have law-and-order—right. You say we've got to save the dollar—right. But anybody who wanted to be President and didn't want to do that —he shouldn't even reach for the job. Because we can have all those things and still be a pretty unhappy country.

He groped about, trying to explain his thinking. Law-and-order? The restoration of order wouldn't be too difficult. There'd still be rioting students and Black Panthers. But there *would* be a new Attorney General, and a change in the attitude of court decisions; the country itself was slowly getting roused to the problem. So that he thought of law-and-order as a temporary crisis, not a long-range crisis.

What was the long-range crisis, then?

He paused and thought for a minute. It was somewhere, something about purpose. The country needed a sense of purpose, a sense of a binding ideal. The trouble, he said, lay rooted somehow in this prosperity, in the affluence itself. The young people, for example—they needed a sense of challenge, and the fact was we were probably doing too much for our young people, they were given too much, too easily; and this weakened them. They needed a sense of common challenge, *needed* it. He thought Kennedy had hit the matter well in his inaugural: "Ask not what your country can do for you, but what you can do for your country." He agreed with that—but the big question was implementing it, to find the *way* to challenge their energies and involve them. But how?

Did I remember the kick-off of the campaign? he asked. The phrase he had used in the opening speech at New Hampshire—"the country needs the lift of a driving dream"? That's what he was looking for.

1968 was a strange year to end talking with a President-Elect about the value of dreams. It had been a year in which 16,511 Americans died in Vietnam, and the year closed as it began with America as powerless to make peace as she was to impose victory. It had been a year when the distant enemy on the battlefields seemed less menacing to millions of Americans than their fellow countrymen at home. It had been a year of nightmares rather than dreams; and the next President of the United

States would face a crisis equal in magnitude to Lincoln's in 1860, or Roosevelt's in 1932. Those crises, however, had been defined—freedom rather than slavery, employment rather than hunger. Richard M. Nixon's crisis was far more complex; it defied definition, thus it was graver.

It is difficult to be precise about the nature of the nightmare year out of which came Nixon's election. No phrase, no thought can catch, hold and bind together in one frame all the roaring events, the blood and disorders, the inflation and uprisings; for underlying them all was the general sense of breakdown—breakdown of control of old instruments, breakdown of manners, breakdown of institutions, breakdown of leadership uncertain of its purposes and unclear in its language, breakdown, above all, of ideas and dreams that once made Americans a community.

One must fall back on clichés to describe the year—for clichés are generally true and describe the action in accepted terms. The cliché for 1968 is, therefore, the cliché of change—not the sudden ripping apart of an ancient system in instant crisis, but the cracking of a system under previous strains and temptations, finally bursting visibly in the streets.

Raw, dislocating change has been moving in America at such speed and with such force that in 1968 it reached the point of overpowering American understanding; and as America outran its comprehension of itself, inherited tradition and inherited knowledge could no longer master reality. "Folk-wisdom," said the late Robert Oppenheimer shortly before he died, "can cry out in pain, but it can't provide solutions."

In America in 1968, folk-wisdom not only ran out of solutions, it ran out of common standards of judgment; and without such common standards, there could be no sense of order, no thongs of discipline to bind individuals to each other, to law, to moralities, to community. At the root of the matter lay a homely fact, so long buried in the past of American politics as to have all but disappeared from serious discussion: nations need dreams, goals they seek in common, within which the smaller dreams of individuals can guide their personal lives. It was as if a master hand had descended and confused the tongues of Americans, made a Babel of their words so that when one group spoke the other could not understand its language. No policeman, no new law-enforcement agency, no new laws can maintain discipline if dreams and ideas do not urge people to go the same way together, with the same civility to others that they expect for themselves.

If change was what caused the cracking of dreams in 1968, the new dynamic was the very pace of change itself. The accelerating rhythm of new perceptions, new technologies, new knowledge had been churning out new opportunities, new appetites, new temptations, new capacities too fast for folk-wisdom to grasp, for dreams to adjust; in 1968 the rhythm rocked all politics, and politics, too, cracked.

We should linger over the rhythm of our time to see how different it is from other times. Change is the law of history itself, moving slowly or rapidly through every era; but in ours it has come almost ungoverned.

In times gone by, decades, centuries, ages were permitted to folk-wisdom to adjust to the pace of novelty. It was sixty years between James Watt's invention of the steam engine in 1769 and Stephenson's first practical steam locomotive in 1829; and another generation before the social laws of England caught up with what steam power did to industry, and industry to people. It was twenty-four years between the first flight of the Wright brothers and Charles Lindbergh's first solo transatlantic flight, then another twenty years before transatlantic flights became common. It was forty years between the time that Einstein announced $E = mc^2$ and the demonstration of that fancy in the sky over Hiroshima in 1945.

But now, in the 1960's, the rhythms of change have burst containment or governance.

§ In 1960 the moon still hung in the skies, a flat disk to some, green cheese to others, a lantern for lovers in the fall—but incredibly remote, beyond man's ken. In 1961 John F. Kennedy announced that Americans in the decade of the sixties would reach the moon. In the years since then, after $24 billion spent, with only three deaths to mourn in the adventure, Americans stand ready to walk on the moon, and may have done so by the time this book is in print.

In the sweep of time, the adventure has occupied a nano-second. Generations passed after Columbus' landing in the New World, before men could accept the thought that the world was *really* round; and centuries before the New World became real in politics as well as in romance. A Pope could attempt to draw a line through the New World, dividing it between Spain and Portugal. There is no universal Pope today, no law-giver. How will outer space be governed? No one knows, for speed has outrun judgment; and no institutions are ready to offer guidance.

§ It was only in May, 1960—while both John F. Kennedy and Richard M. Nixon were struggling toward their final clash—that the Pill was introduced to American life, the first safe oral contraceptive, releasing the ecstasy of sex from the discipline of love or parenthood.

Since then the American birthrate has fallen from 23.7 per thousand to 21 per thousand in 1964, to 17.4 per thousand in 1968. Within five years of the introduction of the pill, one woman in four under thirty was using it; of all married women, 84 percent were using some form of birth control.

The speed of change in this most personal of matters has provoked another crisis of values. Sex without obligation or devotion is a concept so new that decades should pass to let our laws adjust to the new idea, to let institutions accept the value and social use of contraception. Yet time will not wait, and as one of his parting legacies to the new President, Lyndon Johnson left the recommendation of a special Presidential commission that birth control become a positive obligation of the Federal government—implying a new, more formal, governmental discipline over the act of love itself, because the ancient discipline has ceased to run.

§ Pace of change creates insoluble administrative problems.

In October, 1958, the first efficient jet-powered passenger plane, the Boeing 707, carried its first commercial passengers—from New York to Paris. The engineers who designed that aircraft predicted fully and accurately its explosive impact, and the inability of any authority—municipal, federal or local—to prepare for its reception, or adequately to cope with the congestion and turmoil it would create in the skies or in ground access. By the summer of 1968 the growth of air traffic had reduced travel at America's major air terminals in peak hours on peak days to a squalor not equaled since the condition of steerage travel two generations before.

There is now, aloft and flying, the first experimental air bus, the Boeing 747, which can triple the capacity of a single plane to move men at 625 miles an hour, from coast to coast, city to city. The air bus is a quantum jump in aviation. No airport in the United States and no political authority has even remotely adequate plans for ground facilities and terminals to absorb the impact of the new plane. Again a technical innovation has outrun the foresight of political authority. The questions which the air bus poses do not fit easily into American political discourse: Should the introduction of the new plane be forbidden until ground facilities are ready? Should travel be restricted in peak periods by fiat? Should the government's essential resources be conscripted from more important human needs to make ready the facilities that pure technology in aircraft requires to make the new mode of travel manageable?

§ The pace of change erodes every assumption of American foreign policy.

In 1960 Japan, to take one example, was an American satellite. The growth curve of Japan's energy since then is a phenomenon absolutely unprecedented in world history. A nation utterly annihilated in 1945, its industrial centers literally flattened, its merchant marine sunk, its spirit shattered, Japan has come to a capacity which marks it third (and rapidly closing on Russia, which is second) of the world's industrial nations. Its shipyards produce half the world's shipping, nineteen times as much annually as the American shipyards which built the fleet that once destroyed them. Its steel industry, which twenty years ago produced less than one percent of the tonnage of American steel mills, now produces more than half our tonnage. Its universities and colleges—the real seedbeds of strength—have tripled their student enrollment since 1950, to almost 1,200,000; have left European enrollment figures far behind; and are outstripped only by Russia and the United States in proportion of student population to the nation as a whole.

In the decade of the 1970's, realistically, Americans must anticipate that Japan, as one of the three major world powers, will express its own sense of national policy. But nothing has prepared the popular American view of Japan—seen as a defeated, now docile, subordinate power—for the adjustment which the pace of change in Japan will force upon us.

The moon, the pill, air-traffic congestion, Japan are only a few of those areas where the pace of change forces us to decision faster than our ideas can sort out right from wrong; half a dozen other areas of approaching trauma come to mind. Yet Richard Nixon in 1969, and until the end of his term in office, must face problems rushing at him even more swiftly than these. And in each he faces the same conundrum. He must lead a people and guide a Congress, both of them imprisoned in old dreams, conventional wisdom, accepted myths and concepts—yet recognize the assault of newer temptations, newer ideas and the clamor for instant solutions.

What is common among the problems that must lie on the agenda of Richard Nixon is that few of them are amenable any longer to conventional law-making. Endowed by the outgoing administration with the greatest mass of undigested legislation in American history, Nixon is left with problems whose solutions require either revision of the American Constitution or a change in the mood of American culture which he cannot control. All Presidents yearn to make their mark in history, and history awards its laurels to the action men, the bold ones. Nixon's personal heroes in conversation are Winston Churchill and Woodrow Wilson. Yet the problems he confronts permit no bold solutions, no simple strokes, no massive legislation. It is as if, elected President, he must first solve riddles; and it is in this light one must see the agenda before his administration.

In each of the main areas of his concern, one sees problems not as problems of action, but as problems of analysis—a problem either of discarding a time-hallowed idea or saving a still-valid idea from extinction by the blind forces of change that would suffocate it.

§   There is the idea of the City, first.

The word "city" bears its definition in itself. When primitive peasants first gathered together in clusters, they became *"cives,"* or citizens, of a *"civitas,"* or city—and the city was civilization. In the first cities peasants were freed from primitive slavery to the rhythm of the fields, and from the fear of random violence at the hands of marauders. The city offered safety and man-made order, divorced from the cruelty of nature.

The idea of the city grew slowly through the Middle Ages, coating itself slowly with other ideas. The city became the market-place; and in the market-place men talked, gossiped, exchanged thoughts, made learning. The fine word "bourgeoisie," reduced to a term of scorn in the last century, illuminates the growing meaning. The "bourgeoisie" of the city were feudatories to no lord, proud and increasingly arrogant people; but they were mannered people who had learned that when men live together in clusters, there must be sanitation and sewers, gendarmes on the streets, rule and rights and privileges to make living together possible.

Before its transplantation to America, the idea of the city grew even further—chiefly in England under the rising pressures of the industrial revolution. In Manchester, England, for example, the "Commissioners" of that ancient town became concerned about the inrush of the uprooted peasants driven from England's fields to work in the town's cruel factories. Manchester's "Watch Committee" was responsible for public safety; the thought occurred to someone that if streets were lit at night, this would reduce mugging and knifing, purse-snatching and crime in general. The Commissioners assumed the responsibility, thus, for street-lighting; from street-lighting grew the world's first municipal gas service in 1824; and then other services. Service became the key word—the city was a corporation whose function was to provide services. It was not sovereign; it demanded no high and eternal loyalties. It was there to do things for people.

It was in America that the idea of the city as the great provider of first-call services flourished most exuberantly. In Europe, as in England, the duty of the city was to provide policing, lighting, fire-fighting, sewers, thoroughfares; the rest of the services were provided by the sovereign state. In America, however, it was the city—not the state, not the Federal government—that provided all the traditional services of Europe, and more. The city in America provided free education for all; then hospitals for all; then mass transit for all; then welfare for all; then housing for all.

In America, the Federal government makes demands—even to the lives of men. But the city is the organ of government which must itself meet demands. To the city was left the task of Americanizing and civilizing millions of immigrants and their children. Upon the city they vented their bitterness for the hardship of life; the nation became the object of their pride.

Today, quite simply, the old idea of the city in America will not stretch to meet what Americans have come to demand of it. The promises made to millions of underprivileged Americans by the American dream are presented at the city's door, like bank-drafts on a bank that is bankrupt. No city has financial resources, legislative authority or constitutional jurisdiction even remotely adequate to meet the rising demands on it— whether for housing, welfare, hospitals, policing, pollution-control, refuse-disposal or relieving traffic congestion.

What is required now is something revolutionary—a redefinition of the city's function. Most devices suggested, such as Federal-Urban tax-sharing, are palliatives. They are necessary in the present emergency; but they are politically dangerous, for they are so complicated that ordinary people cannot politically comprehend them. They deprive the cities and the people who live in them of clear understanding of responsibility and purpose, of control of their own lives. If one is to save the idea of the city as a self-governing community, there is no way of saving it short of a fundamental revision of the American Constitution—a revision of state and municipal borders, a revision of the levels of sovereignty allowed each community in the nation, a revision of the distribution of the nation's resources. The dream of the city must somehow be preserved—but what new forms must be shaped to let it live?

§   There follows the idea of World Order.

The national dream, ever since World War II, has been of an orderly world—all governments, all races, all men joined in the United Nations, pledged to settle their problems without war. The dream has been fleshed out not only by our commitment to the United Nations but by a series of pacts and alliances which give the shelter of American power to some forty-three nations around the globe. One of these pledges alone has cost over 35,000 American lives in Vietnam. How many more?

The dream rested on national experience valid until the 1950's—an experience based on a warfare of armies, navies and missiles. But while we rested our dream on this experience, other societies prepared for a different kind of warfare—the political warfare of guerrilla, partisan and irregular, which challenges our strength as a flight of stabbing crows challenges a dummy scarecrow. Partisan warfare traces back to the one authentic contribution of Mao Tse-tung to the history of ideas. It is the thought that in war there must be no neutrals, that war recognizes no innocents. Almost a thousand years of barbarous killing passed in Western Europe before war was finally harnessed into those "civilized" rules which distinguish between uniformed men and un-uniformed civilians, which protect, even in the heat of combat, certain values of conduct and forbid certain forms of torture and savagery.

Against the newer concept of partisan warfare, our older Western military tradition has been almost helpless. From the Vietnam war Americans have learned that there is no way to victory in irregular war short of terror or total annihilation—of which the American ethos is incapable. Yet upon the prowess of American arms the entire American dream of an orderly world rests. It is impossible to cast away the dream—yet impossible to pursue it further in the old way. What new invention of American military or political thought must come about to cope with the newer forms of world disorder? What new internal rearrangement of roles must be made in Washington between State Department, Defense Department and CIA in order to bring American strength to buttress world peace and world order without involving us in further death and destruction?

§ There follows the problem of Race.

Race, too, tangles a snarl of ideas that no one can sort out. Black Americans insist they will now dream the same dreams, entertain the same hopes as white Americans. The resistance they find to their legitimate demands comes, however, not from government but from millions of white Americans unable to include blacks in their dreams of America. Government can open the way to dreams—but it can make no guarantee of delivery.

The easy things have all been done; the administrations of John F. Kennedy and Lyndon B. Johnson, supported by the Supreme Court, have all but erased whatever restrictions or discriminations previously bound American blacks by law; a mopping-up of pockets of legal prejudice still remains to be accomplished, but the great legal steps have been taken. It is almost impossible for Richard M. Nixon to suggest new cures for injustices or pass new laws that others have not already suggested and passed. Yet the problem remains, and is aggravated from day to day.

It would be good if the black Americans could agree among themselves on a solution and offer a sharp proposal, to be rejected or accepted. But they cannot, for, even among themselves, their dreams of America clash. Is a black American to be treated as an individual person, privileged as all other Americans are to go as far as his talents will carry him, and burdened as are all other Americans with the obligation to accept the general law? Or is he to be treated as a member of a separate community, under his own separate leaders, under the discipline of his own community, with separate laws, standards and customs?

Over the years of the sixties, the country has learned that legal goodwill alone will not comfort black Americans; it has learned that money alone, poured into the ghettos, will not cure their condition; it has learned that white men, enforcing their standards on black and white alike, will rouse hate rather than respect. All these are, however, negative lessons. The decisive questions are more pointed now than at the beginning of the decade: Is the dynamic of hate—on the part of black and white racists alike—to be accepted as the drive wheels of domestic adjustment? Or are terms of partnership to be worked out reasonably? Is the law to be applied to all alike, or are special exemptions to be made for black intransigence because of white guilt? And, above all, how shall we determine who speaks for the black communities?

For such questions the past offers no answers—just as it has no answers for the questions of the City and of World Order. The answers have passed beyond the reach of ordinary legislation because the old ideas that governed American attitudes have come to the end of their writ, and the new ones are not ready.

So, too, in almost every outburst of American energy in this last third of the century; and one need touch on only two more areas of American development to demonstrate how old ideas are mocked by new development.

§ Education, for example, has been as close to a national religion in this secular society as the American people have permitted themselves.

Yet education today poses the same problem as does aviation. The airlines of America were nursed by romance, their pioneers seen as gallants challenging the skies, deserving of every government favor and support in their conquest of time and space. Since then they have become a monster industry, jealous of every privilege, voracious of public moneys, contemptuous of the communities and people they once promised to serve. In robust maturity, the airlines have totally outgrown the fostering protection given them at birth—but still wail and squawl like infants when deprived of their bottles.

Education in the United States has a longer tradition than aviation, but, like aviation, has completely outrun the thinking of its beginnings. It is not only that higher education, as we have seen,[1] has become the largest industry in America. It is quite possible—though the thought is always branded as heresy—that higher education, swollen and still swelling, has outrun the needs of nation and society. The rhythm of change in college enrollment must be recalled once more: in 1959, a decade ago, only 22.7 percent of all Americans between eighteen and twenty-one were in college; by 1963 this had grown to 26.8 percent; by 1968 to 34.2 percent—and, by extrapolation, may rise to 50 percent in the next decade. Education in America is, as it should be, open to all. But the momentum of past dogma carries the thought on to the belief that all education must be capped by *college* education. This idea of universal *college* education runs, however, directly contrary to another idea ingrained in American folk culture—that college education trains men and women for leadership, and that whoever passes through college (unless it be in the discipline of agriculture) is forever thereafter to be considered above physical labor. Can any nation arbitrarily prepare a full half its population to lead the other half, without grotesquely warping the concept of leadership? Can a nation desperately short of craftsmen, artisans, skilled workers, technicians of service, continue to encourage the growth of unmanageable numbers of educated, semi-educated or under-educated college graduates for whom no useful jobs or responsibilities can be found? How much of the increasing resources and tax moneys going into education should be devoted to the expansion of already swollen university rolls? And how much, by contrast, of those resources should go into the education of underprivileged children in those earliest years of life when deprivation is cruelest?

[1] See Chapters Three and Seven.

Thinking on higher education today is not only perplexed by numbers and physical growth. It is also plagued by problems of quality and privilege. The old idea of a university was that of a sanctuary of the spirit. The university was a quiet place of learning, where scholars pursued knowledge, served the public with research, trained young people to think. Its professors were to be protected from hard pressure and left free and inviolate to concentrate on truth. Its students, who sacrificed years of profitable life on the altar of learning, were to be sheltered from harm.

Both constituent groups have now changed. The corps of lifetime-tenured professors in America has now swollen to over 150,000, a priesthood beyond judgment of ordinary men and as secure from restraint and removal as judges of the Federal Court. Moreover, in their own internal rivalries the most arrogant and aggressive achieve dominance over the more quiet and inwardly creative scholars; and voice their thoughts in public life as if they spoke for all wisdom itself, on campus and beyond. Students, as we have seen, have grown even more rapidly in numbers; and the shelter of privilege given them in a sanctuary of spirit has become the shelter of a fortress from which they may, as citizens, emerge to disturb the peace of other citizens, yet to which they may retreat to claim student immunity from the laws that govern the community.

§ Even more baffling are the erosion of standards and turbulence of ideas that enwrap the conditions of Prosperity.

The prosperity of America today is a unique condition in world history. Always, since the records of man have run, most people were poor and only the few were comfortable. Today, in America most people are comfortable and only the few are poor. No other nation has ever faced this challenge to the oldest political folklore of men; and we have learned there can never be an "absolute" prosperity, or a general contentment. Prosperity and poverty are relative terms, and whatever level any society ever reaches will always contain, by definition, "underprivileged." When, in the Age of Scarcity, the American government attempted to redistribute wealth, the base-line was always an attempt to give every man a "decent, living wage." In the Age of Abundance no one can any longer define what a "decent, living wage" is—how much time off, how many holidays, how much medical care, how much vacation time, how many televisions and automobiles and how much fun it must sustain to be "decent."

Statistics only faintly reflect the change in the condition of American well-being over the past eight years, but they are interesting as measures. Since 1960 the Gross National Product of the United States, even corrected for inflationary price increases, has grown by one half. Indeed, the Gross National Product of the United States in 1968 almost equaled the combined American Gross National Product of 1960 *plus* the entire Gross National Product of the Soviet Union in 1968! Since 1960 the spendable take-home pay of the average American family—even after taxes and price increases—has increased by one third. Ten million new jobs have been created; unemployment, down to 3.3 percent by January, 1969, has fallen by almost 50 percent. Of the 40,000,000 Americans living below the accepted poverty line at the beginning of the decade, the number has fallen to 26,000,000, and by the end of the decade, only two years hence, we will have a society where those who live in poverty are diminished to less than 10 percent of the national total.

The old idea ran that if everyone had an opportunity for a job; if everyone had enough money to buy what he needed; if the specter of hunger and poverty were removed, then men would be free to explore themselves, the nation would flourish, generosity would increase, and all would be well.

Except that it has not worked that way. Like the gold the Spaniards discovered in the New World, the new wealth, when poured into old forms, imperils the life it is supposed to fertilize. In America, as in Castilian Spain, the new abundance has strengthened old appetites—not old values; prosperity has proven almost as unsettling as deprivation. Neither government nor public nor private facilities can keep up with the appetites of prosperity or their effect. Hospitals, schools, colleges cannot keep up with the numbers who seek their services. Streets, highways and bridges cannot accommodate the new flux of movement. And the volcanic outburst of industrial activity in the past decade, the orgiastic consumption which it feeds, increasingly chokes, clogs and fouls the air, the waters, the seas. Prosperity has released millions from fear; it has also released millions of others—particularly the youth of the middle class—from the discipline of work, free to seek their own personality. Only they do not know what it is they seek.

Prosperity has also fostered two other conditions—the first, inflation, being amenable to law; and the other, nameless, being amenable to no control except a new vision of America.

Inflation, in the past four years in American life, has ravaged our standards of behavior. As in other inflations I have lived through, notably those in China during the war, and Germany and France after the war, the beginning ravages are almost unnoticeable, indeed, pleasant. As inflation continues, however, it changes moralities, it destroys reason itself. Prosperity opens opportunities; inflation urges haste in using them. Not saving, but shrewd spending become the mark of wisdom in planning; the "operators," not the creators, thrive. It divides those who can manipulate from those locked into fixed incomes who see their resources dwindling and their savings shrinking, who are helpless to recapture their share of rising well-being. Above all, it victimizes the poor, the old and those who have planned ahead. Inflation is, at the beginning, a technical problem of public finance—and in the end raises problems of morality, of the disciplining of indulgences artificially incubated by the disappearance of values. How deftly and firmly the Nixon government deals with inflation is a matter of politics; it is the most unpleasant task of any government in such a situation, as painful as depriving an alcoholic of his liquor and leaving him to face his hangover sick and stone-cold sober in the morning.

Inflation is probably the only one of all the problems on the Nixon agenda which can be mastered by legislation, cruel as it may have to be.

The second condition of the American prosperity is probably the only one which absolutely cannot be solved by any manmade law. This condition is the attitude of mind, the technique of thought, by which the present prosperity was brought about.

Fundamentally, the present prosperity of America was engineered by the scholarly discipline of economics, whose most eloquent spokesmen succeeded in persuading both the Kennedy and the Johnson administrations to use their wisdom. Their wisdom, brilliantly as it has succeeded in the general economy, is, however, a parochial one, a study of greeds and desires divorced from humanity. Deep within the scholarly discipline of economics is a concept of man's world as a universe of random particles. The desires and greeds that move these random particles are unpredictable for any single individual. But when measured all together as a universe of random particles, they become, as a mass, thoroughly predictable and generally controllable. Economists can graph, chart and predict the influence of almost any government intervention, curb, tax law or stimulus on this universe of random particles. In the getting, making and distribution of material things the wisdom of economics has had stunning success.

But the economists, by their success, have achieved the same sort of cultural imperialism in American life that the nuclear physicists enjoyed shortly after the first bomb worked. It would be extravagant and utterly silly to blame on the economists the emotional and intellectual diseases from which America suffers today. Yet their way of thinking runs as the dominant fashion at every level of American managerial life. Americans are increasingly treated, by administrative bodies both public and private, as random particles, entirely depersonalized, to be data-processed into patterns. Human beings are machine-judged, at shop, at factory and in school. Bills for necessary services come on punch-cards. Questions on telephones are answered by automatic recorded voices repeating over and over again the same mad or irrelevant answers. Grocery stores give way to supermarkets; elevators in great buildings rise and descend without human operators; race relations are measured by recording exclusion and inclusion, achievement and failure, in chromatic percentages; war is measured in digits of killed in action, weapons captured, deserters per month.

The mood of revolt—of blacks in ghettos, of youth in college, of white workingmen in the Wallace movement—moves against the shadow prison of this Digital Society. Yet the revolting groups behave in practice, whether consciously or not, as if the theory of random particles was an irrevocable reality. Thus, the goal of the revolting groups has been either to smash the machinery of government which manipulates the random particles—or to get their own hands on the buttons that control the mechanisms. Thus the assaults—on mayors' offices, on police stations, on deans' offices, on conventions, on all those sensitive command posts where, supposedly, the mythic buttons glow. If the insurgents can but smash their way through to the buttons, the machinery can be stopped, the depersonalized controls they hate turned about. Thus the ultimate paradox—that those who hate restraint of government most, seek most violently to compel government to do their bidding against others.

And it is here that one must come back to Richard Nixon. For if government were indeed only a matter of buttons and legislation, the verdict on his term of office could be written now: nearly hopeless. He has no buttons to push—no military buttons which will give victory in Vietnam, no diplomatic buttons marked "peace," no command buttons which will heal the hates and traumas of America within; and no recent President has entered office with more limited legislative authority, and less control in House and Senate.

Yet if there *is* reason for hope in the Presidency of Richard Nixon, it is precisely because government, in the American tradition, has never been exclusively, or even largely, a matter of buttons and mechanisms. It is a process shared by many men, and the process itself is as important as legislation. The apocalyptic visions of revolutionaries call for sudden, cleaving decisions. But people who live within a time span of individual lives are unwilling to be sacrificed now for results that will be visible only forty years hence. They will follow gratefully, even though hesitantly, any leader who makes his purpose clear by the process and manner of his governing. Thus, the verdict on Richard Nixon must rest not on the measure of his immediate power or his instant achievements, but on the direction in which he turns the instruments of government—and on his ability to control them.

Most Presidents come to the White House as finished portraits. Life has shaped and styled them in advance, and the White House freezes the mold. Lincoln and Roosevelt, Truman and Johnson, Eisenhower and Kennedy were all finished men before they had won their

Presidency. But Richard M. Nixon is still an unfinished portrait. His victory in 1968 can be discussed *ad infinitum* in terms of plans and programs, organization and tactics, strategies and media. Yet his greatest struggle was always with himself, within his personality. His greatest adversary was always a past Richard Nixon whose image stained the minds of millions of Americans; his greatest victory, since 1960, has been his ability to learn, to persist, to master what it was he did not know, and then, finally, to understand himself.

Nor is the process yet finished. No more plastic President, none more open to suggestion and ideas, none more willing to admit mistakes or learn from error, has sat in the White House in recent times. It is only as he learns in the White House, as he reacts to the influences that press and sway him, that we will learn what his vision of America is, and be able to measure him by how well he translates that vision to his people.

There were to be no Hundred Days or Great Society to mark the beginning of the Nixon administration; the style of the Presidency and its goals would become apparent only as the years wore on. But the style of the man, as President, had begun to change within days of the election; and calling on the President, two days after the inauguration, it was as if history itself was now taking a hand in finishing the portrait I had watched so long and seen take shape so slowly.

He seemed, as he waved me into the Oval Office, suddenly on first glance a more stocky man than I had known on the campaign rounds. There was a minute of adjustment as he waved me to a sofa in the barren office, poured coffee, put me at ease; then, watching him, I realized that he was not stockier, but, on the contrary, slimmer. What was different was the movement of the body, the sound of the voice, the manner of speaking—for he was calm as I had never seen him before, as if peace had settled on him. In the past, Nixon's restless body had been in constant movement as he rose, walked about, hitched a leg over the arm of a chair or gestured sharply with his hands. Now he was in repose; and the repose was in his speech also—more slow, studied, with none of the gear-slippages of name or reference which used to come when he was weary; his hands still moved as he spoke, but the fingers spread gracefully, not punchily or sharply as they used to.

We talked first of how it had come to him—how, when, at what moment the Presidency had settled on him. The sense had come gradually, he said. He felt he had won at half past eleven on election night; he knew he had it locked up by three o'clock of election morning. But there had been the comfort of the two months ahead; and yet with that comfort was always a sense of counting off the days, one day less every day, through November and December and into January, when he could still relax. It was Lyndon Johnson who still had to answer that telephone at night, who had to be there with the immediate response in crisis. The moment, the actual moment of burden, he felt, had come just after he had finished his inaugural speech and, walking up the broad stairs back into the Capitol, he had turned around and looked down on the crowd—it was then that it all came to him. Only not as it had come to Churchill, who, when he became Prime Minister in 1940, had felt exultation; Nixon quoted Churchill on that "profound sense of relief—at last I had the authority to give directions over the whole scene." Yet Nixon was not afraid of the authority either; it all would come to rest here in this room, and, he said, he felt ready for it.

I had been looking over the room as he spoke, for I had never been in the Oval Office at such a moment of transition. In the forty-eight hours since the inauguration, all that had made it the home of Lyndon Johnson had vanished—the portraits had vanished, the rocking chair was gone, the news-tickers and television sets were gone, the huge desks, fore and aft, were gone, the bookshelves were empty, the console of telephones was stripped out. Of all that had been Lyndon Johnson's there remained only a shelf and a half of volumes of Presidential papers in their familiar green-and-red bindings, and the two sofas facing each other across the coffee table which Kennedy had installed. The room seemed suddenly bare, and the green-gray rug in the nakedness was filthy with smears of spilled coffee, of Coca-Cola, marks of cigarette butts. It was as shabby as any other office undergoing change of tenants, and was hollow of everything except Richard Nixon, in blue suit, with new gold cufflinks of Presidential eagles, completely relaxed, talking of how he would fill it.

His new desk was still completely bare of papers, but, indulging my curiosity, he took me over to it and showed me the device they had explained to him that morning. He stooped and we both half-knelt to look into the knee-well of the desk; on the inside of the knee-well, just beside his left knee, was an aluminum pronged device. He had but to nudge the device with his knee and the Secret Service guards outside the door would come bursting in; if he had a heart attack, or took ill, or some visitor suddenly went mad in the President's presence, he must nudge the device—and then the Secret Service would rush in to protect the President. This, in his second full day as President, was the chief instruction he had received—and the rest was up to him.

We came back to the sofas and began to talk again. The last time I had spoken to him in New York, before the inaugural, he had talked of his priorities. Now, I asked, how does a President go about them, what, indeed, is it like being President, what were these first hours like?

He reminisced. He had had to visit all six inaugural balls on Monday evening, and that had kept him up late, until 2:30 in the morning. Yet he had woken the next morning shortly after seven and come to his desk by 7:45, escorted by his Secret Service officer, and he was all alone until the others came, as he had told them to, at nine. He had spent the early morning hour by himself simply doing the little thank-yous "that people never have time to do when they get busy"—dictating thanks to the bands who had played in the inaugural parade, the divines who had prayed, the staff which had organized the ceremony. The rest of the morning had been procedural, with the swearing-in of staff; and the business of the Presidency had not begun until the afternoon.

He had called for his schedule of the first two days, and when it was set before him, he described the order of business of President as the schedule recalled it to him. Yet the order of business reflected exactly what he had said in a thousand speeches across the nation, and I was listening to a President translate campaign pledges into program.

First, on Tuesday afternoon, he had called together the National Security Council to review the whole range of problems America faces in the outer world. He had already made one prior decision about the National Security Council before the inauguration: the Council would be the President's Council, he said; it would be a large council, including all the voices of State, Defense, CIA. It would be different from Eisenhower's Security Council, different from Kennedy's—Kennedy had almost let it die—different from Johnson's, which had been reduced finally to a lunch group that met once a week. It would be large, and include powerful men. State had protested his position, and that had been quite a battle—was this to be a strong or a weak council? State wanted the Council weak, wanted to retain its own pre-eminence as the President's chief adviser on foreign affairs. He himself had wanted it strong; insisted on it; had finally sent a directive to the State Department that he would entertain "no further appeal" from decision. He, as President Nixon, would not have his options limited; he wanted to hear the majority voice, but also the minority voice on policy; he wanted no consensus brought to him.

The National Security Council had been briefed by Richard Helms, chief of the CIA. They had, of course, talked mostly about Vietnam and the Middle East situation. But then, he added, "there are trouble spots you never anticipated, the ones I should have thought of but I didn't" —a new crisis in Berlin, the new Peruvian junta, the new aggressiveness of the North Koreans, the new friction between Formosa and Japan, the Biafra problem. When Helms had finished, Nixon asked, "Haven't you got any good news to report?" And then he had spoken his own mind to the Council: they, the Council, were there as an advisory group. He would listen to them. But he would never, as President, make his decision in their presence; he might call in one or two people alone, later, to reflect with him as he decided; but never in Council. "I'll decide," he said.

"That's what I'm hired for, to make the big decisions, not them."

There had followed then a conference with the Chairman of the Joint Chiefs of Staff, General Earle Wheeler, and Presidential adviser Henry Kissinger—about the Armed Forces, about personalities, about the situation in Vietnam, about the morale of the generals of the Pentagon. Another conference had followed with Dr. Arthur Burns, who was trying to package the ideas of the Nixon campaign, all the campaign promises, all the inputs from the new Cabinet appointees, into one large over-all program that would be a Nixon program. And a meeting with Glado Plaza, Secretary-General of the Organization of American States, to signify the new administration's concern with Latin America; and a talk with Secretary of Treasury Kennedy about government policy on balance of payments (which was much worse, said Nixon, than Johnson had last publicly described it), the gold problem and international monetary problem, and, above all, about the inflation.

There had been other appointments; but on the first day it was the National Security Council and America's foreign affairs that had preoccupied him.

That first evening he had been alone in the White House—and he had walked all over the White House, exploring. He had never, in his eight years as Vice-President, been in the East Room of grand ceremony; he had never been upstairs to the living quarters of the President on the third floor. So he had walked in the evening through the corridors, examining his new home. Off the Lincoln bedroom he found a little sitting room he had not known of; he ordered a huge ugly TV set carted off and decided that room would be his personal study; and sat down there to read the reports and problem papers of the first day until he went to bed.

Wednesday, his second day, two major matters had preoccupied him—and again I could mark the thrust of campaign politics carrying through to government. He had had his first lunch with a Cabinet member, John Mitchell, the new Attorney General, and they had discussed law-and-order. "I said," recalled the President, "that I would take personal command in this area. In urban affairs I have a lot of experts—Finch, Romney, Moynihan—and I'll learn. But in this matter I know something myself." The lunch with Mitchell had stretched for two hours, the longest single rendezvous of anyone with the new President in the first two days. They had talked of the law, of judges, of the next Chief Justice of the Supreme Court, of the crime condition in the District of Columbia; he had admonished Mitchell to control wire-tapping with an iron hand ("I want no climate of fear in this country," he had told his Attorney General).

More important was his meeting with his Cabinet, and in discussing his Cabinet one could see a new chamber of the Nixon mind.

He had opened the Cabinet meeting at 8:34. He had walked right into the Cabinet Room, he recalled, and they were sitting there—and started business right away. The President held the agenda of the morning's meeting in his hand and he showed it to me—it was, by now, typed and dittoed but the phrases, the indentations, the categories and sub-categories were so authentically Nixonian that they could have come only from the hand-scrawled yellow legal pads, a personal essay of Richard Nixon to make the government of the United States governable, to put the instruments in their place.

He had broken his thinking into four parts: (a) the functions of the Cabinet, (b) the functions of the smaller Cabinet committees, (c) the role of Cabinet officers and (d) Cabinet officers' communications with the President. In each category were the sub-points of Nixon's thinking, curt and precise; the Cabinet would meet once a month; it had been called together too often in Eisenhower's time, and members had been bored by discussions not relevant to their departments; when it met, it would be to share advice and to "make sure we are doing the right thing for America and Americans know what we are doing." But basically, so ran Point Two, the Cabinet would function in subcommittees that met more frequently, each subcommittee with its own staff, each subcommittee acting on a problem-solving basis. Point Three defined what a Cabinet officer did in his department—they were "Deputy Presidents" in their departments, they ran their own show, referring only key problems to the President; and, finally, Point Four, how they could reach him directly when needed. The outline was clear and crisp —an executive mind at work, with logic, force, and clarity.

It was to be his Cabinet, his government, his administration. Nixon's speech, previously, had always been marked by a somewhat self-deprecating use of the word "I," the politician's use of the pronoun as of a detached and distinct *dramatis persona*. Now, in discussing the Cabinet, the word "I" was used flatly, not as an overbearing man would use it, nor as a pompous man would use it, but as if forty-eight hours in the Presidency had stripped the pronoun bare. "I ran the meeting," he said. "I believe I should run the meetings—all Cabinet meetings. A meeting means more if the President runs it, and I find my attention will stray unless I do run a meeting; it means I have to work to understand matters. The National Security Council will meet twice a week for the first month, and once a week after that; the Urban Affairs Council will meet once a week; the Committee on Economic Policy will meet once a week—and I'm chairman of each committee, I run them." These were the committees that the problems had forced on him. There would later, he hoped, be called into being something he had not yet named —a Committee on Environment and Natural Resources, perhaps. That was the one he was looking forward to. The Committee on Urban Affairs would be looking into the problems of today, the inescapable tangle of housing, traffic, congestion, pollution, "things like that." But the new committee would look to the future; it would, when organized, "think about the lakes, the mountains, the seas." "I know nothing about those things," he added, "it's quite exciting." He spoke as if, once freed from all pressures put on his desk by the past, he anticipated the pressure he, as President, might put on the future.

But that was far away. Nothing would be easy. "You realize," he said, "the days are going to be longer and tougher." There would be no more parties, no more late hours; you realized that a President could not even take a drink; it was so different from being Vice-President, and he knew because he had once been Vice-President himself. The President had to be ready for the phone call at any hour of the day or night; two drinks and the edge of the mind is not quite sharp; supposing the call says they've just blown up an embassy in Lebanon? Or at midnight you must decide to send troops into a troubled area? A President has to be ready—*"semper paratus."*

But he did not seem as worried as his words now suggest on paper. Without any outer show of gaiety or exuberance, he was, quite clearly, enjoying himself in the empty room which he would have to fill with decision and purpose. "It's not what they say about you in the paper now that counts," he said at one point, "it's what they say about you six months from now." We rose, after an hour, when an aide came in to discuss Latin America, and the President stood there in the center of the room, on the dirty rug, against the barren walls, and bade farewell cheerfully. He had to hasten because this afternoon he was going to wander through the White House again—this time escorted by Mr. Ketchum, the curator, who would explain to him where everything was.

But there is more to the White House than any curator can ever explain.

It takes years to evaluate any President; and we will probably sit longer in judgment on Richard Nixon than any other President of recent times.

John F. Kennedy became President calling for movement; it was almost two years before one could catch the first sense of his greatness, as movements tentatively unfurled and the nation discovered he meant what he said and would offer leadership to movement. To the surge of black revolt, he offered clear openings; to the stagnant economy he offered new management that set it on course to prosperity; in the stalemate of cold-war confrontation, he offered, first, resolution in the missile crisis and, next, a détente with our then-greatest adversary, Russia; and to a newly educated people he offered a quality of beauty and elegance that met an unrecognized hunger.

Lyndon Johnson was the most clearly endowed President since Roosevelt. It was his rare good fortune to be mandated to build, and with all good-will he set about to clear away the old and erect the new. His tragedy was multiple—his ego outran his own great achievements; his personality offended those whom he strove most to please; above all, in foreign affairs he accepted war in Asia, having sworn in his campaign to avoid it. He accepted war not out of malice, but in conscience, where war need not have been accepted. Within two years it was quite clear that he had fallen short. History will credit him with many triumphs, but his Party and people repudiated him. He left his leadership with no issues of any clarity, all pendant on the outcome of a war where honor lay on his side and common sense on the other.

Peace, then, is Nixon's first task. If he brings no peace, all other verdicts on his administration will trail off, as the history of Thucydides trails off in that unfinished sentence which closes the account of the destruction of Greek glory: "When the winter after this summer is over, the twenty-first year of the war will be completed. . . ."

Nor will all else fall into place at home, if peace is made abroad. The surges and restlessness that disturb our cultures, the old and the new, are rooted in matters of spirit, not material things. Richard Nixon, who has left far behind the old culture in which he was bred, will probably never be able to speak in the idiom or rhetoric of the new culture which sweeps America today. Thus, he is condemned to be prey to both groups as he tries to broaden the middle between them, at the expense of both; and will receive no mercy from either.

He must make his way, certain of being abused whether rightly or wrongly, before his achievements permit sober judgment to be passed.

And he must do so alone—as he always has. Few Presidents have spent so much of their early lives in the public eye, at the center of controversy, so conspicuously groping to find their own positions on the issues and affairs of their times. Few, in the past century, have come from origins so humble and made their way, solitary, against such odds, to influence so great. None has shown himself, on the way to power, so susceptible to strain, yet apparently learned better how to cope with strain within himself. Richard Nixon has roved across the entire map of the United States geographically, emotionally, spiritually, above all, politically, seeking his own lodestar. But no passage of this public wandering has been more impressive than the transformation of the impulsive, wrathful man of the 1950's, so eager for combat and lustful for vengeance, to the man in the White House, cautious and thoughtful, intent on conciliation.

Richard Nixon's mandate now is what he chooses to make of it, for it is apparent to no outside eye, or from any examination of the year of his victory. But of what he considers his mandate, he spoke best himself, in his inaugural address:

"The greatest honor history can bestow is the title of peacemaker. . . . We find ourselves rich in goods, but ragged in spirit; reaching with magnificent precision for the moon, but falling into raucous discord on earth. We are caught in war, wanting peace. We are torn by divisions, wanting unity. . . . America has suffered from a fever of words; from inflated rhetoric that promises more than it can deliver; from angry rhetoric that fans discontent into hatreds; from bombastic rhetoric that postures instead of persuading. We cannot learn from one another until we stop shouting at one another—until we speak quietly enough so that our words can be heard as well as our voices. . . . The peace we seek, the peace we seek to win is not victory over any other people, but the peace that comes with healing in its wings; with compassion for those who have suffered; with understanding for those who have opposed us. . . ."

APPENDIXES
AND
INDEX

APPENDIX A

THE VOTING OF 1968

The following table of voting results by state and nation is based on the compilation of the Associated Press and is used here by permission. There is still no such things as an official national vote count in the United States; but the Associated Press table, based on official returns state by state, is the closest to accurate that I have found.

State	Electoral Vote	Nixon	Pct.	Humphrey	Pct.	Wallace	Pct.	Others	Pct.
ALABAMA	10	146,923	14.1	*194,388	18.6	689,009	66.0	13,857	1.3
ALASKA	3	37,540	45.2	35,411	42.7	10,024	12.1	—	—
ARIZONA	5	266,721	54.8	170,514	35.0	46,573	9.6	3,128	.6
ARKANSAS	6	189,062	31.0	184,901	30.3	235,627	38.7	—	—
CALIFORNIA	40	3,467,644	47.8	3,244,318	44.7	487,270	6.8	52,335	.7
COLORADO	6	409,345	50.8	331,063	41.0	60,813	7.5	5,762	.7
CONNECTICUT	8	556,721	44.4	621,561	49.5	76,650	6.1	—	—
DELAWARE	3	96,714	45.1	89,194	41.6	28,459	13.3	—	—
DISTRICT OF COLUMBIA	3	31,012	18.2	139,556	81.8	—	—	—	—
FLORIDA	14	886,804	40.5	676,794	30.9	624,207	28.6	—	—
GEORGIA	12	366,611	29.7	334,439	27.0	535,550	43.3	—	—
HAWAII	4	91,425	38.7	141,324	59.8	3,469	1.5	—	—
IDAHO	4	165,369	56.8	89,273	30.7	36,541	12.5	—	—
ILLINOIS	26	2,174,774	47.1	2,039,814	44.2	390,958	8.5	13,878	.2
INDIANA	13	1,067,885	50.3	806,659	38.0	243,108	11.4	5,909	.3
IOWA	9	619,106	53.0	476,699	40.8	66,422	5.7	5,704	.5
KANSAS	7	478,674	54.8	302,996	34.7	88,921	10.2	2,192	.3
KENTUCKY	9	462,411	43.8	397,541	37.6	193,098	18.3	2,843	.3
LOUISIANA	10	257,535	23.5	309,615	28.2	530,300	48.3	—	—
MAINE	4	169,254	43.1	217,312	55.3	6,370	1.6	—	—
MARYLAND	10	517,995	41.9	538,310	43.6	178,734	14.5	—	—
MASSACHUSETTS	14	766,844	32.9	1,469,218	63.0	87,088	3.7	8,602	.4
MICHIGAN	21	1,370,665	41.5	1,593,082	48.2	331,968	10.0	10,535	.3
MINNESOTA	10	658,643	41.5	857,738	54.0	68,931	4.3	3,198	.2
MISSISSIPPI	7	88,516	13.5	150,644	23.0	415,349	63.5	—	—
MISSOURI	12	811,932	44.9	791,444	43.7	206,126	11.4	—	—
MONTANA	4	138,853	50.6	114,117	41.6	20,015	7.3	1,437	.5
NEBRASKA	5	321,163	59.8	170,784	31.8	44,904	8.4	—	—
NEVADA	3	73,188	47.5	60,598	39.3	20,432	13.2	—	—
NEW HAMPSHIRE	4	154,903	52.1	130,589	43.9	11,173	3.8	535	.2
NEW JERSEY	17	1,325,467	46.1	1,264,206	44.0	262,187	9.1	23,536	.8
NEW MEXICO	4	169,692	51.8	130,081	39.7	25,737	7.9	1,771	.6
NEW YORK	43	3,007,938	44.3	3,378,470	49.8	358,864	5.3	44,800	.6
NORTH CAROLINA	13	627,192	39.5	464,113	29.2	496,188	31.3	—	—
NORTH DAKOTA	4	138,669	55.9	94,769	38.2	14,244	5.7	200	.2
OHIO	26	1,791,014	45.2	1,700,586	42.9	467,495	11.8	603	.1
OKLAHOMA	8	449,697	47.4	306,658	32.3	191,731	20.3	—	—
OREGON	6	408,433	49.8	358,865	43.8	49,683	6.1	2,640	.3
PENNSYLVANIA	29	2,090,017	43.9	2,259,403	47.5	387,582	8.1	19,922	.5
RHODE ISLAND	4	122,359	31.8	246,518	64.0	15,678	4.1	383	.1
SOUTH CAROLINA	8	254,062	38.1	197,486	29.6	215,430	32.3	—	—
SOUTH DAKOTA	4	149,841	53.3	118,023	42.0	13,400	4.7	—	—
TENNESSEE	11	472,592	37.8	351,233	28.1	424,792	34.1	—	—

* Includes 141,124 under listing of Alabama Independent Democratic party and 53,264 under listing of National Democratic party of Alabama.

TEXAS	25	1,227,844	39.9	1,266,804	41.1	584,269	19.0	489	—
UTAH	4	238,728	56.5	156,665	37.1	26,906	6.4	180	—
VERMONT	3	85,142	52.8	70,255	43.5	5,104	3.2	873	.5
VIRGINIA	12	590,315	43.4	442,387	32.5	320,272	23.6	6,950	.5
WASHINGTON	9	588,510	45.1	616,037	47.2	96,990	7.5	—	—
WEST VIRGINIA	7	307,555	40.8	374,091	49.6	72,560	9.6	—	—
WISCONSIN	12	809,997	47.9	748,804	44.3	127,835	7.6	4,902	.2
WYOMING	3	70,927	55.8	45,173	35.5	11,105	8.7	—	—
TOTALS		31,770,237	43.4	31,270,533	42.7	9,906,141	13.5	239,908	.4

MINOR PARTY CANDIDATES

E. Harold Munn Sr., Prohibition party—Alabama 3,420, California 59, Colorado 275, Indiana 4,616, Iowa 362, Kansas 2,192, Massachusetts 2,369, Michigan 60, Montana 510, North Dakota 38, Ohio 19, Virginia 599. Total: 14,519.

Eldridge Cleaver, Peace and Freedom party—Arizona 217, California 27,707, Iowa 1,332, Michigan 4,585, Minnesota 935, Washington 1,609. Total: 36,385.

Hennings Blomen, Socialist-Labor party—Arizona 75, California 341, Colorado 3,016, Illinois 13,878, Iowa 241, Massachusetts 6,180, Michigan 1,762, Minnesota 285, New Jersey 6,784, New York 8,432, Ohio 120, Pennsylvania 4,977, Virginia 4,671, Washington 488, Wisconsin 1,338. Total: 52,588.

Fred Halstead, Socialist Worker party—Arizona 85, Colorado 235, Indiana 1,293, Iowa 3,377, Kentucky 2,843, Michigan 4,099, Minnesota 808, Montana 457, New Hampshire 104, New Jersey 8,668, New Mexico 252, New York 11,851, North Dakota 128, Ohio 69, Pennsylvania 4,862, Rhode Island 383, Vermont 294, Washington 270, Wisconsin 1,222. Total: 41,300.

Eugene J. McCarthy, New party—Arizona 2,751; California 20,721, Colorado 305, Minnesota 585, Oregon 1,496. Total: 25,858.

New party without candidate—Montana 470, New Hampshire 431, Vermont 579. Total: 1,480.

Dick Gregory, New party—California 3,230, Colorado 1,393, New Jersey 8,084, New York 24,517, Ohio 372, Pennsylvania 7,821, Virginia 1,680. Total: 47,097.

Charlene Mitchell, Communist party and Free Ballot party—California 260, Minnesota 415, Ohio 23, Washington 377. Total: 1,075.

Others: 19,606.

APPENDIX B

BALLOTING ON REPUBLICAN PRESIDENTIAL NOMINATION

PRESIDENTIAL NOMINATION—FIRST BALLOT VOTING BEFORE SWITCHES

State	Total Delegate Votes	Nixon	N. Rockefeller	Reagan	Rhodes	Romney	Case	Carlson	W. Rockefeller	Fong	Stassen	Lindsay
ALABAMA	26	14		12								
ALASKA	12	11	1									
ARIZONA	16	16										
ARKANSAS	18								18			
CALIFORNIA	86			86								
COLORADO	18	14	3	1								
CONNECTICUT	16	4	12									
DELAWARE	12	9	3									
FLORIDA	34	32	1	1								
GEORGIA	30	21	2	7								
HAWAII	14									14		
IDAHO	14	9		5								
ILLINOIS	58	50	5	3								
INDIANA	26	26										
IOWA	24	13	8	3								
KANSAS	20							20				
KENTUCKY	24	22	2									
LOUISIANA	26	19		7								
MAINE	14	7	7									
MARYLAND	26	18	8									
MASSACHUSETTS	34		34									
MICHIGAN	48	4				44						
MINNESOTA	26	9	15								1	1
MISSISSIPPI	20	20										
MISSOURI	24	16	5	3								
MONTANA	14	11		3								
NEBRASKA	16	16										
NEVADA	12	9	3									
NEW HAMPSHIRE	8	8										
NEW JERSEY	40	18					22					

PRESIDENTIAL NOMINATION—FIRST BALLOT VOTING BEFORE SWITCHES

State	Total Delegate Votes	Nixon	N. Rockefeller	Reagan	Rhodes	Romney	Case	Carlson	W. Rockefeller	Fong	Stassen	Lindsay
NEW MEXICO	14	8	1	5								
NEW YORK	92	4	88									
NORTH CAROLINA	26	9	1	16								
NORTH DAKOTA	8	5	2	1								
OHIO	58	2			55						1	
OKLAHOMA	22	14	1	7								
OREGON	18	18										
PENNSYLVANIA	64	22	41	1								
RHODE ISLAND	14		14									
SOUTH CAROLINA	22	22										
SOUTH DAKOTA	14	14										
TENNESSEE	28	28										
TEXAS	56	41		15								
UTAH	8	2				6						
VERMONT	12	9	3									
VIRGINIA	24	22	2									
WASHINGTON	24	15	3	6								
WEST VIRGINIA	14	11	3									
WISCONSIN	30	30										
WYOMING	12	12										
DIST. OF COLUMBIA	9	6	3									
PUERTO RICO	5		5									
VIRGIN ISLANDS	3	2	1									
TOTAL	1,333	692	277	182	55	50	22	20	18	14	2	1

APPENDIX C

BALLOTING ON DEMOCRATIC PRESIDENTIAL NOMINATION

PRESIDENTIAL NOMINATION—FIRST BALLOT VOTING BEFORE SWITCHES

State	Total Delegate Votes	Humphrey	McCarthy	McGovern	Phillips	Moore	Kennedy	Bryant	Gray	Wallace	Abstain
ALABAMA*	32	23	2	3		½	3½	1½		½	3
ALASKA	22	17	2½	2							
ARIZONA	19	14½									1
ARKANSAS	33	30	2								1
CALIFORNIA	174	14	91	51	17						
COLORADO	35	16½	10	5½	3						
CONNECTICUT	44	35	8		1						
DELAWARE	22	21									1
FLORIDA	63	58	5								
GEORGIA LOYAL.	20½	2½	13½	1	3				½		
GEORGIA REG.	22½	17				2	½				3
HAWAII	26	26									
IDAHO	25	21	3½	½							
ILLINOIS	118	112	3	3							
INDIANA	63	49	11	2	1						
IOWA	46	18½	19½	5			3				
KANSAS	38	34	1	3							
KENTUCKY	46	41	5								
LOUISIANA	36	35									1
MAINE	27	23	4								
MARYLAND	49	45	2	2							
MASSACHUSETTS	72	2	70								
MICHIGAN	96	72½	9½	7½	6½						
MINNESOTA	52	38	11½		2½						
MISSISSIPPI*	24	9½	6½	4	2						2
MISSOURI	60	56	3½		½						
MONTANA	26	23½	2½								
NEBRASKA	30	15	6	9							
NEVADA	22	18½	2½	1							
NEW HAMPSHIRE	26	6	20								

PRESIDENTIAL NOMINATION—FIRST BALLOT VOTING BEFORE SWITCHES

State	Total Delegate Votes	Humphrey	McCarthy	McGovern	Phillips	Moore	Kennedy	Bryant	Gray	Wallace	Abstain
NEW JERSEY	82	62	19		1						
NEW MEXICO	26	15	11								
NEW YORK	190	96½	87	1½	2		3				
NORTH CAROLINA	59	44½	2	½		12					
NORTH DAKOTA	25	18	7								
OHIO	115	94	18	2			1				
OKLAHOMA	41	37½	2½	½	½						
OREGON	35		35								
PENNSYLVANIA	130	103¾	21½	2½	1½		¾				1
RHODE ISLAND	27	23½	2½								
SOUTH CAROLINA	28	28									
SOUTH DAKOTA	26	2		24							
TENNESSEE	51	49½	½	1							
TEXAS	104	100½	2½		1						
UTAH	26	23	2		1						
VERMONT	22	9	6	7							
VIRGINIA	54	42½	5½		2	3					1
WASHINGTON	47	32½	8½	6							
WEST VIRGINIA	38	34	3				1				
WISCONSIN	59	8	49	1	1						
WYOMING	22	18½	3½	1							
CANAL ZONE	5	4									
DIST. OF COLUMBIA	23	2			21						
GUAM	5	5									
PUERTO RICO	8	8									
VIRGIN ISLANDS	5	5									
TOTAL	2,622	1,760¼	601	146½	67½	17½	12¾	1½	½	½	14

* Abstaining votes not counted.

INDEX

THEODORE H. WHITE

Born in Boston, Massachusetts, in 1915, Theodore H. White attended
Boston Latin School and was graduated *summa cum laude* from Harvard University in 1938. That year he received the Frederick Sheldon
Traveling Fellowship and got as far as China, where he became correspondent of *Time* magazine in 1939. He was later named chief of
the China Bureau of *Time* and served in that capacity until 1945. At
the end of World War II he returned to the United States, and in 1946
his first book (written with Annalee Jacoby), *Thunder out of China,*
was published. After serving for a brief time as editor of *The New
Republic,* he edited *The Stilwell Papers.* In 1948 he went to live in
Europe, where he served for a while as European correspondent for
The Reporter, and completed his second book, *Fire in the Ashes,* published in 1953, the year he returned to the United States. The following year he was national correspondent for *The Reporter* and in 1955
became national correspondent for *Collier's* magazine. His first novel,
The Mountain Road, was published in 1958, and his second, *The View
from the Fortieth Floor,* in 1960. In 1961, Theodore H. White pub-
lished *The Making of the President—1960* and for it won the 1962
Pulitzer Prize. *The Making of the President—1964* followed in 1965.
For his writing of the television documentary *The Making of the
President—1960,* Mr. White received an Emmy Award as well as
television's Program of the Year Award. He also wrote the television
documentaries *The Making of the President—1964* and *China: The
Roots of Madness,* for which he won another Emmy. His first play,
Caesar at the Rubicon, was published in 1968. Mr. White lives in New
York City with his wife and two children.

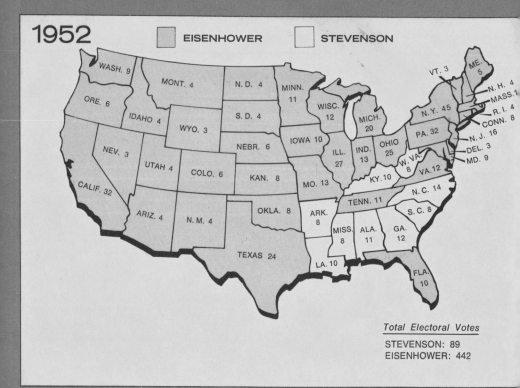

1952

EISENHOWER STEVENSON

WASH. 9
ORE. 6
IDAHO 4
MONT. 4
N. D. 4
MINN. 11
WISC. 12
MICH. 20
VT. 3
ME. 5
N. H. 4
MASS.
N. Y. 45
R. I. 4
CONN. 8
PA. 32
N. J. 16
DEL. 3
MD. 9
NEV. 3
UTAH 4
WYO. 3
S. D. 4
NEBR. 6
IOWA 10
ILL. 27
IND. 13
OHIO 25
W. VA. 8
VA.12
CALIF. 32
COLO. 6
KAN. 8
MO. 13
KY.10
N. C. 14
ARIZ. 4
N. M. 4
OKLA. 8
ARK. 8
TENN. 11
S. C. 8
TEXAS 24
MISS. 8
ALA. 11
GA. 12
LA. 10
FLA. 10

Total Electoral Votes

STEVENSON: 89
EISENHOWER: 442

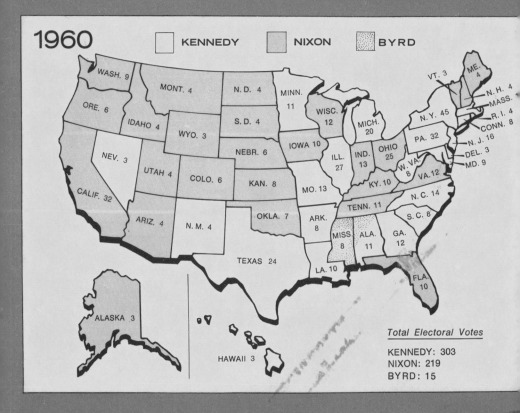

1960

KENNEDY NIXON BYRD

WASH. 9
ORE. 6
IDAHO 4
MONT. 4
N. D. 4
MINN. 11
WISC. 12
MICH. 20
VT. 3
ME. 4
N. H. 4
MASS.
N. Y. 45
R. I. 4
CONN. 8
PA. 32
N. J. 16
DEL. 3
MD. 9
NEV. 3
UTAH 4
WYO. 3
S. D. 4
NEBR. 6
IOWA 10
ILL. 27
IND. 13
OHIO 25
W. VA. 8
VA.12
CALIF. 32
COLO. 6
KAN. 8
MO. 13
KY.10
N. C. 14
ARIZ. 4
N. M. 4
OKLA. 7
ARK. 8
TENN. 11
S. C. 8
TEXAS 24
MISS. 8
ALA. 11
GA. 12
LA. 10
FLA. 10

ALASKA 3

HAWAII 3

Total Electoral Votes

KENNEDY: 303
NIXON: 219
BYRD: 15